Media/Impact

an introduction to mass media

ENHANCED TENTH EDITION

From the Wadsworth Series in Mass Communication and Journalism

General Mass Communication

Biagi, *Media/Impact: An Introduction to Mass Media*, Enhanced Tenth Edition
Fellow, *American Media History*, Third Edition
Hilmes, *Connections: A Broadcast History Reader*
Hilmes, *Only Connect: A Cultural History of Broadcasting in the United States*, Third Edition
Lester, *Visual Communication: Images with Messages*, Fifth Edition
Overbeck, *Major Principles of Media Law*, 2012 Edition
Straubhaar/LaRose/Davenport, *Media Now: Understanding Media, Culture, and Technology*, Enhanced Seventh Edition
Zelezny, *Cases in Communications Law*, Sixth Edition
Zelezny, *Communications Law: Liberties, Restraints, and the Modern Media*, Sixth Edition

Journalism

Bowles/Borden, *Creative Editing*, Sixth Edition
Davis/Davis, *Think Like an Editor: 50 Strategies for the Print and Digital World*
Hilliard, *Writing for Television, Radio, and New Media*, Tenth Edition
Kessler/McDonald, *When Words Collide: A Media Writer's Guide to Grammar and Style*, Eighth Edition
Kessler/McDonald, *Cengage Advantage Books: When Words Collide: A Media Writer's Guide to Grammar and Style + Exercise Book*, Eighth Edition
Rich, *Writing and Reporting News: A Coaching Method*, Seventh Edition

Public Relations and Advertising

Diggs-Brown, *Strategic Public Relations: Audience Focused Approach*
Diggs-Brown, *The PR Styleguide: Formats for Public Relations Practice*, Third Edition
Drewniany/Jewler, *Creative Strategy in Advertising*, Tenth Edition
Hendrix, *Public Relations Cases*, Ninth Edition
Newsom/Haynes, *Public Relations Writing: Form and Style*, Ninth Edition
Newsom/Turk/Kruckeberg, *Cengage Advantage Books: This is PR: The Realities of Public Relations*, Eleventh Edition
Sivulka, *Soap, Sex, and Cigarettes: A Cultural History of American Advertising*, Second Edition

Research and Theory

Baran/Davis, *Mass Communication Theory: Foundations, Ferment, and Future*, Sixth Edition
Sparks, *Media Effects Research: A Basic Overview*, Fourth Edition
Wimmer/Dominick, *Mass Media Research: An Introduction*, Ninth Edition

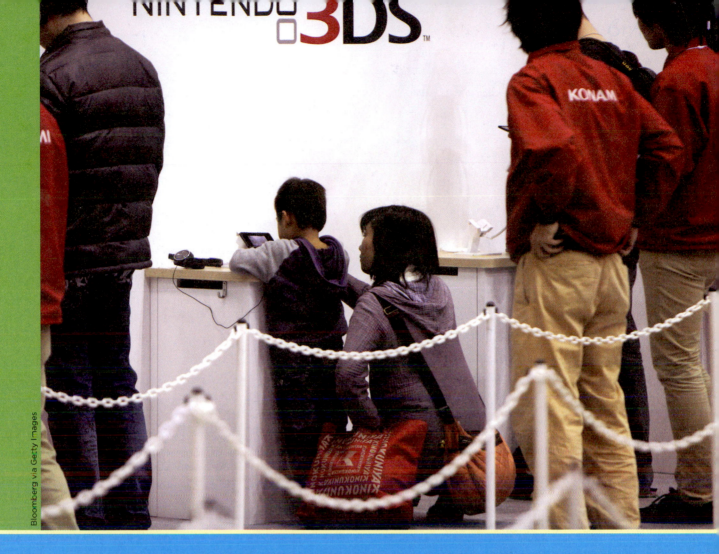

Bloomberg via Getty Images

Media/Impact

an introduction to mass media

ENHANCED TENTH EDITION

Shirley Biagi
California State University, Sacramento

Australia • Brazil • Japan • Korea • Mexico • Singapore • Spain • United Kingdom • United States

Media/Impact: An Introduction to Mass Media, Enhanced Tenth Edition

Shirley Biagi

Senior Publisher: Lyn Uhl

Publisher: Michael Rosenberg

Development Editor: Laurie K. Dobson

Assistant Editor: Erin Bosco

Editorial Assistant: Rebecca Donahue

Media Editor: Jessica Badiner

Marketing Program Manager: Gurpreet Saran

Content Project Manager: Corinna Dibble

Art Director: Marissa Falco

Manufacturing Planner: Doug Bertke

Rights Acquisition Specialist: Mandy Groszko

Production Service/Compositor: Lachina Publishing Services

Text Designer: Riezebos Holzbaur Group

Cover image credits: JOHN G. MABANGLO/epa/Corbis; CBS via Getty Images; Getty Images; Dilip Vishwanat/Getty Images Sport/Getty Images; George Rose/Getty Images News/Getty Images; John M. Heller/Getty Images Entertainment/Getty Images; Christian JENTZ/Gamma-Rapho/Getty Images; Jim Prisching/AP Images for IMAX; CASEY KELBAUGH/*The New York Times*/Redux Pictures; Alberto E. Rodriguez/Getty Images; Bloomberg/Getty Images; Vic Biondi; Bloomberg/Getty Images; Bloomberg/Getty Images; Bloomberg/Getty Images; Pictorial Press Ltd/Alamy; Bloomberg via Getty Images; Vic Biondi; Alberto E. Rodriguez/Getty Images

Library of Congress Control Number: 2012932719

ISBN-13: 978-1-111-83529-3

ISBN-10: 1-111-83529-2

Wadsworth
20 Channel Center Street
Boston, MA 02210
USA

Cengage Learning is a leading provider of customized learning solutions with office locations around the globe, including Singapore, the United Kingdom, Australia, Mexico, Brazil and Japan. Locate your local office at **international.cengage.com/region**.

Cengage Learning products are represented in Canada by Nelson Education, Ltd.

For your course and learning solutions, visit **www.cengage.com**.

Purchase any of our products at your local college store or at our preferred online store **www.cengagebrain.com**.

Instructors: Please visit **login.cengage.com** and log in to access instructor-specific resources.

Printed in the United States of America
1 2 3 4 5 6 7 16 15 14 13 12

Brief Contents

John M. Heller/Getty Images Entertainment/Getty Images

Contents

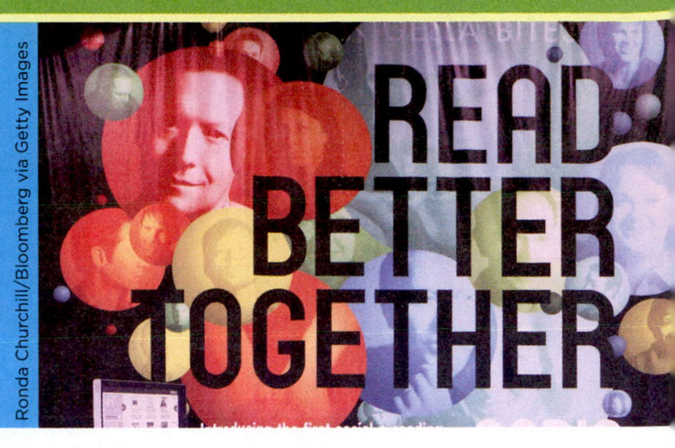

Ronda Churchill/Bloomberg via Getty Images

PART ONE The Mass Media Industries

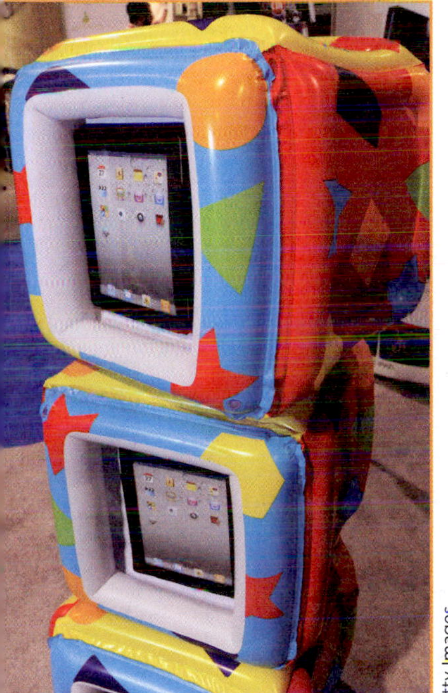
Getty Images

CHAPTER 1

Mass Media and Everyday Life

Photo by Vic Biondi

CHAPTER 2

Books: Rearranging the Page

Bloomberg/Getty Images

CHAPTER 3

Newspapers: Expanding Delivery

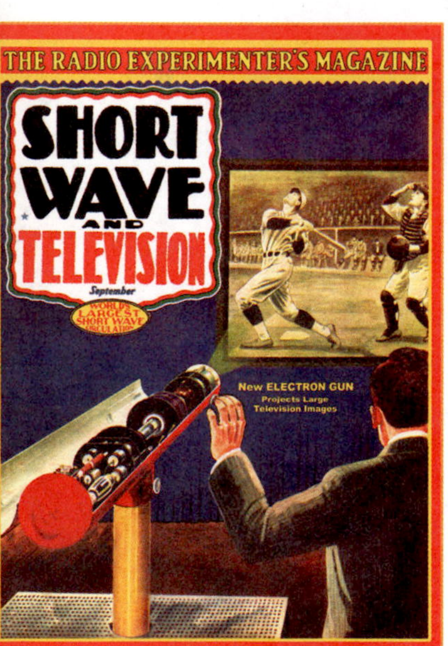

Buyenlarge/Getty Images

CHAPTER 4

Magazines: Targeting the Audience

Photo by Vic Biondi

CHAPTER 5
Recordings: Demanding Choices

Bloomberg/Getty Images

CHAPTER 6

Radio: Riding the Wave

Jim Prisching/AP Images for IMAX

CHAPTER 7

Movies: Picturing the Future

Bloomberg/Getty Images

CHAPTER 8

Television: Changing Channels

Bloomberg/Getty Images

CHAPTER 9
Digital Media: Widening the Web

Dilip Vishwanat/Getty Images Sport/Getty Images

PART TWO Selling the Message

CHAPTER 10

Advertising: Motivating Customers

U.S. Coast Guard/Getty Images

CHAPTER 11

Public Relations: Promoting Ideas

PART THREE Changing Messages

HAZEM BADER/AFP/Getty Images

CHAPTER 12

News and Information: Getting Personal

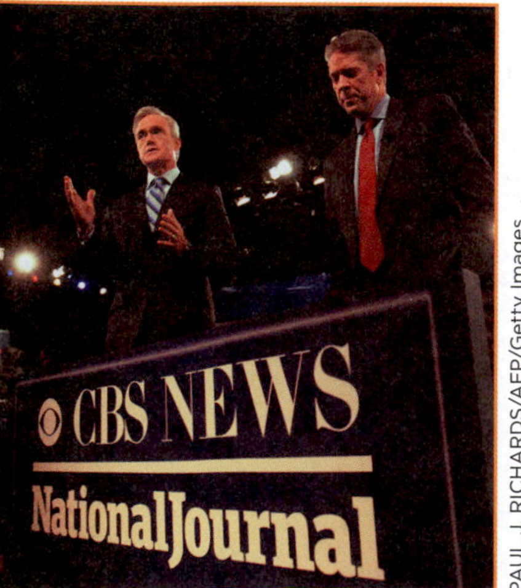

PAUL J. RICHARDS/AFP/Getty Images

CHAPTER 13
Society, Culture and Politics: Shaping the Issues

George Rose/Getty Images News/Getty Images

CHAPTER 14
Law and Regulation: Rewriting the Rules

Fred Vuich/Sports Illustrated/Getty Images

CHAPTER 15
Ethics: Placing Responsibility

Photo by Shirley Biagi

CHAPTER 16
Global Media: Discovering New Markets

Impact Boxes

CHAPTER 8

CHAPTER 9

CHAPTER 10

CHAPTER 11

CHAPTER 12

CHAPTER 13

CHAPTER 14

CHAPTER 15

CHAPTER 16

Foreword

Christian JENTZ/Gamma-Rapho/Getty Images

As I write this, mass media companies continue to grab daily headlines and remain at the center of global events.

Facebook, which claims more than 800 million monthly users worldwide, has announced plans to become a public company, making its founder Mark Zuckerberg a billionaire at age 27. News Corp. has agreed to pay hundreds of thousands of dollars to settle allegations that reporters at one of its newspapers illegally hacked into celebrity e-mails and voicemails.

Borders Books has closed all its stores, citing competition from Internet retailer Amazon. And political candidates are raising record amounts of campaign donations online.

What subject could possibly be more interesting to study than the mass media?

Acknowledging Professional Support

To track fast-moving mass media events and incorporate them into a comprehensive text like *Media/Impact* takes tremendous effort from everyone involved. This process is very complex, and several people deserve extra credit for helping to make this Enhanced Tenth edition the best yet.

The concept for annual editions began three years ago with the supportive, can-do attitude of Cengage Publisher Michael Rosenberg. There is no better publications management company than Lachina Publishing Services, which gave me the patient, gifted assistance of project manager Matthew Orgovan. Laurie Dobson handled the compressed schedule with dedicated, patient zeal. Corinna Dibble, Cengage Content Project Manager, kept us organized and moving forward. And Marissa Falco supervised a wonderful updated design for the new silver cover.

People Who Are Personally Important

The most important personal thank you goes to my closest visual adviser and superb video co-producer, Vic Biondi. The spectacular variety and currency of all the images in this edition, and the professional quality of the new Impact/Action Videos, represent hundreds of hours of his patient, inspired work. Thank you.

The Enhanced Tenth edition of *Media/Impact* also reflects the suggestions, contributions and ideas of hundreds of students and colleagues who write, e-mail, text and stop me on the street to offer new ideas. People from around the world regularly e-mail me, and their comments add an international perspective. *Media/Impact* now is published in Korean, Spanish, Greek and Canadian editions.

After you explore all of *Media/Impact*'s information, images and valuable special features, I'd be interested to know what you think. My e-mail address is sbiagi@csus.edu.

Your comments and ideas are always welcome.

Shirley Biagi

Preface

Al Seib/Los Angeles Times

Begin Your *Media/ Impact* Journey Here.

What Makes the Enhanced Tenth Edition New?

Daily events surrounding today's mass media industries mean it is crucially important to annually update *Media/ Impact* so students have the best, most current information available for their mass media studies.

Companies buy, sell, merge and collapse; corporations change executives, cut salaries and reduce the number of employees; businesses introduce new technologies, services and products; companies challenge regulatory rulings; people create ethics scandals; and industries try to respond to the ever-increasing influence of the Internet and globalization.

Coverage of the impact of all these events—and much more—in this edition of *Media/Impact* makes the Enhanced Tenth edition the best, most current resource available to present essential historical and current information in context—to encourage classroom discussions about the state of the mass media industries today.

Impact/Action Videos

Media/Impact has always been the most current introductory mass media textbook available. So for the first time with this edition, we are excited to announce the addition of four instruction-rich video lessons on important, timely communications topics, produced specifically for *Media/Impact* by Shirley Biagi and Vic Biondi.

These **Impact/Action Videos**—available to students and instructors on the Mass Communication CourseMate for *Media/Impact* through CengageBrain.com—are designed to provoke critical thinking and to visually reinforce and enhance the text. These topical video lessons cover:

1. **Communicating Change: Egypt 2011.** An analysis of the way demonstrators in Cairo, Egypt, used various methods of communication to protest and ultimately topple the government of President Hosni Mubarak.
2. **Reporters at Risk.** A look at why journalists all over the world place their lives in jeopardy every day to cover the news.
3. **Living in 3-D.** A discussion of emerging 3-D technologies, and their impact on today's mass media industries.
4. **Moving Pages.** The economic and social consequences that result when printed media goes digital.

Media/Impact Boxes

The Enhanced Tenth edition also features more than a dozen new *Media/Impact* boxes—highlighting the latest topics, as written by top industry experts and scholars. Presented in five different types of Media/Impact boxes—**Media/Impact: Culture**, **Media/Impact: Money**, **Media/Impact: World**, **Media/Impact: People** and **Media/Impact: Audience**—these boxes emphasize the crucial role that current events play in the ongoing story of mass media in America.

My goal has always been—especially through the *Media/Impact* feature boxes—to help students grasp the central role that the mass media industries play every day in shaping and reshaping their community, their country and their world.

Here's just a sample of more than 30 *Media/Impact* boxes in this edition, many of them new:

Media/Impact: Culture

"How Steve Jobs Put Passion Into Products"
"Murdoch Settles Suits by Dozens of Victims of Hacking"
"Raised on the Web, but Liking a Little Ink"
"Headphones with Swagger (and Lots of Bass)"
"After Recalls, Toyota Monitors Social Media to Protect Its Reputation"
"How Do People Use Social Media to Share News?"

Media/Impact: Money

"For Instant Ratings, Interviews with a Checkbook"
"Hollywood's TV Factory"
"Political TV Ad Spending Sets Record: October 2010 Is the Busiest Month in History for Political Ads on TV"
"How Do Book Publishers Make Their Money?"
"BP Touts Itself as 'Green,' but Faces PR Disaster with 'BP Oil Spill'"
"How Much Does It Cost to Make a Movie? The 10 Most Expensive Movies Ever Made"

Media/Impact: World

"How the Egyptian Government Killed the Internet in January 2011"
"What Would Daniel Ellsberg Do with the Pentagon Papers Today?"
"British TV Ads Flaunt Their Arty Side"
"*Vice* Magazine: A Cult Glossy Spawns a Global Media Empire and Gets a Partnership with CNN"

Media/Impact: People

"Kelly Bush: A Publicist Who Sees No Need to Duck Calls"
"Beaten Russian Reporter Mikhail Beketov Convicted of Slander"
"Keith Olbermann and Joe Scarborough Suspended Over Campaign Donations"
"Artful Entrepreneur Mike Richardson Finds Comic Book Success in Print, Movies and on the Internet"
"Kathryn Bigelow: How Oscar Found Ms. Right"

Media/Impact: Audience

"Screen Time Higher Than Ever for Children"
"There's Little Privacy in a Digital World"
"Amazon Signs Up Authors, Writing Publishers Out of Deal"
"Where Newspapers Thrive"
"Why Marathons Are Hot Spot to Chase Consumers"

Ongoing Features in *Media/Impact*'s Enhanced Tenth Edition That Guarantee Currency

- **Comprehensive coverage of the latest in digital media.** *Media/Impact* details the latest innovations and controversies surrounding the Internet, mobile media, 3-D, video games, intellectual property rights, government regulation, convergence and social media.
- **Analysis of changing delivery systems for news and information.** Chapter 12 chronicles the declining popularity of broadcast news as consumers personalize their information and use the Internet to stay current, as well as the social media's transformative role in gathering and sharing information. First introduced in the sixth edition, when few people understood how consumers' changing news habits would affect news delivery, this chapter has proven extremely popular with faculty and students.
- **Discussion of current media issues.** Beginning with the first page of Chapter 1 ("Mass Media and Everyday Life"), *Media/Impact* presents a realistic picture of today's media, highlighting the latest regulatory, ethical and economic climates affecting the mass media industries.
- **Career information.** Each media industry chapter covers the organizational structure and jobs within each type of media business, giving students a useful introduction to media careers.
- **Picturing the Numbers.** More than 20 graphic illustrations present the most current statistics in an easy-to-understand visual format. Detailed captions also help students make sense of the numbers, enabling them to see what critical media industry data means.
- **Margin definitions.** Designed to help students build a media vocabulary while they read, key terms are listed in the margins of each chapter, giving students concise definitions right where they need them.
- **Comprehensive end-of-chapter review.** Each chapter's concluding materials include these useful resources:
  - **Chapter summaries.** Organized by headings that correspond to the chapter's major topics, the section **Review, Analyze, Investigate** uses bullet points to summarize major concepts.
  - **Key terms.** A list of important terms with corresponding page numbers appears at the end of each chapter and in the comprehensive **Glossary** at the end of the book.
  - **Critical questions.** Following the key terms, five questions enhance students' analysis of each chapter to help deepen their understanding and engage their critical thinking skills.
  - **Working the Web.** Finishing each chapter, a list of 10 Web sites specific to the chapter includes a brief annotation to describe each site and encourages mass media students to pursue further research.
- **Media Information Resource Guide.** This invaluable student reference tool at the end of the book provides hundreds more resources to help students explore media topics, including an alphabetical listing of the 200 Web site references from the text.

Most Important to *Media/Impact*'s Success: Students and Faculty

To all the teachers who use *Media / Impact* in their classes and to the faculty reviewers who provided the formal feedback for the Enhanced Tenth edition, a personal thank you. The Tenth edition's reviewers are:

Philip J. Auter, University of Louisiana at Lafayette
Eric Carlson, Collin College
Patricia A. Holmes, University of Louisiana at Lafayette
Amy K. Lenoce, Naugatuck Valley Community College
Richard Lenoce, Middlesex Community College
Pam Parry, Belmont University
Kristen Perez, Briar Cliff University
Cliff Vaughn, Belmont University

And a special thank you to all the students who have used *Media / Impact* for the last 25 years. You're the most important factor in the book's success.

Accompanying Resources: An Exclusive Teaching and Learning Package

Media / Impact, Enhanced Tenth edition, offers a comprehensive array of print and electronic resources to help students succeed, while making the Introduction to Mass Communication course meaningful and enjoyable for both students and instructors.

Resources for Students

- **Mass Communication CourseMate:** *Media / Impact* includes Mass Communication CourseMate, a complement to your textbook. Mass Communication CourseMate includes these items:
    - An interactive e-book, with highlighting, note-taking and search capabilities.
    - Impact/Action Videos, with specialized narration, images and footage that help expand your understanding of how mass communication is changing the world.
    - Many other interactive teaching and learning tools:
        - Quizzes
        - Flashcards
        - Career podcasts
        - Web resources
        - and more!

  Go to login.cengagebrain.com to access these resources.
- **NewsNow:** Be current and relevant with NewsNow news stories for your Intro to Mass Communication class. Be prepared for instructor lessons based on these stories.

Resources for Instructors

Media / Impact also features a full suite of resources for instructors. The following class preparation, classroom presentation, assessment and course management resources are available:

- **Instructor's Edition (IE):** Examination and desk copies of the Instructor's Edition of *Media / Impact*, Enhanced Tenth edition are available upon request.
- **Instructor's Web site:** The password-protected instructor's Web site includes electronic access to the Instructor's Resource Manual, discussion questions for each of the Impact/Action Videos and downloadable versions of the book's PowerPoint slides.
- **Instructor's Resource Manual:** *Media / Impact*'s Instructor's Resource Manual by Shirley Biagi provides a comprehensive teaching guide featuring the following tools for each chapter: chapter goals and an outline; suggestions for integrating print supplements and online resources; suggested discussion questions and activities and a comprehensive test bank with an answer key that includes multiple choice, true-false, short answer, essay and fill-in-the-blank test questions. The manual also includes discussion questions for each of the Impact/Action Videos. This manual is available on the password-protected instructor Web site and the Power Lecture CD-ROM, which includes ExamView® Computerized Testing. You'll find more information about these teaching tools below.
- **Power Lecture CD-ROM:** This disc contains an electronic version of the Instructor's Resource Manual, ExamView computerized testing and ready-to-use Microsoft® PowerPoint® presentations corresponding with the text and JoinIn™ on Turning Point®. This all-in-one lecture tool makes it easy for you to assemble, edit, publish and present custom lectures for your course. More information about ExamView and JoinIn follows.
- **ExamView® Computerized Testing:** Enables you to create, deliver and customize tests and study guides (both print and online) in minutes using the test bank questions from the Instructor's Resource Manual. ExamView offers both a *Quick Test Wizard* and an *Online Test*

Wizard to guide you step-by-step through the process of creating tests, while its "what you see is what you get" interface allows you to see the test you are creating on-screen exactly as it will print or display online. You can build tests of up to 250 questions, using up to 12 question types. Using the complete word processing capabilities of ExamView, you can even enter an unlimited number of new questions or edit existing ones.

- **JoinIn™ on TurningPoint®:** Transform your classroom and assess your students' progress with instant in-class quizzes and polls. TurningPoint® software lets you pose book-specific questions and display students' answers seamlessly within the Microsoft® PowerPoint® slides of your own lecture, in conjunction with the "clicker" hardware of your choice. Enhance how your students interact with you, your lecture and each other.
- **Mass Communication CourseMate:** *Media/Impact* includes Mass Communication CourseMate, a complement to your textbook. This new multimedia resource offers a variety of rich learning opportunities designed to enhance the learning experience. This product includes chapter-specific tools such as tutorial and sample quizzing, interactive glossaries and timelines, videos, career podcasts and Web resources. Mass Communication CourseMate also includes an interactive e-book, as well as Impact/Action Videos that bring themes and issues to life through narrated multimedia presentations created specifically for *Media/Impact*. Use the Engagement Tracker tracking tools to see progress for the class as a whole or for individual students. Identify students at risk early in the course. Uncover which concepts are most difficult for your class. Monitor time on task. Keep your students engaged.
    - Note to faculty: To give your students access to these online textbook resources, please be sure to order them for your course. This content can be bundled at no additional charge to your students with every new copy of the text. You must specifically order them for your students to have access to these online resources. *Contact your local Cengage Learning sales representative for more details.*
- **NewsNow:** Do you get NewsNow? Grab the attention of your students with current and relevant news stories embedded in a PowerPoint presentation with images, videos, discussion questions and more. A turnkey solution to start a lecture is also fully customizable.
- **WebTutor Toolbox for WebCT and Blackboard:** With the pre-formatted content and total flexibility of WebTutor Toolbox, you can easily create and manage your own custom course Web site. This course management tool includes chapter summaries, chapter glossaries and flashcards, practice quizzing and additional web resources for students and instructor support, including a test bank.

These resources are available to qualified adopters, and ordering options for the student text and supplements are flexible. Please consult your local Cengage sales representative for more information, to evaluate examination copies of any of these instructor or student resources, or product demonstrations. You may also contact the Cengage Learning Academic Resource Center at 800-423-0563, or visit us at http://www.cengagebrain.com.

About the Author

Christopher Briscoe

Shirley Biagi is a professor in the Department of Communication Studies at California State University, Sacramento. Her bestselling text, *Media/Impact*, is also published in Canadian, Greek, Spanish and Korean editions. Biagi has authored several other Wadsworth communications texts, including *Media/Reader: Perspectives on Mass Media Industries, Effects and Issues* and *Interviews That Work: A Practical Guide for Journalists*. She is co-author, with Marilyn Kern-Foxworth, of *Facing Difference: Race, Gender and Mass Media*.

From 1998 to 2000, she was editor of *American Journalism*, the national media history quarterly published by the American Journalism Historians Association.

She has served as guest faculty for the University of Hawaii, the Center for Digital Government, the Poynter Institute, the American Press Institute, the National Writers Workshop and the Hearst Fellowship Program at the *Houston Chronicle*. She has also been an Internet and publications consultant to the California State Chamber of Commerce.

She also was one of eight project interviewers for the award-winning Washington (D.C.) Press Club Foundation's Women in Journalism Oral History Project, sponsored by the National Press Club. Interviewers completed 57 oral histories of female pioneers in journalism, available free on the Press Club's Web site at http://www.wpcf.org.

In 2007, Biagi was nominated and served as a delegate to the Oxford Round Table's conference on Ethical Sentiments in Government at Pembroke College in Oxford, England. Biagi's other international experience includes guest lectureships at Al Ahram Press Institute in Cairo, Egypt, and at Queensland University in Brisbane, Australia.

1

"By watching transactions and clicks we have a massive telescope into human behavior at a scale we've never had before."

—Prabhakar Raghavan, Yahoo Labs

Mass Media and Everyday Life

What's Ahead?

Mass Media Are Everywhere You Are

Mass Communication Becomes Wireless

How the Communication Process Works

What Are the Mass Media Industries?

Three Key Concepts to Remember

Mass Media Are Profit-Centered Businesses

Competition and Convergence Dominate

Why Media Properties Converge

Advertisers and Consumers Pay the Bills

Technology Changes Mass Media Delivery and Consumption

Media Take Advantage of Digital Delivery

How Today's Communications Network Operates

Mass Media Both Reflect and Affect Politics, Society and Culture

Why You Should Understand Mass Media and Everyday Life

Getty Images

An inflatable child-proof iPad holder is displayed at the 2012 Consumer Electronics Show in Las Vegas, Nevada, on January 12, 2012. According to the manufacturer, the cube allows someone to strap an iPad into the recess on one side, making it harder for children to damage it.

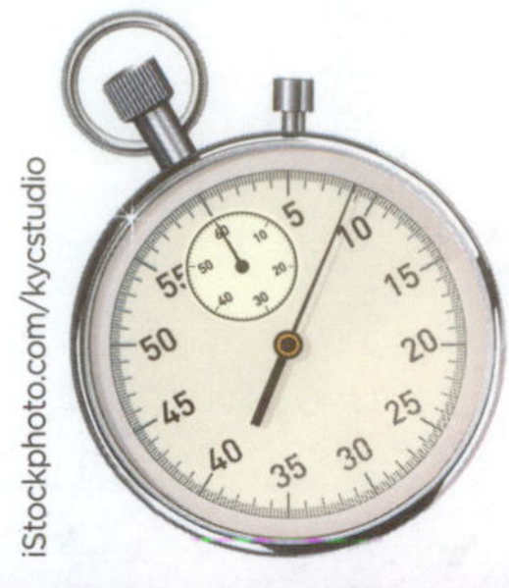
iStockphoto.com/kycstudio

TimeFrame 3500 B.C. — Today

Three Information Communications Revolutions Form the Basis for Today's Digital Media

3500 B.C. The first known pictographs are carved in stone.

2500 B.C. **The Egyptians invent papyrus.**

DEA/De Agostini/ Getty Images

1000 B.C. **The First Information Communications Revolution: Phonetic Writing**

200 B.C. The Greeks perfect parchment.

100 A.D. The Chinese invent paper.

1300 Europeans start to use paper.

1445 The Chinese invent the copper press.

1455 **The Second Information Communications Revolution: Movable Type**

SSPL/Getty Images

1640 The first American book is published.

1690 The first American newspaper is published.

1741 The first American magazine is published.

1877 Thomas Edison first demonstrates the phonograph.

1899 **Guglielmo Marconi first uses his wireless radio.**

Hulton Archive/Stringer/ Archive Photos/ Getty Images

1927 *The Jazz Singer*, the first feature-length motion picture with sound, premieres in New York City.

1939 **NBC debuts TV at the New York World's Fair. On display were 5-inch and 9-inch television sets priced from $199.50 to $600.**

MPI/Stringer/Archive Photos/Getty Images

1951 **The Third Information Communications Revolution: digital computers that can process, store and retrieve information**

1980 The Federal Communications Commission begins to deregulate the broadcast media.

1989 Tim Berners-Lee develops the first Internet Web browser.

2008 Internet advertising income reaches $23 billion annually, more than twice what it was in the year 2000.

2010 Apple introduces the iPad and the iPhone 4.

2011 Apple introduces iCloud.

Today **Wireless digital technology is the standard for all mass media. Mass media is personalized and mobile.**

Ross Kinnaird/Staff/Getty Images

Media/Impact
AUDIENCE

Illustration 1.1

Average Time People Spend Using Mass Media Each Day

On average, people spend more time each day with the mass media than without them.

Source: Veronis Suhler Stevenson Communications Industry Forecast, *http://www.vss.com/news/index.asp?d_News_ID=190.*

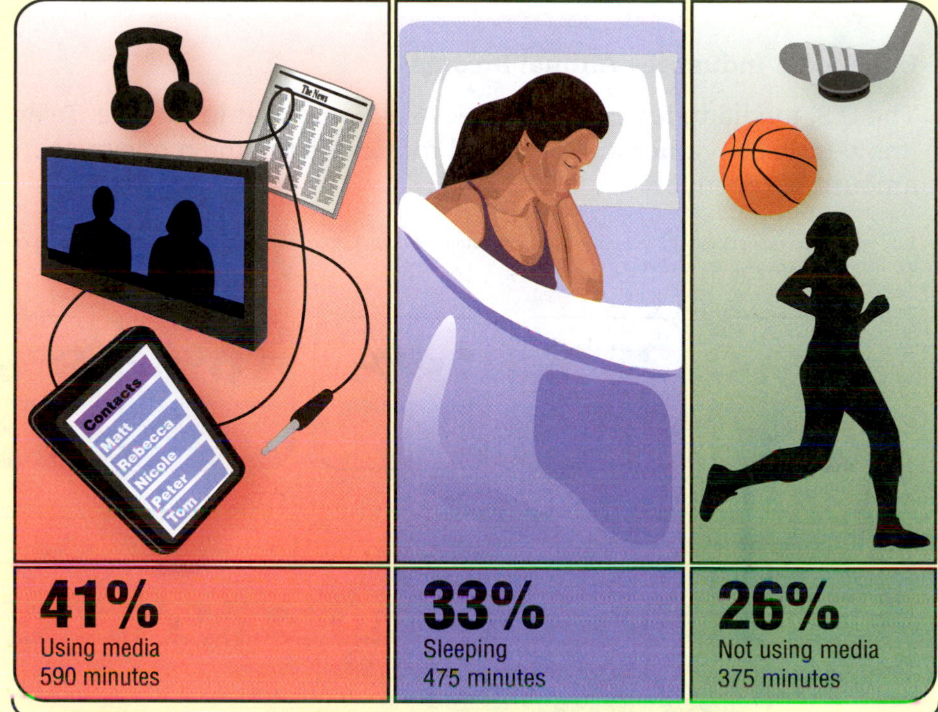

You are *connected.*

In today's world mass media are waiting to bombard you every waking hour. When was the last time you spent 24 hours without the media? From the moment you get up in the morning until the time you go to bed at night, mass media are available to keep you informed, make sure you're entertained, and—most importantly—sell you products.

Mass Media Are Everywhere You Are

Radio news gives you headlines in the shower and traffic reports on the freeway. Internet newspapers offer national and local news and help you follow the latest high school football standings, with constant updates and breaking news stories. Magazines describe new video games, show you the latest fashion trends and help plan your next camping trip.

Should you do your homework now or grab the newest paperback romance novel or stream a video from Netflix? Maybe you should grab your iPhone 4S to download the latest episode of your favorite sitcom or text a friend to ask about dinner tonight. Perhaps you should take some time to answer e-mail from your overseas college friends, while downloading some new songs. All those media choices certainly are more compelling than your homework.

According to industry estimates, today's adults spend more than half their waking lives with the media—more time than they spend sleeping. (See **Illustration 1.1**.) During the day, the average person spends more time with the media than without them. Some form of mass media touches you every day—economically, socially and culturally. The mass media can affect the way you vote and the way you spend your money. Sometimes the mass media influence the way you eat, talk, work, study and relax. This is the impact of mass media on you individually and, collectively, on American society.

The media's wide-ranging global presence means today's mass media capture more time and attention than ever. The media affect almost all aspects of the way people live, and the media collect unprecedented amounts of money for delivering information and entertainment. The American media

Media/Impact
MONEY

Illustration 1.2

U.S. Media Industries Annual Income

The U.S. media industries collect $276 billion a year in income. Television and the entertainment media (movies, video games and recorded music) are the top moneymakers, while radio generates the smallest amount of revenue.

Sources: www.publishers.org, www.hoovers.com, www.naa.org, http://blog.mediaideas.net, www.fmpq.com, http://adage.com, www.forrester.com, www.emarketer.com, www.riaa.org.

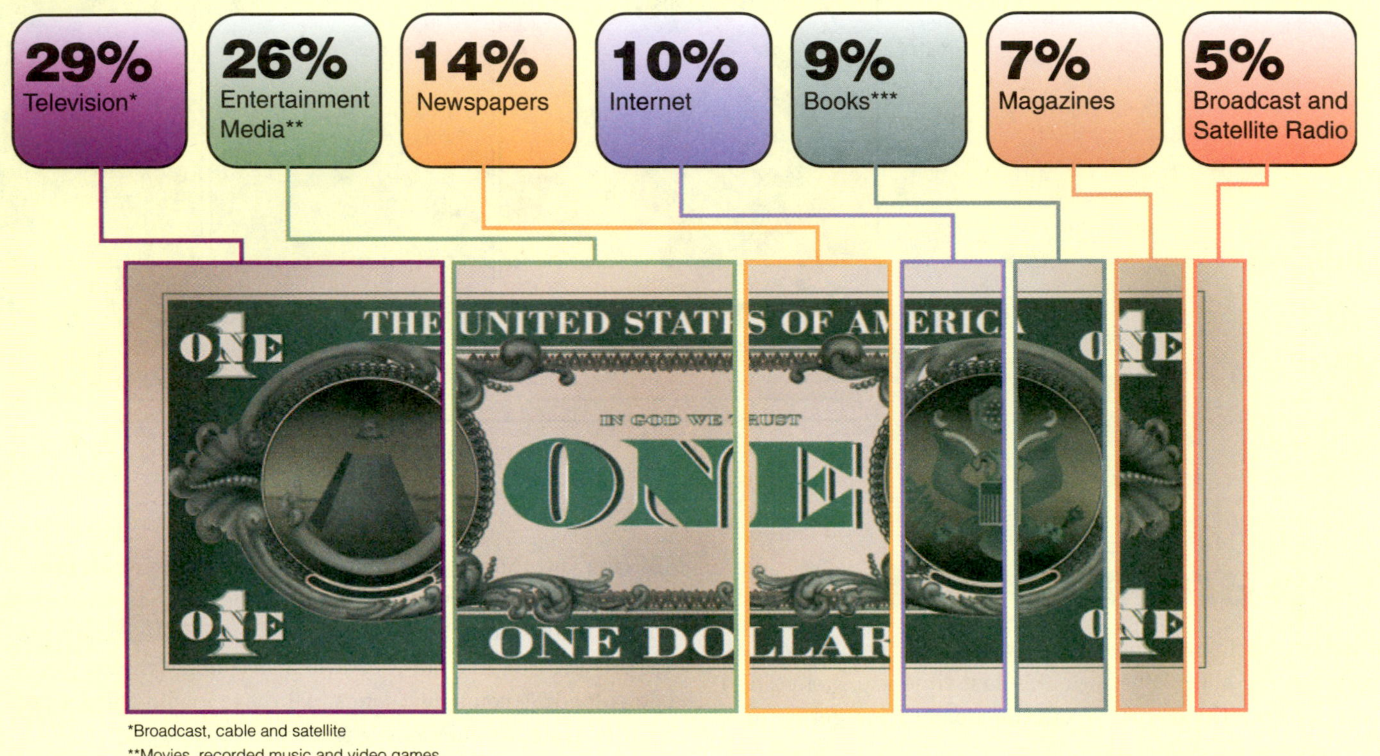

*Broadcast, cable and satellite

**Movies, recorded music and video games

***Trade books, mass market paperbacks, K-12 and college textbooks, and e-books

industries earn about $276 billion a year. (See **Illustration 1.2**.)

Today's American society has inherited the wisdom, mistakes, creativity and vision of the people who work in the mass media industries and the society that regulates and consumes what the mass media produce. Consider these situations:

- You are shopping online at Amazon.com, trying to decide between James Patterson's latest e-book novel and a travel guide to Brazil. What are the economic consequences of your book-buying decision for the book publishing industry? (See **Chapter 2**.)
- You are an entrepreneur with a lot of ideas but very little money. You decide to start an online cooking magazine. What are the chances your new magazine will succeed? (See **Chapter 4**.)
- On the Internet, a friend e-mails you a song from the latest album of your favorite recording artist, which you download and publish on your personal Web site. You get the music you want, but the artist's music company sues you because you haven't paid for the song. Will you be prosecuted? (See **Chapter 5**.)

- You are a reporter for a major news organization. To try to scoop the competition, you hack into a celebrity's cellphone. How does your company respond when it learns what you've done? (See **Chapter 15**.)

People who work in the media industries, people who own media businesses, people who consume media, and people who regulate what the media offer face decisions like these every day. The choices they make continue to shape the future of the American mass media.

Mark Allan/WireImage/Getty Images

If a friend e-mails you a copy of the latest song by Coldplay, and you use the song on your Web site without permission, can you be prosecuted for violating the music copyright?

Mass Communication Becomes Wireless

In the 1930s, to listen to the radio, your house had to have electricity throughout. You plugged your radio into an electrical outlet, with the furniture positioned so the family could listen to the programs. In the 1950s, you put an antenna on the roof so you could watch your new TV set, which was connected at the wall to an electrical outlet and the antenna. To be wired was to be connected. In the 1990s, you still needed an electrical outlet at home and at work to be connected to your computer, and the furniture in your family room still was arranged to accommodate the cable, satellite and/or telephone lines for your television set.

Today's technology makes mass media wireless (often called ***Wi-Fi***, an abbreviation for *Wi*reless *Fi*delity). New technologies give you access to any mass media in almost any location without wires. You can sit on your front porch and watch movies on your laptop, listen to radio by satellite and download music, books, newspapers and video games to the cell phone you carry in your pocket. Today, you and your mass media are totally mobile.

The new mass media are as convenient as your cell phone, complete with graphics and sound, offering massive choices of information, entertainment and services whenever and wherever you want them. You can

- Check Facebook to see what your friends are doing.
- Download a first-run movie, your favorite TV sitcom or new and classic books—even your textbook—to a handheld device you carry with you.
- Play the newest video game on your cell phone with three people you've never met.
- Drink coffee in a Wi-Fi café while you check your family ancestry to create an online family tree, leading you to connect with overseas relatives you didn't know existed.
- Stop on the street corner in a new town and retrieve directions to the closest Italian restaurant on your cell phone, complete with the latest recommendations about the best pizza to order there.

Today's digital environment is an intricate, webbed network of many different types of communications systems that eventually will connect every home, school, library and business in the United States. Most of the systems in this digital environment are invisible. Electronic signals have replaced wires, freeing up people to stay connected no matter where or when they want to communicate.

This global communications system uses broadcast, telephone, satellite, cable and computer technologies to connect everyone in the world to a variety of services.

Wi-Fi An abbreviation for *Wi*reless *Fi*delity.

DON EMMERT/AFP/Getty Images

Wireless technology means you can carry your media with you and freely send and receive messages anytime, just about anywhere you want. A woman uses her cell phone while enjoying the waves in Falmouth, Mass.

Eventually, this communications system will be accessible and affordable everywhere in the world. As futurist George Gilder phrased it: "Who will ride the next avalanche of bits on the information superhighway—and who will be buried under it?"

How the Communication Process Works

To understand mass communication in the digital age, first it is important to understand the process of communication. Communication is the act of sending messages, ideas and opinions from one person to another. Writing and talking to each other are only two ways human beings communicate. We also communicate when we gesture, move our bodies or roll our eyes.

Three ways to describe how people communicate are

- *Intrapersonal communication*
- *Interpersonal communication*
- *Mass communication*

Each form of communication involves different numbers of people in specific ways. If you are in a grocery store and you silently debate with yourself whether to buy an apple or a package of double-chunk chocolate chip cookies, you are using what scholars call *intra*personal communication—communication within one person. To communicate with each other, people rely on their five senses—sight, hearing, touch, smell and taste. This direct sharing of experience between two people is called *inter*personal communication. ***Mass communication*** is communication from one person or group of persons through a transmitting device (a medium) to large audiences or markets.

In *Media/Impact* you will study *mass communication*. To describe the process of mass communication, scholars use a communications model. This includes six key terms: *sender*, *message*, *receiver*, *channel*, *feedback* and *noise*. (See **Illustration 1.3**.)

Pretend you're standing directly in front of someone and say, "I like your San Francisco Giants hat." In this simple communication, you are the sender; the message is "I like your San Francisco Giants hat," and the person in front of you is the receiver (or audience). This example of interpersonal communication involves the sender, the message and the receiver.

In mass communication, the *sender* (or *source*) puts the *message* on what is called a *channel*. The sender (source) could be a local cable provider or satellite company, for example. The channel (or ***medium***) delivers the message (the signal). The channel could be the cable or satellite provider that hooks into the back of your TV set. A medium is the means by which a message reaches an audience. (The plural of the word *medium* is *media*; the term ***media*** refers to more than one medium.) Your television set is the medium that delivers the message simultaneously to you and many other people.

The *receiver* is the place where the message arrives, such as your TV set. ***Noise*** is any distortion (such as static or a briefly interrupted signal) that interferes with clear communication. ***Feedback*** occurs when the receiver processes the message and sends a response back to the sender (source).

As a very simple example, say your satellite company (sender/source) sends an advertisement for a movie-on-demand (the message) through the signal (channel) into

Mass Communication Communication from one person or group of persons through a transmitting device (a medium) to large audiences or markets.

Medium The means by which a message reaches the audience. The singular form of the word *media*.

Media Plural of the word *medium*.

Noise Distortion (such as static) that interferes with clear communication.

Feedback A response sent back to the sender from the person who receives the communication.

Media/Impact CULTURE

Illustration 1.3

Elements of Mass Communication

The process of mass communication works like this: A *sender* (source) puts a message on a channel (medium) that delivers the message to the *receiver*. *Feedback* occurs when the receiver responds, and that response changes subsequent messages from the source. *Noise* (such as static or a dropped connection) can interrupt or change the message during transmission.

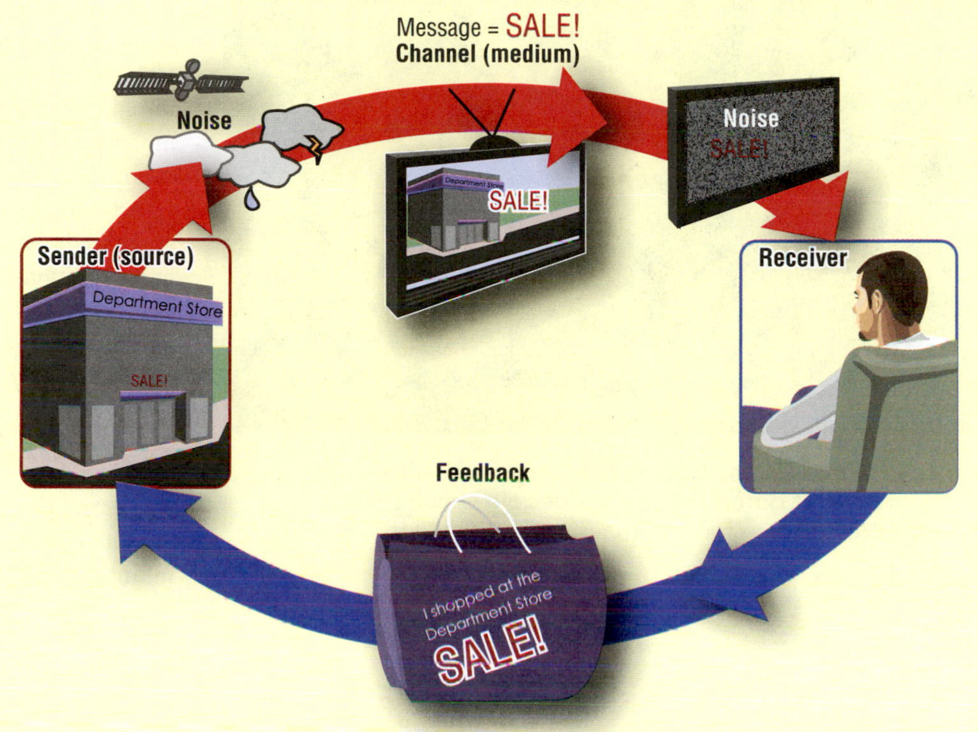

your TV set (medium). If you (the receiver) use the controls on your TV remote to order a movie from Netflix, the order you place (feedback) ultimately will bring you a movie to watch. This entire loop between sender and receiver, and the resulting response (feedback) of the receiver to the sender, describes the process of mass communication.

Using a general definition, mass communication today shares three characteristics:

1. A message is sent out on some form of mass communication system (such as the Internet, print or broadcast).
2. The message is delivered rapidly.
3. The message reaches large groups of different kinds of people simultaneously or within a short period of time.

Thus, a telephone conversation between two people does *not* qualify as mass communication, but a message from the president of the United States, broadcast simultaneously by all of the television networks, would qualify because mass media deliver messages to large numbers of people at once.

What Are the Mass Media Industries?

The term ***mass media industries*** describes eight types of mass media businesses. The word *industries*, when used to describe the media business, emphasizes the primary goal of mass media in America—to generate money. The eight media industries are

- Books
- Newspapers
- Magazines
- Recordings

Mass Media Industries Eight types of media businesses: books, newspapers, magazines, recordings, radio, movies, television and the Internet.

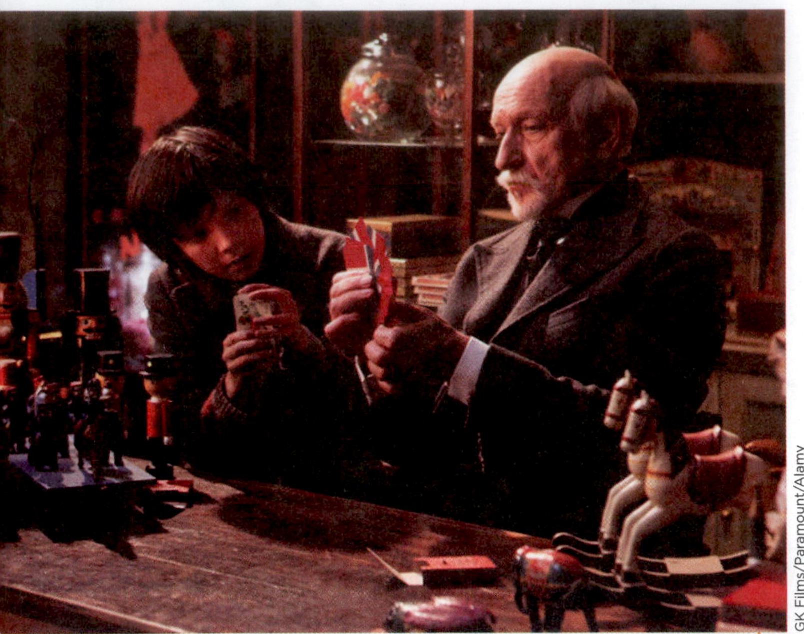

GK Films/Paramount/Alamy

Movies such as *Hugo*, which are available to large groups of different types of people simultaneously, represent one form of mass communication.

- Radio
- Movies
- Television
- The Internet

Books, newspapers and magazines were America's only mass media for 250 years after the first American book was published in 1640. The first half of the 20th century brought four new types of media—recordings, radio, movies and TV—in less than 50 years. The late-20th-century addition to the media mix, of course, is the Internet. To understand where each medium fits in the mass media industries today, you can start by examining the individual characteristics of each media business.

Books

Publishers issue about 150,000 titles a year in the United States, although many of these are reprints and new editions of old titles. Retail bookstores in the United States account for one-third of all money earned from book sales. The rest of book publishing income comes from books that are sold online, in college stores, through book clubs, to libraries and to school districts for use in elementary and high schools. Book publishing, the oldest media industry, is a static industry, with very little growth potential, although book publishers are trying to expand their sales by selling e-books (downloaded copies of books) as an alternative to printed books.

Newspapers

There are about 1,400 daily newspapers in the United States. Newspapers are evenly divided between morning and afternoon delivery, but the number of afternoon papers is declining. Papers that come out in the morning are growing in circulation, and papers that come out in the afternoon are shrinking. The number of weekly newspapers also is declining.

Advertising makes up more than two-thirds of the printed space in daily newspapers. Most newspapers have launched online editions to try to expand their reach, but overall newspaper industry income is shrinking, and many major newspaper organizations have had to cut staff and sell off some of their newspapers to try to stay profitable.

Magazines

According to the Magazine Publishers of America, about 20,000 magazines are published in the United States. To maintain and increase profits, magazines are raising their subscription and single-copy prices and fighting to sustain their advertising income. Many magazines have launched Internet editions, and a few magazines (such as *Slate*) are published exclusively online. Magazine subscriptions and newsstand sales are down. Magazine income is expected to decline over the next decade, primarily because advertising revenue is down substantially.

Recordings

People over age 25 are the most common buyers of recordings today because people under 25 download music from the Internet, both legally and illegally, and buy very few CDs. CDs and online downloads account for almost all recording industry income, with a small amount of money coming from music videos. Industry income has been declining sharply because new technologies allow consumers to share music over the Internet rather than pay for their music. The only growing revenue source for the recording companies among people under 25 is individual music downloads, sold through online sites such as iTunes. In 2010, Apple announced that iTunes had sold its 10 billionth download, becoming the nation's largest music retailer.

Radio

About 14,000 radio stations broadcast programming in the United States, evenly divided between AM and FM stations. About 2,900 radio stations are public stations, most of them FM. Satellite radio, such as Sirius XM, generates revenue through subscriptions, offering an almost unlimited variety of music and program choices without commercials. As a result, over-the-air broadcast radio revenue from commercials is declining because the price of a commercial is based on the size of the audience, which is getting smaller. To expand their audience, more than 6,000 traditional radio stations also distribute their programs online. Pandora is the most successful online radio station, available exclusively on the Internet.

Movies

About 40,000 theater screens exist in the United States. The major and independent studios combined make about 600 pictures a year. The industry is collecting more money because of higher ticket prices, but more people watch movies at home and online than in theaters, so the number of movie theaters is declining. Fewer people are buying DVDs and instead are getting movies through Redbox and streaming through Netflix. The only increases in income to the U.S. movie industry have been from overseas movie sales, movie downloads and the introduction of 3-D movies. Overall movie industry income began declining in 2005, and that trend continues so the movie industry continues to suffer losses.

Television

About 1,700 television stations operate in the United States. One out of four stations is a public station. Many stations are affiliated with a major network—NBC, CBS, ABC or Fox—although a few stations, called *independents*, are not affiliated with any network. More than 90 percent of the homes in the United States are wired for cable or satellite delivery. To differentiate cable and satellite TV from network television, cable and satellite television services are now lumped together in one category, called ***subscription television***.

TV network income is declining while income to cable operators and satellite companies for subscription services is increasing, so all the television networks also have invested heavily in subscription TV programming. The nation's largest cable operator, Comcast Corp., also owns the E! Entertainment cable network. In 2008, AT&T began offering subscription television services using fiber cable through its U-verse system. Total television industry revenue—including cable, satellite and fiber delivery—is expected to grow steadily in the next decade.

The Internet

The newest media industry also is growing the fastest. About 79 percent of all U.S. consumers are online, and the amount of money spent for Internet advertising increased from $8 billion in the year 2000 to $26 billion in 2010. Internet media have become a new mass medium as well as an integrated delivery system for traditional print, audio, and video and interactive media (such as video games). The Internet also offers access to many other consumer services, such as shopping and social networking, and a place for businesses to sell their products using advertising and product promotion.

Three Key Concepts to Remember

The mass media are key institutions in our society. They affect our culture, our buying habits and our politics. They are affected in turn by changes in our beliefs, tastes, interests and behavior. Three important concepts about the mass media can help organize your thinking about mass media and their impact on American society:

Subscription Television A new term used to describe consumer services delivered by cable and satellite program delivery.

ChinaFotoPress/Getty Images

American mass media are very popular overseas, representing substantial income potential for U.S. media companies. Recording artist Usher performs at a concert in Beijing, China, on July 11, 2010.

1. The mass media are profit-centered businesses.
2. Technological developments change the way mass media are delivered and consumed.
3. Mass media both reflect and affect politics, society and culture.

Mass Media Are Profit-Centered Businesses

What you see, read and hear in the mass media may tease, entertain, inform, persuade, provoke and even perplex you. But to understand the American mass media, the first concept to grasp is that the central force driving the media business in America is the desire to make money. American media are businesses, vast businesses.

The products of these businesses are information and entertainment that depend on attracting an audience of media consumers to generate income. Of course, other motives shape the media in America: the desire to fulfill the public's need for information, to influence the country's governance, to disseminate the country's culture, to offer entertainment and to provide an outlet for artistic expression. But American media are, above all, profit-centered.

To understand the mass media industries, it is essential to understand who owns these important channels of communication. In the United States, all media are privately owned except the Public Broadcasting Service (PBS) and National Public Radio (NPR), which survive on government support, private donations and minimal corporate sponsorship. The annual budget for all of public broadcasting (PBS and NPR combined) is less than 2 percent of the amount advertisers pay every year to support America's commercial media.

In some media industries, the same number of companies control ownership today as in the 1950s. There are five major movie studios today, for example, compared to the same number of major studios in the 1940s. The number of broadcast stations and the number of magazines has increased since the 1940s, but the number of newspapers, magazines and recording companies has declined.

Overall, however, American media ownership has been contracting rather than expanding. This is because large companies are buying small companies. The trend is for media companies to cluster together into big groups, which means that a small number of companies now control many aspects of the media business. This trend, called ***concentration of ownership***, takes four different forms: chains, broadcast networks, conglomerates and vertical integration.

CHAINS. Benjamin Franklin established America's first newspaper chain in the 1700s, when he was publishing his own newspaper, the *Pennsylvania Gazette*, as well as sponsoring one-third of the cost of publishing the *South Carolina Gazette*. (He also collected one-third of the *South Carolina Gazette*'s profits.) William Randolph Hearst expanded this tradition in the 1930s. At their peak, Hearst newspapers accounted for nearly 14 percent of total national daily newspaper sales and 25 percent of Sunday sales. Today's U.S. newspaper chain giant is Gannett Co., with 83 daily newspapers, including *USA Today*. The word *chain* is used to describe a company that owns several newspapers.

Concentration of Ownership The current trend of large companies buying smaller companies so that fewer companies own more types of media businesses.

BROADCAST NETWORKS. A broadcast network is a collection of radio or television stations that offers programs during designated program times. Unlike newspaper ownership (which is not regulated by the government), the Federal Communications Commission (***FCC***) regulates broadcast station ownership and operations. The FCC is a government regulatory body whose members are appointed by the president.

The four major TV networks are ABC (American Broadcasting Co.), NBC (National Broadcasting Co.), CBS (originally the Columbia Broadcasting System) and Fox. NBC, the oldest network, was founded in the 1920s. NBC and the two other original networks (CBS and ABC) first were established to deliver radio programming across the country and continued the network concept when television was invented. Fox is the youngest major network, founded in 1986, and was created to deliver only television programming.

NBC Television/Getty Images

NBC's Chet Huntley (left) and David Brinkley were the first national TV network newscast team, presenting the news every weekday night on the Huntley-Brinkley Report. In 1968, Huntley-Brinkley reported the final results of the presidential election, won by Richard Nixon (note the vote percentages displayed behind the news desk).

Time Warner Inc. and Viacom Inc. each launched a TV network in 1996—WB (Warner Bros.) and UPN (United Paramount Network)—but neither of the new networks ever found a large audience.

Broadcast networks can have as many ***affiliates*** as they want. Affiliates are stations that use network programming but are owned by companies other than the networks. No network, however, can have two affiliates in the same geographic broadcast area, due to government regulation of network affiliation.

In 2006, the TV networks announced they would offer shows on demand for downloading. Apple and Disney agreed to make series programming available on video iPods. One month later, CBS and NBC announced they planned to offer series programs on demand for 99 cents an episode through Comcast and DirecTV. Today broadcast network programming also is available on all mobile media, such as cell phones and iPads. To generate revenue, the broadcast networks today take the programming to their viewers instead of waiting for viewers to come to them.

CONGLOMERATES. When you watch a Universal Pictures film, you might not realize that General Electric Co. owns a 49 percent interest in NBC Universal, which produces movies through Universal Pictures. In 2010, General Electric, which had once owned NBC Universal outright, sold a 51 percent interest to the nation's largest cable company, Comcast. General Electric is a ***conglomerate***—a company that owns media companies as well as other businesses that are unrelated to the media business, such as GE's financial services and appliance manufacturing businesses. Media properties are attractive investments, but some conglomerate owners are unfamiliar with the idiosyncrasies of the media industries. Conglomerates often struggle to make the media companies profitable after acquiring them, which is one of the reasons GE sold its majority interest to Comcast in 2010.

VERTICAL INTEGRATION. The most widespread trend among today's media companies is ***vertical integration***—where one company controls several related aspects of the media business at once, with each part of the company helping the others. Many media companies own more than one type of media property: newspapers, magazines, radio and TV stations, for example.

Gannett, which owns the nation's largest chain of newspapers, also owns television and radio stations, so Gannett is a chain that is also vertically integrated. The media

FCC Federal Communications Commission.

Affiliates Stations that use network programming but are owned by companies other than the networks.

Conglomerates Companies that own media companies as well as businesses that are unrelated to the media business.

Vertical Integration An attempt by one company to simultaneously control several related aspects of the media business.

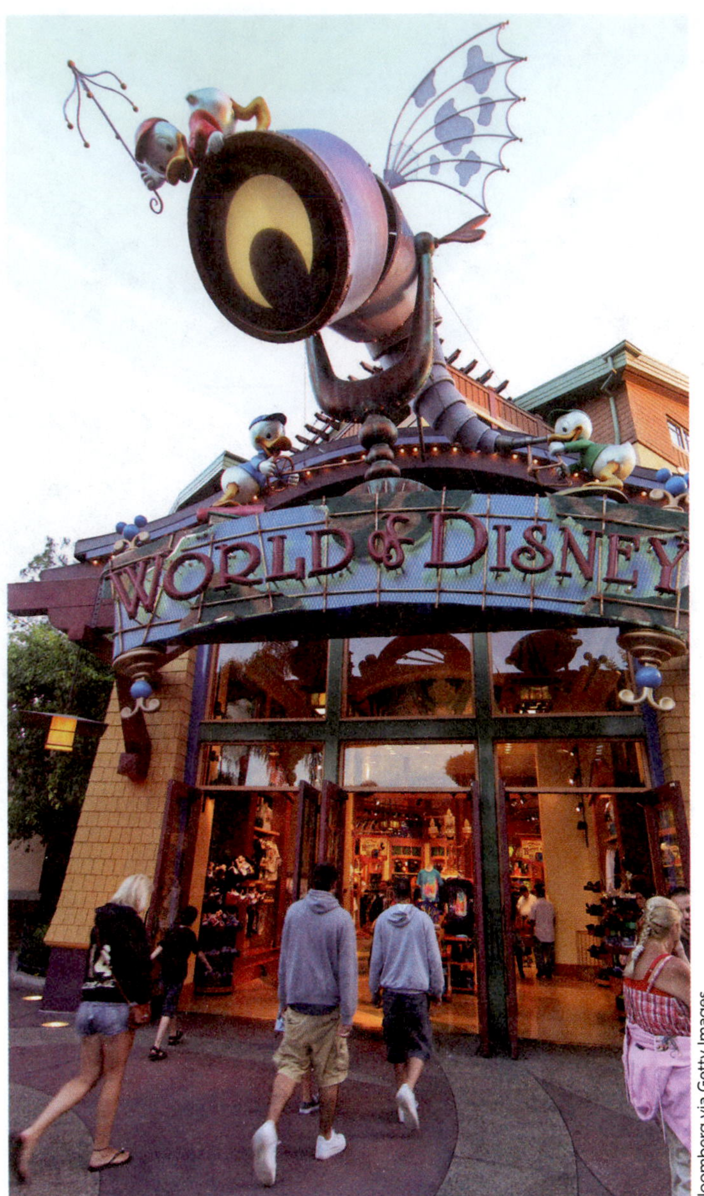

Bloomberg via Getty Images

The Walt Disney Company is a vertically integrated media corporation—a company that owns several different types of media businesses, with each part of the company contributing to the others. Shoppers enter a store at the Disneyland amusement park in Anaheim, Calif. Disney regularly markets characters in its movies as toys for sale in its stores and attractions at its amusement parks—a very successful example of vertical integration.

Convergence The melding of the communications, computer and electronics industries. Also used to describe the economic alignment of the various media companies with each other to take advantage of technological advancements.

company Viacom owns MTV, Comedy Central, Nickelodeon and Black Entertainment Television (BET). The Walt Disney Co. owns Disneyland amusement parks, Walt Disney Motion Pictures Group, the ABC TV network, the ESPN cable network and *ESPN: The Magazine*. Time Warner owns Warner Bros. Pictures, HBO, Turner Broadcasting, CNN, TNT, TBS, *Sports Illustrated*, SI.com and the Cartoon Network.

Competition and Convergence Dominate

To describe the financial status of today's media industries is to talk about intense competition. Media companies are buying and selling each other in unprecedented numbers and forming media groups to position themselves in the marketplace to maintain and increase their income. Since 1986, all three original TV networks (NBC, CBS and ABC) have been sold to new owners—sometimes more than once—making each of the three original networks smaller parts of giant publicly owned media companies. Fox Broadcasting Co. is a part of the larger international media company, Rupert Murdoch's News Corp., which also owns *The Wall Street Journal*, TV stations, magazines, and Twentieth Century Fox Film Corp. Since shares in most of today's media companies are publicly traded, they face heavy pressure to deliver hefty profits to their shareholders.

Media companies today also are driven by media ***convergence***. The word *convergence* describes two developments taking place simultaneously. First, it means the melding of the communications, computer and electronics industries because of advances in digital technology. Second, *convergence* also means the economic alignment of different types of media companies with each other to make sure they can offer the variety of services that technical advancements demand.

The people who manage U.S. media companies today want to make money. As in all industries, there are people who want to make money quickly and people who take the long-term view about profits, but certainly none of them wants to lose money. One way to expand a company to take advantage of technological and economic convergence is to acquire an already established business that's successful. Such media acquisitions have skyrocketed for two reasons—public ownership and deregulation.

PUBLIC OWNERSHIP. Most media companies today are publicly traded, which means their stock is sold on one of the nation's stock exchanges. This makes acquisitions relatively easy. A media company that wants to buy another publicly owned company can buy that company's stock when the stock becomes available.

The open availability of stock in these public companies means any company or individual with enough money can invest in the American media industries, which is exactly how the Australian Rupert Murdoch, owner of Fox Broadcasting, joined the U.S. media business and was able to accumulate so many media companies in such a short time.

DEREGULATION. Beginning in 1980, the Federal Communications Commission gradually deregulated the broadcast media. ***Deregulation*** means the FCC withdrew many regulatory restrictions on broadcast media ownership. Before 1980, for example, the FCC allowed a broadcast company to own only five TV stations, five AM radio stations and five FM radio stations. Companies also were required to hold onto a station for three years before the owners could sell it.

The post-1980 FCC eliminated the three-year rule and raised the number of broadcast holdings allowed for one owner. Today, there are very few FCC restrictions on broadcast media ownership.

Why Media Properties Converge

Ownership turnover is highest in the newspaper and broadcast industries. Six factors have affected the economic alignment of these properties:

1. Media properties can be attractive investments. Many broadcast companies have historically earned profits of 10 percent a year, for example, which is about double the average amount that a U.S. manufacturing company earns.

2. Newspapers and broadcast stations are scarce commodities. Because the number of newspapers has been declining and the government regulates the number of broadcast stations that are allowed to operate, a limited number of established media outlets are available. As with all limited commodities, this makes them attractive investments.

3. Newspapers and broadcast stations have gone through a cycle of family ownership. If the heirs to the founders of the business are not interested in joining the company, the only way for them to collect their inheritance is to sell the newspaper, and the only companies with enough money to buy individual media businesses are large corporations and investment companies.

4. Newspapers and broadcast stations are easier businesses to buy than to create. Because these businesses require huge investments in equipment and people, they are expensive to start up. In broadcasting, the major factor that encouraged ownership changes, beginning in the 1980s, was deregulation. This allowed investors who had never been in the broadcast business before to enter the industry, using bank loans to pay for most of their investment. Some new owners of broadcast media companies see these companies the way they would look at any business—hoping to invest the minimum amount necessary. They hold onto the property until the market is favorable, planning to sell at a huge profit.

5. In the 1990s, the introduction of new technologies, especially the Internet, changed the economics of all the media industries. Each industry had to adapt to the Internet quickly, and the fastest way to gain Internet expertise was to buy a company or to invest in a company that already had created an Internet presence or a successful Internet product.

6. The economic downturn that began in 2007 hit the newspaper business especially hard. Heavily dependent on real estate advertising and classifieds and challenged by the dynamics of the Internet, many publicly owned newspaper companies began losing money at an unprecedented rate. This fall in profits drove down their stock prices to new lows, which made them vulnerable to takeovers and buyouts as the companies struggled to survive. Some newspaper companies, such as the Tribune Company (which publishes the *Chicago Tribune* and the *Los Angeles Times*), have filed for bankruptcy protection.

Supporters of concentrated ownership and convergence say a large company can offer advantages that a small company could never afford—training for the employees, higher wages and better working conditions.

The major arguments against the concentration and convergence of group ownership are that concentration of so much power limits the diversity of opinion and the quality of ideas available to the public and reduces what scholars call ***message pluralism***. Ben H. Bagdikian, dean emeritus, Graduate School of Journalism at the University of California, Berkeley, describes how the loss of message pluralism can affect every aspect of communication:

> It has always been assumed that a newspaper article might be expanded to a magazine article which could become the basis for a hardcover book, which, in turn, could be a paperback, and then, perhaps a TV series and finally, a movie. At each step of change an author and other enterprises could compete for entry into the array of channels for reaching the public mind and pocketbook. But today several media giants own these

Deregulation Government action that reduces government restrictions on the business operations of an industry.

Message Pluralism The availability to an audience of a variety of information and entertainment sources.

arrays, not only closing off entry points for competition in different media, but influencing the choice of entry at the start.

Today, ownership concentration is a continuing trend in the media business.

Advertisers and Consumers Pay the Bills

Most of the $276 billion annual income the American mass media industries collect comes from advertising. Advertising directly supports newspapers, radio and television. Subscribers actually pay only a small part of the cost of producing a newspaper. Advertisers pay the biggest portion. Magazines receive more than half their income from advertising and the other portion from subscriptions. Income for movies, recordings and books, of course, comes primarily from direct purchases and ticket sales.

This means that most of the information and entertainment you receive from the Internet, TV, radio, newspapers and magazines in America is paid for by people who want to sell you products. You support the media industries *indirectly* by buying the products that advertisers sell. General Motors Corp. spends $3 billion a year on advertising. Verizon Communications Inc. spends $800 million a year just on print advertising. Multiply the spending for all this advertising for all media, and you can understand how easily American media industries accumulate $276 billion a year.

You also pay for the media *directly* when you buy a book or a video game or go to a movie. This money buys equipment, underwrites company research and expansion, and pays stock dividends. Advertisers and consumers are the financial foundation for American media industries because different audiences provide a variety of markets for consumer products.

Technology Changes Mass Media Delivery and Consumption

The channels of communication have changed dramatically over the centuries, but the idea that a society will pay to stay informed and entertained is not new. In Imperial Rome, people who wanted to find out what was going on paid professional speakers a coin (a *gazet*) for the privilege of listening to the speaker announce the day's events. Many early newspapers were called *gazettes* to reflect this heritage.

The history of mass communication technology involves three information communications revolutions: phonetic writing, printing and computer technology. (See Time-Frame, p. 4).

Phonetic Writing: The First Information Communications Revolution

Early attempts at written communication began modestly with ***pictographs***. A pictograph is a symbol of an object that is used to convey an idea. If you have ever drawn a heart with an arrow through it, you understand what a pictograph is. The Sumerians of Mesopotamia carved the first known pictographs in stone in about 3500 B.C.

The stone in which these early pictographic messages were carved served as a medium—a device to transmit messages. Eventually, people imprinted messages in clay and then they stored these clay tablets in a primitive version of today's library. These messages weren't very portable, however. Heavy clay tablets don't slip easily into someone's pocket.

In about 2500 B.C., the Egyptians invented papyrus, a type of paper made from a grass-like plant called sedge, which was easier to write on, but people still communicated using pictographs.

Pictographs as a method of communication developed into ***phonetic writing*** in about 1000 B.C. when people began to use symbols to represent sounds. Instead of drawing a picture of a dog to convey the idea of a dog, scholars represented the sounds d-o-g with phonetic writing. The invention of phonetic writing has been called *the first information communications revolution*. "After being stored in written form, *information could now reach a new kind of audience, remote from the source and uncontrolled by it*," writes media scholar Anthony Smith. "Writing transformed knowledge into information."

About 500 years later, the Greek philosopher Socrates anticipated the changes that widespread literacy would bring. He argued that knowledge should remain among the privileged classes. Writing threatened the exclusive use of information, he said. "Once a thing is put in writing, the composition, whatever it may be, drifts all over the place, getting into the hands not only of those who understand it, but equally of those who have no business with it."

In about 200 B.C., the Greeks perfected parchment, made from goat and sheepskins. Parchment was an even better medium on which to write. By about A.D. 100, before

Pictograph A symbol of an object that is used to convey an idea.

Phonetic Writing The use of symbols to represent sounds.

the use of parchment spread throughout Europe, the Chinese had invented paper, which was much cheaper to produce than parchment. Europeans didn't start to use paper until more than a thousand years later, in about A.D. 1300. The discovery of parchment and then paper meant that storing information became cheaper and easier.

As Socrates predicted, when more people learned to write, wider communication became possible because people in many different societies could share information among themselves and with people in other parts of the world. But scholars still had to painstakingly copy the information they wanted to keep or pay a scribe to copy for them. In the 14th century, for example, the library of the Italian poet Petrarch contained more than 100 manuscripts that he himself had copied individually.

Universitatsbibliothek, Gottingen, Germany/Bildarchiv Steffens/The Bridgeman Art Library

The Gutenberg Bible, published by Johannes Gutenberg in Germany in 1455, was the first book printed using movable type. Printing is the second communications revolution.

In Petrarch's day, literate people were either monks or members of the privileged classes. Wealthy people could afford tutoring, and they also could afford to buy the handwritten manuscripts copied by the monks. Knowledge—and the power it brings—belonged to an elite group of people.

Printing: The Second Information Communications Revolution

As societies grew more literate, the demand for manuscripts flourished, but a scribe could produce only one copy at a time. What has been called *the second information communications revolution* began in Germany in 1455, when Johannes Gutenberg printed a Bible on a press that used movable type.

More than 200 years before Gutenberg, the Chinese had invented a printing press that used wood type, and the Chinese also are credited with perfecting a copper press in 1445. But Gutenberg's innovation was to line up individual metal letters that he could ink and then press onto paper to produce copies. Unlike the wood or copper presses, the metal letters could be reused to produce new pages of text, which made the process much cheaper.

The Gutenberg Bible, a duplicate of the Latin original, is considered the first book printed by movable type (47 copies still survive today, 555 years later). As other countries adopted Gutenberg's press, the price for Bibles plummeted. In 1470, the cost of a French, mechanically printed Bible was one-fifth the cost of a hand-printed Bible.

The second information communications revolution—printing—meant that *knowledge, which had belonged to the privileged few, would one day be available to everyone.* The key development of printing was one of the essential conditions for the rise of modern governments, as well as an important element of scientific and technological progress.

Before the Gutenberg press, a scholar who wanted special information had to travel to the place where it was kept. But once information could be duplicated easily, it could travel to people beyond the society that created it. The use of paper instead of the scribes' bulky parchment also meant that books could be stacked end to end. *For the first time, knowledge was portable and storable.*

Libraries now could store vast amounts of information in a small space. And because people could easily carry these smaller, lighter books, all different kinds of people in many different cities could read classical works simultaneously. Another benefit of the development of printing was that societies could more easily keep information to share with future generations. *Knowledge now was accessible to many; knowledge no longer belonged to just the chosen few.*

This effort to communicate—first through spoken messages, then through pictographs, then through the written word and finally through printed words—demonstrates people's innate desire to share information with one another.

Trago/FilmMagic/Getty Images

The introduction of digital delivery represents the third information communications revolution and affects all aspects of American politics, society and culture. In Paris, France, on July 25, 2010, actor Jackie Chan uses a fan's cell phone to take a picture with the crowd, using mobile digital technology.

Storability, portability and accessibility of information are essential to today's concept of mass communication. By definition, *mass communication is information that is available to a large audience quickly.*

Computer Technology: The Third Information Communications Revolution

Today's age of communication has been called the *third information communications revolution* because computers have become the electronic storehouses and transmitters of vast amounts of information that previously relied on the written word.

Computer technology, which processes and transmits information much more efficiently than mechanical devices, is driving the majority of changes affecting today's media. This has become possible with the development of digital computers, beginning around 1950. Digital delivery means that changes in today's media industries happen much faster than in the past. Satellite broadcasts, digital recordings and the international computer network called the Internet are just three examples of the third information communications revolution.

Although each medium has its own history and economic structure, today all of the media industries compete for consumers' attention. Digital technology is transforming the media business more than we can foresee—enabling faster transmission of more information to more people than ever before.

Media Take Advantage of Digital Delivery

The economics of the communications industries makes digital delivery very important. All the industries involved in building and maintaining this interconnected network—broadcast, cable, telephone, computer, software, satellite and the consumer electronics industries—want a piece of the estimated $1 trillion in income that digital delivery represents.

Leaders of the media industries in the United States can be the central driving force in this network because many Americans already have most of the tools that such a system needs and many of the companies that are developing digital products—such as Apple and Microsoft—are based in the United States.

Because the United States already contributes so many of the digital environment's necessary elements, it has become logical—and very profitable—for the media industries in this country to drive the convergence technology to package and deliver information worldwide.

One-Way Versus Two-Way Communication

The classic model of mass communication (see **Illustration 1.3** on page 9) describes a process that begins with a *sender* (or source), who puts a *message* on a *channel* (a medium). The channel then delivers the message to the *receiver*. This is the equivalent of a one-way road—sender to receiver.

Digital delivery begins in the same way. The *channel* carries information and entertainment (*messages*) from many different sources (*senders*) to many different people (*receivers*). The messages that return from the receiver to the sender are called *feedback*. In the digital environment, messages and feedback can occur instantaneously because the sender and the receiver can communicate with each other almost simultaneously. This makes digital systems ***interactive***.

To take advantage of this interactivity, today's delivery system is transforming from a communications system that works like an ordinary television (sending messages and programming one way from the sender to the receiver) into a two-way digital system that can send and receive messages simultaneously and that works more like a combination television, telephone and computer.

dePIXion studios, inc./Mike Keefe/Intoon

Dumb Versus *Smart* Communication

The television set is a "dumb" appliance; it can only deliver programming. You can change the channel to receive different programs, but you can't talk back to the people who send the programming to your television set to tell them when you'd like to see a particular program. You can't watch something when you want to watch it, unless you remember beforehand to record the program. You also can't add anything to the programs on your TV, such as your personal commentary about a football game or a bad movie. This type of mass communication—in which the programs are sent to you on an established schedule and you are a passive receiver (a couch potato) for the program—is *one-way*.

As communications devices, however, telephones are smarter. When you talk on the telephone, the person on the other end of the conversation can listen to you and talk back right away (and, in the case of a teleconference, this can involve several people at the same time). This makes telephone communication interactive, giving you the ability to talk back—to receive as well as to transmit messages. Telephone communications are *two-way*. (See **Media/ Impact: Audience**, "There's Little Privacy in a Digital World," p. 20.)

To communicate rapidly, telephone communication uses a system of digitized information. When you talk, the telephone system uses electronic signals to transform your voice into a series of digits—ones and zeroes—and then reassembles these digits into an exact reproduction of your voice on the other end of the line. This method of storing and transmitting data is called ***digital communication***.

Like telephone communications, computers also operate using digitized information and are interactive. Written words, audio and video are translated and stored as *bits*. These bits can easily be transmitted, using two-way communication. This is the reason that someone can, for instance, connect to the Internet on a computer and receive and send information. To communicate via the Internet, a computer uses a *modem* to connect to a telephone line or a cellular signal, making two-way communication possible.

And, unlike television and telephones, computers can store digital information for future use. This ability to store information makes the computer different from broadcast, cable, telephone and satellite communications. "In the information economy, the best opportunities stem from the exponential rise in the power of computers and computer networks," according to futurist George Gilder.

How Today's Communications Network Operates

Today's communications network combines many different elements from existing media industries. The broadcast industry produces content and delivers one-way communication by antenna and satellite; the cable industry delivers

Interactive A message system that allows senders and receivers to communicate simultaneously.

Digital Communication Data in a form that can be transmitted and received electronically.

Media/Impact AUDIENCE

There's Little Privacy in a Digital World

By David Sarno

During his two-hour morning bike ride, Eric Hartman doesn't pay much attention to his iPhone.

But the iPhone is paying attention to him.

As he traverses the 30-mile circuit around Seal Beach, Hartman's iPhone knows precisely where he is at every moment, and keeps a record of his whereabouts. That data is beamed to Apple Inc. multiple times each day, whether Hartman is using his phone to take pictures, search for gas stations or check the weather.

And it's not just the iPhone that's keeping track.

Buying milk at Ralphs? Playing *World of Warcraft*? Texting dinner plans to friends? Watching an episode of *Glee*? It's all recorded.

Over the course of a day, hundreds of digital traces pile up, each offering more insight into the way Hartman and his family live.

For this kind of surveillance, no fancy spy gadgets are needed. The technological instruments that capture details of the Hartmans' lives are the ones they use most often: their computers, smartphones and TV systems.

The Hartmans' digital devices, like those of millions of other U.S. families, feed into a massive river of personal data that flows back to the servers of technology companies, where it is often kept indefinitely. The data are sifted for behavior patterns that can be of great value to marketers eager to zoom in on the consumers who are most likely to buy their products.

Eric Hartman's iPhone, perhaps the best-known mobile device of all, has been a lightning rod for privacy concerns.

Lawrence K. Ho, *Los Angeles Times*/October 2, 2011

Active Internet users, like the Hartman family—parents Eric and Nia, daughter Emily and sons Spencer and Evan—may unknowingly give up their privacy while providing a rich source of marketing data for advertisers every time they go online.

Data collection can also pop up in surprising places.

When Evan Hartman, 11, logs into *World of Warcraft*, a popular online video game played by millions, Blizzard, the game's maker, records his location, what kind of computer he's using and information about his playing behavior.

When Eric Hartman and his wife, Nia, go grocery shopping, he uses an iPhone application called CardStar that stores digital versions of loyalty cards for a dozen retail stores.

"We've found grocery retail to be a rich and fertile vein," said Matt Keylock, an executive at Dunnhumby, which processes data for dozens of retail chains worldwide, including Home Depot, Best Buy and Ralphs owner Kroger Co.

When Spencer Hartman, 16, . . . clicks on friends' profiles or photographs, or leaves messages on their walls, he may forget what and who he clicked on that day, but Facebook, one of the largest data harvesters in the world, does not.

"By watching transactions and clicks we have a massive telescope into human behavior at a scale we've never had before," said Prabhakar Raghavan, the head of Yahoo! Labs.

David Sarno, "There's Little Privacy in a Digital World," Los Angeles Times*, October 1, 2011. Copyright © 2011,* Los Angeles Times*. Reprinted with Permission.*

Media/Impact
MONEY

Illustration 1.4

How the Communications Network Works

Today's communications network combines different elements of broadcast, cable, telephone, satellite, cellular and computer technology to create an international digital communications service.

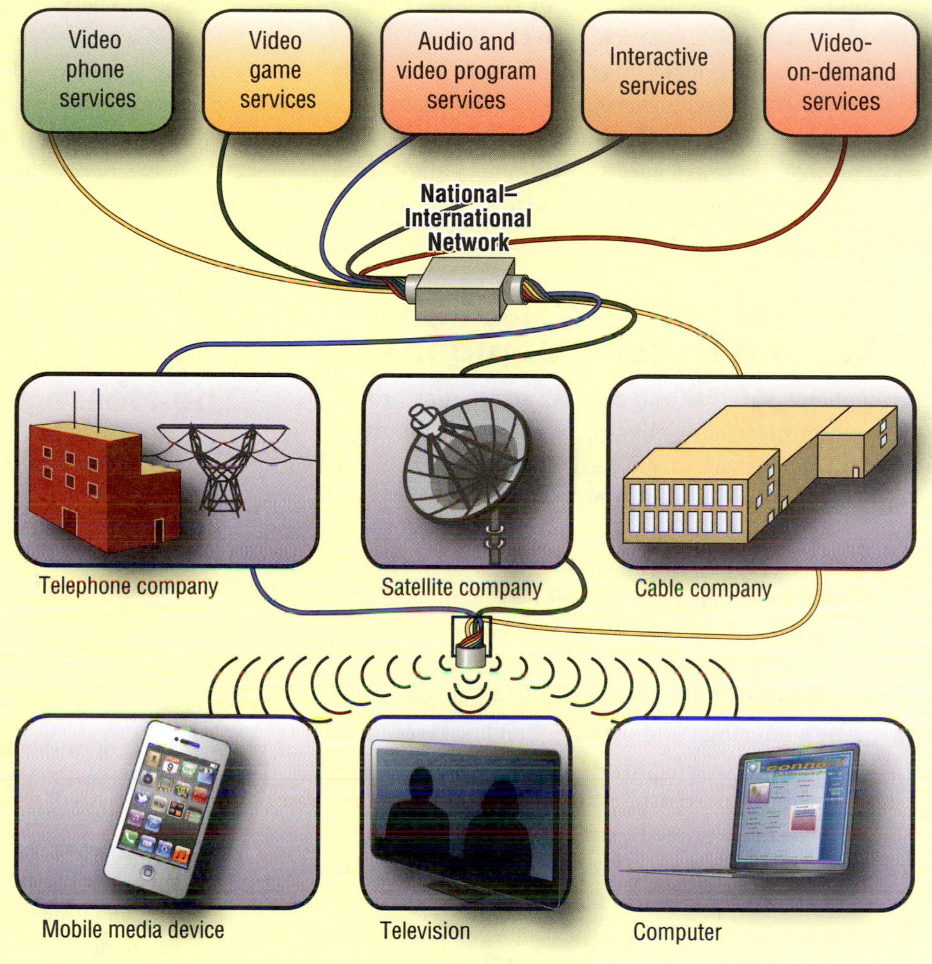

one-way communication and two-way communication by underground (or overhead) cable; the telephone companies deliver digital two-way communication using fiber, satellite and cellular technology; and the computer industry offers digital storage capability.

A digital communications network combines all these elements: content, two-way digital communication and digital storage. **Illustration 1.4** shows how this communications network operates.

The Receiver (You, the Subscriber)

A digital network begins with you, the receiver/subscriber. For example, you go online to check your ***e-mail***, then look around to decide which other services you want, such as

- First-run movie and music downloads
- TV soap opera and sitcom downloads, available and priced per episode
- Worldwide video news feeds, including access to overseas news channels in a variety of languages
- Newspaper and video services, offering a list of today's stories from newspapers and video outlets around the globe on topics you've pre-selected
- Sports, family, travel, shopping and music videos

E-mail Mail that is delivered electronically over the Internet.

- Internet video games and gambling sites
- Bulletin board discussion groups, social networks, blogs and video indexed by subject

You glance through the offerings of each service and make your choices. Your screen shows several windows simultaneously so you can use various services at the same time, each on a different screen. For example, you check your bank balance while you play poker online and check your e-mail messages while you watch overseas news headlines.

All these services, which you take for granted today, weren't available ten years ago. The Internet's digital communications network is what makes all these services possible.

The Channel (Cable, Telephone, Satellite and Cellular Companies)

Cable, telephone, satellite and cellular companies provide Internet communications delivery, acting as a conduit—gathering all the services from national and international networks. Some companies offer only specific services, or they package services together (local, national and international news services, for example), or they offer an unlimited menu of all the available services and let you choose what you want. Cable, telephone, satellite and cellular companies are competing today for consumers' Internet business.

You can choose the type of service you want based on each company's offerings and pricing. Some services are billed as pay-per-use (a $5 charge to view a first-run movie, for example) or per minute (to use a newspaper's archive for research, for example, billed to a credit card).

This international communications network and the satellite system to support it already are in place—long-distance carrier networks run by a communications company such as AT&T or a satellite service such as DirecTV or Dish Network. The ***Internet***, as an international web of computer networks, forms the backbone of this communications network, which is available to any consumer who has a screen and a cable, satellite, cellular or telephone connection to the system.

The Sender (Internet Service Providers)

Internet service providers (***ISPs***), such as America Online (AOL) and MSN, provide a way of organizing the information to help you find what you want. Today's broadcast networks, as well as cable and satellite channels, already have become video program services, offering a group of programs for a specific subscription fee. Telephone companies are also beginning to compete to deliver programs directly to consumers.

Program services are moving toward a different model, however, which eventually will make it possible for you to choose programs from NBC and ABC and not CBS, for example, or pick 10 channels from a list of available channels, rather than having to accept a large number of channels—many that you don't necessarily want to watch—packaged together as they are now. When the complete communications network is in place, the ISP will offer program ***bundles***, and you will be able to select the specific bundle you want.

Internet An international web of computer networks.

ISP Internet service provider.

Bundles A collection of programs and/or media services offered together for a set fee.

The Message (Content)

All text, audio and video that are digitized into bits are potential content for a digitized communications system. In a world of networked, rapid, digitized communications, *any* digitized textbook, novel, movie, magazine article, recording, video segment or news story, for example, qualifies as content.

Information and entertainment that already have been produced, stored and digitized form the basic content for this communications network. Companies that hold the copyrights on information and entertainment can quickly and easily market the content they already own as products, along with the ongoing information/entertainment they are producing, because they own the rights to their content and don't have to buy the rights from someone else.

Today, media companies that traditionally have produced content, such as newspaper publishers, book publishers, TV program producers and movie producers, are busy creating and buying more "inventory" for the online world. "Movie companies have been increasing production," says *The Wall Street Journal*, "because there is a general feeling that as 'content providers' they will be big winners."

Once information and entertainment products are digitized, they are available in many different formats. This is the reason a music video of Disney songs is available online as soon as—even before—Disney releases a new movie; a profile of a well-known musician, complete with video and sound, can be made available on the musician's Internet site during the musician's worldwide concert tour; and a publisher can assemble excerpts and photos from a new book, along with a video interview with the author, and make them available on the Internet to promote the book before it hits the bookstores. With convergence, the availability of digital content means all the mass media industries have become interdependent and interconnected.

Mass Media Both Reflect and Affect Politics, Society and Culture

The media industries provide information and entertainment, but media also can affect political, social and cultural institutions. Although the media actively influence society, they also mirror it, and scholars constantly strive to delineate the differences.

For example, when the advertising industry suddenly started using patriotic themes to market products after the U.S. military moved into Iraq in 2003, was the industry pandering to the public, or were advertisers proudly reflecting genuine American sentiment, or both? Did the spread of patriotic advertising themes silence those who disagreed with the government? What role did the mass media play in setting the political agenda? If you were a scholar studying the mass media, how would you view these developments?

This is an example of the difficulty scholars face when analyzing mass media's political, social and cultural effects. Early media studies analyzed each message in the belief that once a message was sent, everyone would receive and react to the message in the same way. Then studies proved that different people process messages differently—a phenomenon described as ***selective perception***. This occurs because everyone brings many variables—family background, interests and education, for example—to each message.

Complicating the study of mass media's political, social and cultural effects is the recent proliferation of media outlets. The multiplying sources for information and entertainment today mean that very few people share identical mass media environments. This makes it much more difficult for scholars to determine the specific or cumulative effects of mass media on the general population.

Still, scholars' attempts to describe mass media's political, social and cultural roles in society are important because, once identified, the effects can be observed. The questions should be posed so we do not become complacent about media in our lives, so we do not become immune to the possibility that our society may be cumulatively affected by media in ways we cannot yet identify.

"Marketers used to try their hardest to reach people at home, when they were watching TV or reading newspapers or magazines. But consumers' viewing and reading habits are so scattershot now that many advertisers say the best way to reach time-pressed consumers is to try to catch their eye at literally every turn," reports *The New York Times*.

Photo by John Moore/Getty Images

It is important to understand the role that mass media play in the political, social and cultural aspects of society. On May 24, 2010, mass media focused attention on British Petroleum CEO Tony Hayward, who responded to questions from reporters at Port Fourchon, La., after a massive oil spill caused by an accident on a BP oil rig in the Gulf of Mexico. Mass media both reflect and affect the society in which they operate.

According to the market research firm Yankelovich, a person living in a city 30 years ago saw up to 2,000 ad messages a day, compared with up to 5,000 today. According to *The New York Times*, about half the people surveyed by Yankelovich said they thought marketing and advertising today was "out of control."

Why You Should Understand Mass Media and Everyday Life

In the United States and other countries such as Japan and China that have encouraged technological advancements, communication changes are moving faster than ever before.

Selective Perception The concept that each person processes messages differently.

For the media industries, this means increasing costs to replace old equipment. For consumers, this means a confusing array of products that need to be replaced soon after you buy them—DVD players replacing VCRs, HDTV replacing conventional TVs and iPods replacing CD players, for example.

The development of communications technology directly affects the speed with which a society and culture evolve. A town with only one telephone or one radio may be impossible for people in the United States to imagine, but there still are many countries in which 10 families share a single telephone and people consider a television set to be a luxury.

By today's standards, the earliest communications obstacles seem unbelievably simple: how to transmit a single message to several people at the same time and how to share information inexpensively. Yet it has taken nearly 5,500 years to achieve the capability for instant communication that we enjoy today.

After you understand how each type of media business works, you can examine why people who work in the media make the business decisions they do and the effects these decisions have on the U.S. and the world economy. Once you have traced the history of mass media development, you can consider their present-day effects on you and on society as a whole.

With a better grasp of technology's role in the evolving mass media landscape, you can see how technological change affects the media business. Only then can you truly begin to analyze the *impact* of mass media on your everyday life.

Review, Analyze, Investigate

REVIEWING CHAPTER 1

Mass Media Are Everywhere You Are

- ✓ Adults spend more than half of their waking lives with the media.
- ✓ Some form of media touches your life every day—economically, socially and culturally.

Mass Communication Becomes Wireless

- ✓ Historically, to be connected to media meant that you had to be near an electrical outlet.
- ✓ Because of the development of digital communication, most of today's mass media is wireless.
- ✓ Electronic signals have replaced wires, freeing people up to stay connected no matter where or when they want to communicate.

How the Communication Process Works

- ✓ Communication is the act of sending ideas and attitudes from one person to another.
- ✓ *Intra*personal communication means communication within one person.
- ✓ *Inter*personal communication means communication between two people.
- ✓ Mass communication is communication from one person or group of persons through a transmitting device (a medium) to large audiences or markets.
- ✓ By definition, mass communication is information that is made available to a large audience quickly.

What Are the Mass Media Industries?

- ✓ There are eight mass media businesses: books, newspapers, magazines, recordings, radio, movies, television and the Internet.
- ✓ Books were the first mass medium.
- ✓ The Internet is the newest mass medium.

Three Key Concepts to Remember

- ✓ Mass media are profit-centered businesses.
- ✓ Technological developments change the way mass media are delivered and consumed.
- ✓ Mass media both reflect and affect politics, society and culture.

Mass Media Are Profit-Centered Businesses

- ✓ All U.S. media are privately owned except the Public Broadcasting Service and National Public Radio, which survive on government support and private donations.
- ✓ Overall, American mass media ownership has been contracting rather than expanding, with fewer companies owning more aspects of the media business. This trend is called *concentration of ownership*.
- ✓ Concentration of ownership takes four forms: chains, broadcast networks, conglomerates and vertical integration.

- ✓ The mass media industries—books, newspapers, magazines, recordings, radio, movies, television and the Internet—earn about $276 billion a year.
- ✓ Above all, the major goal of the American mass media is to make money. Except for National Public Radio and the Public Broadcasting Service, all U.S. media operate primarily as profit-centered businesses.

Competition and Convergence Dominate

- ✓ Media acquisitions in the United States have skyrocketed because most conglomerates today are publicly traded companies and because, beginning in 1980, the federal government deregulated the broadcast industry.
- ✓ The economic downturn that began in 2007 made publicly owned newspapers especially vulnerable to takeovers and acquisitions.
- ✓ The trend of mergers and acquisitions is expected to continue as changing technology expands the global market for media products.

Why Media Properties Converge

- ✓ U.S. media industries continue to prosper, but the share of profits is shifting among the different types of media industries.
- ✓ Supporters of concentrated ownership and convergence say a large company offers advantages that a small company can never afford; critics say concentrated ownership and convergence interfere with message pluralism.

Advertisers and Consumers Pay the Bills

- ✓ Most of the income the mass media industries collect comes from advertising.
- ✓ People who want to sell you products pay for most of the information and entertainment you receive through the American mass media.
- ✓ Consumers support the media indirectly by buying the products that advertisers sell.

Technology Changes Mass Media Delivery and Consumption

- ✓ The invention of phonetic writing in 1000 B.C. was considered the *first information communications revolution*.
- ✓ The invention of movable type in 1455 marked the *second information communications revolution*.
- ✓ The invention of digital computers in 1951 ushered in the *third information communications revolution*.
- ✓ The new world of mass media uses wireless communications technology, an intricate webbed network of many different types of communications systems.
- ✓ The development of communications technology directly affects the speed with which a society evolves.
- ✓ Storability, portability and accessibility of information are essential to today's concept of mass communication.

Media Take Advantage of Digital Delivery

- ✓ Today's information network uses broadcast, telephone, cable, satellite and computer technology.
- ✓ The traditional delivery system for information and entertainment is primarily a one-way system.
- ✓ The ability to talk back—to receive as well as transmit messages—makes the telephone interactive.
- ✓ Today's communications network is a two-way, interactive system.

How Today's Communications Network Operates

- ✓ The communications network needs content, two-way digital communication and digital storage.
- ✓ Cable companies, satellite services, telephone and cellular companies deliver services on the new communications network.
- ✓ Many Americans already have all the tools that such a digital communications system needs—television, telephone, cellular, cable and satellite services and computers.
- ✓ Information and entertainment that already have been produced, stored and digitized have become the first content on the communications network.
- ✓ Many motives shape the American mass media, including the desire to fulfill the public's need for information, to influence the country's governance, to disseminate the country's culture, to offer entertainment and to provide an outlet for creative expression.
- ✓ Different media expand and contract in the marketplace to respond to the audience.

Mass Media Both Reflect and Affect Politics, Society and Culture

- ✓ The media are political, social and cultural institutions that both reflect and affect the society in which they operate.
- ✓ Multiplying sources of information and entertainment mean that, today, very few people share identical mass media environments.

Why You Should Understand Mass Media and Everyday Life

- ✓ In the United States and other countries such as Japan and China that have encouraged technological advancements, communication changes are moving faster than ever before.
- ✓ For the media industries, this means increasing costs to replace old equipment. For consumers, this means a

confusing array of products that need to be replaced soon after you buy them.

✓ The development of communications technology directly affects the speed with which a society and culture evolve.

✓ It has taken nearly 5,500 years to achieve the capability for instant communication that we enjoy today.

KEY TERMS

These terms are defined in the margins throughout this chapter and appear in alphabetical order with definitions in the Glossary, which begins on page 383.

Affiliates 13
Bundles 22
Concentration of Ownership 12
Conglomerates 13
Convergence 14
Deregulation 15
Digital Communication 19
E-mail 21
FCC 13
Feedback 8
Interactive 19
Internet 22
ISP 22
Mass Communication 8
Mass Media Industries 9
Media 8
Medium 8
Message Pluralism 15
Noise 8
Phonetic Writing 16
Pictograph 16
Selective Perception 23
Subscription Television 11
Vertical Integration 13
Wi-Fi 7

CRITICAL QUESTIONS

1. Explain the differences between one-way and two-way communication, and explain why two-way communication is important for the new communications network.
2. Give three examples of how consumers pay both directly and indirectly for mass media in America.
3. Identify the three communications revolutions and discuss how each one drastically changed the world's mass media.
4. Summarize the advantages and disadvantages of the concentration of ownership in today's mass media business.
5. In traditional media, advertising aimed at consumers pays for delivery of entertainment and information. How has advertising's role changed on the digital communications network?

WORKING THE WEB

This list includes both sites mentioned in the chapter and others to give you greater insight into mass media and everyday life.

CBS Corporation
http://www.cbscorporation.com

CBS Corp. has operations in virtually every field of media and entertainment. The company consists of mass media brands including CBS Television Network, CBS Radio, Showtime, Simon & Schuster publishers, The CW (a joint venture with Warner Bros. Entertainment) and CBS Outdoor (out-of-home advertising). CBS Corp. also owns CBS Outernet (in-store media networks to grocery retailers) and CNET, which is a part of CBS Interactive (its digital division).

Gannett Company, Inc. (owner of *USA Today*)
http://www.gannett.com

The United States' largest newspaper chain, Gannett publishes 83 daily newspapers, including *USA Today,* and 650 magazines. The Web site usatoday.com is one of the most popular news sites on the Web. The company operates 23 U.S. television stations and has made strategic investments and partnerships in online advertising and marketing, including careerbuilder.com, the #1 employment site on the net. Gannett's broadcasting group also delivers news and advertising to specific audiences through video screens in office building elevators and select hotels in North America.

General Electric
http://www.ge.com

This conglomerate has many businesses that include financial, industrial and health care operations in addition to its media and entertainment division. GE began in the 19th century with Thomas Edison's invention of the light bulb and continues to innovate by developing more energy-efficient products and services worldwide. GE has a 49 percent ownership share in NBC Universal.

News Corporation

http://www.newscorp.com

News Corp. is Rupert Murdoch's diversified media empire and home of the various Fox media. Its operations include filmed entertainment, television, cable, satellite TV, magazines, newspapers and books. The company began in Australia and has many media outlets there and in Europe and Asia, as well as in the United States. In 2007 News Corp. bought *The Wall Street Journal*.

Sony Corporation of America

http://www.sony.com

This U.S. subsidiary of Sony Corp. is based in New York City. Its parent company, based in Tokyo, Japan, is a leading manufacturer of audio, video, communications and information technology. In the United States, Sony's principal businesses include Sony Electronics, Sony Pictures and a 50 percent interest in Sony BMG Music Entertainment (50 percent is owned by Bertelsmann AG).

Time Warner Inc.

http://www.timewarner.com

A leading media and entertainment company, Time Warner Inc.'s businesses include cable and broadcast television; interactive services; filmed entertainment; and publishing. In addition to entertainment companies (HBO, CNN and Warner Bros.), Time Warner also owns AOL and investment and global media groups.

Tribune Company

http://www.tribune.com

Tribune Co. operates businesses in publishing, interactive and broadcast media. The company's leading daily newspapers include the *Los Angeles Times*, the *Chicago Tribune* and the *Baltimore Sun*. In 2009, the Tribune Company filed for bankruptcy protection.

Twitter

http://twitter.com

Twitter describes itself as "a real-time information network powered by people all around the world that lets you share and discover what's happening now. Twitter asks 'what's happening' and makes the answer spread across the globe to millions, immediately." Users can follow personal or celebrity blogs, breaking news, find out more about a local traffic jam, sales at their favorite stores, even receive and send messages to friends.

U.S. Census Bureau Statistical Abstract: Information and Communications

http://www.census.gov/compendia/statab/cats/information_communications.html

This source presents statistics on the various information and communications media: publishing, motion pictures, recordings, broadcasting, telecommunications and information services such as libraries. Internet-use statistics also are included.

Viacom Inc. (owner of Nickelodeon, Comedy Central and Nick at Nite)

http://viacom.com

This publicly traded company was formerly known as the Viacom Corporation before it split from CBS in 2005. Its well-known cable networks and entertainment brands include Nickelodeon, Nick at Nite, Comedy Central and CMT: Country Music Television. Viacom Inc. also owns Rhapsody, a membership-based music service, and Shockwave, a library of Web-based and mobile games.

Walt Disney Company (owner of ABC)

http://disney.go.com

This vertically integrated entertainment pioneer began as an animated cartoon studio in 1923. Today, Disney is divided into five major business segments: Studio Entertainment (Walt Disney Pictures and Touchstone Pictures); Parks and Resorts; Consumer Products; Disney Interactive Media Group; and Media Networks (which includes the Disney-ABC Television Group, ESPN and The Walt Disney Internet Group). Disney's latest acquisitions are Pixar and Marvel Comics.

YouTube

http://www.youtube.com

Founded in 2005 and acquired by Google Inc. just a year later, YouTube is the leader in online video. Users can watch anything from current events to quirky and unusual content and can browse categories such as comedy, news and politics, pets and animals, and sports.

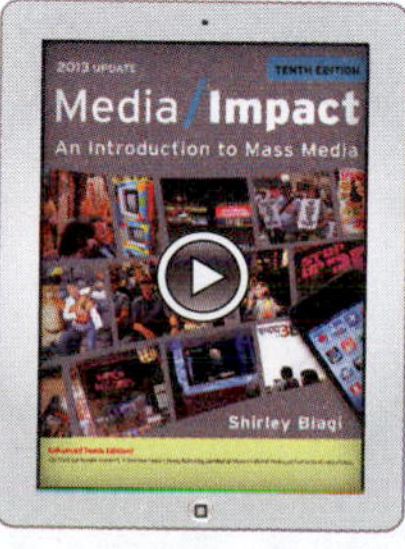

Impact/Action Videos are concise news features on topics covered in this chapter, created exclusively for **Media/Impact**. They are available for students and instructors at CengageBrain.com, and include screen access for classroom viewing and discussion questions.

"The only really necessary people in the publishing process now are the writer and the reader."

—Russell Grandinetti, Amazon executive

Books: Rearranging the Page

What's Ahead?

Publishers Nurture Ideas and Try to Make Money

How American Book Publishing Grew

Cheaper Books Create a Mass Market

Grove Press Tests Censorship

Investors Buy Up Publishing Companies

Book Publishing at Work

Authors and Agents: Where Books Begin

How Do Books Get Published?

Book Industry Has Five Major Markets

Corporations Demand Higher Profits

Chain Bookstores and Internet Retailers Compete

Small Presses Seek Specialized Audiences

New Technologies Affect Production and Consumption

Book Publishing Today Is a Competitive, Complex Business

Photo by Vic Biondi

Blackwell's Books is the largest bookstore in Oxford, England, offering 250,000 volumes. Founded in 1879, Blackwell's boasts that its Norrington Room (shown here) is the biggest single room devoted to book sales in Europe.

TimeFrame 1620 — Today

Book Publishing Becomes Big Business

1620 Imported books arrive in the colonies on the Mayflower.

1640 America's first book, *The Bay Psalm Book*, is printed at Cambridge, Mass.

1731 Benjamin Franklin creates the first lending library.

1776 **Thomas Paine publishes the revolutionary pamphlet *Common Sense*.**

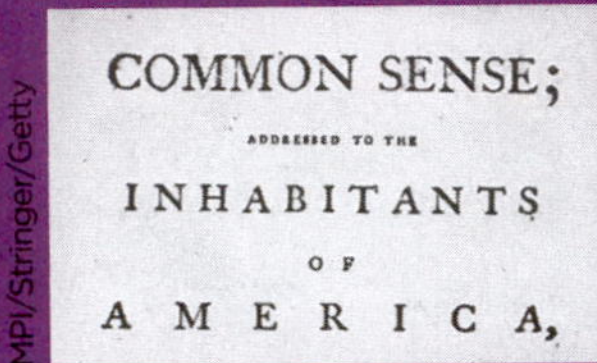
COMMON SENSE; ADDRESSED TO THE INHABITANTS OF AMERICA,

MPI/Stringer/Getty

1891 Congress passes the International Copyright Law of 1891, which requires publishing houses to pay royalties to foreign authors as well as American authors.

1900 **Elementary education becomes compulsory, which means increased literacy and more demand for textbooks.**

Buyenlarge/Archive Photos/Getty Images Images

1926 Book-of-the-Month Club is founded, increasing the audience for books.

1939 **Robert de Graff introduces Pocket Books, America's first series of paperback books. Suddenly, inexpensive books with mass appeal can reach millions of people who have never owned a book before.**

Transcendental Graphics/Getty Images

1948 New American Library begins publishing serious fiction by and about African Americans.

1960 Publishing houses begin to consolidate, concentrating power in a few large corporations, and decreasing the role of small presses and independent booksellers.

1970s The most significant changes in book marketing begin with the growth of retail bookstore chains.

1980s Publishers begin producing audiobooks of popular titles.

1990s Amazon.com begins doing business as an Internet retailer for books.

2000 Publishers launch e-books, electronic versions of paper books, which can be downloaded.

2004 Google announces the Google Book Project to scan the books of major research libraries and make their contents searchable.

2007 Amazon introduces the Kindle e-reader.

2009 **The U. S. Department of Justice opposes a settlement reached by the Google Book Project with authors, citing anti-trust arguments, and a U.S. District Court agrees, putting the project's future in doubt.**

Kim White/Bloomberg/Getty Images

2010 **Apple introduces the iPad, making books available as instant downloads. Google launches Google eBooks, which makes books available on smartphones and computers as well as electronic tablets.**

Jim Wilson/The New York Times/Redux Pictures

Today Most books are sold through Internet retailers and chain bookstores, and independent booksellers are struggling. Publishers are promoting e-books, including e-textbooks, as a cheaper, convenient alternative to traditional printed books.

"I'm not sure I can

explain how to write a book," said essayist and author E. B. White, who wrote 19 of them, including *Charlotte's Web*. "First you have to want to write one very much. Then, you have to know of something that you want to write about. Then, you have to begin. And, once you have started, you have to keep going. That's really all I know about how to write a book." The process of writing a book today is much more complex than White suggests, and every year in the United States publishers produce about 150,000 book titles. This number includes revised editions of previously published books, but most of the books are new.

Publishers Nurture Ideas and Try to Make Money

The publishing industry always has been tugged by what publishing scholars Lewis A. Coser, Charles Kadushin and Walter W. Powell call "the culture and commerce of publishing"—the desire to preserve the country's intellectual ideas versus the desire to make money. But a publisher who doesn't make a profit cannot continue to publish books.

Coser and his colleagues describe the four characteristics of book publishing in America today:

1. The industry sells its products—like any commodity—in a market that, in contrast to that for many other products, is fickle and often uncertain.
2. The industry is decentralized among a number of sectors whose operations bear little resemblance to each other.
3. A mixture of modern mass media production methods and craftlike procedures characterizes these operations.
4. The industry remains perilously poised between the requirements and restraints of commerce and the responsibilities and obligations that it must bear as a prime guardian of the symbolic culture of the nation.

Many new owners of publishing houses try to bring some predictability to the market. Says Coser, "Publishers attempt to reduce . . . uncertainty . . . through concentrating on 'sure-fire' blockbusters, through large-scale promotion campaigns or through control over distribution, as in the marketing of paperbacks. In the end, however, publishers rely on sales estimates that may be as unreliable as weather forecasts in Maine."

How American Book Publishing Grew

Today, the book publishing industry divides responsibilities among many people. But when Americans first started publishing books, one person often did all the work. Aboard the *Mayflower* in 1620, there were two dogs and 70 adults and only a few books. The pilgrims were very practical. They brought a map of Virginia and John Smith's *Description of New England*, but the main books they carried were their Bibles.

The first books in the United States were imports, brought by the new settlers or ordered from England after the settlers arrived. In 1638, the colonists set up a press at Cambridge, Mass., and in 1640 they printed America's first book: *The Bay Psalm Book*. As the only book, it became an instant best-seller. There were only about 3,500 families in the colonies at the time, and the book's first printing of 1,750 sold out.

By 1680, Boston had 17 booksellers, but most of the books still came from England. Between 1682 and 1685, Boston's leading bookseller, John Usher, bought 3,421 books to sell. Among the books he ordered were 162 romance novels.

In 1731, Benjamin Franklin decided that Philadelphia needed a library. So he asked 50 subscribers to pay 40 shillings each to a library company. The company imported 84 books, which circulated among the subscribers. This circulating library was America's first.

The year after he established the circulating library, Franklin published *Poor Richard's Almanack*. Unlike most printers, who waited for someone to come to them with a manuscript, Franklin wrote his own books. The typical author sought a patron to pay for the book's printing and then sold the book at the print shop where it was published.

To expand readership, early publishers sold political pamphlets, novels, poetry and humor. In addition, three events of the 19th century ensured that the book publishing industry would prosper in the 20th century: the International Copyright Law, the creation of publishing houses and the establishment of compulsory education.

Political Pamphlets

The big seller of the 1700s was Thomas Paine's revolutionary pamphlet *Common Sense*, which argued for the colonies' independence from Great Britain. From January to March 1776, colonial presses published 100,000 copies of Paine's persuasive political argument—one copy for every 25 people in the colonies—a true best-seller. Throughout the Revolutionary War, Paine was America's best-read author.

Novels and Poetry

Political pamphlets became much less important once the new nation was established, and printers turned their attention to other popular reading, especially fiction. Historians credit Benjamin Franklin with selling *Pamela* by Samuel Richardson in 1744, the first novel published in the United States, although it was a British import that had first appeared in England in 1740.

Mick Stevens/Cartoonbank.com

Because there was no international copyright law, colonial printers freely reprinted British novels like *Pamela* and sold them. It was cheaper than publishing American authors, who could demand royalties. (See "International Copyright Law of 1891.")

Like other media industries, book publishing has always faced moral criticism. Novels, for example, didn't start out with a good reputation. One critic said the novel "pollutes the imaginations." Women wrote one-third of all the early American novels, and women also bought most of them.

Especially popular after the Civil War and before the turn of the century were dime novels, America's earliest paperbacks. Dime novels often featured serial characters, like many of today's mystery novels. The stories and characters continued from one novel to the next. Most of them cost only a nickel, but some early paperbacks were as expensive as 25 cents.

Poetry generally has been difficult to sell, and it is correspondingly difficult for poets to get published. Literary scholar James D. Hart says that although poetry was never as popular as prose, the mid-1800s was "the great era of poetry. . . . It was more widely read in those years than it has been since."

Humor

Humor has been a durable category in book publishing since the days of humorist Mark Twain. Made famous by his short story "The Celebrated Jumping Frog of Calaveras County," Twain became a one-man publishing enterprise. One reason his books sold well was that he was the first American author to recognize the importance of advance publicity. Like most books, Twain's novels were sold door to door. Sales agents took advance orders before the books were published so the publisher could estimate how many to print. Before 1900, more than three-fourths of the popular books people bought were sold door to door.

International Copyright Law of 1891

Before 1891, publishers were legally required to pay royalties to American authors but not to foreign authors. This hurt American authors because books by American authors cost more to publish.

After the International Copyright Law of 1891, all authors—foreign and American—had to give permission for their works to be published. For the first time, American authors cost publishing houses the same amount as foreign authors. This motivated publishers to look for more American writers. In fact, after 1894, American writers published more novels in the United States than foreign writers did.

Publishing Houses

Many publishing houses that began in the late 18th century or during the 19th century continued into the 20th century. Nineteenth-century book publishing houses were just that—book publishing houses. They were nothing like today's multimedia corporations.

These pioneering companies housed all aspects of publishing under one roof: They sought out authors, reviewed and edited copy, printed and then sold the books.

Compulsory Education

By 1900, 31 states had passed compulsory education laws. This was important to book publishing because schools buy textbooks, and education creates more people who can read. Widespread public education meant that schools broadened their choices, and textbook publishing flourished (see **Media/Impact: Audience,** "Electronic Reading Devices Are Transforming the Concept of a Book," p. 33). Expanded public support for education also meant more money for libraries—more good news for the publishing industry.

Cheaper Books Create a Mass Market

The first quarter of the 20th century enabled still more publishing houses, such as Simon & Schuster and McGraw-Hill, to meet the public's needs. Publishers that specialized

Media/Impact
AUDIENCE

Electronic Reading Devices Are Transforming the Concept of a Book

By Alex Pham and David Sarno

Emma Teitgen, 12, thought the chemistry book her teacher recommended would make perfect bedside reading. Perfect because it might help her fall asleep.

Then she downloaded *The Elements: A Visual Exploration* to her iPad. Instead of making her drowsy, it blossomed in her hands. The 118 chemical elements, from hydrogen to ununoctium, came alive in vivid images that could be rotated with a swipe of the finger.

Tapping on link after link, Teitgen was soon engrossed in a world of atomic weights and crystal structures. Three hours later, the seventh-grader looked up to see that it was 11 p.m., way past her bedtime.

"It was like a breath of fresh air compared to my textbook," said Teitgen, who lives in Pittsford, N.Y. "I was really amazed by all the things it could do. I just kept clicking so I could read more."

More than 550 years after Johannes Gutenberg printed 180 copies of the Bible on paper and vellum, new technologies as revolutionary as the printing press are changing the concept of a book and what it means to be literate. Sound, animation and the ability to connect to the Internet have created the notion of a living book that can establish an entirely new kind of relationship with readers.

As electronic reading devices evolve and proliferate, books are increasingly able to talk to readers, quiz them on their grasp of the material, play videos to illustrate a point or connect them with a community of fellow readers. The same technology allows readers to reach out to authors, provide instant reaction and even become creative collaborators, influencing plot developments and the writer's use of dramatic devices.

Emma Teitgen, 12, downloaded her chemistry textbook to her iPad. Her e-book includes sound, animation and links to the Internet, changing the idea of what constitutes a textbook.

Digital tools are also making it possible for independent authors to publish and promote their books, causing an outpouring of written work on every topic imaginable.

If the upheaval in the music industry over the last decade is any guide, the closing of more bookstores and a decreasing demand for physical books will force authors and their publishers to find new ways to profit from their work.

"There is not a single aspect of book publishing that digital won't touch," said Carolyn Kroll Reidy, chief executive of Simon & Schuster. "It is transformational."

in paperbacks started in the 1930s and 1940s: Pocket Books (1939), Bantam Books (1946) and New American Library (1948). If you drop a product's price drastically, sales can explode. That's exactly what happened to book publishing with the introduction of book clubs and paperbacks, beginning in the 1920s.

Book Clubs

Book clubs replaced door-to-door sales agents as a way to reach people who otherwise wouldn't buy books. Book-of-the-Month Club was founded in 1926, and Literary Guild in 1927. By 1946, there were 50 book clubs in America, and the Book-of-the-Month Club was selling nearly 12 million copies a year.

Paperbacks

In 1939, Robert de Graff introduced America's first series of paperback best-sellers, called Pocket Books, which issued titles that had already succeeded as hardbound books. They were inexpensive (25 cents), and they fit in a pocket or a purse. Suddenly, a book could reach millions of people who had never owned a book before. Paperbacks democratized reading in America.

The books were so small, however, that people at first thought paperback books were shortened versions of the original. So publishers printed messages to readers on the cover to assure them that the paperbacks were the "complete novel, as originally published."

More publishers joined Pocket Books to produce paperbacks: New American Library (NAL), Avon, Popular Library, Signet and Dell. NAL distinguished itself by being the first mass-market publisher willing to issue serious books by and about African Americans—Richard Wright's *Native Son*, Lillian Smith's *Strange Fruit* and Ralph Ellison's *Invisible Man*. Signet's unexpected hit in the 1950s was J. D. Salinger's novel *Catcher in the Rye*, still popular today.

Grove Press Tests Censorship

Book publishers have always resisted any attempts by the government to limit freedom of expression. One of the first publishers to test those limits was Grove Press. In 1959, Grove published the sexually explicit *Lady Chatterley's Lover* by D. H. Lawrence (originally published in Italy in 1928); in 1961, the company published *Tropic of Cancer* by Henry Miller (originally published in Paris in 1934). Both books had been banned from the United States as obscene. The legal fees to defend Miller's book against charges of pornography cost Grove more than $250,000, but eventually the U.S. Supreme Court cleared the book in 1964.

The publisher again challenged conventional publishing in 1965, when it issued in hardback the controversial *The Autobiography of Malcolm X*, the story of the leader of the African American nationalist movement, by Alex Haley, as told by Malcolm X. The book became a best-seller.

Investors Buy Up Publishing Companies

Forecasts for growing profits in book publishing in the 1960s made the industry attractive to corporations looking for new places to invest. Before the 1960s, the book publishing industry was composed mainly of independent companies whose only business was books. Then, rising school and college attendance from the post–World War II baby boom made some areas of publishing, especially textbooks, lucrative investments for media companies that had not published books before.

Beginning in the 1960s, publishing companies began to consolidate. Publishing expert John P. Dessauer says, "Publishing stocks, particularly those of educational companies, became glamour holdings. And conglomerates began to woo every independent publisher whose future promised to throw off even a modest share of the forecast earnings." Dessauer acknowledges that the new owners often brought a businesslike approach to an industry that was known for its lack of attention to making a profit.

But, according to Dessauer, another consequence of these large-scale acquisitions was that "in many cases they also placed the power of ultimate decision and policymaking in the hands of people unfamiliar with books, their peculiarities and the markets." The same pace of acquisitions continued through the end of the 20th century, and today large media corporations own many of the book publishing companies.

Book Publishing at Work

When authors get together, often they tell stories about mistakes publishers have made—about manuscripts that 20 or 30 publishers turned down but that some bright-eyed editor eventually discovered and published. The books, of course, then become best-sellers. Some of the stories are true. But the best publishing decisions are made deliberately, to deliver an awaited book to an eager market. Successful publishing companies must consistently anticipate both their competitors and the market.

Not only must books be written, but they also must be printed, they must be promoted and they must be sold. This whole process usually takes at least 18 months from the time a project is signed by an editor until the book is published, so publishers are always working ahead. The classic publisher's question is, "Will someone pay $25 (or whatever the projected price of the book is) for this book 18 months after I sign the author?"

Authors and Agents: Where Books Begin

Publishers acquire books in many ways. Some authors submit manuscripts "over the transom," which means they send an unsolicited manuscript to a publishing house, hoping the publisher will be interested. However, many of the nation's larger publishers refuse to read unsolicited manuscripts and accept only books that agents submit.

Publishers pay authors a ***royalty*** for their work. A royalty amount is based on an established percentage of the book's price and may run anywhere from 6 to 15 percent of the cover price of the book. Some authors receive an ***advance***, which is an amount the publisher pays the author before the book is published. Royalties the book earns once it is in print are charged against the advance payment, so the book first must sell enough copies to pay off the advance before the author gets additional money.

Agents who represent authors collect fees from the authors they represent. Typically, an agent's fee is 10 to 15 percent of the author's royalty. If a publisher prices a book at $20, for example, the author receives from $2 to $3 per book, depending on the author's agreement with the publisher; the agent then receives 20 cents to 45 cents of the author's $2 to $3, depending on the agent's agreement with the author.

How Do Books Get Published?

In most cases, books start with the *author*, who proposes a book to an acquisitions editor, usually with an outline and some sample chapters. Sometimes an agent negotiates the contract for the book, but many authors negotiate their own contracts. Today the author is only one part of publishing a book. Departments at the publishing house called *acquisitions*, *media*, *design*, *production*, *manufacturing*, *marketing* and *fulfillment* all participate in the process. At a small publishing house, these jobs are divided among editors who are responsible for all the steps.

The *acquisitions editor* looks for potential authors and projects and works out an agreement with the author. The

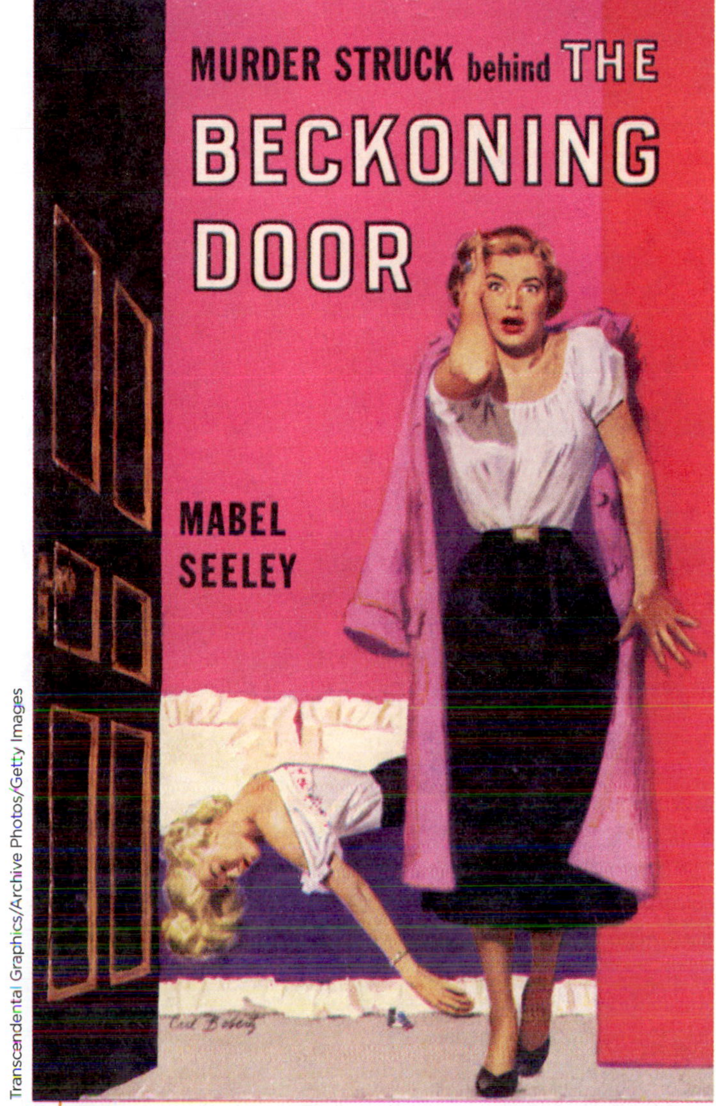

Transcendental Graphics/Archive Photos/Getty Images

Novels with women as central characters have a long history of popularity with American readers, starting with the English novel *Pamela*, first published in the United States in 1744. *The Beckoning Door*, written by Mabel Seeley and published as a paperback in 1952, features a woman fleeing a possible murder scene. Paperbacks, introduced in the United States by Robert de Graff in 1939, priced at 25 cents or less, made books available to millions of readers who had never before owned a book.

Royalty An amount the publisher pays an author, based on an established percentage of the book's price; royalties run anywhere from 6 to 15 percent.

Advance An amount the publisher pays the author before the book is published.

Cengage

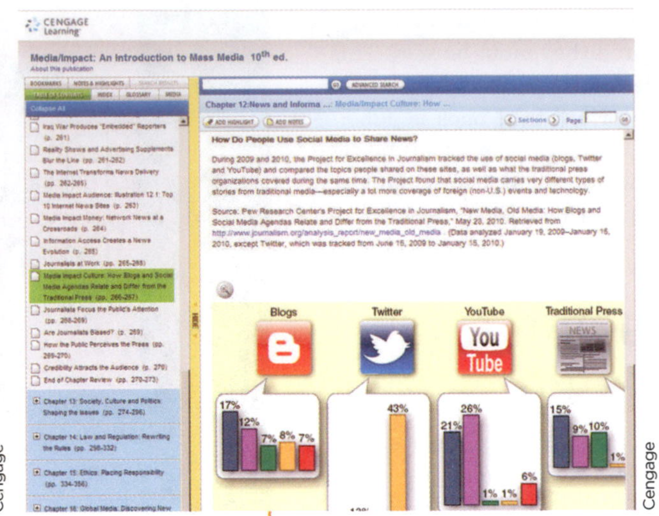

Cengage

Book designers use digital technology to help them create the way a book looks inside and outside. The cover is a vital part of any cover design. Designers also adapt the book's format so it can be viewed and used as an e-book. *Media/Impact* was first published as an e-book in 2010 (see example on right).

acquisitions editor's most important role is to be a liaison among the author, the publishing company and the book's audience. Acquisitions editors also may represent the company at book auctions and negotiate sales of ***subsidiary rights***, which are the rights to market a book for other uses—to make a movie, for example, or to use the image of a character in the book on T-shirts.

The *media editor* works with the author to create electronic materials to enhance the book. This could be simply an e-book version of the printed book or any other type of multimedia (such as archival photographs, slide shows, or video). For textbooks, this might mean a Web site where students can take sample tests and download chapter outlines.

The *designer* decides what a book will look like, inside and out. The designer chooses the typefaces for the book and determines how the pictures, boxes, heads and subheads will look and where to use color. The designer also creates a concept—sometimes more than one—for the book's cover. Designers also must help with the format for the e-book version of a text, which is different from the printed version.

The *production editor* manages all the steps that turn a double-spaced typewritten manuscript into a book. After the manuscript comes in, the production editor sets up a schedule and makes sure that all the production work gets done on time.

The *manufacturing supervisor* buys the typesetting, paper and printing for the book. The book usually is sent outside the publishing company to be manufactured.

Marketing, often the most expensive part of creating a book, is handled by several departments. *Advertising* designs ads for the book. *Promotion* sends the book to reviewers. Sales representatives visit bookstores and college campuses to tell book buyers and, in the case of textbooks, potential adopters about the book.

Fulfillment makes sure that the books get to the bookstores on time. This department watches inventory so that if the publisher's stock gets low, more books can be printed.

Twenty thousand American companies call themselves book publishers today, but only about 2,000 of them produce more than four titles a year. Most publishing houses are small: 80 percent of all book publishers have fewer than 20 employees.

Today, adult and juvenile trade books account for almost half of the books people buy, and textbooks make up about a third of all books sold. The number of new books and new editions has stabilized, but publishers are charging more for each book. Today, paperbacks and hardbacks cost nearly three times what they cost 30 years ago, while e-books typically cost less than hardback editions of new books.

Subsidiary Rights The rights to market a book for other uses—to make a movie or to print a character from the book on T-shirts, for example.

Book Industry Has Five Major Markets

Books fall into five major categories: adult and juvenile trade books, textbooks, book clubs and university press books, mass market paperbacks, audio books and e-books. Originally, many publishing houses were described by these classifications based on the specific type of publisher that produced the books. A company that was called a textbook publisher produced only textbooks, for example. Today, one publishing house often publishes several kinds of books, although it may have separate divisions for different types of books and markets. (See **Illustration 2.1**.)

Media/Impact
MONEY

Illustration 2.1

How Do Book Publishers Make Their Money?

Most of the books people buy are adult and juvenile trade books and professional books, but textbooks (kindergarten through 12th grade and college) account for a substantial percentage of the book market. Today e-books account for a small percentage of the market, but e-book sales are growing rapidly.

Source: Association of American Publishers, "Estimated Book Publishing Industry Net Sales 2002–2009."

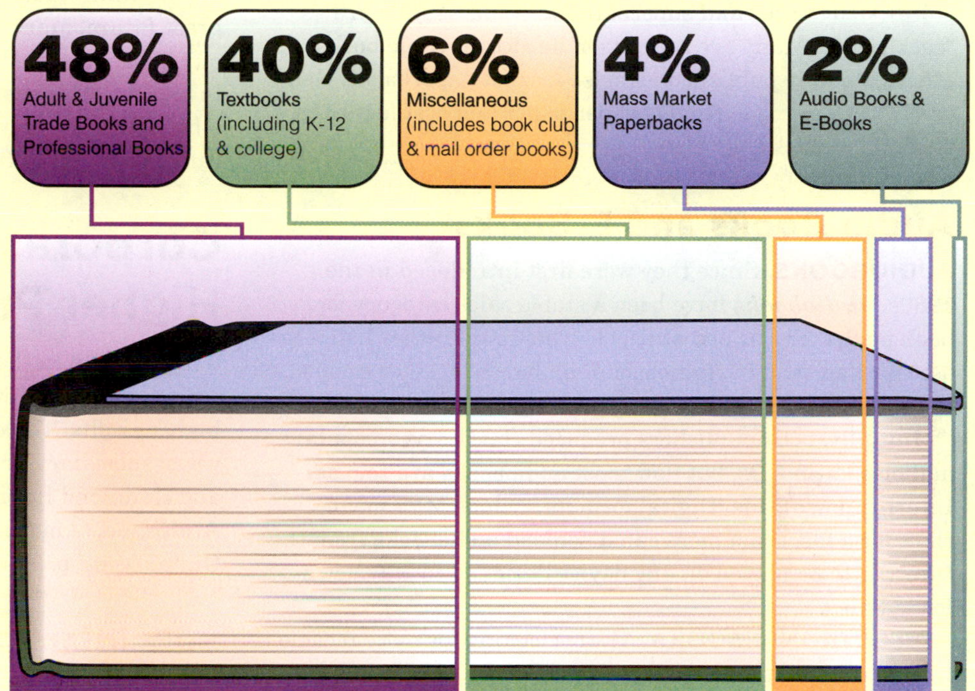

Adult and Juvenile Trade Books

Usually sold through bookstores and to libraries, trade books are designed for the general public. These books include hardbound books and trade (or "quality") paperbound books for adults and children. Typical trade books include hardcover fiction, current nonfiction, biography, literary classics, cookbooks, travel books, art books and books on sports, music, poetry and drama. Many college classes use trade books as well as textbooks. Juvenile trade books can be anything from picture books for children who can't read yet to novels for young adults.

Textbooks

Textbooks are published for elementary and secondary school students (called the "el-hi" market) as well as for college students. Most college texts are paid for by the students but are chosen by their professors.

Very little difference exists between some college texts and some trade books. Often the only real difference is that textbooks include what publishers call *apparatus*—for example, test questions and chapter summaries with extra assignments. The difference in content may be difficult to discern, so the Association of American Publishers classifies these two types of books (that is, trade books and textbooks) according to where they are sold the most. A book that is used mainly in grammar school, high school or college classrooms, for example, is called a textbook.

Book Clubs and University Press Books

University presses publish a small number of books every year and are defined solely by who publishes them: A university press book is one that a university publishes. Most university presses are nonprofit and are connected to a university, museum or research institution. These presses produce mainly scholarly materials in hardcover and softcover. Most university press books are sold through direct mail and in college bookstores.

Book clubs publish and sell books directly to a select audience. Although they were once very popular, book clubs today represent a very shrinking portion of the book market.

Mass Market Paperbacks

Here, definitions get tricky. These books are defined not by their subjects but by where they are sold. Although you can find them in bookstores, ***mass market books*** are mainly distributed through "mass" channels—newsstands, chain stores, drugstores and supermarkets—and usually are "rack-sized." Many are reprints of hardcover trade books; others are only published as mass market paperbacks. Generally, they're made from cheaper paper and cost less than trade paperbacks.

Audio Books and E-Books

AUDIOBOOKS. Since they were first introduced in the 1980s, ***audiobooks*** have been a stable sales category for book publishers, aimed at people who would rather listen to a book than read it. Audiobooks can be abridged or complete versions of the originals.

Initially, book publishers produced classics and popular audiobooks on CDs, but now most audiobooks are sold as Internet downloads. Digital formats such as MP3 mean that, for a fee, consumers can download audiobooks from the Internet to be played on any device designed to play downloaded files.

ELECTRONIC BOOKS. Always looking for more income from the content they own, book publishers today are producing some books only as electronic books (***e-books***) as well as e-book versions of printed books. E-books are downloaded and then read on a screen.

The introduction of e-books is the latest attempt by publishers to expand the market for their products. With the introduction of e-readers such as the Amazon Kindle and Apple's iPad, e-books have become a very popular and portable way to read a book. In 2010, Google launched Google eBooks, which makes e-books available on smartphones and computers as well as electronic tablets.

"As with digital music, multiple books—say, Shakespeare's collected works—can be stored on a memory card the size of a stick of gum, making them popular with travelers, students and professionals," says Reuters columnist Franklin Paul. According to software developer Adobe's Russell Brady, "Two audiences that will benefit best are young people who loathe the idea of a library . . . and aging people who want the convenience of large type on demand, or freedom from lugging heavy hardcover tomes.

"We think that in the long term, e-book technology has a great future. Market acceptance has not taken off quite as quickly as was predicted, but we are certainly continuing to invest in this area." Many publishers now believe that e-books are the only way that the book publishing business can expand in the future.

Mass Market Books Books distributed through "mass" channels—newsstands, chain stores, drugstores and supermarkets.

Audiobooks Abridged or complete versions of classic books and popular new titles on CDs.

E-books Electronic books.

Blockbuster A book that achieves enormous financial success.

Corporations Demand Higher Profits

Consolidation in the book business means the giants in today's publishing industry are demanding increasingly higher profits. The companies look for extra income in three ways: subsidiary and international rights, blockbuster books and chain and Internet marketing. (See **Media/Impact: Audience,** "Amazon Signs Up Authors, Writing Publishers Out of Deal," p. 39.)

Subsidiary and International Rights

Trade and mass market publishers are especially interested in, and will pay more for, books with the potential for subsidiary- and international-rights sales. The rights to make a video game version of a book, for example, are subsidiary rights.

In the 19th century, the number of copies of books that individual readers bought determined a book's profit. Today, profits come from the sale of subsidiary rights to movie companies, book clubs, foreign publishers and paperback reprint houses. The same rights govern whether a character in a book becomes a star on the front of a T-shirt or a video game. For some publishing houses, subsidiary- and international-rights sales make the difference between making a profit and going out of business.

Blockbusters

Selling a lot of copies of one book is easier and cheaper than selling a few copies of many books. This is the concept behind publishers' eager search for ***blockbuster*** books. Publishers are attracted to best-selling authors because usually they are easy to market. Brand loyalty draws loyal readers to buy every book by a favorite author, so publishers try to capitalize on an author's popularity in the same way movie producers seek out stars who have made successful films.

Following are some amounts that publishers recently have paid for potential blockbusters:

Media/Impact AUDIENCE

Amazon Signs Up Authors, Writing Publishers Out of Deal

By David Streitfeld

Amazon.com has taught readers that they do not need bookstores. Now it is encouraging writers to cast aside their publishers.

Amazon will publish 122 books [in fall 2011] in an array of genres, in both physical and e-book form. It is a striking acceleration of the retailer's fledging publishing program that will place Amazon squarely in competition with the New York houses that are also its most prominent suppliers.

It has set up a flagship line run by a publishing veteran, Laurence Kirshbaum, to bring out brand-name fiction and nonfiction. It signed its first deal with the self-help author Tim Ferriss. [In October 2011] it announced a memoir by the actress and director Penny Marshall, for which it paid $800,000, a person with direct knowledge of the deal said.

Publishers say Amazon is aggressively wooing some of their top authors. And the company is gnawing away at the services that publishers, critics and agents used to provide.

Several large publishers declined to speak on the record about Amazon's efforts. "Publishers are terrified and don't know what to do," said Dennis Loy Johnson of Melville House, who is known for speaking his mind.

"Everyone's afraid of Amazon," said Richard Curtis, a longtime agent who is also an e-book publisher. "If you're a bookstore, Amazon has been in competition with you for some time. If you're a publisher, one day you wake up and Amazon is competing with you too. And if you're an agent, Amazon may be stealing your lunch because it is offering authors the opportunity to publish directly and cut you out."

Bloomberg/Getty Images

Amazon, the nation's biggest online bookseller, launched the Kindle Fire, its latest e-book reader, on November 15, 2011. Amazon also announced the company will publish books as well as distribute them.

Amazon executives, interviewed at the company's headquarters here, declined to say how many editors the company employed, or how many books it had under contract. But they played down Amazon's power and said publishers were in love with their own demise.

"It's always the end of the world," said Russell Grandinetti, one of Amazon's top executives.

He pointed out, though, that the landscape was in some ways changing for the first time since Gutenberg invented the modern book nearly 600 years ago. "The only really necessary people in the publishing process now are the writer and reader," he said. "Everyone who stands between those two has both risk and opportunity."

Publishers caught a glimpse of a future they fear has no role for them late last month when Amazon introduced the Kindle Fire, a tablet for books and other media sold by Amazon. Jeffrey P. Bezos, the company's chief executive, referred several times to Kindle as "an end-to-end service," conjuring up a world in which Amazon develops, promotes and delivers the product.

From David Streitfeld, "Amazon Signs Up Authors, Writing Publishers Out of Deal," The New York Times, *October 16, 2011.*

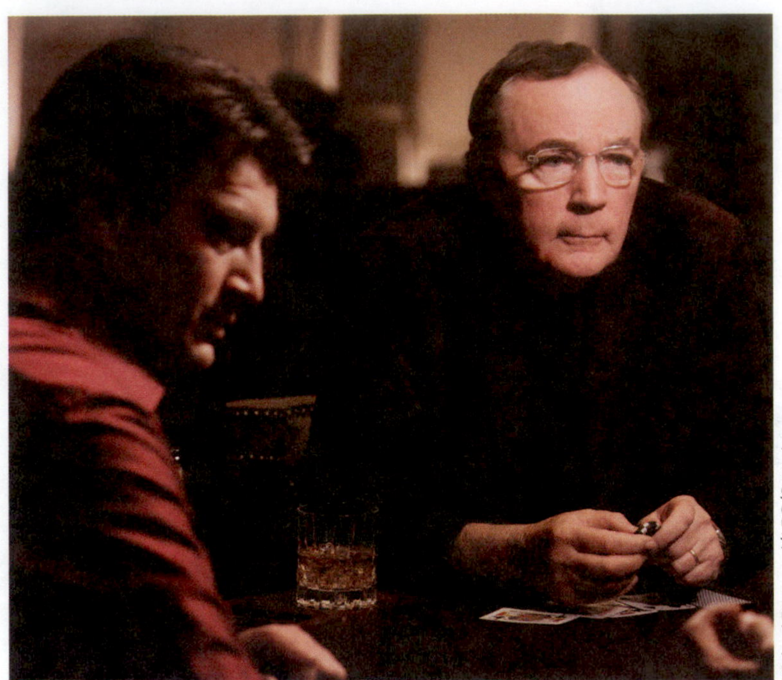
Michael Desmond/ABC/Getty Images

Author James Patterson signed a multi-million dollar book deal in 2009 to produce 17 books by 2012. Patterson is highly sought after because he has a devoted following of readers. In May 2010, Patterson played himself in the season finale of the ABC TV series *Castle*.

- In December 2010, WikiLeaks founder Julian Assange received a $1.3 million advance for American and British rights to write his memoirs.
- Novelist James Patterson signed a 17-book contract with Hachette Book Group USA in September 2009 for an undisclosed amount. The books are due by 2012, but Patterson said he already had finished writing 14 of them. Patterson broadened the market for his books by producing a James Patterson mystery, *Women's Murder Club*, as a video game for Nintendo DSi.
- Little, Brown & Company reportedly signed a $5 million deal with TV comedian Tina Fey in late 2008 for a book called *Bossypants*.

Only the big publishing houses can afford such a bidding game. Some publishers have even developed computer models to suggest how high to bid for a book and still make a profit, but these high-priced properties are a very small part of book publishing, perhaps 1 percent. The majority of editors and writers rarely get involved in an argument over seven-figure advances. Many authors would be pleased to see five-figure advances in a contract.

Some critics believe that what has been called a *blockbuster complex* among publishing houses hurts authors who aren't included in the bidding. One Harper & Row editor told *The Wall Street Journal* that seven-figure advances "divert money away from authors who really need it and center attention on commercial books instead of less commercial books that may nonetheless be better. God help poetry or criticism."

Chain Bookstores and Internet Retailers Compete

The most significant change in book marketing in the past 40 years has been the growth of bookstore chains and Internet retailers. The big chains, such as Borders and Barnes & Noble, account for more than half the bookstore sales of trade books. They have brought mass-marketing techniques to the book industry, offering book buyers an environment that is less like the traditional cozy atmosphere of a one-owner bookstore and more like a department store.

"The large chains are the power behind book publishing today," says Joan M. Ripley, a former president of the American Booksellers Association. "Blockbusters are going to be published anyway, but with a marginal book, like a volume of poetry, a chain's decision about whether to order it can sometimes determine whether the book is published." But in 2010, Barnes & Noble reported declining sales at its retail outlets, and in 2011 Borders shut down 200 stores and filed for bankruptcy protection. The reason? Internet booksellers are rapidly stealing business from the chains.

Online book retailers, such as Amazon, have become a major factor in book marketing. Internet retailers can buy in huge volume, and they buy books only from publishers that give them big discounts. Even books that are published by smaller publishing houses can today easily reach online buyers. For blockbusters and specialty books alike the Internet retailer is a very important outlet.

Like the resistance to book clubs when they first were introduced, the skepticism among book publishers about chain bookstores and Internet retailers has changed into an understanding that they have expanded the book market to people who didn't buy very many books before. But the competitive pricing that the Internet retailers bring emphasizes what can happen when a small number of companies control the distribution of an industry's products, as they do in book publishing.

Small Presses Seek Specialized Audiences

The nation's large publishing houses (those with 100 or more employees) publish 80 percent of the books sold each year, but some of the nation's publishers are small operations with fewer than 10 employees. These publishers are called *small presses*, and they counterbalance the corporate world of large advances and multimedia subsidiary rights.

Small presses do not have the budgets of the large houses, but their size means they can specialize in specific topics, such as the environment or bicycling, or in specific types of writing that are unattractive to large publishers, such as poetry.

Small presses are, by definition, alternative. Many of them are clustered together in locations outside of the New York City orbit, such as Santa Fe, New Mexico, and Berkeley, California. Specialization and targeted marketing are the most important elements of small press success. However, because they have limited distribution capabilities, most small presses today struggle to survive.

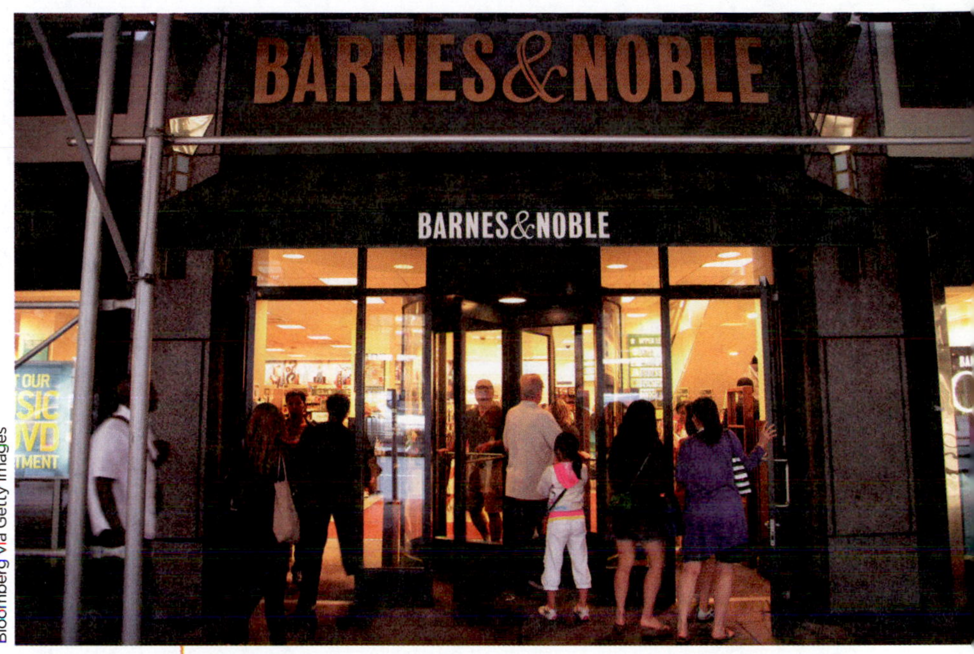

Bloomberg via Getty Images

Chain bookstores, such as Barnes & Noble and Borders, account for more than half of bookstore sales of trade books. But online retailers, such as Amazon .com, have become a major factor in book marketing because they often can sell books cheaper than the chains. Barnes & Noble continues to report declining sales at its retail outlets and in 2011 Borders closed all its stores.

New Technologies Affect Production and Consumption

Technology is a major factor in most aspects of book publishing. Because books cost so much to publish, advances in technology can lower the cost of producing books, which benefits the industry.

Changes in Production

Technological advances in the last 20 years have led to seven important changes in the way books are produced, distributed and promoted.

1. Because computers monitor inventories more closely, publishers can easily order new printings of books that are selling quickly so booksellers can keep the books in stock.
2. Book publishing is an on-screen industry. Publishers now receive most manuscripts from authors electronically via the Internet. Editors process the manuscripts on computers and then send the books into production online. This means books can be printed anywhere, often overseas.
3. Electronic graphics make books more interesting, and many book publishers are using online content to produce expanded versions of traditional books and to add materials that enhance a book's marketability.
4. Publishers are using Web sites to promote their books and to advertise blockbusters.
5. Large publishers are continuing to consolidate, and the number of small publishers is decreasing.
6. Many aspects of the publishing process, such as copyediting, photo research and even editing, are contracted to freelancers who work outside the publishing house. Because publishing can be done online, book projects can be managed from any location. This means that publishers have fewer in-house employees today and much of the work is contracted and sent overseas.
7. To try to maintain and expand the market for books, publishers are exploring all aspects of digital delivery, of which e-books seem the most promising.

Changes in Consumption

Imagine a world in which every book ever written is available to search online. This is the vision of the Google Book Project, which began contracting in 2004 with several of the nation's libraries to scan the contents of the books the libraries hold so that eventually the books' contents could be available through Google online. You could enter the word "romance," for instance, and call up a list of all the books in which the word had appeared. Or you could call up a famous phrase and trace its origin to the author who first used it. Google Inc. began to digitize millions of books to make them

"In preparation for landing, please turn off your books."

Ward Sutton/Cartoonbank.com

searchable. This concept introduced a huge shift in the way books may be consumed in the future.

This project is as controversial as it is ambitious. Authors and publishers have legal questions about copyright and royalties; booksellers wonder whether anyone will buy books if they're all available online; scholars wonder what will happen to the value of knowledge and information once it is searchable on such a wide scale. Still, Google says the company is committed to the project, which certainly will have wide-ranging consequences for the book publishing industry in the future. In 2008, Google paid $125 million to settle two copyright lawsuits brought by publishers and authors over the company's right to digitize books for online use.

However, the settlement still "left unresolved the question of whether Google's unauthorized scanning of copyrighted books was permissible under copyright laws," according to *The New York Times*. In September 2009, the U.S. Department of Justice asked that the settlement be delayed indefinitely, citing anti-trust problems. The U.S. District Court with jurisdiction over the agreement agreed. This leaves unresolved the fate of Google's ambitious project.

Book Publishing Today Is a Competitive, Complex Business

Because book publishing has been part of America's culture for so long, the contrast between its simple beginnings and its complicated future is especially startling. On August 2, 2010, book retailer Amazon.com announced that, for the previous three months, the company had sold more e-books than hardcover printed books—143 Kindle books for every 100 hardcover books.

By the end of 2010, 100 million e-books had been sold, according to Forrester Research. Books are getting smaller and more portable—small enough for more than 100 electronic books to fit on an iPad or a Kindle in a space 9 inches square and 1 inch deep—the same size as a single copy of one hardback book.

"The real competition [at Amazon.com] is not . . . between the hardcover book and the e-book," Amazon executive Russ Grandinetti told *The New Yorker* magazine. "TV, movies, Web browsing, video games are all competing for people's valuable time. And if the book doesn't compete we think that over time the industry will suffer."

Review, Analyze, Investigate

REVIEWING CHAPTER 2

Publishers Nurture Ideas and Try to Make Money

- ✓ U.S. book publishers produce about 150,000 book titles every year.
- ✓ Publishers have always been torn between the goal of preserving the country's intellectual ideas and the need to make money.
- ✓ Many new owners of publishing houses are trying to limit uncertainty by publishing blockbusters and by spending money on promotional campaigns.

How American Book Publishing Grew

- ✓ Early publishers widened their audience by publishing political pamphlets, novels, poetry and humor.
- ✓ The International Copyright Law of 1891 expanded royalty protection to foreign writers, which also benefited American authors.
- ✓ The creation of publishing houses in the 19th and early 20th centuries centralized the process of producing books.

- ✓ The adoption of compulsory education throughout the United States was important for book publishing because schools buy textbooks, and education creates more people who can read.

Cheaper Books Create a Mass Market

- ✓ Beginning in the 1920s, publishers dropped prices and introduced book clubs and paperbacks.
- ✓ Early book clubs, such as Book-of-the-Month, expanded the market for books and widened the audience.
- ✓ The introduction of paperbacks that sold for as little as 25 cents meant the books could reach people who had never owned a book before.

Grove Press Tests Censorship

- ✓ Grove Press challenged book censorship by publishing *Lady Chatterley's Lover* in 1959 and *Tropic of Cancer* in 1961. Both books had been banned in the United States as obscene.
- ✓ The publication by Grove Press of *The Autobiography of Malcolm X* in 1965 was another challenge to censorship. The book became a best-seller.

Investors Buy Up Publishing Companies

- ✓ Before the 1960s, the book publishing industry was composed mainly of independent companies whose only business was books.
- ✓ Publishing company consolidation began in the 1960s, and this pattern of consolidation continues today.

Book Publishing at Work

- ✓ Successful publishers consistently anticipate both their competitors and the market.
- ✓ The process of publishing a book usually takes at least 18 months from the time an author is signed until the book is published.

Authors and Agents: Where Books Begin

- ✓ Publishers acquire books in many ways. Some authors submit unsolicited manuscripts, hoping the publisher will be interested. However, many publishers refuse to read unsolicited manuscripts and accept only books that agents submit.
- ✓ Publishers pay authors a royalty for their work.
- ✓ Agents who represent authors collect fees from the authors they represent.

How Do Books Get Published?

- ✓ Book publishing requires an author, an acquisitions editor, a media editor, a designer, a production editor, a manufacturing supervisor, a marketing department and a fulfillment department.
- ✓ Most publishing houses are small, with fewer than 20 employees.
- ✓ Textbooks account for about one-third of book publishing income.

Book Industry Has Five Major Markets

- ✓ Books fall into five major categories: adult and juvenile trade books; textbooks; book clubs and university press books; mass market paperbacks; audio books and e-books.
- ✓ Audiobooks in MP3 format allow consumers to download and purchase book files on the Internet and listen to books on their computers or a specialized MP3 player.
- ✓ Electronic books (e-books) offer digital copies of thousands of titles instantly.

Corporations Demand Higher Profits

- ✓ Publishers are especially interested in books with subsidiary- and international-rights potential.
- ✓ To reduce their risks, many publishers look for blockbuster books (and best-selling authors) that they can sell through large-scale promotion campaigns.

Chain Bookstores and Internet Retailers Compete

- ✓ Chain bookstores and Internet retailers, such as Amazon, are big factors in book marketing.
- ✓ Chain bookstores and Internet retailers can buy in huge volume, and often they buy books only from publishers that give them big discounts.
- ✓ Internet retailing has expanded the book market but has introduced competitive pricing.

Small Presses Seek Specialized Audiences

- ✓ Small presses are, by definition, alternative.
- ✓ Many small presses exist outside the New York City orbit.
- ✓ Specialization and targeted marketing are important elements of small press success.

New Technologies Affect Production and Consumption

- ✓ Computers monitor inventories more closely.
- ✓ Publishers now receive and process manuscripts electronically via the Internet. Many aspects of the publishing process, such as copyediting and photo research, are contracted to freelancers who work outside the publishing house, including overseas.
- ✓ Electronic graphics make books more interesting to look at, and many book publishers use Web sites to promote books and enhance the content.
- ✓ Large publishers are continuing to consolidate, and the number of small publishers is decreasing.

- ✓ To try to maintain and expand the market for books, publishers are exploring all aspects of digital delivery.
- ✓ Beginning in 2004, the Google Book Project contracted with several of the nation's libraries to scan the contents of books the libraries hold. Google Inc. planned to make the books' contents available online.
- ✓ In 2008, Google Inc. paid $125 million to settle copyright infringement claims, but the copyright issues inherent in the project remain unresolved.
- ✓ In 2009, the U.S. Justice Department and the U.S. District Court with jurisdiction over the case delayed the settlement indefinitely, citing anti-trust objections.

Book Publishing Today Is a Competitive, Complex Business

- ✓ On August 2, 2010, book retailer Amazon.com announced that, for the previous three months, the company had sold more e-books than hardcover printed books—143 Kindle books for every 100 hardcover books.
- ✓ By the end of 2010, book buyers had purchased an estimated 100 million e-books.
- ✓ Book publishing, which had simple beginnings in America that still evoke romantic ideas about the way books were produced and sold, today has become a competitive corporate industry.

KEY TERMS

These terms are defined in the margins throughout this chapter and appear in alphabetical order with definitions in the Glossary, which begins on page 383.

Advance 35
Audiobooks 38
Blockbuster 38
E-books 38
Mass Market Books 38
Royalty 35
Subsidiary Rights 36

CRITICAL QUESTIONS

1. Why was passage of the International Copyright Law of 1891 so important to American authors?
2. List five ways the economics of book publishing changed from Benjamin Franklin's day to today.
3. Will new technologies like e-books replace print books? Why or why not?
4. Why are textbooks so important to the publishing industry?
5. Why is the Google Book Project so controversial?

WORKING THE WEB

This list includes both sites mentioned in the chapter and others to give you greater insight into book publishing.

Amazon

http://www.amazon.com

Since this pioneer Internet bookseller started in 1995, Amazon has expanded its e-commerce offerings to include a wide variety of products in multiple categories including Movies, Music & Games, Digital Downloads and even Grocery. In 2007, Amazon released Kindle, a wireless, portable reading device with instant access to books at more than 50 percent savings from the print price, as well as blogs, newspapers and magazines. Amazon.com operates sites internationally, including the United Kingdom, France, Japan, China, Canada and Germany.

American Booksellers Association

http://www.bookweb.org

This national not-for-profit trade association for independent booksellers exists to protect to protect and promote the interests of its members: independently owned bookstores, large and small, with storefront locations in towns and cities nationwide. The ABA provides "advocacy, education, opportunities for peer interaction, support services and new business models." Its IndieBound program (evolved from Book Sense, http://www.indiebound.org) is a national marketing program to raise consumer awareness of the value of independent bookstores.

American Booksellers Foundation for Free Expression (ABFFE)

http://www.abffe.org

Founded by the American Booksellers Association in 1990, ABFFE is "The bookseller's voice in the fight against censorship." The Foundation opposes book banning and other restrictions on free speech, participates in legal cases about First Amendment rights and provides education on the importance of free expression to many entities including the public, the press and politicians.

Association of American Publishers

http://www.publishers.org

This organization deals with broad issues concerning publishers, as well as specific concerns in particular industry segments. Committees attend to such issues as intellectual property; new technology; First Amendment rights, censorship and libel; funding for education and libraries; postal rates and regulations; and international copyright enforcement.

Barnes & Noble

http://www.barnesandnoble.com

Barnes & Noble.com uses mass-marketing techniques to sell books, DVDs, music and other merchandise. B&N.com maintains that it has one million titles available for immediate delivery as well as used and out-of-print-titles. The Web site features include online Book Clubs, B&N Review and B&N Studio, a video library with hundreds of webcasts where viewers can learn more about authors, musical artists and fellow book lovers.

Biblio

http://www.biblio.com

Based in Asheville, N.C., Biblio is an online marketplace for used, rare and out-of-print books and textbooks. The booksellers are located around the world, and the list of links to specialists is very long (use the Booksellers tab and go to the "Specialist Bookstores" link). Users can search 50 million used and rare books, browse by subject or author, or browse collectible and rare books by featured category.

BookFinder

http://www.bookfinder.com

BookFinder.com is an e-commerce search engine for new, used, rare and out-of-print books and textbooks. It searches all the major online catalogs (such as Amazon and Barnes & Noble) and independent sources. Searches can be conducted in English, French, German or Italian. BookFinder's global network of book search engines includes JustBooks.de, JustBooks.co.uk and JustBooks.fr.

Google Book Search

http://books.google.com

This controversial project between Google and several libraries (including the University of Michigan, Harvard University, Stanford University, New York Public Library and Oxford University) has expanded to include partnerships with book publishers and authors. Google's plan "to digitize the world's books in order to make them easier for people to find and buy" has encountered legal obstacles and its future is in doubt.

IndieBound

http://www.indiebound.org

Evolved from the ABA's Book Sense program, IndieBound "rallies passionate readers around a celebration of independent stores and independent thinking." Independently owned ABA member bookstores are automatically part of the program and are encouraged to use the logos, spirit lines, posters, buttons, T-shirts and more provided by the ABA.

Scholastic Corporation

http://www.scholastic.com

The world's largest publisher of children's books, Scholastic creates a variety of educational and entertainment materials and products for home and school use, and distributes them through various channels including school-based book clubs and book fairs, retail stores, television networks and Scholastic.com.

Impact/Action Videos are concise news features on topics covered in this chapter, created exclusively for **Media/Impact**. They are available for students and instructors at CengageBrain.com, and include screen access for classroom viewing and discussion questions.

"When we engage in these discussions about how to 'monetize' journalism, it's refreshing to remember [there are] weekly newspaper editors and reporters who keep churning out news for the corniest of reasons—because their readers depend on it."

—Judy Muller, University of Southern California Journalism Professor

Newspapers: Expanding Delivery

What's Ahead?

- First Mass Medium to Deliver News
- Publishers Fight for an Independent Press
- Technology Helps Newspapers Reach New Audiences
- Dissident Voices Create the Early Alternative Press
- Newspapers Seek Mass Audiences and Big Profits
- Newspapers Dominate the Early 20th Century
- Unionization Encourages Professionalism
- Television Brings New Competition
- Alternative Press Revives Voices of Protest
- Newspapers Expand and Contract
- Newspapers at Work
- Newspapers Struggle to Retain Readers
- Technology Transforms Production
- Consolidation Increases Chain Ownership
- Today's Newspaper Audience Is a Moving Target

Bloomberg/Getty Images

On January 20, 2011, *The New York Times* began charging for online content. NYTimes.com is the nation's most popular newspaper Web site, with more than 17 million readers a month. Electronic tablets like the iPad offer newspapers a way to maintain their audience and increase revenue.

TimeFrame 1690 — Today

Newspapers Adapt to Try to Maintain Their Audience Share

1690 *Publick Occurrences*, America's first newspaper, is published.

1721 James Franklin publishes *The New England Courant*, the first newspaper to appear without the Crown's "Published by Authority" sanction.

1734 **John Peter Zenger is charged with sedition. While he is in jail, his wife, Anna Zenger, continues to publish *The New York Weekly Journal*, making her America's first woman publisher.**

Bettmann/CORBIS

1808 *El Misisipi*, America's first Spanish-language newspaper, begins publication in Georgia.

1827 John B. Russwurm and the Reverend Samuel Cornish launch *Freedom's Journal*, the nation's first newspaper directed specifically at an African American audience.

1828 Elias Boudinot launches the *Cherokee Phoenix*.

1831 **In Boston, William Lloyd Garrison launches the abolitionist newspaper *The Liberator*.**

Hulton Archive/Stringer/Getty Images

1847 Frederick Douglass introduces the weekly *North Star*, considered America's most important African American pre-Civil War newspaper.

1848 Jane Grey Swisshelm publishes the first issue of the abolitionist newspaper the *Pittsburgh Saturday Visiter*, which also promoted women's rights.

1889 Ida B. Wells becomes part owner of the *Memphis Free Speech and Headlight* and begins her anti-lynching campaign.

1900 One third of the nation's newspapers follow the popular trend toward yellow journalism.

1950 **Newspaper readership begins to decline following the introduction of television.**

CBS Photo Archive/Getty Images

1982 Gannett Co. creates *USA Today*, using a splashy format and color throughout the paper.

1990s **Newspapers launch special sections to appeal to declining audiences—teens and women. Some newspapers launch Spanish-language editions, and existing Spanish-language newspapers expand their audience.**

Tim Boyle/Getty Images

2009 **Tribune Co. files for bankruptcy protection. Denver's *Rocky Mountain News* and the *Seattle Post-Intelligencer* close down.**

Kevin P. Casey/CORBIS

2011 *The New York Times* begins charging for online content.

Today The newspaper business is consolidating as large newspaper companies buy up small newspapers and gather them in groups. To attract younger readers, newspapers have expanded their Internet editions and news-on-demand features. Declining ad revenue has forced many newspapers to close.

In 1882, Harrison Gray Otis bought a 25 percent share of the *Los Angeles Times* for $6,000. In 2000, the Chandler family (Otis' descendants) sold Times Mirror Co., which included the *Los Angeles Times*, *Newsday*, *The Baltimore Sun* newspapers, the *Hartford Courant* and other media properties to Chicago-based Tribune Co. for $8.3 billion. Then in 2007, Chicago real estate tycoon Sam Zell paid $8.2 billion for Tribune Co. (including Times Mirror), less than Tribune Co. had paid for Times Mirror alone seven years earlier. Then one year later, in December 2008, Tribune Co. filed for bankruptcy protection, citing the rapid decline in newspaper revenue.

At the end of 2010, Tribune Co.'s future remained unsettled. The company was still deeply in debt, and investors were in court claiming that Zell's buyout was fraudulent. The purchase of the *Los Angeles Times* by Tribune Co. and then by Zell (two ownership changes in seven years), then the bankruptcy filing and the investors' court fight demonstrate the precarious economics of the newspaper business today.

American newspapers began in colonial America more than three centuries ago as one-page sheets that consisted primarily of announcements of ship arrivals and departures and old news from Europe. Today's large urban newspapers such as the *Los Angeles Times* rely on satellite-fed information, and these papers often run to 500 pages on Sunday. (*The New York Times* holds the record for the largest single-day's newspaper. On November 13, 1987, *The Times* published a 1,612-page edition that weighed 12 pounds.) In most cases, newspapers today also are just one part of large media companies rather than family-run operations.

First Mass Medium to Deliver News

Technological developments in the last century have changed the role of newspapers and the way news is delivered. From 1690 until the introduction of radio in 1920, newspapers were the only mass news medium available, attempting to deliver news and information as soon as it happened. Until 1920, newspapers were the only way for large numbers of people to get the same news simultaneously. There was no competition.

The invention of broadcasting in the early 20th century changed newspapers' exclusive access to news because broadcasting offered quicker access to information. Yet, despite increasing competition for its audience, newspapers continue to be a significant source of information and news.

The newspaper industry also historically has played an important role in defining the cultural concept of an independent press, based on the belief that the press must remain independent from government control to fulfill its responsibility to keep the public informed. Concepts about what the public should know, when they should know it and who should decide what the public needs to know developed in America during a time when newspapers were the main focus of these discussions.

Publishers Fight for an Independent Press

The issue of government control of newspapers surfaced early in the history of the colonies. At first, newspapers were the mouthpieces of the British government, and news was subject to British approval. The British government subsidized many colonial newspapers, and publishers actually printed "Published by Authority" on the first page of the paper to demonstrate government approval.

The first colonial newspaper angered the local authorities so much that the newspaper issued only one edition. This newspaper, *Publick Occurrences*, which was published in Boston on September 25, 1690, often is identified as America's first newspaper.

The first and only edition of *Publick Occurrences* was just two pages, each page the size of a sheet of today's binder paper (then called a half-sheet), and was printed on three

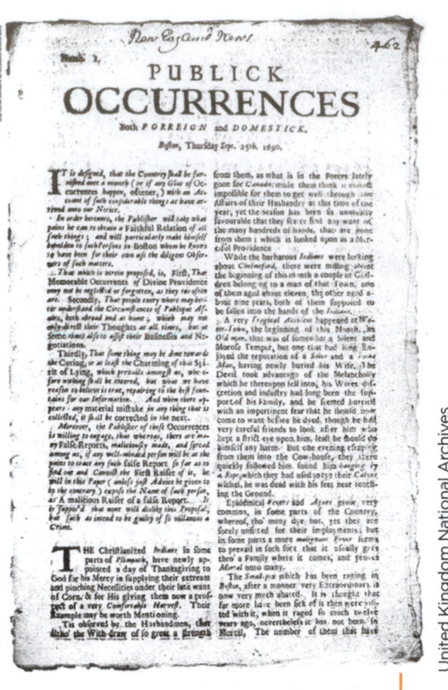

PUBLICK OCCURRENCES

Both FORREIGN and DOMESTICK.

Boston, Thursday Sept. 25th. 1690.

United Kingdom National Archives

Publick Occurrences was America's first newspaper, published in 1690. It was a two-page newspaper, and each page was the size of a sheet of binder paper.

sides. Publisher Benjamin Harris left the fourth side blank so people could jot down the latest news before they gave the paper to friends. Harris made the mistake of reporting in his first issue that the French king was "in much trouble" for sleeping with his son's wife. Harris' journalism was too candid for the governor and council of the Massachusetts Bay Colony, who stopped the publication four days after the newspaper appeared.

The nation's first consecutively issued (published more than once) newspaper was *The Boston News-Letter*, which appeared in 1704. It was one half-sheet printed on two sides. In the first issue, editor John Campbell reprinted the queen's latest speech, some maritime news and one advertisement telling people how to put an ad in his paper. Like many subsequent colonial publishers, Campbell reprinted several items from the London papers.

Seditious Language Language that authorities believe could incite rebellion against the government.

Libel A false statement that damages a person's character or reputation by exposing that person to public ridicule or contempt.

James Franklin's *New England Courant* Establishes an Independent Press Tradition

The next challenge to British control came when James Franklin started his own newspaper in Boston in 1721. His *New England Courant* was the first American newspaper to appear without the crown's "Published by Authority" sanction. *Thus, James Franklin began the tradition of an independent press in this country.*

Benjamin Franklin Introduces Competition

In 1729, Benjamin Franklin, James' younger brother, moved to Philadelphia and bought the *Pennsylvania Gazette* to compete with the only other newspaper in town, the *American Weekly Mercury* published by Andrew Bradford. The *Pennsylvania Gazette* became the most influential and most financially successful of all the colonial newspapers. In the same print shop that printed the *Gazette*, Franklin published *Poor Richard's Almanack* in 1732, an annual book that sold about 10,000 copies a year for the next 25 years. *Benjamin Franklin proved that a printer could make money without government sanctions or support.*

Truth Versus Libel: The Zenger Trial

In New York, John Peter Zenger started the *New York Weekly Journal* in 1733. The *Journal* continually attacked Governor William Cosby for incompetence, and on November 17, 1734, Zenger was arrested and jailed, charged with printing false and seditious writing. (***Seditious language*** is language that authorities believe could incite rebellion against the government.) While Zenger was in jail, his wife, Anna, continued to publish the paper.

Zenger's trial began on August 4, 1735, nine months after his arrest. His defense attorney argued that *truth was a defense against libel*, and that if Zenger's words were true, they could not be libelous. (A ***libelous*** statement is a false statement that damages a person by questioning that person's character or reputation.)

The trial established a *landmark precedent for freedom of the press in America—the concept that truth is the best defense for libel.* If what someone publishes is true, the information cannot be considered libelous. (The issue of libel is explained in **Chapter 14**.)

Women's Early Role as Publishers

Colonial women were not encouraged to work outside the home at all. Therefore, women who published newspapers during the colonial period are especially notable because so few women managed businesses early in the nation's history. Early colonial women printers, such as Anna Zenger, usually belonged to printing families that trained wives and daughters to work in the print shops. By the time the American Revolution began, at least 14 women had worked as printers in the colonies. One of these family-trained printers was the first woman publisher.

Elizabeth Timothy became editor of the weekly *South Carolina Gazette* in Charleston when her husband, Lewis, died unexpectedly and their son, Peter, was only 13. Elizabeth Timothy published her first edition on January 4, 1737, under her son's name. Her first editorial appealed to the community to continue to support the "poor afflicted widow and six small children." Mother and son ran the paper together until 1746, when Peter formally took over the business.

Birth of the Partisan Press

As dissatisfaction with British rule grew in the colonies, newspapers became political tools that fostered the debate that eventually led to the colonies' independence. By 1750, 14 weekly newspapers were being published in the colonies.

The Stamp Act

Opposition to the British Stamp Act in 1765 signaled the beginning of the revolutionary period. The Stamp Act taxed publishers a halfpenny for each issue that was a half-sheet or smaller and one penny for a full sheet. Each advertisement was taxed two shillings. All the colonial newspapers, even those loyal to the crown, fought the act.

Many newspapers threatened to stop publication, but only a few of them did. Most editors published newspapers that mocked the tax. William Bradford III issued the famous tombstone edition of the *Pennsylvania Journal* on October 31, 1765. The front page, bordered in black, showed a skull and crossbones where the official stamp should have been.

The Stamp Act Congress met in New York in October 1765 and adopted the now-familiar slogan "No taxation without representation." Parliament, facing united opposition from all the colonial publishers, repealed the Stamp Act on March 18, 1766.

Getty Images

Furious colonists reacted to the Stamp Act in 1765 by throwing stamped documents onto a bonfire in Boston. Newspaper publishers threatened to stop publication, but instead printed editions that mocked the tax. The Stamp Act was repealed a year later.

The Alien and Sedition Laws

During the early part of the country's history, journalists often used newspapers as a way to oppose the new government. The Alien and Sedition Laws, passed by Congress in 1798, were the federal government's first attempt to control its critics. Congress said that anyone who "shall write, print, or publish . . . false, scandalous and malicious writing or writings against the government of the United States, or either house of the Congress of the United States, or the President of the United States" could be fined up to $2,000 and jailed for two years.

Several journalists went to jail. A Boston publisher was jailed for libeling the Massachusetts legislature. A New York editor was fined $100 and jailed for four months. By 1800, the angry rhetoric had dissipated. The Alien and Sedition Laws expired after two years and were not renewed. However, *throughout American press history, the tradition of an independent press, established by James Franklin in 1721, continued to confront the government's desire to restrain criticism.*

Buyenlarge/Archive Photos/Getty Images

On the frontier, journalists learned to improvise. This press operation, assembled to publish the *New York Herald*, was set up under a tree.

Technology Helps Newspapers Reach New Audiences

Technological advances of the 19th century—such as cheaper newsprint, mechanized printing and the telegraph—meant newspapers could reach a wider audience faster than before. Confined to eastern cities and highly educated urban audiences during the 1700s, newspaper publishers in the 1800s sought new readers—from the frontier, from among the nation's growing number of immigrants and from within the shrinking Native American population. This expansion resulted in three new developments for American newspapers: frontier journalism, ethnic and cultural newspapers and the alternative press.

Frontier Journalism

Gold, silver and adventure lured people to the West, and when the people arrived, they needed newspapers. The *Indiana Gazette*, the *Texas Gazette*, the *Oregon Spectator*, the *Weekly Arizonian* and Colorado's *Rocky Mountain News* met that need, aided by the telegraph, which moved news easily from coast to coast.

The wide-open land beckoned many journalists. The most celebrated journalist to chronicle the frontier was Samuel Clemens, who traveled to Nevada in 1861, prospecting for silver. Clemens didn't find any silver, but a year later Virginia City's *Territorial Enterprise*—the area's largest paper—hired him for $25 a week. Clemens first signed his name as Mark Twain on a humorous travel letter written for the *Enterprise*.

Ethnic and Native American Newspapers

English-language newspapers did not satisfy everyone's needs. In the first half of the 19th century, many newspapers sought to succeed by catering to ethnic and cultural interests. In the early 1800s, Spanish-speaking people in Georgia could read *El Misisipi*. Herman Ridder's German newspaper, *New Yorker Staats-Zeitung*, founded in 1845, was the most successful foreign-language newspaper in the United States. It formed the financial basis for today's Knight Ridder chain, which was bought by McClatchy Co. in 2006.

People outside the mainstream of society, such as Spanish and German immigrants, used newspapers to create a sense of community and ethnic identity. In the 1800s, Native Americans who had been displaced by the settlers also felt a need to express their culture through a newspaper. As a non-mainstream group, they especially wanted to voice their complaints.

On February 21, 1828, the nation's first Native American newspaper appeared. Elias Boudinot, a Native American who had been educated at a northern seminary, launched the *Cherokee Phoenix*. The Cherokee nation held exclusive control over the four-page paper, which was printed half in English and half in an 86-character alphabet that represented the Cherokee language. (Authorities shut down the press in 1832 because they felt Boudinot was arousing antigovernment sentiment.)

Dissident Voices Create the Early Alternative Press

Two strong social movements—emancipation and women's suffrage—brought new voices to the American press. This ***alternative press*** movement signaled the beginning of a significant American journalistic tradition. Newspapers became an outlet for the voices of social protest, a tradition

Alternative, or Dissident, Press Media that present alternative viewpoints that challenge the mainstream press.

that continues today. (The alternative press also is called the ***dissident press***.)

Six early advocates for domestic change who used the press to advance their causes—the abolition of slavery and suffrage for women—were John B. Russwurm, the Reverend Samuel Cornish, Frederick Douglass, William Lloyd Garrison, Jane Grey Swisshelm and Ida B. Wells.

In 1827, Russwurm and Cornish, who were African American, started *Freedom's Journal* in New York City with very little money. They launched their newspaper to respond to racist attacks in several local newspapers. *Freedom's Journal* lasted for two years and reached only a few readers, but it was the beginning of an African American press tradition that eventually created more than 2,700 newspapers, magazines and quarterly journals.

What often has been called the most important African American pre-Civil War newspaper was Frederick Douglass' weekly *North Star*. "Right is of no Sex—Truth is of no Color—God is the Father of us all, and we are all Brethren" read the masthead. Beginning in 1847, Douglass struggled to support the *North Star* by giving lectures. The newspaper eventually reached 3,000 subscribers in the United States and abroad with its emancipation message.

Library of Congress

CHEROKEE PHOENIX.

The Granger Collection, NYC

Elias Boudinot (left) published the first Native American newspaper (right), the *Cherokee Phoenix*, from 1828 to 1832. The newspaper used the Cherokee language.

In 1831, William Lloyd Garrison began publishing *The Liberator*, a weekly abolitionist paper in Boston. As a white man fighting slavery and advocating women's rights, Garrison was attacked by a mob in 1835 but survived when the Boston mayor jailed him for his own protection. Garrison continued to publish *The Liberator* for 30 years.

Like Douglass and Garrison, Ida B. Wells and Jane Grey Swisshelm campaigned for civil rights. Swisshelm's first byline appeared in 1844 in the *Spirit of Liberty*, published in Pittsburgh. Four years later she began her own abolitionist publication, the *Pittsburgh Saturday Visiter*, which also promoted women's rights. (See **Media/Impact: People**, "Ida B. Wells Uses Her Pen to Fight 19th Century Racism," p. 54.)

As a correspondent for Horace Greeley's *New York Tribune* in Washington, D.C., Swisshelm convinced Vice President Millard Fillmore to let her report from the Senate press gallery. The gallery had been open to male journalists for 55 years, and on May 21, 1850, Swisshelm became the first female journalist to sit in the gallery.

These pioneers—Russwurm, Cornish, Douglass, Garrison, Wells and Swisshelm—used newspapers to lobby for

Stock Montage/Archive Photos/Getty Images

Stock Montage/Archive Photos/Getty Images

Frederick Douglass (left) established the weekly newspaper *North Star*, often called the most important African American pre-Civil War newspaper. William Lloyd Garrison (right), a Boston abolitionist, founded the New England Anti-Slavery Society and published *The Liberator*, another important abolitionist newspaper.

Media/Impact PEOPLE

Ida B. Wells Uses Her Pen to Fight 19th Century Racism

By Shirley Biagi

Ida B. Wells didn't start out to be a journalist, but the cause of emancipation drew her to the profession. Wells, who eventually became co-owner of the *Free Speech and Headlight* in Memphis, Tennessee, documented racism wherever she found it. She is known for her pioneering stand against the unjustified lynching of African Americans in the 1890s.

Ida B. Wells, part owner of the *Memphis Free Speech and Headlight*, wrote under the pseudonym Iola. Wells' struggle for social justice represents an early historical example of the role of the dissident press in American history.

In 1878, both of Wells' parents and her infant sister died in a yellow fever epidemic, so 16-year-old Wells took responsibility for her six brothers and sisters, attended Rush College, and then moved the family to Memphis, where she became a teacher.

A Baptist minister who was editor of the Negro Press Association hired Wells to write for his paper. She wrote under the pseudonym Iola.

In 1892, Wells wrote a story about three African American men who had been kidnapped from a Memphis jail and killed. "The city of Memphis has demonstrated that neither character nor standing avails the Negro, if he dares to protect himself against the white man or become his rival," she wrote. "We are outnumbered and without arms." While in New York, she read in the local paper that a mob had sacked the *Free Speech* office.

Wells decided not to return to Memphis. She worked in New York and lectured in Europe and then settled in Chicago, where she married a lawyer, Ferdinand Lee Barnett. Ida Wells-Barnett and her husband actively campaigned for African American rights in Chicago, and she continued to write until she died at age 69 in 1931.

social change. These dissident newspapers offered a forum for protest and reform, which is an important cultural role for an independent press.

Newspapers Seek Mass Audiences and Big Profits

The voices of social protest reached a limited, committed audience, but most people could not afford to subscribe to a daily newspaper. Newspapers were sold by advance yearly subscription for $6 to $10 at a time when most skilled workers earned less than $750 a year. Then, in 1833, Benjamin Day demonstrated that he could profitably appeal to a mass audience by dropping the price of a newspaper to a penny and selling the paper on the street every day.

Benjamin Day's *New York Sun* published sensational news and feature stories for the working class. He was able to lower the price to a penny by filling the paper with advertising and by hiring newsboys to sell the paper on street corners. In its four pages, this first successful penny paper reported local gossip and sensationalized police news and carried a page and a half of advertising.

Newsboys (and some newsgirls) bought 100 papers for 67 cents and tried to sell them all each day to make a profit. Even *The New York Times*, founded by Henry J. Raymond in

1851, was a ***penny paper*** when it began. The legacy of these early penny papers continues in today's gossip columns and crime reporting.

Newspapers Dominate the Early 20th Century

For the first 30 years of the 20th century—before radio and television—newspapers dominated the country. Newspapers were the nation's single source of daily dialogue about political, cultural and social issues. This was also the era of the greatest newspaper competition for readers.

AP Photo

Peter Stackpole/Time & Life Pictures/Getty Images

The battle for New York readers between Joseph Pulitzer (left) and William Randolph Hearst (right) provoked the Spanish-American War and spawned the term *yellow journalism*.

Competition Breeds Sensationalism

In large cities such as New York, as many as 10 newspapers competed for readers at once, so the publishers looked for new ways to expand their audience. Two New York publishers—Joseph Pulitzer and William Randolph Hearst—revived and refined the ***penny press*** sensationalism that had begun in 1833 with Benjamin Day's *New York Sun*. Like Benjamin Day, Pulitzer and Hearst proved that newspapers could reap enormous fortunes for their owners. They also demonstrated that credible, serious reporting is not all that people want in a newspaper. Pulitzer and Hearst promoted giveaways, included gossip and fabricated stories.

An ambitious man who knew how to grab his readers' interest, Joseph Pulitzer published the first newspaper comics and sponsored journalist Nellie Bly on an around-the-world steamship and railroad trip to try to beat the fictional record in the popular book *Around the World in 80 Days*. Bly finished the trip in 72 days, 6 hours and 11 minutes, and the stunt brought Pulitzer the circulation he craved. In San Francisco, young William Randolph Hearst, the new editor of the San Francisco Examiner, sent a reporter to cover Bly's arrival.

In 1887, William Randolph Hearst convinced his father, who owned the *San Francisco Examiner*, to let him run the paper. Hearst tagged the *Examiner* "The Monarch of the Dailies," added a lovelorn column, and attacked several of his father's influential friends in the newspaper. He spent money wildly, buying talent from competing papers and staging showy promotional events.

Yellow Journalism Is Born: Hearst's Role in the Spanish-American War

In New York, Hearst bought the *New York Journal*, hired Pulitzer's entire Sunday staff and cut the *Journal*'s price to a penny, so Pulitzer dropped his price to match it. Hearst bought a color press and printed color comics. Then he stole Pulitzer's popular comic "Hogan's Alley," which included a character named the Yellow Kid.

Hearst relished the battle, as the *Journal* screamed attention-grabbing crime headlines, such as "Thigh of the Body Found," and the paper offered $1,000 for information that would convict the murderer. Critics named this sensationalism ***yellow journalism*** after the Yellow Kid, a term that is still used to describe highly emotional, exaggerated or inaccurate reporting that emphasizes crime, sex and violence. By 1900, about one-third of the metropolitan dailies were following the trend toward yellow journalism.

Beginning in 1898, the Spanish-American War provided the battlefield for Pulitzer and Hearst to act out their newspaper war. For three years, the two newspapers

Penny Press or Penny Paper A newspaper produced by dropping the price of each copy to a penny and supporting the production cost through advertising.

Yellow Journalism News that emphasizes crime, sex and violence; also called jazz journalism and tabloid journalism.

DAILY NEWS EXTRA

DEAD!

RUTH SNYDER'S DEATH PICTURED!—This is perhaps the most remarkable exclusive picture in the history of criminology. It shows the actual scene in the Sing Sing death house as the lethal current surged through Ruth Snyder's body at 11:06 last night. Her helmeted head is stiffened in death, her face masked and an electrode strapped to her bare right leg. The autopsy table on which her body was removed is beside her. Judd Gray, mumbling a prayer, followed her down the narrow corridor at 11:14. "Father, forgive them, for they don't know what they are doing?" were Ruth's last words. The picture is the first Sing Sing execution picture and the first of a woman's electrocution.

New York Daily News/Getty Images

SPORTS • FINAL

DAILY NEWS

MILLION READERS EVERY DAY

Federal prosecutors look ready to come to terms with Madoff

DEAL WITH THE DEVIL

PAGE 5

RIHANNA'S TORMENT

Family wants star to sever ties to Chris Brown - Page 3

Play NEW YORK LOTTO

Jackpot Is Now $21 Million!

NY Daily News Archive/Getty Images

This 1928 photo of Ruth Snyder's execution (left) in the *New York Daily News* exemplifies the screaming headlines and large photographs of early tabloids that still populate today's *Daily News* (right). At the Snyder execution, a reporter from the *Daily News* strapped a small hidden camera to his leg and surreptitiously snapped a picture of Snyder as she was executed. During a sensational trial, fueled by tabloid headlines, an all-male jury convicted Snyder of helping her boyfriend kill her husband.

unrelentingly overplayed events in the Cuban struggle for independence from Spain, each trying to beat the other with irresponsible, exaggerated stories, many of them invented.

The overplayed events that resulted from the sensational competition between Pulitzer and Hearst showed that newspapers could have a significant effect on political attitudes. The Spanish-American War began a few months after the sinking of the U.S. battleship Maine in Havana harbor, which killed 266 crewmembers. The cause of the explosion that sank the ship was never determined, but Pulitzer's and Hearst's newspapers blamed the Spanish.

Hearst dubbed the event "the *Journal*'s War," but in fact Hearst and Pulitzer shared responsibility because both men had inflamed the public unnecessarily about events in Cuba. *The serious consequences of their yellow journalism vividly demonstrated the importance of press responsibility.*

Tabloid A small-format newspaper that features large photographs and illustrations along with sensational stories.

Tabloid Journalism: Selling Sex and Violence

The journalistic legacy of Day, Pulitzer and Hearst surfaced again in the tabloid journalism of the 1920s, also called jazz journalism. In 1919, the publishers of the *New York Daily News* sponsored a beauty contest to inaugurate the nation's first tabloid. A ***tabloid*** is a small-format newspaper, usually 11 inches by 14 inches, featuring illustrations and sensational stories.

The *Daily News* merged pictures and screaming headlines with reports about crime, sex and violence to exceed anything that had appeared before. It ran full-page pictures with short, punchy text. Love affairs soon became big news and so did murders. In the ultimate example of tabloid journalism, a *Daily News* reporter strapped a camera to his ankle in 1928 and took a picture of Ruth Snyder, who had conspired to kill her husband, as she was electrocuted at Sing Sing prison.

Snyder's picture covered the front page, and the caption stated, "This is perhaps the most remarkable exclusive picture in the history of criminology." Photojournalism had taken a sensational turn. Today, yellow journalism's successors are the supermarket tabloids, such as the *National Enquirer*, which feature large photographs and stories about sex, violence and celebrities.

Unionization Encourages Professionalism

The first half of the 20th century brought the widespread unionization of newspaper employees, which standardized wages at many of the nation's largest newspapers. Labor unions were first established at newspapers in 1800, and the International Typographical Union went national in the mid-1850s.

Other unions formed to represent production workers at newspapers, but reporters didn't have a union until 1934, when *New York World-Telegram* reporter Heywood Broun called on his colleagues to organize. Broun became the Newspaper Guild's first president. Today, the Guild continues to cover employees at many of America's urban newspapers. Unions represent roughly one in five newspaper employees.

With the rise of unions, employee contracts, which once had been negotiated in private, became public agreements. In general, salaries for reporters at union newspapers rose, and this eventually led to a sense of professionalism, including codes of ethics.

Television Brings New Competition

The invention of television dramatically affected the newspaper industry. Newspaper publishers had learned how to live with only one other 20th-century news industry—radio. In the 1920s, when radio first became popular, newspapers refused to carry advertising or time logs for the programs, but eventually newspapers conceded the space to radio.

In the 1950s, however, television posed a larger threat: TV offered moving images of the news, along with entertainment programs. The spread of television demonstrated how interrelated the media were. The newspaper industry gave up its position as the number one news medium and was forced to share the news audience with broadcasting. Eventually, television's influence changed both the look and the content of many newspapers.

Francis Miller/Time Life Pictures/Getty Images

In the 1950s, newspaper readership began to decline with the introduction of television, as TV became America's primary source of news and entertainment. Television sets replaced radio receivers as the central piece of living room furniture. In 1958, two orphaned German brothers, adopted by a family in the United States, watch television for the first time on a TV set in their new parents' home.

Alternative Press Revives Voices of Protest

The social movements of the 1960s briefly revived one portion of the early newspaper industry—the alternative press. Like their 1800s predecessors in the abolitionist and emancipation movements, people who supported the revival of the alternative press in the 1960s believed the mainstream press was avoiding important issues, such as the anti-Vietnam War movement, the civil rights movement and the gay rights movement.

In 1964, as a way to pass along news about the antiwar movement, the *Los Angeles Free Press* became the first underground paper to publish regularly. The *Barb* in Berkeley, California, *Kaleidoscope* in Chicago and *Quicksilver Times* in Washington, D.C., soon followed. In 1965, Jim Michaels launched the nation's first gay newspaper, the Los Angeles *Advocate*. What the 1960s underground press proved already had been proven in the 19th century: In America, causes need a voice, and if those voices are not represented in the mainstream press, publications emerge to support alternative views.

Newspapers Expand and Contract

Since the 1970s, the overall number of newspapers has declined. Many afternoon papers died when TV took over the evening news. Other afternoon papers changed to morning papers. Then, newspaper publishers realized television could provide the news headlines, but newspapers could offer the background that television news could not.

Newspaper publishers also began to exploit the popularity of television personalities, and expanded their entertainment, business and sports news. Eventually, advertisers realized that newspapers gave people the broader news that TV couldn't deliver. Also, viewers couldn't clip coupons out of their television sets or retrieve copies of yesterday's TV ads, so advertisers began to use newspapers to complement television advertising campaigns. To try to match television's visual appeal, newspapers introduced advanced graphics and vivid color.

Today newspapers are facing declining readership, especially among young readers, and many major newspapers have announced staff cuts in an attempt to stay as

Media/Impact AUDIENCE

Illustration 3.1

Percentage of Adults Who Say They Use Newspapers as Their Main News Source (includes Internet and cell phone readers)

Adults between 18 and 35 are much less likely to read a daily newspaper—even online—than mature adults (age 45 and above).

Source: The Pew Research Center for People and the Press, "Internet Gains on Television as Public's Main News Source," January 4, 2011.

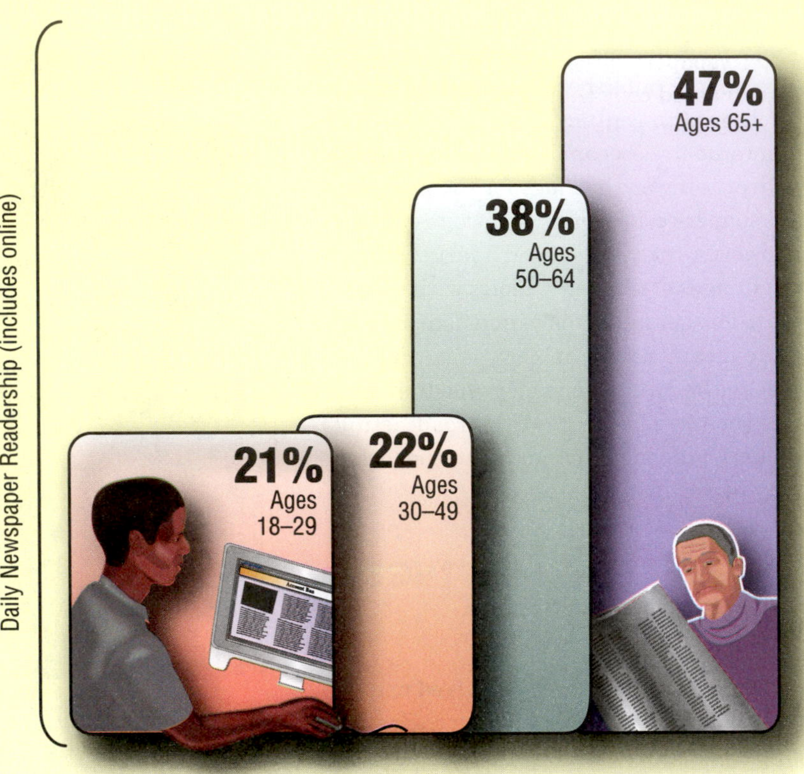

profitable as they have been in the past. (See **Illustration 3.1**). To survive, most of today's dailies have become part of a chain; most cities have only one newspaper.

Newspapers at Work

Many colonial publishers handled all the tasks of putting out a newspaper single-handedly, but today's typical newspaper operation is organized into two separate departments: the editorial side and the business side. The *editorial side* handles everything that you read in the paper—the news and feature stories, editorials, cartoons, photographs and online editions. The *business side* handles everything else—production, advertising, distribution and administration.

On the editorial side at a medium-size daily newspaper, different *editors*—a news editor, a sports editor, a features editor and a business editor, for example—handle different parts of the paper. The managing editor oversees these news departments. A copyeditor checks the reporters' stories before they are set in type, and a layout editor positions the stories. Editorial writers and cartoonists usually work for an editorial page editor. The editorial department usually also manages all aspects of the newspaper's Internet editions. All editorial employees report to the *editor-in-chief* or the *publisher* or both.

A *business manager* and his or her staff run the business side of the paper: getting the paper out to subscribers, selling advertising and making sure the paper gets printed every day. These people also ultimately report to the editor-in-chief or the publisher. Sometimes the publisher also owns the paper. If a corporation owns the paper, the publisher reports to its board of directors.

Almost all newspapers today run Web sites, and many newspapers have created New Media departments to introduce strong graphic and video elements to their Internet editions.

Syndicates News agencies that sell articles for publication to a number of newspapers simultaneously.

Syndicates

Newspapers also can add to their content without having to send their own reporters to stories by using ***syndicates***, which are news agencies that sell articles for publication to a number of newspapers simultaneously. The first syndicated column was a fashion letter distributed in 1857.

Today, many newspapers syndicate their columns and features to try to add income. Syndicates mainly provide columnists such as Dear Abby, as well as comics and editorial cartoons. The price of the syndicated copy for each newspaper is based on the newspaper's circulation. A large newspaper pays more for syndicated copy than a small newspaper, but revenue from syndication is limited.

Newspapers Struggle to Retain Readers

In the 1980s, newspaper companies looking for new ways to make money rediscovered and expanded on some old ideas. Gannett Co. introduced a new national newspaper, *USA Today*, in the 1980s with bold graphics and shorter stories, and more newspaper organizations joined the syndication business. Many newspapers introduced Internet editions in the 1990s, and today online publishing is an essential element of any newspaper business. (See **Media/Impact: Culture**, "The Web Eclipses Print Newspapers as a News Source," p. 60.)

Newspapers depend primarily on advertising for support. Subscriptions and newsstand sales account for only a small percentage of newspaper income.

Today's newspapers are maintaining most of their readership but only because they've added Internet editions. Big-city newspapers lost readers as people moved to the suburbs, and suburban newspapers grew, as well as suburban editions of big-city papers.

But as people stop reading the printed newspaper and migrate to the Internet, and as younger readers abandon newspapers altogether (even online), newspaper revenues are declining very quickly, and some newspapers have been shut down. More than 100 newspapers closed in the U.S. in the first six months of 2009. Seattle lost Washington state's oldest newspaper, the *Seattle Post-Intelligencer*, and Denver lost the *Rocky Mountain News*. "In 2009 and 2010, all the two-newspaper markets will become one-newspaper markets," said Mike Simonton of Fitch Ratings, a company that analyzes the newspaper industry, "and you will start to see one-newspaper markets become no-newspaper markets." By 2011, Simmons' prediction had come true, as the number of newspapers continued to decline.

National Newspapers

In 1982, the Gannett newspaper chain (which owns more newspapers than any other chain) created *USA Today*, which it calls "The Nation's Newspaper." Gannett designed *USA Today* to compete with the country's two other major national newspapers, *The Wall Street Journal* and *The New York Times*. Dubbing it "McPaper" with only "McNuggets" of news, critics called *USA Today* the fast-food approach to news. It features expensive color graphics, a detailed national weather report, comprehensive sports coverage and news stories that rarely run longer than 600 words.

USA Today went after a different audience—people who don't want to spend a lot of time reading but who want to know the headlines. Someone in an airport or someone who likes something to read on a coffee break, Gannett argued, may not need a paper the size of *The Wall Street Journal* or a large metropolitan daily. *USA Today* succeeded, and Gannett's innovations also have influenced many other newspapers, which added graphics and color and shortened the average length of stories.

Today, *The Journal*, *USA Today*, and *The Times* publish regional editions by satellite so that a local bank, for example, can place an ad in a regional edition of a national newspaper. Each area's regional edition is distributed in a defined geographic area, so a local advertiser (such as the bank) pays a lower price than someone who advertises nationwide.

USA Today (owned by Gannett), *The Journal* (owned by Rupert Murdoch's News Corp.) and *The Times* (owned by The New York Times Co.) are in constant competition to become the nation's number one newspaper. Each paper has more than a million daily readers for its print edition, with an expanded audience online. Still, even the expanded online audience is not enough to consistently maintain profits, so they are always trying to find new readers or grab them from their competitors.

In 2010, *The Wall Street Journal* announced that it would add a local news section to its New York edition, in direct competition with *The New York Times*. The same year, Gannett launched HighSchoolSports.net, to offer comprehensive local high school sports coverage throughout the country. For newspapers, high school sports have been a mainstay of local news coverage. Many weekly newspapers focus on high school sports reporting, targeted at a younger audience and their parents to help maintain readership. (See **Media/Impact: Audience**, "Where Newspapers Thrive," p. 61.)

Internet Editions

Newspaper publishing companies first launched Internet editions in the late 1990s to try to capture new audiences for the information they gather. Today, newspapers arriving on-screen are an essential part of newspapers' reader-friendly strategy, but Internet editions generate a lot less revenue than paper editions because a paper edition can carry much more advertising than an online version. Paper editions also generate revenue from newsstand sales and

Media/Impact CULTURE

The Web Eclipses Print Newspapers as a News Source

By Jeff Bercovici

It was inevitable, and now it's official: The Internet has overtaken printed newspapers as a source of news for Americans.

According to the latest edition of the news consumption survey conducted biennially by the Pew Research Center for the People and the Press, 34 percent of those polled said they had gone online for news the previous day, while 31 percent said they had read a newspaper. That represents a reversal from 2008, when 29 percent of respondents had gotten news online the day before while 34 percent had read a newspaper. It's the first time since Pew began asking people about the online news consumption that the Internet outpolled newspapers as a news source.

Justin Sullivan/Getty Images

According to the Pew Research Center for the People and the Press, in 2010 more people read newspapers online than read the printed edition.

That shouldn't necessarily be bad news for newspaper publishers, since presumably many of those who have stopped consuming newsprint are instead reading the same stories on the websites of the same newspapers (even if those publishers haven't yet quite figured out how to effectively monetize their digital audiences). But the rise in online readership of newspapers isn't happening fast enough to offset the precipitous fall in print readership. While the proportion of respondents saying they read newspaper content online the day before nearly doubled between 2006 and 2010, from 9 percent to 17 percent, the proportion reporting having read a newspaper in any format dropped from 43 percent in 2006 to 39 percent in 2008 to 37 percent this year.

Newspapers may be losing audience share, but Americans are nevertheless consuming more news overall, thanks not only to the growing popularity of nontraditional channels including social networks, mobile phones and podcasts but also to a modest increase in TV news viewership. Overall, survey takers reported spending 70 minutes a day with the news, up 3 percent from 2008.

Jeff Bercovici, "The Web Eclipses Print Newspapers as a News Source," AOL DailyFinance, *September 13, 2010. Content © 2010 AOL Inc. AOL and the AOL logo are trademarks of AOL Inc. Used with permission.*

subscriptions but, of course, most Internet editions are available free.

Internet editions publish shorter highlights of the day's news, as well as special features that don't appear in the daily newspaper. Chat rooms offer subscribers the chance to discuss the news, for example, and other interactive features offer Internet links to more information, a list of archived stories on related topics, and updated photos and audio and video clips from breaking news events.

Newspapers also are trying to generate some income from Internet users who are willing to pay a fee for access to their archives. Many larger newspapers offer the current week's news free online, but charge a fee to retrieve the full text of stories that are more than a week old. Some newspapers offer free Internet access only to people who subscribe to their daily print edition. *The Wall Street Journal* charges a subscription fee for access to its complete online edition, and in 2010 *The New York Times* announced that it would begin charging frequent users for content.

Media/Impact AUDIENCE

Where Newspapers Thrive

By Judy Muller

We've been hearing a lot of depressing news in recent years about the dire financial prospects for big daily newspapers, including the one you're now holding. Or watching. Or, in the argot of the digital age, "experiencing."

But at the risk of sounding like I'm whistling past the graveyard, I'd like to point out that there are thousands of newspapers that are not just surviving but thriving. Some 8,000 weekly papers still hit the front porches and mailboxes in small towns across America every week and, for some reason, they've been left out of the conversation. . . .

At a time when mainstream news media are hemorrhaging and doomsayers are predicting the death of journalism (at least as we've known it), take heart: The free press is alive and well in small towns across America, thanks to the editors of thousands of weeklies who, for very little money and a fair amount of aggravation, keep on telling it like it is. . . .

"If we discover a political official misusing taxpayer funds," an editor in Dove Creek, Colo., told me, "we wouldn't hesitate to nail him to a stump. . . ."

Of course, most of these newspapers are not uncovering major scandals on a regular basis. That's not what keeps them selling at such a good clip; it's the steady stream of news that readers can only get from that publication— the births, deaths, crimes, sports and local shenanigans that only matter to the 5,000 or so souls in their circulation area. It's more than a little ironic that small-town papers have been thriving by practicing what the mainstream media are now preaching. "Hyper-localism," "citizen journalism," "advocacy journalism"—these are some of the latest buzzwords of the profession.

Welcome, Sara - | Account Settings • Current Issue |

The Canadian RECORD

Search

Blog Gallery Calendar Contact Sign-out

// archives

Sports

RSS feed for this section

The Sports archive contains 844 articles

ADVERTISEMENT

Turner Energy

Canadian Junior Varsity Results Canadian Junior Varsity Results

by Tyler Bean · February 8, 2012 · Post a comment

The JV Wildcats made their way out of Stinnett with a win on Friday night, beating the Comanches 32-23. Thanks to some tough defending, Canadian was able to hold West Texas to just 11 first half points. "Our guys played well and the entire team contributed on both ends of the court," said coach Jeff [...]

Lady Cats cruise to share of district title

by Tyler Bean · February 8, 2012 · Post a comment

Canadian's Lady Cats capped their regular season campaign with a 69-44 victory Tuesday night over a solid Sunray team. That leaves just one game before the playoffs for coach Kevin Richardson's squad: another battle against Gruver to determine the first and second seeds in the postseason. On Canadian's Senior Night, Autumn Chidester turned in what [...]

CATEGORIES

BUSINESS

CLASSIFIEDS

COMMUNITY

LOCAL NEWS

OPINION

SCHOOL

SPORTS

UNCATEGORIZED

POPULAR TAGS

basketball Blotter

Alan Halt/*The Canadian Record*

In this opinion column, University of Southern California Journalism Professor Judy Muller says that weekly newspapers like the *Canadian Record*, published in Canadian, Texas, are surviving better than dailies because weeklies provide local news their readers can't get anywhere else.

But the concepts, without the fancy names, have been around for ages in small-town newspapers.

The "holy trinity" of weekly papers consists of high school sports (where even losing teams benefit from positive spin), obituaries (where there's no need to speak ill of the dead because everyone in town already knows if the deceased was a jerk) and the police blotter. . . .

And what of the Internet threat? Many of these small-town editors have learned a lesson from watching their big-city counterparts: Don't give it away. Many weeklies [such as] the *Canadian Record* in the Texas Panhandle are charging for their Web content, and, because readers can't get that news anywhere else, they're willing to pay. . . .

I wouldn't be so bold as to predict the future, not in a media landscape that is constantly shifting. But when we engage in these discussions about how to "monetize" journalism, it's refreshing to remember a different kind of bottom line, one that lives in the hearts of weekly newspaper editors and reporters who keep churning out news for the corniest of reasons—because their readers depend on it.

Source: From Judy Muller, "Where Newspapers Thrive" September 13, 2011, latimes.com. © 2011 Judy Muller. Used by kind permission of the author.

Reprinted with permission of *The Dallas Morning News*

Courtesy of the *Siuslaw News*

Large-city newspapers, such as *The Dallas Morning News* (left), and small-town newspapers, such as the *Siuslaw News* (right), published on the Oregon coast, offer Internet editions to attract advertisers and boost their audience.

Technology Transforms Production

Since their colonial beginnings, newspapers have shown their ability to appeal to changing audiences, adapt to growing competition and continue to attract advertisers. The Newspaper Association of America and other newspaper analysts describe these recent advances:

- Reporters and photographers in the field send their stories from laptop computers using wireless technology. Photographers use video and digital cameras, transmitting their pictures to the newsroom electronically. News photography systems can reproduce still pictures for newspapers from video images and digital cameras.
- Newspapers use the Internet to sell more of the information they gather. Once a story is in a digital format, the information and photographs can easily be sold to people who want that information, such as lawyers and researchers.
- Satellite publishing brings customized national newspapers to readers in regional editions so advertisers can choose their audiences more selectively.

Today's technology also means that machines are doing work formerly done by people. For newspaper unions, this shift to technology has meant a consistent effort among newspaper owners to challenge union representation.

Before 1970, newspapers needed typographers to handset metal type, and labor unions represented most of these typographers. With the introduction of photocomposition, newspaper management slowly moved to eliminate the typographers' jobs. The unions fought the transition, and many newspaper workers went on strike—notably at the *New York Daily News* in 1990, at the *San Francisco Chronicle* and *San Francisco Examiner* in 1994 and at the *Detroit News* in 1996.

With the threat of technology eliminating even more jobs, newspaper unions are understandably worried. Membership in the Newspaper Guild (which covers reporters) has remained steady, but most of the other newspaper unions have lost members. Forecasts report that union influence at big-city newspapers will remain stable but that the effort by publishers to diffuse union influence at smaller newspapers will continue.

Consolidation Increases Chain Ownership

Because newspaper circulation is declining, large corporations have bought up many newspapers that once were family-owned. Instead of editors competing locally within a community, like Hearst battling Pulitzer, national chains now compete with one another. (See **Illustration 3.2**.)

Chain ownership doesn't necessarily mean that every newspaper in a chain speaks with the voice of the chain owner. Chains can supply money to improve a newspaper's printing plant and to add more reporters. But critics say the tendency to form chains consolidates and limits the traditional sources of information for readers. (See **Chapter 1** for more discussion of media consolidation.)

Today's Newspaper Audience Is a Moving Target

Although newspapers still hold power for advertisers, recent studies reveal that younger readers are deserting the medium. According to Grant Podelco, arts editor of the Syracuse (New York) *Herald-Journal*, "It dawned on us that if we don't start luring teenagers into the paper and start them reading us now, they may not subscribe in the future."

To stop the slide among young readers, many newspapers have added inserts directed to, and sometimes written by, teenagers. *The Wall Street Journal* introduced a high school classroom edition. At the *Chicago Tribune*, five teenage film reviewers appear in the newspaper every Friday with their choices, and a "Preps Plus" section covers high school sports. *The Dallas Morning News* runs a half-sheet called "The Mini Page," subtitled "Especially for Kids and Their Families," which carries puzzles, explanatory stories about current issues and a teacher's guide.

Female readers also are abandoning newspapers in unprecedented numbers. Karen Jurgensen, editorial page editor of *USA Today*, says that readership surveys show women today are less likely to read a daily newspaper than men. "Women across the board are more likely than men to feel that the paper doesn't speak to them," she says. To attract more female readers, *The Charlotte Observer* created a daycare beat, and some newspapers are attempting to devote more space to women's sports. Newspapers also are experimenting with a section targeted specifically for women. The *Chicago Tribune*, for example, launched a section called "WomaNews." Newspaper executives also blame television and the Internet for the declining audience, but others say people's reading habits reflect the changing uses of family time.

In some cities with large Latino populations, English-language newspapers are expanding the market by publishing Spanish-language editions, and existing Spanish-language newspapers are finding a wider audience. In areas like Dallas-Fort Worth, for example, where about a fifth of the population is Latino, newspaper companies see an ever-increasing audience with a desire for information in Spanish.

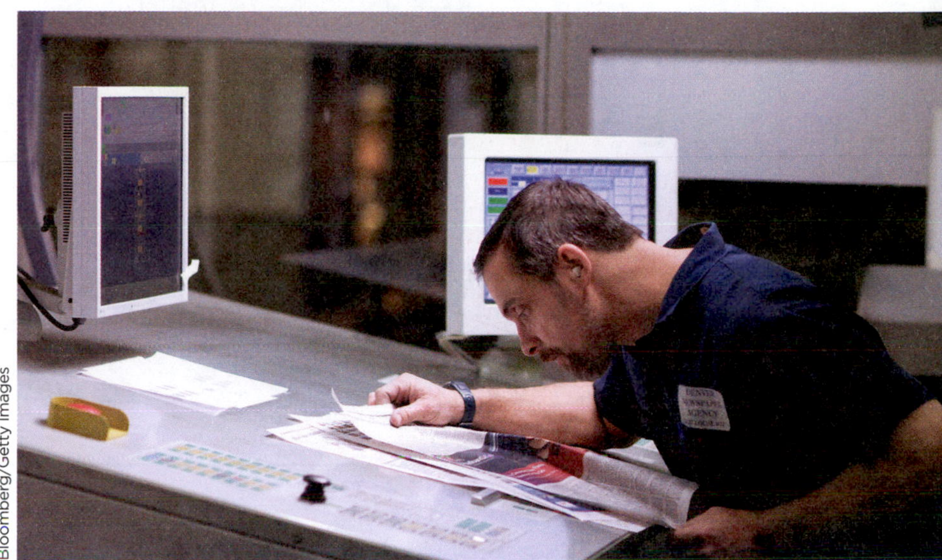

Bloomberg/Getty Images

Unionization of newspaper employees began in the 1800s when printing was entirely mechanical. New technologies have reduced the number of people required to produce a newspaper today, but unions continue to be a big factor among production employees at urban newspapers. Unions are less influential in mid-sized and small cities. On March 2, 2010, a production employee at the Denver Newspaper Agency in Denver, Co., checks a newspaper that just came off the printing press where the *Denver Post*, *USA Today* and *The Wall Street Journal* are printed.

JIMMY MARGULIES © 2005 NORTH AMERICA SYNDICATE

Media/Impact
MONEY

Illustration 3.2

Top 10 U.S. Newspaper Companies

Gannett Co., publisher of *USA Today*, is the nation's biggest newspaper company. Gannett owns more newspapers than any other chain.

Source: *"Top Companies by Medium,"* Advertising Age, *October 3, 2011.*

Newspapers are competing to maintain their audience because audiences attract advertisers—and profits. People who don't read a printed copy of a newspaper may still want to read the news online. Some large newspapers have even introduced free newspapers, hoping the advertising revenue will support the free editions.

The challenge facing newspaper owners today is how to make money with something people can get free—either a free printed newspaper or a newspaper online. The average daily printed newspaper is about two-thirds advertising, and in some printed newspapers advertising runs as high as 70 percent. National advertisers (such as Procter & Gamble) buy much more television time than printed newspaper space, but small community businesses still need local newspapers to advertise their products and services.

Newspapers are racing to figure out how to make a profit by bringing the news to an audience that is distracted by other free media and by the personal demands of their own lives. Newspapers also traditionally have brought the public information about controversies and conflicts that people sometimes would rather ignore. "It's not always our job to give readers what they want," says Dean Baquet, former editor of the *Los Angeles Times*, now at *The New York Times*. The job of newspapers is to help readers understand the world, he told *The New Yorker*. "If we don't do that, who will?"

As the country's first mass medium for news, today's newspaper companies are no longer necessarily the first place people go for information. Today's newspapers are trying to rediscover how they can continue to fulfill their responsibility to keep the public informed and still stay profitable.

REVIEW, ANALYZE, INVESTIGATE

REVIEWING CHAPTER 3

First Mass Medium to Deliver News

✓ Between 1690 and 1920, newspapers were the only mass news medium.

✓ Newspapers are historically important in defining the cultural concept of an independent press.

Publishers Fight for an Independent Press

✓ The issue of government control of newspapers surfaced early in colonial America, when the authorities stopped *Publick Occurrences* in 1690 after a single issue because the paper angered local officials.

✓ The tradition of an independent press in this country began when James Franklin published the first newspaper without the heading "Published by Authority."

✓ The John Peter Zenger case established an important legal precedent: If what a newspaper reports is true, the paper cannot successfully be sued for libel.

✓ By the time the American Revolution began, at least 14 women had worked as printers in the colonies.

✓ As dissatisfaction grew over British rule, newspapers became essential political tools in the effort to spread revolutionary ideas, including opposition to the British Stamp Act and the Alien and Sedition Laws.

Technology Helps Newspapers Reach New Audiences

✓ The technological advances of the 19th century, such as cheaper newsprint, mechanized printing and the telegraph, meant that newspapers could reach a wider audience faster than ever before.

✓ In the 1800s, newspapers sought new readers—Native Americans, immigrants and those on the nation's frontiers.

Dissident Voices Create the Early Alternative Press

✓ The abolitionist and women's suffrage movements fostered the first alternative press movements.

✓ Six early advocates for domestic change were John B. Russwurm, The Rev. Samuel Cornish, Frederick Douglass, William Lloyd Garrison and Ida B. Wells.

Newspapers Seek Mass Audiences and Big Profits

✓ Penny papers made newspapers affordable for virtually every American.

✓ The penny press made newspapers available to the masses.

✓ The legacy of the penny press continues today in gossip columns and crime reporting.

Newspapers Dominate the Early 20th Century

✓ Newspapers were the nation's single source of daily dialogue about politics, culture and social issues.

✓ Intense competition bred yellow journalism.

Unionization Encourages Professionalism

✓ Unions standardized wages at many of the nation's largest newspapers.

✓ Unions raised wages and created a sense of professionalism.

Television Brings New Competition

✓ The introduction of television contributed to a decline in newspaper readership that began in the 1950s.

✓ Newspapers were forced to share their audience with broadcasting.

Alternative Press Revives Voices of Protest

✓ The social causes of the 1960s briefly revived the alternative press.

✓ People who supported the alternative press believed the mainstream press was avoiding important issues such as the anti-Vietnam War movement, the civil rights movement and the gay rights movement.

Newspapers Expand and Contract

✓ Since the 1970s, the overall number of newspapers has declined.

✓ To try to match TV's visual appeal, newspapers introduced advanced graphics and vivid color.

✓ Today newspaper audiences are still declining, especially among young readers.

Newspapers at Work

✓ Newspaper operations are divided into two areas: business and editorial.

✓ The editorial department usually also manages all aspects of the newspaper's Internet editions.

- ✓ Editorial employees report to the editor-in-chief or the publisher or both.
- ✓ Almost all newspapers today produce Web sites.

Newspapers Struggle to Retain Readers

- ✓ Big-city newspapers are losing readers.
- ✓ Newspapers depend primarily on advertising for support.
- ✓ Most newspaper publishing companies have launched Internet editions to capture new audiences for the information they gather.
- ✓ According to the Pew Research Center for the People and the Press, in 2010 more people read newspapers online than read the printed edition.
- ✓ The nation's three national newspapers are *USA Today*, *The New York Times* and *The Wall Street Journal*.
- ✓ In 2010, *The Wall Street Journal* announced that it would add a local news section to its New York edition, in direct competition with *The New York Times*.
- ✓ In 2010, Gannett launched a national local high school sports site, highschoolsports.net, to try to attract younger readers.

Technology Transforms Production

- ✓ Wireless technology has simplified field reporting.
- ✓ Newspapers are using the Internet to sell more of the information they gather.
- ✓ Satellite publishing means national newspapers can publish regional editions.

Consolidation Increases Chain Ownership

- ✓ Large corporations have bought up newspapers that once were family-owned.
- ✓ Instead of competing locally, national chains now compete with one another.

Today's Newspaper Audience Is a Moving Target

- ✓ The future financial success of newspapers depends on their ability to appeal to a shifting audience and meet growing competition.
- ✓ Newspapers still hold power for advertisers, but recent studies reveal that younger readers are deserting the medium faster than any other group. Readership among women also has declined. To stop this slide in readership, many newspapers have introduced features and special sections targeted toward teenagers and women.
- ✓ In cities with large Latino populations, newspapers have introduced Spanish-language editions, and existing Spanish-language newspapers have expanded.
- ✓ Some large newspapers are distributing free editions in order to attract advertisers. The average daily newspaper is about two-thirds advertising.
- ✓ To survive economically, many newspapers may start charging for online content.
- ✓ Newspapers must continue to fulfill their responsibility to keep the public informed yet still stay profitable.

KEY TERMS

These terms are defined in the margins throughout this chapter and appear in alphabetical order with definitions in the Glossary, which begins on page 383.

Alternative, or Dissident, Press 52
Libelous 50
Penny Press or Penny Paper 55
Seditious Language 50
Syndicates 58
Tabloid 56
Yellow Journalism 55

CRITICAL QUESTIONS

1. Describe the circumstances surrounding the John Peter Zenger decision. Which important precedent did the case set for the American mass media? Why is this precedent so important?
2. Describe the contributions of two early colonial American women publishers.
3. Describe the impact on American society of the competition that developed between the Hearst and Pulitzer newspaper empires. Describe the style of news coverage that characterized that competition. Give an example of sensationalized reporting from your experience.
4. Discuss the growing importance of newspapers published in Spanish and other languages and of newspapers published on the Internet. Consider both the informational and the economic impacts of these changing audiences on local communities and the nation.

5. Describe some of the Internet services newspapers offer and discuss how they make newspapers more accessible to readers. Do you read a newspaper online? How often? Under which circumstances, if any, would you be willing to pay for online news content?

WORKING THE WEB

This list includes sites mentioned in the chapter and others to give you greater insight into newspaper publishing.

American Society of Newspaper Editors (ASNE)

http://www.asne.org

This professional organization for daily newspaper editors has committees and annual conventions that address such issues as ethics, diversity and the Freedom of Information Act. ASNE also is concerned about improving journalism training and education.

The Dallas Morning News

http://www.dallasnews.com

One of the major daily newspapers in Texas, *The Dallas Morning News* was a pioneer in creating an online version, DallasNews.com. The paper was the first major news organization to run an exclusive online story of convicted Oklahoma City bomber Timothy McVeigh before the printed version was distributed.

Honolulu Star-Advertiser

http://www.staradvertiser.com

In June 2010, the long-standing competition between Honolulu's two major newspapers—the 128-year-old *Honolulu Star-Bulletin* and the 154-year-old *Honolulu Advertiser*—ended when the two newspapers merged to become the *Honolulu Star-Advertiser*.

Los Angeles Times

http://www.latimes.com

As one of California's major urban newspapers, the *Los Angeles Times* is known for the quality of its reporting and its coverage of entertainment-industry news. Since 1942, it has won 35 Pulitzer Prizes. On the Web site, viewers can personalize their news pages around the content that interests them.

The Miami Herald

http://www.miamiherald.com

South Florida's daily newspaper, owned by McClatchy Co., has developed a reputation for its coverage of Caribbean and Latin American news due to Miami's large Latino population. The paper has published an international edition for readers in the Caribbean and Latin America since 1946 and in Mexico since 2002. When McClatchy Co. bought Knight Ridder in 2006, *The Herald* was the largest paper acquired in the purchase.

The New York Times

http://www.nytimes.com

Long regarded as the nation's most credible and complete newspaper, *The Times* has won over 100 Pulitzer Prizes, more than any other news organization. The New York Times Co. also owns the *International Herald Tribune* and *The Boston Globe*.

Newspaper Association of America (NAA)

http://www.naa.org

As the lobbying organization of the newspaper industry, NAA's goals are to improve newspapers' market shares, advocate their interests to the government, encourage a diverse workforce and provide business and technological guidance.

Topix

http://www.topix.net

A customizable news site founded in 2002 by developers of the Open Directory Project, Topix LLC is a privately held company with investment from Gannett Co., McClatchy Co. and Tribune Co. The Web site links news from 50,000 sources to 360,000 user-generated forums. In 2007, Topix opened its Web site to give all users the power to discuss, edit and share the news important to them.

The Washington Post

http://www.washingtonpost.com

The Post is the major daily newspaper of Washington, D.C., and the preeminent newspaper for national political news. The Washington Post Co. also owns other media, including Cable One and six television stations.

Impact/Action Videos are concise news features on topics covered in this chapter, created exclusively for **Media/Impact**. They are available for students and instructors at CengageBrain.com, and include screen access for classroom viewing and discussion questions.

> *"The 'zine is enjoying something of a comeback. . . . Their creators say 'zines offer a respite from the endless onslaught of tweets, blog posts, I.M.'s and other products of digital media."*
>
> —*Jenna Wortham,* The New York Times

Magazines: Targeting the Audience

What's Ahead?

Magazines Reflect Trends and Culture

Colonial Magazines Compete with Newspapers

Magazines Travel Beyond Local Boundaries

Publishers Locate New Readers

McClure's Launches Investigative Journalism

The New Yorker and *Time* Succeed Differently

Specialized Magazines Take Over

Companies Consolidate Ownership and Define Readership

Magazines Divide into Three Types

Magazines at Work

Magazines Compete for Readers in Crowded Markets

Readers Represent a Valuable Audience for Advertisers

Internet Editions Offer New Publishing Outlets

Magazines' Future Is on the Internet

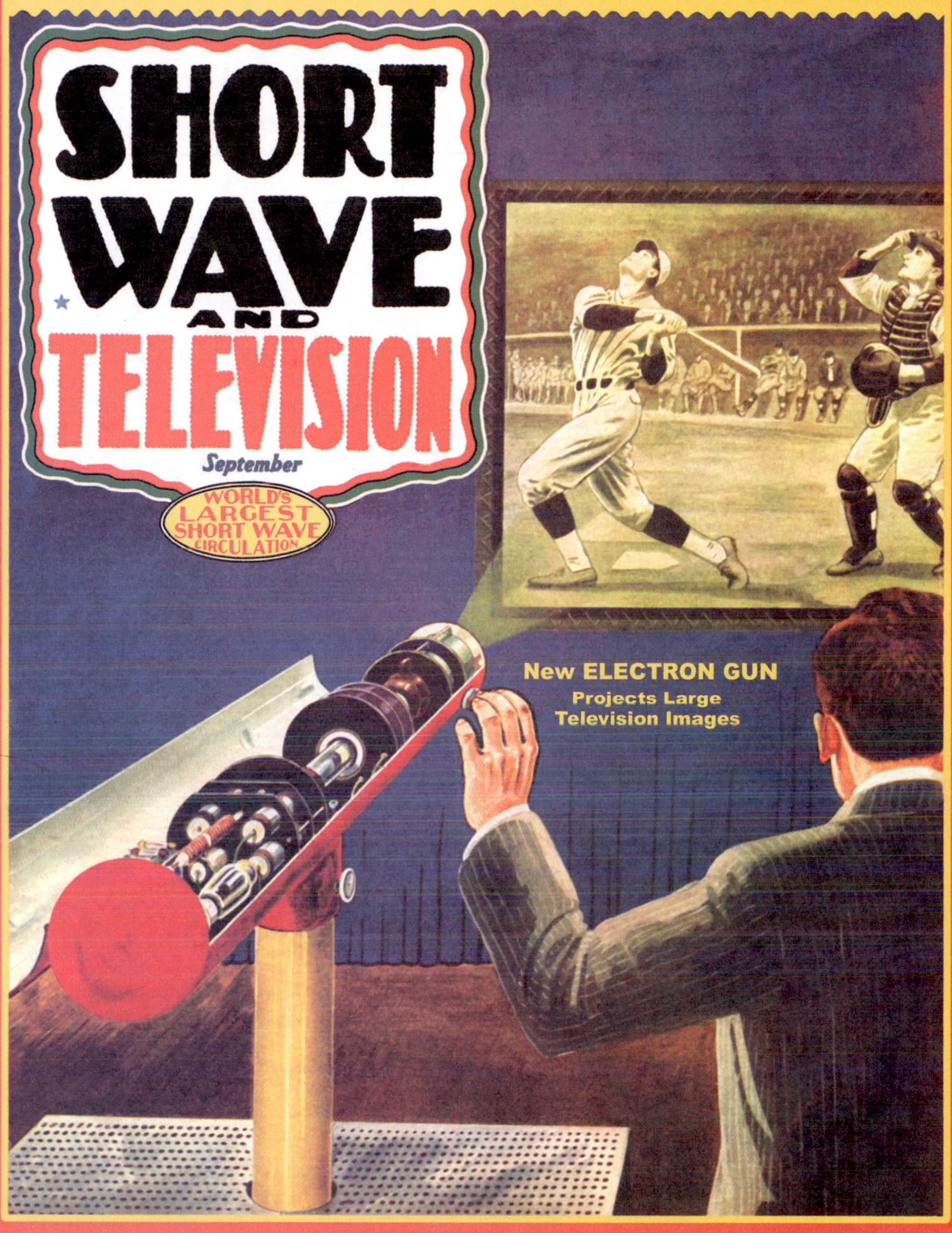

Buyenlarge/Getty Images

Magazines have always sought to serve specialized audiences. In September 1937, magazine illustrator Frank Rudolph Paul created this cover for *Short Wave and Television* magazine, targeted at "radio experimenters." The cover shows an experimental "electron gun" projecting a television image of a baseball game.

TimeFrame 1741 — Today

Magazines Grow as a Specialized Medium That Targets Readers

1741 **Benjamin Franklin and Andrew Bradford publish America's first magazines, *General Magazine* (Franklin) and *American Magazine* (Bradford).**

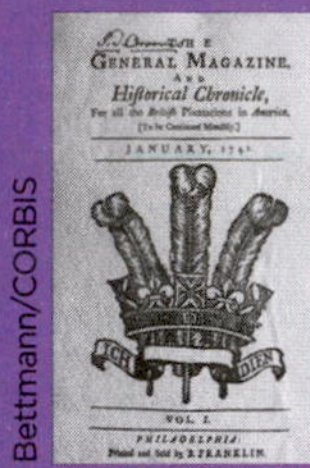

Bettmann/CORBIS

1821 The *Saturday Evening Post* becomes the first magazine to reach a wide public audience.

1830 Louis A. Godey hires Sarah Josepha Hale as the first woman editor of a general circulation women's magazine, *Godey's Lady's Book*.

1865 *The Nation*, featuring political commentary, appears in Boston.

1887 Cyrus Curtis begins publishing *The Ladies' Home Journal*.

1893 **Samuel A. McClure founds *McClure's Magazine*, the nation's first major showcase for investigative magazine journalism, featuring muckrakers Ida Tarbell and Lincoln Steffens.**

Bettmann/CORBIS

1910 W. E. B. Du Bois and the National Association for the Advancement of Colored People (NAACP) start *The Crisis*.

1923 Henry Luce creates *Time*, the nation's first newsmagazine, and then *Fortune* and *Life*, and eventually *Sports Illustrated*.

1925 Harold Ross introduces *The New Yorker*.

1945 **John Johnson launches *Ebony* and then *Jet*. Johnson's company eventually becomes the nation's most successful magazine publisher for African American readers.**

Steven L. Raymer/*National Geographic*/Getty Images

1985 **Advance Publications buys *The New Yorker* for more than $185 million, beginning the era of magazine industry consolidation. Today Condé Nast, owned by Advance Publications, publishes 30 magazines, including *The New Yorker* and *Vogue*.**

Rolls Press/Popperfoto/Getty Images

1993 *Newsweek* launches an Internet edition of the magazine.

1997 Dennis Publishing, which owns *Rolling Stone* magazine, launches *Maxim*, the most successful magazine launch in the last decade.

1999 Time Warner Inc. (publishers of *Time* magazine) merges with America Online to form the media giant AOL Time Warner Inc. (now Time Warner Inc.).

2000 Oprah Winfrey launches the lifestyle magazine *O, The Oprah Magazine*.

2005 *Slate* magazine grows popular as an Internet magazine, one of the first magazine-type publications to be issued exclusively online.

2009 **Magazine publisher Condé Nast shuts down several formerly successful magazines, such as *Gourmet* and *Modern Bride*, because of the drop in advertising revenue caused by the nation's economic downturn.**

Mario Tama/Getty Images

2010 Citing a deep slump in advertising revenue, the owners of *Newsweek* sell the magazine to an investment group. Condé Nast announces it will launch mobile and tablet editions of its most popular printed magazines.

Today Magazines are very specialized, targeting narrow groups of readers for advertisers. Large media companies publish most magazines, and some magazines are published only on the Internet. Magazine income is declining, primarily because of a large drop in overall advertising revenue. Some magazines are charging for online content.

By the early 1950s,

magazine mogul Henry Luce's *Time* and *Fortune* were well established. He often traveled with his wife, Ambassador Clare Boothe Luce, and many of the people Henry Luce met overseas wanted to talk with him about sports instead of international politics.

"Luce knew nothing about sports," says *Los Angeles Times* sports columnist Jim Murray, who in the early 1950s was writing about sports for *Time* magazine. "But every place he'd go, all over the world, the conversation would veer to the World Cup or the British Open or whatever. He got fascinated and irritated, I guess, and finally said, 'Why this all consuming interest in games?' We said, 'Well, that's the way the world is, Henry.' He said, 'Well, maybe we ought to start a sports magazine.'" The result was *Sports Illustrated*, which today is ranked among the nation's most profitable magazine brands and is published by the media giant Time Warner Inc.

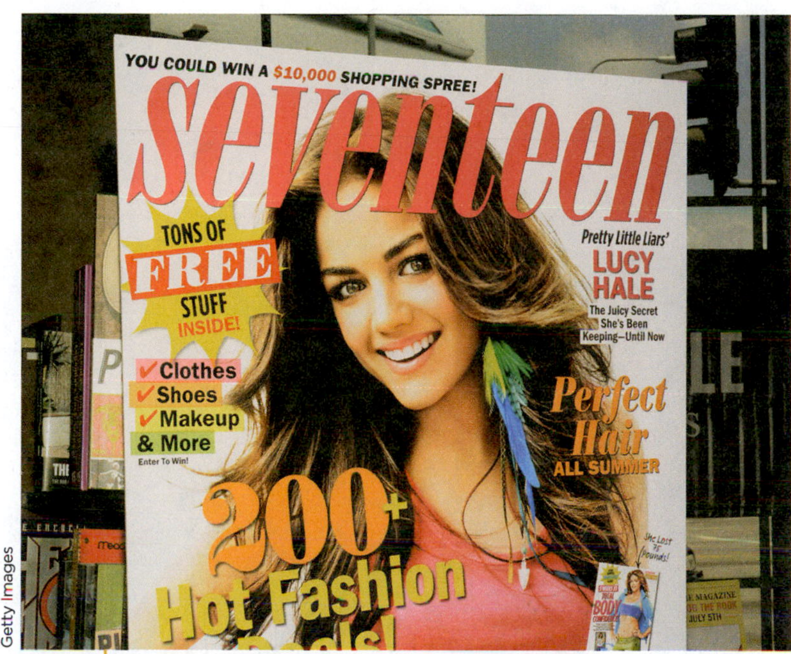

From the beginning, women have been magazines' best audience and *Seventeen* magazine continues today to attract a loyal female audience.

Sports Illustrated was one of the earliest magazines to anticipate today's trend in magazines targeted to a specific audience. Today, successful magazines cater to their audiences with articles and advertising that reflect what each audience wants. What advertisers like most about magazines is that their readers are usually good targets for the products they see advertised around the articles.

You probably have seen a copy of *Sports Illustrated* recently, or perhaps you read *Glamour* or *Maxim*. These publications, ranked among the country's top magazines, give their readers information they can't find anywhere else, and their vast readership might surprise you.

Magazines Reflect Trends and Culture

Glamour, published by Condé Nast, reaches more than 2 million readers every month and is ranked among the nation's top 10 women's magazines. *Parenting*, the nation's most successful family magazine, caters primarily to new parents and parents with small children, and the magazine's readership is very attractive to advertisers. New parents need new products to take care of that new baby. Advertisers pay $200,000 a page to reach its readers.

Maxim, a flashy magazine aimed at young adult males, was one of the most successful magazine launches ever when it debuted in 1997. Published by the same company that produces *Rolling Stone*, *Maxim* has 2.5 million readers. In 2004, *Maxim* launched Maxim Radio on the satellite radio network Sirius (now Sirius XM Radio), to reach the same audience as the magazine, 21- to 34-year-old males, and in the same year expanded the brand to Latin America.

Glamour, *Parenting* and *Maxim* demonstrate a significant fact about the history of the magazine industry: *Magazines reflect the surrounding culture and the characteristics of the society.* As readers' needs and lifestyles change, so do magazines. The current trend toward specialty and Internet magazines, in response to the shrinking number of magazine readers, is the latest development in this evolution.

Colonial Magazines Compete with Newspapers

In 1741, more than 50 years after the birth of the colonies' first newspaper, magazines entered the American media marketplace. Newspapers covered daily crises for local readers, but magazines could reach beyond the parochial concerns of small communities to carry their cultural, political and social ideas to help foster a national identity.

The U.S. magazine industry began in 1741, in Philadelphia, when Benjamin Franklin and Andrew Bradford raced each other to become America's first magazine publisher. Franklin originated the idea of starting the first American magazine, but Bradford issued his *American Magazine* first, on February 13, 1741. Franklin's first issue of *General Magazine* came out three days later. Neither magazine lasted

Bettmann/CORBIS

Pictured is a sample of 1875 clothing displayed in *Godey's Lady's Book*, one of the nation's first fashion magazines. Sarah Josepha Hale served as the magazine's editor for 40 years, beginning in 1837. She fervently supported access to higher education and property rights for women.

very long. Bradford published three issues and Franklin published six, but their efforts initiated a rich tradition.

Because they didn't carry advertising, early magazines were expensive and their circulations remained very small, limited to people who could afford them. Like colonial newspapers, early magazines primarily provided a means for political expression.

Magazines Travel Beyond Local Boundaries

Newspapers flooded the larger cities by the early 1800s, but they circulated only within each city's boundaries, so national news spread slowly. Colleges were limited to the wealthy because they cost too much to attend, and books were expensive. Magazines became America's only national medium to travel beyond local boundaries, and subscribers depended on them for news, culture and entertainment.

The magazine that first reached a large public was *The Saturday Evening Post*, started in 1821. The early *Posts* cost a nickel each and were only four pages, with no illustrations. One-fourth of the magazine was advertising, and it was affordable.

Publishers Locate New Readers

Magazines like *The Saturday Evening Post* reached a wide readership with their general interest content, but many other audiences were available to 19th-century publishers, and they spent the century locating their readership. Four enduring subjects that expanded the magazine audience in the 1800s were women's issues, social crusades, literature and the arts, and politics.

Women's Issues

Because women were a sizable potential audience, magazines were more open to female contributors than were newspapers. A central figure in the history of women's magazines in America was Sarah Josepha Hale. In 1830, Louis A. Godey was the first publisher to capitalize on a female audience. Women, most of whom had not attended school, sought out *Godey's Lady's Book* and its gifted editor, Sarah Josepha Hale, for advice on morals, manners, literature, fashion, diet and taste.

When her husband died in 1822, Hale sought work to support herself and her five children. As the editor of *Godey's* for 40 years beginning in 1837, she fervently supported higher education and property rights for women. By 1860, *Godey's* had 150,000 subscribers. Hale retired from the magazine when she was 89, a year before she died.

Social Crusades

Magazines also became important instruments for social change. *The Ladies' Home Journal* is credited with leading a crusade against dangerous medicines. Many of the ads in women's magazines in the 1800s were for patent medicines like Faber's Golden Female Pills ("successfully used by prominent ladies for female irregularities") and Ben-Yan, which promised to cure "all nervous debilities."

The Ladies' Home Journal was the first magazine to refuse patent medicine ads. Founded in 1887 by Cyrus Curtis, the *Journal* launched several crusades. It offered columns about women's issues, published popular fiction and even printed sheet music.

Editor Edward Bok began his crusade against patent medicines in 1892, after he learned that many of them contained more than 40 percent alcohol. Next, Bok revealed that a medicine sold to soothe noisy babies contained morphine. Other magazines joined the fight against dangerous ads, and partly because of Bok's crusading investigations,

Congress passed the Pure Food and Drug Act of 1906.

Fostering the Arts

In the mid-1800s, American magazines began to seek a literary audience by promoting the nation's writers. Two of today's most important literary magazines—*Harper's* and *The Atlantic*—began more than a century ago. *Harper's New Monthly Magazine*, known today as *Harper's*, first appeared in 1850.

The American literary showcase grew when *The Atlantic Monthly* appeared in 1857 in Boston. The magazine's purpose was "to inoculate the few who influence the many." That formula continues today, with *The Atlantic* and *Harper's* still publishing literary criticism and promoting political debate.

Bettmann/CORBIS

A display of the many types of magazines available to American audiences in the 1800s and early 1900s, including *Harper's New Monthly Magazine* (bottom left) and *McClure's Magazine* (upper middle).

Political Commentary

With more time (usually a month between issues) and space than newspapers had to reflect on the country's problems, political magazines provided a forum for public arguments by scholars and critical observers. Three of the nation's progressive political magazines that began in the 19th and early 20th centuries have endured: *The Nation*, *The New Republic* and *The Crisis*.

The Nation, founded in 1865, is the oldest continuously published opinion journal in the United States, offering critical literary essays and arguments for progressive change. This weekly magazine has survived a succession of owners and financial hardship. It is published by a foundation, supported by benefactors and subscribers.

Another outspoken publication, which began challenging the establishment in the early 1900s, is *The New Republic*, founded in 1914. The weekly's circulation has rarely reached 60,000, but its readers enjoy the role it plays in regularly criticizing political leaders.

An important organization that needed a voice at the beginning of the century was the National Association for the Advancement of Colored People (NAACP). For 24 years, beginning in 1910, that voice was W. E. B. Du Bois, who founded and edited the organization's monthly magazine, *The Crisis*. Du Bois began *The Crisis* as the official monthly magazine of the NAACP. In *The Crisis*, he attacked discrimination against African American soldiers during World War I, exposed Ku Klux Klan activities, and argued for African American voting and housing rights. By 1919, circulation was more than 100,000. Today, *The Crisis* continues to publish quarterly.

Postal Act Helps Magazines Grow

The Postal Act of 1879 encouraged the growth of magazines. Before the Act passed, newspapers traveled through the mail free while magazine publishers had to pay postage. With the Postal Act of 1879, Congress gave magazines second-class mailing privileges and a cheap mailing rate. This meant quick, reasonably priced distribution for magazines, and today magazines still travel on a preferential postage rate.

Aided by lower mailing costs, the number of monthly magazines grew from 180 in 1860 to over 1,800 by 1900. However, because magazines travel through the mail, they are vulnerable to censorship (See **Chapter 14**).

McClure's Launches Investigative Journalism

Colorful, campaigning journalists began investigating big business just before the turn of the 20th century. They became known as ***muckrakers***. The strongest editor in the first 10 years of the 20th century was legendary magazine

Muckrakers Investigative magazine journalists who targeted abuses by government and big business.

Underwood & Underwood/CORBIS

The Crisis, founded by W. E. B. Du Bois in 1910 as the monthly magazine of the National Association for the Advancement of Colored People (NAACP), continues to publish today as a quarterly. This photo, taken around 1910, shows workers in the magazine's offices. W.E.B. DuBois is the man standing on the far right near the door.

publisher Samuel S. McClure, who founded *McClure's Magazine* in 1893.

McClure and his magazine were very important to the Progressive era in American politics, which called for an end to the close relationship between government and big business. To reach a large readership, McClure priced his new monthly magazine at 15 cents an issue, while most other magazines sold for 25 or 35 cents. He hired writers such as Lincoln Steffens and Ida Tarbell to investigate wrongdoing. Ida Tarbell joined *McClure's* in 1894 as associate editor. Her series about President Lincoln boosted the magazine's circulation. Subsequently, Tarbell tackled a series about Standard Oil Co. (See **Media/Impact: People**, "Muckraker Ida Tarbell Targets John D. Rockefeller," page 75.)

Tarbell peeled away the veneer of the country's biggest oil trust. Her 19-part series began running in *McClure's* in 1904. Eventually the series became a two-volume book, *History of the Standard Oil Company*, which established Tarbell's reputation as a muckraker. The muckrakers' targets were big business and corrupt government. President Theodore Roosevelt coined the term *muckraker* in 1906 when he compared reformers like Tarbell and Steffens to the "Man with the Muckrake" who busily dredged up the dirt in John Bunyan's book *Pilgrim's Progress*.

By 1910, many reforms sought by the muckrakers had been adopted, and this particular type of magazine journalism declined. The muckrakers often are cited as America's original investigative journalists.

The New Yorker and *Time* Succeed Differently

Magazines in the first half of the 20th century matured and adapted to absorb the invention of radio and then television. As with magazines today, magazine publishers had two basic choices:

1. Publishers could seek a *definable, targeted loyal audience*, or
2. Publishers could seek a *broad, general readership*.

Harold Ross, founding editor of *The New Yorker*, and Henry Luce, who started Time Inc., best exemplify these two types of American publishers in the first half of the 20th century.

Harold Ross and *The New Yorker*

Harold Ross' *The New Yorker* magazine launched the wittiest group of writers that ever gathered around a table at New York's Algonquin Hotel. The "witcrackers," who met there regularly for lunch throughout the 1920s, included Heywood Broun, Robert Benchley, Dorothy Parker, Alexander Woollcott, James Thurber and Harpo Marx. Because they sat at a large round table in the dining room, the group came to be known as the Algonquin Round Table.

Harold Ross persuaded Raoul Fleischmann, whose family money came from the yeast company of the same name, to invest half a million dollars in *The New Yorker* before the magazine began making money in 1928, three years after its launch. Ross published some of the country's great commentary, fiction and humor, sprinkled with cartoons that gave *The New Yorker* its charm. Ross edited the magazine until he died in 1951, and William Shawn succeeded him.

After one owner—the Fleischmann family—and only two editors in 60 years, *The New Yorker* was sold in 1985 to Advance Publications, the parent company of one of the nation's largest magazine groups, Condé Nast. *The New Yorker* continues today to be the primary showcase for contemporary American writers and artists.

Henry Luce's Empire: *Time*

Henry Luce is the singular giant of 20th-century magazine publishing. Unlike Harold Ross, who sought a sophisticated, wealthy audience, Luce wanted to reach the largest possible

Media/Impact PEOPLE

Muckraker Ida Tarbell Targets John D. Rockefeller

When John D. Rockefeller refused to talk with her, Ida Tarbell sat at the back of the room and watched him deliver a Sunday-school sermon. In her autobiography, *All in the Day's Work,* written when she was 80, Tarbell described some of her experiences as she investigated Standard Oil:

"The impression of power deepened when Mr. Rockefeller took off his coat and hat, put on a skullcap and took a seat commanding the entire room, his back to the wall. It was the head which riveted attention. It was big, great breadth from back to front, high broad forehead, big bumps behind the ears, not a shiny head but with a wet look. The skin was as fresh as that of any healthy man about us. The thin sharp nose was like a thorn. There were no lips; the mouth looked as if the teeth were all shut hard. Deep furrows ran down each side of the mouth from the nose. There were puffs under the little colorless eyes with creases running from them.

"Wonder over the head was almost at once diverted to wonder over the man's uneasiness. His eyes were never quiet but darted from face to face, even peering around the jog at the audience close to the wall. . . .

"My two hours' study of Mr. Rockefeller aroused a feeling I had not expected, which time has intensified. I was sorry for him. I know no companion so terrible as fear. Mr. Rockefeller, for all the conscious power written in face and voice and figure, was afraid, I told myself, afraid of his own kind."

Bettmann/CORBIS

In 1904, muckraker Ida Tarbell targeted oil magnate John D. Rockefeller, who called her "that misguided woman." This photo shows Tarbell working on a story, leaving after an interview.

readership. Luce's first creation was *Time* magazine, which he founded in 1923 with his Yale classmate Briton Hadden. Luce and Hadden paid themselves $30 a week and recruited their friends to write for the magazine.

The first issue of *Time* covered the week's events in 28 pages, minus 6 pages of advertising—half an hour's reading. "It was of course not for people who really wanted to be informed," wrote Luce's biographer W. A. Swanberg. "It was for people willing to spend a half-hour to avoid being entirely uninformed." The brash news magazine became the foundation of Luce's media empire, which eventually also launched *Fortune*, *Life*, *Sports Illustrated*, *Money* and *People Weekly*. Today, *Time* is only a small part of the giant company Time Warner Inc., which includes television stations, movie studios, and book publishing companies, Home Box Office, CNN and America Online.

Luce's magazine fostered a *Life* magazine look-alike called *Ebony*, an African American magazine introduced in the 1940s by John H. Johnson. The Johnson chain also launched *Jet* magazine. At the beginning of the 21st century, *Ebony* and *Jet* had a combined readership of three million people. Johnson groomed his daughter, Linda Johnson Rice, to assume management of the company, a job Rice assumed in 2005 when her father died.

Specialized Magazines Take Over

In the 1950s, television began to offer Americans some of the same type of general interest features that magazines provided. General interest magazines collapsed. Readers

Christoph Niemann/Cartoonbank.com

Published since 1925, *The New Yorker* is one of the nation's most successful magazines and continues today to be the primary showcase for American writers and artists. The August 9, 2010 cover showcases an illustration by Christoph Niemann called "Dropped Call."

wanted specialized information they could not get from other sources. These new targeted magazines segmented the market, which meant each magazine attracted fewer readers.

Very few general interest magazines survive today. The trend, since television expanded the media marketplace, is for magazines to find a specific audience interested in the information that magazines can deliver. This is called *targeting an audience*, which today magazines can do more effectively than any other medium.

Consumer Magazines All magazines sold by subscription or at newsstands, supermarkets and bookstores.

Trade, Technical and Professional Magazines Magazines dedicated to a particular business or profession.

Companies Consolidate Ownership and Define Readership

In 1984, for the first time, the price paid for individual magazine companies and groups of magazines bought and sold in one year reached $1 billion. *U.S. News & World Report* sold for $100 million. *Billboard* sold for $40 million. Like other media industries, magazines are being gathered together under large umbrella organizations, and this trend continues today. A single magazine publishing company, such as Condé Nast, may publish 200 or more different magazines each month.

These companies tend to seek more refined audience targeting. As the audience becomes more segmented, magazine publishers envision a time when they will deliver to each reader exactly what he or she wants to read. This means an infinitely defined readership, so advertisers will be able to reach only the people they want.

Magazines Divide into Three Types

Today's magazines can be categorized into three types:

1. Consumer magazines
2. Trade, technical and professional magazines
3. Company magazines

You probably are most familiar with ***consumer magazines***, which are popularly marketed: *Time*, *Glamour*, *Parenting* and *Maxim* are examples. In the magazine business, consumer magazines are not just those that give buying advice. This term refers to all magazines sold by subscription or at newsstands, supermarkets and bookstores. As a group, consumer magazines make the most money because they have the most readers and carry the most advertising. (See **Illustration 4.1**).

People in a particular industry read ***trade, technical and professional magazines*** to learn more about their business. *Veterinary Practice Management*, for example, is a trade magazine, published as "a business guide for small animal practitioners." Other examples of trade magazines are the *Columbia Journalism Review* (published by Columbia University) and *American Medical News* (published by the American Medical Association).

Media companies issue these magazines for their specific subscribers (*Veterinary Practice Management*, for example); universities or university-connected organizations, for their subscribers (*Columbia Journalism Review*, for example); or professional associations, for their members (*American

Medical News, for example). Most trade, technical and professional magazines carry advertising directed at the professions they serve.

Company magazines are produced by businesses for their employees, customers and stockholders. These magazines usually don't carry advertising. Their main purpose is to promote the company. Chevron Corp., for instance, publishes a company magazine called *Chevron USA Odyssey*.

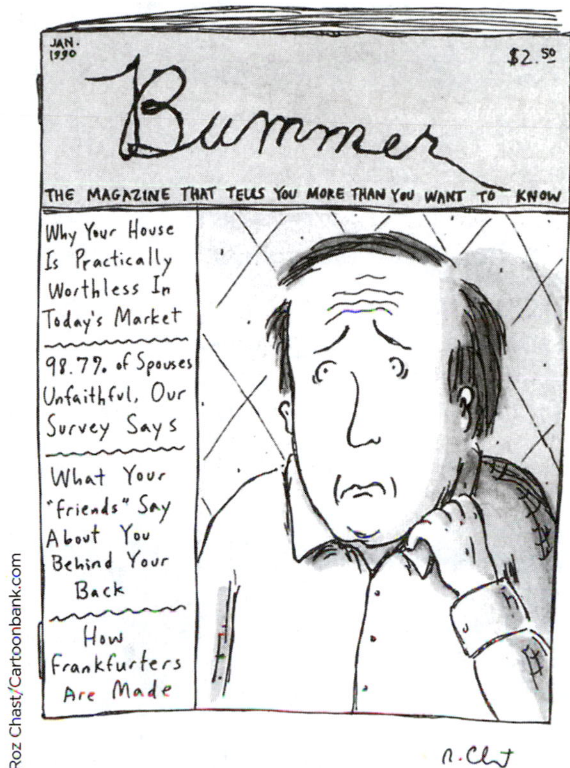

Roz Chast/Cartoonbank.com

Magazines at Work

Magazine employees work in one of five divisions:

1. Editorial
2. Circulation sales
3. Advertising sales
4. Manufacturing and distribution
5. Administration

The *editorial* department handles everything regarding the content of the magazine, except the advertisements. Magazine editors work in this department, and they decide the subjects for each magazine issue, oversee the people who write the articles and schedule the articles for the magazine. Designers who determine the "look" of the magazine also are considered part of the editorial department, as well as the artists and photographers who provide the magazine's illustrations and photographs.

The *circulation* department manages the subscription information. Workers in this department enter new subscriptions and handle address changes and cancellations, for example. The *advertising* department is responsible for finding companies that would like to advertise in the magazine. Advertising employees often help the companies design their ads to be consistent with the magazine format.

Manufacturing and *distribution* departments manage the production of the magazine and get it to readers. This often includes contracting with an outside company to print the magazine. Many magazine companies also contract with an outside distribution company rather than deliver the magazines themselves.

Administration, as in any media company, takes care of the organizational details—the paperwork of hiring, paying bills and managing the office, for example.

Because advertisers provide nearly half a magazine's income, tension often develops between a magazine's advertising staff and its editorial staff. The advertising staff may lobby the editor for favorable stories about potential advertisers, but the editor is responsible to the audience of the magazine. The advertising department might argue with the editor, for example, that a local restaurant will not want to advertise in a magazine that publishes an unfavorable review of the restaurant. If the restaurant is a big advertiser, the editor must decide how best to maintain the magazine's integrity.

The Audit Bureau of Circulations (***ABC***), an independent agency of print media market research, verifies and publishes circulation figures for member magazines. Advertisers use ABC figures to help them decide which magazines will reach their audience. Circulation figures (how many readers each magazine has) determine how much each magazine can charge for ads in the magazine.

Putting the magazine together and selling it (circulation, advertising, administration, manufacturing and distribution) cost more than organizing the articles and photographs that appear in the magazine (editorial). Often a managing editor coordinates all five departments.

The magazine editor's job is to keep the content interesting so people will continue to read the magazine. Good magazine editors can create a distinctive, useful product by carefully choosing the best articles for the magazine's audience and ensuring the articles are well written.

Company Magazines Magazines produced by businesses for their employees, customers and stockholders.

ABC Audit Bureau of Circulations.

Media/Impact AUDIENCE

Illustration 4.1

Top 10 U.S. Consumer Magazines

Magazines that are targeted toward women have always been the most successful type of magazine. Half the nation's top 10 magazines are considered women's magazines (*Better Homes and Gardens*, *Good Housekeeping*, *Woman's Day*, *Family Circle* and *Ladies' Home Journal*. In 2010, *Game Informer Magazine* joined the list for the first time, a reflection of the growing interest in video games.

Source: Audit Bureau of Circulation figures for 6-month period ending June 30, 2011.

Full-time magazine staffers write many of the articles, such as a food editor who creates recipes or a columnist who writes commentary. Nearly half the nation's magazines, however, use articles by ***freelancers***. Freelancers do not receive a salary from the magazine; instead, they are paid for each article published in the magazine. Many freelancers write for several magazines simultaneously. Some freelancers specialize—just writing travel articles, for example. Other freelancers work just as the tradition of their name implies: They have a pen for hire, and they can write about any subject a magazine editor wants.

Freelancers Writers who are not on the staff of a magazine but who are paid for each individual article published.

Magazines Compete for Readers in Crowded Markets

Today, trends in magazine publishing continue to reflect social and demographic changes, but magazines no longer play the cutting-edge social, political and cultural role they played in the past. Instead, most magazines are seeking a specific audience, and many more magazines are competing for the same readers.

Newsweek and *U.S. News & World Report* compete with *Time* in the newsweekly category to serve the reader who wants a weekly news roundup. *Fortune* is no longer alone; joining *Fortune* in the category of business magazines are *Bloomberg Businessweek* and *Nation's Business* among others. Some new men's magazines, such as *Maxim* and *Men's Vogue*, have been launched successfully to appeal to a younger audience. However, magazine audiences have grown older and today read magazines like *Yachting* and *Better Homes and Gardens*. Younger readers are less likely to read magazines than their parents. In 1990, for the first time, the number of magazines published in the United States stopped growing, and today the number is declining.

Still, women continue to be the single most lucrative audience for magazines. *Family Circle* and *Woman's Day* are called ***point-of-purchase magazines*** because they are sold mainly at the checkout stands in supermarkets and are one part of the women's market. *Vogue*, *Glamour* and *Cosmopolitan* cater to the fashion-conscious, and women's magazines have matured to include the working women's audience with *Savvy*, *Self* and *Working Woman*, for example. The market is divided still further by magazines like *Essence*, aimed at professional African American women, and the specifically targeted *Today's Chicago Woman* for female executives who live in Chicago.

Bryan Bedder/Getty Images

Photographers are considered part of a magazine's editorial staff. A magazine photographer sets up a photo shoot at Cooper Square in New York City on September 21, 2010.

Segmenting the Audience

The newest segment of the magazine audience to be targeted by special-interest magazines is the young men's audience, represented by *Maxim*, *Men's Vogue* and the international magazine *Vice*. (See **Media/Impact: World**, "*Vice* Magazine: A Cult Glossy Spawns a Global Media Empire and Gets a Partnership with CNN," p. 80.) The need for magazines to specialize based on current cultural trends and interests is reflected in the very different audience targets for two of today's fastest growing magazines, *Off-Road Adventures* and *Women's Health*.

Magazine publishers are seeking readers with a targeted interest and then selling those readers to the advertisers who want to reach that specific audience—skiers, condominium owners, motorcyclists and toy collectors. Besides targeting a special audience, such as gourmets or computer hackers, magazines also can divide their audience further with regional and special editions that offer articles for specific geographic areas along with regional advertising, or they can use ***webzines*** (also called ***zines***), which are online magazines available on the Internet. The newsweeklies, such as *Time* and *Newsweek*, can insert advertising for a local bank or a local TV station next to national ads. This gives the local advertiser the prestige of a national magazine at a lower cost than a national ad.

Readers Represent a Valuable Audience for Advertisers

The average magazine reader is a high school graduate, is married, owns a home and works full-time. This is a very attractive audience for advertisers. Advertisers also like magazines because people often refer to an ad weeks after they first see it. Many readers say they read a magazine as much for the ads as they do for the articles. This, of course, is also very appealing to advertisers. ***MPA***—The Association of Magazine Media—estimates that people keep a magazine issue an average of 17 weeks and that each issue has at least four adult readers on average. This magazine sharing is called ***pass-along readership***.

Point-of-Purchase Magazines Magazines that consumers buy directly, not by subscription. They are sold mainly at checkout stands in supermarkets.

Webzines (also called **zines**) Online magazines available on the Internet.

MPA The Association of Magazine Media, originally the Magazine Publisher's Association.

Pass-Along Readership People who share a magazine with the original recipient.

Media/Impact

WORLD

Vice Magazine: A Cult Glossy Spawns a Global Media Empire and Gets a Partnership with CNN

By Simon Dumenco

NEW YORK—It'd be easy to dismiss *Vice* as a cultish niche title—a street-smart youth-culture magazine with a famously ribald editorial sensibility. But a growing number of major players—including CNN, which this spring [2010] partnered with *Vice*'s online broadcast offshoot, VBS.TV—are recognizing that the ultimate glossy outsider has quietly spawned a global media empire while becoming an unlikely journalistic powerhouse.

Headquartered in New York since 1999 (it was born in Canada as *Voice of Montreal* in 1994, then rebranded in 1996), *Vice* is published in 24 editions distributed in 27 countries, with worldwide circulation of 1.1 million. It is the first primarily free magazine to make *Ad Age*'s A-List (paid subs aside, *Vice* is mostly distributed at boutiques, bookstores and other hot spots in urban areas).

That CNN deal, which puts VBS content on CNN.com, is recognition of *Vice*'s unwavering devotion to global reporting. In print, hands-on co-founders Suroosh Alvi and Shane Smith, together with editor in chief Jesse Pearson, somehow manage to comfortably interweave hard-hitting reports from Afghanistan and Uganda with outré fashion spreads and sassy pop-cultural coverage. Think *Rolling Stone* in its heyday crossed with Tibor Kalman–era *Colors* crossed with a cracked-out *National Geographic*. On VBS.TV, led by creative director Spike Jonze (of *Being John Malkovich* and *Where the Wild Things Are* fame), you can click from a report on the gun markets of Pakistan to a show called *Skate Europe*. The site got 2.2 million U.S. visitors in August [2010], according to ComScore.

Francois G. Durand/Getty Images

In 2010, *Vice* magazine created a partnership with Spike Jonze, Creative Director of VBS.TV, the Internet broadcast site. *Vice*, which has become well known worldwide for its investigative reporting, represents a new approach to magazine publishing. By creating partnerships with Internet and broadcast outlets like VBS.TV, the magazine can expand its audience and its revenue beyond the printed edition.

Once (and still) known for its ads from edgy street-fashion labels, *Vice* increasingly also pulls in major marketers like Nike, Diesel, HBO and Levi's. And this year, *Vice* launched The Creators Project, a co-branded effort with Intel. "It's a new global initiative to identify leading artists who are pushing creative boundaries through technology," explains Smith.

The empire of cool has also spawned record label Vice Music, Vice Films, Vice Books and Virtue Worldwide, a 50-person communications agency.

Dumenco, Simon, "Vice is No. 9 on Ad Age's Magazine A-List," Advertising Age, October 4, 2010, http://adage.com/u/P4z3wb.

Advertisers can target their audiences better in magazines than in most other media because magazines can divide their audiences for advertisers by geography, income, interests and even zip code. This means that advertisers can promote special offers in separate portions of the country or market expensive products in regional issues of the magazine that go to wealthy zip codes.

John Gress/Getty Images

Weekly news magazines, such as *Newsweek*, are losing their audience because of the instant availability of news on the Internet. To try to maintain revenue, magazines such as *Essence* target a more specific audience.

Magazines' High Failure Rate

Most new magazines are small-scale efforts produced on a computer and financed by loyal relatives or friends. Sex is a favorite category for new magazines, followed by lifestyle, sports, media personalities and home improvement. In 2000, television personality Oprah Winfrey launched a lifestyle magazine called *O, The Oprah Magazine.*

But only a few new magazines succeed. Today, only one in three new magazines will survive more than five years. The reason most magazines fail is that many new companies do not have the money to keep publishing long enough to be able to refine their editorial content, sell advertisers on the idea and gather subscribers—in other words, until the magazine can make a profit. Today, many well-established magazines are struggling to survive. In 2009, Condé Nast Publications (which publishes *Vogue, Vanity Fair* and *The New Yorker*) announced that it was shutting down *Gourmet* and *Modern Bride*, which had been publishing for more than half a century.

All magazines are vulnerable to changing economic and even technology trends. In 2005, *TV Guide* announced that it was discontinuing the magazine's role as a publisher of local TV schedules and, instead, re-launching the magazine in a new format exclusively devoted to celebrity news. Changing technology, and the expansion of TV channels, made it too hard for the magazine to keep up with TV programming, so the magazine chose to focus on the most popular part of the magazine—celebrity features.

Today's consumers are buying fewer magazines, and advertising revenues are declining. Although magazines once were very inexpensive and advertising paid for most of the cost of production, publishers gradually have been charging more, even charging for online content, to see if subscribers will be willing to pay more for specific content they want. For example, some magazines like *Rolling Stone* have recently announced plans to charge for online content. (See **Media/Impact: Money**, "*Rolling Stone*, Acme of Counterculture, Announces That It Will Charge for Web Site," p. 82.)

CSL, CartoonStock Ltd.

"It's a novel based on a movie adapted from a magazine article that was inspired by a video game."

Even though the audiences are smaller, magazines have increased the price they charge advertisers because magazine readers are a very good consumer audience. They're

Media/Impact
MONEY

Rolling Stone, Acme of Counterculture, Announces That It Will Charge for Web Site

By London Times Online

Rolling Stone magazine, the U. S. Bible of 1960s counterculture and music that went on to launch some big names in journalism, is to charge for its Web site. . . . The fortnightly publication, founded in 1967 by Jann Wenner, will become one of the best-known magazines to place a "pay wall" around its content, in an attempt to make money from the Web.

The move is sure to be closely watched by media industry observers who are divided between those who believe that charging for content is the only way to sustain expensive, high-quality journalism and those who fear that asking readers to pay for online content will drive them straight into the arms of free rivals. . . .

"We're taking control of our digital destiny," Mr. [Steven] Schwartz [*Rolling Stone* Chief Digital Officer] told the Associated Press. "This is not, 'Let's rush to the Web because print isn't strong.' This is our brand's ability to tap into a new medium," he added.

Although the magazine, like the rest of the publishing industry, had a lean year in 2009, selling nearly 20 percent fewer ad pages than the year before, its privately owned publisher says it is still profitable.

Its print circulation is running at a record 1.5 million, up from 1.3 million in 2000. Despite its association with the baby boomer generation, a spokesman for the company says it does not have an aging readership, claiming that the average age of readers is 30.

NC1 WENN Photos/Newscom

In 2010, *Rolling Stone* magazine announced plans to charge for content on its Internet site. Stung by declining advertising revenue for their print editions, magazines are looking for new ways to maintain profits.

The fact remains, however, that *Rolling Stone* faces stiff competition for the attention of younger music fans from a range of popular Web sites, such as Pitchfork.com.

The magazine became known for its political coverage in the 1970s, running long and controversial articles by the gonzo journalist Hunter S. Thompson. Other famous contributors include Tom Wolfe and the photographer Annie Leibovitz.

Having changed its format in the 1990s to appeal to a younger readership, it was criticized for losing some of its radical appeal, but has since returned to its more traditional roots.

Times Online, "Rolling Stone, Acme of Counterculture, Charges for Web Site," April 16, 2010, timesonline.co.uk. Reprinted with permission of The Times/nisyndication.com.

more likely to be interested in the specific products advertised in a magazine that's devoted to a subject that interests them.

However, today's changing economic outlook means that people are less willing to buy magazines when they believe they can find most of the information they want for free on the Internet. In 2009, when he announced that Condé Nast Publications was shutting down several popular magazines, including *Gourmet* and *Modern Bride*, CEO Chuck Townsend said, "In this economic climate it is important to narrow our focus to titles with the greatest prospects for long-term growth." Townsend's comment described the challenge facing the magazine industry as a whole—how to maintain the audience that advertisers want.

Yet even though *Gourmet* shut down, the same year the cable channel Food Network launched *Food Network Magazine* with a circulation target of 400,000. One year later the magazine had 1.25 million readers.

Food Network Magazine. Reprinted with permission.

In 2009, the cable channel Food Network launched the *Food Network Magazine*, designed to capitalize on the popular show. Magazines with a tie-in to other media, such as television or the Internet, seem to have a better chance to survive. In April 2010, Food Network parked its Sweet Truck outside ad agencies in New York to promote the magazine.

Internet Editions Offer New Publishing Outlets

The way magazines do business in the future will be affected by technology as well as by the shifting economics of the industry. The latest innovation in magazine publishing is Internet editions as a way to expand readership and give advertisers access to an online audience.

As early as 1993, *Newsweek* launched an Internet edition of its weekly magazine; in 1994, *Business Week* began offering its magazine online, including a feature that gives readers access to Internet conferences with editors and newsmakers and forums where readers can post messages related to topics covered in each issue of the magazine. Many major consumer magazines today publish Internet editions. (See **Illustration 4.2**.)

The economics of Internet publishing also make it possible for someone using a personal computer, a scanner, a digital camera and desktop publishing software to publish a magazine just online, dedicated to a fairly small audience, with none of the expense of mail distribution. Some large magazine publishing companies have launched literary-political online magazines, such as Salon.com and Slate, which have attracted a very loyal Internet readership. (See **Media/Impact: Culture**, "Raised on the Web, but Liking a Little Ink," p. 85.)

In 2005, *Slate* editor Michael Kinsley launched online ***podcasts***, available by subscription on *Slate's* Web site. Kinsley said *Slate* would offer "weekday podcasts of one or more of our articles read aloud (mostly by me, *Slate's* resident radio guy). Think of this as books on tape—only without the books and without the tape." With podcasts, Kinsley said, readers would be able to "listen to some of your favorite *Slate* features while you're commuting or working out or sitting in a tedious meeting (make sure the boss can't see your earbuds)." Podcasts are the latest way the Internet has helped magazines and newspapers expand their audiences beyond the printed page.

Magazines' Future Is on the Internet

Magazines complement other media yet have their own special benefits. Magazines' survival has always depended on their ability to adapt to new trends. To maintain their audience and revenue, the magazine industry today can integrate magazines with other mass media in three ways: expand their presence on the Internet, such as *People en Español*;

Podcast An audio or video file made available on the Internet for anyone to download, often available by subscription.

Media/Impact
MONEY

Illustration 4.2

Top 10 Web Sites Associated with Magazine Brands

Women are the largest audience for printed magazines, and they are also the biggest users of magazine Web sites. Six out of ten of the Top 10 magazine Web sites originate from women's interest magazines.

Source: *Media Industry Newsletter, www.minonline.com.*

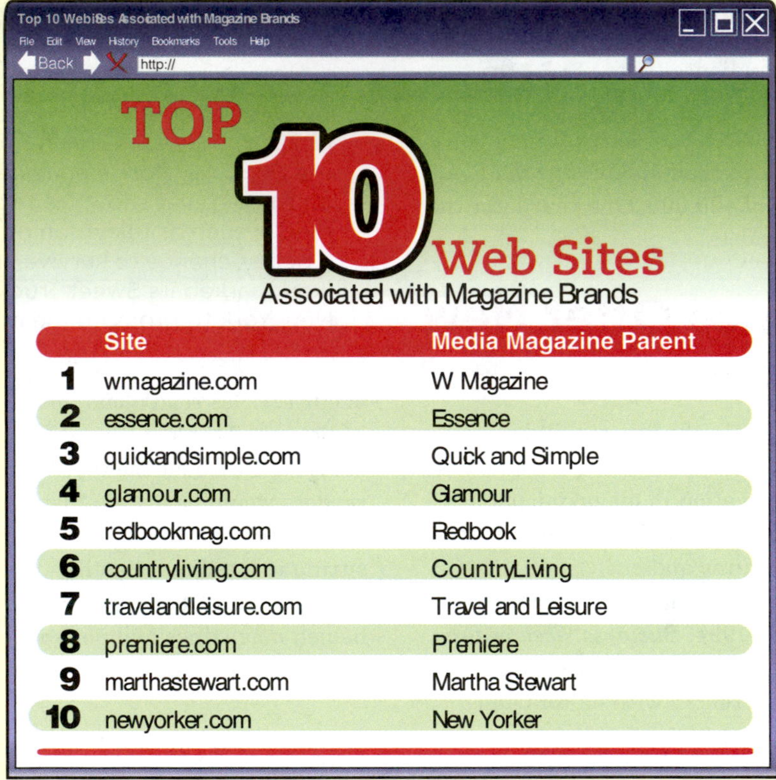

TOP 10 Web Sites Associated with Magazine Brands

	Site	Media Magazine Parent
1	wmagazine.com	W Magazine
2	essence.com	Essence
3	quickandsimple.com	Quick and Simple
4	glamour.com	Glamour
5	redbookmag.com	Redbook
6	countryliving.com	CountryLiving
7	travelandleisure.com	Travel and Leisure
8	premiere.com	Premiere
9	marthastewart.com	Martha Stewart
10	newyorker.com	New Yorker

create partnerships, such as *Vice* magazine; and find new niche audiences, such as Nomad. "There is clear demand for good content on mobile devices as evidenced by the amazing growth of e-books and the terrific response to the magazine apps launched on the iPad," says Mark Edmiston, Nomad's CEO. "We believe that there is even greater potential for content designed from the ground up for mobile rather than taking an existing format and converting it to mobile."

In 2010, magazine giant Condé Nast announced plans to create tablet versions of some of its top magazines, such as *GQ*, *Vanity Fair* and *Wired*. "We feel confident enough that consumers will want our content in this new format that we are committing the resources necessary to be there," says Charles H. Townsend, President and Chief Executive of Condé Nast. "How large a revenue stream digitized content represents is an answer we hope to learn through this process."

Media/Impact
CULTURE

Raised on the Web, but Liking a Little Ink

By Jenna Wortham

On a trip to an indie bookstore in Brooklyn in the summer, I came across a curious creation: a small, black-and-white publication that consisted entirely of snapshots of Lindsay Lohan. . . This print tribute to Ms. Lohan, called Lindzine, reignited my obsession with zines—mini-magazines that are generally made by hand and are available only in small quantities. . . .

DANIEL ROSENBAUM/*The New York Times*/Redux Pictures

Zines—special interest magazines printed in small quantities and also published on the Web—are enjoying new popularity. Malaka Gharib works on her food zine, The Runcible Spoon, at home in Washington.

I began to hunt for zines, both in small shops and on the Web, and was thrilled to discover a flourishing industry of quirky, clever do-it-yourself publications that touched on almost everything, with topics as varied as local food, art, short fiction, music reviews and comics. . . .

The word "zine" is a shortened form of the term fanzine, according to the Oxford English Dictionary. Fanzines emerged as early as the 1930s among fans of science fiction. Zines also have roots in the informal, underground publications that focused on social and political activism in the '60s. By the '70s, zines were popular on the punk rock circuit. In the '90s, the feminist punk scene known as riot grrrl propelled the medium.

Lately, it seems, the zine is enjoying something of a comeback among the Web-savvy, partly in reaction to the ubiquity of the Internet. Their creators say zines offer a respite from the endless onslaught of tweets, blog posts, I.M.'s, e-mail and other products of digital media.

"There's nothing more joyous than having a little publication in your hands," said Malaka Gharib, a social media coordinator for a nonprofit organization in Washington. In her spare time, she publishes a colorful food zine called The Runcible Spoon with her friend Claire O'Neill. . . .

Although working on The Runcible Spoon is a refreshing change of pace, Ms. Gharib still makes much use of technology to create and distribute the zine, employing software to design each issue, Twitter to attract readers, and Etsy, an online marketplace, to sell the publication.

Most zines are labors of love, done as side projects and hobbies. The goal isn't to turn a profit, but rather to capture a cultural moment, which in turn, offers the creators the freedom to explore and experiment.

It's hard to track exactly how many zines are in circulation at any time. Some are handwritten sheets that are photocopied a few dozen times, stapled and distributed by hand. Others, more upscale, are printed professionally in runs of several hundred and may be sold online.

But Karen Gisonny, a librarian at the New York Public Library who has specialized in collecting and cataloging periodicals for the last 25 years, said she has seen a resurgence of interest in zines and other D.I.Y. publications.

"We're seeing a flowering of print," she said. "There's definitely been a renaissance in the last 10 years."

Review, Analyze, Investigate

REVIEWING CHAPTER 4

Magazines Reflect Trends and Culture

- ✓ Magazines mirror the society.
- ✓ Today, magazines target specific audiences.
- ✓ Internet editions expand magazines' traditional reach.

Colonial Magazines Compete with Newspapers

- ✓ American magazines began in 1741 when Andrew Bradford published *American Magazine* and Benjamin Franklin published *General Magazine.*
- ✓ Like colonial newspapers, early magazines provided a means for political expression.
- ✓ *The Saturday Evening Post*, first published in 1821, was the nation's first general interest magazine.
- ✓ Early magazines were expensive and had small circulations.

Magazines Travel Beyond Local Boundaries

- ✓ The Postal Act of 1879 encouraged the growth of magazines because it ensured quick, reasonably priced distribution for magazines. Today's magazines still travel on a preferential postal rate.
- ✓ The *Saturday Evening Post* was the first national magazine with a large circulation.

Publishers Locate New Readers

- ✓ Magazines widened their audience in the 1800s by catering to women, tackling social crusades, becoming a literary showcase for American writers and encouraging political debate.
- ✓ Sarah Josepha Hale and Edward Bok were central figures in the development of early magazines in the United States.
- ✓ In 1910, W. E. B. DuBois launched *The Crisis*, published for an African American audience.

McClure's Launches Investigative Journalism

- ✓ McClure's Magazine pioneered investigative reporting in the United States early in the 20th century. *McClure's* published the articles of Ida Tarbell, who was critical of American industrialists.
- ✓ Early investigative magazine reporters were called muckrakers.

The New Yorker and *Time* Succeed Differently

- ✓ Magazines in the first half of the 20th century adapted to absorb the invention of radio and television. To adapt, some publishers sought a defined, targeted audience; others tried to attract the widest audience possible. *The New Yorker* and *Time* magazines are media empires that began during the early 20th century.

Specialized Magazines Take Over

- ✓ Magazines in the second half of the 20th century survived by targeting readers' special interests.
- ✓ Specialization segments an audience for advertisers, making magazines the most specific buy an advertiser can make.
- ✓ Publishers can target their magazines by geography, income and interest group, as well as by zip code.

Companies Consolidate Ownership and Define Readership

- ✓ Magazines are consolidating into large groups just like other media.
- ✓ Magazine publishers envision a time when their readership will be even more specialized than today.

Magazines Divide into Three Types

- ✓ There are three types of magazines: consumer magazines; trade, technical and professional magazines; and company magazines.
- ✓ Consumer magazines make the most money because they have the most readers and carry the most advertising.

Magazines at Work

- ✓ Magazine employees work in one of five areas: editorial, circulation sales, advertising sales, manufacturing and distribution, and administration.
- ✓ The Audit Bureau of Circulations (ABC) monitors and verifies readership.
- ✓ Advertisers provide nearly half of a magazine's income.

Magazines Compete for Readers in Crowded Markets

- ✓ The audience for magazines is growing older, and young readers are less likely to read magazines.
- ✓ The number of magazines being published in the United States has been declining since 1990.
- ✓ Women continue to be the single most lucrative audience for magazines.

Readers Represent a Valuable Audience for Advertisers

- ✓ Each issue of a magazine, according to the Magazine Publishers Association, has at least four adult readers on average, and people keep an issue an average of 17 weeks.
- ✓ Magazines can target readers better than other media because they can divide their readers by geography, income and interests.

Internet Editions Offer New Publishing Outlets

- ✓ Many magazines have launched Internet sites to expand their readership.
- ✓ Today's Internet technology means people can start an online magazine without the production and mailing expense of a printed publication.
- ✓ Some magazines, such as *Salon.com* and *Slate*, are published only on the Internet.

Magazines' Future Is on the Internet

- ✓ Magazines complement other media.
- ✓ Magazines are a very personal product.
- ✓ To maintain their audience and revenue, the magazine industry today can integrate magazines with other mass media in three ways: expand their presence on the Internet; create partnerships; and find new niche audiences.

KEY TERMS

These terms are defined in the margins throughout this chapter and appear in alphabetical order with definitions in the Glossary, which begins on page 383.

ABC 77
Company Magazines 77
Consumer Magazines 76
Freelancers 78
MPA 79
Muckrakers 73
Pass-Along Readership 79
Podcast 83
Point-of-Purchase Magazines 79
Trade, Technical and Professional Magazines 76
Webzines (also called zines) 79, 85

CRITICAL QUESTIONS

1. What important tradition in magazine journalism did Ida Tarbell and other muckrakers establish? Describe how Tarbell reported on Standard Oil Co. Why is her reporting important?
2. Why do today's magazines target specialized audiences for readership? Give at least three specific examples of this phenomenon and the reasons for each.
3. Discuss the role that magazines like *Ebony* and *Jet*, targeted to a specific audience, play in the development of American society.
4. If you started a magazine, what kind would you launch? How would you fund it? Who would read and advertise in it? Would you print it or put it just on the Internet or publish both printed and Internet editions? Using lessons from this chapter, how would you ensure its success?
5. What impact are developing media technologies having on magazines' future direction? Consider the audience for magazines, the way in which magazines are delivered to their readers, and the impact on advertisers and advertising.

WORKING THE WEB

This list includes both sites mentioned in the chapter and others to give you greater insight into the magazine industry.

AllYouCanRead.com

http://www.allyoucanread.com

The largest database of magazines and newspapers on the Internet, AllYouCanRead.com lists more than 22,000 media sources from all over the world. Listings are organized by topic and country of origin, and they can also be searched by name or keyword. Registered users can personalize their news collections, and visitors can read their favorite sources online. Subscriptions to printed materials are also available.

American Society of Journalists and Authors (ASJA)

http://www.asja.org

The ASJA is a national organization for freelance writers where members can share information about writing rates, publishing contracts, editors and agents. It also provides a referral service where editors and others can search the membership list to hire experienced authors and journalists, as well as health insurance plans for members and a writers' emergency fund.

CondéNet—Web site for Condé Nast Publications

http://www.condenet.com

An Internet unit of Condé Nast publications, CondéNet is the leading creator and developer of upscale lifestyle brands online. It serves as a portal for prestigious online publications in fashion, men's lifestyle, food, travel and more. Users can link to style.com (the online home of *Vogue*), men.style.com (*Details* and *GQ*) and epicurious.com ("for people who love to eat").

Folio: The Magazine for Magazine Management

http://www.foliomag.com

This online magazine for managers in all sectors of the magazine publishing industry reports industry trends and news. Information topics range from Audience Development to Sales and Marketing. The site also includes a Careers section, Industry Events and Webinars, and its own professional and social network, Folio: MediaPro.

MPA—The Association of Magazine Media and the American Society of Magazine Editors (ASME)

http://www.magazine.org

As the "Definitive Resource for the Magazine Industry," MPA (formerly Magazine Publishers of America) represents more than 300 domestic and international publishing companies from AARP to Time Warner. Departments include Government and International Affairs, Consumer Marketing, and Professional Development. ASME supports the editorial division of the site and serves its members through awards, internship programs, forums and career development workshops.

Newsweek

http://www.newsweek.com

First published in 1933, *Newsweek* holds more National Magazine Awards (given by the ASME) than any other newsweekly. Its global network of correspondents, editors and reporters cover national and international affairs, business, science and technology, society, and arts and entertainment. Newsweek.com offers Web-only columns from the print magazine's top writers, as well as podcasts, mobile content and archives. In 2010, Washington Post Co. sold *Newsweek* to investor Sidney Harman, who has no previous magazine publishing experience.

O, The Oprah Magazine

http://www.oprah.com/omagazine.html

The lifestyle magazine launched in 2000 by the popular talk-show host is now a minimal part of Oprah.com. The site itself is formatted as an online magazine, with featured daily content from the *Oprah Winfrey Show*, as well as articles in categories such as Spirit and Self, and Beauty and Style.

Salon

http://www.salon.com

This pioneer online magazine, headquartered in San Francisco with offices in New York City and Washington D.C., was founded in 1995. Because of the quality of its content, it has won many online journalism awards (such as the Webby).

Slate

http://www.slate.com

This online magazine of Washington Post Co. includes links to news stories in current issues of *The Washington Post* and *Newsweek*. Selected *Slate* stories can be heard on National Public Radio on "Day to Day." SlateV.com is an extensive webcast library of entertaining editorials from various interviewers as well as advice from "Dear Prudence." Users can also customize their news through "build your own Slate."

Sports Illustrated

http://sportsillustrated.cnn.com

Known for its use of color photos shot from dramatic perspectives and its talented sportswriters, *Sports Illustrated* is the preeminent weekly sports magazine owned by Time Warner. Its online counterpart, SI.com, offers scores, news, schedules, stats and more, all organized by sport. Users can personalize their views by favorite professional or college teams.

Impact/Action Videos are concise news features on topics covered in this chapter, created exclusively for **Media/Impact**. They are available for students and instructors at CengageBrain.com, and include screen access for classroom viewing and discussion questions.

"As an industry we've fought back from near collapse."

—Paul McGuinness, manager of the Irish rock band U2

Recordings: Demanding Choices

What's Ahead?

Edison Introduces His Amazing Talking Machine

Peter Goldmark Perfects Long-Playing Records

William S. Paley Battles David Sarnoff for Record Format

Hi-Fi and Stereo Rock In

Recording Industry at Work

Concerts Bring In Important Revenue

Four Major Companies Dominate

Music Sales and Licensing Drive Industry Income

Industry Struggles to Protect Content Labeling

Recording Industry Association Sues Downloaders

U.S. Supreme Court Rules Against File Sharing

Music Industry Wins Legal Action

Changing Technology Transforms Delivery

Internet Brings New Obstacles and New Opportunities

Photo by Vic Biondi

Ranch Records in Bend, Oregon, is a rare sight today—a thriving retail music store. Ranch Records sells new music and old CDs as well as collector vinyls.

TimeFrame 1877 — Today

The Recording Industry Caters to a Young Audience

1877 Thomas Edison first demonstrates the phonograph.

1943 **Ampex develops tape recorders, and Minnesota Mining and Manufacturing perfects plastic recording tape. Singer Bing Crosby was one of the first recording artists to use tape.**

Courtesy of 3M

1947 Peter Goldmark develops the long-playing record.

1956 Stereophonic sound arrives.

1958 **Motown, promoted as "Hitsville USA," introduces the Detroit Sound of African American artists, including the Supremes, popularizing rock 'n' roll.**

RB/Redferns/Getty Images

1979 Sony introduces the Walkman as a personal stereo.

1985 The recording industry begins to consolidate into six major international corporations. Only one of these companies is based in the United States.

1999 **MP3 technology, developed by Michael Robertson, makes it easy for consumers to download music files from the Internet.**

Courtesy of Michael Robertson

2001 Napster, which used file-sharing software designed to download music on the Internet, shuts down after the Recording Industry Association of America (RIAA) sues for copyright infringement.

Apple introduces the iPod portable music player.

2003 Apple opens the online music store iTunes, offering music downloads for 99 cents per song.

2005 **The U.S. Supreme Court says that the makers of file-sharing software can be sued for helping people violate recording industry copyright protections.**

NICHOLAS KAMM/AFP/Getty Images

2007 RIAA sues online music consumer Jammie Thomas for copyright infringement and a jury fines her $222,000. In September 2008, the judge orders a retrial. In 2009, a second jury awards recording companies $1.92 million.

2009 **Virgin Music closes all of its U.S. Megastores, marking the end of large-store music retailing.**

Justin Sullivan/Getty Images

2010 A judge reduces the judgment against Jammie Thomas to $54,000 and RIAA asks for a third trial.

Today Four major companies dominate the recording industry. The industry earns most of its revenue from popular music. The industry is fighting copyright infringement and illegal Internet file sharing, but industry income is rapidly declining. The iTunes online music store is the nation's dominant music retailer.

For its recent 360

Degree Tour, the Irish rock band U2 designed a stage that allowed the audience to surround the band on all sides. The set design for their performance at Pasadena's Rose Bowl and the other stops on the tour used massive projection screens above the stage to showcase the performance for the audience. "By removing the hulking backdrop that usually defines a stadium show and relocating all those tons of gear above the band's playing area," according to the *Los Angeles Times*, "the designer said he's been able to create the illusion that the gear isn't there at all."

The new stage also made it possible to expand the Rose Bowl's seating capacity by 20 percent, which meant the band could sell more tickets. More than 95,000 people attended the performance, setting a record. "We've broken a lot of attendance records," said U2 manager Paul McGuinness, "usually ones we've set ourselves."

The sudden decline in music sales, primarily because of illegal downloading, means that musicians can no longer rely on music sales to support their music. Concert performances that can draw a huge audience have become a necessity, as the recording business today struggles to find a financial model to sustain the industry.

Most of the music people listen to each year is categorized as popular music—rock, rap/hip-hop, urban, country and pop—according to the Recording Industry Association of America (RIAA). Other types of music—religious, classical, big band, jazz and children's recordings—make up the rest, but most of the profits and losses in the recording business result from the mercurial fury of popular songs.

Of all the media industries, the recording industry is the most vulnerable to piracy and has suffered the biggest losses as a result of Internet technology. Like the radio and television industries, the recording industry is challenged by rapidly changing technology. The recording industry also is at the center of recent debates over the protection of artistic copyright. In 2003, RIAA sued 261 people for downloading music from the Internet, saying CD shipments were down 15 percent from the year before. In 2009, a jury found one of the plaintiffs in the downloading case guilty of copyright infringement, and the case is still pending.

But in 1877, when Thomas Edison first demonstrated his phonograph, who could foresee that the music business would become so complicated?

Jeff Fusco/Getty Images

More than half the music people buy each year, and a majority of recording industry profits, come from sales of popular artists such as Bruno Mars, performing in Philadelphia, Penn., on September 25, 2010.

Hulton Archive/Getty Images

Today's recording industry would not exist without Thomas Edison's invention of the phonograph in 1877. Edison is shown in 1901 in his laboratory in West Orange, N.J.

Eric Schaal/*Time Magazine*/Time & Life Pictures/Getty Images

Engineer Peter Goldmark invented the long-playing record format. LPs could play for 23 minutes and offered better sound quality than 78 rpm records.

Edison Introduces His Amazing Talking Machine

Today's recording industry would not exist without Thomas Edison's invention, more than a century ago, of what he called a phonograph (which means "sound writer"). In 1877, *Scientific American* reported Edison's first demonstration of his phonograph. Edison's chief mechanic had constructed the machine from an Edison sketch that came with a note reading, "Build this."

In 1887, Emile Berliner developed the gramophone, which replaced Edison's cylinder with flat discs. Berliner and Eldridge Johnson formed the Victor Talking Machine Company (later to become RCA Victor) and sold recordings of opera star Enrico Caruso. Edison and Victor proposed competing technologies as the standard for the industry, and eventually the Victor disc won. Early players required large horns to amplify the sound. Later the horn was housed in a cabinet below the actual player, which made the machine a large piece of furniture.

In 1925, Joseph Maxfield perfected the equipment to eliminate the tinny sound of early recordings. The first jukeboxes were manufactured in 1927 and brought music into restaurants and nightclubs.

By the end of World War II, 78 ***rpm*** (*r*evolutions *p*er *m*inute) records were standard. Each song was on a separate recording, and "albums" in today's sense did not exist. An album in the 1940s consisted of a bound set of 10 envelopes about the size of a photo album. Each record, with one song recorded on each side, fit in one envelope. (This is how today's collected recordings got the title "album," even though they no longer are assembled in this cumbersome way.) Each shellac hard disc recording ran three minutes.

Peter Goldmark, working for Columbia Records (owned by CBS), changed that.

Peter Goldmark Perfects Long-Playing Records

In 1947, engineer Peter Goldmark was listening with friends to Brahms' Second Piano Concerto played by pianist Vladimir Horowitz and led by the world-famous conductor Arturo Toscanini. The lengthy concerto had been recorded on 6 records, 12 sides.

Goldmark hated the interruptions in the concerto every time a record had to be turned over. He also winced at the eight sound defects he detected. After several refinements, Peter Goldmark created the long-playing (***LP***) record, which could play for 23 minutes, but LPs were larger than 78 rpm records.

William S. Paley Battles David Sarnoff for Record Format

William Paley, who owned CBS radio and also CBS records, realized he was taking a big risk by introducing LP records

RPM Revolutions per minute.

LP Long-playing record.

when most people didn't own a record player that could play the bigger 33-1/3 rpm discs. While the LP record was being developed, Paley decided to contact RCA executive David Sarnoff, since RCA made record players, to convince Sarnoff to form a partnership with CBS to manufacture LPs. Sarnoff refused.

Stubbornly, Sarnoff introduced his own 7-inch, 45 rpm records in 1948. Forty-fives had a quarter-size hole in the middle, played one song on a side and required a different record player, which RCA started to manufacture. Forty-fives were a perfect size for jukeboxes, but record sales slowed as the public tried to figure out what was happening. Eventually Peter Goldmark and classical music conductor Arturo Toscanini convinced Sarnoff to manufacture LPs and to include the 33-1/3 speed on RCA record players to accommodate classical-length recordings.

Michael Ochs Archives/Getty Images

Berry Gordy founded Motown Records in 1958 and popularized the Detroit sound of singers like Marvin Gaye (in the middle, above) and Martha & the Vandellas, shown backstage at the Apollo Theater in 1962.

CBS, in turn, agreed to use 45s for its popular songs. Later, players were developed that could play all three speeds (33-1/3, 45 and 78 rpm). A limited number of jazz artists were recorded, but most of the available recorded music was big band music from artists like Tommy Dorsey, Broadway show tunes and songs by popular singers like Frank Sinatra.

Hi-Fi and Stereo Rock In

In the 1950s, the introduction of rock 'n' roll redefined the concept of popular music. Contributing to the success of popular entertainers like Elvis Presley were the improvements in recorded sound quality that originated with the recording industry. First came *high fidelity*, developed by London Records, a subsidiary of Decca. Tape recorders grew out of German experiments during World War II.

Ampex Corp. built a high-quality tape recorder, and Minnesota Mining and Manufacturing (3M) perfected the plastic tape. The use of tape meant that recordings could be edited and refined, something that couldn't be done on discs.

Stereo arrived in 1956, and soon afterward came groups like Marvin Gaye and Martha & the Vandellas with the Motown sound, which featured the music of African American blues and rock 'n' roll artists. With an $800 loan from his family, songwriter Berry Gordy, 29, founded Motown studios in 1958 in a small two-story house in Detroit. He named the label after Detroit's nickname Mo(tor)town and called the building "Hitsville, U.S.A."

"Everything was makeshift," he told *Fortune* in 1999. "We used the bathroom as an echo chamber." In July 1988, Gordy sold Motown Records for $61 million. The Detroit house where Motown began is now a historical museum, and Motown Records is part of Universal Music Group.

During the same time that Berry Gordy was creating Motown, the Federal Communications Commission (FCC) approved "multiplex" radio broadcasts so that monaural (one source of sound) and stereo (two sound sources) could be heard on the same stations. The development of condenser microphones also helped bring truer sound.

In the 1960s, miniaturization resulted from the transistor. Portable transistor radios that could be carried around meant that people could listen to radio wherever they wanted—on the beach, at the park, even in the shower. Eventually the market was overwhelmed with tape players smaller than a deck of playing cards. Quadraphonic (four-track) and eight-track tapes seemed ready to become the standard in the 1970s, but cassette tapes proved more adaptable and less expensive.

In 1979, Sony introduced the Walkman as a personal stereo. (The company is Japanese, but the name Sony comes from the Latin *sonus* for "sound" and *sunny* for "optimism.") Walkmans were an ironic throwback to the early radio crystal sets, which also required earphones.

Today's compact discs (CDs) deliver crystal-clear sound, transforming music into digital code on a 4.7-inch plastic and aluminum disc read by lasers. Discs last longer than records and cassettes ever did, making CDs a much more adaptable format.

Launched in the year 2000, CD players that included a *CD recorder* (also known as a CD writer or CD burner)

Bernard Gotfryd/Getty Images

Improvements in recorded sound quality—hi-fi and stereo—contributed to the success of recording artists like the Beatles, performing on *The Ed Sullivan Show* on February 9, 1964.

and computers with ***CD-RW*** (*Re*-Writable) ***drives*** meant consumers could burn data to a blank CD, allowing them to copy music, play it and then re-record on the same disc. Recordable discs gained widespread acceptance quickly after they were introduced, and these players and computer drives made it even harder for the recording industry to police unauthorized use of copyrighted material.

Music videos, the music channels MTV and VH1 and the availability of iPod music downloads also have expanded the audience and potential income for music artists. The Apple iPod portable music player, first introduced in 2001, allows users to store and play music downloads. Apple launched iTunes, its online music store, in 2003, charging 99 cents per song.

The Apple iPhone, launched in 2007, combined mobile phone technology with the capabilities of the iPod, expanding Apple's dominance in music retailing. Today, the iTunes online music store has become the dominant consumer source for contemporary music. In February 2010, the iTunes store recorded its 10 billionth download, the song "Guess Things Happen That Way" by Johnny Cash. And rather than rely on music sales, some music artists have begun selling equipment. [See **Media/Impact: Culture**, "Headphones with Swagger (and Lots of Bass)" p. 98.]

CD-RW Drives Computer drives that are used to read data and music encoded in digital form and can be used to record more than once.

Recording Industry at Work

Recordings, like books, are supported primarily by direct purchases. But a recording company involves five separate levels of responsibility before the public hears a sound:

1. Artists and repertoire
2. Operations
3. Marketing and promotion
4. Distribution
5. Administration

Artists and repertoire (or A&R) functions like an editorial department in book publishing; it develops and coordinates talent. Employees of this division are the true talent scouts. They try to find new artists and also constantly search for new songs to record.

Operations manages the technical aspects of the recording, overseeing the sound technicians, musicians, even the people who copy the discs. This work centers on creating the master recording, from which all other recordings are made. Before stereophonic recording was developed in 1956, a recording session meant gathering all the musicians in one room, setting up a group of microphones and recording a song in one take. If the first take didn't work, the artists all had to stay together to do another, and then another.

It was common in the 1950s for a recording group to go through 50 takes before getting the right one. Today, artists on the same song—vocals, drums, bass, horns and guitars—can be recorded individually, and then the separate performances are mixed for the best sound. They don't have to be in the same room or even in the same country because the sound can be mixed after each of the artists has recorded his or her portion.

The producer, who works within the operations group, can be on the staff of a recording company or a freelancer. Producers coordinate the artist with the music, the arrangement and the engineer,

Marketing and promotion decides the best way to sell the recording. These employees oversee the cover design and the copy on the cover (jacket or sleeve). They also organize giveaways to retailers and to reviewers to find an audience for their product. Marketing and promotion might decide that the artist should tour or that the group should produce and distribute a music video on Facebook to succeed. Recording companies also often use promoters to help guarantee radio play for their artists. This has led to abuses such as payola (see **Chapter 6**).

Distribution gets the recording into the stores. There are two kinds of distributors: independents and branches. Independents contract separately with different companies to deliver their recordings. But independents, usually responsible for discovering music that is outside of the mainstream, are disappearing as the big studios handle distribution through their own companies, called branches. Because branches are connected with the major companies, they typically can offer the music retailer better discounts.

Administration, as in all industries, handles the bills. *Accounting* tracks sales and royalties. *Legal departments* handle wrangles over contracts.

All these steps are important in the creation of a recording, but if no one hears the music, no one will buy it. This makes *marketing* and *promotion* particularly important. Live concerts have become the best way for artists to promote their music. Many recording artists say that music sales alone don't make them any money and that the only way to make a living is to perform before a live audience.

Michael Caulfield/Getty Images

Live concerts demand expensive digital engineering, using new technologies to create a memorable audience experience. On December 3, 2010 in Miramar, Calif., Nicki Minaj (left) and Katy Perry perform during the "VH1 Divas Salute the Troops" concert.

Concerts Bring In Important Revenue

Concerts have become high-profile showcases for technological innovation and provide an essential source of revenue for today's big bands. For example, the group Coldplay performed in 2008 at the three-day Pemberton Music Festival in Pemberton, British Columbia, along with Jay-Z, Tom Petty and the Heartbreakers and 40 other music acts. A three-day pass for the festival cost $239.50.

The Pemberton concert staging for Coldplay is an example of the importance of today's complex digital engineering, which integrates new technologies to help showcase a band's music. Today someone who pays more than $200 for a concert ticket demands a spectacular experience.

"While the recording industry frets about the financial impact of music trading over the Internet, innovative bands . . . are embracing the latest technologies to create spectacular live concerts and phantasmagoric festival experiences that are more like computer-controlled theme parks than like the rock festivals of yesteryear," reports *The New York Times*.

Richard Goodstone, a partner at Superfly Productions, told *The New York Times*, "The real difference between your normal rock festival like Lollapalooza and Ozzfest is that there's a lot of music, but now we're trying to make it a complete experience in terms of the activities that really interact with the patrons out there, so it's not just a one-element kind of event." Digital technology has become an important element of selling a band to its fans, as well as selling the band's music. (See **Illustration 5.1**.)

CSL, CartoonStock Ltd.

"With so little free time, you have to learn to multi-task your TV watching, ipod listening, and texting with your homework."

Four Major Companies Dominate

About 5,000 companies in the United States produce music, but four companies dominate the global music business: EMI, Sony/BMG, Universal and Warner. Together these four companies, on average, have sold more than two billion recordings each year. The main recording centers in the United States are Los Angeles, New York and Nashville,

Media/Impact
CULTURE

Headphones with Swagger (and Lots of Bass)

By Andrew J. Martin

Dr. Dre, the sonic architect of gangsta rap, is surrounded by a gaggle of slack-jawed journalists and micro-skirted cocktail waitresses. It's not quite 5 in the afternoon, and already the scene is a testosterone fantasy of swaggering grooves and flowing vodka.

Dr. Dre, however, is here on business.

Born Andre Young, he was a founding member of N.W.A. and honed the sound of Snoop Dogg, Eminem and 50 Cent. But now what began as a sideline has turned into multimillion-dollar business.

Mr. Young is the pitchman for the hot new sound in—headphones. On this October day, he is headlining a media party in the Chelsea neighborhood of Manhattan for his creations, Beats by Dr. Dre.

To the surprise of almost everyone, except him and his partners, Beats have redefined the lowly headphone, as well as how much people are willing to pay for a pair of them. A typical pair of Beats sell for about $300—nearly 10 times the price of ear buds that come with iPods. And, despite these lean economic times, they are selling surprisingly fast.

Whether Beats are worth the money is open to debate. Reviews are mixed, but many people love them. The headphones are sleekly Apple-esque, which is no surprise, since they were created by a former designer at Apple. Beats also offer a celebrity vibe and a lot of *boom*-a-chick-a-*boom* bass.

Time was, manufacturers marketed high-priced audio equipment by emphasizing technical merits like frequency response, optimum impedance, ambient noise attenuation and so on. The audience was mostly a small cadre of audiophiles tuned to the finer points of sound quality.

But, three years ago, Beats by Dr. Dre set out to change all that by appealing to more primal desires: good looks, celebrity and bone-rattling bass. Annual sales are approaching $500 million, and Beats have transformed headphones into a fashion accessory.

CASEY KELBAUGH/*The New York Times*/Redux Pictures

Although revenue in the music business is plunging, rapper Dr. Dre found a way to make money by creating designer headphones called Beats, priced at $300 each. In New York, a young customer tries on the latest style.

This unlikely success has touched off a scramble in the industry. The rappers Ludacris and 50 Cent have backed their own headphone brands.

The entire industry is riding a wave. Sales of headphones in the United States nearly doubled in the year ended in August (2011), to $2 billion, according to the NPD Group's Retail Tracking Service.

Beats by Dr. Dre "set off a free-for-all among companies entering the category, many of which relied on celebrity endorsements or style, as opposed to focusing on audio quality per se," said Ross Rubin, the executive director of industry analysis at NPD.

"What Beats did," Mr. Rubin added, "was dramatically expand the market and make the price premium acceptable, as much as for the design and the brand as for the audio quality."

Media/Impact
MONEY

Illustration 5.1

What Types of Music Do People Buy?

The recording industry's success rests on trends in popular music. For more than 50 years, rock music has maintained its lead as the most popular type of music.

Source: Recording Industry Association of America, Consumer Profile, www.riaa.com.

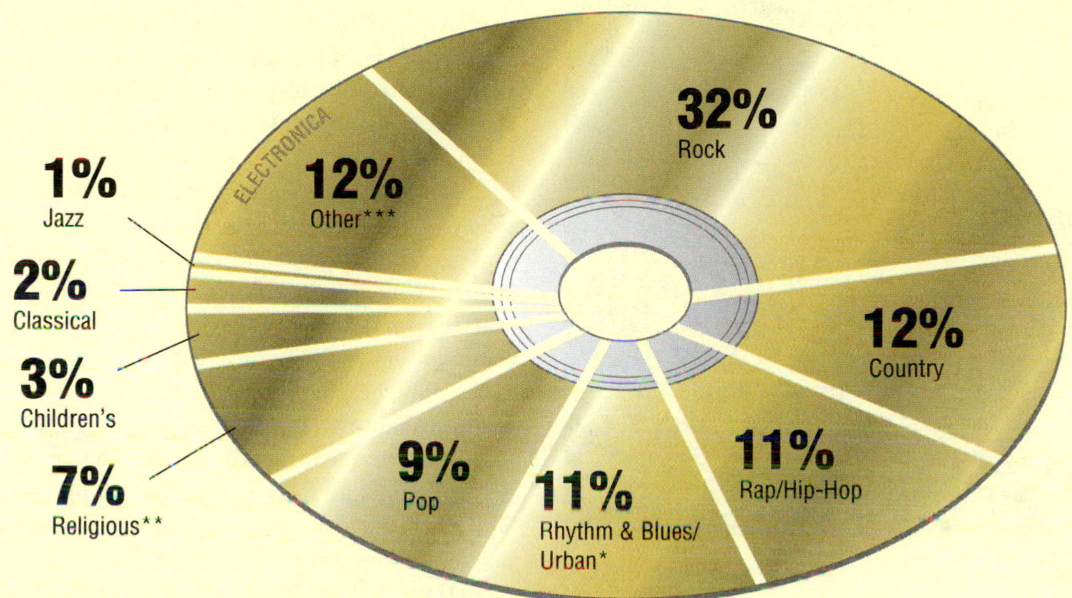

*Includes R&B, Blues, Dance, Disco, Funk, Fusion, Motown, Reggae, Soul.
**Includes Christian, Gospel, Inspirational, Religious, Spiritual.
***Includes Soundtracks, Oldies, New Age, Big Band, Broadway Shows, Comedy, Ethnic, Folk, Holiday Music.

but many large cities have at least one recording studio to handle local productions.

The recording industry, primarily concentrated in large corporations, generally chooses to produce what has succeeded before. "Increasingly, the big record companies are concentrating their resources behind fewer acts," reports *The Wall Street Journal*, "believing that it is easier to succeed with a handful of blockbuster hits than with a slew of moderate sellers. One result is that fewer records are produced."

Most radio formats today depend on popular music, and these recordings depend on radio to succeed. The main measurement of what is popular comes from *Billboard*, the music industry's leading trade magazine. *Billboard* began printing a list of the most popular vaudeville songs and the best-selling sheet music in 1913. In 1940, the magazine began publishing a list of the country's top-selling records.

Today, *Billboard* offers more than two dozen charts that measure, for example, airplay and album sales for popular artists such as Alison Krauss and Jennifer Hudson. Radio, governed by ratings and what the public demands, tends to play proven artists, so new artists are likely to get more radio attention if their recordings make one of the *Billboard* lists. This radio play, in turn, increases the artists' popularity and promotes their music.

Tony R. Phipps/Getty Images

Recording artist Taylor Swift regularly makes it to the Top 10 Country Music Artists List in *Billboard* magazine. This listing keeps her music on radio stations that feature country music. Radio stations must license the music they play. Swift performed in Nashville at the Grand Ole Opry's 85th birthday party on October 9, 2010.

Music Sales and Licensing Drive Industry Income

The industry also collects income from direct sales and from music licensing for radio, television and movies.

ASCAP American Society of Composers, Authors and Publishers.

BMI Broadcast Music, Inc.

Direct Sales

The promotional tour once was the only way a company sold recordings. But in the 1980s, music videos became a very visible form of promotion for an artist. This shift changed the industry's economics. Jennifer Lopez, for example, is attractive to music companies because she is a recording artist who can perform well in videos and also makes movies.

Music Licensing: ASCAP Versus BMI

For the first 30 years of commercial radio, one of the reasons broadcasters used live entertainment was to avoid paying royalties to the recording companies. Today, two licensing agencies handle the rights to play music for broadcast: the American Society of Composers, Authors and Publishers (ASCAP) and Broadcast Music, Inc. (BMI).

ASCAP, founded in 1914, was the first licensing organization. As noted in **Chapter 6**, ASCAP sued radio stations in the 1920s that were playing recorded music. Eventually some radio stations agreed to pay ASCAP royalties through a blanket licensing agreement, which meant that each station that paid ASCAP's fee could play any music that ASCAP licensed.

Throughout the 1930s, many stations refused to pay ASCAP because they didn't have enough money. These stations agreed to explore the idea of forming a separate organization so they could license the music themselves.

In 1939, broadcasters came together to establish a fund to build their own music collection through ***BMI***. ASCAP and BMI became competitors—ASCAP as a privately owned organization and BMI as an industry-approved cooperative. BMI used the same blanket licensing agreement, collecting payments from broadcasters and dividing royalties among its artists. ASCAP licensed the majority of older hits, but rhythm and blues and rock 'n' roll gravitated toward BMI. Today, most broadcasters subscribe to both BMI and ASCAP. They also agree to play only licensed artists, which makes getting on the air more difficult for new talent. BMI and ASCAP, in turn, pay the authors, recording artists, producers and sometimes even the recording companies—whoever owns the rights to use the music.

Recording industry income received a boost from the widespread prices charged for music CDs. (See **Media/Impact: People**, "Independent Label Concord Music: CEO Glen Barros Believes in CDs," p. 101.) However, Internet piracy and file sharing on the Internet are the main reasons recording income is declining.

Industry Struggles to Protect Content Labeling

Three issues face today's recording industry: content labeling, overseas piracy and artists' copyright protection from file sharing on the Internet.

Media/Impact PEOPLE

Independent Label Concord Music: CEO Glen Barros Believes in CDs

By Joseph Plambeck

The waters might be choppy for the music business right now, but the Concord Music Group is happy to ride those waves.

In April, Concord, an independent label, announced two deals, one to distribute Paul McCartney's post-Beatles catalog and another to buy Rounder Records, the roots label from Boston whose "Raising Sand" won a Grammy for best album in 2009.

Those two additions are the latest in a years-long period of growth for Concord, which is based in Beverly Hills. And they come at a time when many other labels are shrinking or battling for survival.

The success has Glen Barros, Concord's chief executive, singing a tune not always heard around the industry.

"The future of the music business is very bright," Mr. Barros said. "People want to listen to great music."

He thinks people will pay for that music, too, especially the fans he calls the adult audience. Concord has focused its attention on that group, trying to lure people less inclined to chase the latest pop sensation and more interested in music Mr. Barros describes as "timeless and authentic"—more McCartney and less Justin Bieber. . . .

Typically—and especially at the major labels—a company's fortunes rest on a bet that a tiny number of artists will reap huge sales, supporting the rest of its roster.

Concord, however, focuses on getting steady sales from its catalog of 13,000 master recordings and releasing new albums by artists—like James Taylor and Chick Corea—who all pull their own weight. . . .

In 2007, Concord and Starbucks released Mr. McCartney's "Memory Almost Full," starting a relationship that led to last month's announcement. . . .

"Their passion for jazz and music that stands the test of time is the same focus we have," said Chris Bruzzo, a vice president at Starbucks who oversees music for the company. "They're right in our sweet spot."

That sweet spot—the adult market—is less inclined to illegally download music and more inclined to buy a CD. This is especially true for baby boomers. According to the NPD Group, a market research firm, people 50 and older buy 16 percent of all albums and singles but buy 28 percent of all the physical music sold. . . .

While the company continues to grow, the artists and managers working with it say they still get a personal, indie-label treatment. Of course, with just 1 percent market share in the United States, it still is very much an independent.

Todd Heisler/The New York Times/REDUX

Glen Barros, Chief Executive of independent label Concord Music, says there's money to be made licensing classic pop singers, such as James Taylor and Paul McCartney.

"This next block of silence is for all you folks who download music for free, eliminating my incentive to create."

CSL, CartoonStock Ltd.

In 1985, the Parents Music Resource Center (PMRC) called for recording companies to label their recordings for explicit content. The new group was made up primarily of the wives of several national political leaders, notably Susan Baker, wife of then-Treasury Secretary James A. Baker III, and Tipper Gore, wife of then-Senator Al Gore.

Saying that recordings come under the umbrella of consumer protection, the PMRC approached the National Association of Broadcasters and the Federal Communications Commission with their complaints. "After equating rock music with the evils of 'broken homes' and 'abusive parents,' and labeling it a 'contributing factor' in teen pregnancy and suicide, they single[d] out Madonna, Michael Jackson, Mötley Crüe, Prince, Sheena Easton, Twisted Sister and Cyndi Lauper for their 'destructive influence' on children," reported journalism law professor Louis P. Sheinfeld.

The result was that, beginning in January 1986, the ***Recording Industry Association of America*** (RIAA; whose member companies account for 95 percent of U.S. recording sales) officially urged its members either to provide a warning label or to print lyrics on albums that have potentially offensive content. Like the movie industry when it adopted its own ratings system (see **Chapter 7**), the recording industry favored self-regulation rather than government intervention.

In 1990, the nation's two largest record retailers ordered all their outlets to stop stocking and selling sexually explicit recordings by the controversial rap group 2 Live Crew. A Florida judge ruled that the group's album *As Nasty As They Wanna Be* was obscene, even though it carried a warning about explicit lyrics. The Luke Skywalker record label, which produced the album, said the controversy increased sales, but the ban meant that more than 1,000 stores nationwide refused to sell the music. Eventually, the decision was overturned, but sales of the album already had plummeted.

RIAA (Recording Industry Association of America) Industry association that lobbies for the interests of the nation's major recording companies. Member companies account for 95 percent of all U.S. recording company sales.

File Sharing The peer-to-peer distribution of copyrighted material on the Internet without the copyright owner's permission.

Overseas Piracy

Overseas pirates who copy prerecorded music that is then sold in the United States cost the recording industry a lot of money. RIAA says pirates control 18 percent of album sales, and this represents a billion dollars a year in lost income.

Besides the lost revenue, counterfeit copies can easily fool consumers and usually are inferior quality, which doesn't truly represent the artist's music. This is a continuing battle for the music industry because many of the countries responsible for the counterfeit copying do not have agreements with the United States to force them to honor U.S. copyrights and prosecute the pirates.

File Sharing on the Internet

Portable MP3 players—electronic devices that allow users to download music to a computer chip–based player—were introduced in 1999. "They are the hottest new thing in portable audio players," Amy Hill, spokesperson for the Consumer Electronics Manufacturing Association, said in 1999. "Every teenager I know wants one of these things."

In 1999, a software-sharing program available at a Web site called Napster.com skyrocketed into popularity. With the program, computer users could download music over the Internet for free, called ***file sharing***. Then, using MP3 technology (which provides high-quality sound and requires very little computer storage space), users could keep and use the music. RIAA immediately sued Napster, claiming violation of copyright.

In April 2000, the heavy-metal rock group Metallica sued Napster for copyright infringement. Rapper Dr. Dre filed suit two weeks later. In July 2000, an appeals court ordered Napster to shut down the site, but Napster delayed. Napster finally shut down in 2001.

Recording Industry Association Sues Downloaders

In 2003, Apple opened its online iTunes Music Store, offering a place where consumers could download music legally for 99 cents per song. Still, people continued to download free music, aided by new free online music services such as Kazaa and Grokster. (See **Illustration 5.2**.) So in 2003, RIAA sued 261 individual music downloaders across the United States, intensifying its efforts to stop music piracy. On average, each defendant had shared 1,000 songs each.

"A lot of people think they can get away with what they are doing because peer-to-peer file sharing allows them to hide behind made-up screen names," the president of RIAA told *The New York Times*. "They are not anonymous. The law is very clear. What they are doing is stealing." Copyright laws allowed the industry to seek \$750 to \$150,000 for each violation.

The lawsuits included copies of screen shots of many users' entire online music-sharing accounts, showing the names of each song and how many times the user downloaded music. RIAA offered not to pursue the individual lawsuits for people who were willing to sign a notarized statement saying they would stop sharing music files and delete files they now had. A subsequent court ruling stopped the prosecution of people who downloaded free music, but the case headed to the U.S. Supreme Court.

Jason Kempin/Getty Images

In 2003, Apple opened its online iTunes Music Store, offering a place where consumers could download music legally for 99 cents per song. In August 2010, iTunes sponsored a performance of musician David Gray at the Apple Store in New York City.

U.S. Supreme Court Rules Against File Sharing

In June 2005, the U.S. Supreme Court announced a decision that eventually shut down many free music software providers. In *MGM Studios v. Grokster*, the court said the makers of Grokster, which allowed Internet users to browse freely and copy songs from each other, could be sued for their role in helping people violate recording industry copyright protections.

This Supreme Court decision gave the recording companies the legal ammunition they needed to shut down file-sharing services, and the services quickly closed.

Music Industry Wins Legal Action

In 2007, a federal jury ruled that a Minnesota woman, Jammie Thomas, was liable for copyright infringement because she had shared music online. The jury imposed a penalty against Thomas of \$222,000—calculated at \$9,250 in damages for each of the 24 songs involved in the trial. In September 2008, the judge set aside the original verdict and ordered a retrial.

The verdict represented the first time a federal jury had imposed a legal fine on someone for music piracy. Earlier in the summer, however, a judge dismissed record labels' claims that an Oklahoma woman had used an Internet address to share music.

According to evidence presented at the Thomas trial, the music downloads were linked to a Kazaa account user name that belonged to Thomas. Thomas denied she had a Kazaa account. Bringing the charges against Thomas were Capitol Records, the Universal Music Group, Sony BMG Entertainment and the Warner Music Group.

In late 2008, however, RIAA announced that it was dropping the legal actions it had initiated against about 35,000 other people for music downloading. Instead, the association said it planned primarily to pursue agreements with Internet service providers where RIAA would notify the provider when RIAA learns that the provider's customers are making music available online to share with others. The provider would then, after notification, cancel the customers' account.

Media/Impact AUDIENCE

Illustration 5.2

Who Pays for Music?

Because many younger listeners download shared music for free, people who are 30 and older account for almost two-thirds of the recording industry's annual income.

Source: Recording Industry Association of America, Consumer Profile, riaa.com.

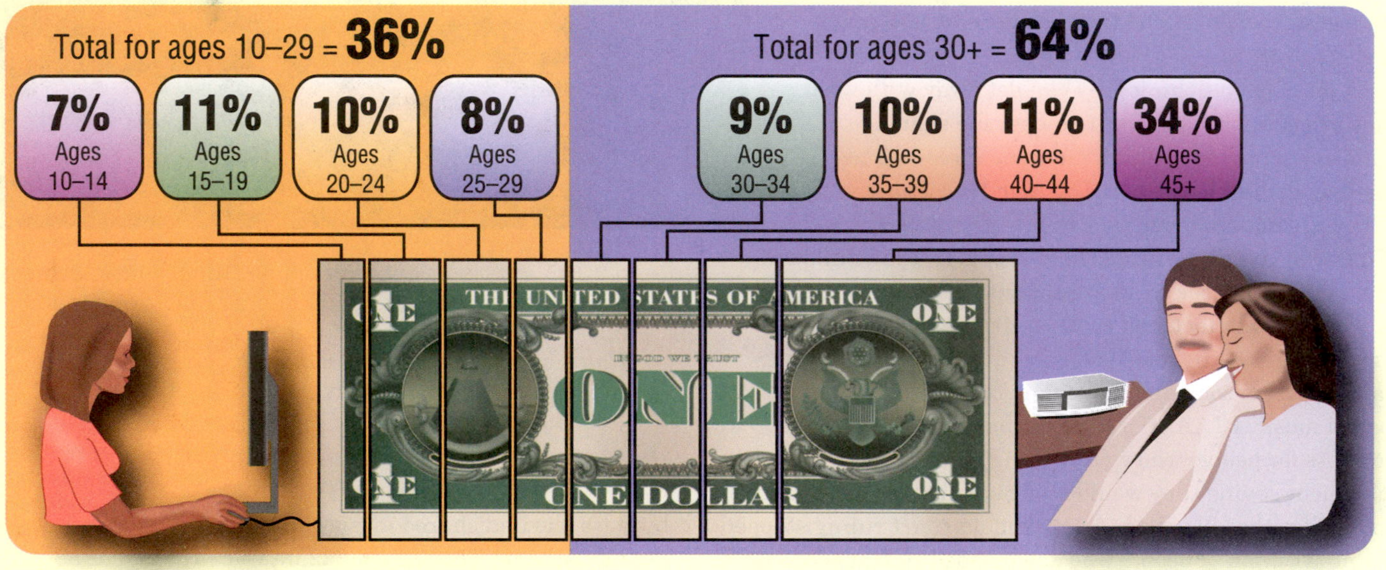

The decision to drop the suits originally was viewed as an admission by RIAA that their initial legal strategy had failed to stop online file sharing. However, RIAA continued to pursue the Thomas case. In 2009, a federal jury found Jammie Thomas guilty of violating the copyright on the 24 songs and awarded the recording companies $1.92 million, or $80,000 a song. In January 2010, a judge reduced the award to $2,250 per song, or $54,000. In June 2010, the court ordered the two sides to try to reach a settlement. One month later, after the two sides could not agree, RIAA asked for a third trial. No date has been set.

Changing Technology Transforms Delivery

From the beginning, profits in the recording industry have been tied to technology. Ever since William S. Paley and David Sarnoff decided to produce LPs and 45s, the consumer has followed equipment manufacturers, looking for better, more convenient sound. The recent expansion of MP3 digital technology signaled a new era for music lovers, making quality music available on the Internet.

But recording companies claim that people's ability to download and copy digitized music on the Internet will financially ruin the industry. Once digitized, the music is available to anyone and can be sent over the Internet around the world.

Music company executives originally thought that the way to protect their music was to develop new technology that would make free downloads impossible. Yet despite aggressive attempts by RIAA to stop music file sharing, it is still a widespread practice with vast copyright and income implications for recording artists and music companies.

Aware of the potential damage to recording company income, officials of RIAA have joined an international crackdown on overseas companies that sell pirated music and people who download copyrighted music on the Internet. But policing the international community for music piracy and monitoring the Internet for illegal music sharing is difficult and expensive. (See **Media/Impact: World**, "Is Spotify the Answer to Illegal Music Downloads?" p. 105.)

Media/Impact WORLD

Is Spotify the Answer to Illegal Music Downloads?

By Alexi Mostrous, Media Editor

It's 4 a.m. in a hotel room far from home and you've just broken up with your lover. Aside from the minibar, there's no empathy on offer; not a soul to talk to, no shoulder to cry on.

You update your Facebook status with news of the split. Seconds later someone on the other side of the world sends our smart phone a digital version of "What Difference Does It Make?," allowing you and Morrissey to wallow together in self-pity. Someone else sends you Paul Simon's "Fifty Ways to Leave Your Lover," which cheers you up a bit.

This may sound far-fetched, but the hope of the music industry rests upon such connections. A future where songs are not bought, but accessed via telephones, sent across cyberspace, and passed around friends through platforms such as Twitter, is what is hoped will save music from the twin ravages of illegal downloading and a lack of strategic direction. . . .

The Internet is the big battleground. Piracy remains rampant, with more than seven million illegal file-sharers in Britain alone. . . .

"As an industry we've fought back from near collapse," said Paul McGuinness, the U2 manager who masterminded the Irish band's current multimillion-pound sponsorship deal with RIM's Blackberry.

For the right band, Mr. McGuinness, said, "Record label funding can be replaced by the right corporate sponsor. And falling CD sales can—hopefully—be made up for by subscription packages. . . ."

Daniel Ek, 27, the founder of Spotify, the online music site, told *The Times* that he expected his company to be one of a few players in a $50 billion industry in five years' time.

Robert Marquardt/Getty Images

Daniel Ek, co-founder of the international music company Spotify, says subscription music sites can return the recording business to profitability.

Spotify currently has seven million users in Britain, Spain, France, Sweden, Norway and Finland, of which about 5 percent pay a monthly subscription fee to listen to advert-free music. . . .

"By 2012 half of all telephones will be smart phones and we'll see impressive growth in 'access' music services such as Spotify," Mr. Ek said. "The overall industry will be worth $40 to $50 billion and, if you look at how Internet companies develop, there will be only a couple of really dominant players. We hope to be one of them. . . ."

Spotify is also looking to introduce new "household" subscription services, allowing a parent to pay for the family's content, as well as partnering with more Internet service providers and telephone companies.

In a few years time, Mr. Ek predicts, "I will be able to update my status on Twitter to 'I'm feeling lonely' and someone will send me a track to cheer me up. But we're only at the beginning. This will only work if there's massive adoption of people paying for music."

Alexi Mostrous, "Music Industry Needs Clear Strategy and Control Over Illegal Downloads," TimesOnline, March 1, 2010. Reprinted with permission of The Times/nisyndication.com.

Internet Brings New Obstacles and New Opportunities

Because of the Internet, music can be shared globally in an instant, which is a huge benefit for artists and consumers. Yet the Internet also makes music piracy so easy that many people consider it a harmless act, and the economic implications for recording artists are substantial. In 2007, RIAA estimated the industry had lost nearly $1 billion in revenue just from illegal music downloads. In 2009, RIAA announced that music sales were down 18 percent worldwide from 2007 to 2008—the lowest level ever. In 2010, RIAA estimated that "globally only one of 20 downloads is authorized, and online piracy rates in many markets is in the vicinity of 99 percent."

No industry could survive for long on such a rapid loss of income. So the recording companies have no choice but to pursue copyright infringement wherever they find it. Licensed music is governed by national and international copyright law, and the recording industry continues to aggressively pursue all the legal remedies available to curtail illegal music downloads in the United States and reduce piracy, especially overseas. The industry, of course, also encourages all legal music download services, such as iTunes, and subscription sites, such as Spotify.

By April 2008, the iTunes store had become the largest music retailer in the United States. By 2010, according to Apple, customers had downloaded 10 billion songs. Spotify has 7 million users in Britain, Spain, France, Sweden, Norway and Finland. Because of the Internet, music artists today can find a bigger audience than Thomas Edison could have ever imagined—through music downloads and subscription services. However, the music business cannot escape the challenges of Internet. The recording companies must learn how to produce music consumers want to hear using a format and/or a service they're willing to buy.

When Edison demonstrated his phonograph for the editors of *Scientific American* in 1877, the magazine reported that "Mr. Thomas Edison recently came into this office, placed a little machine on our desk, turned a crank, and the machine inquired as to our health, asked how we liked the phonograph, informed us that it was very well, and bid us a cordial good night. These remarks were not only perfectly audible to ourselves, but to a dozen or more persons gathered around."

None of the discoveries by Edison's successors has been a new invention, only refinements. Berliner flattened the cylinder; Goldmark and Sarnoff slowed down the speed; hi-fi, stereo and quadraphonic sound increased the fidelity; cassettes, compact discs, digital recorders and MP3 players refined the sound further; and file-sharing software allowed people to share copyrighted music. While advances in technology have dramatically improved the quality of recordings, they have also made free copying possible, robbing the recording companies of their profitability.

Still, the basic foundation of the recording industry today is the same as it was for Thomas Edison in 1887. Reflecting on the movie version of Edison's life, Robert Metz describes the development of the phonograph: An Edison employee was tinkering with "a makeshift device consisting of a rotating piece of metal with a pointed piece of metal scratching its surface. The device was full of sound and fury—and signified a great deal. . . . And thus, supposedly through idle play, came the first permanent 'record' of ephemeral sound. By any measure, it was an invention of genius."

Review, Analyze, Investigate

REVIEWING CHAPTER 5

Edison Introduces His Amazing Talking Machine

✓ Thomas Edison first demonstrated his phonograph in 1877.

✓ Emile Berliner developed the gramophone in 1887.

✓ Berliner and Eldridge Johnson formed the Victor Talking Machine Company (later RCA Victor) to sell recordings.

✓ Joseph Maxfield perfected recording equipment to eliminate the tinny sound.

✓ The first standard records were 78 rpm.

Peter Goldmark Perfects Long-Playing Records

✓ Peter Goldmark, working for CBS' William S. Paley, developed the long-playing (LP) record (33 rpm).

✓ The first long-playing records played for 23 minutes and were larger than 78s.

William S. Paley Battles David Sarnoff for Record Format

✓ David Sarnoff's staff at RCA developed the 45 rpm record.

- ✓ Eventually record players that could play all the different speeds—33-1/3 rpm, 45 rpm and 78 rpm—were sold.

Hi-Fi and Stereo Rock In

- ✓ Rock 'n' roll redefined the concept of popular music.
- ✓ Recording industry efforts to improve recorded sound quality contributed to the success of rock 'n' roll entertainers like Marvin Gaye, Martha & the Vandellas and the Supremes.
- ✓ The introduction of transistor radios in the '60s and the Walkman in the late '70s made music personal and portable.
- ✓ CD-RWs, compact discs that could record as well as play, meant consumers could create their own CDs.
- ✓ The Apple iPod music player, first introduced in 2001, allowed users to store and play music downloads.
- ✓ Apple launched iTunes, its online music store, in 2003, charging 99 cents per song and allowing legal music downloads.
- ✓ The Apple iPhone, introduced in 2007, combined mobile phone technology with the capabilities of the iPod, expanding Apple's dominance in music retailing.
- ✓ Today, Apple's iTunes store has become the primary consumer source for contemporary music.

Recording Industry at Work

- ✓ A recording company is divided into artists and repertoire, operations, marketing and promotion, distribution and administration.
- ✓ CD sales alone don't generate enough revenue to support most music groups.

Concerts Bring In Important Revenue

- ✓ Concerts require high-tech innovation.
- ✓ Concert ticket sales are an essential source of revenue for large bands.

Four Major Companies Dominate

- ✓ About 5,000 labels produce recordings in the United States, but four large corporations dominate the recording industry.
- ✓ Recording companies sell over two billion recordings a year.
- ✓ Radio depends on popular music to succeed.

Music Sales and Licensing Drive Industry Income

- ✓ The recording industry collects income from direct sales, music licensing, music videos and music downloads, but recording income today is declining.
- ✓ Today two licensing agencies—ASCAP and BMI—handle the rights to play music for broadcast.

Industry Struggles to Protect Content Labeling

- ✓ Three issues facing today's recording industry are attempts to control music content through labeling, overseas piracy and copyright protection for music file sharing.
- ✓ The recording industry responded to threats of government regulation of music lyrics by adopting its own standards for music labeling.
- ✓ MP3 digital technology, perfected in 1999, allowed consumers to download and store good-quality music directly from the Internet.
- ✓ Music-sharing company Napster was sued in 1999 for copyright infringement by the Recording Industry Association of America and shut down in 2001.
- ✓ Consumers continued to use music-sharing sites such as Kazaa and Grokster, even though the downloaded songs were covered by copyright.

Recording Industry Association Sues Downloaders

- ✓ In 2003, the Recording Industry Association of America sued 261 individual music downloaders, hoping to stop the flow of free music on the Internet, but people still continue to download.
- ✓ The lawsuits included specific names of people who had downloaded music.

U.S. Supreme Court Rules Against File Sharing

- ✓ In June 2005, the U.S. Supreme Court in *MGM Studios v. Grokster* ruled that the makers of Grokster, which allowed Internet users to browse freely and copy songs from each other, could be sued for helping people violate recording industry copyright protections.
- ✓ *MGM Studios v. Grokster* gave the recording industry the legal standing it needed to try to stop illegal file sharing.

Music Industry Wins Legal Action

- ✓ In 2007, a federal jury imposed a penalty for file sharing of $222,000 against a woman named Jammie Thomas—calculated at $9,250 in damages for each of the 24 songs involved in the trial. In September 2008, the judge in the case ordered a retrial. The verdict against Thomas represented the first time a federal jury had imposed a legal fine on someone for music piracy.
- ✓ In late 2008, RIAA dropped suits against 35,000 downloaders and said it primarily would pursue downloaders through their Internet service providers.
- ✓ In 2009, a federal jury reaffirmed the decision against Thomas and awarded the recording companies $1.92

million, or $80,000 per downloaded song. Thomas appealed. In January 2010, a judge reduced the award to $2,250 per song, or $54,000. The case is still pending.

Changing Technology Transforms Delivery

- ✓ Apple introduced the iPod portable music player in 2001.
- ✓ Apple's iTunes music store, launched in 2003, provides a legal way for people to download music.
- ✓ Despite aggressive attempts by RIAA to stop music file sharing, the practice is still widespread.

Internet Brings New Obstacles and New Opportunities

- ✓ The Apple iPhone, introduced in 2007, combines the functions of the Apple iPod and a mobile phone, making Apple the dominant music retailer.
- ✓ In 2007, RIAA estimated the industry had lost nearly $1 billion in revenue just from illegal music downloads.
- ✓ By April 2008, the iTunes store had become the largest music retailer in the United States.
- ✓ In 2010, RIAA estimated that "globally only one of 20 downloads is authorized, and online piracy rates in many markets is in the vicinity of 99 percent."
- ✓ The recording companies have no choice but to pursue copyright infringement wherever they find it. Licensed music is governed by national and international copyright law, so the recording industry aggressively pursues all the legal remedies available to curtail illegal music downloads in the United States and reduce piracy, especially overseas.
- ✓ The industry also encourages all legal music download services, such as iTunes, and subscription sites, such as Spotify.

KEY TERMS

These terms are defined in the margins throughout this chapter and appear in alphabetical order with definitions in the Glossary, which begins on page 383.

ASCAP 100
BMI 100
CD-RW Drives 96
File Sharing 102
LP 94
RIAA 102
RPM 94

CRITICAL QUESTIONS

1. Describe the competition between William Paley's 33-1/3 records and David Sarnoff's 45s. How was that battle resolved? What does that battle tell you about the role that technology plays in the media industries?
2. Why are the recording industry and the radio industry so interdependent?
3. Give a brief history of Motown. Why was the company so important in the history of the music industry?
4. Discuss the response of the music recording industry to file sharing, and evaluate the extent to which it has been successful in protecting recording artists and recording companies. Do you believe file sharing will stop after the federal court's decision in the Jammie Thomas case? Explain.
5. How have recent technologies, such as the iPod and the iPhone, affected the music recording and performance industries in ways other than file sharing? Discuss.

WORKING THE WEB

This list includes both sites mentioned in the chapter and others to give you greater insight into the recording industry.

American Top 40 with Ryan Seacrest

http://www.at40.com

Along with America's longest-running popular music weekend countdown, AT40 offers music news, artist pictures and podcasts, and user contests and blogs. The Web site AT40.com features a search, "Where to Listen," that allows users to find local radio stations that play current music hits.

AOL Music

http://music.aol.com

The music division of America Online, AOL Music offers streaming radio, music downloads from a variety of genres and entertainment news. Users can watch live performances on Sessions and connect with other fans on Spinner and Popeater.

Apple.com/iTunes

http://www.apple.com/itunes

iTunes provides "music jukebox" software used to store music on a computer or a hand-held digital player such as an iPod. Apple's online music service opened in 2003, and its popularity has proven the feasibility of online music sales. In addition to music, the iTunes Store features audio books, TV shows, movies, iPod games and cell phone ringtones. The iPod is currently rivaled by Apple's own iPhone, which has all the iPod's capabilities plus Internet access, GPS mapping, cell phone service and more.

Billboard

http://billboard.biz and http://billboard.com

Billboard.biz is the official business Web site of *Billboard* magazine, the music industry's bible. It includes breaking news about the music business, top-selling charts in all music categories and even a job bulletin board to lead readers to jobs in the music industry. The companion Web site, Billboard.com, offers samples from best-selling music albums and singles; news articles on artists, products and awards; interactive blogs, games and contests; and even a Billboard fashion store. Billboard.com is also available in Spanish at billboardenespanol.com.

Insound

http://www.insound.com

Developed in 1999 by "a bunch of indie rock kids" determined to improve the music mail-order business, Insound presents a wide variety of independent music. The Web site offers CDs, music downloads and vinyl records as well as T-shirts, posters and other merchandise. Favorite music lists created by staff, bands and guests are also available.

Napster

http://www.napster.com

One of the first music file-sharing services, Napster offers a subscription service, free legal on-demand music through freenapster.com, and a fast-growing mobile music platform. Originally (in 1999), the Web site simply provided an index to music files in other users' computers. Because much of the music was copyrighted, the music industry sued. After almost closing in 2001, Napster gained a new owner and was turned into a subscription service that pays royalties to the music companies.

Pandora: Radio from the Music Genome Project

http://pandora.com

With the belief that each listener has an individual relationship with music, Pandora provides a customizable online listening experience. Users enter favorite artist or song names and Pandora's software analyzes melody, harmony, rhythm and more to identify and recommend similar music.

Recording Industry Association of America (RIAA)

http://www.riaa.com

As the trade group representing U.S. music companies, RIAA protects intellectual property rights and First Amendment rights globally, conducts consumer and technical research and monitors governmental regulations and policies. It also issues the awards for Gold and Platinum best-selling recordings.

Universal Music Group (UMG)

http://www.universalmusic.com

Owned by Vivendi, Universal Music Group has worldwide operations that cover recorded music and music publishing. UMG offers the world's largest digital music catalog and holds recording labels including Interscope Geffen A & M, Universal Motown and Nashville groups, and Universal Music Latino. Its Web site hosts videos in all music genres.

Impact/Action Videos are concise news features on topics covered in this chapter, created exclusively for **Media/Impact**. They are available for students and instructors at CengageBrain.com, and include screen access for classroom viewing and discussion questions.

6

"Of the 20 hours a week that an average American spends listening to music, only three of it is stuff you own. The rest is radio."

—Tim Westergren, Founder, Pandora Internet Radio

Radio: Riding the Wave

What's Ahead?

Radio Sounds Are Everywhere

Radio Takes a Technological Leap

Broadcasting Is Born

Federal Government Regulates the Airwaves

Radio Audience Expands Quickly

Radio Grows into a Powerful Force

"War of the Worlds" Challenges Radio's Credibility

Radio Networks Expand

Radio Adapts to Television

Radio at Work

Congress Creates National Public Radio

Portability and Immediacy Help Radio Survive

Telecommunications Act of 1996 Overhauls Radio

Are Radio Ratings Accurate?

Radio Depends on Ready-Made Formats

Audience Divides into Smaller Segments

Competition Brings Back Payola

Digital Audio Delivers Internet and Satellite Radio

Digital Delivery Splits Radio Industry Income

Bloomberg/Getty Images

At Bloomberg Radio on September 7, 2010, financial experts discuss the economy with host Tom Keene (far right). Bloomberg Radio, based in New York City, is available simultaneously on AM WBBR-AM (1130), Sirius XM, and on the Internet at http://www.bloomberg.com/radio.

TimeFrame 1889 — Today

Radio Technology and Format Programming Chase the Audience

1899 Guglielmo Marconi introduces his wireless radio to the U.S. with a report of the America's Cup race.

1907 **Lee de Forest introduces the Audion tube, which improves the clarity of radio signal reception. Reginald Aubrey Fessenden transmits the first voice and music broadcast.**

Hulton Archive/Archive Photos/Getty Images

1920 Station KDKA in Pittsburgh goes on the air, the nation's first commercial radio station.

1934 Congress establishes the Federal Communications Commission to regulate broadcasting.

1936 Edwin H. Armstrong licenses frequency modulation (FM).

1938 *Mercury Theater on the Air* broadcasts "War of the Worlds," demonstrating how quickly broadcast misinformation can cause a public panic.

1948 **First transistor radios are sold, making radio portable and expanding radio's reach to audiences outside of the home and the car.**

Lawrence Manning/Corbis

1959 Gordon McLendon introduces format radio at KABL in San Francisco.

1960 **The Manhattan grand jury indicts disc jockey Alan Freed for payola.**

AP Photo

1970 National Public Radio (NPR) goes on the air. By design, public radio was created as an alternative to commercial radio.

1996 Congress passes the Telecommunications Act of 1996, which encourages unprecedented consolidation in the radio industry.

2001 **Sirius Satellite Radio and XM Radio begin offering digital satellite radio service.**

Gary Gershoff/ WireImage/Getty Images

2005 New York Attorney General Eliot Spitzer charges that payola still is pervasive in the radio industry.

Radio broadcasters form the HD Digital Radio Alliance to promote HD radio.

Internet radio pioneer Tim Westergren launches Internet radio service Pandora, which offers free and subscription music online.

Courtesy of Pandora Media, Inc.

2008 Satellite radio companies XM and Sirius merge into a company called Sirius XM.

The Nielsen Company, which provides ratings for television, launches a radio ratings service, ending Arbitron's monopoly on radio ratings.

2009 Pandora Internet radio reaches a royalty-fee agreement with a group representing artists and record labels, which frees Pandora to legally expand its Internet radio services.

Today The radio industry has consolidated primarily into large groups of stations that use standardized formats, but satellite and Internet radio also are splitting the audience into smaller pieces.

Today, the nation's

collective memory and impressions about events that happened in the first half of the 20th century are directly tied to radio. Newspapers offered next-day reports and occasional extras, and magazines offered long-term analysis. But radio gave its listeners an immediate news record at a time when world events demanded attention. Radio also gave people entertainment: sports, big bands, Jack Benny, George Burns and Gracie Allen, Abbott and Costello, Bob Hope, and the original radio character, the Shadow ("The weed of crime bears bitter fruit. Crime does not pay! The Shadow knows!").

Radio transformed national politics by transmitting the sounds of public debate, as well as the words, to the audience. Radio also expanded Americans' access to popular as well as classical culture. Opera played on the same dial as slapstick comedy; drama and music shared the airwaves with sports—all supported by advertising.

Radio Sounds Are Everywhere

The legacy of news and music remains on radio today, but the medium that once was the center of attention in everyone's front room has moved into the bedroom, the office, the car and the shower. Radio wakes you up and puts you to sleep. Radio goes with you when you run on the trail or sit on the beach. Internet radio even follows you to your desk at work. Consider these industry statistics about radio today:

- 99 percent of America's homes have radios.
- 95 percent of America's cars have radios, and radio reaches four out of five adults in their cars at least once each week.
- 40 percent of Americans listen to the radio sometime between 6 a.m. and midnight.
- 7 percent of America's bathrooms have radios.
- More than 6,000 radio stations are available on the Internet.

Although radio is more accessible today, what you hear is not the same as what your great-grandparents heard. Advertisers, who once sought radio as the only broadcast access to an audience, have many more places to put their ads. For audiences, radio has become an everyday accessory rather than a necessity. No one had envisioned radio's place in today's media mix when radio's pioneers began tinkering just before the turn of the 20th century. All these pioneers wanted to do was figure out a way to send sounds along a wire, not through the air.

Radio Takes a Technological Leap

Today we are so accustomed to sending and receiving messages instantaneously that it is hard to imagine a time when information took more than a week to travel from place to place. In the early 1800s, the pony express took ten and a half days to go from St. Joseph, Mo., to San Francisco. Stagecoaches had to travel 44 hours to bring news from New York to Washington.

Technological advances brought rapid changes in how quickly information could move throughout the country. First came the invention of the telegraph and the telephone, which depended on electrical lines to deliver their messages, and then wireless telegraphy, which delivers radio signals through the air.

In 1835, *Samuel F. B. Morse* first demonstrated his electromagnetic telegraph system in America. In 1843, Congress gave him $30,000 to string four telegraph lines along the Baltimore & Ohio Railroad right-of-way from Baltimore to Washington. Morse sent the first official message—"What hath God wrought?"—from Baltimore to Washington, D.C., on May 24, 1844.

Telegraph lines followed the railroads, and for more than 30 years Americans depended on Morse's coded messages printed on tape, sent from one railroad station to another. On March 10, 1876, *Alexander Graham Bell* sent a message by his new invention, the telephone, to his associate Thomas A. Watson in an adjoining room of their Boston laboratory: "Mr. Watson, come here. I want you." Both Morse's telegraph and Bell's telephone used wires to carry messages.

Then in Germany in 1887, the physicist *Heinrich Hertz* began experimenting with radio waves, which became known as Hertzian waves—the first discovery in a series of refinements that led eventually to the development of radio broadcasting.

Broadcasting Is Born

Broadcasting was truly a revolutionary media development. Imagine a society in which the only way you can hear music or enjoy a comedy is at a live performance or by listening to tinny noises on a record machine. The only way you can hear a speech is to be in the audience. Movies show action but no sound.

Without the inventions of broadcasting's early pioneers such as Heinrich Hertz, you could still be living without the sounds of media that you have come to take for granted. Four pioneers besides Hertz are credited with advancing early radio broadcasting in America: Guglielmo Marconi, Reginald Aubrey Fessenden, Lee de Forest and David Sarnoff.

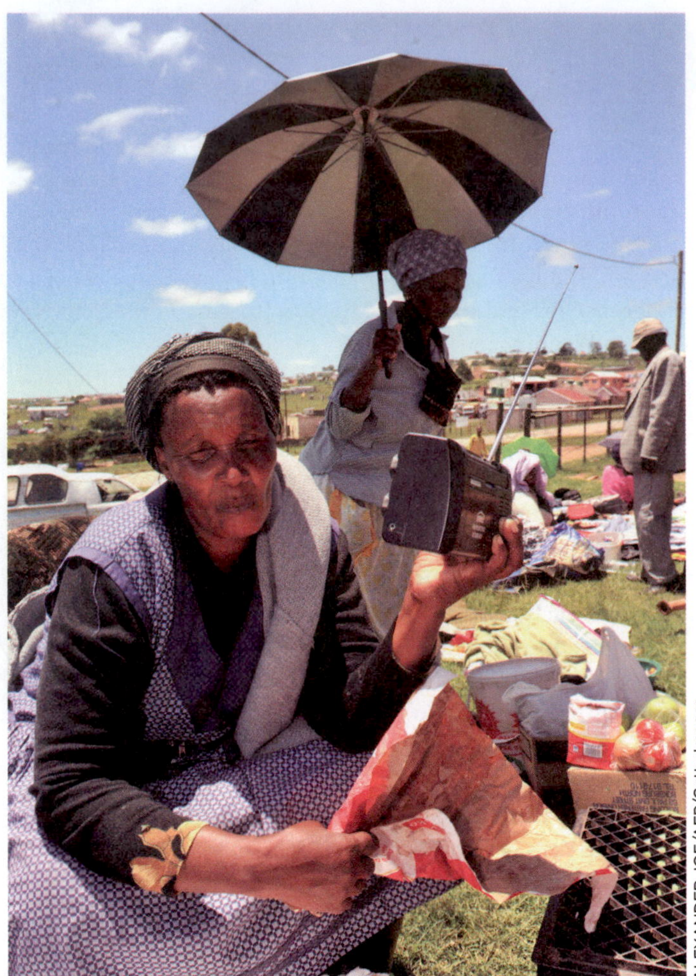

ALEXANDER JOE/AFP/Getty Images

In many parts of the world today, radio is a necessity rather than an accessory. On January 28, 2011, a street vendor in South Africa listens for news about the release of former South African President Nelson Mandela from the hospital.

Wireless Breakthrough: Guglielmo Marconi

Twenty-year-old Guglielmo Marconi, the son of wealthy Italian parents, used the results of three discoveries by Morse, Bell and Hertz to expand his idea that messages should be able to travel across space without a wire. Marconi became obsessed, refusing food and working at home in his locked upstairs room, trying to make his invention work. Soon Marconi could ring a bell across the room or downstairs without using a wire. Eventually Marconi was able to broadcast over a distance of nine miles. "The calm of my life ended then," Marconi said later.

The *New York Herald* invited Marconi to the United States to report the America's Cup race in October 1899. Marconi reported "by wireless!" American business people, intrigued by the military potential of Marconi's invention, invested $10 million to form American Marconi.

To experiment with the new discovery, amateur radio operators created radio clubs. Two experimenters, Reginald Aubrey Fessenden and Lee de Forest, advanced the Marconi discovery to create today's radio.

Experimental Broadcasts: Reginald Aubrey Fessenden

Reginald Aubrey Fessenden, a Canadian, began wireless experiments in the United States in 1900 when he set up his National Electric Signaling Company to attempt sending voices by radio waves. On Christmas Eve 1906, "ship wireless operators over a wide area of the Atlantic . . . were startled to hear a woman singing, then a violin playing, then a man reading passages from Luke. It was considered uncanny; wireless rooms were soon crowded with the curious," wrote broadcast historian Erik Barnouw.

The noises were coming from Fessenden's experimental station at Brant Rock, Massachusetts. Fessenden's 1906 experiment is considered the world's first voice and music broadcast.

Detecting Radio Waves: Lee de Forest

Lee de Forest called himself the father of radio because in 1907 he perfected a glass bulb called the Audion that could detect radio waves. "Unwittingly then," wrote de Forest, "had I discovered an invisible Empire of the Air." Besides being an inventor, de Forest was a good publicist. He began what he called "broadcasts" from New York and then from the Eiffel Tower.

In 1910, de Forest broadcast Enrico Caruso singing at the Metropolitan Opera House. Later his mother broadcast an appeal to give women the vote. Gradually, the Audion became the technical foundation of modern broadcasting.

A Household Utility: David Sarnoff

In 1912, 21-year-old wireless operator David Sarnoff relayed news from Nantucket Island, in Massachusetts, that he had received a distress call from the *Titanic* on his Marconi wireless. Four years later, when Sarnoff was working for the Marconi Company in New York, he wrote a visionary memo that predicted radio's future, although in 1916 his ideas were widely ignored.

"I have in mind a plan of development which would make radio a household utility. The idea is to bring music into the home by wireless," Sarnoff wrote. Eventually, as commercial manager and then president of RCA, Sarnoff watched his early vision for radio come true, and RCA became the nation's primary radio distributor.

Federal Government Regulates the Airwaves

The federal government decided to regulate broadcasting almost as soon as it was invented. This decision to regulate broadcasting separated the broadcast media, which are regulated by the federal government, from the print media, which are not regulated directly by any federal government agency.

As amateurs competed with the military for the airwaves, Congress passed the Radio Act of 1912 to license people who wanted to broadcast or receive messages. The federal government decided to license people to transmit signals because there only were a certain number of frequencies available to carry broadcast signals. Many amateurs, trying to send signals on the same frequency, were knocking each other off the air. The government intervened to try to keep the operators out of each other's way.

Then, during World War I, the federal government ordered all amateurs off the air and took control of all privately owned stations, and the military took over radio broadcasting. After the war, the federal government lifted the freeze, and the Navy argued that the military should maintain the monopoly over the airwaves that it had enjoyed during the war.

Underwood & Underwood/CORBIS

The nation's first commercial radio station, KDKA in Pittsburgh, went on the air in 1920. KDKA announcer Louis Kaufman stands with members of the Pittsburgh Pirates baseball team in 1925, the year the Pirates won the World Series.

Government Approves Commercial Broadcasting

Faced with strong arguments by the amateurs that they should be able to return to the airwaves, Congress decided against a Navy monopoly. Instead, the government sanctioned a private monopoly formed by General Electric, Westinghouse, AT&T, Western Electric Company and United Fruit Company. General Electric bought out American Marconi and its patents, and in 1919, these five sympathetic interests pooled the patents they controlled to form Radio Corporation of America (RCA).

David Sarnoff became RCA's general manager in 1921. Because of this early monopoly, RCA dominated radio development for many years, but eventually smaller operations formed all over the country as radio fever spread from coast to coast.

Experimental Stations Multiply

A plaque in San Jose, Calif., celebrates the 1909 founding of the experimental station FN: "On this site in 1909, Charles D. Herrold founded a voice radio station which opened the door to electronic mass communication. He conceived the idea of 'broadcasting' to the public, and his station, the world's first, has now served Northern California for half a century." Today, KCBS is based in San Francisco.

Various other stations claim they were among the earliest radio pioneers. Station 9XM broadcast music and weather reports from Madison, Wis.; 6ADZ broadcast concerts from Hollywood, Calif.; 4XD sent phonograph music from a chicken coop in Charlotte, N.C.; and 8MK in Detroit, operated by *Detroit News* publisher William E. Scripps, transmitted election returns.

These stations were run by amateur radio operators who broadcast messages to each other and their friends but not to the general public; nevertheless, they are early examples of broadcast entrepreneurs. They were tinkerers, fascinated with an invention that could carry sounds through the air. One of these tinkerers, Frank Conrad, is credited with creating the beginnings of the nation's first *commercial* radio station.

KDKA Launches Commercial Broadcasting

An ad in the September 29, 1920, *Pittsburgh Sun* changed broadcasting from an exclusive hobby to an easy-to-use medium available to everyone. The ad described a 20-minute evening concert broadcast from the home of Frank Conrad, a "wireless enthusiast" who worked for Westinghouse.

Conrad often broadcast concerts from his garage on his station, 8XK, but his boss at Westinghouse, Harry P. Davis, had an idea: Why not improve the broadcasts so more people would want to buy radios? Davis talked Conrad into setting up a more powerful transmitter at the Westinghouse plant by November 2, so Conrad could broadcast election returns.

On October 27, 1920, using the powers of the 1912 Radio Act, the U.S. Department of Commerce licensed station KDKA as the nation's first *commercial* radio station. The broadcast began at 8 p.m. on November 2, 1920, and continued past midnight, reporting that Warren G. Harding was the nation's next president. KDKA immediately began a daily one-hour evening schedule, broadcasting from 8:30 to 9:30 p.m.

Radio Audience Expands Quickly

The crude KDKA broadcasts proved that regular programming could attract a loyal audience. KDKA was just the beginning of what eventually became radio networks. The radio craze led almost immediately to a period of rapid expansion as entrepreneurs and advertisers began to grasp the potential of the new medium. Almost as quickly, government was compelled to step in to expand its regulation of radio broadcasting.

Radio's potential as a moneymaker for its owners fueled competition for the airwaves. Three important developments for radio's future were the

1. Blanket licensing agreement
2. Decision that radio would accept commercial sponsors
3. Radio Act of 1927

Blanket Licensing

At first, stations played phonograph records; then they invited artists to perform live in their studios. Some of the nation's best talent sought the publicity that radio could give them, but eventually the performers asked to be paid.

In 1923, the American Society of Composers, Authors and Publishers (***ASCAP***) sued several stations for payment. ASCAP claimed that if radio aired ASCAP-licensed music, people would buy less sheet music, so ASCAP members would be cheated out of royalties. Station owners argued that playing the songs on their stations would publicize the sheet music, which would mean ASCAP members would make more money.

Eventually the stations agreed to pay royalties to ASCAP through a ***blanket licensing agreement***, which meant the stations paid ASCAP a fee ($250 a year at first). In exchange, the stations could use all ASCAP-licensed music on the air. (ASCAP licenses its music to stations the same way today.) Eventually another licensing organization, Broadcast Music, Inc., or ***BMI***, also would collect broadcast royalties (see "Licensed Recordings Launch Disc Jockeys," p. 120).

Commercial Sponsorship

Once station owners agreed to pay for their programs, they had to figure out where they would get the money. AT&T had the answer with an idea pioneered at its station WEAF in New York. WEAF started selling advertising time to sponsors. Its first sponsored program cost the advertiser $100 to sponsor a 10-minute program.

The success of commercial sponsorship as a way to support radio settled the issue of who would pay the cost of airing the programs. Advertisers paid for programs through their advertising; the American public paid for the programs indirectly by supporting the advertisers who supported radio.

Federal Radio Commission

As more stations began to crowd the air, their signals interfered with one another. With only so many good radio frequencies available, the provisions of the Radio Act of 1912 (see "Federal Government Regulates the Airwaves," p. 115) began to seem inadequate. Congress passed the Radio Act of 1927, which formed the Federal Radio Commission under the jurisdiction of the Department of Commerce. The president appointed the commission's five members, with the Senate's approval.

The shortage of air space required that broadcasting in the United States operate under a type of government regulation unknown to newspaper and magazine publishers. The federal government licensed the stations for three years, and the commission mandated that the stations operate *"as a public convenience, interest or necessity requires."*

The commission, created to protect the stations by allocating frequencies, also became the license holder. The

ASCAP American Society of Composers, Authors and Publishers.

Blanket Licensing Agreement An arrangement whereby radio stations become authorized to use recorded music for broadcast by paying a fee.

BMI Broadcast Music, Inc., a cooperative music licensing organization.

stations could operate only with the government's approval, and the stations needed commission approval to be sold or transferred. The Radio Act of 1927, including the concept that broadcasters must operate in the "*public convenience, interest or necessity*," became the foundation for all broadcast regulation in the United States.

In 1934, Congress established the Federal Communications Commission (***FCC***) to regulate the expanding wireless medium, making the FCC a separate agency of government and no longer a part of the Department of Commerce. It is important to remember that the commission's original purpose was to allocate the broadcast spectrum so station broadcast signals would not interfere with one another. The FCC was not originally envisioned to oversee broadcast content.

The FCC began work on July 11, 1934, with seven commissioners appointed by the president, with Senate approval. This same basic structure and purpose govern the commission's actions today, but now there are only five commissioners. The establishment of the FCC in 1934 also set the precedent for the later regulation of television.

R. Gates/Archive Photos/Getty Images

Radio in the 1930s and 1940s became a powerful cultural and political force, offering people an inexpensive source of information and entertainment. In December 1944, Westinghouse advertised these small models as Your Personal Radio, manufactured with a new, cheaper material for the case called Bakelite. Inexpensive, smaller models meant that families could afford to have more than one radio at home.

Radio Grows into a Powerful Force

Most radio stations mixed entertainment, culture and public service. Radio created a new kind of collective national experience. Radio in the 1930s and 1940s became a powerful cultural and political force and gave millions of people a new, inexpensive source of information and entertainment (see **Illustration 6.1**).

The commercialization of American broadcasting also gave advertisers access to this audience at home. Radio's massive group of listeners sat enraptured with sponsored programming of many types: comedy, music, serials, sports, drama and news. Eventually, all these types of programming migrated to television.

"War of the Worlds" Challenges Radio's Credibility

On Halloween Eve, October 30, 1938, the *Mercury Theater on the Air* broadcast a play based on the H. G. Wells novel *War of the Worlds*. The live 8 p.m. broadcast played opposite the very popular Edgar Bergen program on NBC, and the *Mercury Theater* broadcast rarely had even 4 percent of the audience. Very few people heard the announcement at the beginning of the program that the Mercury Theater was performing a version of the Wells story.

The program began with the announcer introducing some band music. A second voice then said, "Ladies and gentlemen, we interrupt our program of dance music to bring you a special bulletin. At 20 minutes before 8 o'clock Central Time, Professor Farrell of Mount Jennings Observatory, Chicago, reports observing several explosions of incandescent gas occurring at regular intervals on the planet Mars."

FCC Federal Communications Commission.

Bettmann/CORBIS

The fear created by Orson Welles' "War of the Worlds" broadcast in 1938 demonstrated how easily unsubstantiated information could be misinterpreted on the radio. Orson Welles (center) met with reporters on October 31, 1938 to answer questions about the broadcast.

More dance music followed and then more bulletins about a meteor, with the startling news that 1,500 people near Princeton, N. J., had died when the meteor hit the town. Then the announcer said it was not a meteor but a spaceship carrying Martians armed with death rays.

Two professors from the Princeton geology department actually set out to locate the "meteors." In Newark, N. J., more than 20 families rushed out of their homes, covering their faces with wet handkerchiefs to protect them from the "gas." After a burst of horrified calls, CBS began repeating the announcement that the program was just a play, but the damage had been done.

The episode demonstrated how easily alarming information could be innocently misinterpreted, especially because the listeners had no other source than radio to check the reliability of what they were hearing. Radio listeners truly were a captive audience.

Radio Networks Expand

The formation of radio networks as a source of programming and revenue is a crucial development in the history of American radio. A ***network*** is a collection of stations (radio or television) that offers programs, usually simultaneously, throughout the country, during designated times.

Media/Impact AUDIENCE

Illustration 6.1

Where Do People Listen to the Radio?

Adults tune into the radio more at work and in the car than they do at home. Advertisers, such as car dealers, use this demographic information to help target radio audiences with their messages. (Because people listen to the radio in more than one place, the percentage total exceeds 100%.)

Source: Radio Advertising Bureau, 2010.

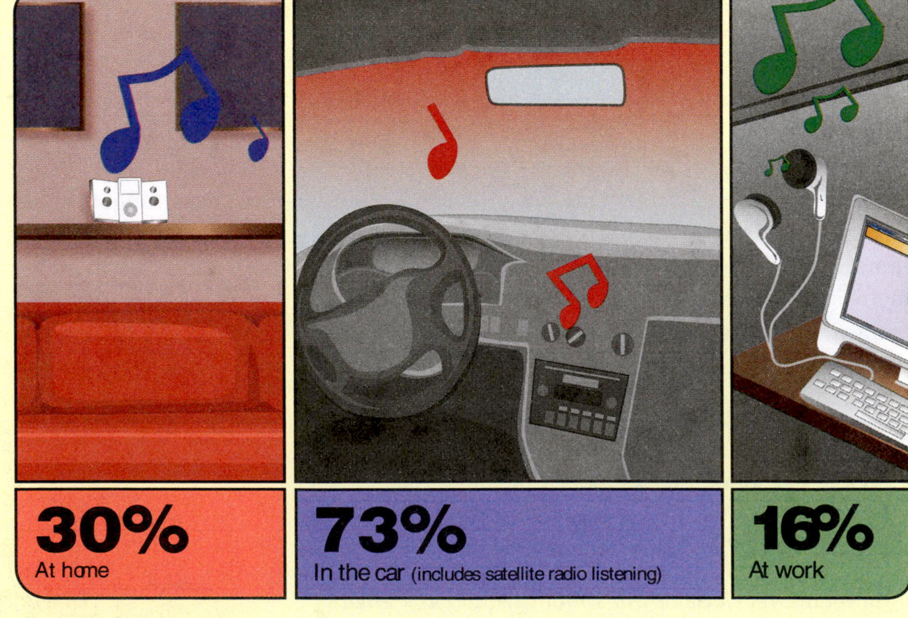

As the radio networks stretched across the country, they provided a dependable source of programming. Most stations found it easier to affiliate with a network and receive and distribute network programming than to develop local programs.

David Sarnoff Launches NBC

NBC grew out of the government's original agreement with RCA. RCA, GE and Westinghouse formed the National Broadcasting Company in 1926. By January 1927, NBC, headed by David Sarnoff, had formed two networks: the Red network (fed from WEAF in New York) and the Blue network (originating from station WJZ in Newark). Station engineers drew the planned hookups of the two networks with red and blue colored pencils, which is how the networks got their names. RCA faced criticism about its broad control over the airwaves because it continued to be the world's largest distributor of radios, which were made by Westinghouse and General Electric.

Hulton Archive/Getty Images

Bettmann/CORBIS

David Sarnoff (left), who began his broadcast career as a wireless operator, eventually became president of Radio Corporation of America (RCA). William S. Paley (right), who launched CBS radio, often battled with Sarnoff. The continuing competition between Sarnoff and Paley shaped the early development of American broadcasting.

William S. Paley Starts CBS

Twenty-six-year-old William S. Paley, heir to a tobacco fortune, bought the financially struggling Columbia Phonograph Company in 1929. He changed the name to Columbia Broadcasting System, and put his CBS network on the air with 25 stations. Programming originated from WABC in New York. Paley became the nemesis of NBC, then controlled by David Sarnoff, and this early competition between Sarnoff and Paley shaped the development of American broadcasting.

Edward Noble Buys ABC

In 1941, the FCC ordered RCA to divest itself of one of its networks. In 1943, RCA sold NBC-Blue to Edward J. Noble (who had made his fortune as head of the company that produced LifeSavers candy). Noble paid $8 million for the network that became the American Broadcasting Company (ABC), giving the country a three-network radio system.

Radio Adapts to Television

Radio networks prospered from the 1940s to the 1980s, when NBC sold its radio network, and CBS and ABC devoted more attention to their television holdings. When television initially was launched in the 1940s, it seemed it would cause the death of radio. As soon as television proved itself, advertisers abandoned radio, said comedian Fred Allen, "like the bones at a barbecue."

The entertainers fled to television, too—original radio talents such as Bob Hope, Milton Berle and Jackie Gleason soon dropped their radio programs and devoted themselves to TV. Public affairs programs like *Meet the Press* made the move from radio to TV, as did Edward R. Murrow's radio news program, *Hear It Now*, which on television became *See It Now*.

Network A collection of stations (radio or TV) that offers programs, usually simultaneously, throughout the country.

Five developments in the 1940s, 1950s and 1960s transformed the medium of radio as well as guaranteed radio's survival alongside television:

1. FM radio frequency was accepted by the public.
2. Disc jockeys hosted music shows.
3. Radio formats streamlined broadcasts.
4. People started buying clock and car radios.
5. The payola scandals focused on broadcast ethics.

Bettmann/CORBIS

Edwin H. Armstrong's invention of FM made radio signals clearer. For nearly 20 years, Armstrong battled RCA's David Sarnoff for royalties. Disheartened by the legal battle, Armstrong committed suicide, but his widow eventually won the royalty payments. In 1923, Armstrong shows off one of his inventions—radio in a suitcase—on the beach.

Inventor Edwin H. Armstrong Pioneers FM

After working for more than a decade to eliminate static from radio broadcasts, engineer Edwin H. Armstrong applied to the FCC in 1936 to broadcast using his new technique, frequency modulation (FM). Because of the way FM signals travel through the air, FM offered truer transmission than AM (amplitude modulation) with much less static. Armstrong faced difficult opposition from David Sarnoff at RCA, who had been an early Armstrong sponsor.

The FCC received 150 applications for FM licenses in 1939, but then froze licensing during World War II. After the war, Armstrong again faced Sarnoff, but this time Armstrong lost. RCA was using Armstrong's frequency modulation in its TV and FM sets but refused to pay Armstrong royalties, so Armstrong sued RCA.

RCA fought Armstrong for four years, saying that RCA had been among the early developers of FM and citing RCA's sponsorship of Armstrong's beginning experiments. In 1953, Armstrong became ill and suffered a stroke; then he committed suicide. RCA quickly settled the suit with Armstrong's widow for $1 million. Eventually FM became the spectrum of choice for music lovers, far surpassing the broadcast quality of AM.

Licensed Recordings Launch Disc Jockeys

Early radio station owners avoided playing records because they would have had to pay ASCAP royalties. The FCC also required stations that played records to remind their audiences every half-hour that the audience was listening to recorded music, not a live orchestra. This discouraged record spinning.

In 1935, newscaster Martin Block at New York's independent station WNEW began playing records in between his newscasts, and then he started a program called *Make Believe Ballroom*. He is generally considered America's first disc jockey. In 1940, the FCC ruled that once stations bought a record, they could play it on the air whenever they liked, without the half-hour announcements.

To counteract ASCAP's insistence on royalties, broadcasters formed a cooperative music licensing organization called Broadcast Music, Inc. Most rhythm and blues, country and rock 'n' roll artists eventually signed with BMI, which charged stations less for recording artists than ASCAP did. This inexpensive source of music also created a new type of media personality—the disc jockey.

Clock, Car and Transistor Radios Make Radio a Necessary Accessory

Clock and car radios helped ensure radio's survival by making it an everyday accessory. Transistor radios, first sold in 1948 for $40, were more reliable and cheaper than tube radios. Clock radios, introduced in the 1950s, woke people up and caused them to rely on radio for the first news of the day.

William Lear, who also designed the Lear jet, invented the car radio in 1928. Early car radios were enormous, with spotty reception, but the technology that was developed during World War II helped refine them.

In 1946, 9 million cars had car radios. By 1963, the number was 50 million. A radio station owner coined the term ***drive-time audiences*** to describe people who listened in their cars on the way to work from 6 to 9 a.m. and on the way home from 4 to 7 p.m.

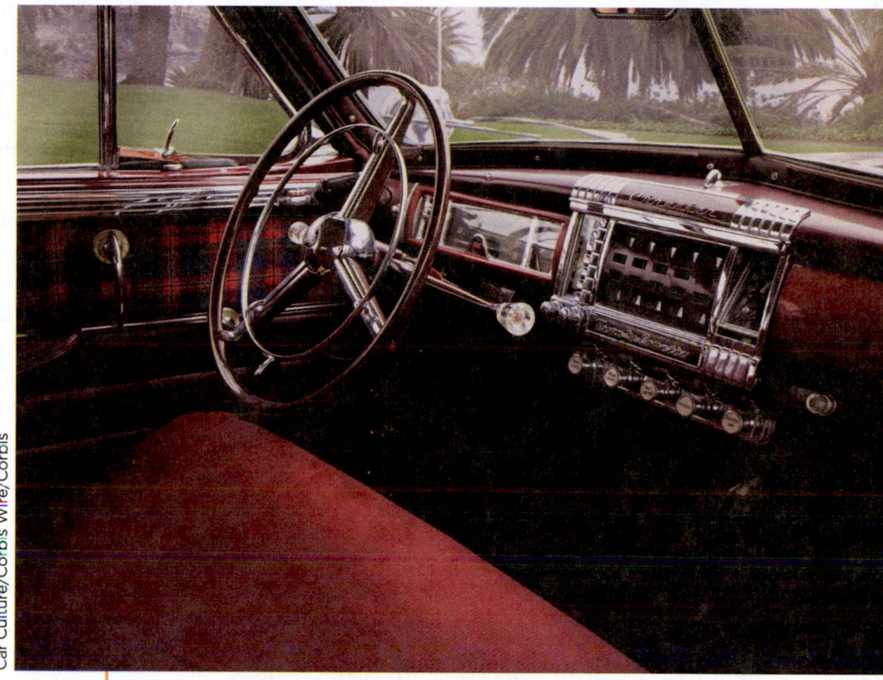

Car Culture/Corbis Wire/Corbis

William Lear invented the first car radio in 1928. By 1946, nine million cars had radios. Shown here is a 1947 Chrysler Town and Country luxury model, complete with wood trim, plaid interior and a luxurious chrome radio on the dashboard.

Gordon McLendon Introduces Format Radio

How would the stations know which mix of records to use and who would play them? The answer came from Gordon McLendon, the father of format radio. At KLIF in Dallas, McLendon combined music and news in a predictable rotation of 20-minute segments, and eventually KLIF grew very popular. Next he refined the music by creating the Top-40 format.

Top 40 played the top-selling hits continually, interrupted only by a disc jockey or a newscast. By 1959, McLendon launched the beautiful-music format at KABL in San Francisco. In 1964, he created a 24-hour news format for Chicago's WNUS, using three news vans with "telesigns" that showed news on the roofs in lights as the vans drove around town.

Formats meant stations could share standardized programs instead of producing programs individually. Eventually, formatted programming spread, which made network programming and the networks themselves less important to individual stations.

Payola Scandals Highlight Broadcast Ethics

The rise of rock 'n' roll coincided with the development of transistor and portable radios, which meant radio played a central role in the rock revolution. "Rock and radio were made for each other. The relationship between record companies and radio stations became mutually beneficial. By providing the latest hits, record companies kept stations' operating costs low. The stations, in turn, provided the record companies with the equivalent of free advertising," wrote radio historian David MacFarland.

Eventually this relationship would prove too close. On February 8, 1960, Congress began hearings into charges that disc jockeys and program directors had accepted cash to play specific recordings on the air. To describe this practice, the term ***payola*** was coined from the combination of *pay* and *Victrola* (the name of a popular record player).

In May 1960, the Manhattan grand jury charged eight men with commercial bribery for accepting more than $100,000 in payoffs for playing records. The most prominent among them was Alan Freed, who had worked in Cleveland (where he was credited with coining the term *rock 'n' roll*) and at New York's WABC.

In February 1962, Freed pleaded guilty to two counts of accepting payoffs, paid a $300 fine and received six months

Drive-Time Audiences People who listen to the radio in their cars during 6 to 9 a.m. and 4 to 7 p.m.

Payola The practice of accepting payment to play specific recordings on the air.

AP Photo/Matty Zimmerman

Gordon McLendon introduced format radio in 1959, which meant stations could share standardized formats that they previously had to produce individually.

probation. Then he was found guilty of income tax evasion. He died in 1965 while awaiting trial, at age 43. In September 1960, Congress amended the Federal Communications Act to prohibit the payment of cash or gifts in exchange for airplay; nevertheless, the issue of payola surfaced again in 2005 and resulted in stiff fines in 2007 (see "Competition Brings Back Payola," p. 127).

Radio at Work

A Columbia University report, commissioned by NBC in 1954, defined radio's role after television. "Radio was the one medium that could accompany almost every type of activity. . . . Where radio once had been a leisure-time 'reward' after a day's work, television was now occupying that role. Radio had come to be viewed less as a treat than as a kind of 'companion' to some other activity." Like magazines, radio survived in part because the medium adapted to fill a different need for its audience.

Today, about 10,800 broadcast radio stations are on the air in the United States. They are about evenly divided between FM and AM. Network programming plays a much smaller role than when radio began because most stations play music and so don't need network programming to survive. National Public Radio is the only major public network. Many commercial stations today use *program services*, which provide satellite as well as formatted programming.

Most stations are part of a *group*, which means that a company owns more than one station in more than one broadcast market. Some stations are part of a combination AM/FM (*a combo*), which means that a company owns both AM and FM stations in the same market. A few stations remain family-owned, single operations that run just like any other small business.

The management structure at a radio station usually includes a general manager, a program manager, account executives, the traffic department, production department, engineering department and administration.

The *general manager* runs the radio station. The *program manager* oversees what goes on the air, including the news programs, the station's format and any on-air people. Salespeople, who are called *account executives*, sell the advertising for programs.

The *traffic department* schedules the commercials, makes sure they run correctly and bills the clients. The *production department* helps with local programming, if there is any, and produces local commercials for the station. *Engineering* keeps the station on the air. *Administration* pays the bills, answers the phones and orders the paper clips. A small station requires five employees, or fewer, to handle all these jobs.

Congress Creates National Public Radio

The Public Broadcasting Act of 1967 created the Corporation for Public Broadcasting and included funding for public radio and TV stations. National Public Radio launched a national program on FM in 1970, but many radios still didn't have an FM dial. Most public stations—owned by colleges and universities and staffed by volunteers—were staffed irregularly.

Then NPR started the program *All Things Considered* for the evening drive-time and in 1979 launched *Morning*

"By the way, that's not just my opinion. It also happens to be the opinion of some guy on NPR."

David Sipress/Cartoonbank

Edition, hosted by Bob Edwards until 2004. Today, *Morning Edition* and *All Things Considered* have a very loyal audience for their long interviews on topical issues and international reports. By design, public radio is an alternative to commercial radio. Today, NPR still receives some public funding, but it depends primarily on private donations to survive.

Johnny Vy/NBAE/Getty Images

On September 25, 2010, Andrew Bynum of the Los Angeles Lakers is interviewed by local radio station AM 710 in El Segundo, California. Sports is one of radio's most popular formats.

Portability and Immediacy Help Radio Survive

Instead of dying after the spread of television, radio managed to thrive by adapting to an audience that sought the portability and immediacy that radio offers. Nothing can beat radio for quick news bulletins or the latest hits. Radio also delivers a targeted audience much better than television, because the radio station you prefer defines you to an advertiser much better than the television station you watch.

The advertising potential for an intimate medium like radio is attracting entrepreneurs who have never owned a station and group owners who want to expand their holdings, given the FCC's deregulation. When you listen to the radio in your car or through earphones while you jog, for instance, radio is not competing with any other medium for your attention. Advertisers like this exclusive access to an audience. Three important issues for people in radio today are:

1. Deregulation
2. Ratings
3. Formats

Telecommunications Act of 1996 Overhauls Radio

The Telecommunications Act of 1996 was the first major overhaul of broadcast regulation since the Federal Communications Commission was established in 1934. Today the legacy of the act is that commercial radio is regulated much less than it was in the 1970s. This is called a policy of ***deregulation***.

Before the 1996 act passed, the FCC limited the number of radio stations that one company could own nationwide. The Telecommunications Act removed the limit on the number of radio stations a company can own, and in each local market the number of stations that one owner can hold depends on the size of the market. (For a complete discussion of the Telecommunications Act, see **Chapter 14**.)

The Telecommunications Act also allows ***cross-ownership***, which means that companies can own radio and TV stations in the same market and broadcast and cable outlets in the same market. As soon as the act passed in February 1996, radio station sales began to soar.

Today many radio companies each own hundreds of stations. Supporters of the changes say radio could become more competitive because these larger companies can give the stations better financial support than small, single owners. Opponents point out that consolidation in the radio

Deregulation Government action that reduces government restrictions on the business operations of an industry.

Cross-Ownership The practice of one company owning radio and TV stations in the same broadcast market.

Larry Marano/FilmMagic/Getty Images

Popular singers like Enrique Iglesias make Spanish programming a very popular format. Critics say that radio ratings do not accurately reflect the large number of non-English-speaking listeners.

industry will lead to less program variety for consumers and too much power for companies that own large numbers of radio stations nationwide.

Are Radio Ratings Accurate?

Radio station owners depend on ratings to set advertising rates, and the stations with the most listeners command the highest ad rates. A company called Arbitron gathers ratings for the radio business. To find out what radio stations people are listening to, Arbitron requests that selected listeners complete and return diaries the company sends them.

Arbitron often is criticized because minorities, non-English-speaking listeners, and people ages 18 to 24 don't return the diaries in the same proportion as other people that Arbitron surveys. The critics contend that Arbitron's ratings hurt rock and urban formats, such as rap/hip-hop and Spanish language programming, while aiding the contemporary and news/talk/information formats, whose audiences are older and more responsive to the diaries. Arbitron acknowledges the problems and has tried filling out diaries for people over the phone and adding bilingual interviewers.

Still, questions persist, and radio stations are very dependent on ratings to set their rates for advertising.

In November 2008, the Nielsen Company, which provides ratings for TV, launched a radio ratings service, in direct competition with Arbitron.

Radio Depends on Ready-Made Formats

Today's radio station owners, looking for an audience, can use one of several ready-made formats. By adjusting their formats, radio managers can test the markets until they find a formula that works to deliver their target audience to advertisers. (See **Illustration 6.2**.)

If you were a radio station manager today, and you wanted to program your station, you could choose from several popular formats:

NEWS/TALK/INFORMATION/SPORTS. A station with this format devotes most of its airtime to different types of talk shows, which can include call-in features, where listeners question on-the-air guests. Its typical audience is 35 and older. It is difficult for a small radio station to survive on news alone, so most of these stations are in big cities because of the continuing source of news stories. The immediacy of the live news/talk format also can create problems for broadcasters because talk show hosts sometimes push the limits of commentary with outrageous, potentially libelous statements.

The news/talk category also includes live sports broadcasts (see **Media/Impact: People**, "Vin Scully: A City Hangs on His Every Word," p. 126), which are very popular because radio is a convenient way to follow live sports in the car and at work.

ADULT CONTEMPORARY. This program format includes adult rock and light rock music from the 1970s to today and aims to reach 25- to 40-year-olds in all types of markets.

CONTEMPORARY HIT/TOP 40. Playing songs on *Billboard*'s current hits list, a Top 40 station closely follows trends among listeners, especially teenagers.

SPANISH. Spanish stations are the fastest-growing radio format, as radio owners target the nation's expanding Latino population. Spanish-language radio usually features news, music and talk. Many Spanish-language stations are

Media/Impact MONEY

Illustration 6.2

Which Radio Formats Are Most Popular?

The most popular radio formats are country music, news/talk, Spanish, sports, oldies and adult contemporary.

Source: The Radio Marketing Guide, Radio Advertising Bureau Format Analysis, The Radio Book 2010–2011.

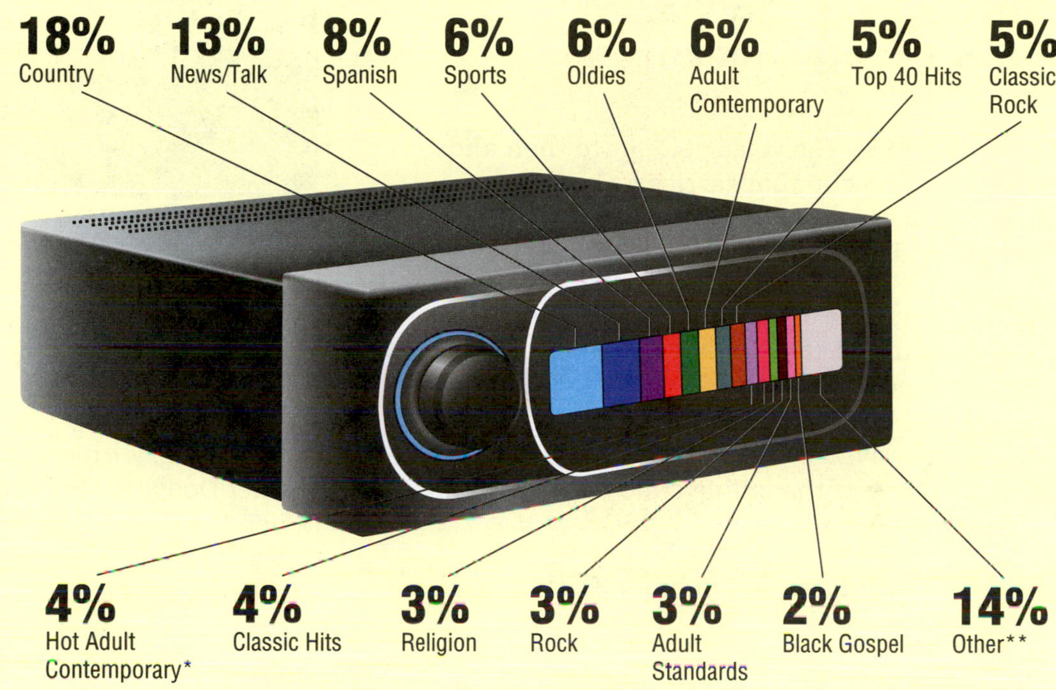

AM stations that recently have been converted from less-profitable formats.

COUNTRY. The Grand Ole Opry first broadcast country music on WSM in Nashville in 1925. This radio format is aimed at 25- to 45-year-olds in urban as well as rural areas.

The most popular radio formats are country music and news/talk/information/sports programs. Although news/talk radio is very popular in Los Angeles, the most-listened-to radio station in the Los Angeles area is now a Spanish-language station. Its popularity in an area with an expanding Spanish-language population shows how cultural changes in urban areas can affect the economics of local radio. Stations can also divide traditional formats into subcategories: Adult contemporary is splitting into modern rock and oldies; some Spanish-language stations play only love songs.

The use of recorded program formats means that a station can specialize its programming simply by what it chooses to play. Many stations operate without any disc jockeys or limit personality programming to morning and evening drive-time. At these stations, engineers and announcers carry the programming. Today, radio networks, which once dominated radio programming, mainly exist to provide national news to their affiliates.

Station managers can program their own stations, mixing local news, music and announcements. Stations also can get programming from syndicated and satellite program services. Syndicates provide pre-packaged program formats. Satellites make program distribution easier; satellite networks, such as Satellite Music Network, promise the broadcaster original, up-to-date programming without a large local staff.

Audience Divides into Smaller Segments

The most significant trend in radio is the move toward more segmentation of the audience, similar to the division of audiences in the magazine industry. Identifying a

Media/Impact PEOPLE

Vin Scully: A City Hangs On His Every Word

By Christine Daniels

LOS ANGELES—His voice belongs to then and now, an audio clip that carries us back to a bygone era even as it keeps us up-to-the-minute updated.

It has been there as long as big-league baseball has been in this city, actually pre-dating the Los Angeles Dodgers by several years, which was the biggest advantage the Dodgers had when they first arrived in 1958, certainly more important than any of the fading stars on the playing roster.

When Vin Scully settled in behind his microphone at the Coliseum 50 years ago, Los Angeles had the narrator it needed and the Dodgers had the pitchman they required to break the ice, to melt any pockets of resistance that might have been scattered around the Southland. . . .

Scully represents more than an era in Los Angeles sports history; he also represents an era in sports broadcasting when announcers were as indelibly linked to the teams they covered as the logo on the players' caps.

When Scully was hired by the Brooklyn Dodgers in 1950, his contemporaries included Mel Allen with the Yankees and Russ Hodges with the Giants. They were icons, with larger-than-life personas, as they served as the immediate conduits of information and news to fans hungry for details about their teams.

Over time, that part of the job description changed. More teams meant more job movement among announcers. New media, such as the Internet, meant more sources for information.

What has Scully meant to the Dodgers since 1958?

Noel Vasquez/FilmMagic/Getty Images

Perhaps the finest radio sportscaster ever, Vin Scully has been the voice of the Dodgers on radio for more than 60 years. In November 2009, the Hollywood Radio Television Society (HRTS) honored Scully as a broadcast legend.

"Everything, with an exclamation point," former Dodgers owner Peter O'Malley said. When the Dodgers first arrived in Los Angeles, O'Malley said, Scully was "the face of the Dodgers. It wasn't the manager. It wasn't a player. It wasn't the owner. It wasn't where they played. It wasn't any of those things. He was the face and the voice of the Dodgers. And he made so many friends for us, then and now."

More than just defining L.A. baseball culture, Scully invented it. For a city perpetually on the move, Scully became essential listening for harried freeway drivers who, once grounded, continued the habit with portable transistor radios—and today with audio supplied via satellite and the Internet.

Al Michaels listened to Scully as a kid growing up in Brooklyn, then followed the Dodgers to Los Angeles in 1958 when his father had to relocate because of work.

"I never missed a beat," Michaels said. "I've listened to Vinny almost since Vinny started. . . .

"To be able to do it over that period of time, and to still watch a game and broadcast a game with a sense of wonderment . . . to me that's the most astonishing thing about Vin Scully."

Excerpted from Christine Daniels, "A City Hangs On His Every Word," Los Angeles Times, March 31, 2008.

specific audience segment and programming for it is called ***narrowcasting***.

"With narrowcasting, advertising efficiency goes way up as overall costs go down. . . . We are approaching the unstated goal of all radio programmers: to create a station aimed so perfectly that the listener will no longer have to wait, ever, for the song that he wants to hear," says radio historian Eric Zorn.

Competition Brings Back Payola

As radio technology grows more complex and companies test new formats and different program delivery systems, the competition for your ear expands the choices that advertisers can make to reach you. However, as the competition among stations intensifies, some stations look for profits from a familiar but unethical source.

In 2005, New York Attorney General Eliot Spitzer announced he was investigating the four major music companies to examine their practice of paying independent promoters to influence which songs the stations played on the air. The practice often was criticized as a way for stations to get around laws prohibiting payola that date from the 1960s. (See "Payola Scandals Highlight Broadcast Ethics," p. 121.) Some record labels paid individual stations as much as $100,000 to help promote their songs, Spitzer said. Other companies gave the stations luxury travel for station employees or gifts to use in station giveaways.

"To disguise a payoff to a radio programmer at KHTS in San Diego, Epic Records called a flat-screen television a 'contest giveaway,' " reported *The New York Times*. "Epic . . . used the same gambit in delivering a laptop computer to the program director of WRHT in Greenville, N.C.—who also received PlayStation 2 games and an out-of-town trip with his girlfriend."

After more payoffs like these were uncovered, Sony agreed to a $10 million settlement and fired the top promotion executive at its Epic label. Radio executives at some of the other corporations said they already had stopped paying independent promoters, but Spitzer said, "This is not a pretty picture; what we see is that payola is pervasive." In 2007, the stations agreed to pay an additional $12.5 million to the Federal Communications Commission to settle the complaints.

Digital Audio Delivers Internet and Satellite Radio

A recent technology known as ***digital audio broadcast*** (DAB) eliminates all the static and hiss of current broadcast signals and means infinite program choices for consumers as all radio digital signals share the same delivery system. Today digital stations can send their digital signals over the Internet as well as over the air.

Robb Armstrong/Cartoonbank

"Starting Monday, this radio station will switch from classical music to hard-core rap."

SATELLITE RADIO. Another recent technology in the radio business is ***satellite radio***. Launched in 2001, satellite radio offers more than 200 channels of varied music and talk, with limited advertising on some stations and no advertising on others. For a subscription fee, two companies—Sirius Satellite Radio (based in New York) and XM (based in Washington)—began offering the service. The companies charged $9.95 to $12.95 a month to hear uninterrupted programming, without commercial announcements.

Satellite radio service requires special radios containing a miniature satellite radio receiver. In 2002, General Motors began offering satellite radios as a factory-installed option on some models. Ford and DaimlerChrysler began

Narrowcasting Segmenting the radio audience.

Digital Audio Broadcast A new form of audio transmission that eliminates all static and makes more program choices possible.

Satellite Radio Radio transmission by satellite, with limited or no advertising, available by subscription.

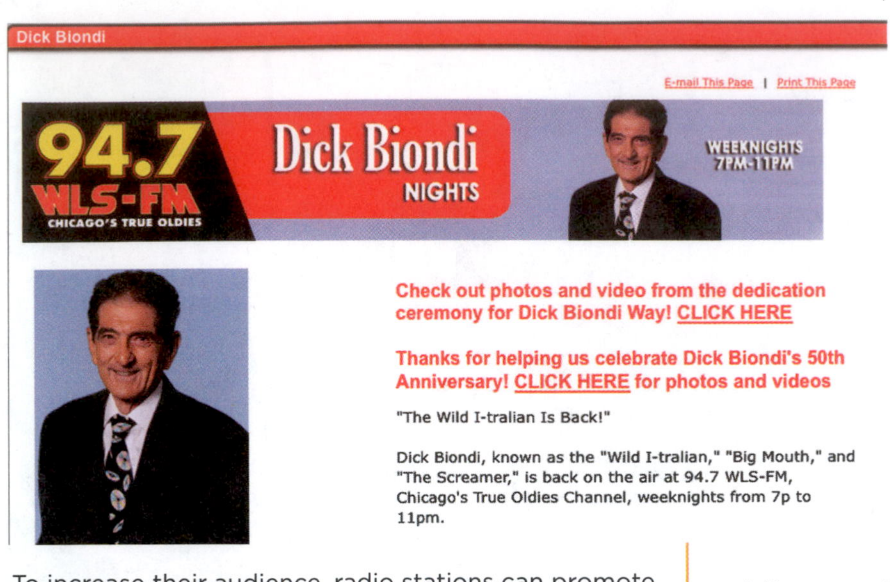

Courtesy of Citadel Broadcasting Corporation

To increase their audience, radio stations can promote themselves and broadcast their programming on the Internet. WLS-FM (94.7), Chicago, features legendary disc jockey Dick Biondi on its oldies station every weeknight. Biondi, who was the nation's number one disc jockey in the 1960s, has been a radio D.J. for more than 50 years.

offering the feature in 2003. New car buyers bundled the subscription fee with their automobile financing.

By 2005, XM boasted 4 million subscribers, and the company said it planned to have 10 million subscribers by 2010. In 2008, the Justice Department approved the merger of XM and Sirius, to become Sirius XM. Today, the two program services combined have about 18 million subscribers.

INTERNET RADIO. More than 6,000 stations now send their programming over the Internet. The Internet offers unlimited possibilities for radio to be distributed free beyond the bounds of a local radio audience, and people in the United States can easily hear overseas stations, such as the ***BBC*** (British Broadcasting Corporation), as well as stations based in the United States but outside their local area, such as WLS-FM.

Even low-power stations such as IBDAA Radio 194, originating from Palestine, can be rebroadcast over the Internet. The streaming Internet radio service Pandora, launched in 2005, allows users to select the programs and music they want to hear, free and by subscription (see **Media/Impact: Culture**, "You, the D.J.: Online Music Moves to the Cloud," p. 129).

BBC British Broadcasting Corporation.

HD Radio Hybrid digital technology that improves sound quality and makes it possible for radio stations to transmit real-time text messaging along with their programming.

Digital Delivery Splits Radio Industry Income

The more stations and digital radio services (such as satellite digital radio and Internet radio) that are available for customers, the harder every station and delivery service must compete for advertising. This means less revenue for each station because each station's potential audience becomes smaller.

Satellite and Internet radio delivery systems change the entire revenue equation for the radio industry as people pay subscription fees to hear radio on satellite without commercials and go to the Internet for access to new channels they couldn't hear before, offering listener-specific programming that isn't available on commercial radio in the United States.

Meanwhile, commercial radio is trying to stay afloat using the same commercial model that has served the industry for more than 80 years. In 2005, commercial radio introduced the concept of ***HD Radio***, hybrid digital technology that improves sound quality and also makes it possible for radio stations to transmit real-time text-based information services along with their programming. HD Radio can display song titles and artists' names, weather, news and traffic alerts as a digital readout accompanying the audio programming.

HD Radio is easier to engineer for FM stations than for AM stations, so more FM than AM stations have HD. "Only a core number of mostly big-wattage, large-market stations are broadcasting in AM digital," says the industry publication *Radio World*. The conversion to HD is more expensive and complicated for AM stations, and many station owners aren't willing to spend the money without a guaranteed return. To receive HD audio and text, consumers must have an HD-enabled radio, so car manufacturers will have to be willing to install HD radios to receive the signal; so far there has been very little consumer demand, so the conversion to HD has been slow.

In the 1930s, radio learned how to compete with newspapers. In the 1950s, radio learned how to compete with television. Today the radio industry must learn how to compete with itself.

Media/Impact CULTURE

You, the D.J.: Online Music Moves to the Cloud

By Sasha Frere-Jones

No one knows what the future of the music business will look like, but the near future of *listening* to music looks a lot like 1960. People will listen, for free, to music that comes out of a stationary box that sits indoors; they'll listen to music that comes from an object that fits in the hand; and they'll listen to music in the car. That box was once a radio or a stereo; now it's a computer. The handheld device that was once a plastic AM radio is now likely to be a smartphone. The car is still a car, though its stereo now plays satellite radio and MP3s.

"Of the 20 hours a week that an average American spends listening to music, only three of it is stuff you own. The rest is radio," Tim Westergren told me. Westergren is the founder of Pandora, one of several firms that have brought the radio model to the Internet. Pandora offers free, streaming music, not so different from the radio stations that many people grew up with, except that the D.J. is you, more or less. The company does not sell music—like normal radio, Internet radio is considered a promotional tool for recordings, even though the fees that it pays to labels are currently higher than those paid by terrestrial stations.

If you go to Pandora, on the Web or on a phone, you begin by picking a song or an artist, which then establishes a "station." Pandora's proprietary algorithm, in which a panel of musicians assesses about four hundred variables, like "bravado level in vocals" and "piano style," for each song, leads you from what you chose to a song that seems to fit with it, musically. You also have the option to teach the algorithm, by giving a song a thumbs up or a thumbs down. The company has captured a very large chunk of the Internet-radio audience—the service now has 50 million users, who listen an average of more than eleven hours a month.

Thor Swift/*The New York Times*/Redux Pictures

Tim Westergren launched the Internet streaming-music site Pandora in 2000. Listeners can customize their online streaming music. Pandora Internet Radio offers both a free ad-supported site and a subscription ad-free site. Pandora has 50 million users.

In Europe, the most prominent such service is Spotify, a Swedish company that has grown rapidly in the past year. In America . . . one of the biggest on-demand players is MOG, a new service that offers a wide array of listening options, the least expensive of which costs five dollars a month. MOG offers the option of streaming 320-kilobyte-per-second files, the highest available digital quality, though customers have been reluctant to pay extra for greater audio fidelity.

With MOG, you can play entire albums, create playlists, or let the service perform the same kind of algorithmic radio function that Pandora provides. (While listening to a song, you pull a slider all the way to the right; the software suggests related artists and tracks.) You can also share playlists with other users.

The anonymous programmers who write the algorithms that control the series of songs in these streaming services may end up having a huge effect on the way that people think of musical narrative—what follows what, and who sounds best with whom. Sometimes we will be the D.J.s, and sometimes the machines will be, and we may be surprised by which we prefer.

Excerpted from Sasha Frere-Jones, "You, the D.J.: Online Music Moves to the Cloud," The New Yorker, *June 14, 2010.*

Review, Analyze, Investigate

REVIEWING CHAPTER 6

Radio Sounds Are Everywhere

✓ Radio transformed national politics and also expanded Americans' access to popular, as well as classical, culture.

✓ Radio is a commercial medium, supported almost entirely by advertising.

Radio Takes a Technological Leap

✓ Radio history began with Samuel F. B. Morse's invention of the telegraph, first demonstrated in 1835.

✓ Alexander Graham Bell invented the telephone, demonstrated in 1876, and Heinrich Hertz first described radio waves in 1887.

Broadcasting Is Born

✓ Guglielmo Marconi's promotion of wireless radio wave transmission began in 1899 with the America's Cup race.

✓ Reginald Fessenden advanced wireless technology, but Lee de Forest called himself the father of radio because he invented the Audion tube to detect radio waves.

✓ David Sarnoff and William S. Paley made radio broadcasting a viable business in the United States.

Federal Government Regulates the Airwaves

✓ The federal government intervened to regulate broadcasting almost as soon as it was invented.

✓ Early regulation separated the broadcast media from the print media, which are not regulated directly by the federal government.

Radio Audience Expands Quickly

✓ Three important developments for commercial radio were blanket licensing, commercial sponsorship and the Radio Act of 1927.

✓ Blanket licensing meant that radio owners could use recorded music inexpensively.

✓ Commercial sponsorship established the practice of advertisers underwriting the cost of American broadcasting.

✓ The Radio Act of 1927 established the concept that the government would regulate broadcasting "as a public convenience, interest or necessity requires."

✓ The Radio Act of 1927 is the foundation for all broadcast regulation in the United States, including the establishment of the Federal Communications Commission (FCC) in 1934.

Radio Grows into a Powerful Force

✓ In the 1930s, radio programming expanded to include comedy, music, serials, drama and news.

✓ Radio also indirectly created a collective national experience that had not existed before.

✓ Commercials gave advertisers access to an audience at home.

"War of the Worlds" Challenges Radio's Credibility

✓ On Halloween Eve, October 30, 1938, *Mercury Theater on the Air* broadcast "War of the Worlds."

✓ The "War of the Worlds" broadcast demonstrated the vulnerability of a captive audience.

Radio Networks Expand

✓ Originally, the three radio networks (NBC, CBS and ABC) provided most radio programming. Today, most stations use a variety of sources to program themselves.

✓ David Sarnoff launched NBC radio in 1927, William S. Paley started CBS radio in 1929 and Edward Noble bought NBC-Blue, which became ABC, in 1941.

Radio Adapts to Television

✓ Edwin H. Armstrong is responsible for the invention of FM radio. Today, FM stations are three times as popular as AM stations.

✓ Clock, car and transistor radios expanded radio's audience, but the role of radio changed with the advent of TV, which meant radio had to compete with visual entertainment and TV news.

✓ Gordon McLendon launched format radio in 1959.

✓ In the 1960s, Congress uncovered the unethical practice of payola in the radio industry. Recording companies were paying station disc jockeys to play their songs on the air. These complaints resurfaced in 2005 when the New York attorney general filed payola charges against the four major music companies.

Radio at Work

✓ Radio is a portable medium that can accompany almost every activity.

✓ Today the 10,800 broadcast radio stations in the U.S. are about evenly divided between AM and FM.

- ✓ There is one major public network. Many commercial stations are part of a group or a combo and use program services instead of doing original programming.
- ✓ The management structure at a radio station includes a general manager, a program manager, account executives, the traffic, production, and engineering departments, and administration.

Congress Creates National Public Radio

- ✓ The federal government began funding National Public Radio in 1967, and NPR began broadcasting national programming in 1970.
- ✓ Today, NPR programs such as *Morning Edition* and *All Things Considered* still attract a very loyal audience, and public radio depends on private donations to survive.

Portability and Immediacy Help Radio Survive

- ✓ Radio is the best medium for quick news bulletins and the latest hits.
- ✓ Because it is an intimate medium, radio delivers a targeted audience to advertisers much better than TV.
- ✓ Radio is also portable—you can listen to it in your car or take it with you anywhere.

Telecommunications Act of 1996 Overhauls Radio

- ✓ The Telecommunications Act of 1996 was the first major overhaul of broadcast regulation since the FCC was established in 1934.
- ✓ The act removed the limit on the number of stations one company can own, and in each local market the number of stations one owner can hold depends on the size of the market.

Are Radio Ratings Accurate?

- ✓ Arbitron historically has been the primary ratings service for radio.
- ✓ Stations use ratings to set their rates for advertising.
- ✓ In November 2008, the Nielsen Company launched a radio ratings service, in direct competition with Arbitron.

Radio Depends on Ready-Made Formats

- ✓ Formats systematize radio broadcasts.
- ✓ Stations use formats to target a specific type of radio listener and define the audience for advertisers.
- ✓ The most popular radio formats are country music and news/talk.

Audience Divides into Smaller Segments

- ✓ The most significant trend in radio today is the move toward more segmentation of the audience, similar to the division of audiences in the magazine industry.
- ✓ Identifying a specific audience segment and programming for it is called *narrowcasting*.

Competition Brings Back Payola

- ✓ Payola resurfaced in 2005 when New York's attorney general charged that the four major recording companies paid private promoters to get their songs on the air.
- ✓ Sony paid $10 million to settle the charges against it, and in 2007 the radio stations paid the FCC an additional $12.5 million.

Digital Audio Delivers Internet and Satellite Radio

- ✓ Digital audio broadcast, Internet radio and satellite radio mean more program choices for listeners.
- ✓ Streaming Internet radio services like Pandora, launched in 2005, are the latest development in radio delivery systems.

Digital Delivery Splits Radio Industry Income

- ✓ Today radio listeners have more choices than ever.
- ✓ The addition of new sources for radio programming, such as satellite and Internet radio, are changing the economics of radio today.
- ✓ In 2005, commercial radio introduced the concept of HD Radio, digital technology that improves sound quality and also makes it possible for radio stations to transmit real-time text-based information services along with their programming.

KEY TERMS

These terms are defined in the margins throughout this chapter and appear in alphabetical order with definitions in the Glossary, which begins on page 383.

ASCAP 116
BBC 128
Blanket Licensing Agreement 116
BMI 116
Cross-Ownership 123
Deregulation 123
Digital Audio Broadcast 127
Drive-Time Audiences 121
FCC 117
HD Radio 128
Narrowcasting 127
Network 119
Payola 121
Satellite Radio 127

CRITICAL QUESTIONS

1. How did the Radio Act of 1912 set a precedent for American broadcasting?
2. How did the following developments in radio affect the industry? Why is each of them so important?
   a. Blanket licensing
   b. Commercial sponsorship
   c. Establishment of networks
3. Discuss the "War of the Worlds" broadcast and its effects upon its audience. How did it change people's perceptions of radio?
4. Discuss the ethics issues involved in the payola scandals.
5. Briefly discuss the present-day state of radio program delivery, including satellite programming and Internet radio.

WORKING THE WEB

This list includes both sites mentioned in the chapter and others to give you greater insight into the radio industry.

The Broadcast Archive

http://www.oldradio.com

This is a site for radio historians, with an emphasis on radio technology. The site includes an archive of manuals and schematics, as well as historical narratives and biographies of people who worked in early broadcasting.

Canadian Broadcasting Corporation (CBC) Radio-Canada

http://www.cbc.ca/radio

The radio division of Canada's national public broadcasting system, the CBC was created in 1936 in response to concern about the growing U.S. influence in radio. Now encompassing television and new media services, the CBC has a mandate to provide a wide range of programming that informs, enlightens and entertains and that is predominantly and distinctively Canadian. The Web site provides live radio streams from CBC Radio One (news and talk) and Radio 2 (jazz, blues and classical music), as well as program schedules, podcasts and forums. It also has links to CBC Radio 3 (rock, pop, hip hop, electronica and alt-country music) and Sirius XM.

CBS Radio

http://www.cbsradio.com

As one of the largest U.S. major-market radio operators, CBS provides broadcast, digital and on-demand radio. In addition to operating 130 radio stations, it is home to more than two dozen professional sports franchises.

Friday Morning Quarterback (FMQB)

http://www.fmqb.com

Recently celebrating 40 years of serving the music and radio industries with high-quality content, insightful articles and news, FMQB is the self-proclaimed "premier destination for music and radio industry professionals." The production division is renowned for its one-hour National Radio Series that feature major artists premiering new music. Web site features include breaking radio industry and music news, a voice talent vault, music available for airplay, ratings and job information, and industry links.

Inside Radio

http://www.insideradio.com

This radio industry publication features industry news, ratings and classifieds. Inside Radio also publishes *Who Owns What* (a weekly update on station ownership), *Radio Journal* (featuring FCC updates and technical news) and *The Radio Book* (a directory of radio stations in the U.S. and Canada).

National Public Radio

http://www.npr.org

NPR distributes and produces noncommercial news, talk and entertainment programs. Its more than 860 independently operated local stations mix national and local programming to fit the needs of their communities. Audio archives are available for a growing number of nationally produced shows.

Radio Advertising Bureau

http://www.rab.com

The goal of the RAB, the promotional arm of the commercial radio industry, is to increase the use of radio advertising and develop the skills of radio marketing representatives.

Radio Lovers

http://www.radiolovers.com

Radiolovers.com offers hundreds of vintage radio shows online for free. Its goal is to bring the world of Old Time Radio to a new generation of listeners. Users can browse by show genre or search by title. The site includes a disclaimer stating that the creators believe all show copyrights have expired or never existed and that they will remove any recording that is shown to violate a copyright.

Radio Time

http://radiotime.com

This electronic guide to radio allows users to find local programming by zip code; browse stations by location, genre and subcategories; listen to radio; and search by station, program or personality name. Also available by subscription is Red-Button, software that records and pauses live radio.

Sirius XM

http://www.siriusxm.com

Sirius XM offers over 200 channels of satellite radio, including commercial-free music as well as sports, news and talk shows. Radios must be Sirius XM-ready. Programming top names include CNN, Martha Stewart and Howard Stern. Sirius XM also provides Internet radio and Backseat TV, the first live in-vehicle television network.

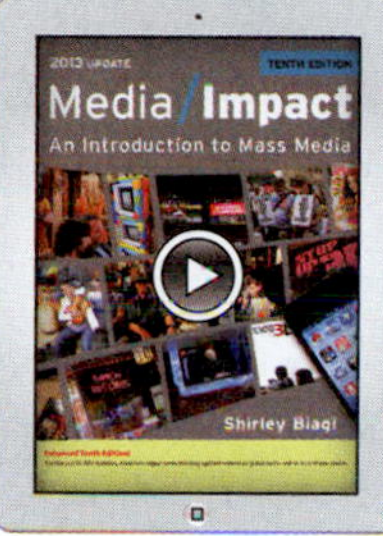

Impact/Action Videos are concise news features on topics covered in this chapter, created exclusively for **Media/Impact**. They are available for students and instructors at CengageBrain.com, and include screen access for classroom viewing and discussion questions.

7

"We are finally at the tipping point where digital is becoming relevant."

—Curt Marvis, President of Digital Media, Lionsgate

Movies: Picturing the Future

What's Ahead?

Movies Mirror the Culture

Inventors Capture Motion on Film

Filmmakers Turn Novelty into Art

Studio System and Independent Moviemakers Flourish

Movies Become Big Business

Big Five Studios Dominate

Labor Unions Organize Movie Workers

Movies Glitter During the Golden Age

Congress and the Courts Change Hollywood

Movies Lose Their Audience to Television

Movies and Money Today

Movies at Work

Digital Technology Drives the Business

International Markets Bring Concentrated Power

Jim Prisching/AP Images for IMAX

Movie industry revenue in the U.S. has been declining. 3-D movies provide the only growing source of revenue because today's audiences are willing to pay a premium to watch 3-D movies.

TimeFrame 1877 — Today

Movies Mature as a Popular Medium

1877 **Eadweard Muybridge catches motion on film when he uses 12 cameras to photograph a horse's movements for Leland Stanford in Palo Alto, Calif.**

Eadweard Muybridge/CORBIS

1915 Director D. W. Griffith introduces the concept of the movie spectacular with *The Birth of a Nation.*

1916 Brothers Noble and George Johnson launch Lincoln Films, the first company to produce movies called "race films," serious narrative movies for African American audiences.

1919 **Oscar Micheaux releases *Within Our Gates*, a response to D. W. Griffith's controversial, anti-black epic *The Birth of a Nation.***

Hulton Archive/Moviepix/Getty Images

1927 *The Jazz Singer*, the first feature-length motion picture with sound, opens in New York City.

1930 The Motion Picture Producers and Distributors Association adopts a production code to control movie content.

1947 The House Un-American Activities Committee calls The Hollywood Ten to testify.

1948 **The U.S. Supreme Court breaks up the large studios' control of Hollywood by deciding in the case of *United States v. Paramount Pictures, Inc., et al.* that the studios are a monopoly.**

Louie Psihoyos/Terra/Corbis

1966 The Motion Picture Association of America introduces a voluntary content-ratings system for the movies.

1994 **Steven Spielberg, Jeffrey Katzenberg and David Geffen launch DreamWorks SKG, the first independent movie studio created in the U.S. since United Artists.**

Daniel Acker/Bloomberg/Getty Images

2001 To attempt to stop movie piracy, the Motion Picture Association of America challenges the availability of recordable DVD technology, but eventually DVD-Rs reach the marketplace.

2006 DreamWorks is sold to Viacom, Inc., leaving the U.S. without a major independent movie studio.

2011 **3-D movies begin to generate higher revenue for the industry.**

Alberto E. Rodriguez/Getty Images

Today **Movie theaters collect about 1 billion tickets a year, but more people see movies on video than in theaters. The market for American movies continues to grow overseas. Movie downloads are an expanding source of revenue. Some movie distribution companies send their movies to theaters and directly to consumers' homes via video streaming.**

The movie industry

has been called "an industry based on dreams" because it has been such an imaginative, creative medium. It also would be easy to assume the movie industry is one of the biggest media businesses because the publicity surrounding movie celebrities captures a great deal of attention. So it often surprises people to learn that the movie industry makes less money each year than the newspaper, television or book businesses.

Movies and movie stars thrive on public attention because the size of the audience has a direct effect on whether movies succeed. Movies are expensive to make, and most movies lose money. Investors, therefore, often favor "bankable" talent that brings fans to a movie, rather than new, untested talent. But even movies featuring established talent can fail; no one in the movie industry can accurately predict which movies will be hits.

Movies Mirror the Culture

Perhaps more than any other medium, movies mirror the society that creates them. Some movies offer an underlying political message. Other movies reflect changing social values. Still other movies are just good entertainment. And all movies need an audience to succeed. (See **Media/Impact: Culture**, "A Second Act for Independent Film: Tight-Fisted Experiments Wring Profits from Small Movies," p. 138.)

Like other media industries, the movie business has had to adapt to changing technology. Before the invention of television, movies were the nation's primary form of visual entertainment. The current use of special effects—something you seldom get from television—is one way the movie industry competes with television for your attention and dollars. But special effects don't fit every movie, and they are very expensive. Today, as always, the economics of moviemaking is very important.

Inventors Capture Motion on Film

Movies were invented at a time when American industry welcomed any new gadget, and inventors wildly sought patents on appliances and electrical devices. The motion picture camera and projector were two of the Industrial Revolution's new gadgets.

Early Inventors Nurture the Movie Industry

Movies were not the invention of one person. First, a device to photograph moving objects had to be invented, followed by a device to project those pictures. This process involved six people: Étienne-Jules Marey, Eadweard Muybridge, Thomas Edison, William K. L. Dickson, and Auguste and Louis Lumière.

Marey and Muybridge

Étienne-Jules Marey, a scientist working in Paris, sought to record an animal's movement by individual actions—one at a time—to compare one animal to another. He charted a horse's movements on graphs and published the information in a book, *Animal Mechanism*.

Unknown to Marey, photographer Eadweard Muybridge was hired by railroad millionaire and horse breeder Leland Stanford to settle a $25,000 bet. Stanford had bet that during a trot, all four of a horse's feet simultaneously leave the ground. In 1877, Muybridge and Stanford built a special track in Palo Alto, Calif., with 12 cameras precisely placed to take pictures of a horse as it moved around the track. The horse tripped a series of equidistant wires as it ran, which in turn tripped the cameras' shutters. Stanford won his $25,000—one photograph showed that all four of the horse's feet did leave the ground—and the photographic series provided an excellent study of motion.

Muybridge expanded to 24 cameras, photographed other animals and then took pictures of people moving. He traveled throughout Europe showing his photographs.

Eadweard Muybridge/Hulton-Deutsch Collection/Corbis

This dancing woman is one of the early images photographed by Eadweard Muybridge, who captured motion on film. Muybridge's experiments led to the development of the first motion picture camera.

Media/Impact AUDIENCE

A Second Act for Independent Film: Tight-Fisted Experiments Wring Profits from Small Movies

By Michael Cieply

. . . For more than a decade, the indie film movement centered in New York flourished, at times almost eclipsing the output of the mainstream Hollywood studios in terms of impact and accolades. But the financial collapse and the credit crisis had a deep impact on all of the movie world, which has responded with fewer expensive releases and safer bets. . . .

"The world is different now," Richard Abramowitz, a new-wave film distributor, said last week. . . . There are, however, signs of life. The struggling indie scene is getting a boost from fleet-footed, penny-pinching guerrilla operations that are trying to resuscitate the business by spending less on production, much less on marketing and embracing all forms of distribution, including the local art house and the laptop. . . .

While many in Los Angeles continue to struggle with the studio system and the emerging intricacies of 3-D, New York has locked on a different challenge: how to wring even the tiniest profit from that enormous investment in smaller movies. . . .

Independent distributors that survived the great shakeout include Focus Features, a Universal Studios unit that is anchored in Manhattan, and Sony Pictures Classics, a specialty film label based in New York that has consistently released about 20 movies a year with a staff of just 25. Along with the survivors, there are some newly established companies, like Apparition.

For many of these companies, austerity is a given, and that means looking at digital distribution.

At Tribeca Enterprises, a sponsor of its namesake festival, the chief creative officer, Geoffrey Gilmore, in March joined the company's co-founder Jane Rosenthal and others to announce a new distribution unit focused on video-on-demand—where the dollars are small, but the potential audience is vast.

Nicole Bengiveno/*The New York Times*/REDUX

Independent filmmakers are trying to revive an interest in small-budget movies. In 2010, a crew shoots the film *East Fifth Bliss* in New York City on a budget of less than $2 million.

Already, Rainbow Media, which operates IFC Entertainment, is feeding about 120 films a year to cable television systems, while perhaps 50 of those movies are shown in one or more theaters. The company, led by Joshua Sapan, also operates an independent theater complex.

Producers cannot recoup their investment from the marginal payout from on-demand showings, but a run on IFC's channels or those of other services brings recognition that helps increasingly entrepreneurial filmmakers make money on DVDs—from foreign release, sales to airlines and, often, at screenings for political, religious or other groups, often with appearances by the writer, director and cast.

"The business is coming back smarter," said Marian Koltai-Levine, a veteran of Fine Line and Picturehouse, who is now a marketing and distribution adviser through Zipline Entertainment.

Excerpted from Michael Cieply, "A Second Act for Independent Film: Tight-Fisted Experiments Wring Profits from Small Movies," The New York Times, *April 25, 2010, page B-1.*

Eventually, Muybridge and Marey met. In 1882, Marey perfected a photographic gun camera that could take 12 photographs on one plate—the first motion picture camera.

Thomas Edison

Thomas Edison bought some of Muybridge's pictures in 1888 and showed them to his assistant, William K. L. Dickson. Edison then met with Marey in Europe, where Marey had invented a projector that showed pictures on a continuous strip of film, but the strip of film moved unevenly across the projector lens, so the pictures jumped.

William K. L. Dickson

Back in America, Dickson perforated the edges of the film so that, as the film moved through the camera, sprockets inside the camera grabbed the perforations and locked the film in place, minimizing the jumps.

Dickson looped the strip over a lamp and a magnifying lens in a box 2 feet wide and 4 feet tall. The box stood on the floor with a peephole in the top so people could look inside. Edison named this device the kinetoscope. On April 11, 1894, America's first kinetoscope parlor opened in New York City. For 25 cents, people could see 10 different 90-second black-and-white films, including *Trapeze*, *Horse Shoeing*, *Wrestlers* and *Roosters*.

Auguste and Louis Lumière

In France, the Lumière brothers, Auguste and Louis, developed an improved camera and a projector that could show film on a large screen. The first public Lumière showing was on December 28, 1895: 10 short subjects with such riveting titles as *Lunch Hour at the Lumière Factory*, which showed workers leaving the building, and *Arrival of a Train at a Station*. Admission was 1 franc and the Lumières collected 35 francs.

Edison Launches American Movies

Four months after the Lumière premiere in France, Edison organized the first American motion picture premiere with an improved camera developed by independent inventor Thomas Armat. Edison dubbed the new machine the Vitascope, and America's first public showing of the motion picture was on April 23, 1896, at Koster and Bial's theater in New York. Edison sat in a box seat, and Armat ran the projector from the balcony.

At first, movies were a sideshow. Penny-arcade owners showed movies behind a black screen at the rear of the arcade for an extra nickel. But soon the movies were more popular than the rest of the attractions, and the arcades were renamed *nickel*odeons. In 1900, there were more than 600 nickelodeons in New York City, with more than 300,000 daily admissions. Each show lasted about 20 minutes. The programs ran from noon until late evening, and many theaters blared music outside to bring in business.

By 1907, Edison had contracted with most of the nation's movie producers, as well as the Lumière brothers and the innovative French producer Georges Méliès, to provide movies for the theaters. Licensed Edison theaters used licensed Edison projectors and rented Edison's licensed movies, many of which Edison produced at his own studio. The important exception to Edison's licensing plan was his rival, the American Mutoscope and Biograph Company, commonly called Biograph.

Biograph manufactured a better motion picture camera than Edison's, and Edison was losing business. In 1908, Biograph signed an agreement with Edison, forming the Motion Picture Patents Company (MPPC).

Filmmakers Turn Novelty into Art

All the early films were black-and-white silent movies. Sound was not introduced to the movies until the 1920s, and color experiments did not begin until the 1930s. Two innovative filmmakers are credited with turning the novelty of movies into art: Georges Méliès and Edwin S. Porter.

Georges Méliès

French filmmaker Georges Méliès added fantasy to the movies. Before Méliès, moviemakers photographed theatrical scenes or events from everyday life. But Méliès, who had been a magician and a caricaturist before he became a filmmaker, used camera tricks to make people disappear and reappear and to make characters grow and then shrink.

His 1902 film, *A Trip to the Moon*, was the first outer-space movie adventure, complete with fantasy creatures. When his films, which became known as *trick films*, were shown in the United States, American moviemakers stole his ideas.

Edwin S. Porter

Edison hired projectionist/electrician Edwin S. Porter in 1899, and in the next decade Porter became America's most important filmmaker. Until Porter, most American films were trick films or short documentary-style movies that showed newsworthy events (although some filmmakers used titillating subjects in movies such as *Pajama Girl* and *Corset Girl* to cater to men, who were the movies' biggest fans). In 1903, Porter produced *The Great Train Robbery*, an action movie with bandits attacking a speeding train.

Bettmann/CORBIS

Georges Méliès created fanciful creatures for his 1902 film, *A Trip to the Moon*, introducing fantasy to motion pictures. In a scene from the movie, an explorer searches the moon landscape from the top of his shell rocket capsule.

Instead of using a single location like most other moviemakers, Porter shot 12 different scenes. He also introduced the use of dissolves between shots, instead of abrupt splices. Porter's film techniques—action and changing locations—foreshadowed the classic storytelling tradition of American movies.

Studio System and Independent Moviemakers Flourish

None of the players in the early movies received screen credit, but then fans began to write letters addressed to "The Biograph Girl," who was Biograph star Florence Lawrence. In 1909, Carl Laemmle formed an independent production company, stole Lawrence from Biograph and gave her screen credit. She became America's first movie star.

Biograph was the first company to make movies using the studio system. The ***studio system*** meant that a studio hired a stable of stars and production people who were paid a regular salary. These people signed contracts with that studio and could not work for any other studio without their employer's permission.

In 1910, Laemmle lured Mary Pickford away from Biograph by doubling her salary. He discovered, says film scholar Robert Sklar, "that stars sold pictures as nothing else could. As long as theaters changed their programs daily—and the practice persisted in neighborhood theaters and small towns until the early 1920s—building up audience recognition of star names was almost the only effective form of audience publicity." (Mary Pickford became one of the most influential women in early Hollywood, and helped finance the independent studio United Artists. See page 142.)

The ***star system***, which promoted popular movie personalities to lure audiences, was nurtured by the independents. This helped broaden the movies' appeal beyond their original working class audience. Movie houses began to open in the suburbs. In 1914, President Woodrow Wilson and his family watched a popular movie at the White House. From 1908 to 1914, movie attendance doubled.

In 1915, the first real titan of the silent movies, director D. W. Griffith, introduced the concept of spectacular entertainment. Most early movies were two reels long, 25 minutes. Griffith expanded his movies to four reels and longer, pioneering the feature-length film. In his best-known epic, *The Birth of a Nation* (1915), the Southern-born Griffith presented a dramatic view of the Civil War and Reconstruction, portraying racial stereotypes and touching on the subject of sexual intermingling of the races. The movie's cost—about $110,000—was five times more than that of any American film until that time.

In 1916, brothers Noble and George Johnson launched Lincoln Motion Picture Company, the first company to produce serious narrative movies for African American audiences, called "race films," paving the way for African American film stars Paul Robeson and Josephine Baker.

Moviemakers like the Johnson brothers and Oscar Micheaux proved that movies produced for specialized audiences could succeed. From 1910 to 1950, filmmakers produced more than 500 movies directed at African American audiences. (See **Media/Impact: Culture**, "Lighting Up a Black Screen: Early 'Race Films' Pioneered the Art of Breaking Stereotypes," p. 141.)

With *The Birth of a Nation* and his subsequent epics, Griffith showed the potential that movies had as a mass medium for gathering large audiences. He also proved that

Studio System An early method of hiring a stable of salaried stars and production people under exclusive contracts to a specific studio.

Star System Promoting popular movie personalities to lure audiences.

Media/Impact
CULTURE

Lighting Up a Black Screen: Early "Race Films" Pioneered the Art of Breaking Stereotypes

By Teresa Moore

The halcyon age for African Americans on the big screen was the period between 1910 and 1950 when blacks—and some whites—produced more than 500 "race movies," showcasing all-black casts in a variety of genres, including Westerns, mysteries, romances and melodramas. . . .

In the naturally sepia-toned world of race movies, African Americans could—and did—do just about anything.

Lena Horne shone as the *Bronze Venus*. Crooner Herb Jeffries was the *Bronze Buckaroo*. There were black millionaires and black detectives, black sweethearts and socialites. Black heroines who swooned—tender, wilting ladies who never swept a broom or donned a do-rag. Black heroes who could be gentle and genteel, tough and smart. Black villains of both genders, out to separate black damsels and grandees from their virtue or fortune.

Race movies were so called because they were made for black Southern audiences barred from white-owned theaters. The films were shown either in the black-owned movie palaces of the urban North and Midwest or in "midnight rambles"—special midnight-to-2 a.m. screenings in rented halls or segregated theaters of the South.

Under segregation, the moviemakers created an onscreen world that not only reflected the accomplishments of the rising black middle class but also transformed reality into a realm where race was no impediment to love, power or success. . . .

The leading directors and producers—Oscar Micheaux and the brother team of Noble and George Johnson—wanted to uplift African Americans. Besides presenting black images more appealing to black audiences, they also offered black perspectives on racial injustice.

Science, Industry & Business Library, The New York Public Library, Astor, Lenox and Tilden Foundations

Oscar Micheaux (center) was a pioneering African American filmmaker who produced "race movies," showing all-African American casts in a variety of roles. Micheaux's *Within Our Gates* was designed to counter the racism in D. W. Griffith's epic *The Birth of a Nation*.

"In some ways these filmmakers were more free because they were making the movies for themselves," said Michael Thompson, a professor of African American history at Stanford. In *Within Our Gates*, Micheaux's filmic response to D. W. Griffith's controversial, anti-black epic *The Birth of a Nation*, a white man tries to rape a young black woman—stopping only when he recognizes her as his illegitimate daughter. . . .

According to *Midnight Ramble*, Bestor Cram and Pearl Bowser's 1994 documentary on the black film industry, that industry developed alongside—and initially in reaction against—the white film industry. Virtually shut out of Hollywood, where a handful of black actors were usually cast as Indians and in various "ethnic" or "exotic" roles while whites in blackface cavorted onscreen, African Americans formed their own production companies, making hundreds of features and shorts.

Press Agency/Moviepix/Getty Images

PETER MORGAN/Reuters/Corbis

(Left) Mary Pickford, D. W. Griffith, Charlie Chaplin and Douglas Fairbanks founded United Artists in 1919. (Right) In 1994, David Geffen, Jeffrey Katzenberg and Steven Spielberg launched DreamWorks SKG, the first major independent movie studio created in the United States since United Artists. In 2006, the media conglomerate Viacom bought DreamWorks, leaving the United States without a major independent studio.

people would pay more than a nickel or a dime to see a motion picture. The Johnson brothers and Oscar Micheaux demonstrated that films also could succeed with specialized audiences. Movies clearly had arrived as a popular, viable mass medium, moving from the crowded nickelodeon to respectability.

Movies Become Big Business

The movie business was changing quickly. Five important events in the 1920s transformed the movie industry:

1. The move to California
2. The adoption of block booking
3. The formation of United Artists
4. The industry's efforts at self-regulation
5. The introduction of sound

Block Booking The practice of requiring theaters to take a package of movies instead of showing the movies individually.

Studios Move to Hollywood

During the first decade of the 20th century, the major movie companies were based in New York, the theater capital. Film companies sometimes traveled to Florida or Cuba to chase the sunshine because it was easier to build sets outdoors to take advantage of the light, but soon they found a new home in California.

In 1903, Harry Chandler, who owned the *Los Angeles Times*, also owned a lot of Los Angeles real estate. He and his friends courted the movie business, offering cheap land, moderate weather and inexpensive labor. Soon the moviemakers moved to Hollywood.

Distributors Insist on Block Booking

People who owned theater chains soon decided to make movies, and moviemakers discovered they could make more money if they owned theaters, so production companies built theaters to exhibit their own pictures. The connection between production, distribution and exhibition grew, led by Paramount's Adolph Zukor, who devised a system called ***block booking***.

Block booking meant a company, such as Paramount, would sign up one of its licensed theaters for as many as 104 pictures at a time. The movie package contained a few "name" pictures with stars, but the majority of the movies in the block were lightweight features with no stars. Because movie bills changed twice a week, the exhibitors were desperate for something to put on the screen. Often, without knowing which movies they were getting in the block, exhibitors accepted the package and paid the distributor's price.

United Artists Champions the Independents

In 1919, the nation's five biggest movie names—cowboy star William S. Hart, Mary Pickford, Charlie Chaplin, Douglas Fairbanks and D. W. Griffith—rebelled against the strict studio system of distribution and formed their own studio. Eventually Hart withdrew from the agreement, but the remaining partners formed a company called United Artists (UA). They eliminated block booking and became a distributor for independently produced pictures, including their own.

In its first six years, UA delivered many movies that today still are considered classics, including *The Mark of Zorro*, *The Three Musketeers*, *Robin Hood* and *The Gold Rush*. These movies succeeded even though UA worked outside the traditional studio system, proving that it was possible to distribute films to audiences without using a major studio.

Victoria Roberts/Cartoonbank

I've been in three documentaries, but I've never been nominated."

Moviemakers Use Self-Regulation to Respond to Scandals

In the 1920s, the movie industry faced two new crises: scandals involving movie stars and criticism that movie content was growing too provocative. As a result, the moviemakers decided to regulate themselves.

The star scandals began when comedian Roscoe "Fatty" Arbuckle hosted a marathon party in San Francisco over Labor Day weekend in 1921. As the party was ending, model Virginia Rappe was rushed to the hospital with stomach pains. She died at the hospital, and Arbuckle was charged with murder. Eventually the cause of death was listed as peritonitis from a ruptured bladder, and the murder charge was reduced to manslaughter. After three trials, two of which resulted in hung juries, Arbuckle was acquitted.

Then director William Desmond Taylor was found murdered in his home. Mabel Normand, a friend of Arbuckle's, was identified as the last person who had seen Taylor alive. Normand eventually was cleared, but then it was revealed that "Taylor" was not the director's real name, and there were suggestions he was involved in the drug business. Hollywood's moguls and businesspeople were shocked. The Catholic Legion of Decency announced a movie boycott. Quick to protect themselves, Los Angeles business leaders met and decided that Hollywood should police itself.

Los Angeles Times owner Harry Chandler worked with movie leaders to bring in Will Hays, a former postmaster general and Republican Party chairman, to respond to these and other scandals in the movie business. Hays' job was to lead a moral refurbishing of the industry. In March 1922, Hays became the first president of the Motion Picture Producers and Distributors Association (MPPDA), at a salary of $100,000 a year. A month later, even though Arbuckle had been acquitted, Hays suspended all of Fatty Arbuckle's films, ruining Arbuckle's career.

Besides overseeing the stars' personal behavior, Hays decided that his office also should oversee movie content. The MPPDA, referred to as the Hays Office, wrote a code of conduct to govern the industry. In 1930, the MPPDA adopted a production code, which began with three general principles:

1. No picture shall be produced which will lower the moral standards of those who see it. Hence the sympathy of the audience shall never be thrown to the side of crime, wrongdoing, evil or sin.
2. Correct standards of life, subject only to the requirements of drama and entertainment, shall be presented.
3. Law, natural or human, shall not be ridiculed, nor shall sympathy be created for its violation.

The code then divided its rules into 12 categories of wrongdoing, including

- Murder: "The technique of murder must be presented in a way that will not inspire imitation."
- Sex: "Excessive and lustful kissing, lustful embraces, suggestive postures and gestures are not to be shown."
- Obscenity: "Obscenity in word, gesture, reference, song, joke, or by suggestion (even when likely to be understood only by part of the audience) is forbidden."
- Costumes: "Dancing costumes intended to permit undue exposure or indecent movements in the dance are forbidden."

An acceptable movie displayed a seal of approval in the titles at the beginning of the picture. Producers balked at the interference, but most of them, afraid of censorship from outside the industry, complied with the monitoring.

Although standards have relaxed, the practice of self-regulation of content still operates in the motion picture industry today in the form of the movies ratings system.

New Technology Brings the Talkies

By the mid-1920s, silent movies were an established part of American entertainment, but technology soon pushed the industry into an even more vibrant era—the era of the talkies. MPPDA President Will Hays was the first person to appear on screen in the public premiere of talking pictures on August 6, 1926, in New York City. Warner Bros. and Western Electric had developed the movie sound experiment, which consisted of seven short subjects, called *The Vitaphone Preludes*.

The Warner brothers—Sam, Harry, Jack and Albert—were ambitious, upstart businessmen who beat their competitors to sound movies. On October 6, 1927, *The Jazz Singer*, starring Al Jolson, opened at the Warners' Theater in New York and was the first feature-length motion picture with sound. The movie was not an all-talkie but instead contained two sections with synchronized sound.

The success of *The Jazz Singer* convinced Warners' competitors not to wait any longer to adopt sound. By July 1, 1930, 22 percent of theaters still showed silent films. By 1933, fewer than 1 percent of the movies shown in theaters were silents.

Big Five Studios Dominate

In the 1930s, the Big Five—Warner Bros., Metro-Goldwyn-Mayer, Paramount, RKO and Twentieth Century Fox—dominated the movie business. They collected more than two-thirds of the nation's box office receipts. United Artists remained solely a distribution company for independent producers.

The Big Five all were vertically integrated: They produced movies, distributed them worldwide and owned theater chains, which guaranteed their pictures a showing. The studios maintained stables of stars, directors, producers, writers and technical staff. Film scholar Tino Balio calls the studios at this point in their history a "mature oligopoly"—a group of companies with so much control over an industry that any change in one of the companies directly affected the future of the industry.

In the 1930s, Walt Disney was the only major successful Hollywood newcomer. He had released *Steamboat Willie* as "the first animated sound cartoon" in 1928. Disney was 26 years old, and he had sold his car to finance the cartoon's soundtrack. After some more short-animated-feature successes, Disney announced in 1934 that his studio would produce its first feature-length animated film, *Snow White and the Seven Dwarfs*. The film eventually cost Disney $2.25 million, more than MGM usually spent on a good musical. *Snow White* premiered December 21, 1937, at the Cathay Circle Theater in Hollywood and became an instant hit.

Box office receipts sagged in the 1930s as the Depression settled into every aspect of America's economy. Facing bankruptcy, several theaters tried to buoy their profits by adding bingo games and cut-rate admissions. The one innovation that survived the 1930s was the double feature: two movies for the price of one.

Labor Unions Organize Movie Workers

The Depression introduced one more factor into motion picture budgets: labor unions. Before the 1930s, most aspects of the movie business were not governed by union agreements. But in 1937, the National Labor Relations Board held an election that designated the Screen Actors Guild to bargain for wages, working conditions and overtime.

The Screen Writers Guild was certified in 1938 and the Screen Directors Guild soon afterward. Unionization limited the studios' power over the people who worked for them, and by the late 1930s all the major studios had signed union agreements. Union agreements also introduced professionalism into the movie business. Then the Depression ended, and the studios once again prospered.

Movies Glitter During the Golden Age

With glamorous stars and exciting screenplays, supported by an eager pool of gifted directors, producers and technical talent, plus an insatiable audience, the movie industry reached its apex in the late 1930s and early 1940s. The most successful studio in Hollywood was MGM, which attracted the best writers, directors and actors. MGM capitalized on its star lineup with movies such as *The Great Ziegfeld*, *The Wizard of Oz* and *Gone with the Wind*.

Not only did *Gone with the Wind*'s phenomenal success demonstrate the epic character that movies could provide, but the movie also was a technological breakthrough, with its magnificent use of color. The movie business was so profitable that even MGM's dominance didn't scare away the competition. Many other studios, such as RKO, created enduring stars, such as Fred Astaire and Ginger Rogers, in films with light plots but stunning production numbers.

Congress and the Courts Change Hollywood

Before television arrived throughout the country in 1948, two other events of the late 1940s helped reverse the prosperous movie bonanza that began in mid-1930:

1. The hearings of the House Un-American Activities Committee (HUAC)
2. The 1948 antitrust decision of the U.S. Supreme Court in *United States v. Paramount Pictures, Inc., et al.*

The House Un-American Activities Committee

In October 1947, America was entering the Cold War. This was an era in which many public officials, government employees and private citizens seemed preoccupied with the threat of Communism and people identified as "subversives." The House of Representatives Committee on Un-American Activities, chaired by J. Parnell Thomas, summoned 10 "unfriendly" witnesses from Hollywood to testify about their Communist connections. (Unfriendly witnesses were people whom the committee classified as having participated at some time in the past in "un-American activities." This usually meant that the witness had been a member of a left-wing organization in the decade before World War II.) These eight screenwriters and two directors came to be known as the Hollywood Ten.

The Ten's strategy was to appear before the committee as a group and to avoid answering the direct question "Are you now or have you ever been a member of the Communist Party?" Instead, the Ten tried to make statements that questioned the committee's authority to challenge their political beliefs. In a rancorous series of hearings, the committee rejected the Ten's testimony; the witnesses found themselves facing trial for contempt. All of them were sentenced to jail and some were fined. By the end of November 1947, all the Hollywood Ten had lost their jobs. Many more movie people would follow.

In an article for the *Hollywood Review*, Hollywood Ten member Adrian Scott reported that 214 movie employees eventually were ***blacklisted***, which means that many studio owners refused to hire people who were suspected of taking part in subversive activities. The movie people who were not hired because of their political beliefs included 106 writers, 36 actors and 11 directors. This effectively gutted Hollywood of some of its best talent.

United States v. Paramount Pictures, Inc.

The U.S. Justice Department began an antitrust suit against the studios in 1938. In 1940, the studios came to an agreement with the government, while admitting no guilt. They agreed to

1. Limit block booking to five films.
2. Stop ***blind booking*** (the practice of renting films to exhibitors without letting them see the films first).

Al Freni/Time & Life Pictures/Getty Images

The late 1930s and early 1940s have been called the Golden Age of Movies. Fred Astaire and Ginger Rogers never won Oscars for the 10 dancing movies they made together, such as the 1936 RKO Studio film *Follow the Fleet*, but they enjoyed enormous box office success.

Blacklisting Studio owners' refusal to hire someone who was suspected of taking part in subversive activities.

Blind Booking The practice of renting films to exhibitors without letting them see the films first.

Bettmann/CORBIS

The Hollywood Ten, targeted in 1947 by the House Un-American Activities Committee, eventually went to jail for refusing to answer questions before the committee about their political beliefs. In October 1947, a group of Hollywood stars, representing 500 of their colleagues, traveled to Washington, D. C., to protest the way the investigation was being conducted. Front row, left to right: Geraldine Brooks, June Havoc, Marsha Hunt, Lauren Bacall, Richard Conte, Evelyn Keyes. Back row, left to right: Paul Henreid, Humphrey Bogart (group spokesman), Gene Kelly and Danny Kaye.

3. Stop requiring theaters to rent short films as a condition of acquiring features.

4. Stop buying theaters.

After this agreement, the Justice Department dropped its suit with the stipulation that the department could reinstitute the suit again at any time.

By 1944, the government still was unhappy with studio control over the theaters, so it reactivated the suit. In 1948, *United States v. Paramount Pictures, Inc., et al.* reached the Supreme Court. Associate Justice William O. Douglas argued that although the five major studios—Paramount, Warner Bros., MGM-Loew's, RKO and Twentieth Century Fox—owned only 17 percent of all theaters in the United States, these studios held a *monopoly* over first-run exhibition in the large cities. As a result of the Supreme Court decision, by 1954 the five studios had given up ownership or control of all their theaters. Production and exhibition were now split; vertical integration was crumbling.

When the movie companies abandoned the exhibition business, banks grew reluctant to finance film projects because the companies could not guarantee an audience—on paper. Soon the studios decided to leave the production business to the independents and became primarily distributors of other peoples' pictures. The result was the end of the studio system.

Movies Lose Their Audience to Television

In the 1950 Paramount movie *Sunset Boulevard*, aging silent screen star Norma Desmond (played by Gloria Swanson) romances an ambitious young screenwriter (played by William Holden) by promising him Hollywood connections.

> *"You're Norma Desmond. You used to be in silent pictures. You used to be big," says the screenwriter.*
> *"I am* big*," says Desmond. "It's the pictures that got small."*

Desmond could have been talking about the movie business itself, which got much smaller after 1948, when television began to offer home-delivered entertainment across the nation. The House hearings and the consent decrees in the Paramount case telegraphed change in the movie business, but television truly transformed Hollywood forever. In the 1950s, the number of television sets people owned grew by 400 percent, while the number of people who went to the movies fell by 45 percent.

Theaters tried to make up for the loss by raising their admission prices, but more than 4,000 theaters closed between 1946 and 1956. Attendance has leveled off or risen briefly a few times since the 1950s, but the trend of declining movie attendance continues today. The movie industry has tried several methods to counteract this downward trend.

Wide Screen and 3-D Movies

Stunned by television's popularity, the movie business tried technological gimmicks in the 1950s to lure its audience back. First came 3-D movies, using special effects to create the illusion of three-dimensional action. Rocks, for example, seemed to fly off the screen and into the audience. To see the

3-D movies, people wore special plastic glasses. The novelty was fun, but the 3-D movie plots were weak, and most people didn't come back to see a second 3-D movie.

Next came Cinerama, CinemaScope, VistaVision and Panavision—wide-screen color movies with stereophonic sound. All these techniques tried to give the audience a "you are there" feeling—something they couldn't get from television.

John Kobal Foundation/Getty Images

In the 1950s, the movie business used technological gimmicks, such as very primitive 3-D, to try to compete with television. In 1954, Universal produced *Creature from the Black Lagoon,* a 3-D feature about an underwater monster with "centuries of passion pent up in his savage heart."

Changes in Censorship

On May 26, 1952, the Supreme Court announced in *Burstyn v. Wilson* that motion pictures were "a significant medium for the communication of ideas," designed "to entertain as well as to inform." The effect of this decision was to protect movies under the First Amendment, which meant fewer legal restrictions on what a movie could show.

In 1953, Otto Preminger challenged the movies' self-regulating agency, the Production Code Administration (PCA). United Artists agreed to release Preminger's movie *The Moon Is Blue,* even though the PCA denied the movie a certificate of approval because it contained such risqué words as *virgin* and *mistress.* Then, in 1956, United Artists released Preminger's *Man with the Golden Arm,* a film about drug addiction, and the PCA restrictions were forever broken.

Buoyed by the *Burstyn* decision and the United Artists test, moviemakers tried sex and violence to lure audiences away from television. In the 1950s, Marilyn Monroe and Jayne Mansfield offered generously proportioned examples of the new trend. Foreign films also became popular because some of them offered explicit dialogue and love scenes.

Spectaculars

One by one, the studio moguls retired, and they were replaced by a new generation of moviemakers. This second generation "inherited a situation where fewer and fewer pictures were being made, and fewer still made money," says film historian Robert Sklar, "but those that captured the box office earned enormous sums. It was as if the rules of baseball had been changed so that the only hit that mattered was a home run."

Spectaculars like *The Sound of Music* (1965) and *The Godfather* (1971) and its sequels rewarded the rush for big money. But then a few majestic flops taught the studios that nothing demolishes a studio's profits like one big movie bomb.

Movie Ratings

In 1966, Jack Valenti, former adviser to President Lyndon Johnson, became president of the Motion Picture Producers Association (MPPA) and renamed it the Motion Picture Association of America (MPAA). The MPAA protects the business interests of movie companies by lobbying Congress about issues that are important to the movie business, such as freedom from government censorship. One of Valenti's first acts was to respond to continuing public criticism about shocking movie content. (Valenti ran the MPAA until his retirement in 2004.)

The MPAA began a rating system modeled on Great Britain's: G for general audiences, M (later changed to PG)

Jason Squires/WireImage/Getty Images

Because of its broad appeal, *Star Wars* is the most enduring and successful movie project ever produced, with sequels and ancillary rights generating unprecedented income for the movies' creator, George Lucas. In 2009, *Star Wars: In Concert* went on tour throughout the U.S. and England. Here, at the tour's stop in Kansas City, Mo., John Williams conducts The Royal Philharmonic Orchestra performing the movies' music in front of a three-story screen showing *Star Wars* scenes.

for mature audiences, R for restricted (people under 17 admitted only with an adult), and X for no one under 18 admitted. The PG-13 rating—special parental guidance advised for children under 13—was added, and the X rating was changed to NC-17. Standards for the R rating have eased since the ratings system began, further blurring the effectiveness of the ratings system for the public.

Movies and Money Today

In today's system of moviemaking, each of the major studios (such as Disney, Viacom/Paramount and Sony Pictures Entertainment) usually makes fewer than 20 movies a year. The rest come from independent producers, with production, investment, distribution and exhibition each handled by different companies. Most of these independently produced movies are distributed by one of the large studios.

In an attempt to counteract the strong influence of the traditional movie studios, Steven Spielberg, Jeffrey Katzenberg and David Geffen launched a company called DreamWorks SKG in 1994. DreamWorks was the first major independent movie studio created in the United States since United Artists was formed in 1919 (see page 142). The company survived as an independent studio for 11 years, but in 2006 DreamWorks was sold to Viacom, leaving the United States without a major independent movie studio.

In 2004, the animation division of DreamWorks, DreamWorks Animation, had been spun off as a publicly traded company, with Katzenberg as CEO, and Viacom/Paramount kept the live-action portion of the studio. Geffen left the live-action studio in 2008, and in 2009, Spielberg, with two partners, bought back the live-action part of the original studio from Paramount. So today there is DreamWorks Animation, a publicly traded company, and DreamWorks Studios, which is owned by Spielberg and his partners.

Today's movies are created by one group (the writers and producers), funded by another group (the investors), sold by a third group (the distributors) and shown by a fourth group (the exhibitors). No other mass media industry is so fragmented.

Today, the dream merchants aim at a mature audience. Movies are targeted at people of all ages, but especially children and people over 30. Today's moviemakers try to appeal to an over-30 audience and to children (who typically bring their parents with them to the show), with films such as *Megamind* and *Toy Story 3*.

Losing Money: Ticket Sales Drop

In 1946, the movies' best year, American theaters collected more than 4 billion tickets. Today, as more people watch more movies on video and DVD, the number of theater admissions has dropped to about 1 billion. Exhibitors believe that if they raise their admission prices, they'll lose more patrons. This is why exhibitors charge so much for refreshments, which accounts for 10 to 20 percent of their income.

The movie studios claim they lose money on *most* of the pictures they underwrite. Producers claim that, by hiding behind complicated financing schemes, the studios are able to keep exorbitant profits on the movies they distribute, which raises the cost of making movies for producers.

Movie finance is an important part of the movie business today because movies, like other media industries, are part of publicly owned corporations where loyalty to stockholders comes first. Studios tend to choose safer projects and seek proven audience-pleasing ideas rather than take risks (see **Illustration 7.1**).

Media/Impact MONEY

Illustration 7.1

How Much Does It Cost to Make a Movie? The 10 Most Expensive Movies Ever Made

The average cost to make a movie today is $107 million, but an average is just that—many movies cost less, and a few movies cost a lot more. Even if a movie is a big box-office success, a movie is a financial success only when it brings in more money than it costs to make.

Source: [London] TimesOnline, Money Central, March 5, 2010.

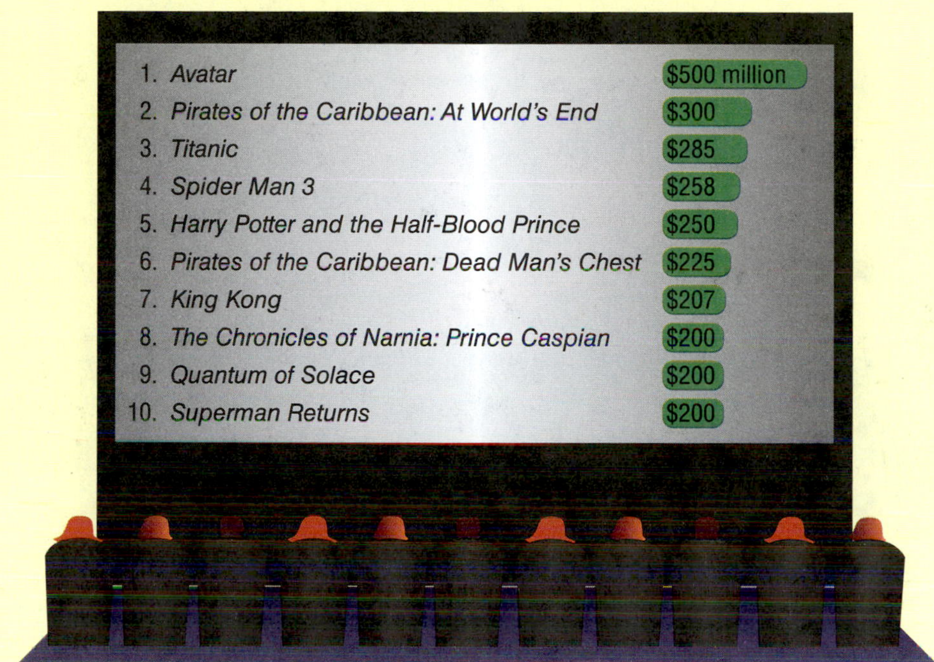

1. Avatar $500 million
2. Pirates of the Caribbean: At World's End $300
3. Titanic $285
4. Spider Man 3 $258
5. Harry Potter and the Half-Blood Prince $250
6. Pirates of the Caribbean: Dead Man's Chest $225
7. King Kong $207
8. The Chronicles of Narnia: Prince Caspian $200
9. Quantum of Solace $200
10. Superman Returns $200

One way the movie industry collects predictable income is to make movies for television. Half the movies produced every year are made for television and are underwritten by the TV networks. Video sales also bring reliable revenues. Another important factor in movie funding is the sale of ancillary rights.

Ancillary Rights Fund Projects

In 1950, a ticket to a movie cost about 50 cents. Today you can still see a movie for 50 cents if you rent a DVD for $3 or download a movie for $2.99 and invite five friends to join you at home to watch it. The explosion of video rentals and sales since the VCR was first marketed in 1976 has had a powerful effect on how the movie business operates today. The sale of movies on video and movie downloads are part of the ***ancillary rights*** market, which means marketing opportunities that are related to a movie (such as video games), in addition to direct income from the movie itself.

Today, the average cost to make a theatrical movie (as opposed to a made-for-television movie) is $107 million, and the studios claim that only two out of 10 theatrical movies make money. "Some pictures make a lot of money," says movie analyst David V. Picker, "and a lot of pictures make no money."

Before a theatrical movie starts shooting, the investors want some assurances that they'll make their money back. Moviemakers use the sale of ancillary rights to try to guarantee investors a return on their investment. Ancillary rights include the following:

- Subscription television rights
- Network television rights
- Syndication rights (sales to independent TV stations)
- Airline rights for in-flight movies
- Military rights (to show films on military bases)
- College rights (to show films on college campuses)
- Song rights for soundtrack albums

Ancillary Rights Marketing opportunities related to a movie, in addition to direct income from the movie itself.

Andrew Cooper/Walt Disney Studios Motion Pictures/Everett Collection

Because movies cost so much to produce, filmmakers generate income by selling ancillary rights to create media products that are related to each other, such as a video game based on a movie. In 2010, producer Jerry Bruckheimer reversed the process by making a movie, *Prince of Persia: The Sands of Time*, based on the 2003 version of the video game. The movie stars Jake Gyllenhaal, shown on location, shooting a scene for the movie.

- Book publishing rights (for original screenplays that can be rewritten and sold as books)
- DVD reproduction rights
- Product placement
- Video game rights
- Internet downloads

Movies are commercialized in the sense that they are tied to products, which are another way of advertising a movie. A movie that can be exploited as a package of ancillary rights, with commercial appeal, is much more attractive to investors than a movie with limited potential.

Often the only choice for a filmmaker who wants to make a film that doesn't have substantial ancillary-rights potential is to settle for a low budget. Once the film is made, the independent filmmaker must then find a way to distribute the movie. This severely limits the number of independent films that make it to the box office. (See **Media/Impact: Audience**, "A Second Act for Independent Film: Tight-Fisted Experiments Wring Profits from Small Movies," p. 138.)

Movies at Work

Today the center of the movie industry is movie production. Independent companies produce most of the movies that are distributed by the major studios and exhibited at your local theater under agreements with individual studios. Although these production companies work independently, and each company is organized differently, jobs in movie production fall mainly into the following categories:

1. Screenwriters
2. Producers
3. Directors
4. Actors
5. Technical production
6. Marketing and administration

Every movie begins with a story idea, and these ideas come from *screenwriters*. Screenwriters work independently, marketing their story ideas through agents, who promote their clients' scripts to the studios and to independent producers.

Typically, *producers* are the people who help gather the funding to create a movie project. Financing can come from banks or from individuals who want to invest in a specific movie. Sometimes producers or actors help finance the movies they make.

Once the funding for the story is in place, a *director* organizes all the tasks necessary to turn the script into a movie. The director works with the producer to manage the movie's budget. (See **Media/Impact: People**, "Kathryn Bigelow: How Oscar Found Ms. Right," p. 152.)

Obviously, *actors* are important to any movie project. Sometimes the producer and director approach particular stars for a project even before they seek funding, to attract interest from the investors and also to help assure the investors that the movie will have some box office appeal.

Technical production includes all the people who actually create the movie—camera operators, set designers, film editors, script supervisors and costumers, for example. Once the movie is finished, the *marketing* people seek publicity for the project. They also design a plan to advertise and promote the movie to the public.

As in any media industry, people who work in *administration* help keep all the records necessary to pay salaries and track the employees' expenses, as well as keep track of the paperwork involved in organizing any business.

Digital Technology Drives the Business

New digital technologies affect three aspects of today's movie business:

1. Production
2. Distribution
3. Exhibition

Production

Smaller, portable cameras mean a camera operator can move more easily through a crowd. New types of film mean that filmmakers can shoot more scenes at night and in dark places with less artificial lighting. Directors digitally record scenes as they shoot them and immediately play back the scene to be sure they have the shot they want. Computer technology offers exciting special effects possibilities. Filmmakers also are experimenting with the holograph, which uses lasers to make a computer-generated three-dimensional image from a flat picture.

The ability to digitize color also means the images in movies can be intensified, adjusted and totally transformed after the movie is shot, in a way that was impossible even 15 years ago.

Film studios today use the Internet to attract an audience for their movies. Movie Web sites include movie trailers, downloads, posters, screen savers, show times and other product promotion. But sometimes traditional publicity works best, such as this appearance by actor Antonio Banderas promoting his 2011 movie, *Puss in Boots*.

Distribution

Reproducing copies of films to send to theaters and guaranteeing their arrival is one of the costliest aspects of moviemaking. In the future, distribution companies plan to send their movies by satellite-to-satellite dishes on top of each theater and directly to consumers' homes. Live performances, such as a symphony concert or a major sports event, already are available by satellite at many local theaters, and eventually they will be sent directly to your home.

The theater industry is poised to replace the traditional film projector, invented more than 100 years ago, with digital projectors, which can show movies that are sent by satellite or recorded on optical discs. Digital movies are cheaper to distribute and can be shown on more screens or removed quickly from distribution, depending on audience demand.

"It strayed too far from the video game."

Media/Impact PEOPLE

Kathryn Bigelow: How Oscar Found Ms. Right

By Manohla Dargis

Kathryn Bigelow's two-fisted win at the [2010] Academy Awards for best director and best film for *The Hurt Locker* didn't just punch through the American movie industry's seemingly shatter-proof glass ceiling; it has also helped dismantle stereotypes about what types of films women can and should direct. It was historic, exhilarating, especially for women who make movies and women who watch movies, two groups that have been routinely ignored and underserved by an industry in which most films star men and are made for and by men. It's too early to know if this moment will be transformative—but damn, it feels so good. . . .

Ms. Bigelow was the first woman in Oscar's 82 years to win for best directing. Real discussions about sexual politics don't usually enter the equation during the interminable Oscar "season," which is why her nomination was almost as important as her double win. . . .

One of the lessons of Ms. Bigelow's success is that it was primarily achieved outside of the reach of the studios. She had help along the way, including from male mentors like James Cameron, her former husband, who helped produce *Strange Days*. But that movie did poorly at the box office, as did her next two features. . . . It wasn't until she went off to the desert to shoot *The Hurt Locker*, just as she had when she directed *Near Dark*, her 1987 cult vampire western, that she found a movie that hit on every level.

It was a long time coming, as Ms. Bigelow suggested when she appeared on *60 Minutes* on Feb. 28 [2010]. . . . She insisted that there was no difference between what she and a male director might do, even as she also conceded that "the journey for women, no matter what venue it is—politics, business, film—it's, it's a long journey. . . ."

Her cool has disturbed some, who have scrutinized Ms. Bigelow up and down, sometimes taking suspicious measure of her height and willowy frame, partly because these are the only personal parts of her that are accessible to nosy interviewers. . . . All that Ms. Bigelow freely gives of herself for public consumption is intelligent conversation and her work. Her insistence on keeping the focus on her movies is a quiet yet profound form of rebellion. She might be a female director, but by refusing to accept that gendered designation—or even engage with it—she is asserting her right to be simply a director.

Michael Caulfield/WireImage/Getty Images

In 2010, Kathryn Bigelow won two Academy Awards, for best director and best film for *The Hurt Locker*. It was the first time in the Academy Award's 82-year history that a woman won the Best Director award.

One of the strange truths of American cinema is that women thrived in the silent era—Mary Pickford was one of the first stars and helped start a studio, United Artists—but soon after the movies started to talk in the late 1920s, women's voices started to fade, at least behind the scenes. Hollywood might have been partly built on the hard work and beauty of its female stars, but it was the rare female director, Dorothy Arzner starting in the 1920s, Ida Lupino beginning in the 1940s, who managed to have her say behind the camera. It hasn't gotten better. According to Martha M. Lauzen, an academic who annually crunches numbers about women in American movies: "Women comprised 7 percent of all directors working on the top 250 films of 2009. Ninety-three percent of the films had no female directors."

From Manohla Dargis, "Kathryn Bigelow: How Oscar Found Ms. Right," The New York Times, *March 14, 2010.* © 2010 The New York Times. *All rights reserved. Used by permission and protected by the Copyright Laws of the United States. The printing, copying, redistribution, or retransmission of this content without express written permission is prohibited.*

The Internet also allows independent moviemakers to produce movies inexpensively and transfer them to the Internet for downloading.

As computer video technology grew faster and more accessible, established movie studios and independent moviemakers devised a whole new distribution system, based on digital movie downloads delivered directly to consumers. In 2008, Apple iTunes launched online movie rentals, which allows customers to download first-run movies to their Macs, PCs, iPods and iPhones for $2.99 each—designed to increase movie revenue by creating another distribution network.

In 2010, Netflix announced agreements with Paramount, Lionsgate and MGM for its "watch instantly" streaming service for new feature films. Subscription TV services, such as DirecTV and cable companies, also are stockpiling movies so they can set up a complete system of video-on-demand, available at home by subscription or pay-per-view.

Merrick Morton/© Columbia Pictures/Courtesy Everett Collection

Most movies today are independently produced and then distributed through a major studio. *The Social Network*, a story about Facebook founder Mark Zuckerberg, opened on October 4, 2010, distributed through Columbia Pictures. The film cost an estimated $50 million to produce, and two weeks after opening it had earned an estimated $62 million. Cast members (left to right): Joseph Mazzello, Jesse Eisenberg, Andrew Garfield, Patrick Mapel.

Exhibition

Theaters are turning to the picture-palace environment that enchanted moviegoers in the 1930s. "The movie theater will have to become an arena; a palace to experience the full grandeur and potential of the theatrical motion picture," says futurist and electronic technology consultant Martin Polon.

In 1994, some of the nation's theater chains began offering "motion simulation" in a few of their theaters. Specially controlled seats moved in conjunction with a "ridefilm" to give the feeling of space travel or other adventures. Many of the nation's theme parks, such as Dollywood, already offer ridefilms to their patrons. "We're looking to marry the moviegoing experience to different kinds of technological experiences, thereby enhancing the attractiveness of the whole complex," said United Artists chairman Stewart Blair. Movie chains also have introduced stadium seating so that every moviegoer has a clear, unimpeded view of the movie.

To draw people back into theaters, New Line Cinema and DreamWorks began developing a new digital version of 3-D technology similar to what theaters tried in the 1950s. The new process, called RealD, uses a single projector to merge two images—one for each eye—to give the movie its realistic effect. To exhibit 3-D movies, theaters must buy new digital projection systems, which cost $75,000 per screen, but they can charge more for a RealD ticket, sometimes twice as much as a regular admission.

By 2009, RealD was available in selected theaters. *Avatar*, released late in 2009, was the first big 3-D hit. Disney released 3-D versions of *Toy Story 3* and *Alice in Wonderland* in 2010, and DreamWorks Studios released *How to Train Your Dragon* and *Megamind*. The new technology did bring people out of their homes to see the movies and added more than $1 billion to 2010 industry income. Although the movie industry produced fewer movies in 2010 and DVD sales dropped, the higher ticket prices for 3-D features helped to maintain their profitability.

International Markets Bring Concentrated Power

Today's movie industry is undergoing two major changes. One recent trend in the movie business is global ownership and global marketing. The second trend is the merging of the movie industry with the television industry.

Global Influence

Overseas companies own two of the major studios (Sony owns Sony Pictures Entertainment and Rupert Murdoch's

MAX NASH/AFP/Getty Images

The overseas market for American movies, such as *Toy Story 3*, accounts for one-third of the movie industry's profits. In July 2010, the four main characters (Jessie, Woody, Buzz and Lots-O'-Huggin' Bear) promoted the film in London's Leicester Square.

News Corporation owns Twentieth Century Fox). Foreign ownership gives these companies easier access to overseas markets.

American motion pictures are one of America's strongest exports, and income from foreign sales accounts for more than one-third of the movie industry's profits. "If Hollywood has learned anything the past few years," says *Business Week*, "it's that the whole world is hungry for the latest it has to offer."

Concentrating Media Power

Today, people in the television business are buying pieces of the movie business, and people in the movie business want to align themselves with television companies. In 1993, the Federal Communications Commission voted to allow the TV networks to produce and syndicate their own programs. This opened the door for TV networks to someday enter the movie business.

The result today is consolidated companies that finance movies, make movies and show those movies in their own theaters, on their own television stations and on video. By controlling all aspects of the business, a company can have a better chance to collect a profit on the movies it makes.

Sound familiar? The studios held this type of controlling interest in their movies before the courts dismantled the studio system with the 1948 consent decrees (see "*United States v. Paramount Pictures, Inc., et al.*," p. 146). Today's major studios are trying to become again what they once were: a mature oligopoly in the business of dreams.

Review, Analyze, Investigate

REVIEWING CHAPTER 7

Movies Mirror the Culture

✓ Before the invention of TV, movies were the nation's primary form of entertainment.

✓ Like other industries, the movie business has had to adapt to changing technology.

Inventors Capture Motion on Film

✓ Eadweard Muybridge and Thomas Edison contributed the most to the creation of movies in America. Muybridge demonstrated how to photograph motion, and an Edison employee, William K. L. Dickson, developed a projector, the kinetoscope.

✓ Auguste and Louis Lumière developed an improved camera and a projector to show film on a large screen.

✓ Edison also organized the Motion Picture Patents Company to control movie distribution.

Filmmakers Turn Novelty into Art

✓ French filmmaker Georges Méliès envisioned movies as a medium of fantasy.

✓ Edwin S. Porter assembled scenes to tell a story.

Studio System and Independent Moviemakers Flourish

✓ Biograph became the first studio to make movies using what was called the studio system.

✓ The studio system put the studio's stars under exclusive contract, and the contract could not be broken without an employer's permission.

✓ The star system promoted popular movie personalities to lure audiences.

- ✓ D. W. Griffith mastered the full-length movie. Griffith's best-known movie is a controversial view of the Civil War, *The Birth of a Nation*.
- ✓ From 1910 to 1950, filmmakers like Noble and George Johnson and Oscar Micheaux produced movies specifically directed at African American audiences, called "race films."

Movies Become Big Business

- ✓ The movie studios move from New York to Hollywood, where the climate is more favorable.
- ✓ The practice of block booking, led by Adolph Zukor, obligated movie houses to accept several movies at once, usually without previewing them first.
- ✓ The formation of United Artists by Mary Pickford, Charlie Chaplin, Douglas Fairbanks and D. W. Griffith was a rebellion against the big studios.
- ✓ UA distributed films for independent filmmakers.
- ✓ In the 1920s, the movie industry faced two crises: scandals involving movie stars and criticism that movie content was growing too explicit.
- ✓ The movie industry responded to the scandals and criticism about content by forming the Motion Picture Producers and Distributors Association under the direction of Will Hays.
- ✓ In 1930, the MPPDA adopted a production code, which created rules that governed movie content.
- ✓ Although standards have relaxed, the practice of self-regulation of content continues today.
- ✓ The Jazz Singer, the first feature-length motion picture with sound, premiered in New York City on October 6, 1927.

Big Five Studios Dominate

- ✓ As the studio system developed, the five largest Hollywood studios were able to control production, distribution and exhibition.
- ✓ In the 1930s, Walt Disney premiered the first feature-length animated film, *Snow White and the Seven Dwarfs*.
- ✓ Box office receipts sagged during the Depression, so theaters introducued the double feature—two movies for the price of one.

Labor Unions Organize Movie Workers

- ✓ In the 1930s, labor unions challenged studio control and won some concessions.
- ✓ Union agreements limited the studios' power over their employees.

Movies Glitter During the Golden Age

- ✓ The movies' golden age was the 1930s and 1940s, supported by the studio system and an eager audience.
- ✓ The most successful Hollywood studio was MGM, which concentrated on blockbuster movies such as *The Wizard of Oz* and *Gone with the Wind*.

Congress and the Courts Change Hollywood

- ✓ Three factors caused Hollywood's crash in the 1950s: the House Un-American Activities Committee hearings, the U.S. Justice Department's antitrust action against the studios, and television.
- ✓ At least 214 movie employees eventually were blacklisted as a result of the hearings of the House Un-American Activities Committee (HUAC).
- ✓ In 1948, the U.S. Supreme Court decision in *United States v. Paramount Pictures* ended the studio system.

Movies Lose Their Audience to Television

- ✓ People abandoned the movies for television, and the trend of declining movie attendance continues today.
- ✓ Hollywood tried to lure audiences back to the movies in the 1950s with technological gimmicks, sultry starlets and spectaculars, but the rewards were temporary.
- ✓ Movie ratings were originally a response to criticism about immoral movie content, but the standards for these ratings have become blurred.

Movies and Money Today

- ✓ DreamWorks SKG, launched in 1994 by Steven Spielberg, Jeffrey Katzenberg and David Geffen, was the first major independent movie studio created in the United States since United Artists was formed in 1919. In 2006, DreamWorks was sold to Viacom, leaving the United States without a major independent movie studio.
- ✓ Today the number of moviegoers continues to decline, although DVD sales and rentals, as well as video game development, add to movie industry income.
- ✓ Most movies are funded in part by ancillary rights sales.
- ✓ The median cost to make a movie today is $107 million, and only two out of 10 theatrical movies make money.
- ✓ Most movies are sold as packages, with all their potential media outlets underwriting the movie before it goes into production. This makes independent filmmaking difficult.

Movies at Work

- ✓ Movie production is the heart of the movie industry today.

- ✓ Screenwriters begin the moviemaking process; other jobs include producer, director, actor, technical production, marketing and administration.

Digital Technology Drives the Business

- ✓ New digital technologies affect production, distribution, and exhibition of movies
- ✓ Independent moviemakers can use computers to create movies inexpensively and distribute them on the Internet.
- ✓ In the future, distribution companies plan to send movies by satellite to satellite dishes on top of each theater and directly to consumers' homes.
- ✓ In 2008, Apple made first-run movie downloads available on its iTunes Web site for $2.99 each.
- ✓ In 2010, Netflix announced agreements with major studios to offer streaming service for new feature films. Subscription TV services also are developing a system to offer video-on-demand, available at home by subscription or pay-per-view.
- ✓ New Line Cinema and DreamWorks developed a new digital version of 3-D technology called RealD, which added more than $1 billion to industry income in 2010.

International Markets Bring Concentrated Power

- ✓ Overseas sales of American movies account for more than one-third of movie industry income.
- ✓ In 1993, the FCC voted to allow the TV networks to make and syndicate their own programs. This means that, in the future, the movie industry and the television industries may align themselves more closely. Eventually one company could control all aspects of moviemaking.

KEY TERMS

These terms are defined in the margins throughout this chapter and appear in alphabetical order with definitions in the Glossary, which begins on page 383.

Ancillary Rights 149
Blacklisting 145
Blind Booking 145
Block Booking 142
Star System 140
Studio System 140

CRITICAL QUESTIONS

1. Which audience age category is most attractive to today's moviemakers? Why?
2. What were race movies? Discuss the ways in which these films changed the perspective of African Americans in the films and for their audiences.
3. What was the effect of the practice of block booking on the movie industry? How and why did the practice end?
4. Why do you believe the Hollywood Ten became a target of the House Un-American Activities Committee? Could the same thing happen today? Why? Why not? Explain.
5. Describe how today's digital technologies are changing moviemaking, distribution and exhibition.

WORKING THE WEB

This list includes both sites mentioned in the chapter and others to give you greater insight into the movie industry.

Academy of Motion Picture Arts and Sciences

http://www.oscars.org

This honorary association of over 6,500 motion picture professionals is the home of the Oscars. The organization's goals include advancing the arts and sciences of motion pictures, recognizing outstanding achievement and promoting technical research of methods and equipment. The Web site includes Academy publications, information on the Academy Film Archive and an Academy Awards database.

DEG Digital Entertainment Group

http://www.dvdinformation.com

DEG is a nonprofit trade consortium composed of electronics manufacturers, movie studios and music companies whose goal is to explore opportunities in other digital technologies and represent all aspects of the home entertainment industry. Members include Philips Consumer Electronics, Paramount Home Entertainment and Sony BMG Music Entertainment.

The Internet Movie Database (IMDB)

http://www.imdb.com

Owned by Amazon.com, IMDB says its mission is to provide "useful and up to date movie information freely available online across as many platforms as possible." What started as a hobby project by movie fans has grown into a database of over 15 million film and TV credits. Search capabilities include name, character, keyword and quote. The site also has movie and TV listings, trailers and interactive sections such as trivia, polls and message boards.

Lucasfilm

http://www.lucasfilm.com

This film and entertainment company founded by George Lucas in 1971 has produced such hits as *American Graffiti* and the *Star Wars* and *Indiana Jones* series. In addition to motion picture and television production, the company's businesses include Industrial Light & Magic (visual effects), Skywalker Sound and LucasArts (video games).

Motion Picture Association of America (MPAA) and Motion Picture Association (MPA)

http://www.mpaa.org

Advocates for the motion picture, home video and television industries, the MPAA and its international counterpart the MPA are responsible for the movie ratings and also work to protect copyrights and stem piracy of filmed works.

Netflix

http://www.netflix.com

The world's largest online movie rental source, Netflix provides subscribers access to more than 100,000 DVD titles and more than 10,000 instant downloads. DVDs are delivered free to subscriber households with a postage-paid return envelope, and there are no due dates or late fees.

Screenwriters Federation of America (SFA)

http://www.screenwritersfederation.org

Formerly the Screenwriters Guild of America, the SFA is an organization to promote the common interests of industry professionals. Its goals are to educate screenwriters about their craft and about the entertainment business, to create a network for screenwriters and to administer standards for marketing scripts. The Web site includes news excerpts and links to Indiwire.com, the independent film community's news, information and social networking site. Users can also search IMDb.com with one mouse click.

Sundance Institute

http://www.sundance.org

This nonprofit organization dedicates itself to discovering and developing independent moviemakers. Founder Robert Redford began hosting labs in 1981 where emerging filmmakers could work with leading writers and directors to develop their original projects. The Institute is now an internationally recognized independent artist resource and the host of the annual Sundance Film Festival.

United Artists

http://www.unitedartists.com

Formed in November 2006 under a partnership between Tom Cruise, Paula Wagner and MGM, United Artists Entertainment LLC plans to revive the historic UA brand initially founded by movie greats Douglas Fairbanks, Charlie Chaplin, Mary Pickford and D. W. Griffith. The "new" independent studio will allow artists to "pursue their creative visions outside of the traditional studio system."

Warner Bros.

http://www.warnerbros.com

This company founded by the four Warner brothers began as a silent-film distributor in 1903 and became a successful producer of "talkies" and animated cartoons. The company, now a division of Time Warner Inc., also produces television shows, animation, DVDs and interactive entertainment.

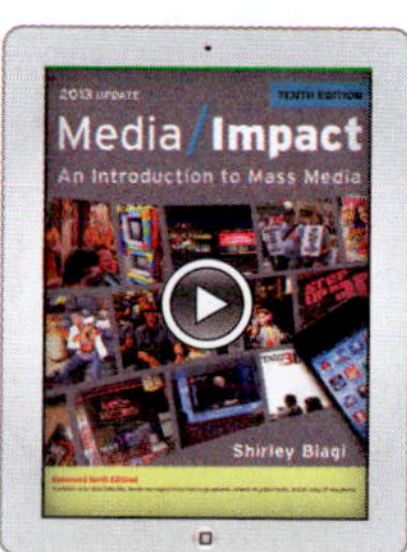

Impact/Action Videos are concise news features on topics covered in this chapter, created exclusively for **Media/Impact**. They are available for students and instructors at CengageBrain.com, and include screen access for classroom viewing and discussion questions.

> *"3-D is an effort by the industry to come up with something that will motivate consumers to trade up."*
>
> *—Van Baker, TV industry analyst, Gartner Research*

Television: Changing Channels

What's Ahead?

Television Transforms Daily Life

TV Delivers an Audience to Advertisers

Visual Radio Becomes *Television*

Television Outpaces Radio

Quiz Shows Bring Ethics Scandals

Ratings Target the Audience

Newton Minow Criticizes TV as a "Vast Wasteland"

Public Television Finds an Audience

Satellites Make Transatlantic TV and Live Broadcasts Possible

Television Changes National Politics

TV News Images Bring Global Events into View

Television at Work

Audiences Drive TV Programming

New Technology Expands TV's Focus

Television Offers a New Vision

Bloomberg/Getty Images

On Sept. 4, 2011, at the Consumer Electronics Fair in Berlin, Germany, LG Electronics launched a new 3-D TV called Pentouch, which allows users to draw on their TV screen with a stylus.

TimeFrame 1884 — Today

Television Becomes the Nation's Major Medium for News and Entertainment

1884 **In Germany, Paul Nipkow patents the Nipkow disk, which he calls an "electrical telescope." The Nipkow disk forms the basis for TV's development through the 1920s.**

SSPL/Getty Images

1907 The word *television* first appears in the June 1907 issue of *Scientific American*.

1939 NBC's David Sarnoff debuts television at the World's Fair in New York City. President Franklin D. Roosevelt, whose blurry image is broadcast at the fair, becomes the first U.S. president to appear on television.

1947 NBC and CBS begin broadcasting television news on the *Camel News Caravan* (NBC) and *Television News with Douglas Edwards* (CBS).

1951 **CBS launches *I Love Lucy*, a situation comedy, which would prove to be TV's most durable type of entertainment program.**

CBS Photo Archive/Getty Images

1962 *Telstar I* sends the first transatlantic satellite broadcast.

1963 Network television provides nonstop coverage of the assassination and funeral of President John F. Kennedy.

Public television begins broadcasting as National Educational Television, featuring programs like *Sesame Street*, which is still on the air today.

John Lamparski/WireImage/Getty Images

1973 The television networks present live broadcasts of the Watergate hearings.

1979 Ted Turner starts Cable News Network. CNN's global reach gives the U.S. audience instant access to news about international events.

1983 120 million people tune in for the final episode of *M*A*S*H*, the highest rated program ever.

1987 TV broadcasts the Iran-Contra hearings.

1993 More than 80 million people tune in for the final episode of *Cheers*.

2001 **Television news offers non-stop, commercial-free coverage of the terrorist attacks at the World Trade Center, the Pentagon and in rural Pennsylvania.**

James Devaney/WireImage/Getty Images

2003 TV again becomes a focus of nationwide attention during the live news coverage of the Iraq War.

2006 Congress mandates that TV broadcasters switch totally to digital high-definition signals by February 17, 2009.

2008 More than 70 million people watch President-elect Barack Obama's election night victory on television on November 4, a record audience for a presidential election night.

2009 The U.S. changes to a national high-definition television transmission standard (HDTV).

2010 **Television manufacturers introduce 3-D television.**

EVERETT KENNEDY BROWN/EPA/Landov

Today Television programming is delivered on more than 500 channels by over-the-air broadcast, cable, satellite and the Internet. HD is the standard.

Television Outpaces Radio

By 1945, 10 television stations were on the air in the United States. According to media historian Eric Barnouw, "By the late 1940s, television began its conquest of America. In 1949, the year began with radio drawing 81 percent of all broadcast audiences. By the year's end, television was grabbing 41 percent of the broadcast market. When audiences began experiencing the heady thrill of actually seeing as well as hearing events as they occurred, the superiority of television was established beyond doubt."

Black-and-white television replaced radio so quickly as the nation's major advertising medium that it would be easy to believe television erupted suddenly in a surprise move to kill radio. But remember that the two major corporate executives who developed television—Sarnoff and Paley—also held the country's largest interest in radio. They used their profits from radio to develop television, foreseeing that television eventually would expand their audience and their income.

News with Pictures

Broadcast news, pioneered by radio, adapted awkwardly at first to the new broadcast medium—television. According to David Brinkley, a broadcast news pioneer who began at NBC, "When television came along in about 1947–1948, the big time newsmen of that day—H. V. Kaltenborn, Lowell Thomas—did not want to do television. It was a lot of work, they weren't used to it, they were doing very well in radio, making lots of money. They didn't want to fool with it. So I was told to do it by the news manager. I was a young kid and, as I say, the older, more established people didn't want to do it. Somebody had to."

In 1947, CBS launched *Television News with Douglas Edwards* and NBC broadcast *Camel News Caravan* (sponsored by Camel cigarettes) with John Cameron Swayze (see **Chapter 12**). Eventually, David Brinkley joined Swayze for NBC's 15-minute national newscast. He recalled, "The first broadcasts were extremely primitive by today's standards. It was mainly just sitting at a desk and talking. We didn't have any pictures at first. Later we began to get a little simple news film, but it wasn't much.

"In the beginning, people would call after a program and say in tones of amazement that they had seen you. 'I'm out here in Bethesda, and the picture's wonderful,'" Brinkley said. "They weren't interested in anything you said. They were just interested in the fact that you had been on their screen in their house."

At first, network TV news reached only the East Coast because there was no web of national hookups to deliver television across the country. By 1948, AT&T's coaxial cable linked Philadelphia with New York and Washington, D.C. The 1948 political conventions were held in Philadelphia and broadcast to 13 eastern states. When the 1952 conventions were broadcast, AT&T's national coaxial hookups joined 108 stations across the country.

CBS had developed a strong group of radio reporters during World War II, and by 1950 many of them had moved to the new medium. CBS News also made a practice, more than the other networks, of using the same reporters for radio and television news. The major early news figure at CBS was Edward R. Murrow, who, along with David Brinkley at NBC, created the early standards for broadcast news. (See **Media/Impact: People**, "Edward R. Murrow (1908–1965) Sets the Standard for Broadcast News," p. 165.)

Public affairs programs like Murrow's *See It Now* continued to grow along with network news, and in 1956 NBC teamed David Brinkley with Chet Huntley to cover the political conventions. The chemistry worked, and after the convention, NBC put Huntley and Brinkley together to do the evening news, *The Huntley-Brinkley Report*. Brinkley often called himself "the other side of the hyphen."

Entertainment Programming

Early television entertainment also was the same as radio with pictures: It offered variety shows, situation comedies, drama, Westerns, detective stories, Hollywood movies, soap operas and quiz shows. The only type of show television offered that radio did not (besides movies, of course) was the talk show. (However, radio eventually created call-in programs, radio's version of the TV talk show.)

VARIETY SHOWS. The best radio stars jumped to the new medium. Three big variety show successes were Milton Berle's *Texaco Star Theater*, *The Admiral Broadway Revue* (later *Your Show of Shows*) with Imogene Coca and Sid Caesar, and Ed Sullivan's *Toast of the Town* (later *The Ed Sullivan Show*). These weekly shows featured comedy sketches and appearances by popular entertainers. *The Ed Sullivan Show*, for example, is where most Americans got their first glimpse of Elvis Presley and the Beatles. All of the shows were done live.

The time slot in which these programs were broadcast, 7 to 11 p.m., is known as ***prime time***. Prime time simply means that more people watch television during this period than any other, so advertising during this period costs more. Berle's 8 p.m. program on Tuesday nights often gathered 85 percent of the audience. *Texaco Star Theater* became so

Prime Time The TV time period from 7 to 11 p.m. when more people watch TV than at any other time.

"Television is the

pervasive American pastime," writes media observer Jeff Greenfield. "Cutting through geographic, ethnic, class and cultural diversity, it is the single binding thread of this country, the one experience that touches young and old, rich and poor, learned and illiterate. A country too big for homogeneity, filled by people from all over the globe, without any set of core values, America never had a central unifying bond. Now we do. Now it is possible to answer the question, 'What does America do?' We watch television."

Television is turned on in today's American household, on average, more than eight hours a day, according to the A. C. Nielsen Company, which monitors television usage for advertisers. (See **Illustration 8.1**.) Even though people in your household may not watch TV this much, the percentage of households in the United States that use television a lot counterbalances the smaller amount of time people at your house spend with their television sets.

Media/Impact
CULTURE

Illustration 8.1

How Much Time Each Day Do People Watch Television?

The time people spend watching TV has increased every year since 1950. These statistics reflect total viewing per household, which means the total combined time that all people in the average household have the TV turned on each day.

Source: nielsenwire, "Average TV Viewing for 2008–09 TV Season at All-Time High," http://blog.nielsen.com/nielsenwire/media_entertainment/average-tv-viewing-for-2008-09-tv-season-at-all-time-high/.

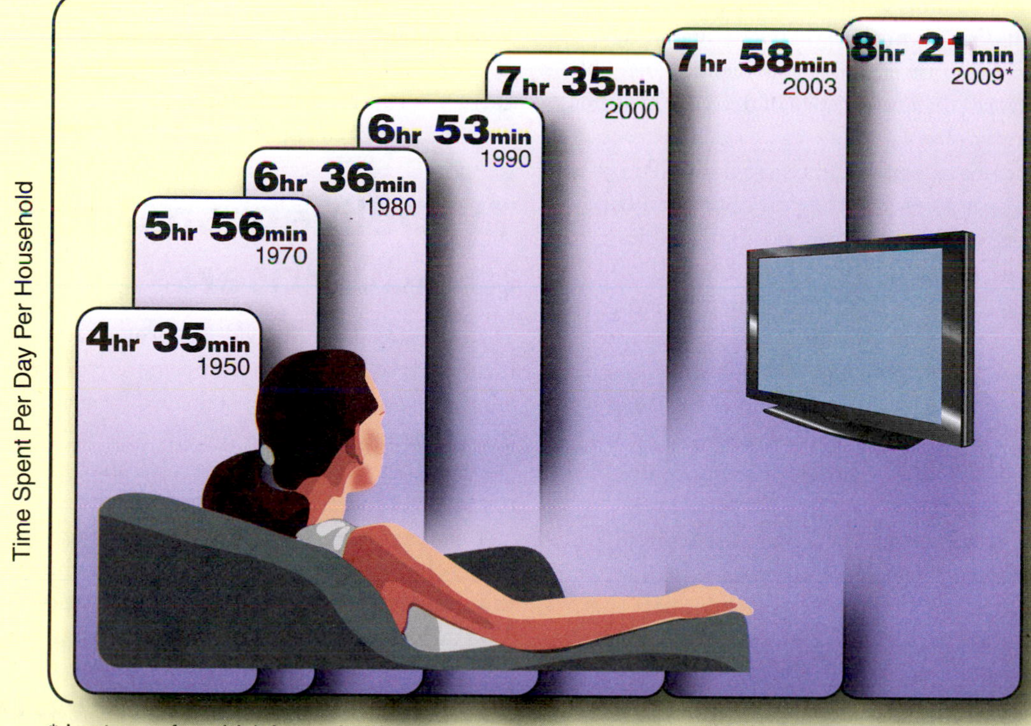

* Last year for which household viewing statistics are available.

Television Transforms Daily Life

It's not surprising that the effects of such a pervasive medium have attracted so much attention from parents, educators, social scientists, religious leaders, public officials and anyone else who wants to understand society's habits and values. TV has been blamed for everything from declines in literacy to rises in violent crime to the trivialization of national politics. Every once in a while it is praised, too, for giving viewers instant access to world events and uniting audiences in times of national crisis.

An industry with this much presence in American life is bound to affect the way we live. Someone who is watching television is not doing other things: playing basketball, visiting a museum, or looking through a telescope at the planets, for instance. Television can, however, bring you to a museum you might never visit or to a basketball game you cannot attend or to the surface of a planet you can only see through a telescope.

Matthew Diffee/Cartoonbank

"The post-season coverage ended yesterday. This is the pre-season coverage."

Television technology, by adding pictures to the sounds of radio, truly transformed Americans' living and learning patterns. The word *television*, which once meant programs delivered by antennas through over-the-air signals, now means a *television screen*, where several different types of delivery systems bring viewers a diversity of programs.

The programs Americans watch today are delivered by antennas, cables and satellites, but they all appear on the same television screen, and as a viewer, you can't tell how the program arrived at your television set and probably don't care. What you do know is that television gives you access to all types of programs—drama, comedy, sports, news, game shows and talk shows. You can see all types of people—murderers, public officials, foreign leaders, reporters, soldiers, entertainers, athletes, detectives and doctors. The television screen is truly, as scholar Erik Barnouw observed, a "tube of plenty."

About 1,600 television stations operate in the United States. Three out of four of these are commercial stations, and the others are noncommercial stations. About half the commercial stations are affiliated with a network.

According to TV commentator Jeff Greenfield, "The most common misconception most people have about television concerns its product. To the viewer, the product is the programming. To the television executive, the product is the audience. Strictly speaking, television networks and stations do not make any money by producing a program that audiences want to watch. The money comes from selling advertisers the right to broadcast a message to that audience. The programs exist to capture the biggest possible audiences."

TV Delivers an Audience to Advertisers

To understand why we get the programming we do, it is important to remember that *commercial television exists primarily as an advertising medium*. Programming surrounds the advertising, but it is the advertising that is being delivered to the audience. Commercial television, from its inception, was created to deliver audiences to advertisers.

Because television can deliver a larger audience faster than other mass media, television can charge higher rates than any other medium for its advertising—which makes TV stations rich investments. During a widely watched TV program like the 2012 Super Bowl (with an estimated audience of half the U.S. population and an even larger audience worldwide), a 30-second ad can cost as much as $3.5 million. Today, even the smallest independent television station is a multimillion-dollar operation. However, the television era began much more humbly, and with very little excitement, around the turn of the 20th century.

Visual Radio Becomes Television

The word *television* first appeared in the June 1907 issue of *Scientific American*. Before then, experiments in image transmission had been called "visual wireless," "visual radio" and "electric vision." Alexander Graham Bell's telephone and Samuel F. B. Morse's telegraph contributed to the idea of sending electrical impulses over long distances.

The first major technological discovery to suggest that pictures also could travel was the *Nipkow disk*. Twenty-four-year-old *Paul Nipkow* patented the Nipkow disk, which he called the "electrical telescope," in Germany in 1884. This disk, which formed the basis for television's development through the 1920s, was about the size of a phonograph record, perforated with a spiral of tiny holes.

Also crucial in television's (and radio's) development were *Guglielmo Marconi* and *Lee de Forest*. Marconi eliminated sound's dependence on wires and put sound on airwaves. De Forest contributed the Audion tube, which amplified radio waves so that people could hear the sound clearly.

In 1927, Secretary of Commerce Herbert Hoover appeared on a 2-inch screen by wire in an experimental AT&T broadcast. On September 11, 1928, General Electric broadcast the first dramatic production, "The Queen's Messenger"—the sound came over station WGY, in Schenectady, N.Y., and the picture came from experimental television station W2XAD. All the pictures were close-ups, and their quality could best be described as primitive.

Two researchers, one working for a company and one working alone, brought television into the electronic age. Then the same man who was responsible for radio's popularity, RCA's David Sarnoff, became television's biggest promoter.

Vladimir Zworykin was working for Westinghouse when he developed an all-electronic system to transform a visual image into an electronic signal that traveled through the air. When the signal reached the television receiver, the signal was transformed again into a visual image for the viewer.

Philo T. Farnsworth, working alone in California, developed the cathode ray tube (which he called a dissector tube). Farnsworth's cathode ray tube used an electronic scanner to reproduce the electronic image much more clearly than Nipkow's earlier mechanical scanning device. In 1930, 24-year-old Farnsworth patented his electronic scanner.

Archive Photos/Getty Images

In 1939, NBC's David Sarnoff introduced TV with a broadcast at RCA's Hall of Television at the New York World's Fair. RCA displayed its TV sets inside the building, priced from $199.50 to $600.

NBC television's commercial debut was at the 1939 World's Fair in New York City at the Hall of Television. On April 30, 1939, President Franklin D. Roosevelt formally opened the fair and became the first president to appear on television. Sarnoff also spoke, and RCA displayed its 5-inch and 9-inch sets, priced from $199.50 to $600 (equivalent to $2,950 to $8,870 in today's dollars).

NBC and CBS were the original TV networks. A ***network*** is a collection of radio or television stations that offers programs, usually simultaneously, throughout the country, during designated program times.

In 1943, ABC, the third major network, grew out of NBC's old Blue network. ABC labored from its earliest days to equal the other two networks but didn't have as many affiliates as NBC and CBS. The two leading networks already had secured the more powerful, well-established broadcast outlets for themselves. David Sarnoff and William Paley controlled the network game.

Network A collection of radio or TV stations that offers programs, usually simultaneously, throughout the country, during designated program times.

Media/Impact CULTURE

Edward R. Murrow (1908–1965) Sets the Standard for Broadcast News

By Theodore H. White

Note: Edward R. Murrow had established a reputation for excellence as a CBS radio news broadcaster when he migrated to television news in 1951. In this profile, veteran journalist Theodore H. White outlines Murrow's broadcast career and its impact on television audiences.

CBS Photo Archive/Getty Images

In the 1950s, Edward R. Murrow (right) established a very high standard for TV news. Murrow is shown here in 1950 with his long-time radio and television program producer Fred Friendly.

It is so difficult to recapture the real Ed Murrow from the haze that now shrouds the mythical Ed Murrow of history.

Where other men may baffle friends with the infinite complexity of their natures, Ed was baffling otherwise. He was so straightforward, he would completely baffle the writers who now unravel the neuroses of today's demigods of television. When Ed was angry, he bristled; when he gave friendship, it came without withholding.

He could walk with prime ministers and movie stars, GIs and generals, as natural in rumpled GI suntans as in his diplomatic homburg. But jaunty or somber, to those of us who knew him he was just plain old Ed. In his shabby office at CBS cluttered with awards, you could loosen your necktie, put your feet up and yarn away. The dark, overhanging eyebrows would arch as he punctured pretension with a jab, the mouth would twist quizzically as he questioned. And then there were his poker games, as Ed sat master of the table, a cigarette dangling always from his lips—he smoked 60 or 70 a day—and called the bets.

Then—I can hear him now—there was the voice. Ed's deep and rhythmic voice was compelling, not only for its range, halfway between bass and baritone, but for the words that rolled from it. He wrote for the ear—with a cadence of pauses and clipped, full sentences. His was an aural art but, in Ed, the art was natural—his inner ear composed a picture and, long before TV, the imagination of his listeners caught the sound and made with it their own picture.

We remember the voice. But there was so much more to Ed. He had not only a sense of the news but a sense of how the news fit into history. And this sense of the relation of news to history is what, in retrospect, made him the great pioneer of television journalism. . . .

He is very large now, for it was he who set the news system of television on its tracks, holding it, and his descendents, to the sense of history that give it still, in the schlock-storm of today, its sense of honor. Of Ed Murrow it may be said that he made all of us who clung to him, and cling to his memory still, feel larger than we really were.

Excerpted from "When He Used the Power of TV, He Could Rouse Thunder," TV Guide 34, no. 3 (Jan. 18, 1986), pages 13–14. Reprinted by permission of Heyden White Rostow and David F. White.

Paramount Pictures/Hulton Archive/Getty Images

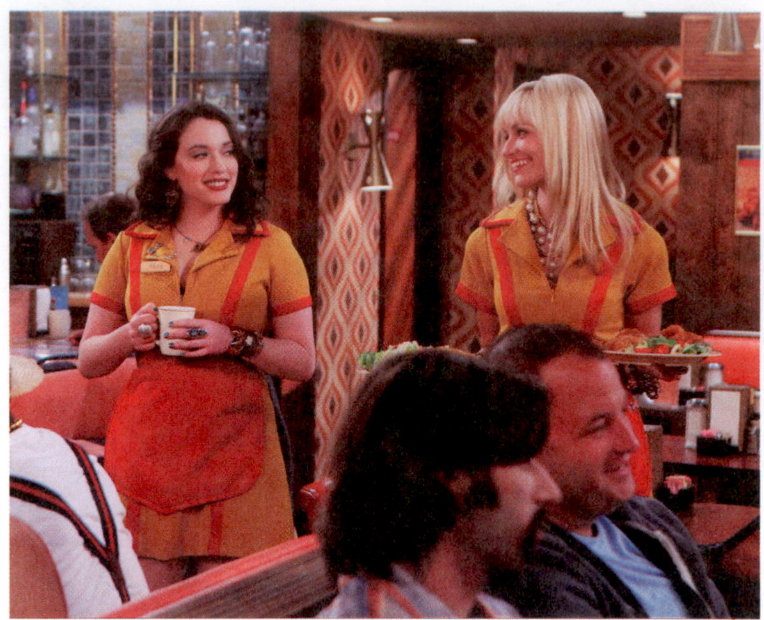

CBS via Getty Images

The Honeymooners, which ran from 1955 to 1956 on CBS, is an early example of one of the most durable types of prime-time TV programming—the situation comedy (Left to right: Jackie Gleason, Art Carney, Joyce Randolph and Audrey Meadows). *2 Broke Girls* is today's version of early TV sitcoms.

popular that one Laundromat installed a TV set and advertised, "Watch Berle while your clothes twirl."

SITUATION COMEDIES. Along with drama, the ***situation comedy*** (sitcom) proved to be one of TV's most durable types of programs. The situation comedy established a regular set of characters in either a home or work situation. *I Love Lucy*, starring Lucille Ball and Desi Arnaz, originated from Los Angeles because the actors wanted to live on the West Coast. In 1951, Ball began a career as a weekly performer on CBS that lasted for 23 years.

In 1955, Jackie Gleason launched *The Honeymooners*, a show based on his childhood experiences growing up in New York. *The Honeymooners* was only on for two years, but Gleason maintained the characters and featured them in skits on his variety program, *The Jackie Gleason Show*, beginning in 1961.

In 1960, CBS launched *The Andy Griffith Show*, which followed the adventures of widower and Mayberry sheriff Andy Taylor, who was raising his young son, Opie. Ron Howard played Opie, and Don Knotts played Andy's nervous cousin, Barney Fife. *The Andy Griffith Show*, a spin-off of another sitcom, *The Danny Thomas Show*, ran for eight seasons, and is still shown today on the TV Land cable television network. *Modern Family* and *2 Broke Girls* are examples of current situation comedy successes. (See **Media/Impact: Money**, "Hollywood's TV Factory," p. 173.)

Situation Comedy A TV program that establishes a regular cast of characters typically in a home or work situation. Also called a sitcom.

DRAMA. *The Loretta Young Show* offered noontime drama—broadcast live—every day in the 1950s. *The Hallmark Hall of Fame* established a tradition for high-quality, live dramatic presentations. For many years, TV dramas were limited to 1- or 2-hour programs. But in the 1970s, encouraged by the success of Alex Haley's *Roots*, which dramatized Haley's search for the story of his African ancestry, television began to broadcast as many as 14 hours of a single drama over several nights. Today, the series *CSI* is an example of a popular prime-time drama.

WESTERNS. TV went Western in 1954, when Jack Warner of Warner Brothers signed an agreement with ABC to provide the network with a program called *Cheyenne*. The outspoken Warner had openly criticized TV's effect on the movie business, but when ABC asked Warner to produce programs for them, Warner Brothers became the first movie company to realize that the studios could profit from television.

DETECTIVE STORIES. *Dragnet*, with Sergeant Friday, was an early TV experiment with detectives, starting in 1951 and running for eight seasons. The genre became a TV staple: *Dragnet*'s successors today are programs like *Law and Order* and *CSI*.

MOVIES. The movie industry initially resisted the competition from TV, but then it realized there was money to be made in selling old movies to TV. In 1957, RKO sold 740 pre-1948 movies to television for $25 million. The other studios followed. Through various distribution agreements, movie reruns and movies produced specifically for television were added to television's program lineup.

SOAP OPERAS. Borrowed from radio serials, soap operas filled morning television programming. Today, game shows and reruns are more popular choices, but some soaps still survive. Soap operas have their own magazines, and some newspapers carry weekly summaries of plot development. Soap operas (*telenovelas*) also are an important feature of today's Spanish-language television.

TALK SHOWS. Sylvester "Pat" Weaver (actress Sigourney Weaver's father) created and produced television's single original contribution to programming: the talk show. Weaver's *Tonight Show* (originally *Jerry Lester's Broadway Open House*) first appeared in 1954. Through a succession of hosts from Lester to Steve Allen to Jack Paar to Johnny Carson to Jay Leno and (briefly) Conan O'Brien, *The Tonight Show* has lasted longer than any other talk show on television. Modern-day successors of the late-night talk show format include David Letterman and Jimmy Kimmel.

QUIZ SHOWS. In the mid-1950s, all three TV networks introduced quiz shows, on which contestants competed with each other for big-money prizes. Soon, the quiz shows were mired in controversy because of charges that the contestants had been given answers.

Donna Svennevik/ABC/Getty Images

Talk shows are a very profitable TV program format. In May 2010, George Lopez (center), late-night host of *Lopez Tonight*, appeared as a guest on the daytime talk show *The View*, along with (left to right) Whoopi Goldberg, Joy Behar, Sherri Shepherd, comedian Vernard "Bone" Hampton and Elisabeth Hasselbeck.

Quiz Shows Bring Ethics Scandals

CBS's *$64,000 Question* premiered June 7, 1955, and was sponsored by Revlon. Contestants answered questions from a glass "isolation booth." Successful contestants returned in succeeding weeks to increase their winnings, and Revlon advertised its Living Lipstick. By September, the program was drawing 85 percent of the audience, and Revlon had to substitute an ad for another product because its factory supply of Living Lipstick had completely sold out.

As the most popular quiz show on early television, *$64,000 Question* engendered imitation: *Treasure Hunt*, *Giant Step* and *Twenty-One*. Winnings grew beyond the $64,000 limit; Charles Van Doren won $129,000 on *Twenty-One*. In the fall of 1955, CBS replaced Murrow's *See It Now* with a quiz program.

Sponsors produced many network quiz shows like *$64,000 Question* for the networks, and these programs usually carried the sponsor's name. In the 1958–1959 quiz show

Everett Collection

Charles Van Doren (far left) won $129,000 on the quiz show *Twenty-One,* facing contestant Herb Stempel (far right). Contestants appeared in "isolation booths," allegedly to keep them from hearing quiz answers from the audience. Van Doren and Stempel, who were fed answers beforehand by the show's producers, were central figures in the 1950s quiz show ethics scandals.

PEDRO UGARTE/AFP/Getty Images

Live sporting events are among the most profitable types of TV programming today because of their high audience ratings. In 2010, a huge worldwide television audience watched the FIFA World Cup finals live from Soweto, near Johannesburg, South Africa. Spain celebrates its win over the Netherlands on July 11, 2010.

scandals, Revlon was implicated when a congressional subcommittee investigated charges that the quiz shows were rigged to enhance the ratings. Charles Van Doren admitted before the subcommittee that *Twenty-One*'s producer had fed him the answers. Staff members from other quiz shows confirmed Van Doren's testimony.

The quiz show scandals caused the networks to reexamine the relationship between advertisers and programs. Before the scandals, advertisers and their agencies produced one-quarter to one-third of network programming. As a result of the quiz show scandals, the networks turned to other sources, such as independent producers, for their programming.

By the late 1960s, advertisers provided less than 3 percent of network programming, and soon advertisers provided no network shows. The networks programmed themselves. They also used reruns of newly acquired studio movies to replace the quiz shows, but quiz shows resurfaced in 1983 with *Wheel of Fortune* and, in the 1990s, *Who Wants to Be a Millionaire?*, and today's *Are You Smarter Than a Fifth Grader?*

Ratings Target the Audience

After the quiz show scandals, the networks were criticized for being motivated only by ratings. Ratings give sponsors information about the audience they're reaching with their advertising—what advertisers are getting for their money.

By the late 1950s, the A. C. Nielsen Company dominated the television ratings business. The national Nielsen ratings describe the audience to advertisers; based on the Nielsens, advertisers pay for the commercial time to reach the audiences they want.

Today, Nielsen provides two types of numbers, known as rating and share. The ***rating*** is a percentage of the total number of households with television sets. If there are 95 million homes with TV sets, for example, the rating shows the percentage of those sets that were tuned in to a specific program. The share (an abbreviation for share-of-audience) compares the audience for one show with the audience for another. ***Share*** means the percentage of the audience with TV sets turned on that is watching each program.

For example, if TV sets in 50 million homes were turned on at 8 p.m. on Friday night, and 25 million homes were tuned to Program A, that program would have a rating of 26 (25 million divided by 95 million, expressed as a percentage) and a share of 50. (See **Illustration 8.2**.)

The most concentrated ratings periods for local stations are "sweeps" months—February, May and November. (Ratings are taken in July, too, but the numbers are not considered accurate because so many people are on vacation.) The sweeps provide an estimate of the local TV audience, and advertisers use that information when they decide where to place their commercials.

Sweeps are the months when the ratings services gather their most important ratings, so the networks and local stations often use these important months to showcase their best programs. This is when you are most likely to see a

Rating The percentage of the total number of households *with TV sets* tuned to a particular program.

Share The percentage of the audience *with TV sets turned on* that is watching a particular program.

Sweeps The months when TV ratings services gather their most important ratings—February, May and November.

Media/Impact AUDIENCE

Illustration 8.2

Measuring the Audience: What TV Ratings Mean

Suppose that at 8 p.m. on Friday TVs are on in 50 million out of 95 million households and that 25 million TVs are tuned to Program A. Program A's rating is 26, meaning 26 percent of all TV households are tuned to Program A. Program A's share is 50, meaning that 50 percent of the total number of TV households watching TV are watching Program A.

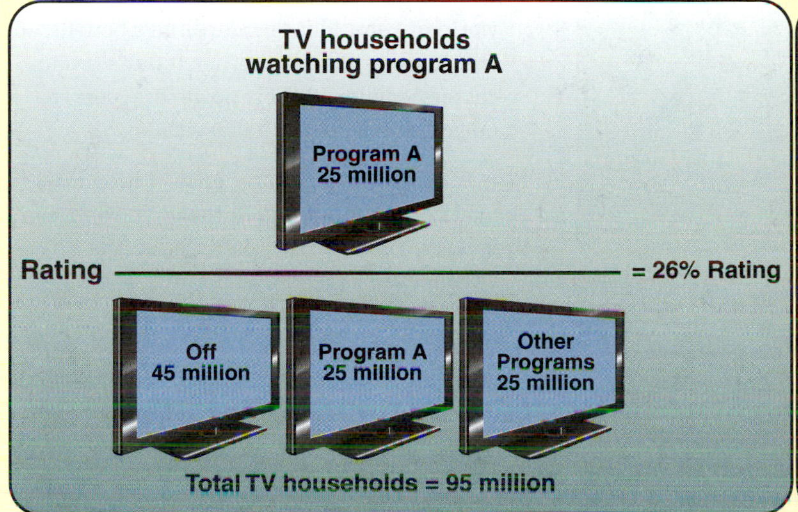

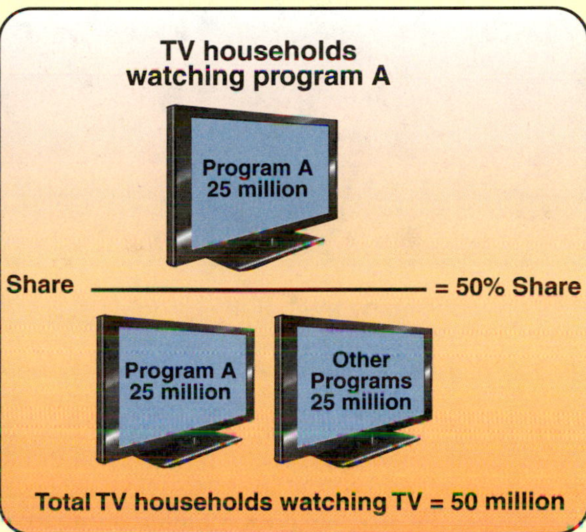

special one-hour episode of a popular series, for example, or a lavishly produced made-for-TV movie.

Today's Nielsen ratings work essentially the same as they did in the 1950s, except that the Nielsens now deliver very specific information on ***demographics***—age, occupation and income, for instance—and Nielsen can deliver daily ratings information to any client willing to pay for it.

In 2007, the Nielsen Company expanded its tracking service to count people who watch TV outside the home, in places like bars, restaurants, airports, offices and retail stores. Nielsen also plans to track viewership on computers, iPods, cell phones and other mobile devices. "Nielsen has a mandate to follow the video wherever it goes," said Sara Erichson, executive vice president for client services at Nielsen Media Research North American, a unit of the Nielsen Company.

Advertisers use this ratings information to target their most likely consumers. Nike shoes might choose to create a new advertising campaign for the NBA playoffs, for instance, and Nielsen could tell Nike, judging from previous NBA championships, all about the people the company will reach with its ads.

Criticism about the ratings persists. The main flaw today, critics contend, is the way the broadcast community religiously follows and uses ratings to determine programming.

Newton Minow Criticizes TV as a "Vast Wasteland"

The 1950s were a trial period for television, as the networks and advertisers tested audience interest in various types

Demographics Data about consumers' characteristics, such as age, occupation and income level.

pbs.org/wgbh/masterpiece/downtownabbey

PBS provides many memorable programs, like *Masterpiece Classic*, yet PBS attracts less than 3 percent of the national TV audience. At the Golden Globe Awards on January 15, 2012, *Downtown Abbey* writer and creator Julian Fellowes (center) accepts the award for the Best Mini-Series Made for Television, a British series co-produced by the BBC and PBS. (L-R actors Hugh Bonneville, Elizabeth McGovern; PBS producer Rebecca Eaton; Fellowes; co-producer Gareth Neame.)

of programming. Captured by the miracle that television offered, at first audiences seemed insatiable; they watched almost anything that TV delivered. But in the 1960s, audiences became more discriminating and began to question how well the medium of television was serving the public.

Once it established itself throughout the country, television needed a public conscience. That public conscience was Newton Minow. An unassuming soothsayer, Minow was named chairman of the Federal Communications Commission in 1961 by newly elected President John F. Kennedy. On May 9, 1961, speaking to the National Association of Broadcasters in his first public address since his appointment, Minow told broadcast executives what he believed were the broadcasters' responsibilities to the public. According to Minow, in his book *Equal Time*, he told the broadcasters:

> Your license lets you use the public's airwaves as trustees for 180 million Americans. The public is your beneficiary. If you want to stay on as trustees, you must deliver a decent return to the public—not only to your stockholders. . . .
>
> Your industry possesses the most powerful voice in America. It has an inescapable duty to make that voice ring with intelligence and with leadership. In a few years this exciting industry has grown from a novelty to an instrument of overwhelming impact on the American people. It should be making ready for the kind of leadership that newspapers and magazines assumed years ago, to make our people aware of their world.
>
> Ours has been called the jet age, the atomic age, the space age. It is also, I submit, the television age. And just as history will decide whether the leaders of today's world employed the atom to destroy the world or rebuild it for mankind's benefit, so will history decide whether today's broadcasters employed their powerful voice to enrich the people or debase them.

Minow then asked his audience of broadcast station owners and managers to watch their own programs. He said that they would find a "vast wasteland," a phrase that resurfaces today during any critical discussion of television.

Public Television Finds an Audience

The concept of educational television has been alive since the 1950s, when a few noncommercial stations succeeded in regularly presenting public service programs without advertisements, but the shows were low budget.

The educational network NET (National Educational Television) emerged in 1963 to provide some national programming (about 10 hours a week), sponsored mainly by foundations, with some federal support. Then in 1967, the Ford Foundation agreed to help pay for several hours of live evening programming.

Also in 1967, the Carnegie Commission on Educational Television released its report *Public Television: A Program for Action*, which included a proposal to create the Corporation for Public Broadcasting (CPB). CPB would collect money from many sources—including the enhanced federal funds the Carnegie report suggested—and disburse the money to the stations.

President Lyndon Johnson's administration and several foundations added money to CPB's budget. The Public Broadcasting Service (PBS) was created to distribute programs. The extra money underwrote the creation of programs like *Sesame Street* and *The French Chef.* PBS also began to buy successful British television programs, which were broadcast on *Masterpiece Theatre*. PBS programs actually started to show up in the ratings.

In 1995, members of Congress called for the "privatization" of public television, with the idea that eventually PBS would become completely self-sustaining. Today, the CPB, which oversees public television, still receives funding from the federal government. Local funding supplements this government underwriting, but within the past 10 years, public donations to public television have been declining. This decline in funding has led public broadcasters to seek underwriting from more corporate donors, but companies accustomed to advertising on commercial networks are reluctant to advertise on a network that commonly attracts less than 3 percent of the national audience.

For the first time, public television began to pay attention to ratings. This attention to an audience of consumers means the pressure is building on public television executives to make each program profitable.

The FCC began liberalizing its rules for commercial announcements on public television in 1981. Now, corporate sponsors often make announcements, including graphics and video, at the beginning and the end of PBS-produced programs. The announcements often look the same as advertisements on commercial television. Critics of this commercialization of public television are calling for more government funding, but Congress seems unwilling to expand its underwriting. Today, public television is struggling to reinvent itself, and it still remains commercial television's stepchild.

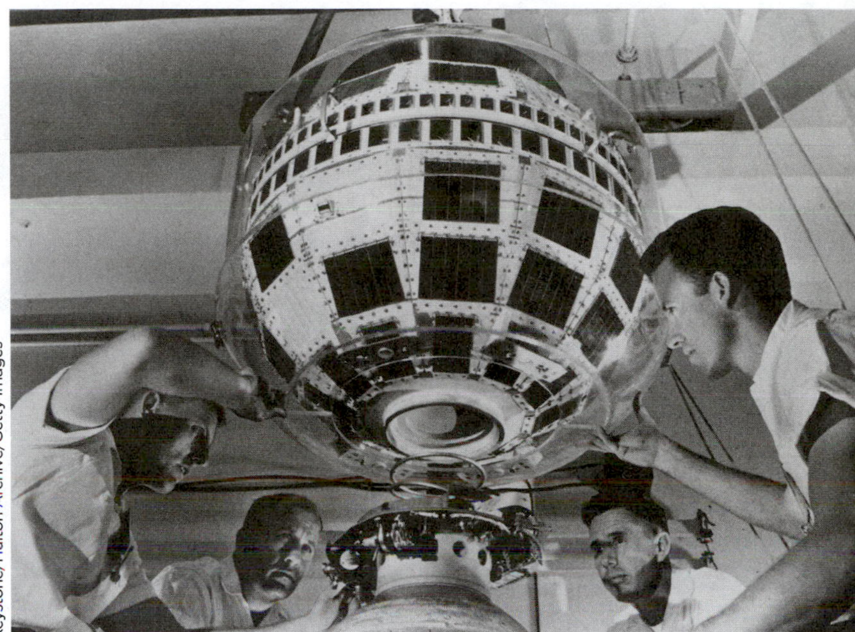

Keystone/Hulton Archive/Getty Images

In 1962, technicians readied the *Telstar I* communications satellite for launch. *Telstar I* enabled the first transatlantic satellite broadcast. Today's modern satellites, the successors to *Telstar I*, make television delivery systems like DirecTV possible.

Satellites Make Transatlantic TV and Live Broadcasts Possible

On July 10, 1962, *Telstar I* sent the first transatlantic satellite broadcast. Before *Telstar*, copper cable linked the continents, film footage from overseas traveled only by plane, and in most homes a long-distance telephone call was a special event. Today, *Telstar*'s descendants orbit at a distance of more than 22,000 miles. A single modern communication satellite can carry more than 30,000 telephone calls and three television channels. (Modern satellites make program services like CNN and satellite systems like DirecTV possible.)

By 1965, all three networks were broadcasting in color. Television demonstrated its technological sophistication in December 1968 with its live broadcast from the *Apollo* spacecraft while the spacecraft circled the moon, and seven months later television showed Neil Armstrong stepping onto the moon.

Television Changes National Politics

Just as radio was first an entertainment medium and then expanded to cover important news events, television first established itself with entertainment and then developed a serious news presence. Franklin D. Roosevelt had been the first president to understand and use radio, and John F. Kennedy became the country's first television president. Some of Kennedy's predecessors had appeared on television, but he instinctively knew how to *use* television to promote his agenda.

Observers claimed Kennedy's 1960 presidential victory was partly due to his success in the televised presidential debates with Richard Nixon. Kennedy also was the first president to hold live televised news conferences. In July 1962, he oversaw the launch of the first communications satellite, *Telstar I*. One year later news organizations used that same satellite technology to broadcast live coverage of the news events following President Kennedy's assassination on November 22, 1963.

Television received credit for uniting the nation with its news coverage of the Kennedy assassination, but it also was blamed for dividing it. President Lyndon Johnson, beleaguered by an unpopular war in Vietnam, used television to

Asahi Shimbun via Getty Images

Originally a very small part of television programming, television news today gives audiences access to 24-hour coverage of global events. In March 2011, news coverage of a 9.0 magnitude earthquake and tsunami in Japan riveted television viewers around the world.

make an announcement to the nation in 1968 that he would not run for a second term.

Johnson's successor, President Richard Nixon, had always been uncomfortable with the press. The Nixon administration often attacked the press for presenting perspectives on world affairs that the administration did not like. Upset with the messages being presented, the Nixon administration battled the messenger, sparking a bitter public debate about the role of a free press (especially television) in a democratic society.

Ironically, television's next live marathon broadcast chronicled the ongoing investigation of the Nixon presidency—Watergate. The Watergate scandal began when burglars broke into the offices of the Democratic Party's national headquarters in the Watergate complex in Washington, D.C., on June 17, 1972. Some of the burglars had ties to President Nixon's reelection committee as well as to other questionable activities originating in the White House.

In the months following the break-in, the president and his assistants sought to squelch the resulting investigation. Although Nixon denied knowledge of the break-in and the cover-up, the U.S. Senate hearings about the scandal, televised live across the country, created a national sensation. (See also **Chapter 12**.) Eventually, faced with the prospect of impeachment, Nixon announced his resignation on television on August 8, 1974.

In 1987, television repeated its marathon coverage of an important national investigation with the Iran-Contra hearings, a congressional investigation of the Reagan administration's role in illegally selling weapons to Iran and using the money to secretly finance Nicaraguan rebels, called contras.

TV News Images Bring Global Events into View

Television news has matured from its early beginnings as a 15-minute newscast to today's 24-hour international coverage of events around the world.

On September 11, 2001, U.S. TV network news offered nonstop coverage of the terrorist events at New York's World Trade Center, the Pentagon and in rural Pennsylvania. Two years later, TV networks brought viewers even closer to events when TV reporters and photographers sent live battlefield images and stories during the Iraq War. On October 13, 2010, worldwide live news coverage chronicled the rescue of 33 miners trapped in a mine near Santiago, Chile.

Television at Work

A typical television station has eight departments:

1. Sales
2. Programming (which includes news as well as entertainment)
3. Production
4. Engineering
5. Traffic
6. Promotion
7. Public affairs
8. Administration

People in the *sales* department sell the commercial slots for the programs. Advertising is divided into national and local sales. Advertising agencies, usually based on the East Coast, buy national ads for the products they handle. An ad agency may buy time on a network for the Ford Motor Company, for instance, for a TV ad that will run simultaneously all over the country.

But local Ford dealers, who want you to shop at their showroom, buy their ads directly from the local station. These ads are called local (or spot) ads. For these sales, salespeople (called account executives) at each station negotiate packages of ads based on their station's advertising

Media/Impact MONEY

Hollywood's TV Factory

By Amy Chozick

BURBANK, CA—*Casablanca* was shot at the Warner Bros. studio lot here, as were *Rebel Without a Cause* and *Million Dollar Baby*. But while movies may confer glamour and prestige, it's television that pays the bills. . . .

Today, the Warner lot is Hollywood's most prolific TV factory, cranking out dozens of shows a year. This collection of 30 soundstages on 112 acres is the epicenter of Warner Bros. Television Group, the largest TV supplier in the U.S. by a wide margin, and a robust exporter of television all over the world. Currently, it produces 56 shows for American television, 26 of which will be on the broadcast networks this fall.

"Movies come in and they're like a rich visiting uncle, but we know where our bread is buttered," says Jon Gilbert, president of Warner Bros. Studio Facilities.

This is where *Friends* and *The West Wing* were made. Active shows from Warner Bros. Television include *Two and a Half Men*, on CBS, TNT's Southland, Fox's *Fringe*, NBC's *The Voice*, ABC's *The Bachelor* and, in daytime, *The Ellen DeGeneres Show*. . . .

Warner Bros. has a costume department the size of two football fields, with four miles of pipe rail on which hang hundreds of Samurai outfits, Hawaiian shirts and cheerleading garb (college and pro). There's also a sizable section devoted to wicked stiletto heels labeled "hooker shoes."

Producers have access to a 150,000-square-foot props and upholstery department. Warner boasts that more than 60% of all upholstery on TV comes from here.

Other studios depend on the steady cash flow of television production, and some have bigger hits. But Warner's operations, by sheer vol-

Bloomberg via Getty Images

Warner Bros. Studios in Burbank, California, houses a costume department as large as two football fields. As the nation's largest TV program supplier, Warner Bros. TV produces 56 different shows for American audiences, including *Two and Half Men*, *The Big Bang Theory*, and *2 Broke Girls*.

ume and infrastructure, make it the standard of manufacturing efficiency, if not sexiness: General Motors in the 1960s.

Warner's perennial success in television is especially notable because unlike four of its five major competitors, it is unattached to a major broadcast network.

The Big Four networks have a huge incentive to buy programs from their corporate siblings, so they can profit both from advertising revenue and from owning the shows, which down the line translates into the real pot of gold: revenue from reruns, foreign and DVD sales, on-demand and streaming. The share of new network shows produced by sibling studios rose from 50 percent in 2006 to a record 77 percent in 2010, according to a study by Nomura Equity Research.

So Warner TV sells to everybody, and must hustle extra hard to do so.

"You have to be everybody's second-favorite supplier," says Bruce Rosenblum, president of Warner Bros. Television Group.

rates. These rates are a direct reflection of the station's position in the ratings.

The *programming* department selects the shows that you will see and develops the station's schedule. Network-owned stations, usually located in big cities (KNBC in Los Angeles, for example), are called ***O & Os***, which stands for "owned and operated." O & Os automatically carry network programming. ***Affiliates*** are stations that carry network programming but that the networks do not own. The networks pay affiliates to carry their programming, for which the networks sell most of the ads and keep the money. An affiliate is allowed to insert into the network programming a specific number of local ads, for which the affiliate keeps the income.

Because affiliates can make money on network programming and don't have to pay for it, many stations choose to affiliate themselves with a network. When they aren't running what the network provides, affiliates run their own programs and keep all the advertising money they collect from them.

Some of the nation's commercial TV stations operate as independents. Independent stations must buy and program all their own shows, but independents also keep all the money they make on advertising. Independents run some individually produced programs and old movies, but most of their programming consists of reruns such as *I Love Lucy* and *The Andy Griffith Show* that once ran on the networks. Independents buy these reruns from program services called ***syndicators***.

Syndicators also sell independently produced programs such as *The Oprah Winfrey Show*. Independent programs are created and sold either by non-network stations or by independent producers. Stations pay for these first-run syndication programs individually; the price is based on the size of the station's market.

Local news usually makes up the largest percentage of a station's locally produced programming. In some large markets, such as Los Angeles, local news programming runs as long as two hours.

The *production* department manages the programs the station creates in-house. This department also produces local commercials for the station. The *engineering* department makes sure all the technical aspects of a broadcast operation are working: antennas, transmitters, cameras and any other broadcast equipment. The *traffic* department integrates the advertising with the programming, making sure that all the ads that are sold are aired when they're supposed to be. Traffic also handles billing for the ads.

The *promotion* department advertises the station—on the station itself, on billboards, on radio and in the local newspaper. These people also create contests to keep the station visible in the community. The *public affairs* department helps organize public events, such as a fun run to raise money for the local hospital. *Administration* handles the paperwork for the station—paychecks and expense accounts, for example.

O & Os TV stations that are owned and operated by the networks.

Affiliates Stations that use network programming but are owned by companies other than the networks.

Syndicators Services that sell programming to broadcast stations and cable.

Audiences Drive TV Programming

Today's most-watched television programs are situation comedies, sports and feature movies. More than 120 million people tuned in for the final episode of the situation comedy *M*A*S*H* in 1983, making it the highest-rated television program ever. In 1993, the final episode of the sitcom *Cheers* garnered an audience of 80 million. Super Bowls generally grab about half the homes in the United States. In 2008, the surprise ratings leader was President-elect Barack Obama. More than 70 million people watched his election victory the night of November 4, 2008, a record number of viewers for a presidential election night.

Six developments promise to affect the television industry over the next decade: station ownership changes, the shrinking role of the networks, the accuracy of ratings, the growth of cable and satellite delivery, the profitability of sports programming and the growing audience for Spanish-language TV.

Station Ownership Changes and Mergers

The Telecommunications Act of 1996 (see **Chapter 14**) used a station's potential audience to measure ownership limits. The Act allowed one company to own TV stations that reach up to 35 percent of the nation's homes. Broadcasters also are no longer required, as they once were, to hold onto a station for three years before selling it. Today, stations may be sold as soon as they are purchased.

In 1999, the Federal Communications Commission (FCC) adopted new regulations that allow media companies to own two TV stations in one market, as long as eight separately owned TV stations continue to operate in that market after the merger. The rules said the four top-rated stations in one market cannot be combined under the same ownership,

Media/Impact AUDIENCE

Illustration 8.3

Top Rated U.S. Regularly Scheduled Television Programs, 2010–2011 Season

Because there are so many sources of TV programming available to today's viewers, even the most popular shows attract a relatively small percentage of the overall audience (as reflected in their audience ratings, shown here).

Source: "Ratings: How Every Broadcast Show Ranked This Season," May 25, 2011. http://insidetv.com/2011/05/2010-11-season-tv-ratings/.

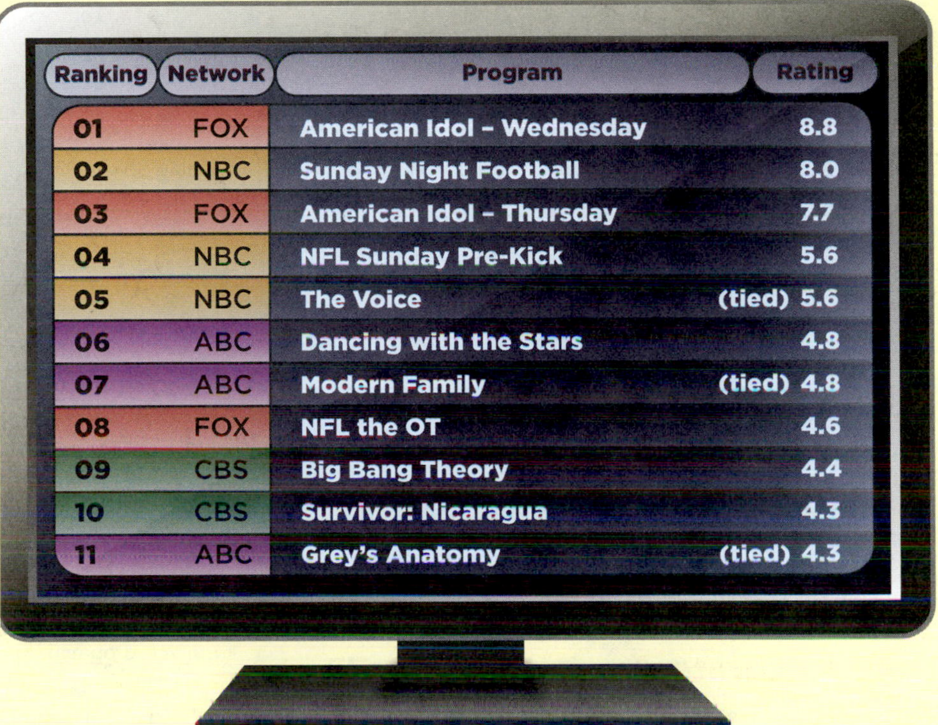

Ranking	Network	Program	Rating
01	FOX	American Idol - Wednesday	8.8
02	NBC	Sunday Night Football	8.0
03	FOX	American Idol - Thursday	7.7
04	NBC	NFL Sunday Pre-Kick	5.6
05	NBC	The Voice	(tied) 5.6
06	ABC	Dancing with the Stars	4.8
07	ABC	Modern Family	(tied) 4.8
08	FOX	NFL the OT	4.6
09	CBS	Big Bang Theory	4.4
10	CBS	Survivor: Nicaragua	4.3
11	ABC	Grey's Anatomy	(tied) 4.3

but a station that is among the four top-rated stations can combine with one that is not in the top four.

In 2003, the FCC relaxed ownership rules even further, leaving few restrictions on network ownership. Like radio, fewer companies are putting together larger and larger groups of TV stations. Today, most local TV stations are not owned by local companies, as they once were. Television is *concentrating* ownership, but it is also *shifting* ownership, as stations are bought and sold at an unprecedented rate. This has introduced instability and change to an industry that until 1980 witnessed very few ownership turnovers.

The Networks' Shrinking Role

Advertisers always have provided the economic support for television, so in 1986 the networks were disturbed to see the first decline in advertising revenues in 15 years. New and continuing developments—such as cable, satellite broadcast, VCRs and DVD players—turned the television set into a smorgasbord of choices. Audiences—and advertisers—began to desert the networks, and network ratings declined as a result.

Today, because there are so many sources of TV programming available, even the most popular shows attract a relatively small percentage of the overall audience. (See **Illustration 8.3**.)

The networks' share of the audience for the evening news also is shrinking. The story is familiar, paralleling the decline in radio listening in the late 1940s when television first replaced radio and then television began competing with itself. Today more stations and more sources of programming mean the TV networks must expand their audience beyond the traditional prime-time evening time slot to stay profitable.

Michael Loccisano/Getty Images

Cable channels began offering their own programming, separate from the networks, in 1972. Today, more than 500 program services, including HBO (owned by Time Warner) are available by satellite. In 2010, HBO launched an expensive new drama, *Boardwalk Empire*, set in Atlantic City in the 1920s.

How Accurate Are TV Ratings?

People meters, first used in 1987 by the A. C. Nielsen Company to record television viewing, gather data through a 4-inch-by-10-inch box that sits on the television set in metered homes. People meters monitor the nation's Nielsen families (about 4,000 of them, which Nielsen says are a cross section of American viewers), and the results of these recorded viewing patterns are the ratings that establish the basis for television advertising rates.

Nielsen family members each punch an assigned button in the set-top box when they begin to watch television. The system's central computer, linked to the home by telephone lines, correlates each viewer's number with information about that person stored in its memory.

Network ratings have plunged since people meters were introduced as a ratings system, and the networks have complained that the people meters underestimates specific audiences, especially African Americans and Latinos. Still, Nielsen is the only company in the United States offering TV audience measurement.

CATV Community antenna television or cable television.

DBS Direct broadcast satellite.

Subscription Television A new term used to describe consumer services delivered by cable and satellite program delivery.

Cable and Satellite Delivery

Today's cable giants, ESPN (Entertainment and Sports Programming Network) and CNN, are descendents of America's first cable TV system, which was established in Pennsylvania and Oregon to bring TV signals to rural areas that couldn't receive an over-the-air signal. Soon, this community antenna television (***CATV***) system spread to remote areas all over the country where TV reception was poor.

By 1970, there were 2,500 CATV systems in the United States, and commercial broadcasters were getting nervous about what they called "wired TV." Cable operators were required by the FCC to carry all local broadcast programming, and programs often were duplicated on several channels. The FCC also limited the programs that cable could carry. One FCC ruling, for example, said that movies on cable had to be at least 10 years old.

Believing that cable should be able to offer its own programming, Home Box Office (owned by Time Warner) started operating in Manhattan in 1972, offering a modest set of programs. Ted Turner's Turner Network Television (TNT) first relayed programs by satellite in 1976, and in 1979 Turner started Cable News Network (CNN). Today, more than 500 different program services, ranging from ESPN to the concert sounds of VH-1 to classic 1930s and 1940s movies on American Movie Classics (AMC), are available by satellite.

Cable television as an alternative to the traditional networks moved to the center of the national news agenda in 1991 when CNN offered 24-hour coverage of the Gulf War in Iraq. CNN's fast response to world events underlined the new global role that CNN and many other cable companies will play in future television developments.

In 1982, the FCC authorized direct broadcast satellite (***DBS***), making direct satellite-to-home satellite broadcasts possible. In 1994, a company called DirecTV began offering services directly to the home by satellite. For a monthly fee, DirecTV and other DBS companies provide access to more than 500 different worldwide channels. The monthly fee is about the same as, or cheaper than, a monthly cable bill.

Today, the number of satellite subscribers is increasing, and the number of cable subscribers is declining. Cable and satellite program delivery systems now are collectively called ***subscription television*** services.

Cable and satellite programming, which divides viewers into smaller segments than the networks, makes it easier for advertisers to target a specific audience. Programs like National Geographic's *The Dog Whisperer* starring Cesar Millan, for instance, bring dog lovers to any advertiser that wants to sell dog-related products.

ATTENTION
THE WILSONS NEXT DOOR JUST BOUGHT A MUCH BIGGER TV THAN THIS ONE.
CONSUMER ALERT

Mick Stevens/Cartoonbank

TV Changes Professional Sports

One of the most profitable types of television programming is sports. In 1964, CBS paid $28 million for television rights to the 1964–1965 National Football League (NFL) games. In 1990, the networks paid $3.6 billion to broadcast NFL football. Today the price is much higher.

Television fees fund most of the cost of organized sports. Today's televised sports have become spectacularly complex entertainment packages, turning athletes as well as sports commentators into media stars. The expansion of sports programming beyond the networks to cable channels such as ESPN means even more sports programming choices for viewers and more money for American sports teams.

Spanish-Language Television Brings a New Audience

During the summer of 2005, Univision, the nation's largest Spanish-language network, drew more prime-time viewers in the 18–34 age group than all the traditional broadcast networks—NBC, CBS, ABC and Fox. This was the first time Spanish-language TV had surpassed the networks, and the main draw was *telenovelas*, or soap operas in Spanish.

This Spanish-language lead in prime time had been building for several years, as the nation's Latino population increased. According to *The New York Times*: "Market researchers say that Latinos—no matter their age or dominant language—tend to tune in to Spanish-language television for two main staples: newscasts, because networks like Univision and Telemundo cover Latino issues and Latin America with more breadth and resources than English-language networks; and telenovelas, which function like a kind of cultural touchstone.

"Whether you're U.S.-born and you're introduced to it by a parent or grandparent or whether you're foreign-born and you grew up with it, it's the kind of thing that's inherent in the culture," multicultural marketing consultant Derene Allen told the *Times*. "It's as Mexican as eating tortillas and as Venezuelan or Colombian as eating arepas."

As traditional audiences shrink, and advertisers try to find new ways to sell their products, Spanish-language TV is emerging as one of the few promising markets for programming.

New Technology Expands TV's Focus

When technological developments move like a rocket, as they have in the past decade, program delivery becomes easier and less expensive. New technologies have brought more competition. Several new delivery systems have been developed to bring more choices to consumers than ever before—from the size of the screen to the clarity of the picture—and to change further the way people use television.

Digital Video Recorders

Digital video recorders (***DVRs***) download programming, using a set-top box that looks like a cable box and sits on or near the TV. DVRs use electronic storage to receive information from any program service (including the broadcast networks and satellite and cable programmers) to send viewers up-to-date information about what's on TV. DVRs transfer

DVR Digital video recorders.

the information to an on-screen program guide, where viewers can decide what to watch and when, a practice called ***time-shifting***.

One of the biggest features of a DVR is that it allows viewers to press the pause button during a show they're watching, leave the TV set on and then resume the program when they return or fast-forward through the recorded portion.

Because DVRs change viewers' control over which programming they watch (and, most importantly, which commercials, if any), all the major TV networks have invested in the companies that produce this technology, such as TiVo. The networks want to be able to influence what consumers can record and when, but total viewer control is one of DVRs' most attractive features for consumers.

High-Definition Television

A traditional television picture scans 525 lines across the screen. ***High-definition television*** (***HDTV***) scans 1,125 lines. CBS first demonstrated HDTV in the United States in 1982. HDTV, which offers a wider, sharper digital picture and better sound, requires more spectrum space than conventional television signals.

Digital TV also makes it easier for manufacturers to combine the functions of TV and the functions of a computer in the same piece of equipment. HDTV became the national industry standard in 2009.

Video Streaming and 3-D TV

In September 2010, Apple announced a push into the television market with Apple TV, a new device that uses video streaming and allows people to rent TV shows over the Internet for 99 cents each. Fox and Walt Disney will make the shows available the day after they are broadcast over the air. The service requires users to buy a $99 Apple TV box, and Apple TV was called an "elementary effort" by Apple to enter the television business. Still, this is one more outlet for broadcast programming that wasn't available before. TV program downloads already are available on Apple's other devices, such as the iPad and the iPhone, and through iTunes.

In a more aggressive move that could change television viewing, in 2010 major television manufacturers started selling 3-D TVs, and several programmers announced plans to create 3-D shows to feed the new market. (See **Media/Impact: Culture**, "Television Begins a Push into the 3rd Dimension," p. 179.) "Now that almost two-thirds of American homes have ditched their old tube televisions for flat-screens and high-definition sets, TV makers are trying to lure consumers back into the stores for the next big thing—3-D TV," reports *The New York Times*.

In July 2010, ESPN showed some of the 2010 FIFA World Cup soccer games in 3-D and shot a New York Yankees–Seattle Mariners game in 3-D and set up 3-D televisions at the Mariners stadium so people could see what 3-D looked like. The Discovery Channel plans to launch a 3-D network in January 2011 to show various action sports, such as motocross, in 3-D.

To see most 3-D television, consumers must have a 3-D set ($2,300), 3-D glasses ($150 each) and a special 3-D receiver box, although Toshiba announced plans late in 2010 to sell a 3-D TV that didn't require special glasses. Still, the cost for consumers will be a barrier to the new technology, especially since many households have just absorbed the cost of their new HD sets. So far, 3-D TV accounts for just 2.5 percent of new television sales in the U.S.

Television Offers a New Vision

Forecasts for the future of television parallel the forecasts for radio—a menu board of hundreds of programs and services available to viewers at the touch of a remote-control button. In the 1990s, regional telephone companies (abbreviated as ***telcos***) rushed to merge with cable TV companies to form giant telecommunications delivery systems.

To try to maintain their audience dominance, the TV networks have invested heavily in satellite TV and Internet program services to develop the capability to deliver programs to screens as small as a cell phone, and these new financial powerhouses can spend large sums of money for research to reach the audiences they want.

In one vision of the future, for example, your television will serve not only as a program service with unlimited channels but also as an artificial reality machine, says *The Wall Street Journal*. This machine would use "remarkably crisp pictures and sound to 'deliver' a viewer to a pristine tropical beach, to a big football game or to a quiet mountain-top retreat. Japanese researchers envision golfers practicing their swings in front of three-dimensional simulations of courses."

In 2006, when Congress passed a law that required TV broadcasters to switch totally to digital signals by 2009, only about 60 percent of U.S. households were capable of receiving a digital TV signal, according to the Consumer

Time-Shifting Recording a television program on a DVR to watch at a more convenient time.

High-Definition Television (HDTV) The industry standard for digital television transmission as of 2009; it provides a picture with a clearer resolution than earlier TV sets.

Telcos An abbreviation for telephone companies.

Media/Impact
CULTURE

Television Begins a Push into the 3rd Dimension

By Brian Stelter and Brad Stone

Ralph Kramden can finally buy a television.

It was more than half a century ago, in a 1955 episode of *The Honeymooners*, that Kramden, the parsimonious bus driver played by Jackie Gleason, told his wife, Alice, that he had not yet bought a new television because "I'm waiting for 3-D."

The wait will soon be over. A full-fledged 3-D television turf war is brewing in the United States, as manufacturers unveil sets capable of 3-D and cable programmers rush to create new channels for them.

Many people are skeptical that consumers will suddenly pull their LCD and plasma televisions off the wall. Beginning at around $2,000, the 3-D sets will, at first, cost more than even the current crop of high-end flat-screens, and buyers will need special glasses—techie goggles, really—to watch in 3-D. . . .

But programmers and technology companies are betting that consumers are almost ready to fall in love with television in the third dimension. "The stars are aligning to make 2010 the launch year of 3-D," said John Taylor, a vice president for LG Electronics USA. "It's still just in its infancy, but when there is a sufficient amount of content available—and lots of people are working on this—there will be a true tipping point for consumers." . . .

It took high-definition television about a decade to catch on—to the point where it has become part of the entertainment mainstream, with an adequate stock of HD programming and the sets now cheap enough to entice middle-class buyers. Analysts expect 3-D television to go through the same curve, initially attracting first adopters for whom price is little or no object and gradually moving out to other affluent and then middle-class homes as sets become cheaper and programmers create enough 3-D fare.

Al Messerschmidt/Getty Images

In September 2010, a 3-D cameraman shot the preaseason game between the New York Giants and the New England Patriots, the first 3-D broadcast of an NFL game. A 3-D television divides picture images into two sets, one for each eye, so 3-D picture transmission requires a camera that shoots through two lenses simultaneously.

Or, of course, the technology could be a total flop.

For decades 3-D was a gimmick for B-movies and occasionally on television (in bad quality with flimsy paper glasses), but newer technology has largely erased those memories. Peter M. Fannon, a vice president at Panasonic, called the new sets "totally different than what one had seen over the last 20 to 30 years."

In 3-D, television makers see an opportunity to persuade households that have already bought HDTVs to return to the electronics store. Though television sales jumped 17 percent in 2009, the industry needs new innovations to keep the cash register ringing.

"3-D is an effort by the industry to come up with something that will motivate consumers to trade up," said Van Baker, an analyst at Gartner Research.

Electronics Association. Broadcasters resisted the 2009 deadline because they were afraid they would lose part of their audience—people without a digital TV—but the conversion happened without any major problems. Today, digital television is the new national standard. Television audiences seem to welcome new technology, even seek it out.

Digital technology makes high-quality television images available on screens as big as 100 inches and as small as a cell phone. New HDTV screens offer movie-quality pictures and CD-quality sound. Internet delivery offers programming that's mobile and can follow you wherever and whenever you want to view it.

The definition of what we call "television" is exploding. Lanny Smoot, an executive at Bell Communications Research, calls the future of television a *telepresence*. "This," he says, "is a wave that is not possible to stop."

Review, Analyze, Investigate

REVIEWING CHAPTER 8

Television Transforms Daily Life

✓ The word *television*, which once meant programs delivered by antennas through over-the-air signals, today means a *television screen*, where a variety of delivery systems brings viewers a diversity of programs.

✓ Many groups are concerned that, because of its pervasiveness, television influences the nation's values, habits and behavior.

✓ About 1,600 television stations operate in the United States. Three out of four of these are commercial stations and about half of U.S. stations are affiliated with a network.

TV Delivers an Audience to Advertisers

✓ More than any other media industry today, commercial television exists primarily as an advertising medium.

✓ A 30-second ad during Super Bowl 2012 costs an advertiser as much as $3.5 million.

Visual Radio Becomes *Television*

✓ Guglielmo Marconi put sound on airwaves. Lee de Forest invented the Audion tube. Vladimir Zworykin turned an electronic signal into a visual image. Philo T. Farnsworth added the electronic scanner.

✓ The rivalry between David Sarnoff (RCA) and William S. Paley (CBS) is central to the early history of television.

✓ The ABC network was formed when the Federal Communications Commission (FCC) ordered David Sarnoff to sell one of his two networks (Red and Blue). The Blue network became ABC.

Television Outpaces Radio

✓ The first television news broadcasts were primitive compared to today's broadcasts. Television news, like radio news, developed its own standard of excellence, led by news pioneers Edward R. Murrow and David Brinkley.

✓ Most television entertainment programming was derived from radio.

✓ The only type of program that didn't come from radio was the talk show, which appeared on television first and then moved to radio. The situation comedy proved to be one of television's most durable types of programming.

Quiz Shows Bring Ethics Scandals

✓ A congressional investigation revealed that several 1950s TV quiz shows were rigged to enhance their ratings.

✓ The 1950s quiz show scandals caused the networks to eliminate advertiser-produced programming.

✓ Charles Van Doren, who admitted that he cheated, was a central figure in the quiz show scandals.

Ratings Target the Audience

✓ The Nielsen ratings determine the price that TV advertisers pay to air their commercials.

✓ TV audiences are measured as ratings and shares.

Newton Minow Criticizes TV as a "Vast Wasteland"

✓ In the 1960s, audiences grew more discriminating and began to question how well the medium of television was serving the public.

✓ An influential person who outlined TV's responsibility to its audience was then-FCC Chairman Newton Minow, who coined the phrase "vast wasteland" to describe television.

Public Television Finds an Audience

✓ National Educational Television (NET) is the predecessor of today's Corporation for Public Broadcasting (CPB).

✓ In 1981, the FCC loosened the rules for commercials on public television.

Satellites Make Transatlantic TV and Live Broadcast Possible

✓ In 1982, *Telstar I* sent the first transatlantic satellite broadcast.

✓ Modern satellites make CNN and DirecTV possible.

Television Changes National Politics

✓ In the 1960s, television drew criticism for the way it was perceived to influence politics and the dialogue about national issues.

✓ Television broadcast nonstop coverage of the Watergate hearings, President Nixon's resignation and investigations of the Iran-Contra scandal.

TV News Images Bring Global Events into View

✓ In 2001, U.S. TV network news offered nonstop coverage of the terrorist attacks at New York's World Trade Center, the Pentagon and in rural Pennsylvania.

✓ In 2003, the TV networks brought viewers even closer to events when TV reporters and photographers sent live battlefield images and stories to viewers during the Iraq War.

✓ In 2010, people around the world saw live television coverage of the rescue of 33 Chilean miners who had been trapped underground for over two months.

Television at Work

✓ A typical TV station has eight departments: sales, programming, production, engineering, traffic, promotion, public affairs and administration.

✓ Many TV stations are affiliated with a network.

Audiences Drive TV Programming

✓ The most-watched TV programs are situation comedies, sports and feature movies.

✓ Deregulation, with relaxed ownership rules, means that instability, mergers and change have become major characteristics of the television industry.

✓ Network ratings have plunged since people meters were introduced as a ratings system, and the TV networks also must compete with the huge variety of program options vying for consumers' attention.

✓ More than 200 program services now offer alternatives to network programming.

✓ Television licensing fees fund most of the cost of the nation's college and professional sports.

✓ Spanish-language networks draw increasing numbers of prime-time viewers.

New Technology Expands TV's Focus

✓ Several technological developments are changing the way programs are delivered to consumers, including digital video recorders, high definition television and the Internet.

✓ HDTV offers better pictures, clearer sound and a flatter screen than traditional TV and became the national industry standard in 2009.

✓ Digital TV makes it easier for manufacturers to combine the functions of TV and the functions of a computer in the same TV set.

✓ In 2010 major television manufacturers started selling 3-D TVs, and several programmers announced plans to create 3-D shows to feed the new market.

Television Offers a New Vision

✓ Cable, satellite and Internet program services have developed the capability to deliver programs to screens as small as a cell phone.

✓ In the future, TV will serve as a program service with unlimited channels, including separate 3-D programming.

KEY TERMS

These terms are defined in the margins throughout this chapter and appear in alphabetical order with definitions in the Glossary, which begins on page 383.

CRITICAL QUESTIONS

1. Explain what media observer Jeff Greenfield means when he says, "To the television executive, the product [of television] is the audience." Give examples of why this is true.

2. How did the quiz show scandals of the 1950s affect the relationship between advertisers and the networks? Is the relationship between advertisers and the networks different or the same today? Explain.

3. Discuss the economic challenges facing public broadcasting and the various sources of funding on which individual public broadcast stations, as well as CPB and PBS rely. Summarize how public broadcasting has responded to the problems.

4. Explain the role of the Nielsen ratings in television, including such factors as ratings accuracy, advertiser dependence on ratings, the effect of ratings on programming, and the importance of ratings to commercial and public broadcasting networks.

5. Describe how new technologies (such as program downloads, video streaming and 3-D TV) will affect the television industry.

WORKING THE WEB

This list includes both sites mentioned in the chapter and others to give you greater insight into the television industry.

Disney-ABC Television Group

http://www.disneyabctv.com

Home to Disney's international entertainment and news properties, the Disney-ABC Television Group includes the ABC Television Network (Daytime, Entertainment and News divisions), Disney Channels World-wide, ABC Studios and Hyperion Books. The Group also manages the Radio Disney Network and the company's equity interest in Lifetime Entertainment Services and A&E Television Networks.

National Association of Broadcasters (NAB)

http://www.nab.org

The trade association for over-the-air radio and television broadcasters, the NAB provides networking opportunities, a career center and information about communication law. It also represents industry interests to government officials and provides research grants.

National Cable & Telecommunications Association

http://www.ncta.com

The principal trade association of the U.S. cable television industry, NTCA provides a unified voice for its members on all issues affecting cable and telecommunications. Its Web site includes information on other industry-related organizations, resources and services, as well legislative issues, filings and publications. Key issues for consumers include Internet regulation, TV parental controls and the digital television transition.

Nielsen Media Research

http://www.nielsenmedia.com

This research company provides the Nielsen ratings, which measure the popularity of various television programs. Its founder, Arthur C. Nielsen, was one of the fathers of modern marketing research. Its data play a large part in determining how much can be charged for ads. Useful features on the Web site include a TV History Timeline and a searchable glossary of media industry acronyms and terms.

Northwestern University Library: Broadcast, Cable and Satellite Resources on the Internet

http://www.library.northwestern.edu/media/resources/broadcast.html

This site offers a long list of links to useful media Web sites including the All in One Media Directory and the United States Information Agency.

Parental Media Guide

http://parentalguide.org/movies.html

Sponsored by major entertainment industry associations such as the MPA, NAB and Entertainment Software Rating Board, this Web site provides a central resource for parents and caregivers seeking information on the voluntary parental guideline systems in place for television, movies, video games and recorded music.

Public Broadcasting (PBS)

http://www.pbs.org

This network of more than 350 noncommercial television stations reaches nearly 73 million viewers per week with content on air and online. PBS.org includes a program search, TV schedules and links to online-featured topics such as History, Life & Culture and News & Views. PBS Kids Online (http://pbskids.org) provides educational entertainment for children as well as comprehensive sections for parents and teachers.

Television Bureau of Advertising (TVB)
http://www.tvb.org

This trade association for broadcast groups, advertising sales reps, syndicators, international broadcasters and individual television stations provides audience analyses and a business databank. The Web site also offers advice for selling smarter, a job center and information on electronic business processes.

TV.com
http://www.tv.com

Powered by CNET, this fan-run site includes information about programs, episodes, actors, lines and trivia for TV shows from the 1940s to today. It has a wide variety of online forums sorted by show genre as well as news, celebrity photos, downloads and podcasts.

Impact/Action Videos are concise news features on topics covered in this chapter, created exclusively for **Media/Impact**. They are available for students and instructors at CengageBrain.com, and include screen access for classroom viewing and discussion questions.

"Stay hungry. Stay Foolish"

—Apple CEO Steve Jobs, Stanford University Commencement speech, June 12, 2005.

Digital Media: Widening the Web

What's Ahead?

Digital Communication Transforms Media

Digital Media Support Convergence

20th-Century Discoveries Made Internet Possible

Web Opens to Unlimited Access

What Happens to Old Media?

Transformation Takes 30 Years

Web Access Leaves Some People Behind

Internet Combines Commerce, Information and Entertainment

Mobile Media Chase the Audience

Government Attempts to Coordinate and Control the Net

Protection Sought for Intellectual Property Rights

FCC Proposes Internet Neutrality

Internet Faces Four Challenges

New Technologies Mix with Old Ideas

Bloomberg/Getty Images

Visitors try out Nintendo's 3DS at Nintendo World 2011 in Chiba, Japan, on January 9, 2011. The largest single source of new revenue generated by the Internet comes from the development and sale of video games.

TimeFrame 1978 — Today

Digital Media Covers the Globe

1978 Nicholas Negroponte at the Massachusetts Institute of Technology first uses the term *convergence* to describe the intersection of the media industries.

SSPL/Getty Images

1988 **Less than one-half of 1 percent of U.S. households are online.**

1989 Tim Berners-Lee develops programming languages that allow people to share all types of information online and the first browser, which allows people to view information online.

1994 Marc Andreessen and his colleagues at the University of Illinois introduce Mosaic, a browser that allows people to combine pictures and text in the same online document. Congress names the new effort to coordinate all the different senders, channels and receivers in the United States the National Information Infrastructure (NII).

1995 David Filo and Jerry Yang launch Yahoo! as a search engine company.

1996 Internet advertising reaches $200 million. Congress passes the Communications Decency Act, an unsuccessful attempt to control Internet content.

1998 One in four U.S. households is online. Congress passes the Digital Millennium Copyright Act, which makes it illegal to share copyrighted material on the Internet.

Larry Page and Sergey Brin create Google as a company to create a better search engine for the Web.

Michael Nagle/Getty Images

1999 The Recording Industry Association of America (RIAA) sues Internet file-sharing company Napster for copyright infringement.

2000 **The number of Internet businesses explodes.**

TORU YAMANAKA/AFP/Getty Images

2001 Napster shuts down. The number of Internet startups begins to shrink and many existing companies close.

2003 The RIAA and the Motion Picture Association of America announce campaigns to aggressively fight online piracy.

2004 **Mark Zuckerberg launches Facebook as a social networking Web site. MySpace is launched the same year.**

For the first time, bloggers cover a presidential election.

© Mike Kepko/San Francisco Chronicle/Corbis

2005 File-sharing company Grokster shuts down, settling a landmark intellectual property case. After the success of Apple's online subscription music service, Apple announces online pay-per-view subscription access to first-run video.

2006 Internet advertising reaches $17 billion. Google fights a U.S. Justice Department subpoena for records of its customers' online searches. Google eventually agrees to a limited government request for information.

2007 Apple introduces the iPhone, making digital media more mobile than ever before.

2008 Google, the dominant search engine company, celebrates its 10th anniversary.

2009 The Federal Communications Commission proposes an open network policy for the United States, which means Internet service providers must share access to their networks with each other.

2010 **Apple introduces the iPad and the iPhone 4.**

2011 Apple launches iCloud. Apple CEO Steve Jobs dies.

TORU YAMANAKA/AFP/Getty Images

Today 79 percent of adult Americans use the Internet. Internet advertising is approaching $26 billion a year. The Internet is causing an explosion of digital media development, as new and existing companies compete for consumers' attention in a global online marketplace.

"Today's world has

become so wired together, so flattened, that you can't avoid seeing just where you stand on the planet—just where the caravan is and just how far ahead or behind you are," says *New York Times* columnist Thomas L. Friedman. The main reason for today's flattened planet, of course, is the Internet. Within the last 30 years, the emergence of the Internet as a media delivery system has transformed the structure and the economics of the media business in the United States and throughout the world.

Before the 1970s, media were defined by the systems that delivered them. Paper delivered the print media—newspapers, magazines and books. Antennas carried broadcast signals—radio and television. Movies required film, and music traveled on round discs. These traditional media each were specifically connected to their own method of delivery and organized into different types of companies—newspaper, magazine and book publishers; recording and movie studios; radio and TV stations.

KAREN BLEIER/AFP/Getty Images

Today the Internet offers people wireless access to information just about wherever and whenever they want it, including Chicago's O'Hare Airport.

Digital Communication Transforms Media

Today, the Internet delivers all types of media—print, broadcast, movies and recordings—using a single delivery system without barriers. You can receive all types of media just about anywhere you want, delivered by many different types of companies, carried on invisible electronic signals you can't see. The Internet has caused the emergence of new media products and new competition in the media business that were impossible to foresee when the Internet as a place for consumers first emerged in 1978, originally designed by a group of scientists who were simply hoping to share information.

The Internet combines millions of computer networks sending and receiving data from all over the world—competing interests joined together by a common purpose but no common owner. "No government or commercial entity owns the Net or directly profits from its operation," notes information designer Roger Fidler. "It has no president, chief executive officer or central headquarters."

In its global size and absence of central control, the Internet is completely different from traditional media. Originally developed to help researchers, scientists and educators communicate, the Internet has "evolved in a way no one planned or expected," says Fidler. "It is the relationships among people that have shaped the medium."

The term ***digital media*** describes all forms of communications media that combine text, pictures, sound and video using computer technology. Digital media read, write and store data electronically in numerical form—using numbers to code the data (text, pictures, sound and video). Because all digital media use the same numbered codes, digital media are ***compatible***, which means they can function well with one another to exchange and integrate text, pictures, sound and video. This compatibility is the main reason digital media are growing so fast. Because of its rapid growth, digital communications has become the biggest factor in the development of all of today's mass media industries.

Rather than the one-way communication of traditional media, communication on today's compatible digital networks means someone can receive and send information simultaneously, without barriers. Digital networks "free

Digital Media All emerging communications media that combine text, graphics, sound and video using computer technology.

Compatible Media that can function well with one another to exchange and integrate text, pictures, sound and video.

individuals from the shackles of corporate bureaucracy and geography and allow them to collaborate and exchange ideas with the best colleague anywhere in the world," said futurist George Gilder. "Computer networks give every hacker the creative potential of a factory tycoon of the industrial [turn-of-the-century] era and the communications power of a TV magnate of the broadcasting era."

In an interconnected digital world, the speed and convenience of the network redefines the mass media industries and erases all previous notions of how mass communications should work. Today's media are constantly evolving. Digital media forms "do not arise spontaneously and independently from old media," says media scholar Roger Fidler. Digital media are related and connected to old media. Fidler says today's media are members of an interdependent system, with "similarities and relationships that exist among past, present and emerging forms."

Digital media are similar to traditional media yet different in ways that make them distinct from their predecessors. Because of the interdependence of mass media today, all the media industries are transforming simultaneously.

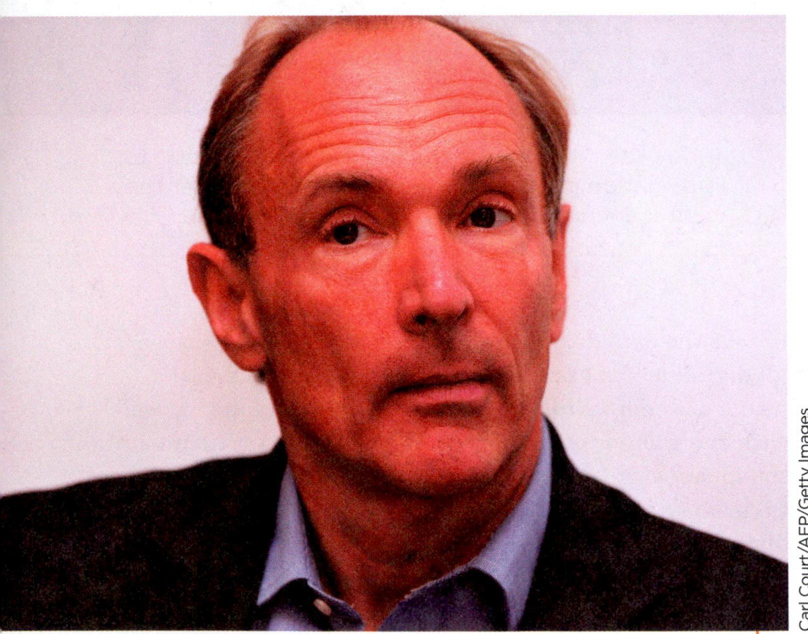

Carl Court/AFP/Getty Images

British computer scientist Tim Berners-Lee invented the World Wide Web and gave the Web its name. In 2008, Berners-Lee launched the World Wide Web Foundation to expand use of the Internet to developing countries.

Convergence The melding of the communications, computer and electronics industries.

Digital Media Support Convergence

In 1978, Nicholas Negroponte at the Massachusetts Institute of Technology was the first to identify a theory called ***convergence***. This theory gave a name to the process by which the various media industries in the late 1970s were beginning to intersect, and MIT was among the first places to foresee and identify this trend. (The concept of *convergence* also is discussed in **Chapter 1**.)

The media industries not only were combining economically, as media companies began to buy and sell each other, but the technology of the industries also was merging, according to MIT. This convergence meant that eventually the products the media companies produced began to resemble each other.

Negroponte also said that the combination of the traditional media industries with the computer industry would create a new type of communication.

To identify what was happening to the media industries, Negroponte created two models (see **Illustration 9.1**) to show the position of the media industries in 1978 and his projected vision for those industries in the year 2000. He listed three segments of the media business: (1) print and publishing, (2) broadcast and motion pictures and (3) the computer industry.

The first diagram in Negroponte's model displays the alignment of the media industries in 1978, which shows them with a small amount of integrated territory. In the second diagram, which shows Negroponte's predictions for the year 2000, the three segments of the media industries completely overlap. Negroponte's forecast was a very accurate prediction, and it helped establish the framework for today's thinking about the Internet.

This early economic and technological convergence in the media industries is the most important reason for the development of today's digital media. By the year 2000, every media industry was equally well positioned to take advantage of new developments, and every media industry benefits from convergence today.

20th-Century Discoveries Made Internet Possible

Several technological developments were necessary for people to be able to share text, graphics, audio and video online. These developments made the creation of the World Wide Web possible. The person most responsible for the World Wide Web is Tim Berners-Lee, a British native with an Oxford degree in physics. Working in 1989 in Geneva, Switzerland, at the CERN physics laboratory, Berners-Lee created several new programming languages.

Media/Impact
MONEY

Illustration 9.1

The Evolution of Today's Convergence: 1978 to 2012

The diagram on the left displays the alignment of the media in 1978, showing each media industry with very little overlapping territory. The middle diagram shows what MIT's Nicolas Negroponte predicted would happen by 2000, with the three types of industries—broadcast/motion pictures, printing/publishing and computers—merging further. The 2012 diagram shows what convergence looks like today—all three media segments have completely converged, with print, broadcast and movie industry products available through the Internet on a laptop computer, a tablet reader and a smartphone.

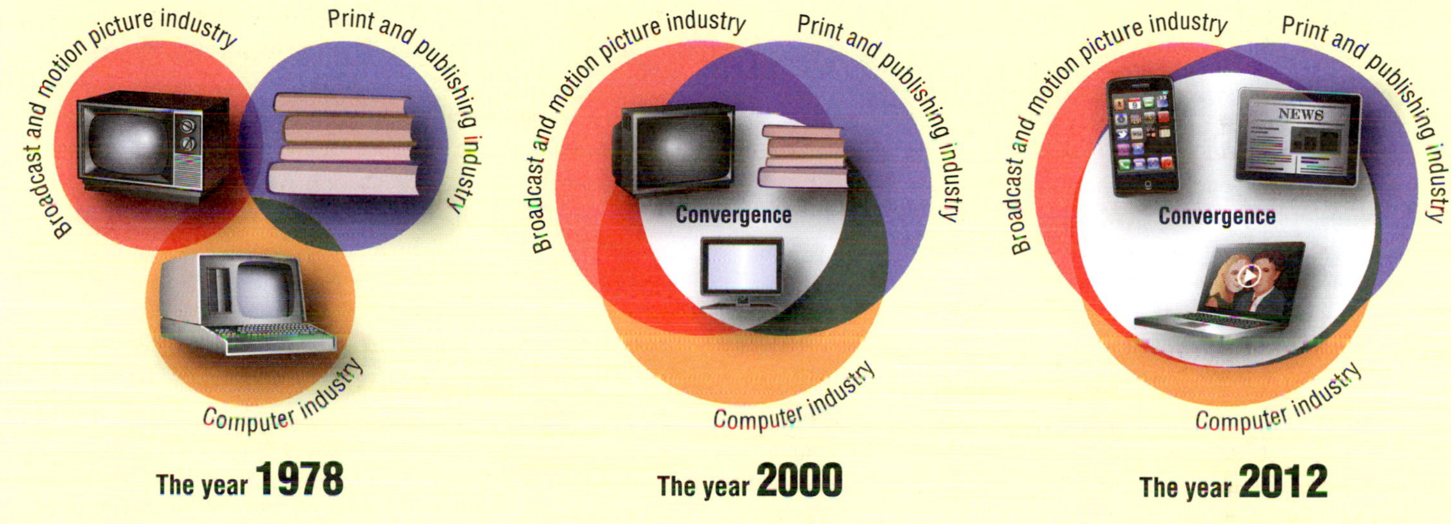

One of these new computer-programming languages was ***HTML*** (hypertext markup language). Hypertext transfer protocol (***HTTP***) allowed people to create and send text, graphics and video information electronically and also to set up electronic connections (called ***links***) from one source of information to another. These developments were very important in the Web's early days, and today people can create their own Web pages without knowing the programming language that made the Web possible.

After he invented the language and mechanisms that would allow people to share all kinds of information electronically, Berners-Lee gave this invention its name—the World Wide Web. "The original goal was working together with others," says Berners-Lee. "The Web was supposed to be a creative tool, an expressive tool." Berners-Lee also created the first ***browser***, which allows people to search electronically among many documents to find what they want.

Today, Berners-Lee still is involved in the Web's development, as founder of the World Wide Web Foundation, which promotes access to the Web throughout the world. "When you think about how the Web is today and dream about how it might be, you must, as always, consider both technology and people," says Berners-Lee. "Future technology should

HTML Hypertext markup language.

HTTP Hypertext transfer protocol.

Links Electronic connections from one source of information to another.

Browser Software that allows people to display and interact with information on Web pages.

"Cell phones! Get yer cell phones here! Cell phones!"

Liza Donnelly/Cartoonbank

be smarter and more powerful, of course. But you cannot ethically turn your attention to developing it without also listening to those people who don't use the Web at all, or who could use it if only it were different in some way. The Web has been largely designed by the developed world for the developed world. But it must be much more inclusive in order to be of great value to us all."

Marc Andreessen and his colleagues at the University of Illinois further defined the browser, and in 1994 they introduced software called Mosaic, which allowed people to put text and pictures in the same online document. Two of the successors to Mosaic are Mozilla Firefox and Internet Explorer, among the most widely used commercial browsers.

Another level of help for Web access is the ***search engine***. This tool locates information in computer databases. Two familiar search engines are Google and Yahoo! These systems turn your typed request for information into digital bits that then search for what you want and return the information to you. Yahoo!, founded in 1995 as a search engine company, today makes money through subscriptions, advertising and classified ads and employs more than 8,000 people around the world. Google, which has 20,000 employees, celebrated its tenth anniversary in 2008. Launched by entrepreneurs Larry Page and Sergey Brin in 1998 with four computers and $100,000, Google is now worth more than $150 billion.

To encourage people to use their systems, both Berners-Lee and Andreessen placed their discoveries in the ***public domain***, which means that anyone with a computer and a modem can download them from the Internet and use them for free. *This culture of free information access, coupled with a creative, chaotic lack of direction, still permeates the Web today.*

The process of putting documents on the Web drew its terminology from print, the original mass medium. That's why placing something on the Web is called ***publishing***, and the publication begins with a ***home page***, the front door to the site—the place that welcomes the user and explains how the site works. However, even though Web sites are similar to published documents in the way they work, what is created on the Web has few of the legal limitations or protections that apply to other published documents. (See **Chapter 14**.)

Search Engine The tool used to locate information in a computer database.

Public Domain Publications, products and processes that are not protected by copyright and thus are available free to the public.

Publishing Placing items on the Web.

Home Page The first page of a Web site, which welcomes the user.

Web Opens to Unlimited Access

Once Tim Berners-Lee had created the tools for access so that all types of text and video images could become available on the Web, it was left to anyone who could use the tools to create whatever they wanted and make it available to anyone who wanted it.

"Nobody ever designed the Web," says Canadian sociologist Craig McKie, who maintains his own Web site. "There are no rules, no laws. The Web also exists without national boundaries." Any type of information—video, audio, graphics and text—can travel virtually instantly to and from anyone with a computer and access to the Internet anywhere in the world.

Universal access, limited only by the available technology, is what gives the Web the feeling and look of what has been called "anarchy"—a place without rules. The Web is a new medium, but its growth as a true *mass medium* for people seeking information and entertainment is limited only by digital technology and economics. The large media companies have huge amounts of money available to bankroll new technologies. These companies also have a shared interest in seeing their investments succeed. So convergence is continuing at a very rapid pace, which is the main

Media/Impact CULTURE

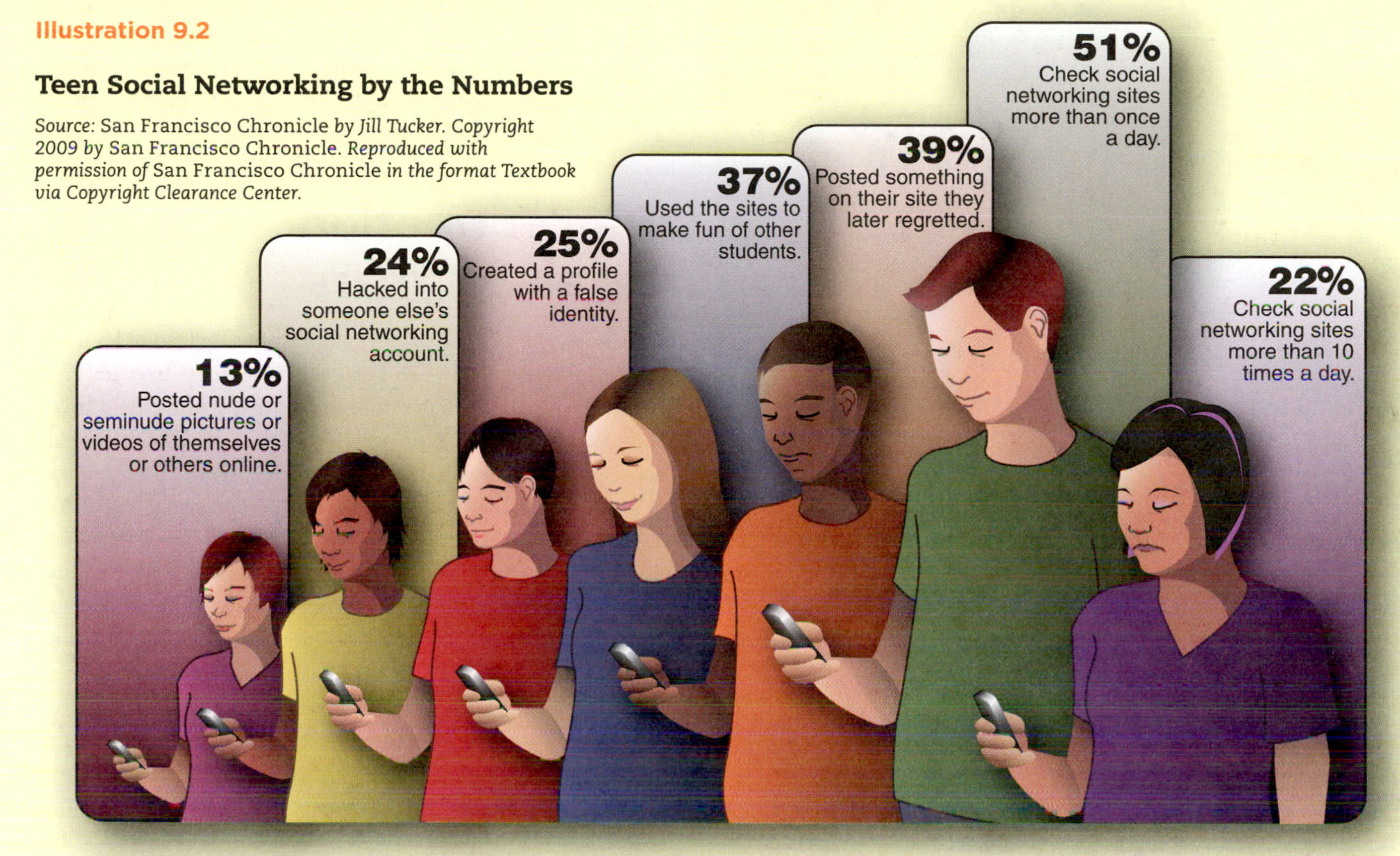
13%
Posted nude or seminude pictures or videos of themselves or others online.
24%
Hacked into someone else's social networking account.
25%
Created a profile with a false identity.
37%
Used the sites to make fun of other students.
39%
Posted something on their site they later regretted.
51%
Check social networking sites more than once a day.
22%
Check social networking sites more than 10 times a day.

Illustration 9.2

Teen Social Networking by the Numbers

Source: San Francisco Chronicle by Jill Tucker. Copyright 2009 by San Francisco Chronicle. Reproduced with permission of San Francisco Chronicle in the format Textbook via Copyright Clearance Center.

reason new digital media products are being introduced so quickly.

Some of the digital media products that flood the marketplace succeed, and many do not. However, the potential reward if consumers adopt a digital media product is so large that all types of media companies are willing to take the risks associated with developing new products. For consumers, this means an array of products bombarding the marketplace simultaneously, such as the iPad and Internet TV.

Media and computer entrepreneurs try to capitalize on fast-moving developments to be the first to deliver new creative products that large numbers of people will want to use, and society struggles to adjust to the access to communication that new products create. For example, some social networking sites, such as Facebook and MySpace, create a hazardous online environment for teenagers. (See **Illustration 9.2**.)

There are many parallels between the development of the Internet and the early history of traditional media, such as movies. Like traditional media, today's emerging technologies are being used to try to create a new popular product the public craves that will result in new consumer uses.

In the early 1900s, when movies first were introduced as flickering images on a small screen, the moving images were something consumers hadn't seen before, but many people thought the silent movies were just a passing fad (see **Chapter 7**). The inventions Thomas Edison and his colleagues introduced at the time made the movies technologically possible, but the movies also needed creative minds like director D. W. Griffith and stars like Mary Pickford to create epic stories that people wanted to see. When new inventions brought sound to the movies, the success of the new medium was unstoppable.

This combination of technological development, creative expression and consumer demand was crucial for the movies' enduring prosperity. The same collision of economics, technology and creativity that drove the early days of the movie industry is behind today's race to develop digital media.

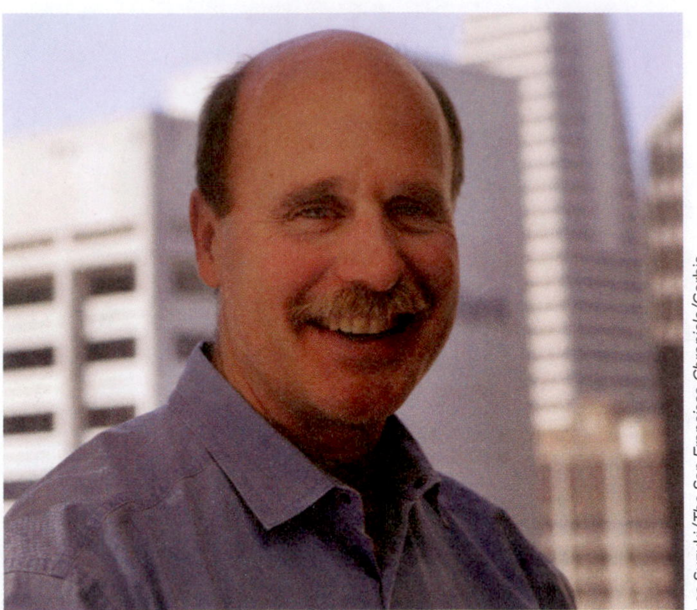
Lea Suzuki/The San Francisco Chronicle/Corbis

Forecaster Paul Saffo devised the 30-year-rule, which describes three stages of development for new technologies, from they time they are introduced to the time they are completely adopted by a culture.

What Happens to Old Media?

How does the development of digital media affect older, traditional media? Some observers have predicted, for example, that print media are dead, yet book sales continue to be steady and publishers have developed e-books to take advantage of the digital form. The history of the evolution of media shows that the introduction of a new medium or a new delivery system does not mean the end of the old. The continuous expansion of the media industries during the 20th century demonstrates this evolution.

When television was introduced, for example, radio did not disappear. Instead, radio adapted to its new place in the media mix, delivering music, news and talk. Today, radio exists very comfortably alongside television. Movies, which also were threatened by the introduction of television, responded by delivering more spectacular and more explicit entertainment than people could see on television, and today movies still play an important role in the business of media.

"When newer forms of communication media emerge, the older forms usually do not die—they continue to evolve and adapt," says Roger Fidler. The different media compete for the public's attention and jockey for positions of dominance, but no medium disappears. Instead, each medium contributes to the development of its successors. Together, all media that now exist will contribute to media forms that are yet to be invented.

30-Year Rule Developed by Paul Saffo, the theory that it takes about 30 years for a new technology to be completely adopted within a culture.

E-mail Mail that is delivered electronically over the Internet.

Transformation Takes 30 Years

Just how quickly consumers adopt new technologies is predictable, according to Paul Saffo, former director of the Institute for the Future in Menlo Park, Calif. Saffo theorizes that for the past five centuries the pace of change has always been 30 years, or about three decades, from the introduction of a new technology to its complete adoption by the culture.

Saffo calls his theory the ***30-year rule***, which he has divided into three stages, with each stage lasting about 10 years. In the first stage, he says, there is "lots of excitement, lots of puzzlement, not a lot of penetration." In the second stage, there is "lots of flux, penetration of the product into society is beginning." In the third stage, the reaction to the technology is, "Oh, so what? Just a standard technology and everybody has it." By Saffo's standard, American society is beginning the third stage of acceptance of online technology because use of the Internet by consumers began in 1988, when less than one-half of 1 percent of the U.S. population was on the Internet. Today, 79 percent of the U.S. population is online.

Saffo's description of the third decade of acceptance coincides with the adaptability of today's media marketplace. New media is more familiar, and people seem better able to incorporate combinations of new and existing media technology into their lives. (See **Media/Impact: People**, "Artful Entrepreneur Mike Richardson Finds Comic Book Success in Print, Movies and on the Internet," p. 193.) The technological transformation is starting to stabilize.

Web Access Leaves Some People Behind

The initial sign of the expansion of the Internet to consumer and educational users in the first decade of change—the early 1990s—was the adoption by businesses and private users of electronic mail, or ***e-mail***, technology. With a computer, a modem and a telephone line, just about anyone could learn how to communicate electronically online.

Media/Impact PEOPLE

Artful Entrepreneur Mike Richardson Finds Comic Book Success in Print, Movies and on the Internet

By Sarah E. Needleman

Dark Horse Comics

Conan Properties International, LLC.

Mike Richardson publishes Dark Horse Comics, which began in 1986 as a comic book store in a small Oregon town, and today is an integrated company that publishes comics, makes movies, and produces comic book downloads on the Internet, such as Conan.

Having studied art in college, as opposed to business, Mike Richardson considered himself an unlikely entrepreneur when he launched Dark Horse Comics in 1986. . . . The privately held concern, located in remote Milwaukie, OR, has become the third largest comics publisher in the U.S., raking in about $30 million in sales [in 2009]. . . .

And through its film division, Dark Horse Entertainment Inc., the company has produced more than two dozen movies, including *The Mask* and *Timecop*.

Dark Horse Comics evolved out of Mr. Richardson's first enterprise, a 400-square foot bookstore in Bend, Ore., that sold mostly comic books and sci-fi novels, which he funded with a credit card. . . .

Q: You used earnings from your stores to launch Dark Horse. What was your strategy for success in retail?

A: Back then, if you were an adult who read comics, you'd drive up to a 7-Eleven and wait until no one was there to buy them. You'd pay as fast as you could, put them in a paper bag and run out to your car. . . . So I tried to make a comics store that was comfortable for adults to walk into. . . .

Q: How did you go about producing your first comic book, *Dark Horse Presents*?

A: In mid-1985 I brought together a group of writers and artists I had met over the years and said I was planning to start publishing comics. It seemed like a screwy idea to most people that someone in Oregon could start a comics company, so as a show of good faith, I said I'd give them 100% of the profits of Dark Horse issue No. 1. We hoped to sell 10,000 copies and we sold 50,000.

Q: Consumers are increasingly reading books on electronic devices like the iPad. Has Dark Horse adapted accordingly?

A: We certainly had to come up with a way for our comics to be easily read on the iPad and we accomplished that by adapting material into single panels. You can enlarge the panels to the size you need, whatever feels comfortable. Those of us who remember buying comics off the rack when we were kids hang onto the old format. Now the kids coming up don't have the same affinity for a paper product and they're happy to get their comics on some kind of downloading device. . . .

Q: What advice do you have for aspiring entrepreneurs?

A: You need a great deal of optimism, almost to the point of blindness to the facts of reality. And you need confidence to get around whatever it is that's blocking you. . . . I was told growing up I could do anything I wanted. I worry sometimes that that message isn't out there anymore, because it really is true.

Sarah E. Needleman, "An Artful Entrepreneur Finds Comic Book Success," The Wall Street Journal, September 15, 2010. Reprinted with permission of The Wall Street Journal,

JOSHUA LOTT/*The New York Times*/Redux Pictures

Even though Internet access is everywhere, 21 percent of the U.S. population still have never gone online. The gap between people who have used the Internet and people who haven't is called the *digital divide*. Jerod Reyes (left) and Dylan Powell use their bus' Wi-Fi to do homework on their way to school.

"The driving force for achieving large subscriber gains is the incorporation of the Internet by consumers as part of their routine," according to Veronis Suhler Stevenson, a media research company. "The Internet has become a tool that allows users to economize on what has become their scarcest resource—time. Virtually all of the leading Internet applications allow users to accomplish tasks more quickly than they can through alternative means."

E-mail and text messaging at school, work or home still is the way most people first experience communicating in an electronic environment. Just as telephone answering machines in the 1970s changed voice communication by allowing people to send and receive messages on their own time schedule, e-mail and text messaging allow people to communicate and receive information at their convenience.

E-mail and text messaging are easy to use, and they are text-based systems, which means that people type in messages on a keyboard, a familiar tool. Familiarity and convenience are very important in the adoption of new technologies because people's fear of something they don't understand and misunderstandings about how new technologies work can keep them from changing their established habits.

Digital Divide The lack of access to digital technology among low-income, rural and minority groups.

ISP Internet service provider, also called an Internet access provider.

About 21 percent of all Americans still do not go online—either because they can't afford it or they're afraid of it or they don't have access. This gap between people who have online access and those who don't is called the ***digital divide***. According to the Pew Internet and American Life Project, one out of five American adults say they have never used the Internet or e-mail and do not live in an Internet-connected household.

Pew calls these people "truly disconnected adults"—people with less than a high school education, or who are over 65, or who live in a rural area. "Americans who are over the age of 65 or who have less education are the most likely to be completely disconnected from the Internet," says Susannah Fox, associate director of the Pew Internet Project. "If they needed to get information from a Web site or other online source, they probably could not easily do so."

Internet Combines Commerce, Information and Entertainment

What makes the Web as a mass medium different from traditional media is its capacity to combine commerce with access to information and entertainment. People not only can buy products on the Web, but they can also learn new things and enjoy themselves.

Most people use an Internet service provider (***ISP***, also called an Internet access provider), such as a telephone, satellite or cable company, to organize and deliver Internet information and entertainment. Today, the largest single source of Web income is the money people pay their ISP to connect to the Web. There are three other potential sources of income on the Web: promoting commerce (connecting sellers with potential buyers), accepting advertising and providing online content.

Promoting Commerce

"Millions of Internet users are forsaking yard sales and the local dump for the prospect of selling their hand-me-downs and unwanted gear online," according to a report by the Pew Internet and American Life Project. "About one in six Internet-using adults have sold something online." This recent success of the Internet as a way for people to sell things is only one example of the Internet's potential as a marketplace.

The most resilient commercial Internet operation is *Amazon*. It began as a place where people could buy media products such as books, CDs and DVDs, but today consumers also can shop on Amazon for just about anything—clothes, cosmetics and sports equipment, for example—often at discount prices from individuals as well as large retailers, such as Target. Amazon has grown into an Internet department store.

Small retailers and even individual consumers also can use the Web to sell products directly, without setting up a store or spending a lot of money on expensive advertising. Another Internet commerce success story is *eBay*, a Web site that began about 25 years ago as a place where individual sellers offered products—mostly collectibles—in an online auction atmosphere.

Today, eBay is another vast marketplace where individuals sell collectibles, but eBay also promotes direct consumer-to-consumer sales for products as varied as cars, houses, even used jeans. Most individual sellers on the site do not have retail stores. Their only outlet is eBay, yet the Internet gives eBay sellers access to buyers all over the world.

Convenience, reliability and affordability sustain both these Web sites as successful commercial ventures—two examples of new businesses that could not survive without the Internet. "On the Internet, consumers looking for a particular product or service can shop over the entire country—the entire world—looking at photographs and comparing prices, features and terms, and then buy what they want with a credit card and arrange to have the purchase delivered to their home," says *Los Angeles Times* media critic David Shaw.

Accepting Advertising

When television was introduced to the public in the late 1940s, people assumed from the beginning that it would be a commercial medium—that is, advertisers who bought the commercials surrounding the programs would pay for the programming. This concept of using advertising to underwrite TV programs was a natural evolution from radio, where commercials also paid for the programming.

Advertisers follow the audience, so as consumers migrated to the Web, advertisers have tried to figure out how to follow them. Advertising is the second potential source of income on the Web. (See **Illustration 9.3**.)

Most commercial Web sites now carry some form of advertising. These appear as banners across the top of the Web site or run as borders alongside the site's pages. But just like traditional media, advertising can crowd out the original message and turn away consumers, and entrepreneurs continue to test the market to develop a Web site advertising structure and design that eventually will help pay the bills.

Because the Web is such a targeted medium—the seller can know exactly who the buyer is—the Web holds better potential for monitoring consumers' buying habits than traditional methods of advertising. Ultimately, Web advertisers hope to "achieve the merchandiser's dream—targeting an audience far more precisely than it can with either newspapers or television by advertising a product only on sites that draw people likely to be interested in that product," says media critic David Shaw, with "nearly instantaneous electronic feedback on whether their ads are effective: How many people saw the ad? How many 'clicked' on it and went on to a more detailed presentation? How many bought the product right then, online?"

Internet "tracking" offers advertisers information about the audiences for their ads. Many sites give advertisers information about how many "hits" the sites receive—how many times people look at the site and how much time they spend. This information-gathering is so sophisticated that the data can even show an advertiser which specific user bought which specific products that were advertised on a specific site.

Companies also have developed "ad robots" that allow a business to, in effect, eavesdrop on chat room conversations while the user is online. If someone mentions a car problem online, for example, the robot recognizes the pattern of words in the discussion and sends the person an ad for car repair.

Always looking for new ways to target specific audiences, advertising agencies now offer services for ***search marketing***, which means placing client ads next to consumers' online search results so that when someone starts a search for SUVs, for example, the SUV car manufacturer's ad immediately appears on the screen next to the user's search results. Appearing within the SUV ad, of course, is a link to a Web site where the user can customize and order a car. By connecting consumers directly to advertisers, search marketers say, they can better trace and document the connection between Internet ads and their audiences, something many advertisers are demanding before they invest in the Internet audience.

Ad robots and search marketing are just two examples of the refined tools advertisers are developing so they can more accurately track and target the Internet consumer.

Paying for Online Content

The culture of the Web began with the idea that content on the Web would be free, so it has taken a long time for

Search Marketing Positioning Internet advertising prominently next to consumers' related online search results.

Media/Impact MONEY

Illustration 9.3

How Much Do Businesses Spend Annually to Advertise on the Internet (in billions)?

Since 2000, advertisers have been racing to reach consumers by advertising products and services on the Internet. The amount that companies spend to advertise on the Internet today has more than tripled since the year 2000.

Source: D. Chmielewski, "Online Advertising to Reach $31 Billion in 2011," June 8, 2011, Latimes.com.

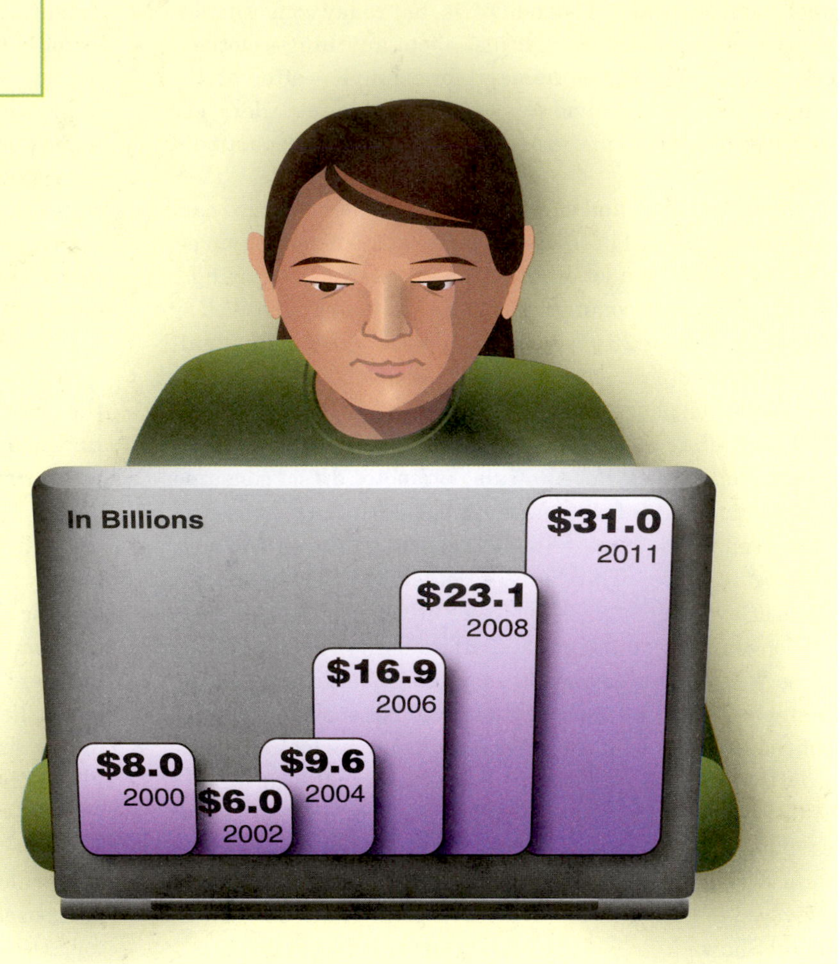

consumers to embrace the idea that they should pay for media content on the Web.

Slate, the online literary magazine, tried to start charging subscribers in 1997, but then decided against it. Editor Michael Kinsley said, "It would be better to establish a brand name with wide readership first." *Slate* celebrated its fifteenth anniversary in 2010 and still does not charge subscribers.

Some explicit Web sites charge for access, and some news and information sites, such as *The Wall Street Journal*, charge subscribers an annual fee for access to archived online content older than seven days—beyond what's available free on the main *Journal* news site. *The New York Times* began charging for access to its site in 2011. Other sites, such as the sports network ESPN, give away some information and then charge for "premium" services. Internet game-makers, who offer video games on the Web, charge by the hour or use a tiered pricing structure—free, basic and premium.

In 2003, consumers showed they were willing to pay for music downloads when Apple founder Steve Jobs introduced iTunes, a music service for subscribers that allows people to download popular songs for a fee. Less than a year after its launch, iTunes celebrated its one-billionth music download. (See **Media/Impact: Culture,** "How Steve Jobs Put Passion Into Products," p. 199.)

In 2010, when Apple introduced the iPad, a tablet, offering many more functions than its predecessor from Amazon, the Kindle, Apple sold 500,000 iPads in the first week. Tablet devices offer another outlet for purchased media. Book downloads sell for about $10, bringing a new source of revenue for book publishers.

The largest single source of new revenue generated by the Internet comes from the development and sale of video games. The video game industry is a hybrid that combines equipment (such as Xbox and PlayStation), software and Internet downloads. According to the Entertainment Software Association, computer and video game sales in the

U.S. generated $10.5 billion in 2009, and more than two-thirds of all American households own video games.

Originally appealing to a younger audience, offering war games for adults and other animated products for children, today's video game companies recently broadened their audience significantly by producing nonviolent kinetic games, such as Nintendo's Wii and Microsoft's Kinect. "The industry is saying we care about hard-core fans, but we have to go after the wide audience," says Brian Crescente, editor in chief of gaming Web site Kotaku.

The shift is also economic—a way to escape the industry's reputation for exploiting violence by producing only "shooter" games. One of the reasons for expansion to establish a wider consumer base is that the industry is facing a precedent-setting challenge before the U.S. Supreme Court. In 2005, the California legislature passed a law that banned the sale of violent video games to minors. The video game industry portrayed the law as a threat to First Amendment freedoms, and in 2011 the court ruled that the ban violated free speech rights.

Justin Sullivan/Getty Images

On April 20, 2010, customers at an Apple store in San Francisco get their first look at the new iPad. Increasingly, Internet entrepreneurs are catering to mobile media users.

Mobile Media Chase the Audience

Internet receivers have grown smaller and smaller, and the latest big target for expanding Internet media sales is the cell phone. Much like radio broadcasters who followed radio listeners from their homes into their cars when car radios were invented, Web site businesses are chasing today's consumers right to their cell phones.

The nation's millions of cell phone users make mobile media consumers an inviting target. Consumers use cell phones to send text messages, take pictures, access the Internet and record video. This makes Smartphones and other mobile media devices attractive media markets. (See **Illustration 9.4**.)

Mobile media content has restrictions—content must be audible and/or clearly visible in the small viewing space of a cell phone screen. News and sports bulletins, short video clips, podcasts, blogs and personalized Web pages are perfectly suited for this media environment. "Advances in high-speed data networks, along with powerful new cell phones, are unlocking the promise of mobile television," reports the *San Francisco Chronicle*. Subscription video services charge customers a fee and offer stored content such as one-minute soap operas and animated cartoons.

All four of the major TV networks and most subscription channels now offer most of their entertainment programs and news video online, on demand, for computer and cell phone viewing.

Podcasts

Podcasting is the distribution of an audio or video file by online syndication, usually by subscription. With very little equipment, people can create and syndicate their own ***podcasts***. Many news organizations, such as PBS and *The New York Times*, have added podcasts to their Web sites as a way to expand their offerings.

A podcast often enhances and expands discussion on a topic. There also are podcast networks that feature several shows on the same feed, similar to a radio station. Consumers can download podcasts and listen to them whenever and

Podcast An audio or video file made available on the Internet for anyone to download, often available by subscription.

Media/Impact AUDIENCE

Illustration 9.4

How Do People Use Mobile Media?

Consumer use of mobile media is the fastest-growing area of media use. People most often use mobile media, such smartphones and cell-phones, to send and receive text messages, take pictures, access the Internet, play games and listen to music.

Source: The Pew Research Center's Internet & American Life Project, April 26–May 22, 2011, Spring Tracking Survey. http://pewinternet.org/Reports/2011/.

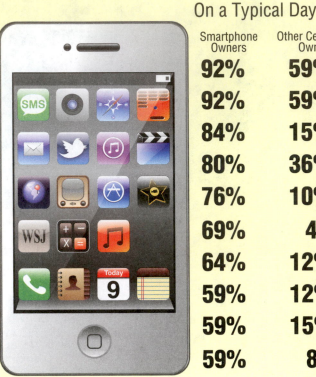

On a Typical Day . . .

Smartphone Owners	Other Cell phone Owners	
92%	59%	Send or Receive Text Messages
92%	59%	Take Still Pictures
84%	15%	Access the Internet
80%	36%	Send a Photo or Video to Someone
76%	10%	Send or Receive E-mail
69%	4%	Download an App
64%	12%	Play a Game
59%	12%	Play Music
59%	15%	Record Video Clips
59%	8%	Access a Social Networking Site

wherever they want, which also makes podcasts an ideal way to reach a mobile audience.

Blogs

By one estimate, 80,000 new blog sites are launched daily, and the blog search engine Technorati tracks 29 million blog sites. A ***blog*** (short for Web log) is an online discussion group where people can post comments about a topic in a running conversation with each other.

The text of the blog runs in reverse chronological order, with the most recent comments posted at the top of the blog so people can choose to read through the previous postings for background on the topic, or they can start reading what follows after they join the group. Typically blogs do not carry advertising and are created as a way to enhance other content on the Web.

Blogs also have become frequent sources of information for news organizations seeking public reaction to ongoing events. The 2004 presidential election was the first time bloggers actually were accredited as part of the presidential press corps, indicating the importance of the bloggers' role as commentators on topical issues.

Blog Short for Web log. A running Internet discussion group, where items are posted in reverse chronological order. Blogs usually focus on a specific topic.

Avatar An icon or a representation of a user—a digital stand-in—that people create to represent their online identity.

Personalized Web Pages

While businesses and tech-savvy Internet users can easily create Web sites, new technology now allows neophytes to create personal Web sites, using prepackaged programs, in less than five minutes. MySpace and Facebook, currently the most successful personal Web site spaces, are aimed primarily at teens and young adults who want to join a social network. In 2010, Facebook announced that it had 500 million users.

Using click technology, users can create an ***avatar***, an online personality complete with a "look" that personalizes

Media/Impact CULTURE

How Steve Jobs Put Passion into Products

By James B. Stewart

...How did [Steve Jobs] take a commodity—to borrow from the novelist Tom Wolfe, the "veal gray" plastic boxes that once weighed so heavily on both our desks and spirits—and turn it into one of the most iconic and desirable objects on the planet?

Bloomberg via Getty Images

On October 6, 2011, a man in Hong Kong, China, watches a TV screen reporting the death of Apple CEO Steve Jobs at age 56.

"Steve Jobs and Apple never—ever—wanted to be a low-margin commodity producer," Donald Norman, a former vice president for advanced technology at Apple and author of *Living With Complexity*, told me this week.... Steve was always, if not an artist, then someone who was charmed by style. He had this dream of something beautiful. If it was going to cost more, it didn't matter. This was in his genes."

Paola Antonelli, senior curator of architecture and design at the Museum of Modern Art in New York, recalled buying a 1990 Macintosh Classic and taking it back to Italy. "When I got home, I took it out of that brown, padded carrying case with the rainbow-colored Apple logo on it and put it on my desk in Milan. It was like a little pug dog looking at me. It wasn't just something I worked with; it kept me company. It had such personality and such life."

Mr. Jobs "had an exceptional eye for design, and not just an eye, but an intelligence for design," Ms. Antonelli said. "We don't talk just about the looks, but how objects communicate: The specific shape, how it feels in the hand, under the fingers, how you read it in the eye and the mind. This is what Steve cared passionately about...."

"Most people underestimate his grandeur and his greatness," Gadi Amit, founder and principal designer of New Deal Design in San Francisco, told me. "They think it's about design. It's beyond design. It's completely holistic, and it's dogmatic. Things need to be high quality; they have to have poetry and culture in each step. Steve was cut from completely different cloth from most business leaders. He was not a number-crunching guy; he was not a technologist. He was a cultural leader, and he drove Apple from that perspective. He started with culture; then followed with technology and design. No one seems to get that."

Mr. Amit says he believes Mr. Jobs's legacy will be "the blending of technology and poetry. It's not about design per se; it's the poetic aspect of the entire enterprise. Compared to Bill Gates or Warren Buffett, he's in a different class. I think this is a revolutionary shift. Jobs is a revolutionary character. He shifted the industry and changed our lives through this amalgamation of culture and technology. If you're looking for CEOs of this caliber, you have to look outside the engineering and business schools. That is truly revolutionary."

"He was really unique, brilliant, demanding and difficult," Mr. Norman said. "Like him or not, it doesn't matter; he redefined the music industry, the cell phone industry, computers and animation. You cannot deny the impact he had on the company, the industry and our culture."

the page, and create a short blog to post personal messages. Avatar images fit perfectly on a cell phone screen to accompany a teen's short diary-style postings about daily life. The ad-supported sites also offer custom features, such as music downloads and games.

Podcasts, blogs and personal Web sites are the latest ways the media business is working to expand its audience. It's important to remember that, in the history of the media business, advertisers always have followed consumers. To be successful, Internet providers know they must attract customers to be able to capitalize on the advertising potential the audience brings with it.

Government Attempts to Coordinate and Control the Net

The federal government has attempted to coordinate and regulate the Internet in the same way government traditionally coordinated and regulated the broadcast media in its early days. However, the U.S. government has learned the hard way that it can exercise only limited control over the Internet, especially its content.

In 1994, in its first attempt to coordinate the growing presence of the Internet, the U.S. Congress named the effort to coordinate the nation's various senders, channels and receivers in the United States the National Information Infrastructure (***NII***). This congressional intervention in the structure of the Internet was based on the history of radio and TV in the United States, which the government had regulated since the 1920s.

Three principles guided the creation of the nation's telecommunications structure, Congress said:

1. Private industry, not the government, would build the digital network.
2. Programmers and information providers would be guaranteed access to the digital network to promote a diversity of consumer choices.
3. Steps would be taken to ensure universal service so that the digital network did not result in a society of information "haves" and "have-nots."

NII National Information Infrastructure.

CDA Communications Decency Act.

Intellectual Property Rights The legal right of ownership of ideas and content published in any medium.

Then two years later, in its first attempt to control Internet content, Congress passed the Telecommunications Act of 1996. Included in that legislation was the Communications Decency Act (***CDA***), which outlined content that would be forbidden on the Internet. As soon as the act passed, civil liberties organizations challenged the law, and in 1997 the U.S. Supreme Court upheld the concept that the U.S. government could not control Internet content. (For more information about Congress and the U.S. Supreme Court's view of the Internet, see **Chapter 14**.)

A recent challenge to Internet content came in 2005, when California passed a law prohibiting video game sales to minors. Federal courts declared the law unconstitutional, saying that the law interfered with freedom of expression, but the state appealed the law to the U.S. Supreme Court, which heard the case in November 2010. The court's decision, which will be announced in 2011, should have a wide-ranging effect on the video game industry.

Protection Sought for Intellectual Property Rights

Money is the main reason the government wants to supervise the development of the Internet. Digitized bits, once they are widely available, can be easily stolen and reproduced for profit, which can means billions of dollars in lost revenue for the companies and individuals who produce media content. Writers, moviemakers, singers and other creative people who provide the content for the media industries are especially concerned about their ideas being reproduced in several different formats, with no compensation for their property.

This issue, the protection of what are called ***intellectual property rights***, is a crucial part of the U.S. government's interest in the design of the Internet as a communications network. To protect online content, the various copyright holders have used court challenges to establish their legal ownership, but some groups still are trying to avoid detection by keeping their online activities hidden from government scrutiny.

With access to copyrighted digital content, someone could capture video from a Disney movie sent over the Internet and join sections of that video with comedy bits from an episode of *Saturday Night Live*, putting the two casts together in a newly digitized program, for example. Once this content is captured and stored, it would be available to anyone who wants to use it.

The protection of content is one of the dilemmas created by digitized files that can be transmitted to anyone's storage system over an international network. The creative people who contribute this content, and the people who produce and own these programs, want laws and regulations structured to protect intellectual property rights.

Court Copyright Challenges

The issue of who owns copyrighted material that already exists, such as recordings and movies, is particularly tricky on a medium like the Internet with few controls and global access. In 1998, Congress passed the Digital Millennium Copyright Act (***DMCA***) to make it illegal to share copyrighted material on the Internet. (For more information about the DMCA, see **Chapter 14**.) Using this law and provisions of existing copyright law, industries with a big stake in content ownership have sued to stop people from sharing copyrighted content on the Internet.

William Haefeli/Cartoonbank

"Don't look. It's the people we steal Wi-Fi from."

The Recording Industry Association of America (***RIAA***) and the Motion Picture Association of America (***MPAA***) have been especially aggressive in seeking to prosecute people who make copyrighted content available on the Web. In 1999, RIAA sued Napster, a company that provided a music-swapping service on the Internet. In 2001, after several appeals, the courts found that Napster was liable for "vicarious copyright infringement." Napster eventually shut down and then reopened as a subscription music service that pays royalties to companies that own rights to music available on the site.

MP3 technology allows users to convert songs on their CDs to MP3 files, which can be circulated freely on the Internet. The Web site MP3.com began as an underground movement in San Diego in 1999 among college students and spread fiercely. The major recording companies quickly began an all-out assault on MP3.com, suing for copyright infringement, and in November 2000, in a series of settlements, MP3.com agreed to pay more than $70 million in damages to the recording companies for the rights to license their music.

In 2001, the MPAA sued to stop publication of the code that allows a person to copy DVDs and place digital copies of the movies on the Internet. The court agreed with the MPAA, saying that even if people possess the code but don't use it, they are committing piracy. This was an important legal precedent for content sharing on the Web and has led to more corporate attempts to seek wider protections over copyrighted content.

In 2003, Apple launched iTunes, a service that charges a fee to download songs legally. iTunes was created to respond to the various court actions since 1999 designed to end illegal ***file sharing***, which means downloading files placed on the Internet by another person, not necessarily the original copyright holder.

In 2005, the music-file-sharing network, Grokster shut down after reaching a settlement with the movie and music industries about online piracy. Grokster replaced its popular Web site with the message "There are legal services for downloading music and movies. This service is not one of them."

In 2010, a federal judge ordered the major remaining music-file-sharing service, LimeWire, to shut its Web site. The court order required that LimeWire disable "searching, downloading, uploading, file trading and/or file distribution functionality." The same day, LimeWire posted a legal notice that said "This is an official notice that LimeWire is under a court-ordered injunction to stop distributing and supporting its file-sharing software. Downloading or sharing copyrighted content without authorization is illegal." (For more information about file sharing and iTunes, see **Chapter 14**.)

DMCA Digital Millennium Copyright Act.

RIAA Recording Industry Association of America.

MPAA Motion Picture Association of America.

File Sharing The peer-to-peer distribution of copyrighted material on the Internet without the copyright owner's permission.

Mark Wilson/Getty Images

FCC chairman Julius Genachowski has proposed Net neutrality rules to ensure that telecommunications companies maintain open Internet access for consumers.

FCC Proposes Internet Neutrality

In October 2009, the Federal Communications Commission (FCC) outlined proposed rules for Internet service providers that require that they keep their networks open and available to carry all legal content from all carriers. These provisions, called Internet neutrality (often referred to as ***Net neutrality***), mean that telecommunications companies, such as AT&T and Verizon, would have to maintain an open network. They could not restrict access by other providers to their network nor could they limit the type or delivery of content they carry.

The FCC said the new rules would mean that an Internet service provider

1. Would not be allowed to prevent any of its users from sending or receiving the lawful content of the user's choice over the Internet.
2. Would not be allowed to prevent any of its users from running the lawful applications or using the lawful services of the user's choice.
3. Would not be allowed to prevent any of its users from connecting to and using on its network the user's choice of lawful devices that do not harm the network.
4. Would not be allowed to deprive any of its users of the user's entitlement to competition among network providers, application providers, service providers and content providers.
5. Would be required to treat lawful content, applications and services in a nondiscriminatory manner.
6. Would be required to disclose such information concerning network management and other practices as is reasonably required for users and content, application, and service providers to enjoy the protections specified in this rule-making.

These proposed rules would mean, for example, that manufacturers such as Apple could not require iPhone users to sign up exclusively with AT&T. People with iPhones and Blackberries would be able to use any carrier they chose. In announcing the neutrality rules, FCC Chairman Julius Genachowski said, "Government should not be in the business of running or regulating the Internet." This signals that, under the Obama administration, the federal government plans minimal interference with consumer access to Internet content, a shift from earlier government attempts to restrict it.

Net Neutrality Rules for Internet service providers that require them to keep their networks open and available to carry all legal content. Under these rules, providers cannot restrict access to their network by other providers nor can they limit the type or delivery of content they carry.

Spam Unsolicited bulk e-mail.

Internet Faces Four Challenges

Today, the Internet has evolved into a wireless delivery system, but the system faces at least four major challenges: open access, storage capacity, compatible delivery and consumer privacy.

Open Access

To protect their subscribers from too much unsolicited e-mail (called ***spam***) or to weed out offensive e-mails, many

Internet service providers (ISPs) use spam filters—technology that allows the ISP to block messages using software that tags suspicious messages, which the ISP filters before delivering, or stopping, them. Of the 135 billion e-mail messages sent every day in 2005, two-thirds of them were spam, according to Radicati Group, a technology research firm. However, many nonprofit organizations and political groups use bulk e-mail to solicit donations and support.

Like many other Internet service providers, AOL uses spam filters to block unwanted mail, but in 2006 AOL announced that it would start offering a service that would allow bulk e-mailers to send e-mail directly to users' mailboxes without passing through AOL's spam filters. AOL said bulk e-mailers who paid the fee would receive a label alerting recipients that the messages were legitimate. Immediately, several interest groups—including the conservative activist group RightMarch.com, the liberal activist group MoveOn.org and the U.S. Humane Society—joined an alliance to fight the fee, calling it a tax on free expression and free access.

In another instance of commercial expediency, online search leader Google agreed in 2006 to censor online search results for its Chinese clients. According to Associated Press, Google was "adhering to the country's [China's] free-speech restrictions in return for better access in the Internet's fastest growing market." Google agreed to omit Web content that the Chinese government found objectionable.

Yahoo! and MSN previously had agreed to similar restrictions in China. Reporters Without Borders criticized the practice, saying, "When a search engine collaborates with the government like this, it makes it much easier for the Chinese government to control what is being said on the Internet."

Fox-Walden/Everett Collection

Data-compression technology reduces the electronic storage space necessary to store full-length animated movies such as *The Chronicles of Narnia: The Voyage of the Dawn Treader*. This makes it possible for consumers to download first-run original movies to view online.

Storage Capacity

The main technological advance that makes today's communications network possible is that electronic systems transform text, audio and video communication into the same type of digital information. However, no single consumer system exists to transfer all the text, audio and video information the Internet delivers from so many different sources. Digital systems theoretically should be compatible, but many places in the world and many media systems have not yet totally converted to the technology that efficient digital delivery requires.

For example, digital delivery requires a huge amount of electronic storage space. To try to eliminate the need for so much storage, researchers are developing a process called ***data compression***. A copy of a major movie, such as *Up*, contains about 100 billion bytes of data. Compression squeezes the content down to about 4 billion bytes. But the time it takes to download a movie on a personal computer and the electronic storage space movies need can make it impractical for the average consumer. Researchers' work on data compression should solve the space requirement problem.

As soon as researchers perfect data compression, it will mean that a movie program service, for example, will need much less storage space to keep movies available for use on demand. This helps make the movie affordable for a

Data Compression The process of squeezing digital content into a smaller electronic space.

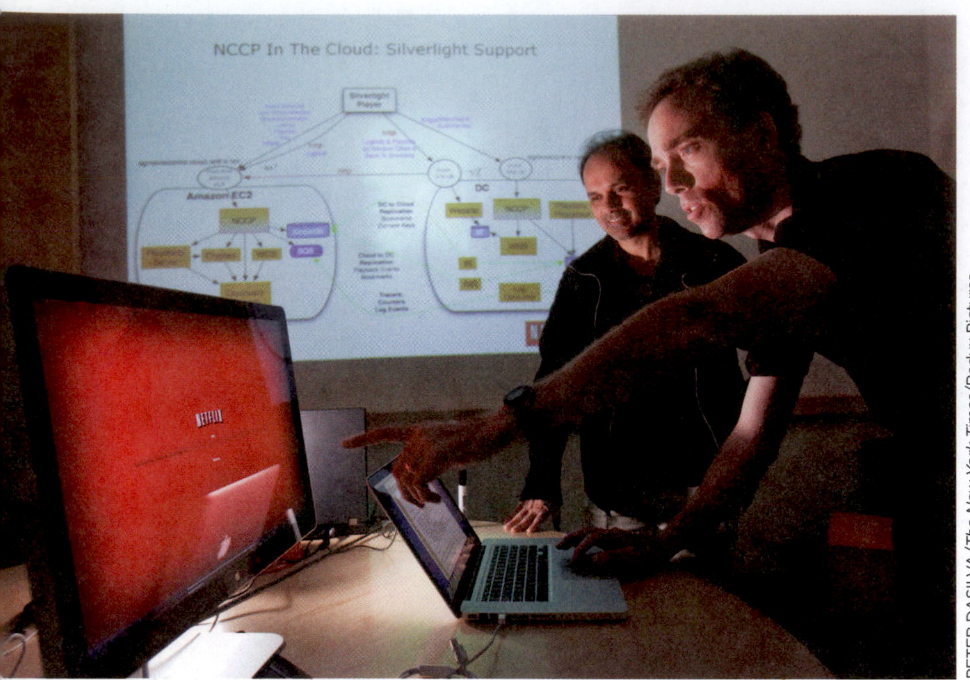

PETER DASILVA/*The New York Times*/Redux Pictures

The latest innovation in data storage is *cloud computing*. This allows one company to use another company's computer system, transferring their information through the Internet to a "cloud"—the second company's secure online network. Netflix systems engineers Kevin McEntee (left) and Santosh Rau, use Amazon's cloud network to manage Netflix's program delivery.

program service to deliver and usable for the customer, who won't need as much data space to view the movie.

Once the data is compressed, the company that delivers the service also must store the data. The next step in the process is a machine that grabs a movie the consumer has selected from a storage area and delivers it to the customer on request. This transfer machine is called a ***server*** because it must be able to serve thousands of programs to millions of subscribers, on demand, all at the same time.

The newest innovation in data storage is called ***cloud computing***, which allows one business to rent remote use of another company's computer space, operating "in the cloud." In 2011, Apple launched iCloud. Other large companies like Microsoft and Google, that can handle massive amounts of data over an online network, now provide cloud computing services to users who would rather share someone else's computer hardware than build their own.

Compatible Delivery

Today's communication system is a mixture of old and new technologies. The current delivery system is a combination of coaxial cable, copper wire, fiber optics and cellular technology. Before the new communications network will be complete, new technology must completely replace old technology throughout the system. Many broadcasters, for example, still send pictures and sounds over airwaves using the same technology they have used since the 1930s, when broadcasting was first introduced. This technology is called ***analog***.

Analog technology encodes video and audio information as continuous signals. Then these signals are broadcast through the air on specific airwave frequencies to your TV set, which translates them into pictures and sounds. Analog technology is a very cumbersome way to move information from one place to another because the analog signal takes up a lot of space on the airwaves. However, because analog signals travel through the air by transmitters, consumers can receive them free by using an antenna.

At least 10 million homes in the United States still receive only over-the-air broadcasts. They do not subscribe to cable or satellite. And although the federal government mandated that TV stations in large cities digitize their signals by 2009, by 2011 some smaller stations still had not made the costly transition to digital.

Cable companies eliminated the need for antennas by using coaxial cable, buried underground or strung from telephone poles. Many coaxial cable systems still use analog technology. Cable operators capture programming, such as HBO, from satellite systems and put these together with analog broadcast signals from your local TV stations and then deliver all this programming to you, using a combination of coaxial cable, copper wire and optical fiber.

Optical fiber is composed of microscopic strands of glass that transmit messages in digitized "bits"—zeroes and ones. Each fiber-optic strand can carry 250,000 times as much information as one copper wire. It can transmit the entire contents of the *Encyclopaedia Britannica* in one second. A fiber-optics communication system is very efficient because fiber can carry digitized information easily and quickly from one place to another.

Server The equipment that delivers programs from their source to the programs' subscribers.

Cloud Computing The remote use by one business of another company's computer space, operating "in the cloud."

Analog In mass communications, a type of technology used in broadcasting, whereby video or audio information is sent as continuous signals through the air on specific airwave frequencies.

Satellite program services use digital signals to carry their programming. Programs that are delivered to a home satellite dish follow a wireless electronic journey from the program source through one of the many telecommunications satellites hovering around the globe. Satellite delivery, however, still requires a telephone line connection to deliver the programs and the menus for the programs to your home receiver.

Telephone companies have converted almost all their major communications delivery systems from coaxial cable and copper wire to fiber optics and cellular technology. However, the incompatibility between analog and digital technology means that all analog signals must be converted first to digital signals to be able to travel smoothly to everyone. Conversion is very expensive.

Digital technology is the most efficient method of delivery, but making the same system available throughout the nation using a standardized delivery system is very complicated, and each competing system wants to control the entire delivery system because control of the delivery system means billions of dollars in revenue for whichever system consumers eventually adopt.

Alistair Baker/CORBIS

The transition to total digital delivery must overcome the incompatibility of traditional media systems with new technology. For example, at least 10 million homes in the U.S. still receive television over the air by antenna, which accounts for the mix of satellite dishes and antennas on this roof. Until all equipment is compatible and digital, the delivery system remains a mix of old and new technologies.

Personal Privacy

With all these media services and programs available, consumers must be able to use them without compromising their personal privacy. Telephone companies already have in place a fairly complex system that matches people with the phone calls they make and carries conversations on secure lines all over the world. To be effective, security for digital communications on the Internet must be at least as private as telephone communications.

Commercial operations, such as banks and retailers, have developed fairly secure systems for transferring transaction records on the Internet. Internet services such as PayPal offer buyers a way to protect their credit card information from being circulated to sellers by processing the transaction without sharing the consumers' credit card information with the seller.

To protect consumers' banking records, for example, banks use codes to secure the transactions from Internet hackers. Software companies have developed reliable systems to ensure that the personal records and content contained in interactive transactions are safe. An entirely new industry has evolved dedicated to the issue of Internet data security.

In 2006, however, questions erupted about government access to Internet communications. The U.S. Justice Department subpoenaed Google Inc., asking the company to provide records of millions of its customers' Internet search requests. The government said it needed the records to prove that existing Internet spam filters were preventing children from accessing online pornography and potentially offensive Web sites.

Yahoo!, MSN and Time Warner already had provided some of the search engine information the government wanted, but Google initially refused, setting the stage for another confrontation pitting the government against at least one Internet service provider. "If users believe that the text of their search queries into Google's search engine may become public knowledge, it only logically follows that they will be less likely to use the service," Google's lawyers argued.

In March 2006, in the first court hearing about the government's request, the government reduced its initial request to a sample of 5,000 search queries instead of its earlier request for a week's worth of searches, which would have totaled close to a billion items. The Justice Department also offered to pay Google's costs to provide the data, and eventually Google agreed to provide the 5,000-item search sample.

MANUEL BRUQUE/epa/Corbis

Virtual reality systems give the user the experience of being somewhere else by creating a digital environment and then placing the digital representative (an avatar) in the new reality. In 2010, a woman uses a virtual reality setup at Valencia College in Spain to take a simulated trip to Mars.

The case shows how tempting and accessible digital data can be—for the government agencies and for attorneys. The judge in the Google case said he tried to balance privacy concerns with the government's request for information, but privacy advocates worry that relinquishing private data to companies like Google and Yahoo! erodes citizen confidentiality on the Internet.

"The mere fact that Google has stood up to the government is a positive thing," Aden J. Fine, an American Civil Liberties Union lawyer, told *The New York Times*. "The government cannot simply demand that third parties give information without providing a sufficient justification for why they need it."

Google made these arguments against U.S. government surveillance at the same time the company was being criticized for allowing the Chinese government to censor Google's search engine in China, just one example of the complexity of doing business in a worldwide environment.

RSS Really Simple Syndication. Allows a person to create a personal set of Internet programs and services to be delivered to a single Web site.

Wiki Technology that allows many users to collaborate to create and update Internet pages.

New Technologies Mix with Old Ideas

The new communications network requires that everyone have access to digitized technology. Today, broadcasters and cable operators have access to the programming and the services, but many of these companies still use a mixture of old and new technologies. No one yet has created a storage system large enough to store and deliver every service consumers may want on demand.

While businesses have been able to develop secure systems for online data transfer, some government officials have tried to get access to consumers' communications records without the consumers' knowledge, challenging the basic concept of consumer privacy. The rules that are developing to govern the new communications network will have a profound impact on individuals, businesses and the media industries.

For consumers, the Internet already affects many everyday activities—the way people shop, get their news, study, manage their money, even how they socialize with friends. For businesses, national and even global information already is instantly available to more companies simultaneously, making communication much easier, but bringing more intense competition.

For the media industries, the Internet places every element of the media business in transition. Today, owners and managers of the companies that make up the media industries are deciding daily how to invest in equipment, employees, and research and development to protect current income while trying to ensure their companies will be able to adapt to the Internet's new demands.

Since the definition of digital media is so broad, people who hope to get attention and financial support for new products throw around the term very easily. Some digital media inventions succeed, some are transitional products that will help develop new products and many already have failed. Until the digital media landscape is clearer, however, it is important to follow ongoing developments because no one can predict exactly where digital media are headed. Three ongoing technologies to watch are virtual reality avatars, personalized channels and wikis.

Virtual Reality Systems

In the 1960s, computer flight simulators began to be used to train military pilots. These simulators were predecessors of today's virtual reality (VR) systems. Virtual reality systems give the user the experience of being somewhere by creating a digital representation of reality and then placing a digital representative in that digital reality. In the Internet world, someone's digital representation is called an avatar. The name comes from Hindu mythology, describing a deity who takes on human form.

An Internet avatar is simply an icon or a representation of a user—a digital stand-in—that people create to represent their online identity. A horse or a rabbit or a cartoon figure, for example, becomes their representative, their signature. Internet sites such as MySpace encourage users to create avatars—an online persona. This new technology is especially promising in the field of medicine, where medical students and doctors can simulate an operation using virtual reality avatars, for example, before using the procedure on a patient.

Personalized Channels

RSS technology (which stands for ***Really Simple Syndication***) allows people to select a personal set of Internet programs and services to be delivered to a single Web site location. The user can pull together free automatic feeds from several Web sites, which eliminates the need to visit each Web site individually. The technology uses an RSS aggregator, or news reader.

To use an RSS service, available from places like NewsGator and Bloglines, a user registers for the service and then chooses from a list of links that connect the user to the desired sites. The aggregator then gathers these links in one place, to be viewed whenever the user wants. RSS aggregators hope to make money from advertising on the RSS site that users see when they go to the site to view the information that's been compiled for them.

Wikis

The term ***wiki*** derives from a Hawaiian word that means "fast." This technology allows many users to collaborate to create and update an Internet page. A wiki Web site allows registered users to add and edit content on a specific topic. The best-known wiki is *Wikipedia*, an online encyclopedia where registered contributors may post additions and changes to any entry.

Wiki technology records the original material plus the material that contributors add over time. Wikis have great potential to gather in one place contributions worldwide from all the specialists on one subject, for example, but there are not any safeguards that the material placed on the site is guaranteed accurate or reliable.

The future of digital media is bound only by the needs of consumers and the imaginations of media developers, as diverse as the people who are online today and going online tomorrow. The new media universe could become a purer reflection of the real universe than any medium yet created, with unprecedented potential, like all mass media, to both reflect and direct the culture.

"The Internet is still in its infancy, and its potential is enormous," writes media critic David Shaw. The Internet, says Shaw, could "revolutionize human communication even more dramatically than Johann Gutenberg's first printing press did more than 500 years ago."

Review, Analyze, Investigate

REVIEWING CHAPTER 9

Digital Communication Transforms Media

✓ The emergence of the Internet within the last 30 years has transformed the structure and economics of the U.S. media business.

✓ The Internet today offers people wireless access to information just about wherever and whenever they want it.

✓ The Internet delivers all types of media using a single delivery system.

✓ The Internet is a combination of millions of computer networks sending and receiving data from all over the world.

✓ In its global size and absence of central control, the Internet is completely different from traditional media.

Digital Media Support Convergence

✓ Nicholas Negroponte at the Massachusetts Institute of Technology was the first person to identify the theory of convergence.

✓ The theory of convergence helped shape today's thinking about the Internet.

✓ Every media industry benefits from convergence.

20th-Century Discoveries Made Internet Possible

✓ The person most responsible for creating the World Wide Web is Tim Berners-Lee, who created the first browser and also gave the World Wide Web its name.

- ✓ Marc Andreessen at the University of Illinois created Mosaic, which allowed people to put text and pictures in the same online document.
- ✓ Both Andreessen and Berners-Lee placed their creations in the public domain, which meant that anyone with a computer and a modem could download them free.
- ✓ A culture of free information access, coupled with a creative, chaotic lack of direction, still permeates the Web today.

Web Opens to Unlimited Access

- ✓ Universal access, limited only by the available technology, is what gives the Web the feeling and look of what has been called "anarchy"—a place without rules.
- ✓ Today's media companies have a shared interest in seeing their investments in new technologies succeed.

What Happens to Old Media?

- ✓ The introduction of a new medium such as the Internet does not mean the end of the old.
- ✓ Older media forms continue to evolve and adapt to the new media environment.

Transformation Takes 30 Years

- ✓ Paul Saffo says the pace of change has consistently been about 30 years from the introduction of a new technology to its complete adoption by the culture.
- ✓ By Saffo's standard—the 30-year rule—American society is beginning to enter the third stage of acceptance, where the majority of the population has adapted to the new technology.

Web Access Leaves Some People Behind

- ✓ About 21 percent of Americans still do not go online—either because they can't afford it or they're afraid of it or they don't have access.
- ✓ The gap between people with online access and those who do not is called the *digital divide*.

Internet Combines Commerce, Information and Entertainment

- ✓ The largest single source of Web income is the money people pay their Internet service provider.
- ✓ Three other potential sources of income on the Web are promoting commerce, accepting advertising and providing online content.
- ✓ Most commercial Web sites now carry some form of advertising.
- ✓ Tablet devices, such as the iPad, offer another outlet for purchased media.
- ✓ The largest single source of new revenue generated by the Internet comes from the development and sale of video games. The video game industry is a hybrid that combines equipment (such as Xbox and PlayStation), software and Internet downloads.
- ✓ Computer and video game sales in the U.S. generated $10.5 billion in 2009.
- ✓ More than two-thirds of all American households own video games.
- ✓ Internet tracking tells advertisers about the audience's behavior.

Mobile Media Chase the Audience

- ✓ The latest big target for expanding Internet media use are mobile media—cell phones and Smartphones.
- ✓ Podcasts, blogs and personal Web pages are perfectly suited for the mobile media environment.

Government Attempts to Coordinate and Control the Net

- ✓ The federal government has attempted to coordinate and regulate the Internet, but the U.S. government has limited control over the Internet, especially its content.
- ✓ In 1994, the U.S. Congress named the effort to coordinate the nation's various senders, channels and receivers the National Information Infrastructure (NIII).
- ✓ In 1997, the U.S. Supreme Court upheld the concept that the U.S. government could not control Internet content.
- ✓ The most recent challenge to Internet content started with the 2005 passage of a law in California that prohibited video game sales to minors. Federal courts declared the law unconstitutional. The state appealed the law to the U.S. Supreme Court, which ruled in 2011 that the ban was a violation of freedom of speech.

Protection Sought for Intellectual Property Rights

- ✓ Legal protections for digital content are called *intellectual property rights*.
- ✓ In 1998, Congress passed the Digital Millennium Copyright Act to make it illegal to share copyrighted material on the Internet.
- ✓ The Recording Industry Association of America and the Motion Picture Association of America have aggressively pursued copyright infringement.
- ✓ In 2003, Apple introduced iTunes, which allows people to download music legally.
- ✓ In 2005, the free music file-sharing network Grokster shut down after reaching a settlement with the movie and music industries about online piracy.

- ✓ In 2010, a federal judge ordered the major remaining music-file-sharing service, LimeWire, to shut its Web site. The court ordered LimeWire to disable "searching, downloading, uploading, file trading and/or file distribution functionality."

FCC Proposes Internet Neutrality

- ✓ In 2009, FCC chairman Julius Genachowski proposed Internet neutrality rules to ensure that telecommunications companies maintain open Internet access.
- ✓ The FCC's actions signal that the federal government plans minimal interference with Internet content.

Internet Faces Four Challenges

- ✓ Four major challenges facing the Internet are open access, storage capacity, compatible delivery and consumer privacy.
- ✓ In 2006, Google agreed to let the Chinese government censor its online search results for Chinese customers. Yahoo! and MSN previously had agreed to similar restrictions in China.
- ✓ Researchers are developing a process called *data compression*, which collapses the size of data files so they are easier to download.
- ✓ The newest innovation in data storage is called *cloud computing*, which allows one business to rent remote use of another company's computer space, operating "in the cloud."
- ✓ Today's communications system is a mixture of analog and digital technologies.
- ✓ At least 10 million homes in the United States still receive only over-the-air broadcasts. They do not subscribe to cable or satellite.
- ✓ In 2006, the U.S. Justice Department subpoenaed online search records from Google, Yahoo!, MSN and Time Warner. Eventually Google agreed only to give the government a small number of Web site addresses from customer searches, temporarily ending a legal battle over the government's right to have access to consumer Internet records.

New Technologies Mix with Old Ideas

- ✓ For the media industries, the Internet places every element of the media in transition.
- ✓ Three ongoing technologies that are affecting consumers' use of the Internet are virtual reality systems, personalized channels driven by RSS and wikis.

KEY TERMS

These terms are defined in the margins throughout this chapter and appear in alphabetical order with definitions in the Glossary, which begins on page 383.

Analog 204
Avatar 198
Blog 198
Browser 189
CDA 200
Cloud Computing 204
Compatible 187
Convergence 188
Data Compression 203
Digital Divide 194
Digital Media 187
DMCA 201
E-mail 192
File Sharing 201
Home Page 190
HTML 189
HTTP 189
Intellectual Property Rights 200
ISP 194
Links 189
MPAA 201
Net Neutrality 202
NII 200
Podcast 197
Public Domain 190
Publishing 190
RIAA 201
RSS 206
Search Engine 190
Search Marketing 195
Server 204
Spam 202
30-Year Rule 192
Wiki 206

CRITICAL QUESTIONS

1. Explain the concept of the digital divide as outlined in this chapter. Why does the digital divide exist? List and explain three actions by government, corporations or individuals that would help eliminate the divide.
2. If only a few Web businesses have been commercially successful so far, why do experts predict that the Web has remarkable potential for revenue growth? Be specific.
3. Discuss Tim Berners-Lee's contributions to the development of the World Wide Web. What did he do, specifically? What was his basic philosophy for use of the Web? Do you agree? Why or why not?

4. Discuss some of the advantages of Internet file sharing. What is the core issue? How was it resolved? What is the future of file sharing?

5. Discuss the role of the U.S. government in regulating activity on the Internet, including issues relating to copyright, intellectual property, pornography and children's content. Discuss areas where the government has been both successful and unsuccessful in regulating the Internet.

WORKING THE WEB

This list includes both sites mentioned in the chapter and others to give you greater insight into the Internet industries.

Apple Inc.

http://www.apple.com

The main home page of Apple, this site's sections include Apple Store, iPod and iTunes, iPhone, Mac computers and software, Downloads and Support. Apple.com Worldwide allows users to shop internationally from Belgium to Portugal to Taiwan.

CNET

http://www.cnet.com

A CBS Interactive site, CNET provides electronic technology news and reviews and does comparison-shopping for products. Its Tips & Tricks section includes more than 1,000 searchable tips with streaming video, online articles, forums and buying guides. Tips are designated by user level: all, beginner, intermediate and advanced.

Electronic Frontier Foundation (EFF)

http://www.eff.org

This nonprofit organization was created in 1990 to protect digital rights. EFF tackles issues including Free Speech (online anonymity), Innovation (patents) and Transparency (e-voting rights). The site lists legal cases with descriptions, outcomes, related documents, press releases and other resources.

Facebook

http://facebook.com

Founded in February 2004, Facebook is a social Web site with about 500 million users and 1,400 employees. The Palo Alto–based company uses Web-based technologies to help people create an online presence so they can share information with people who sign up to be "friends." Anyone can sign up for a free Facebook account.

iVillage

http://www.ivillage.com

iVillage Inc., a division of NBC Universal, is the first and largest media company dedicated exclusively to connecting women at every stage of their lives. Content ranges from health, parenting, beauty and style to fitness, relationships, food and entertainment. Interactive features include social networking and message boards that allow women to connect with others and to seek advice and support.

Journal of Electronic Publishing (JEP)

http://www.journalofelectronicpublishing.org

The Scholarly Publishing Office (SPO), a unit of the University of Michigan Library, produces this forum for research and discussion of contemporary publishing. When JEP began in 1995, it recognized the significant changes in print communication and the growing role of digital communication in transmitting published information. Journal articles present innovative ideas, best practices and progressive thinking about all aspects of publishing, authorship and readership.

MIT Media Lab Project

http://www.media.mit.edu

This innovative multidisciplinary research laboratory at the Massachusetts Institute of Technology explores human/computer interaction. Now in its third decade of operation, the Lab is focusing on "human adaptability" projects including initiatives to treat Alzheimer's disease and depression, sociable robots that can monitor the health of children or the elderly, and the development of prostheses that can mimic the capabilities of biological limbs.

Online Publishers Association (OPA)

http://www.online-publishers.org

A not-for-profit industry trade organization founded in 2001, the OPA represents online content providers to the advertising community, the press, the government and the public. Members, from ABCNews.com to *The Washington Post*, agree to abide by standards of quality and credibility. It also publishes the biweekly OPA Intelligence Report, which summarizes important news and research for the online publishing industry.

Pew Internet & American Life Project

http://www.pewinternet.org

Solely supported by the privately held Pew Charitable Trust, the Pew Internet Project explores the effect of the Internet on various aspects of life: children, families, communities, the work place, education, health care, and civic and political life.

Information available on the site includes reports, presentations, data sets and current trends.

Whatis.com
http://whatis.techtarget.com

This self-education tool contains more than 4,500 individual information technology (IT) definitions, especially about the Internet and computers. Although the majority of its audience is IT professionals, even the layperson can search the site's encyclopedia for the most basic acronyms and terms. Users can find everything from a list of text messaging abbreviations to the definition of a zip drive.

Impact/Action Videos are concise news features on topics covered in this chapter, created exclusively for **Media/Impact**. They are available for students and instructors at CengageBrain.com, and include screen access for classroom viewing and discussion questions.

> "What's interesting is that, with all the talk of recession and cutting back, America still loves its indulgences—we still love our entertainment."
>
> —Denise Larson, principal-founder, NewMediaMetrics

Advertising: Motivating Customers

What's Ahead?

Advertising Supports Mass Media

Ads Share Three Characteristics

Ads Must Grab Your Attention

Advertisers Use Demographics

Advertising Feeds Consumerism

Advertising at Work

Mass Media Depend on Advertising

Media Industries Compete Fiercely for Clients

Federal Government Regulates Advertisers

TV Accepts Hard Liquor Ads

Advertising Business Delivers New Markets

Dilip Vishwanat/Getty Images Sport/Getty Images

In America, advertising is everywhere you look. Against a background of advertising messages in Busch Stadium, the St. Louis Cardinals celebrate after defeating the Texas Rangers in Game 7 of the World Series on October 28, 2011.

American consumers pay for most of their media (newspapers, magazines, radio and television) by watching, listening to and reading advertisements. The American Marketing Association defines *advertising* as "any paid form of non-personal presentation and promotion of ideas, goods or services by an identified sponsor."

You pay directly for books, movies and recordings, although these media use advertising to sell their products. But the broadcast programs you want to hear and see, the articles you want to read and the Internet sites you use every day are filled with advertisements placed by companies that want to sell you products. In 2009, businesses spent a total of $354 billion to advertise their products to American consumers.

Advertising Supports Mass Media

Advertising is not a mass medium. Advertising carries the messages that come to you from the people who pay for the American mass media. Advertising is at least 3,000 years old. In 1200 B.C., the Phoenicians painted messages on stones near paths where people often walked. In the sixth century B.C., ships that came into port with products on board sent criers around town with signboards to announce their arrival.

In the 13th century A.D., the British began requiring trademarks to protect buyers and to identify the makers of quality products. The first printed advertisement was prepared by printer William Caxton in England in 1478 to sell one of his books.

Advertising became part of the American experience even before the settlers arrived. "Never was there a more outrageous or more unscrupulous or more ill-informed advertising campaign than that by which the promoters for the American colonies brought settlers here," writes historian Daniel J. Boorstin. "Brochures published in England in the 17th century, some even earlier, were full of hopeful overstatements, half-truths, and downright lies, along with some facts which nowadays surely would be the basis for a restraining order from the Federal Trade Commission. Gold and silver, fountains of youth, plenty of fish, venison without limit, all these were promised, and of course some of them were found."

"Visit my website."

Joseph Farris/CartoonStock Ltd

Advertising in Newspapers

The nation's first newspaper advertisement appeared in *The Boston News-Letter*'s first issue in 1704 when the newspaper's editor included an ad for his own newspaper. The penny press of the 1800s counted on advertising to underwrite its costs. In 1833, the *New York Sun* candidly said in its first issue: "The object of this paper is to lay before the public, at a price within the means of everyone, all the news of the day and at the same time afford an advantageous medium for advertising." Three years later, the *Philadelphia Public Ledger* reported that "advertising is our revenue, and in a paper involving so many expenses as a penny paper, and especially our own, the only source of revenue."

Because they were so dependent on advertisers, newspapers in the 1800s accepted any ads they could get. Eventually, customers complained, especially about the patent medicines that advertised cures for every imaginable disease and often delivered unwelcome hangovers. (Many of these medicines contained mostly alcohol.) Products like Anti-Corpulence pills claimed they would help someone lose 15 pounds a month: "They cause no sickness, contain no poison and never fail." Dr. T. Felix Couraud's Oriental Cream guaranteed it would "remove tan, pimples, freckles, moth patches, rash and skin diseases and every blemish on beauty."

The newspaper publishers' response to complaints was to develop an open advertising policy, which meant newspapers would accept advertising from anyone who paid for it. This allowed the publishers to continue accepting the ads and then criticize the ads on their editorial pages. The *Public Ledger* described its policy this way: "Our advertising columns are open to the 'public, the whole public, and nothing but the public.' We admit any advertisement of any thing or any opinion, from any persons who will pay the price, excepting what is forbidden by the laws of the land, or what, in the opinion of all, is offensive to decency and morals."

But some editors did move their ads, which had been mingled with the copy, to a separate section. Advertising historian Stephen Fox says: "Advertising was considered an embarrassment . . . the wastrel relative, the unruly servant kept backstairs and never allowed into the front parlor. . . . A firm risked its credit rating by advertising; banks might take it as a confession of financial weakness.

"Everyone deplored advertising. Nobody—advertiser, agent or medium—took responsibility for it. The advertiser only served as an errand boy, passing the advertiser's message along to the publisher: the medium printed it, but surely would not question the right of free speech by making a judgment on the veracity of the advertiser."

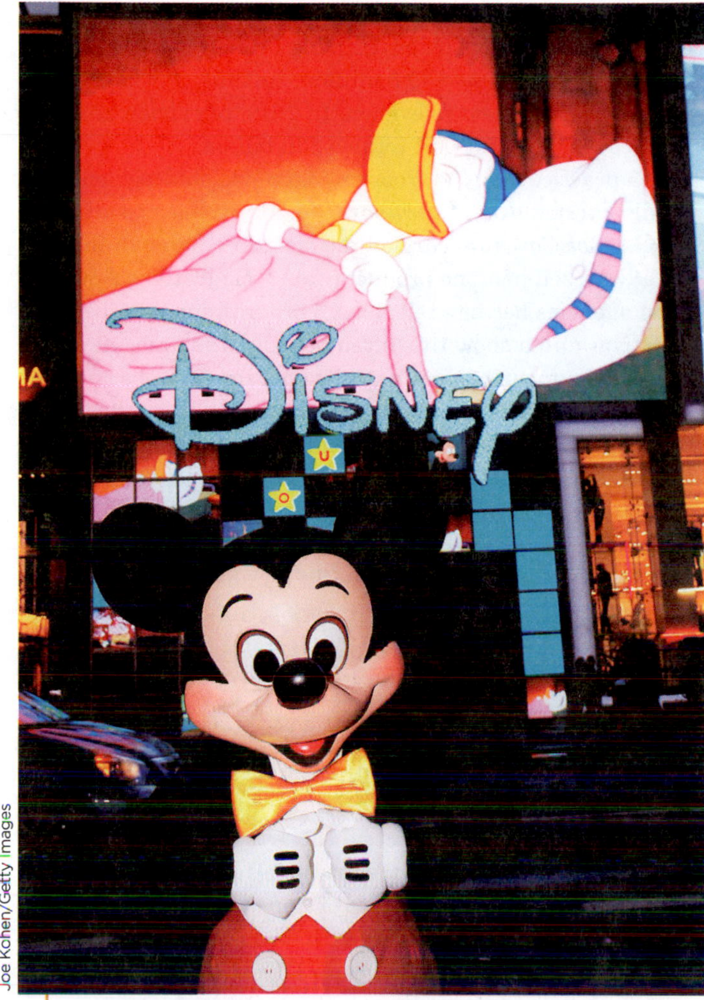

Joe Kohen/Getty Images

Total U.S. advertising revenue for all media totaled $354 billion in 2009. The Walt Disney Co. ranks 7th among the nation's top 10 advertisers. On October 21, 2010, Mickey Mouse unveiled a state-of-the-art digital billboard outside the new Disney retail store in the heart of New York City's Times Square.

Advertising in Magazines

Until the 1880s, magazines remained wary of advertising, but Cyrus H. K. Curtis, who founded *The Ladies' Home Journal* in 1887, promoted advertising as the way for magazines to succeed.

Once when he was asked what made him successful, he answered, "Advertising. That's what made me whatever I am. . . . I use up my days trying to find men who can write an effective advertisement." When Curtis hired Edward Bok as editor, Bok began a campaign against patent medicine ads and joined with *Collier's* and the American Medical Association to seek government restraints. Congress created the Federal Trade Commission (FTC) in 1914, and part of its job was to monitor deceptive advertising. The FTC continues today to be the major government watchdog over advertising (see "Federal Government Regulates Advertisers," p. 227).

Advertising on Radio

WEAF in New York broadcast its first advertisement in 1922, selling apartments in New Jersey. B. F. Goodrich, Palmolive and Eveready commercials followed. In September 1928, the Lucky Strike Dance Orchestra premiered on NBC, and Lucky Strike sales went up 47 percent. More cigarette companies moved to radio, and Camel cigarettes sponsored weekly, then daily, programs.

Sir Walter Raleigh cigarettes sponsored the Sir Walter Raleigh Revue. In one hour, the sponsor squeezed in 70 references to the product, according to Stephen Fox in *The Mirror Makers: A History of American Advertising and Its Creators*. "The theme song ('rally round Sir Walter Raleigh') introduced the Raleigh Revue in the Raleigh Theater with the Raleigh Orchestra and the Raleigh Rovers; then would follow the adventures of Sir Walter in Virginia and at Queen Elizabeth's court, with ample mention of his cigarettes and smoking tobacco," according to Fox. In 1938, for the first time, radio collected more money from advertising than magazines did.

Advertising on Television

Television began as an advertising medium. Never questioning how television would be financed, the TV networks assumed they would attract commercial support. They were right. In 1949, television advertising totaled $12.3 million. In 1950, the total was $40.8 million. In 1951, advertisers spent $128 million on television. In 2010, television advertising revenue in the U.S. totaled $70 billion.

In a practice adopted from radio, television programs usually carried ***direct sponsorship***. Many shows, such as *Camel News Caravan*, carried the sponsor's name in the title and advertised just one product (Camel cigarettes). Advertising agencies became television's programmers. "Given one advertiser and a show title often bearing its name, viewers associated a favorite show with its sponsor and—because of a 'gratitude factor'—would buy the products," writes Fox.

Alfred Hitchcock became legendary for leading into his show's commercials with wry remarks about the sponsor: "Oh dear, I see the actors won't be ready for another 60 seconds. However, thanks to our sponsor's remarkable foresight, we have a message that will fill in here nicely." But Hitchcock's sarcasm was the exception, and the television industry today relies heavily on advertising support.

Advertising on the Internet

Advertisers flocked to major Internet sites when they first were established. They expected quick returns, as consumer use of the Internet skyrocketed. Advertisers primarily used banner advertising, which meant their advertising messages scrolled across a Web site or appeared in a box on the site.

Internet sites also tried ***pop-up*** advertisements, which meant an ad popped up either behind a Web site screen when someone left the site or on top of the Web site home page when someone first visited. Advertisers quickly learned, however, that no matter how they packaged the message, advertising on an Internet site didn't necessarily bring increased sales for their products.

What advertisers call the ***click-through rate*** (the rate at which someone who sees an advertising message on an Internet site actually clicks through to learn more) is less than 1 percent. This is a very disappointing return, especially because Web site advertising can be expensive. By 2011, Internet ad spending reached $31 billion. Advertisers today are still trying to figure out the magic formula to reach consumers on the Internet, and they're willing to spend a lot of money to try to find out what works.

Ford, BMW, Coca-Cola and Absolut Vodka created "advertainments" on their Web sites—short movies (2 to 11 minutes) featuring lots of action and familiar movie stars. Many marketers are using ***viral marketing*** to try to reach younger audiences. Viral marketing means creating an online message that is so entertaining or interesting that consumers pass it along through social networking sites, such as Facebook and MySpace, and by e-mail links. The message becomes an online "virus" that promotes a product without the expense of a paid commercial.

These new approaches are meant to make Internet advertisements seem less like advertisements—further blurring the line between information, entertainment and advertising.

Direct Sponsorship A program that carries an advertiser's name in the program title.

Pop-Up An advertisement on a Web site that appears on the screen either behind a Web page when someone leaves the site or on top of the Web site home page when someone first visits.

Click-Through Rate The rate at which people who see an ad on an Internet site click through to learn more.

Viral Marketing Creating an online message that is entertaining enough to get consumers to pass it on over the Internet like a virus.

Ads Share Three Characteristics

The word *advertise* originally meant to take note or to consider. By the 1700s, the word's meaning had changed. *To advertise* meant "to persuade." "If we consider democracy not just a political system," says Daniel J. Boorstin, "but as a set of institutions which do aim to make everything available to everybody, it would not be an overstatement to describe advertising as the characteristic rhetoric of democracy."

Boorstin says that advertising in America shares three characteristics: repetition, style and ubiquity.

Repetition

In 1851, when Robert Bonner bought the *New York Ledger*, he wanted to advertise his newspaper in the competing *New York Herald*, owned by James Gordon Bennett. Bennett limited all his advertisers to the same type size, so Bonner paid for an entire page of the *Herald*, across which he repeated the message "Bring home the *New York Ledger* tonight." This is an early example of advertising's widespread practice of repeating a simple message for effect.

An Advertising Style

At first, advertising adopted a plain, direct style. Advertising pioneer Claude Hopkins, says Boorstin, claimed: "Brilliant writing has no place in advertising. A unique style takes attention from the subject. . . . One should be natural and simple . . . [I]n fishing for buyers, as in fishing for bass,

Media/Impact WORLD

British TV Ads Flaunt Their Arty Side

By Chloe Veltman

In a recent British television commercial for the Barclaycard credit card, an office worker strips down to his briefs, saunters past his co-workers and enters a storage closet, where he jumps down a chute and sets off on a wild water-slide ride across an urban landscape, sailing down the sides of buildings, whizzing past shoppers and sloshing through a public library to the sound of the 1976 Bellamy Brothers hit "Let Your Love Flow." When his joyously soggy ride comes to an end, he says, "Can you get me a towel?"

The Advertising Archives

British television commercials are known for creative artistry. In a 2010 Barclays Bank campaign, the company created a virtual roller coaster ride in the middle of downtown Manhattan.

In contrast, in this country Bank of America—showing considerably less inspiration than Barclays—is advertising its bill-payment service with a tinny jingle and statically shot images of people spilling coffee on their paper bills.

British commercials have long been known for their creativity and innovation. But from an artistic standpoint, most American advertising, perhaps except for those made for the Super Bowl or the Web, pale in comparison with their British counterparts. And unsurprisingly, British ads have long attracted a huge following in America. . . .

"In general, TV advertising has always been a high form of public art in the U.K.," said Richard Silverstein, co-chairman and creative director of the San Francisco-based advertising firm Goodby, Silverstein & Partners. "People over there watch commercials as if they are entertainment."

On occasion, the American advertising industry is equally capable of producing inspiring commercials. Google's recent "Parisian Love" ad simply communicates the company's services. The 52-second spot tells the story of a young man who travels to France, meets the woman of his dreams and settles down solely through displaying search terms on screen like "impress a French girl" and "how to assemble a crib." The spot doesn't feature any actors or dialogue, yet it manages to imbue something as sterile as a Web search with emotional force. . . .

Yet such creative efforts are not part of this country's standard TV advertising lexicon. Television ads in the United States tend to be more sales-driven and less focused on aesthetics. . . .

A commercial is principally a sales tool. But it can also be art. Perhaps if the American advertising industry were allowed to create more imaginative, aesthetically engaging and thought-provoking commercials, viewers would be less inclined to fast-forward their way through commercial breaks.

From Chloe Veltman, "British TV Ads Flaunt Their Arty Side," The New York Times, *March 13, 2010.*

one should not reveal the hook." The plain-talk tradition is a foundation of what advertisers call modern advertising. But advertising today often adopts a style of hyperbole, making large claims for products. Boorstin calls this "tall-talk."

The tall-talk ad is in the P. T. Barnum tradition of advertising. Barnum was a carnival barker and later impresario who lured customers to his circus acts with fantastic claims. You may recognize this approach in some of the furniture and car ads on television, as an announcer screams at you that you have only a few days left until all the chairs or all the cars will be gone.

Both plain talk and tall-talk combine, Boorstin says, to create advertising's new myth. "This is the world of the neither true nor false—of the statement that 60 percent of the physicians who expressed a choice said that our brand of aspirin would be more effective in curing a simple headache than any other brand. . . . It is not untrue, and yet, in its connotation it is not exactly true."

Ubiquity

In America, advertising is everywhere. Advertisers are always looking for new places to catch consumers' attention. Ads appear on shopping carts, on video screens at sports stadiums, atop parking meters. Says Daniel Boorstin, "The ubiquity of advertising is, of course, just another effect of our uninhibited efforts to use all the media to get all sorts of information to everybody everywhere. Since the places to be filled are everywhere, the amount of advertising is not determined by the needs of advertising, but by the opportunities for advertising, which become unlimited."

In some cases, this ubiquity works to advertising's disadvantage. Many advertisers shy away from radio and TV because the ads are grouped so closely together. In 1986, in an attempt to attract more advertisers, TV began selling the "split-30" ad, which fits two 15-second ads into a 30-second spot. Even 10-second ads are available. Wherever these shorter commercials are sold, the station runs twice or three times as many ads for different products, crowding the commercial time even more. Too many ads that run together makes it hard for one ad to grab consumers' attention.

Ads Must Grab Your Attention

To sell the products, advertisers must catch your eye or your ear or your heart (preferably all three). A study by the Harvard Graduate School of Business Administration reported that the average American is exposed to 500 ads a day.

With so many ads competing for your attention, the advertiser must first get you to read, to listen or to watch one ad instead of another. "The immediate goal of advertising [is to] tug at our psychological shirt sleeves and slow us down long enough for a word or two about whatever is being sold," says humanities and human sciences professor Jib Fowles in *Mass Advertising as Social Forecast*. Research shows that there are at least 15 common ways ads appeal to consumers.

15 Ways Ads Appeal to Consumers

You make your buying decisions based on several sources of information besides advertising: friends, family and your own experience, for example. To influence your choices, the advertising message must appeal to you for some reason as you sift through the ads to make judgments and choose products. Fowles enumerated 15 appeals, which he calls an "inventory of human motives" that advertisers commonly use in their commercials:

1. **Need for sex.** Surprisingly, Fowles found that only 2 percent of the television ads he surveyed used this appeal. It may be too blatant, he concluded, and often detracts from the product.
2. **Need for affiliation.** The largest number of ads uses this approach: You are looking for friendship. Advertisers can also use this negatively, to make you worry that you'll lose friends if you don't use a certain product.
3. **Need to nurture.** Every time you see a puppy or a kitten or a child, the appeal is to your maternal or paternal instincts.
4. **Need for guidance.** A father or mother figure can appeal to your desire for someone to care for you, so you won't have to worry. Betty Crocker is a good example.
5. **Need to aggress.** We all have had a desire to get even, and some ads give you this satisfaction.
6. **Need to achieve.** The ability to accomplish something difficult and succeed identifies the product with winning. Sports figures as spokespersons project this image.
7. **Need to dominate.** The power we lack is what we can look for in a commercial: "Master the possibilities."
8. **Need for prominence.** We want to be admired and respected, to have high social status. Luxury car ads and ads for diamond rings offer this potential.
9. **Need for attention.** We want people to notice us; we want to be looked at. Cosmetics are a natural for this approach.
10. **Need for autonomy.** Within a crowded environment, we want to be singled out, to be "a breed apart." This

can also be used negatively: You may be too ordinary without a particular product.

11. **Need to escape.** Flight is very appealing; you can imagine adventures you cannot have. The idea of escape is pleasurable.
12. **Need to feel safe.** To be free from threats, to be secure is the appeal of many insurance and bank ads.
13. **Need for aesthetic sensations.** Beauty attracts us, and classic art or dance makes us feel creative, enhanced.
14. **Need to satisfy curiosity.** Facts support our belief that information is quantifiable, and numbers and diagrams make our choices seem scientific.
15. **Physiological needs.** Fowles defines sex (item no. 1) as a biological need, and so he classifies our need to sleep, eat and drink as physiological. Advertisements for juicy pizza are especially appealing late at night.

YOU KNOW YOU LOVE IT and the "smiling noodle" are trademarks of Kraft Foods

Advertisers use at least 15 different types of appeals to attract consumers. In 2010, Kraft Macaroni and Cheese unveiled this billboard to sell its product. Which one of the 15 ad appeals listed by Jib Fowles does the ad use?

Advertisers Use Demographics

Advertisers target their messages to an audience according to the audience's needs. But an advertiser also seeks to determine the audience's characteristics. This analysis of observable audience characteristics is called ***demographics***.

Demographics are composed of data about a target audience's gender, age, income level, marital status, geographic location and occupation. These data are observable because they are available to advertising agencies through census data and other sources. Advertising agencies use demographic audience analysis to help advertisers target their messages.

A motorcycle dealer certainly wouldn't want to advertise in a baby magazine, for example; a candy manufacturer probably wouldn't profit from advertising in a diet and exercise magazine. Advertising agencies try to match a client's product to a thoroughly defined audience so each advertising dollar is well spent, such as matching an upscale bank with well-educated, high earners (see **Media/Impact: Audience**, "Why Marathons Are Hot Spot to Chase Consumers," p. 220).

Defining the audience is very important because the goal of advertising is to market a product to people who have the desire for the product and the ability to buy it. Audience analysis tells an advertiser whether there are enough people who can be targeted for a product to make the advertising worthwhile.

Advertising Feeds Consumerism

According to Louis C. Kaufman, author of *Essentials of Advertising*, critics of advertising make three main arguments:

1. **Advertising adds to the cost of products.** Critics of advertising maintain that advertising, like everything that is part of manufacturing a product, is a cost. Ultimately, the consumer pays for the cost of advertising. But the industry argues that advertising helps make more goods and services available to the consumer and that the resulting competition keeps prices lower.
2. **Advertising causes people to buy products they do not need.** Says media scholar Michael Schudson, "Most blame advertising for the sale of specific consumer goods, notably luxury goods (designer jeans), frivolous goods (pet rocks), dangerous goods (cigarettes), shoddy goods (some toys for children), expensive goods that do not differ at all from cheap goods (non-generic over-the-counter drugs), marginally differentiated products that

Demographics Data about consumers' characteristics, such as age, gender, income level, marital status, geographic location and occupation.

Media/Impact
AUDIENCE

Why Marathons Are Hot Spot to Chase Consumers

By Aris Georgiadis

With interest in marathons at an all-time high, marketers are increasingly trying to keep pace and get in front of what's considered a highly desirable consumer. Nowhere is this more apparent than during [the] ING New York City Marathon.

Just how hot have marathons become? Last week [October 24, 2010], the registration for the 2011 Boston Marathon was over in eight hours, and that's for a race [that] runners have to qualify for. According to *Running USA*, about 467,000 runners crossed the finish line at U.S. marathons in 2009. Last year an estimated 470 marathons were held, up 5.6 percent from 2008.

For the ING New York City Marathon, which takes place Nov. 7 [2010], more than 120,000 people paid an application fee just to enter a lottery for a shot at running. Of that, about 45,000 are expected to finish. Last year's 43,660 finishers made the race's 40th edition the largest marathon ever.

And by all accounts, those finishers are a sought-after demo: They're highly educated, high earners and in most cases they travel and spend on hospitality. Almost a third of New York's field is from abroad.

The benefit to sponsors, said Bob Boland, a professor of sports business at New York University's Preston Robert Tisch Center for Hospitality, Tourism and Sports Management, is marathoners are "a pre-qualified demo: You're getting interest and commonality, as opposed to having to attract them on their own."

For ING, which became the New York Marathon's first title sponsor in 2003, the race has been an ideal way for the marketer to reach its target consumer. "The parallels between running and preparing for your financial future speaks to our customers," said ING America's chief marketing officer, Ann Glover. ING translates that attribute in its messaging, often featuring images of runners. The point is to remind those planning for their retirement that, like running a marathon, "You're in it for the long haul," she said.

Andrew Burton/Getty Images

Gebre Gebremariam of Ethiopia runs with the Ethiopian flag after winning the New York City Marathon on November 7, 2010. Participants and fans are a desirable demographic for advertisers—highly educated and in the upper income brackets.

From a demographic and psychographic standpoint, the marathon touches all quadrants, she said. But runners in particular are "planners and deliberate and they do their best to achieve their goals," which is the type of customer ING is trying to reach, she added.

The return on ING's investment, which it declined to reveal, has been the brand's increased presence in New York. Ms. Glover said: "Our research has shown that, following the event, there is an increase in attributes such as brand recognition and trust, interest in doing business with ING and the intent to recommend our products and services to others."

Mr. Boland said ING's sponsorship is one of the better alignments in sports, based on what he calls ROO, or return on objective. "They could do a zillion commercials and never reach this kind of audience."

Aris Georgiadis, "Why Marathons Are Hot Spot to Chase Consumers," Advertising Age, November 1, 2010. Copyrighted 2011 Crain Communications.

do not differ significantly from one another (laundry soaps), and wasteful goods (various un-ecological throw-away convenience goods)." The advertising industry contends the ultimate test of any product is the marketplace and that advertising may stimulate consumers to try a new product or a new brand, but consumers will not continue to buy an unsatisfying product.

3. **Advertising reduces competition and thereby fosters monopolies.** Critics point to the rising cost of advertising, especially on television, which limits which companies can afford to launch a new product or a new campaign. The industry argues that advertising is still a very inexpensive way to let people know about new products.

Tom Williams/Roll Call/Getty Images

Critics of advertising claim that it causes consumers to buy products they don't need. The advertising industry contends the ultimate test of any product is the marketplace because consumers won't continue to buy an unsatisfying product. In Washington, D.C., morning commuters at Union Station were greeted in 2010 with a giant replica of a high heel shoe as an eye-catching advertisement for Mastercard, advertising luxury shoes as an item you could buy with your Mastercard.

"The cost of launching a nationwide advertising campaign may be formidable," writes Louis C. Kaufman, "but the cost of supporting larger, nationwide sales forces for mass-marketed goods would be greater still." Does advertising work? According to Schudson, "Apologists are wrong that advertising is simply information that makes the market work more efficiently—but so too are the critics of advertising who believe in its overwhelming power to deceive and to deflect human minds to its ends."

"Evaluating its impact," Kaufman says, "is more difficult than these simplicities of apology and critique will acknowledge."

Advertising at Work

Several worldwide advertising agencies are based in the United States, but many advertising agencies are small local and regional operations, earning less than $1 million a year. Advertising agencies buy time and space for the companies they represent. For this, they usually earn a commission (commonly 15 percent). Many agencies also produce television and radio commercials and print and Internet advertising for their clients.

Depending on the size of the agency, the company may be divided into as many as six departments:

1. Marketing research
2. Media selection
3. Creative activity
4. Account management
5. Administration
6. Public relations

Marketing research examines the product's potential, where it will be sold and who will buy the product. Agency researchers may survey the market themselves or contract with an outside market research company to evaluate potential buyers.

Media selection suggests the best combination of buys for a client—television, newspapers, magazines, billboards and/or Internet.

Creative activity thinks up the ads. The "creatives" write the copy for TV, radio, print and Internet. They design the graphic art, and often they produce the commercials. They also verify that the ad has run as many times as it was scheduled to run.

Account management is the liaison between the agency and the client. Account executives handle client complaints and suggestions and also manage the company team assigned to the account.

Administration pays the bills, including all the tabs for the account executives' lunches with clients. *Public relations* is an extra service that some agencies offer for companies that don't have a separate public relations office.

Media/Impact
CULTURE

Leggo My iPod: Yes, We're Cutting Back, but Indulgences Stay

Leap Index Reveals Brands to Which Consumers Are Most Attached; Entertainment Still Rocks

By Jennifer Rooney

iPod. iPhone. Xbox. Wii. These are the brands feeling the love—consumers' love, that is, according to NewMediaMetrics' first annual Leap Index (Leveraging Emotional Attachment for Profit), a ranking weighing the relative emotional attachment of consumers to brands in various categories.

Leave it to hard, plastic boxes to get all the warm fuzzies. "What's interesting is that in 2010, [based on] the top 100, with all the talk of recession and cutting back, America still loves its indulgences—we still love our entertainment: iPod, iPhone, Disney, Xbox; we love our communications devices, we love shopping. Even if it is cutting back at a Walmart, still, things are being bought," said Denise Larson, NewMediaMetrics principal-founder. "What struck us is if you go and look, in 2010, Hellman's comes up at 72 out of 100," she said. "Twenty years ago, Hellman's was always the No. 1 brand. So what happened to mayonnaise? It got displaced by iPods and iPhones and Xbox." (See **Illustration 10.1**.)

Also topping this year's list are Honda, Sony PlayStation, iPad and Google. NewMediaMetrics has been creating syndicated databases that measure emotional attachment to brands and media for the past five years, linking the high-value buyers of tracked brands to media they're most attached to. This year the company compiled the brand data into the Leap Index (Leveraging Emotional Attachment for Profit), which enables marketers to compare their brands' strength vs. competitors. To compile this year's index, NewMediaMetrics surveyed online a representative sample of the U.S. population—3,500 people ages 13 through 54, with annual income of at least $35,000. The survey ran from March 17 to March 26, 2010.

Consumers who are most emotionally attached to brands—those most unwilling to give up a given brand, designated as those who select 9 or 10 on a 0 to 10 scale to indicate emotional attachment (or "9/10s")—are obviously most valuable to marketers. They represent the consumers with the greatest likelihood to purchase that brand's products or services, go deeper into a product line, and spend more to get the brand.

"In other words, they're not as likely to buy on the cheap," said Gary Reisman, NewMediaMetrics' principal-founder. "There's a tipping point, but they're less likely to be deterred by an increase in price. They'll spend more to get the premium package. They are two-and-a-half-times more likely to pay attention to an ad for that brand."

And, he said, each percent of emotional attachment will equal revenue potential for a brand.

Jennifer Rooney, "Leggo My iPod: Yes, We're Cutting Back, but Indulgences Stay: Leap Index Reveals Brands to Which Consumers Are Most Attached; Entertainment Still Rocks," Advertising Age, October 11, 2010, *page* 4. *Copyrighted 2011 Crain Communications.*

All these departments work together on an ad campaign. An ***advertising campaign*** is a planned advertising effort, coordinated for a specific time period. A campaign can last anywhere from a month to a year, and the objective is a coordinated strategy to sell a product or a service. (See **Media/Impact: Culture**, "Leggo My iPod: Yes, We're Cutting Back, but Indulgences Stay," and **Illustration 10.1**.)

Advertising Campaign A planned advertising effort, coordinated for a specific time period.

Typically, the company assigns the account executive a team of people from the different departments to handle the account. The account executive answers to the people who control the agency, usually a board of directors. The members of the campaign team coordinate all types of advertising—print and broadcast, for example—to make sure they share consistent content. After establishing a budget based on the client's needs, the campaign team

Media/Impact CULTURE (CONTINUED)

Illustration 10.1

U.S. Consumers' Top 10 Brand Attachments

In 2010, MediaMetrics created its first annual Leap Index, a database that ranks the relative attachment of U.S. consumers to brands in various categories. (*Leap* stands for "leveraging emotional attachment for profit.") Here is a ranked list of the brands with the highest emotional loyalty. (*Note that most of the Top 10 brands are media-related.*)

Source: MediaMetrics as published in Advertising Age, October 11, 2010.

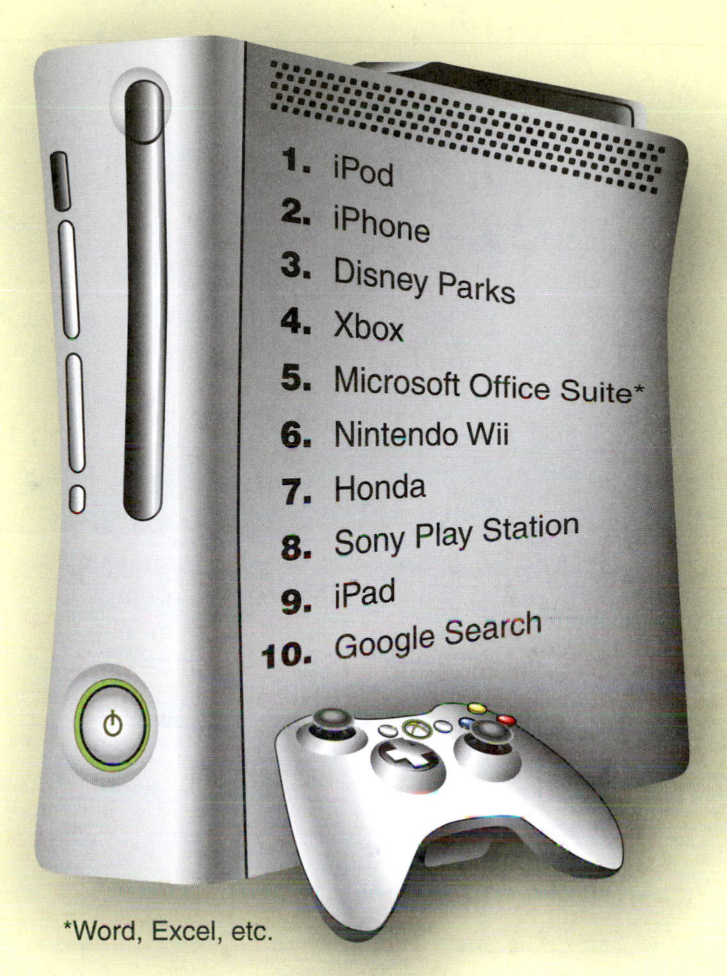

creates a slogan, recommends a strategy for the best exposure for the client, approves the design of print and broadcast commercials and then places the ads with the media outlets.

Advertising agencies tend to be clustered in big cities such as New York, Los Angeles, San Francisco and Chicago. In part, this is by tradition. The agencies may want to be near their large clients in the cities. They also have access to a larger pool of talent and facilities such as recording studios, but today Internet technology enables greater flexibility for agency locations.

Mass Media Depend on Advertising

The advertising business and the media industries are interdependent—that is, what happens in the advertising business directly affects the media industries. The advertising business is very dependent on the nation's economic health. (See **Illustration 10.2**, p. 225.) If the national economy is expanding, the advertising business and the media industries prosper.

If the nation's economy falls into a recession, advertisers typically reduce their ad budgets, which eventually may lead to a decline in advertising revenue for the agencies and also for the media industries where the agencies place their ads. During a recession, advertisers also may change their advertising strategies—choosing the Internet over television, for example, because the Internet is much less expensive.

The advertising industry today, therefore, must be very sensitive to economic trends. The success of an ad agency is best measured by the results an ad campaign brings. The agency must analyze the benefits of different types of advertising—broadcast, print, Internet—and recommend the most efficient combinations for their clients.

Tom Uhlman/Bloomberg/Getty Images

Spending by the nation's biggest advertisers supports the mass media. Procter & Gamble, the world's largest consumer products business, spends more money on advertising than any other company in the U.S. In 2010, Procter & Gamble used vintage boxes of Tide detergent and Ivory soap to promote its new franchise across the U.S., Tide Dry Cleaners.

Commercials on Television

Even though the cost seems exorbitant, sponsors continue to line up to appear on network television. "Advertisers must use television on whatever terms they can get it, for television is the most potent merchandising vehicle ever devised," writes TV producer Bob Shanks in his book *The Cool Fire: How to Make It in Television*. Shanks is talking about national advertisers who buy network time—companies whose products can be advertised to the entire country at once.

Advertising minutes within every network prime-time hour are divided into 10-, 15- and 30-second ads. If an advertiser wants to reach the broad national market, television is an expensive choice because the average price for the TV time for a 30-second commercial is $100,000. The price tag for a 30-second commercial reaches $3.5 million for a widely watched program such as the 2012 Super Bowl.

National advertising on programs like CBS's *NCIS* is bought by national advertising agencies, which handle the country's biggest advertisers—Procter & Gamble and McDonald's, for example. These companies usually have in-house advertising and public relations departments, but most of the advertising strategy and production of commercials for these companies is handled by the agencies. National agencies buy advertising space based on a careful formula, calculated on a cost-per-thousand (***CPM***) basis—the cost of an ad per 1,000 people reached (M is the Roman numeral for 1,000).

CPM Cost-per-thousand, the cost of an ad per 1,000 people reached. (M is the Roman numeral for 1,000.)

Making a TV commercial for national broadcast is more expensive per minute than making a television program because each company wants its ads to be different from the rest. The price to create a TV commercial can run as much as $1 million a minute. That may be why, as one producer said, "the commercials are the best things on TV." Network television commercials certainly are the most visible type of advertising, but not everyone needs the reach of network television. The goal of well-placed advertising is to deliver the best results to the client for the lowest cost, and this may mean looking to other media.

Using Print and Radio

Different types of media deliver different types of audiences. Advertising agencies may buy time and space on local radio, and in newspapers and magazines to target a specific audience by demographics: age, education, gender and income. A radio station with a rock format delivers a different audience than an easy-listening station does. *The New York Times* delivers a different reader than the *Honolulu Advertiser*. *Sports Illustrated* targets a different group than *Ladies' Home Journal*.

Language also can be a targeting factor. Some agencies use Spanish-language media to target Latino consumers, for example, on a Spanish-language radio station or in a Spanish-language newspaper.

With newspaper and magazine circulation declining, and over-the-air radio audiences migrating to satellite radio or listening to their iPods, Internet advertising is quickly becoming the fastest growing avenue to consumers.

Internet Delivers Display and Search Advertising

The Internet offers the largest potential audience, but consumers also can quickly click past ads on the Web so advertisers have become clever at placing Internet ads within and around the sites themselves. Internet ads are display ads, banners that run at the top of the page or alongside the copy.

Media/Impact MONEY

Illustration 10.2

Top 10 Advertisers in the United States

Auto manufacturers, such as General Motors, have always spent a lot of money to advertise their products, but in 2010 telecommunications companies such as Verizon and AT&T spent as much to advertise their products as General Motors (which ranked No. 3). Also ranked in the top 10 was media company Time Warner Inc. (8).

Source: "*100 Leading National Advertisers 2011,*" Advertising Age, *June 20, 2011, 10.*

1. Procter & Gamble Co.
2. AT&T Inc.
3. General Motors Corp.
4. Verizon Communications Inc.
5. American Express
6. Pfizer Inc.
7. Walmart Stores
8. Time Warner Inc.
9. Johnson & Johnson
10. L'Oréal USA

But the most successful method of access to consumers today through the Internet is called ***search advertising***, often called simply *search*. Advertisers pay Internet companies fees to list and/or link their company's site domain name to a specific search word or phrase. In 2010, search accounted for nearly half of all Internet advertising revenue, according to the Internet Advertising Bureau, which divides search advertising into four types:

1. Paid listings—places links at the top or side of the screen next to search results.
2. Contextual search—places text links in the article based on the context of the content.
3. Paid inclusion—guarantees that a search engine indexes a marketer's URL, so that when someone searches for something, the marketer's URL shows up.
4. Site optimization—fixes a site so search engines can more easily index the site.

"Interactive advertising revenue is on a strong upward trajectory," according to Sherrill Mane of the Internet Advertising Bureau. "Nearly all types of ad formats are showing positive movement and marketers across all advertising categories, most notably consumer packaged goods and pharmaceuticals, are increasing their investment in digital media."

Media Industries Compete Fiercely For Clients

The competition among the media industries for advertisers is fierce:

- A study commissioned by the American Newspaper Publishers Association reveals that only one in five

Search Advertising Advertising in the form of a list and/or link to a company's site domain name through a specific online search word or phrase.

Courtesy of Lithia Motors

Auto dealers are among the biggest spenders on local radio and TV advertising as well as the Internet. With Internet advertising, auto dealers like Lithia Motors in Boise, Idaho, can reach consumers outside their local market.

prime-time adult viewers could remember the last ad they had seen on television.

- Print advertisers claim that because viewers can so easily change channels and skip the ads, TV commercials are an unreliable way to deliver an audience.
- *Time* advertises that more airline customers read its magazine than read *Newsweek*.
- *Newsweek* advertises that it delivers more people for the money than *Time*.
- "Radio is the medium working women don't have to make time for," boasts the Radio Advertising Bureau (RAB). Whereas working women spend 15 percent of their daily media time reading a newspaper, they spend half of their media time with radio, says the RAB.
- AT&T launches a talking Internet site to "express themselves better" to consumers.

Rep Firm A company of advertising sales representatives who sell advertising time and space in their market to companies outside their geographic area.

Advertising agencies gather demographic information provided by Nielsen and Arbitron for broadcast and the Internet and by the Audit Bureau of Circulations for print; the audience is converted into numbers. Based on these numbers, agencies advise advertisers about ways to reach buyers for their products by advertising locally or through an advertising sales representative, for example.

Advertising Locally

Kaitlyn's health and fitness salon, a small downtown business, does not need to advertise on the *Late Show with David Letterman* or in *The New York Times*. Kaitlyn and other local business owners need to reach only their neighbors. Businesses larger than the fitness salon, such as a car dealer or a furniture store, may buy local television or radio time, but most of the local advertising dollar goes to newspapers.

A local advertising agency can design a campaign, produce the ad and place the ad just like the national agencies, but on a much smaller scale. Some small companies design and place their own ads directly with the local media. To attract customers, local media often help companies design their ads. Newspapers, for example, will help a small advertiser prepare an ad using ready-made art.

A radio or television station may include the services of an announcer or access to a studio in the price for a series of spot ads. Broadcast stations sometimes trade ads for services offered by the advertiser—dinner for two at the local restaurant in return for two spot ads, for example. Then the station gives the dinners away on one of its programs.

Advertising Sales Representatives

What if you manufacture sunglasses in Dubuque, Iowa, and you hire a local advertising agency to sell your product nationally? The agency tells you they've found a good market for your product on the West Coast. How is the agency going to find out the most efficient way to sell your sunglasses in Los Angeles?

In this situation, many advertising agencies would contact a ***rep firm***—a company of advertising sales representatives who sell advertising time and space in their market to companies outside the area. The agency in Dubuque would first decide who were the most likely customers for your sunglasses. If the agency decided that L.A.-area males age 18 to 24 are the best potential customers, the agency would budget a certain amount of money for advertising in the Los Angeles area and then call the ad reps there.

The rep firm, in return, takes a percentage (usually 15 percent) of the advertising dollars for the ads they place. Ad reps are, in effect, brokers for the media in their markets. Each rep firm handles several clients. Some ad reps sell only broadcast advertising, and some specialize in print ads, but many rep firms sell all types of media.

In this case, each L.A. ad rep would enter the demographics ("demos") for your product into a computer. Based on ratings, readership and the price for the ads, each rep would come up with a CPM (cost per thousand people reached) for your product. The rep then would recommend the most efficient buy—how best to reach the people most likely to buy your sunglasses.

Each rep then presents an L.A. advertising plan for your product to the agency in Dubuque. Usually the buy is based on price: The medium with the lowest CPM gets the customer. But a rep who cannot match the lowest CPM might offer incentives for you to choose his or her plan. If you agree to provide 50 pairs of sunglasses, for example, the rep's radio station will give away the glasses as prizes during a local program, each time mentioning the name of your product. So even though the ad time you buy will cost a little more, you also will get promotional announcements every time the station gives away a pair of sunglasses. Other ad reps might offer different packages.

The agency in Dubuque then would decide which package is the most attractive and would present that proposal to you. This entire process can take as little as 24 hours for a simple buy such as the one for your sunglasses account, or as long as several weeks for a complicated campaign for a big advertiser.

Farley Katz/Cartoonbank.com

"'Killer Whale' is terrible branding. From now on, people will call you 'Happy Silly Fun Fish.'"

Federal Government Regulates Advertisers

Government protection for consumers dates back to the beginning of the 20th century when Congress passed the Pure Food and Drug Act in 1906, mainly as a protection against patent medicine ads. The advertising industry itself has adopted advertising standards, and in some cases the media have established their own codes.

Government oversight is the main deterrent against deceptive advertising. This responsibility is shared by several government agencies: The Federal Trade Commission, the Food and Drug Administration and the Federal Communications Commission.

The Federal Trade Commission

The Federal Trade Commission (FTC), established in 1914, can "stop business practices that restrict competition or that deceive or otherwise injure consumers," according to *Essentials of Advertising*. If the FTC determines an ad is deceptive, the commission can order the advertiser to stop the campaign.

The commission also can require corrective advertising to counteract the deception. In 1993, for example, the FTC launched an investigation of the nation's weight-loss clinics, charging that they were using deceptive advertising.

The Food and Drug Administration

The Food and Drug Administration (FDA) oversees claims that appear on food labels or packaging. If the FDA finds a label is deceptive, the agency can require the advertiser to stop distributing products with that label. Orange juice that is labeled "fresh," for example, cannot be juice that has been frozen first.

The Federal Communications Commission

The Federal Communications Commission (FCC) enforces rules that govern the broadcast media. The FCC's jurisdiction

Tim Boyle/Bloomberg/Getty Images

Ads for hard liquor, such as Cruzan Raspberry Rum, did not start running on TV until 1996, when Seagram's challenged a 30-year voluntary Distilled Spirits Council policy of not advertising on television. The FTC and the BATF regulate the liquor industry, but neither agency has the authority to ban hard liquor ads on television. Hard liquor ads are a lucrative source of revenue and now are commonplace on TV.

over the broadcast industry gives the commission indirect control over broadcast advertising. In the past, the FCC has ruled against demonstrations of products that were misleading and against commercials the FCC decided were tasteless.

TV Accepts Hard Liquor Ads

Although beer and wine advertisements have appeared on TV for decades, the TV networks traditionally did not advertise hard liquor. For three decades, the Distilled Spirits Council of the United States, operating under a voluntary Code of Good Practice, did not run television ads. In 1996, some liquor companies decided to challenge the voluntary ban by placing ads on local television.

Seagram's, the first company to challenge the ban, advertised Crown Royal whiskey on a local TV station in Texas. "We believe distilled spirits should have the same access to electronic media, just the same way beer and wine do," said Arthur Shapiro, executive vice president in charge of marketing and strategy for Seagram's in the United States.

The Federal Trade Commission (FTC) and the Bureau of Alcohol, Tobacco and Firearms (BATF) regulate the spirits industry, but neither agency has the authority to ban hard liquor ads on television. Because the TV networks can gain a great deal of income from advertising hard liquor, the TV networks now accept hard liquor ads.

Other government agencies, such as the Environmental Protection Agency and the Consumer Product Safety Agency, also can question the content of advertisements. Advertising agencies have formed the National Advertising Review Board (NARB) to hear complaints against advertisers. This effort at self-regulation among advertising agencies parallels those of some media industries, such as the movie industry's ratings code and the recording industry's record labeling for lyrics.

Advertising Business Delivers New Markets

The future of advertising will parallel changes in the media, in technology and in demographics. As more U.S. products seek international markets, advertising must be designed to reach those markets. American agencies today collect nearly half of the *world's* revenue from advertising. Three factors will affect the future of the advertising business: international markets, changing technology and shifting demographic patterns.

International advertising campaigns are becoming more common for global products, such as Coca-Cola and McDonald's, and this has meant the creation of international advertising markets. Cable News Network (CNN) sells advertising on CNN worldwide, so that any company in any nation with CNN's service can advertise its product to a worldwide audience. Overall, billings outside the United States are commanding an increasing share of U.S. agencies' business.

A second factor in the future of advertising is changing technology. As new media technologies create new outlets, the advertising community must adapt. Advertisers are trying to figure out how to reach consumers on the Internet. A tennis instructional video, for example, could include advertising for tennis products. One company is using lasers to create advertising in the evening sky. Many companies have created ads that are delivered directly to consumers' cell phones.

A third factor in the future of advertising is shifting demographic patterns. As the ethnicity, education and wealth of a nation shifts, marketing programs have to adapt quickly to reach their target audiences. Some television ads already include dialogue in both English and Spanish, and many national ad campaigns already include multilingual versions of the same ad, targeted for different audiences. Advertisers also will look for new ways to discern what creates product loyalty. Even when the economic outlook is uncertain, there are some brands and products consumers will buy, even if it means waiting awhile or cutting back on necessities to save for what they want.

The challenges for the advertising business are as great as the challenges for the media industries. The advertising industry will do what it has always done to adapt—follow the audience. The challenge for advertising will be to learn how to efficiently and effectively match the audience to the advertising messages the media deliver.

SHAWN BALDWIN/*The New York Times*/Redux Pictures

International advertising campaigns are becoming more common for global products, like Toshiba, advertised here on a wall of billboards in Cairo, Egypt.

Review, Analyze, Investigate

REVIEWING CHAPTER 10

Advertising Supports Mass Media

✓ Advertising carries the messages that come to you from the sponsors who pay for the American media.

✓ In 2009, businesses spent a total of $354 billion to advertise their products to American consumers

✓ As early as 1200 B.C., the Phoenicians painted messages on stones to advertise.

✓ In the sixth century B.C., ship captains sent criers around to announce that their ships were in port.

✓ In the 13th century A.D., the British began requiring trademarks to protect buyers.

✓ In 1704, newspapers were the first medium to use advertising. Magazines, radio, television and the Internet followed in the 19th and 20th centuries.

✓ Advertisers flocked to major Internet sites when they first were established. They expected quick returns as consumer use of the Internet skyrocketed. Advertisers quickly learned, however, that no matter how they packaged the message, advertising on an Internet site didn't necessarily bring increased sales.

✓ What advertisers call the *click-through rate* (the rate at which someone who sees an advertising message actually clicks through to learn more) is less than 1 percent.

✓ In 2011, Internet ad spending reached $31 billion.

✓ Viral marketing is a form of advertising that involves creating an online message that consumers pass on—an online "word of mouth."

✓ Advertisers today are still trying to figure out the magic formula to reach consumers on the Internet. New approaches are meant to make advertisements seem less like advertisements—further blurring the line between information, entertainment and advertising.

Ads Share Three Characteristics

✓ Daniel Boorstin says that advertising in America shares three characteristics: repetition, an advertising style and ubiquity.

✓ The sheer number of ads sometimes works to advertisers' disadvantage because they can crowd each other so much that no individual ad stands out in consumers' minds.

Ads Must Grab Your Attention

- ✓ To influence consumers, an advertising message must appeal to you for some reason.
- ✓ Advertising can catch your attention, according to Jib Fowles, in 15 ways, including playing on your need to nurture, your need for attention and your need for escape.

Advertisers Use Demographics

- ✓ Advertisers target their messages according to an audience's characteristics.
- ✓ Demographics are composed of data about a target audience's gender, age, income level, marital status, geographic location and occupation.

Advertising Feeds Consumerism

- ✓ Advertising provokes three main criticisms: It adds to the cost of products; it causes people to buy products they do not need; and it reduces competition and thereby fosters monopolies.
- ✓ Because the audience is increasingly fragmented, advertisers have used other tactics—from the Internet to viral marketing.

Advertising at Work

- ✓ Most advertising agencies are small, local operations.
- ✓ Depending on the size of the company, an advertising agency may be divided into as many as six departments: marketing research, media selection, creative activity, account management, administration and public relations.

Mass Media Depend on Advertising

- ✓ The advertising business and the media industries are interdependent—what happens in the advertising business directly affects the media industries.
- ✓ The advertising business is very dependent on the nation's economic health.
- ✓ The average price for the TV time for a 30-second commercial is $100,000. The price tag for a 30-second commercial can reach $3.5 million for a widely watched program such as the 2012 Super Bowl.
- ✓ The price to create a TV commercial can run as much as $1 million a minute.
- ✓ Different types of media deliver different types of audiences.
- ✓ The most successful method of access to consumers today through the Internet is called *search advertising*, often called simply *search*.
- ✓ There are four types of search advertising: paid listings, contextual search, paid inclusion and site optimization.

Media Industries Compete Fiercely for Clients

- ✓ Advertising is divided into national and local categories.
- ✓ Advertising sales representatives broker local accounts to out-of-town advertisers.
- ✓ The media compete with each other for the advertising dollar, and some media are better than others for particular products.

Federal Government Regulates Advertisers

- ✓ Government protection for consumers dates back to the beginning of the 20th century.
- ✓ Protection for consumers from misleading advertising comes from government regulation (the Federal Trade Commission, Food and Drug Administration and Federal Communications Commission, for example), from advertising industry self-regulatory groups (National Advertising Review Board, for example), and from codes established by the media industries.

TV Accepts Hard Liquor Ads

- ✓ In 1996, the distilled spirits industry challenged the 30-year-old industry-wide voluntary ban on hard liquor advertising on TV. The liquor industry placed the ads on local TV stations, and hard liquor ads are now commonplace on television.
- ✓ Neither the Federal Trade Commission nor the Bureau of Alcohol, Tobacco and Firearms, which regulate the spirits industry, has the power to stop liquor ads from appearing on TV.

Advertising Business Delivers New Markets

- ✓ The future of advertising will parallel the development of international markets, the refinement and expansion of new media technologies (especially the Internet) and changing demographics.
- ✓ Today's advertising agencies use sophisticated technology to track demographics to help deliver the audience the advertiser wants.
- ✓ International advertising campaigns are becoming more common for global products, such as Coca-Cola and McDonald's, and this has meant the creation of international advertising campaigns.
- ✓ As the ethnicity of the nation evolves, marketing programs must adapt to reach new audiences.

KEY TERMS

These terms are defined in the margins throughout this chapter and appear in alphabetical order with definitions in the Glossary, which begins on page 383.

Advertising Campaign 222
Click-Through Rate 216
CPM 224
Demographics 219
Direct Sponsorship 216
Pop-Up 216
Rep Firm 226
Search Advertising 225
Viral Marketing 216

CRITICAL QUESTIONS

1. Why is advertising not a medium? What role does advertising play in the mass media?
2. What are the three main arguments given by advertising's critics and by its supporters?
3. What are the benefits to an advertiser of TV instead of print? Of radio instead of TV? Of the Internet instead of broadcast and print?
4. Discuss three of Jib Fowles' 15 psychological appeals for advertising in some detail, and present an example of an ad that demonstrates each of the three appeals you discuss.
5. Discuss government regulation and industry self-regulation of advertising. Which government agencies are involved in advertising regulation? Do you think government regulation or industry self-regulation is more effective at protecting consumer interests? Explain.

WORKING THE WEB

This list includes both sites mentioned in the chapter and others to give you greater insight into the advertising business.

Adrants

http://www.adrants.com

Adrants provides marketing and advertising news "with an attitude" through its Web site and daily e-mail newsletter. No-holds-barred commentary on the state of the advertising and media industries includes emerging advertising trends, effects of demographic shifts on advertising strategies, and examination of paradigm shifts in the industry.

Advertising Age

http://www.adage.com

Adage.com is the Internet arm of *Advertising Age*, the weekly paper of advertising news. Other AdAge platforms include electronic newsletters, events and conferences, streaming video, audio webinars, podcasts and blogs. The news on the Web site is updated throughout the day.

Advertising Council

http://www.adcouncil.org

Leading producer of public service announcements, the nonprofit Ad Council has sponsored such familiar campaigns as "Friends Don't Let Friends Drive Drunk" and Smokey Bear's "Only You Can Prevent Forest Fires." Its clients are both nonprofit and governmental organizations.

American Advertising Federation

http://www.aaf.org

With 100 corporate members, as well as clubs around the United States and about 225 college chapters, AAF is the oldest national advertising trade association in the country. "The Unifying Voice for Advertising," AAF educates members about the latest trends, honors advertising excellence, promotes diversity in advertising and "applies the communication skills of its members to help solve community concerns."

American Association of Advertising Agencies

http://www.aaaa.org

This management-oriented trade association provides research, media advice and information, and benefit programs such as liability insurance and retirement savings plans for its members. The Web site provides members with industry news, events (including webinars and speech transcripts), career development opportunities and advice, and links to publications and research.

American Marketing Association

http://www.marketingpower.com

Originally created in 1937 through a merger of the national teachers of advertising and the American marketing association, the AMA is a marketing association for individuals and organizations involved in the practice, teaching and study of marketing worldwide. AMA members are connected to a network of nearly 40,000 experienced marketers in academics, research and practice. Its Web site offers marketing data, articles, case studies, best practices and a job bank.

Association of Hispanic Advertising Agencies

http://www.ahaa.org

With the goal to "grow, strengthen and protect the Hispanic marketing advertising industry," the AHAA aims to raise awareness in the value of the Hispanic market to advertisers. Member agencies range from Acento (Los Angeles) to Zubi Advertising Services (Coral Gables, Fla.).

Clio Awards

http://www.clioawards.com

The most recognized global competition for advertising, the Clio Awards has celebrated excellence in a broad range of mediums for more than 50 years. Founded in 1959 by Wallace Ross, the program's name originates in Greek mythology: Clio was "the muse of history and the recorder of great deeds." Award categories include Interactive, Content & Contact, Billboard, Print, Radio and Television/Cinema/Digital. Students are awarded in limited categories, and Network, Agency, Production Company and Advertiser of the Year are also honored.

Federal Trade Commission (FTC)

http://www.ftc.gov

Created in 1914 to "bust the trusts," the FTC is the only U.S. government agency that protects consumers against fraud and misleading advertising and handles antitrust matters, through its Bureaus of Consumer Protection, Competition and Economics. It does not resolve individual disputes but rather looks for patterns of law violations. Mail order, telemarketing and used cars are among the businesses it regulates. Much of the information on the Web site is also available in Spanish.

MediaPost Communications

http://www.mediapost.com

An integrated publishing and content company, MediaPost is the leading advertising and media Internet portal providing news, events, directories and a social network to help members better plan and buy both traditional and online advertising. The site's media directory includes information on more than 35,000 publications, stations, networks, Web sites and more.

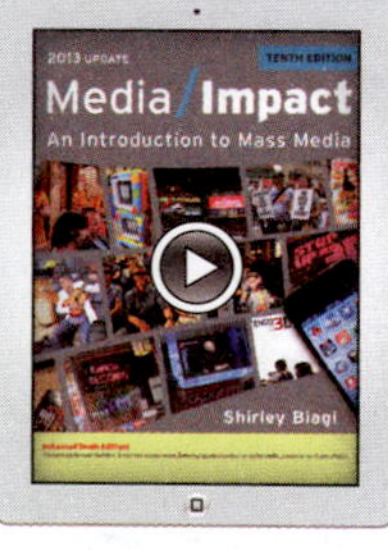

Impact/Action Videos are concise news features on topics covered in this chapter, created exclusively for **Media/Impact**. They are available for students and instructors at CengageBrain.com, and include screen access for classroom viewing and discussion questions.

11

"[BP] was one of the worst PR approaches that I've seen in my 56 years of business. Right away they should have accepted responsibility and recognized what a disaster they faced. They basically thought they could spin their way out of catastrophe. It doesn't work that way."

—Public relations expert Howard Rubinstein

Public Relations: Promoting Ideas

What's Ahead?

PR Helps Shape Public Opinion

PR Pioneer Issues "Declaration of Principles"

Government Recruits PR Professionals

Women Join PR Firms

Professionals Promote Ethics Codes

Public Relations at Work

Public Relations Adapts to the Internet

Public Relations Joins Ad Agencies

Variety of Clients Use Public Relations

Public Relations Organizations Offer Many Services

Publicity Means Free Media

Public Relations Grows Globally

U.S. Coast Guard/Getty Images

According to public relations experts, executives for BP (formerly British Petroleum) made many mistakes in the way they responded to the explosion on April 20, 2010, of their leased offshore rig near New Orleans, La. Eleven people died and four people were critically injured.

You may think

today's cash rebate programs from car manufacturers are relatively new, but in 1914, Henry Ford announced that if he sold 300,000 Model Ts that year, each customer would receive a rebate. When the company reached its goal, Ford returned $50 to each buyer. This was good business. It also was good public relations. Like Henry Ford, public relations people today work to create favorable images—for corporations, public officials, products, schools, hospitals and associations.

There are three ways to encourage people to do what you want them to do: power, patronage and persuasion. Power involves ruling by law, but it also can mean ruling by peer pressure—someone does something because his or her friends do. Patronage is a polite term for bribery—paying someone with favors or money to do what you want. The third method—persuasion—is the approach of public relations. ***Persuasion*** is the act of using argument or reasoning to induce someone to do something.

Like advertising, the public relations business is not a mass medium. Public relations is a media support industry. In the classic definition, ***public relations*** involves creating an understanding for, or goodwill toward, a company, a person or a product.

PR Helps Shape Public Opinion

One of the first political leaders to realize the importance of public relations was Augustus Caesar, who in the first century commissioned statues of himself to be erected throughout the Roman Empire to enhance his image. Since then, many political leaders have ordered heroic images of themselves printed on coins and stamps.

Today's public relations approach can be traced to the beginning of the 20th century. Journalists were an important reason for the eventual emergence of the public relations profession.

Before 1900, businesses believed they could work alongside the press, or even ignore it. Many stories that appeared in the press promoted companies that bought advertising. Then the Industrial Revolution arrived, and some industrialists exploited workers and collected enormous profits. Just before the turn of the 20th century, Ida Tarbell and Lincoln Steffens began to make businesspeople uncomfortable, writing stories for magazines like *McClure's* about the not so admirable characteristics of some companies, such as Standard Oil (see Chapter 4, p. 74).

According to *This Is PR: The Realities of Public Relations*, "No longer could the railroads butter up the press by giving free passes to reporters. No longer would the public buy whitewashed statements like that of coal industrialist George F. Baer, who in 1902 told labor to put their trust in 'the Christian men whom God in His infinite wisdom has given control of the property interests of the country.'"

President Theodore Roosevelt fed public sentiment—public opinion—against the abuses of industry when he started his antitrust campaigns. According to *Effective Public Relations*, "With the growth of mass-circulation newspapers, Roosevelt's canny ability to dominate the front pages demonstrated a new-found power for those with causes to promote.

"He had a keen sense of news and knew how to stage a story so that it would get maximum attention. His skill forced those he fought to develop similar means. He fully exploited the news media as a new and powerful tool of presidential leadership, and he remade the laws and the presidency in the process." Roosevelt used his skills at swaying public opinion to gain support for his antitrust policies.

PR Pioneer Issues "Declaration of Principles"

The first publicity firm was called The Publicity Bureau and opened in Boston in 1900 to head off the growing public criticism of the railroad companies. The best-known early practitioner of public relations was Ivy Lee, who began his PR career by opening an office in New York with George F. Parker.

Lee and Parker represented coal magnate George F. Baer when coal workers went on strike. A former newspaper reporter, Lee issued a "Declaration of Principles" that he mailed to newspaper city editors. This declaration became a manifesto for early public relations companies to follow.

Reacting to criticism that The Publicity Bureau worked secretly to promote the railroads, Lee wrote in 1906 in *American Magazine*, "This [the firm of Lee & Parker] is not a secret press bureau. All our work is done in the open. We aim to supply news. . . . In brief, our plan is, frankly and openly, on behalf of business concerns and public institutions, to supply to the press and public of the United States prompt and accurate information concerning subjects which it is of value and interest to the public to know about."

Lee and Parker dissolved their firm in 1908, when Lee went to work as a publicity agent for the Pennsylvania

Persuasion The act of using argument or reasoning to induce someone to do something.

Public Relations Creating understanding for, or goodwill toward, a company, a person or a product.

Railroad. Eventually, John D. Rockefeller hired Lee to counteract the negative publicity that began with Tarbell's investigation of Standard Oil. (Lee worked for the Rockefellers until he died in 1934.)

The idea of in-house corporate public relations grew as Chicago Edison Company and American Telephone & Telegraph began promotional programs. The University of Pennsylvania and the University of Wisconsin opened publicity bureaus in 1904, and the YMCA of Washington, D.C., hired a full-time publicist to oversee fundraising in 1905—the first time someone hired a publicist to do fundraising.

Bettmann/CORBIS

Edward L. Bernays wrote the first book on public relations, *Crystallizing Public Opinion,* and taught the first course on the subject.

Government Recruits PR Professionals

During World War I (1914–1918), the U.S. government set up the Committee on Public Information, organized by former newspaper reporter George Creel, blurring the line between propaganda and publicity. Creel recruited journalists, editors, artists and teachers to raise money for Liberty Bonds and to promote the nation's participation in the war. One of the people who worked for Creel was Edward L. Bernays. Both Bernays and Ivy Lee have been called the father of public relations.

In 1923, Bernays wrote the first book on public relations, *Crystallizing Public Opinion*, and taught the first course on the subject. Bernays was interested in mass psychology —how to influence the opinions of large groups of people. Procter & Gamble, General Motors and the American Tobacco Company were among his clients. "Public relations," Bernays wrote in 1955, "is the attempt, by information, persuasion and adjustment, to engineer public support for an activity, cause, movement or institution." In 1985, Bernays further defined public relations as "giving a client ethical advice, based on research of the public, that will win the social goals upon which the client depends for his livelihood."

To sell the New Deal in the 1930s, Franklin D. Roosevelt used every tactic he knew. Comfortable with the press and the public alike and advised by PR expert Louis McHenry Howe, FDR "projected an image of self-confidence and happiness—just what the American public wanted to believe in. He talked to them on the radio. He smiled for the cameras. He was mentioned in popular songs. He even allowed himself to be one of the main characters in a Rodgers and Hart musical comedy (played by George M. Cohan, America's favorite Yankee Doodle Dandy)," according to *This Is PR*.

To gain support for the nation's entry into World War II (1939–1945), the federal government mounted the largest public relations drive in its history, centered at the Office of War Information, led by former newscaster Elmer Davis.

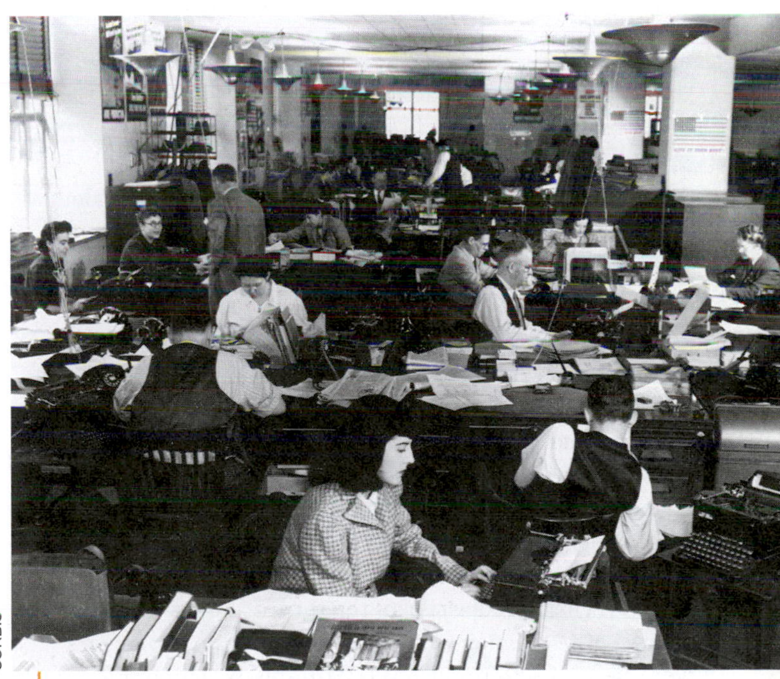

CORBIS

In what was the largest public relations drive of its time, the Office of War Information promoted the role of the United States in World War II. Today, the federal government is the largest single employer of public relations people.

Bettmann/CORBIS

Doris Fleischman, a public relations pioneer, began her career in the 1920s. Fleischman was an early advocate of public relations as a profession for women.

After the war, the public relations business boomed along with the postwar economy.

Women Join PR Firms

Doris E. Fleischman became one of the first women in public relations when she joined her husband, Edward L. Bernays, in his PR firm. Fleischman was an equal partner with Bernays in their public relations business. An early advocate of public relations as a profession for women, in 1931 Fleischman wrote that "one finds women working side by side with men in forming the traditions and rules that will govern the profession of the future."

Two other women who were public relations pioneers were Leone Baxter and Anne Williams Wheaton. Baxter formed Baxter and Whitaker in San Francisco with her husband, Clem Whitaker—the first public relations agency to specialize in political campaigns. In 1957, President Dwight Eisenhower appointed Anne Williams Wheaton as his associate press secretary.

Professionals Promote Ethics Codes

In the 1930s, the requirements to work in public relations were loose, and many people who said they worked in public relations were press agents who often used tricks to get attention for their clients. Henry Rogers, co-founder of what was then the world's largest entertainment PR firm, Rogers & Cowan (based in Beverly Hills), admitted that in 1939 he created a "best-dressed" contest to promote little-known actress Rita Hayworth.

There had been no contest, but Rogers dubbed Hayworth the winner of this fictional event. *Look* magazine gave Hayworth a ten-page spread. "Press agents, and that's what we were, would dream up all sorts of phony stories," he said. "Journalists knew they were phony but printed them because they looked good in print."

During the 1950s, the question of ethics in public relations arose publicly when Byoir and Associates, hired by a railroad company to counteract the expansion of trucking, was charged with creating "front" organizations to speak out against the trucking industry. In court, Byoir's agency argued they were exercising free speech. In 1961, the U.S. Supreme Court upheld Byoir's right to represent a client even if the presentation was dishonest, but this left the ethical issue of honesty unresolved.

The Public Relations Society of America (PRSA) established its first code of ethics in 1954 and expanded that code in 1959 with a Declaration of Principles. That ethics code still exists today to guide the business of public relations. (Excerpts from the PRSA code are in **Chapter 15**.) PR professionals continue to argue among themselves about the differences between the profession's beginnings as press agentry (which often meant fabricating stories) and the concept of ethically representing a client's business, as Edward L. Bernays described.

Public relations grew throughout the 1960s and 1970s with the encouragement of television, the federal government and corporate America. In 1961, for example, the federal government had about 1,000 people working as writer-editors and public affairs specialists. Today, *the total number of people working in federal government public information jobs is nearly 4,000, making the federal government the nation's largest single employer of public information people*. ("Public information" is the name given to the job of government public relations.)

Public Relations at Work

Public relations is an industry of specialties. The most familiar public relations areas are financial public relations, product public relations and crisis public relations, but there are many other specialty areas.

Financial Public Relations

People in financial public relations provide information primarily to business reporters. "Business editors like a PR staff that can provide access to top management," wrote James K. Gentry in the *Washington Journalism Review*, "that knows its company well or can find needed information quickly, that demonstrates ethics and honesty and that knows and accepts the difference between news and fluff." Gentry then listed comments gathered from editors about what makes a bad PR operation:

Robert Mankoff/Cartoonbank.com

"Let's never forget that the public's desire for transparency has to be balanced by our need for concealment."

- "Companies that think they can hide the truth from the public or believe it's none of the public's business."
- "I despise it when a PR person intercepts our calls to a news source but then isn't capable of answering our questions."
- "When they hire an outside PR firm to handle the job."
- "The 'no-comment' attitude. When they have little or no interest in going beyond the press release."
- "People who either get in the way of you doing your job, complain too much or are no help at all."

Product Public Relations

Product PR uses public relations techniques to sell products and services. Many companies have learned that seeking publicity for a product often is less expensive than advertising the product. Public relations "is booming partly because of price," reports *The Wall Street Journal*. A PR budget of $1 million for a substantial client is considered huge, whereas an ad budget that size is considered tiny.

Public relations often works better than advertising. For example, the Wieden & Kennedy agency in Seattle contracted Bigger Than Life, Inc., which makes large inflatables, to manufacture a 21-story pair of Nike tennis shoes. The company attached the shoes to the Westin Copley Place Hotel during the Boston Marathon and to the Westin Hotel in downtown Cincinnati during the March of Dimes walk-a-thon. Pictures of the shoes appeared in *The New York Times*, in *The Cincinnati Enquirer* and in newspapers as far away as Japan. Wieden & Kennedy estimated that buying the same advertising would have cost $7 million.

Crisis Public Relations

This aspect of public relations goes back as far as Edward Bernays responding to the charges against Standard Oil. The term *crisis public relations* (sometimes called ***crisis communication***) describes the response to a public relations emergency facing a company because of an unexpected event that could seriously hurt the company's reputation.

In October 1996, beverage maker Odwalla Inc., faced a public relations crisis when *E. coli* bacteria was traced to unpasteurized apple juice that had been sold by the natural juice company. The death of a 16-month-old girl in Colorado and more than 50 cases of severe illness were eventually traced to the bacteria. Odwalla, the leading manufacturer of unpasteurized juices, had made its reputation on natural, unfiltered products. But as soon as Odwalla detected the bacteria, the company announced an immediate recall of 13 products in the seven western states and British Columbia.

Crisis Communication A timely public relations response to a critical situation that could cause damage to a company's reputation.

Bloomberg/Getty Images

Akio Toyoda, president of Toyota Motor Corp., speaks at a press conference after a meeting of Toyota executives in Toyota City, Japan, on March 30, 2010. Toyota used crisis communications to try to overcome the public relations problems created by the massive recall of some of its vehicles for accelerator flaws linked to at least 51 deaths.

Then the company worked with the Food and Drug Administration to scour the Odwalla processing facilities, which were found to be free of the bacteria. The company continued the investigation, including the processors who supplied fruit for the juice. At the same time, Odwalla Chief Executive Officer Stephen Williamson said the company was exploring all methods of processing the juice to kill the bacteria. One month after the outbreak, Odwalla took out full-page ads in several newspapers, an "open letter" to its customers, thanking them for their support and offering sympathy for people diagnosed with *E. coli*–related illnesses after drinking Odwalla juices. The Odwalla case is often used as an example of effective crisis public relations.

The year 2010 offered two classic corporate crisis public relations challenges—Toyota Motor Corp. and BP PLC (formerly called British Petroleum). Toyota and BP "exacerbated their woes by either declining to fess up promptly, casting blame elsewhere or striking adversarial postures with the public, the government and the news media," wrote Peter S. Goodman in *The New York Times*.

In January 2010, Toyota recalled more than 2 million vehicles for accelerator flaws, a potentially huge public relations blow to its reputation for vehicle quality. The accelerator problems were linked to at least 51 deaths. There were reports that Toyota had known about the gas pedal problems much earlier but did not admit the problem publicly until the National Highway Traffic Safety Administration (NHTSA) issued a public alert. Then, after the NHTSA disclosure, Toyota employed public relations techniques to try to contain the damage to its reputation.

"Toyota blew it," communications expert Brad Burns told *The New York Times*. "It's been the proverbial death by a thousand cuts. They knew they had problems long ago, whether it was a mechanical issue or operator error, but they knew they had an issue they had to deal with. And rather than put public safety over profits, they appear to have listened to the product liability lawyers and they totally lost it. It's brand damage."

Then on April 20 the British Petroleum Deepwater Horizon drilling platform exploded in the Gulf of Mexico, the biggest oil spill in the gulf's history. Eleven people died, four were critically injured, and millions of gallons of oil spilled into the gulf. (See **Media/Impact: Money**, "BP Touts Itself as 'Green,' but Faces PR Disaster with 'BP Oil Spill,'" p. 241.)

"It [BP] was one of the worst PR approaches that I've seen in my 56 years of business," said public relations expert Howard Rubinstein. "They tried to be opaque. They had every excuse in the book. Right away they should have accepted responsibility and recognized what a disaster they faced. They basically thought they could spin their way out of catastrophe. It doesn't work that way."

These three examples—Odwalla, Toyota and British Petroleum—indicate how important the specialty of crisis public relations is within the public relations business.

Public Relations Adapts to the Internet

Because of its ability to deliver information quickly and directly, the Internet offers many benefits for public relations companies. Public relations people, in fact, often are very much involved in creating and modifying Web sites for their clients—creating a public face. News releases, product announcements and company profiles can be made available

Media/Impact
MONEY

BP Touts Itself as "Green," but Faces PR Disaster with "BP Oil Spill"

By Paul Farhi

What do you call a gigantic man-made disaster that is threatening to despoil the ecosystems and wreck the economies of the Gulf Coast? The answer is important, if you happen to be one of the companies responsible for it.

The massive slick spreading toward Louisiana has gone by several names since crude oil began gushing from a damaged drilling rig on April 20 [2010]. Media accounts have referred to it as "the Gulf oil spill," "the Deepwater Horizon spill" and the "Gulf Coast Disaster."

President Obama, leaving little doubt about whom he considers responsible for the epic mess, put a brand name on it in remarks in Louisiana on Sunday. The president dubbed it "the BP oil spill," after the company (formerly British Petroleum) that leased the now-damaged drilling platform. The Environmental Protection Agency refers to it the same way in its official pronouncements.

The name of a disaster can be critical, both as a historic matter and the more immediate matters of image, public relations and legal liability. BP has said it will honor "legitimate" claims from people and businesses seeking compensation from disruption caused by the spill. But since there are likely to be many disputed claims ("This is America—come on," BP chief executive Tony Hayward told *The Times* of London on Wednesday), having your company's name inextricably linked to a disaster can't help when a jury begins assigning damages. . . .

BP has been careful not to invoke its name in regard to the spill. "We refer to it as Gulf of Mexico Response," said Andrew Gowers, the company's spokesman. BP's Web site avoids the linkage, calling it "the spill" or "Gulf of Mexico response," or "BP's MC252 response," a reference to the rig known formally as Mississippi Canyon 252. . . .

Joe Raedle/Getty Images

On July 3, 2010, workers clear off oil washing on to Louisiana's Fourchon Beach. Public relations experts criticized BP for the way it handled public relations aspects of the oil spill.

Ultimately, public anger at BP may be tempered by the company's earlier efforts to polish its environmental image, said Larry Parnell, who directs the master's degree program in public relations at George Washington University. Parnell, a former consultant to an oil-industry company, said BP has invested in a "green" image with ads that featured its sunflower logo and the slogan "Beyond Petroleum." . . .

But the Sierra Club's [Kristina] Johnson isn't buying it. "They're the ones who have profited from oil and from our oceans. They're the ones who put the Gulf Coast at risk so that they could rake in record profits. A few ads don't change the fact that they're responsible for this now."

From Paul Farhi, "BP Touts Itself as 'Green,' but Faces PR Disaster with 'BP Oil Spill,'" The Washington Post, May 6, 2010, page C1.

online, to be captured on demand by the press, stockholders and anyone else who is interested.

The Internet also brings hazards. Disgruntled customers, pranksters and competitors can create their own sites to immediately challenge and even undermine a client's site. "In the pre-Internet days we used to say that a satisfied customer will tell one or two prospects but a dissatisfied customer will tell 10 or more," wrote G. A. Andy Marken, a public relations adviser, in *Public Relations Quarterly*. "With the Internet and the Web those same dissatisfied customers can tell millions of people . . . and they're doing it every day around the globe."

Marken says these attacks, which he calls ***cybersmears***, include anti-Disney, anti-McDonald's and anti-gun regulation sites, as well as chat rooms, discussion groups and online forums. To counter these negative messages, many businesses and organizations hire public relations firms to continuously monitor the Internet and alert their clients when negative information appears so the client can decide the best way to counter the information.

"It's a tedious task but any organization that isn't monitoring Internet traffic and Web activity could find itself in serious trouble," says Marken. "Companies and agencies spend hundreds and thousands of dollars on audio, video and print clipping services to analyze how their messages are being picked up, interpreted and used by the conventional media. They spend little or no time finding out what people are saying in real-time in cyberspace about them. . . . What you don't hear can hurt you . . . and it could be fatal."

For example, Toyota used a public relations company to monitor comments posted on social networking sites after the company recalled more than 2 million cars in 2010 for accelerator problems. By using public relations techniques, such as monitoring Internet social media like Facebook and Twitter for negative comments about the company, public relations people often play a central role in attempting to protect their clients from unfavorable publicity. (See **Media/Impact: Culture**, "After Recalls, Toyota Monitors Social Media to Protect Its Reputation," p. 243.)

Public Relations Joins Ad Agencies

More than 150,000 people in the U.S. work in public relations and about 4,000 firms throughout the nation offer PR-related services. The largest public relations firms employ more than 1,000 people. Several major corporations have 100 to 400 public relations specialists, but most public relations firms have fewer than four employees.

Public relations people often deal with advertising agencies as part of their job, and because PR and advertising are so interrelated, several large public relations firms have joined several large advertising agencies. For example, J. Walter Thompson (advertising) joined Hill & Knowlton (public relations), and the London firm WPP Group PLC bought Young & Rubicam and now owns more than 250 public relations, advertising and marketing companies.

Combined agencies can offer both public relations and advertising services to their clients, and the trend toward advertising/public relations combinations continues today. The difference between public relations and advertising at the nation's largest agencies can be difficult to discern. Advertising is an aspect of marketing that aims to sell products. People in advertising usually *aren't* involved in a company's policy making. They implement the company's policies after company executives decide how to sell a product, a corporate image or an idea.

Public relations people, in comparison, usually are involved in policy. A PR person often contributes to decisions about how a company will deal with the public, the press and its own employees.

Variety of Clients Use Public Relations

Public relations people work for several types of clients, including governments, educational institutions, nonprofit organizations, industry and business.

Government

The federal government is the nation's largest single employer of public information people. State and local governments also hire people to handle PR. Related to government are PR people who work for political candidates and for lobbying organizations. Media consultants also are involved in political PR. These people counsel candidates and officeholders about how they should present themselves to the public through the media.

Education

Universities, colleges and school districts often hire public relations people to promote these educational institutions and to handle press attention from the consequences of decisions that educators make.

Cybersmears Negative information organized and presented on the Internet as continuing attacks against a corporation.

Media/Impact CULTURE

After Recalls, Toyota Monitors Social Media to Protect Its Reputation

By Michael Bush

According to Doug Frisbie, Toyota Motor Sales USA's national social media and marketing integration manager, the automaker has actually grown its Facebook fan base more than 10 percent since late January [2010], around the time of the marketer's Jan. 21 recall announcement and its Jan. 26 stop-sale date. . . .

That's a testament to the resilience of the brand, but also to Toyota's ability to quickly pick up one of the most important tools in a crisis-communications handbook: social media.

Toyota has been faulted for communicating too little and too late in traditional media, but it's gone all out when it comes to Twitter, Facebook, blogs and other social-media channels. Prior to the recall, Toyota didn't have a reputation as an aggressive social-media adopter, yet it's managed to increase the number of fans on its main Facebook presence (from 71,600 to 79,500) over the past five weeks and, starting Jan. 21, it became a far more active user on Twitter. On Feb. 22 alone, it tweeted 34 messages (by contrast, Honda has more than 300,000 Facebook fans).

Toyota's been able to be so aggressive in social media largely because around Feb. 1 [2010] it created a social-media response room, always staffed with six to eight people monitoring the online conversation and responding at all times. It's answering consumers on its four Facebook pages; it created a Twitter chat with Jim Lentz, Toyota Motor Sales USA president–chief operating officer; and it created two new platforms, one with Digg and the other on Tweetmeme called "Toyota Conversations" to aggregate online chatter and allow Toyota to respond directly. . . .

ChinaFotoPress/Getty Images

In 2010, faced with several recalls of its vehicles for a variety of problems, Toyota Motor Sales used social media such as Facebook and Twitter to monitor Internet conversations about its products.

Mr. Frisbie recalls seeing the first tweets about the automaker's unintended acceleration issue toward the end of 2009, when Toyota recalled more than 4 million cars to fix and replace accelerator pedals. "The minute news hits the wires, it becomes a conversation," Mr. Frisbie said. "It's just a question of how high [the] volume [of] that conversation will become."

It didn't take long for Toyota to figure that out. According to Radian6, on Jan. 22, the day after the recall, buzz within the social web skyrocketed, with the number of posts about the automaker going from less than 100 to over 3,200. With the stop-sale announcement four days later, online chatter shot from about 500 posts that morning to more than 3,000 by that afternoon.

"Just by virtue of the volume of conversation you see out there online, [social media] is probably the most important [crisis-communication] element in many cases," said Mr. Frisbie. "How you respond and react to those [social-media] conversations really has become perhaps the most important platform for dealing with a crisis like this."

Michael Bush, "The Cult of Toyota," Advertising Age, March 1, 2010, page 1. Crain Communications Copyrighted 2011.

CRIS BOURONCLE/AFP/Getty Images

Public relations for nonprofit organizations, such as UNICEF, is growing especially fast around the world as charities compete for donations. On October 20, 2010, actor and UNICEF Goodwill Ambassador Danny Glover waves during a press conference in Lima, Peru, as he puts on a clown nose to promote UNICEF Peru's "Good Vibes" (Buena Onda) campaign. Rubber clown noses are the symbol of the annual campaign to raise money for daycare centers in poor neighborhoods and schools in remote areas.

Nonprofit Organizations

Nonprofit organizations include hospitals, churches, museums and charities. Public relations organizations help raise money for charities such as Habitat for Humanity, which builds and remodels homes for low-income communities. Public relations for nonprofit organizations is growing especially fast as different charities compete with each other for donations.

Industry

Chicago Edison's early use of promotion was one type of industry PR. Many industries are government-regulated, so this often means that the industry PR person works with government agencies on government-related issues that affect the industry, such as utility rate increases or energy conservation programs.

Business

This is the best-known area of public relations. Large companies keep an in-house staff of public relations people, and these companies also often hire outside PR firms to help on special projects. Product publicity is one of the fastest-growing aspects of business-related public relations.

Within many large businesses are people who handle corporate PR, sometimes called financial PR. They prepare annual reports and gather financial data on the company for use by the press. They also may be assigned directly to the executives of a corporation to help establish policy about the corporation's public image. Many companies also sponsor charity events to increase their visibility in the community.

Athletic Teams and Entertainment Organizations

A professional sports team needs someone to travel with them and handle the press requests that inevitably come at each stop. Sports information people also are responsible for the coaches', the owner's and the team's relationship with the fans. College and university sports departments often hire public relations people to handle inquiries from the public and from the press. Organizations such as the U.S. Tennis Association also sponsor events, such as the Arthur Ashe Kids' Day at the U.S. Open.

As described earlier, in 1939 Henry Rogers learned how to use press agentry to gather publicity for actress Rita Hayworth. Today, entertainment public relations agencies promote movies and also handle TV personalities and well-known athletes who appear on the lecture circuit.

International

As the nation's consumer market broadens, more attention is being given to developing business in other countries. This means more opportunities in international PR. Hill & Knowlton and Burson-Marsteller, for example, are two big U.S. public relations firms that now also operate in Japan.

Public Relations Organizations Offer Many Services

Responsibilities of PR people include writing, editing, media relations and placement, special events, public speaking, production tasks, research, programming and counseling, training and management.

- Writing: Writing news releases, newsletters, correspondence, reports, speeches, booklet texts, radio and TV copy, film scripts, trade paper and magazine articles, institutional advertisements, product information and technical materials and developing content for Web sites.
- Editing: Editing special publications, employee newsletters, shareholder reports and other communications for employees and for the public.
- Media Relations, Placement and Internet Services: Contacting news media, magazines, Sunday supplements, freelance writers and trade publications with the intent of getting them to publish or broadcast news and features about or originated by clients; responding to media requests for information or spokespersons; charting Web site activity and monitoring social media for comments about clients.
- Special Events: Arranging and managing press conferences, convention exhibits, open houses, anniversary celebrations, fundraising events, special observances, contests and award programs.
- Public Speaking: Appearing before groups and arranging platforms for others before appropriate audiences by managing a speaker's bureau.
- Production Tasks: Creating art, photography and layout for brochures, booklets, reports, institutional advertisements and periodicals; recording and editing audio and Internet materials.
- Research: Gathering data to help an organization plan programs; monitoring the effectiveness of public relations programs. This fast-growing area of public relations includes focus groups to test message concepts; research to target specific audiences; surveys of a company's reputation for use in improving the company's image; employee and public attitude surveys; and shareholder surveys to improve relations with investors.
- Programming and Counseling: Establishing a program for effective public relations within the company.
- Training: Working with executives and other people within the organization to prepare them to deal with the media.
- Management: Overseeing the costs of running the public relations program; paying the bills.

CSL, CartoonStock Ltd

"Nobody likes me. I need a media advisor."

Publicity Means Free Media

Public relations work often means finding ways to attract the attention of the press. Seymour Topping, former managing editor of *The New York Times*, said, "PR people do influence the news, but really more in a functional manner rather than in terms of giving new editorial direction. We get hundreds of press releases every day in each of our departments. We screen them very carefully for legitimate news, and very often there are legitimate news stories. Quite a lot of our business stories originate from press releases. It's impossible for us to cover all of these organizations ourselves."

People in public relations provide ***publicity***, which creates events and presents information so the press and the public will pay attention. Publicity and advertising differ: An advertising message is *paid for*; publicity is *free*. Advertising is a *controlled* use of media, because the person or company that places the ad governs the message and where it will appear. Publicity is considered an *uncontrolled* use of the media, because the public relations person provides

Publicity Uncontrolled free use of media by a public relations firm to create events and present information to capture press and public attention.

Matt Cardy/Getty Images

On November 2, 2010, gorilla keeper Simon Robinson from the Bristol Zoo in England clowns with an interactive, animatronic gorilla. The furry gorilla and his life-size gorilla sculpture friends were distributed around Bristol to bring attention to threats facing gorillas in the wild, an imaginative use of publicity. Publicity is considered an uncontrolled use of media because the public relations person has no control how the press will portray the subject (in this case, giant gorillas).

information to the press but has no control over how the information will appear—the press presents the story.

"We know how the media work," says David Resnicow of the PR firm Ruder Finn & Rotman, "and we make judgments on that, providing access to events as it becomes necessary." It is precisely because people in the media and people in PR know how each other work that they argue about the role of public relations in the news. (See **Media/Impact: People**, "Kelly Bush, a Publicist Who Sees No Need to Duck Calls" p. 247.)

The *Columbia Journalism Review* (*CJR*) studied the relationship between corporate public relations and *The Wall Street Journal* by examining the stories in *The Journal* on a specific day and comparing the stories to press releases issued by PR people. Specific companies were mentioned in 111 articles. More than one-third of the news stories in *The Journal* that day, *CJR* reported in its analysis, were based solely on press releases. In 32 of the stories that were based on press releases, reporters paraphrased the releases almost verbatim; in the 21 remaining cases, only a small amount of additional reporting had been done.

The Journal's executive director, Frederick Taylor, responded to *CJR*'s analysis by saying, "Ninety percent of daily coverage is started by a company making an announcement for the record. We're relaying this information to our readers."

Public Relations Grows Globally

Clever ways to attract attention are trademarks of today's successful public relations professional. Like advertising, the future of public relations is tied closely to the future of the media industries. The basic structure of the business will not change, but public relations practitioners find themselves facing the same challenges as people in the advertising business.

Growing international markets mean that many U.S. public relations firms have expanded overseas and that overseas companies seek help from American companies when faced with a challenge to their international reputation. Global communications mean that public relations agencies often work internationally on some projects, and the agencies have to adjust to the cultural differences that global exposure brings.

"To be successful they need an education on how our market works, what is reputation and how do you build it and who are the people they need to know to have 'permission to operate' in both a formal and informal sense," according to Margery Kraus, global CEO of the independent agency APCO. "Many of these companies also have to overcome the fact that they are from countries that are misunderstood or feared by the U.S., such as Russia and China."

New technologies, especially the Internet, mean more ways to deliver public relations messages and to monitor public relations efforts globally. Satellite technology has streamlined delivery of print, audio and video, giving PR agencies the same access to distributing information to news organizations that the news organizations themselves possess. As in the advertising industry, shifting demographic patterns mean growing potential markets for public relations services.

Media/Impact
PEOPLE

Kelly Bush: A Publicist Who Sees No Need to Duck Calls

By Michael Cieply and *Brooks Barnes*

LOS ANGELES—[Kelly Bush] and her company [ID] have been rattling the clubby world of entertainment public relations with their agile efforts to stay in front of a culture that can chew up a client in an instant. Red carpets, photo shoots and tiffs with the tabloids are still the stuff of Hollywood publicity. But Ms. Bush has been pushing her company—which employs about 75 people in Los Angeles, New York and London—to use every tool in its kit.

That can mean playing the Internet fixer. Ms. Bush claimed in an interview that she knew how to get Google to make nasty, wrong headlines instantly disappear.

"A lot of publicists still see their job as blocking the press—when you call they either run for the hills or lie—and Kelly is smart enough, in the age of the Internet, to know that never works," said Lisa Gregorisch, who runs the syndicated celebrity news program "Extra."

Not that Ms. Bush is easy. "She's a grizzly bear," Ms. Gregorisch said.

Her manner is shockingly direct, though tempered by the occasional funny take-back. Asked about her ultimate goal for ID, Ms. Bush didn't blink: "World domination."

A beat later, she pointed to a reporter's notebook and added, "she said sarcastically."

Ms. Bush knows she's a tough customer but prides herself on never resorting to one tool: the screaming phone call. "It's O.K. to say no to someone, but you should do it with respect," she said.

Her fans include Tobey Maguire, who credits Ms. Bush with helping persuade Sony to cast him as the lead in *Spider-Man* by lining up a sexy magazine spread.

J. EMILIO FLORES/*The New York Times*/Redux Pictures

Kelly Bush owns an entertainment public relations firm called ID that specializes in celebrity PR. Instead of protecting her clients when bad news breaks, she aggressively confronts the criticism.

"I like crystal clarity," Mr. Maguire said, "and that is always what I get from her."

Success inevitably brings detractors. One common criticism is that ID has grown by cutting fees.

Nonsense, Ms. Bush says. Everybody on the list—Amy Adams, Josh Brolin, Natalie Portman, Javier Bardem—pays fees comparable with those charged by competitors. The most basic services start at $4,500 a month and escalate toward what she calls "the high six figures" annually for corporate clients, which recently have included Nintendo, Tiffany & Company, the Weinstein Company and *Elle* magazine. . . .

ID, like most large competitors, has been expanding its brand-related business, partly to stabilize income from sources more reliable than actors, who may pay a retainer only for a few months when they have a television show or a movie to promote. . . .The company is owned exclusively by Ms. Bush, who said she financed its growth completely from cash flow. . . .

The name, ID, is meant to connote "identity," Ms. Bush said.

Review, Analyze, Investigate

REVIEWING CHAPTER 11

PR Helps Shape Public Opinion

- ✓ There are three ways to encourage someone to do what you want them to do: power, patronage and persuasion.
- ✓ Public relations people use persuasion to form public opinion about their clients.
- ✓ Modern public relations emerged at the beginning of the 20th century as a way for business to respond to the muckrakers and to Theodore Roosevelt's antitrust campaign.

PR Pioneer Issues "Declaration of Principles"

- ✓ President Roosevelt successfully used public relations to influence public opinion.
- ✓ The first U.S. publicity firm, called The Publicity Bureau, opened in Boston in 1900.
- ✓ The best-known practitioner of early public relations was Ivy Lee, who wrote a "Declaration of Principles" to respond to the secret publicity activities of The Publicity Bureau.
- ✓ The Chicago Edison Company and American Telephone & Telegraph were the first companies to begin in-house promotional programs.

Government Recruits PR Professionals

- ✓ Both Edward L. Bernays and Ivy Lee have been called the father of public relations.
- ✓ The Committee on Public Information, headed by George Creel, promoted the war effort during World War I.
- ✓ The Office of War Information, headed by newscaster Elmer Davis, promoted the country's efforts during World War II.
- ✓ Edward L. Bernays wrote the first book on public relations, *Crystallizing Public Opinion*.
- ✓ Franklin Roosevelt, assisted by public relations expert Louis McHenry Howe, successfully used public relations to promote the New Deal.

Women Join PR Firms

- ✓ Among the pioneering women in the public relations business were Doris E. Fleischman, Leone Baxter and Anne Williams Wheaton.
- ✓ Doris Fleischman and Edward L. Bernays were equal partners in their public relations firm.
- ✓ Doris Fleischman was an early advocate of public relations as a career for women.

Professionals Promote Ethics Codes

- ✓ The Public Relations Society established the profession's first code of ethics in 1954.
- ✓ Public relations expanded quickly in the 1960s and 1970s to accommodate television, the federal government and corporate America.
- ✓ The federal government is the largest single employer of public relations ("public information") people.

Public Relations at Work

- ✓ Three of the most common public relations specialties are financial public relations, product public relations and crisis public relations.
- ✓ Crisis public relations successfully repaired the public image of Odwalla Inc.
- ✓ Public relations experts criticized Toyota Motor Corp. and BP PLC for the way they handled their public relations crises in 2010.

Public Relations Adapts to the Internet

- ✓ Negative PR can spread very quickly on the Web, where anyone is free to post damaging comments about a company, organization or product.
- ✓ Toyota monitored social media to try to counteract negative comments about its auto recall in 2010.
- ✓ Companies and agencies must be continually vigilant to monitor how their messages are being used and interpreted on the Internet.

Public Relations Joins Ad Agencies

- ✓ Today, more than 150,000 people work in public relations nationwide and about 4,000 firms in the U.S. offer PR-related services.
- ✓ Because PR and advertising are so interrelated, public relations people and advertising agencies often work together in the same company to offer advertising and marketing communications services.

Variety of Clients Use Public Relations

- ✓ Public relations people work in government, education, nonprofit agencies, industry, business, athletic teams, entertainment companies and international business.

Public Relations Organizations Offer Many Services

- ✓ Responsibilities of PR people include writing, Web site development, editing, media relations and placement, Internet monitoring, special events, public speaking, production tasks, research, programming and counseling, training, and management.

Publicity Means Free Media

- ✓ The main difference between advertising and public relations is that advertising messages are controlled and public relations messages are uncontrolled.
- ✓ Public relations people create publicity, which is considered an uncontrolled use of media.

Public Relations Grows Globally

- ✓ New technologies, especially the Internet, mean new ways to deliver public relations messages.
- ✓ Satellite technology has streamlined print, audio and video delivery, giving PR the same access to information distribution as news organizations.
- ✓ Global communications mean many public relations agencies work internationally on some projects and must adjust to cultural differences that global exposure brings.
- ✓ Growing international markets mean that many U.S. public relations firms have expanded overseas.
- ✓ The Chinese company Foxconn hired a U.S. public relations company in 2010 to counteract negative publicity associated with suicides among its employees, an example of global public relations.
- ✓ Shifting demographic patterns mean growing potential markets for public relations services.

KEY TERMS

These terms are defined in the margins throughout this chapter and appear in alphabetical order with definitions in the Glossary, which begins on page 383.

Crisis Communication 239
Cybersmears 242
Persuasion 236
Publicity 245
Public Relations 236

CRITICAL QUESTIONS

1. How did each of the following people contribute to the development of public relations?
   a. Ivy Lee and George F. Parker
   b. Edward L. Bernays
   c. Doris E. Fleischman
2. Explain in some detail how the Office of War Information contributed to positive public relations for World War II.
3. When is it necessary for a company to apply crisis public relations techniques? Give an example from the public relations crises that developed at Toyota, BP or Foxconn.
4. Describe the ways that advertising and public relations are different. Describe the ways they are similar.
5. Describe one or more examples of how negative information on the Internet can create problems for public relations practitioners.

WORKING THE WEB

This list includes both sites mentioned in the chapter and others to give you greater insight into the public relations industry.

All About Public Relations

http://www.aboutpublicrelations.net

This site provides information and links to PR jobs, careers and internships as well as desk references, agencies and PR basics. Subject links range from a How-to PR Toolkit to online public relations campaigns and strategies.

Center for Media and Democracy: PRWatch.org

http://www.prwatch.org

This nonprofit, nonpartisan organization investigates and exposes "corporate and industrial public relations spin and government propaganda," and promotes media literacy and citizen journalism. The Center projects include *PR Watch*, a quarterly publication dedicated to investigative reporting on the PR industry; Latest News, Web-based daily reporting on PR propaganda and media spin; and SourceWatch, an online collaborative encyclopedia of people, groups and issues that shape the public agenda.

Chartered Institute of Public Relations

http://www.cipr.co.uk

The "eyes, ears and voice of the public relations industry," this professional organization for the British public relations industry provides training and events, a professional development program, PR news and research, and a PR jobs board. Its members sign an enforced code of conduct.

Institute for Public Relations

http://www.instituteforpr.com

This independent nonprofit organization sponsors and disseminates scientific research about public relations and sponsors the Commission on Public Relations Measurement and Evaluation, which establishes standards and methods for PR research and issues best-practices white papers. The Commission on Global Public Relations Research was formed in 2005 to study the practice of PR across regions, countries and cultures. The Institute also offers several awards for excellence in PR practice and research, including one for a master's thesis.

Online Public Relations

http://www.online-pr.com

This straightforward Web site provides free online resources for public relations professionals. It is developed and maintained by James L. Horton, a PR executive and educator who specializes in using technology and the Internet to enhance client service. This list of media, reference and PR resources contains thousands of links to reliable sources categorized by subject and alphabetically indexed.

PR Newswire

http://prnewswire.com

This association provides electronic distribution, targeting, measurement, translation and broadcast services for government, association, labor and nonprofit customers worldwide. PRNewswire provides search engine optimization, a professional community, user tracking, and multimedia and multicultural services to customers.

PRWeb

http://www.prweb.com

Founded in 1997 to help small businesses use the Internet to communicate their news to the public, PRWeb pioneered the direct-to-consumer news release. Clients can create a free account, access the site's search engine optimization tools and upload a press release for online distribution. PRWeb has helped more than 40,000 organizations of all sizes maximize the online visibility of their news. The service is owned by Vocus, a leader in on-demand PR software.

PRWeek

http://www.prweekus.com

A publication of Haymarket, producer of more than 100 international trade magazines, *PRWeek* is the company's first weekly in the United States. The magazine provides timely news, reviews, profiles, techniques and groundbreaking research for PR professionals. As the companion Web site for the magazine, PRWeek.com offers a searchable archive of editorials, news, features, industry research and special reports.

Public Relations Society of America (PRSA)

http://www.prsa.org

The world's largest organization for public relations professionals, PRSA was established in 1947 and has nearly 21,000 professional members organized into more than 110 chapters. Representing for-profit and not-for-profit organizations from areas including business and industry, government, health and education, its primary objectives are to advance the standards of the profession by providing members with professional development opportunities, to strengthen the society by increasing members and enriching member services, and to establish global leadership in PR.

Public Relations Student Society of America (PRSSA)

http://www.prssa.org

An organization founded by the Public Relations Society of America for students, the PRSSA's goal is to make students aware of current theories and procedures of the profession, to appreciate ethical ideals and principles, and to understand what constitutes an appropriate professional attitude. It has more than 10,000 members at over 300 chapters on college campuses throughout the country and offers a number of scholarships and travel opportunities.

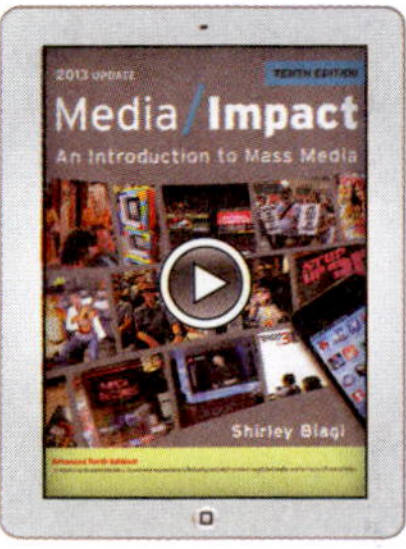

Impact/Action Videos are concise news features on topics covered in this chapter, created exclusively for **Media/Impact**. They are available for students and instructors at CengageBrain.com, and include screen access for classroom viewing and discussion questions.

12

"News today is increasingly a shared, social experience. Half of Americans say they rely on the people around them to find out at least some of the news they need to know."

—Pew Research Center's Project for Excellence in Journalism

News and Information: Getting Personal

What's Ahead?

Early News Organizations Cooperate to Gather News

Civil War Brings Accreditation and Photojournalism

Tabloid News Takes Over

Newsreels Bring Distant Events to American Moviegoers

Newspapers and Radio Personalize World War II

TV News Enters Its Golden Age

TV News Changes the Nation's Identity

TV News Expands and Contracts

Iraq War Produces "Embedded" Reporters

Reality Shows and Advertising Supplements Blur the Line

The Internet Transforms News Delivery

Information Access Creates a News Evolution

Journalists at Work

Journalists Focus the Public's Attention

Are Journalists Biased?

How the Public Perceives the Press

Credibility Attracts the Audience

HAZEM BADER/AFP/Getty Images

Journalists throughout the world often face serious danger in the field, gathering information for a story. On October 2, 2010, Palestinian journalists reporting on Jewish settlements on the West Bank cover their faces to escape tear gas aimed at the settlements.

Today the public's appetite for news means there are more news outlets gathering more types of news than ever before. On September 30, 2010, journalists photograph Tour de France champion Alberto Contador answering questions after he was suspended for failing a doping test. On February 6, 2012, the Court of Arbitration for Sport ruled that he was guilty of doping, stripped his wins in the 2010 Tour and 12 races since then and banned him from the sport for 2 years.

Because the First Amendment to the U.S. Constitution prescribes freedom of the press, it is important to understand the development of news reporting in this country. Today's news delivery is the result of a tug of war between audiences as they define the types of news they want and the news media that try to deliver it.

Publick Occurrences, the nation's first newspaper, published only one issue in 1690 before the authorities shut it down. The nation's first *consecutively issued* newspaper (published more than once) was *The Boston News-Letter*, which appeared in 1704. In the first issue, editor John Campbell reprinted the queen's latest speech, some maritime news and one advertisement telling people how to put an ad in his paper.

From 1704 until the Civil War, newspapers spread throughout New England, the South and across the frontier.

Cooperative News Gathering Member news organizations that share the expense of getting the news.

The invention of the telegraph, in 1844, meant news that once took weeks to reach publication could be transmitted in minutes.

Early News Organizations Cooperate to Gather News

In 1848, six newspapers in New York City decided to share the cost of gathering foreign news by telegraph from Boston. Henry J. Raymond, who subsequently founded *The New York Times*, drew up the agreement among the papers to pay $100 for 3,000 words of telegraph news. Soon known as the New York Associated Press, this organization was the country's first ***cooperative news gathering*** association.

Being a cooperative meant the member organizations shared the cost of getting the news, domestic and foreign, returning any profits to the members. Today's Associated Press (AP) is the result of this early partnership. United Press, founded in 1884 to compete with AP, devised a different way of sharing information. United Press, which eventually became United Press International (UPI), was established not as a cooperative but as a privately owned, for-profit wire service. (Today wire services are called news services.)

Because news services now use satellites and computer terminals instead of the original telegraph machines, cooperative and for-profit news gathering has become virtually instantaneous. Most American newspapers and broadcast news operations subscribe to at least one news service, such as AP. Many other news services send stories and broadcasts worldwide: Agence France-Presse (France), Reuters (Great Britain), ITAR-TASS (Russia), Agenzia-Nationale Stampa Associate (ANSA; Italy), Deutsche-Presse Agentur (Germany) and Xinhua (China).

The news services especially help small newspapers and broadcast stations that can't afford overseas correspondents. Large dailies with their own correspondents around the world still rely on news services when they can't get to a story quickly. AP today is still a cooperative, as it was when it began in New York. UPI had several owners and declined financially. Today, Associated Press serves as the nation's primary news service, constantly feeding stories to newspapers, broadcast outlets and Internet news services.

Some newspaper organizations in the United States—*The New York Times*, *The Washington Post* and the *Chicago Tribune*—also run their own news services. Subscribers publish each other's news service stories. For many newspapers, news service stories provide information at a relatively low cost because the newspaper doesn't need as many staff reporters to cover the news.

Civil War Brings Accreditation and Photojournalism

In the 1860s, interest in the emotional issues of the Civil War sent many reporters to the battlefront. Hundreds of correspondents roamed freely among the soldiers, reporting for the North and the South. Two important results of Civil War reporting were the accreditation of reporters and the introduction of photographs to enhance written reports.

Mathew B. Brady/CORBIS

Mathew Brady's photojournalism during the Civil War created a standard for future photojournalists to follow—using photo images to help capture a story's realism. Mathew Brady photographed this group of men of the 71st New York Infantry outside their tent at Camp Douglas in 1861.

Government Accredits Journalists

The issue of government interests versus press freedom surfaced early in the Civil War. In 1861, Union General Winfield Scott forbade telegraph companies from transmitting military information because he was afraid some stories would help the South. At the Battle of Bull Run in 1861, *New York Times* editor Henry J. Raymond, reporting the war from the front, mistakenly telegraphed a story that said the North had won. When he followed up with the correct story, military censors blocked the news, arguing the information should be kept secret. Then Union General William T. Sherman ordered *New York Herald* correspondent Thomas E. Knox arrested and held as a spy for sending sensitive military information.

President Lincoln intervened to reach a compromise that would balance the needs of the press with the needs of the nation through a process called ***accreditation***. This meant that the federal government certified members of the press to cover the war. Accredited journalists were required to carry press passes issued by the military. The practice of accreditation continues today as the government's method of certifying war-reporting journalists. This concept of accreditation—that a journalist is someone who could be credentialed—served to add to a sense of professionalism among journalists.

Photojournalism Is Born

Also at the Battle of Bull Run was photographer Mathew Brady, who convinced President Lincoln that a complete photographic record of the war should be made. Until the Civil War, photography had been confined primarily to studio portraits because of the cumbersome equipment and slow chemical processing. Brady photographed the battles of Antietam and Fredericksburg and sent photographic teams to other battles.

Newspapers did not yet have a method to reproduce the photographs, but Brady's pictures were published in magazines, making Brady the nation's first news photographer. His 3,500 photographs demonstrated the practicality and effectiveness of using photographs to help report a news story, although newspaper photographs did not become widely used until the early 1900s.

The marriage of photographs and text to tell a better story than either text or photographs could tell alone formed the beginnings of today's concept of ***photojournalism***. It was photojournalism that made *Life* magazine, founded by *Time*'s Henry Luce, such a success and created stars

Accreditation The process by which the government certifies members of the press to cover government-related news events.

Photojournalism Using photographs to accompany text to capture a news story.

Margaret Bourke-White/Time & Life Pictures/Getty Images

Photojournalist Margaret Bourke-White photographed stories for *Fortune* and *Time* magazines, establishing a 20th-century standard for photojournalism. Bourke-White, dressed in a military uniform, sits on top of a B-17 bomber in Northamptonshire, England, in 1942. Bourke-White covered World War II and the Korean War as a photojournalist.

out of gifted photographers like Margaret Bourke-White. The perfect image to accompany the words—the best photojournalism—has become an essential part of any good journalistic news story.

Tabloid News Takes Over

The beginning of the 20th century brought the expansion of newspapers—New York City once had more than 10 daily newspapers—and intensified competition. The introduction of the penny papers meant newspapers had to grab a bigger audience to survive. And, as described in **Chapter 3**, the race for readers ushered in yellow journalism—featuring stories about grisly crimes and illicit sex, often illustrated with large, startling photographs. Substantial newspapers, covering important stories, were being published all over the country, but today people still think first about tabloid journalism when they think about this period in newspaper history.

In the 1930s, people began to turn to radio for instant news headlines and information. Newspapers still flourished, but where they once had an exclusive corner on news, now they shared their audiences with radio. When World War II began, both radio and newspapers were in place to bring home news of the war.

Newsreels Bring Distant Events to American Moviegoers

Beginning at the turn of the 20th century and lasting until television took over news coverage, movie newsreels showed audiences distant locations and newsworthy events. Produced by companies including British Pathé (from 1900 until 1970) and Fox Movietone News (between 1919 and 1960), newsreels were shown in movie theaters to audiences hungry for the pictures that radio couldn't provide. Newsreels and news features, such as *March of Time*, were usually no longer than 10 minutes, with running commentary by a narrator, and were updated every week.

Because it took time to assemble the stories and develop the film, newsreel footage usually reached audiences a week or more after the events took place. Movietone News offered the most popular newsreel in the United States, produced by Fox, using more than 1,000 camera operators who roamed the globe to cover the news each day.

Besides serious news stories, the photographers captured Hollywood celebrities, scoured exotic travel locations and produced sports and feature stories. Another newsreel company, All-American News, produced newsreels directed at African American audiences; these were often shown before feature movies in addition to, or instead of, Movietone newsreels.

Newsreels offered an important realistic glimpse at worldwide news and information events that audiences couldn't get anywhere else.

Newspapers and Radio Personalize World War II

The most honored print journalist during World War II was Ernie Pyle, who worked for the Scripps Howard news organization. His reporting, which focused on the men who were fighting the war rather than battles and casualty counts, reached deep into the emotions of people who were stateside waiting for word from the front. (See **Media/Impact: People**, "Ernie Pyle: The War Correspondent Who Hated War," p. 258.)

Radio is the news medium that began to shine during World War II because radio news broadcasts meant that, for the first time, people could hear the action as it was happening. Imagine the date is September 8, 1940. World War II has begun its second year in Europe. You don't have a television set. You are sitting at home in the United States, listening to your radio. CBS announces a special bulletin from journalist Edward R. Murrow, reporting the first bombing of London: 626 bombers have pounded the city, leaving more than 1,000 people dead and 2,000 people injured. You and your family listen intently in your living room as Murrow describes "men with white scarves around their necks instead of collars . . . dull-eyed, empty-faced women. . . . Most of them carried little cheap cardboard suitcases and sometimes bulging paper shopping bags. That was all they had left. . . .

"A row of automobiles with stretchers racked on the roofs like skis, standing outside of bombed buildings. A man pinned under wreckage where a broken gas main sears his arms and face. . . .

". . . the courage of the people, the flash and roar of the guns rolling down streets . . . the stench of air-raid shelters in the poor districts."

This was radio news reporting at its best. For 26 years, from 1921 until the advent of television news in 1947, broadcast reporters like Murrow painted pictures with words. (For more information about Murrow's career in television, see **Chapter 8**.)

During the first half of the 20th century, radio reporters described Prohibition and its repeal, the stock market crash, the Depression, the election of Franklin D. Roosevelt, the New Deal, the bombings of London and Pearl Harbor, the Normandy invasion, Roosevelt's funeral and the signing of the armistice that ended World War II.

Most radio stations maintained their own radio news departments, until the advent of format radio. Today, very few radio stations maintain full-time news departments, and radio stations with news formats tend to be concentrated in the nation's big cities. Still, the heritage of colorful, exciting radio news formed the foundation for TV news, which began to blossom in the 1950s.

Bettmann/CORBIS

Before TV news existed, newsreels and news features were very popular with movie audiences. Shown in movie theaters before the main feature, newsreels, such as Movietone News, brought viewers closer to distant locations and newsworthy events. On November 2, 1932, Governor Franklin D. Roosevelt was interviewed for newsreel cameras at the executive mansion in Albany, N.Y.

Bettmann/CORBIS

During World War II, radio became the most immediate way for people to learn about current events. On July 5, 1942, radio commentators (left to right) Mark Hawley, William Shirer and John Charles Daly report on the day's war news from New York City.

TV News Enters Its Golden Age

The first network TV newscasts in the 1950s lasted only 15 minutes, but by the 1960s, TV network evening news had expanded to half an hour—the same amount of time the networks dedicate to national news today. Radio news

Media/Impact
PEOPLE

Ernie Pyle: The War Correspondent Who Hated War

By Dan Thomasson

Note: Ernie Pyle worked for Scripps Howard. Dan Thomasson, the editor of Scripps Howard News Service, wrote this reflection on Pyle's work to accompany a collection of Pyle's dispatches that was published in 1986.

The other day while going through some old files in our library, I came upon a yellowed and tattered dispatch.

It made me cry.

It was about the death of a Capt. Waskow during the Italian campaign of 1944. And it probably is the most powerful treatise on war and death and the human spirit I have ever read.

I took it out and had it treated and framed and I hung it in the office in a prominent position where now and then one of the younger reporters will come by and read it and try to hide the inevitable tear.

The man who wrote it, Ernest Taylor Pyle, is but a memory as distant as the war he covered so eloquently and ultimately died in.

But unlike so many who perished beside him, Pyle's contribution to what Studs Terkel calls "the last good war" remains with us in his work—thousands of words that will forever memorialize brave men and debunk the "glory" of war.

The column that says it best perhaps is the one drafted for the end of the fighting in Europe. It was found in his pocket by the foot soldiers who had risked their lives to retrieve his body on the Japanese island of Ie Shima in 1945:

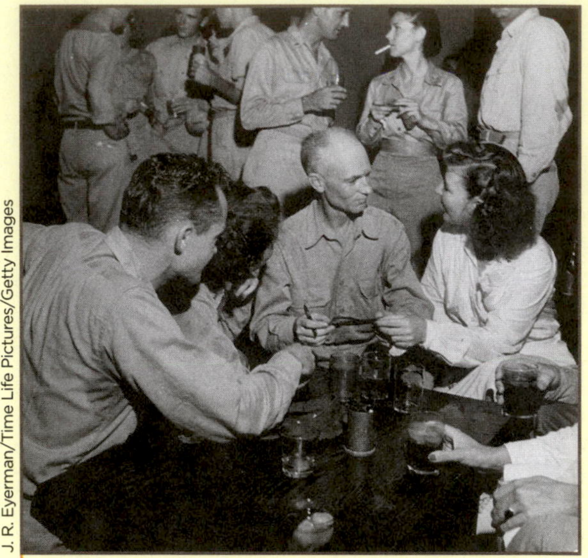

J. R. Eyerman/Time Life Pictures/Getty Images

War correspondent Ernie Pyle (1900–1945), the most honored journalist in the United States, died during the last days of World War II. Pyle (center) visits with a group of soldiers on April 1, 1945. He was killed by sniper fire on the Japanese island of Ie Shima on April 18, 1945.

"Dead men by mass production—in one country after another—month after month and year after year. Dead men in winter and dead men in summer.

"Dead men in such familiar promiscuity that they become monotonous.

"Dead men in such infinity that you come almost to hate them."

. . . When I was a kid starting out in this business, the trade magazines were full of job-seeking ads by those who claimed they could "write like Ernie Pyle." This was 10 years after his death and he was still everyone's model.

From "Why They Still Write Ernie Pyle Books," Honolulu Advertiser, *June 20, 1986, page A-1. Reprinted by permission of Scripps Howard News Service.*

stars like Edward R. Murrow moved from radio to television news, and eventually the TV networks created large news departments with bureaus and correspondents spread throughout the United States and overseas.

What has been called the Golden Age of Television News was the decade that began in 1961, with President John F. Kennedy's inauguration. The Kennedy family was very photogenic, and they invited press coverage. Kennedy's victory as president, in fact, had been credited to his on-camera presence during the Kennedy-Nixon debates in 1960. So it was fitting that Kennedy would be the first president to play Cold War brinkmanship on television, when TV news grew to become a part of politics, not just a chronicler of political events.

New York Daily News Archive/Getty Images

Television news provided a sense of collective national experience covering the events that followed the assassination of President Kennedy. On November 25, 1963, a crowd gathers in front of a giant television set in Grand Central Terminal to watch the funeral procession. The network news broadcasts during the events surrounding the Kennedy assassination have been called the finest four days of television news.

TV and the Cold War

President Kennedy asked all three networks to clear him time on Monday, October 22, 1962, at 7 p.m. Eastern time. The president had learned that missile sites were being built in Cuba with Russian help. Kennedy used television to deliver his ultimatum to dismantle the missile bases.

"Using the word *nuclear* 11 times, Kennedy drew a panorama of devastation enveloping the whole hemisphere," according to media historian Eric Barnouw. "The moves that had made such things possible, said Kennedy, could not be accepted by the United States 'if our courage and our commitments are ever to be trusted again by either friend or foe.'"

Kennedy admonished Russian Premier Nikita Khrushchev and urged him to stop the ships the Soviet Union was sending to Cuba to help build the missile sites. Faced with such a visible challenge, the Soviet Union turned its ships around in the Atlantic and sent conciliatory messages in order to reach a settlement. The Cuban missile crisis had in fact been a carefully constructed live television drama, in which Kennedy performed well.

TV News as a Window on the World

In 1963, television news was forced into an unexpected role as it conveyed a sense of collective national grief following President Kennedy's assassination. For four days beginning at 1:30 p.m. Eastern time on Friday, November 22, 1963, the country witnessed the aftermath of the assassination of the president. At 2:38 p.m., Vice President Lyndon Johnson was sworn in as president on television.

On Saturday, TV viewers watched the world's diplomats arrive for Kennedy's funeral. On Sunday, viewers watched the first murder ever broadcast live on television, as Jack Ruby killed assassination suspect Lee Harvey Oswald. Then, on Monday, November 25, 1963, came the president's funeral.

As many as nine out of ten television sets were turned on during the marathon events surrounding the president's funeral. The networks canceled all commercials. "Some television employees had slept as little as six hours in three nights," wrote media historian Eric Barnouw. "They went on, almost welcoming the absorption in the task at hand." The network news broadcasts during the events surrounding the Kennedy assassination were called the finest four days of television news. Television had become the nation's "window on the world," wrote Barnouw. "The view it offered seemed to be *the* world. They trusted its validity and completeness."

Eddie Martinez/Bettman/Corbis

On March 29, 1973, news cameras recorded the last U.S. serviceman to leave Vietnam, Army Chief Master Sergeant Max Bielke. Graphic TV coverage of the Vietnam War shook American viewers as no previous war coverage had. It also gave them an appetite for live news coverage—instant information about events as they were happening.

TV News Changes the Nation's Identity

In the late 1960s and early 1970s, television played a defining role in two very important stories—the war in Vietnam and the Watergate hearings.

Vietnam Coverage Exposes Reality

The longest-running protest program in the nation's history began appearing on television news as anti-Vietnam War marchers showed up on camera daily in the late 1960s. During live coverage of the Chicago Democratic Convention in 1968, demonstrators faced police in a march toward the convention hall. Television covered the resulting violence, which caused injuries to hundreds of protesters and to 21 reporters and photographers.

"When the war in Vietnam began to escalate in 1965," wrote TV critic Jeff Greenfield, "it was the television networks, covering the war with few official restrictions, that brought to American homes pictures of the face of war that had never been shown before: not friendly troops welcomed by the populace, but troops setting fire to villages with cigarette lighters; troops cutting off the ears of dead combat foes; allies spending American tax money for personal gain."

Candid reporting from the war itself shook viewers as previous war reporting never had, but it also gave Americans an appetite for news and for live news coverage—instant information about events as they were happening.

Wally McNamee/Corbis

Through live coverage of the Senate Judiciary Committee's Watergate hearings from May–August 1973, TV viewers got a close look inside the Nixon presidency as committee members examined evidence against the president. Nixon resigned in 1974.

Watergate Hearings Reveal Politics at Work

In 1973, live television news took another leap with the continuous broadcast of the U.S. Senate's Watergate hearings to investigate allegedly illegal activities of the Republican Committee to Re-elect the President (CREEP). A parade of government witnesses and political appointees fascinated viewers with descriptions of the inner workings of the Nixon presidency.

According to media scholars Christopher Sterling and John Kittross, "Running from May through August 1973, and chaired by North Carolina's crusty Sam Ervin, these hearings were a fascinating live exposition of the political process in America, and were 'must' television watching as a parade of witnesses told—or evaded telling—what they knew of the broad conspiracy to assure the reelection of Nixon and then to cover up the conspiracy itself." For more than a year the political drama continued to unfold on television's nightly news.

Ultimately, the Judiciary Committee of the House of Representatives began a televised debate on whether to impeach the president. For the first time in its history, the nation faced the prospect of seeing a president brought to trial live on national television. On August 8, 1974, President Nixon brought the crisis to an end by announcing his resignation—on television.

News Expands and Contracts

Because viewers were hungry for news and wanted to *watch* it, local TV news operations expanded—some stations offering as much as two hours of local news plus the national news broadcasts. Throughout the 1970s and 1980s, networks and local news departments expanded. Then came broadcast deregulation in the 1980s. The networks were sold and consolidated, and local stations, many of which had been locally owned, became pieces of larger corporations.

In 1980, Ted Turner founded Cable News Network (CNN), which offered round-the-clock news on cable. CNN established overseas bureaus and the concept that all-news-all-the-time would grab an audience. Audiences responded, and CNN became an alternative to network news, often the first place audiences turned whenever there was a crucial international story that required constant updating.

In general, however, in the 1990s, the American public read fewer newspapers and watched less news on television. Network and local TV news audiences declined. News departments began to shrink. Soon, another medium replaced the public's seemingly insatiable need for instant news and information—the Internet.

Iraq War Produces "Embedded" Reporters

Since the Vietnam War, access to battlefield locations has been a battle between the press' aggressive need-to-know and the military's need-to-keep-secret. In 2003, military press relations took a new turn when the United States declared war on Iraq.

Before the battles began, the U.S. military announced a plan to ***embed*** more than 600 reporters with American troops. Embedding offered the reporters access to the frontlines but also kept them within the military's control. Still, it was a reversal of past Pentagon policy makers, who often had sought to keep the press far from military operations.

Scott Peterson/Getty Images

In 2003, during the Iraq War, the Pentagon embedded more than 600 reporters with American troops. Reporters prepared for Iraq duty by attending boot camp. Embedded photographer Shawn Baldwin of *The New York Times* (left) and reporter Carol Rosenberg of *The Miami Herald* ride in the back of a U.S. Marine vehicle on May 1, 2004, on the edge of Fallujah, Iraq.

CNN and the major television networks offered nonstop coverage in the early days of the war, and people watched. "A lot of people have been surprised at the access and cooperation we've had in the field," said Tony Maddox, Senior Vice President Europe, Middle East and Africa for CNN International. "It's produced some remarkable images."

In 2005, the Bush administration sought to influence coverage of the United States in Iraq by paying news outlets to publish stories written by American troops. Congress criticized the practice, saying the U.S. government should not attempt to manage the press.

Reality Shows and Advertising Supplements Blur the Line

TV reality shows, such as *Undercover Boss*, blur the distinction between what is news and what is re-created drama.

Embedded During the Iraq War, a term used to describe journalists who were allowed to cover the war on the frontlines, supervised by the U.S. military.

CBS Photo Archive/Getty Images

Documentary-style TV reality shows, such as *Undercover Boss*, imitate news coverage, even though the video footage is heavily edited and the events are manufactured, which further blurs the distinction between news and entertainment. Each week *Undercover Boss* follows a corporate executive who joins the company "undercover" as a regular employee. In the 1-800-Flowers.com episode, company president Chris McCann (left) tries to arrange flowers as part of his "undercover" assignment.

"And, when we come back, Liz will be here with lots more lip gloss."

Michael Crawford/Cartoonbank.com

Advertorial Paid advertising supplements in newspapers and magazines that often look similar to the regular news pages.

These shows use interviews and cover live action in a documentary style that imitates news stories. Reality shows, or docudramas, make it difficult for an audience to distinguish between packaged entertainment and spontaneous events.

Infomercials—programs that pretend to give viewers information but that are really advertisements for the sponsors' products—also are making it harder to discern what is reporting and what is advertising. The line between news and entertainment on television becomes even trickier when advertisers produce programs that look like news but are really advertisements. Paid advertising supplements in newspapers and magazines—called ***advertorials***—also blur the line between news content and advertising. Although these supplements usually are labeled as advertising, they often look similar to the regular news pages.

This merging of news with entertainment and advertising, as well as the entertaining graphics and the lighthearted presentation style of most local TV newscasts, makes it more difficult for viewers and readers to separate fact from fiction, reality from reenactment, and news from advertising. The result may be a decline in the audience's trust in the news media to deliver accurate information. This makes it important that so-called pseudo-news be properly labeled so it doesn't mislead the public.

The Internet Transforms News Delivery

The immediacy of the Internet brought several changes to the news business. News became more personalized, and the Internet began to replace broadcast news because it is more immediate. The Internet also changed the way journalists work because often they are required to deliver several different types of stories simultaneously for print, broadcast and Internet formats.

Internet Personalizes the News

According to the most recent study from the Pew Research Center, Internet news is attracting a large segment of the national audience. At the same time, many people are losing the news habit, according to the study. They pay attention to the news only when something important happens, and many watch broadcast news with the remote control nearby to skip uninteresting stories and move on to something they would rather watch.

Today, the Internet is a nonstop news and information machine. (See **Illustration 12.1**.) Anyone with access to

Media/Impact AUDIENCE

Illustration 12.1

Top 10 Internet News Sites

The audience for news is migrating from newspapers and television to the Internet. Here are the top 10 Internet sites people use to find the news.

Source: Pew Project for Excellence in Journalism, State of the News Media 2011. *Retrieved from http://www.stateofthemedia.org/2011/.*

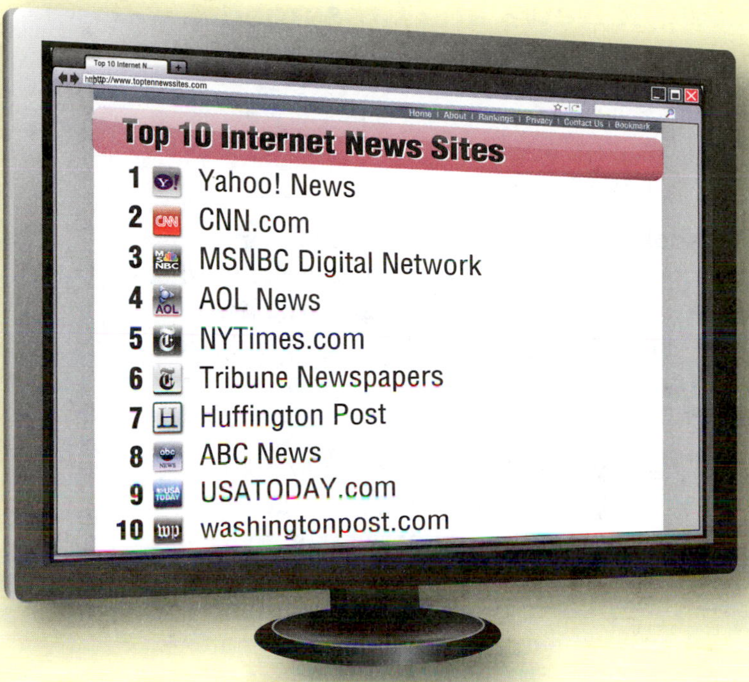

the Internet can choose the sources and subjects to investigate. Yahoo! News, with a significant number of online subscribers, compiles headlines from television and print news outlets—photos and stories from major news organizations—as well as updated headline stories from news magazines like *Time* and *Bloomberg Businessweek*. For specialty information, and for more background, you can visit any corporation's, association's or nonprofit organization's Web site.

You can choose what to look for and also *when* you look. The Internet is available on your schedule—independent of any TV network or local broadcast time schedule. News rotates through CNN Headline News (HLN) on television at 15-minute intervals, but you can check your computer or your cell phone and find just about anything you want to know—sports scores, the weather, international headlines—whenever you want to know it.

The Internet, unlike any other form of news and information delivery, is completely self-directed news and information—targeted to individual needs and not connected to a specific time of day or night. The Internet also is the place where people can get all the news in one location that they previously had to gather from several sources.

Today, one of four Americans lists the Internet as a main source of news (compared to just 15 percent in 2000), and 44 percent say they receive news reports from the Internet at least once a week. At the same time, network evening television news viewership for the major TV networks has continued to drop. In general, the study also found that people who are interested in the news online tend to watch less network TV news.

There were other important findings of the Pew study:

- As large numbers of Americans under age 30 turn to the Internet for news, people of all ages read the news online. Thirty-three percent of people under age 30 go online for news every day, but so do 27 percent of people in their 40s and 25 percent of people in their 50s.
- People who read online newspapers have a far less favorable view of network and local TV news programs than do people who read the print version of the daily newspaper.

More than half the TV audience say they turn to TV cable news, such as CNN, instead of the broadcast TV networks for breaking news, but the audience for cable news is not

Media/Impact MONEY

Network News at a Crossroads

By Brian Stelter and Bill Carter

ABC News is making no secret about what is behind the sweeping staff cuts it now faces: raw survival instinct.

"I just looked out at the next five years and was concerned that we could not sustain doing what we were doing," said David Westin, the president of ABC News, as he explained the decision last week to jettison up to 400 staff members, a quarter of the news staff, in the coming months.

The same compelling motive already instigated strategic retrenchment at ABC's broadcast competitors. NBC, the one network with a cable news channel, MSNBC—and, not coincidentally, the only network in a sound position of profitability—has drastically pared down its operations over the last few years. So has CBS, which is losing money already and has cut about 70 jobs this year [2010].

But with news available more places than ever, on cable channels and Internet sites, and with revenue challenged by heavy dependence on shrinking advertising dollars, the future for the news divisions at ABC and CBS remains deeply insecure.

"Long term, it's going to get harder for these guys to exist as they are currently constructed, with the exception of NBC because it can offload the costs on MSNBC," Michael Nathanson, an industry analyst for Sanford C. Bernstein & Company, said.

The economic problems facing ABC News and CBS News in many ways mirror those faced by newspapers, which have been similarly afflicted by a drop in advertising revenue. The reaction—severe cuts in personnel and other costs—also looks to be the same. . . .

The easy answer would seem to lie in NBC's structure, because in contrast to its competitors, that news organization is flush, making an estimated $400 million in profit a year.

CHRISTIAN HANSEN/*The New York Times*

Viewership for television network news is declining as more people migrate to the Internet for information, and in 2010 there were a series of staff cutbacks in the news departments at the networks. Producer Rick Kaplan is shown working in a CBS News control room.

"We actually think we have a completely different model," Steve Capus, the president of NBC News, said. That model: win every significant ratings competition on the broadcast side and rely on MSNBC's revenue stream of advertising plus cable subscriber fees to subsidize the high costs of news gathering.

The effectiveness of that formula inevitably resurrects predictions that a marriage with a cable news organization is imperative for CBS and ABC. The obvious partner is CNN, and both those networks have been in courtships with it before. To date, the cultural challenges have been insurmountable. CNN, which says last year was its most profitable since its founding in 1980, would seem to have little incentive to rush to the aid of a network. And neither network wants to cede editorial control to CNN.

"If it were easy or obvious, it would have happened by now," Mr. Heyward said.

From Brian Stelter and Bill Carter, "Network News at a Crossroads," The New York Times, *February 28, 2010, page B1.*

growing. (See **Media/Impact: Money**, "Network News at a Crossroads," p. 264.)

Information Access Creates a News Evolution

This evolution in people's news habits has taken nearly a century and required several technological innovations. From print to radio to television to the Internet, as each new system of delivery emerged, the old systems still stayed in place. This means that today there's more news available from more news sources and delivered with more types of technology than ever before.

People can select the kinds of information they want, when they want it, creating personal news. The news business is becoming even more competitive because consumers now have many sources—local, national and international plus the enormous variety of resources available on the Internet, such as social media sites—where they can look for what they want and need to know. (See **Media/Impact: Culture**, "How Blogs and Social Media Agendas Relate and Differ from the Traditional Press," p. 266, and **Illustration 12.2**, p. 267.)

FETHI BELAID/AFP/Getty Images

News organizations like CNN and ABC News increasingly hire "all-platform journalists"—reporters who use laptops and shoot video to file articles for the Internet and TV simultaneously. Reporter Mohamed Hammi uses a still camera, a video camera, a laptop and a cell phone to file his stories from Tunis.

Journalists at Work

The audience for news is shifting and in many cases declining (especially print news sources, such as newspapers and magazines). With so many sources of news available, news organizations must each be satisfied with a smaller piece of the audience. In a practical sense, this means lower revenues for media whose advertising rates are based on audience size—fewer readers, listeners or viewers means less money to hire people to write and report the news.

In today's media business, reporters often must work as ***"all-platform" journalists***. They must be able to write the story and take photographs as well as produce video. In 2008, CNN assigned "digital journalists" to ten cities in the U.S. to report local stories. These journalists report live, using laptops and cell phone cameras. "We are harnessing technology that enables us to be anywhere and be live from anywhere," said Nancy Lane, senior vice president for newsgathering for CNN/U.S. "It completely changes how we can report."

"Today, as they confront new competition on the Web, television networks are increasingly embracing portable—and inexpensive—methods of production," reports *The New York Times*. "A new breed of reporter, sometimes called a 'one-man band,' has become the new norm. Though the style of reporting has existed for years, it is being adopted more widely as these reporters act as their own producer, cameraman and editor, and sometimes even transmit live video."

The Pew Project for Excellence in Journalism has called today's transformation in the way journalists work "epochal, as momentous as the invention of television or the telegraph, perhaps on the order of the printing press itself."

In its 2011 *State of the News Media* report, the Project for Excellence in Journalism outlined six major trends that are affecting the news media today. (Excerpted from *The State of the News Media 2011: An Annual Report on American Journalism*, Project for Excellence in Journalism, www.journalism.org.)

1. **The news industry is turning to executives from outside.** With the old revenue model broken, more

All-Platform Journalists Broadcast journalists who act as their own producer, cameraperson and editor, and sometimes even transmit live video.

Media/Impact CULTURE

How Blogs and Social Media Agendas Relate and Differ from the Traditional Press

By Pew Research Center's Project for Excellence in Journalism

News today is increasingly a shared, social experience. Half of Americans say they rely on the people around them to find out at least some of the news they need to know. Some 44 percent of online news users get news at least a few times a week through emails, automatic updates or posts from social networking sites. . . .

The Pew Research Center's Project for Excellence in Journalism has gathered a year of data on the top news stories discussed and linked to on blogs and social media pages and seven months' worth on Twitter. We also have analyzed a year of the most viewed news-related videos on YouTube. Several clear trends emerge.

Most broadly, the stories and issues that gain traction in social media differ substantially from those that lead in the mainstream press. But they also differ greatly from each other. Of the 29 weeks that we tracked all three social platforms, blogs, Twitter and YouTube shared the same top story just once. . . .

Each social media platform also seems to have its own personality and function. In the year studied, bloggers gravitated toward stories that elicited emotion, concerned individual or group rights or triggered ideological passion. Often these were stories that people could personalize and then share in the social forum—at times in highly partisan language. And unlike in some other types of media, the partisanship here does not lean strongly to one side or the other. . . .

On Twitter, by contrast, technology is a major focus—with a heavy prominence on Twitter itself—while politics plays a much smaller role. The mission is primarily about passing along important—often breaking—information in a way that unifies or assumes shared values within the Twitter community. . . .

YouTube has still other characteristics that set it apart. Here, users don't often add comments or additional insights but instead take part by selecting from millions of videos and sharing. Partly as a result, the most watched videos have a strong sense of serendipity. They pique interest and curiosity with a strong visual appeal. The "Hey you've got to see this," mentality rings strong. Users also gravitate toward a much broader international mix here as videos transcend language barriers in a way that written text cannot.

Across all three social platforms, though, attention spans are brief. Just as news consumers don't stay long on any Web site, social media doesn't stay long on any one story. On blogs, 53 percent of the lead stories in a given week stay on the list no more than three days. On Twitter that is true of 72 percent of lead stories, and more than half (52 percent) are on the list for just 24 hours.

And most of those top weekly stories differ dramatically from what is receiving attention in the traditional press. Blogs overlap more than Twitter, but even there only about a quarter of the top stories in any given week were the same as in the "mainstream media."

Instead, social media tend to home in on stories that get much less attention in the mainstream press. And there is little evidence, at least at this point, of the traditional press then picking up on those stories in response. (See **Illustration 12.2**.)

Excerpted from: Project for Excellence in Journalism, "New Media, Old Media: How Blogs and Social Media Agendas Relate and Differ from the Traditional Press," May 23, 2010. Retrieved from http://www.journalism.org/analysis_report/new_media_old_media.

Media/Impact CULTURE (CONTINUED)

Illustration 12.2

How Do People Use Social Media to Share News?

During 2009 and 2010, the Project for Excellence in Journalism tracked the use of social media (blogs, Twitter and YouTube) and compared the topics people shared on these sites, as well as what the traditional press organizations covered during the same time. The Project found that social media carries very different types of stories from traditional media—especially a lot more coverage of foreign (non-U.S.) events and technology.

Source: Pew Research Center's Project for Excellence in Journalism, "New Media, Old Media: How Blogs and Social Media Agendas Relate and Differ from the Traditional Press," May 23, 2010. Retrieved from http://www.journalism.org/analysis_report/new_media_old_media. (Data analyzed January 19, 2009–January 15, 2010, except Twitter, which was tracked from June 15, 2009 to January 15, 2010.)

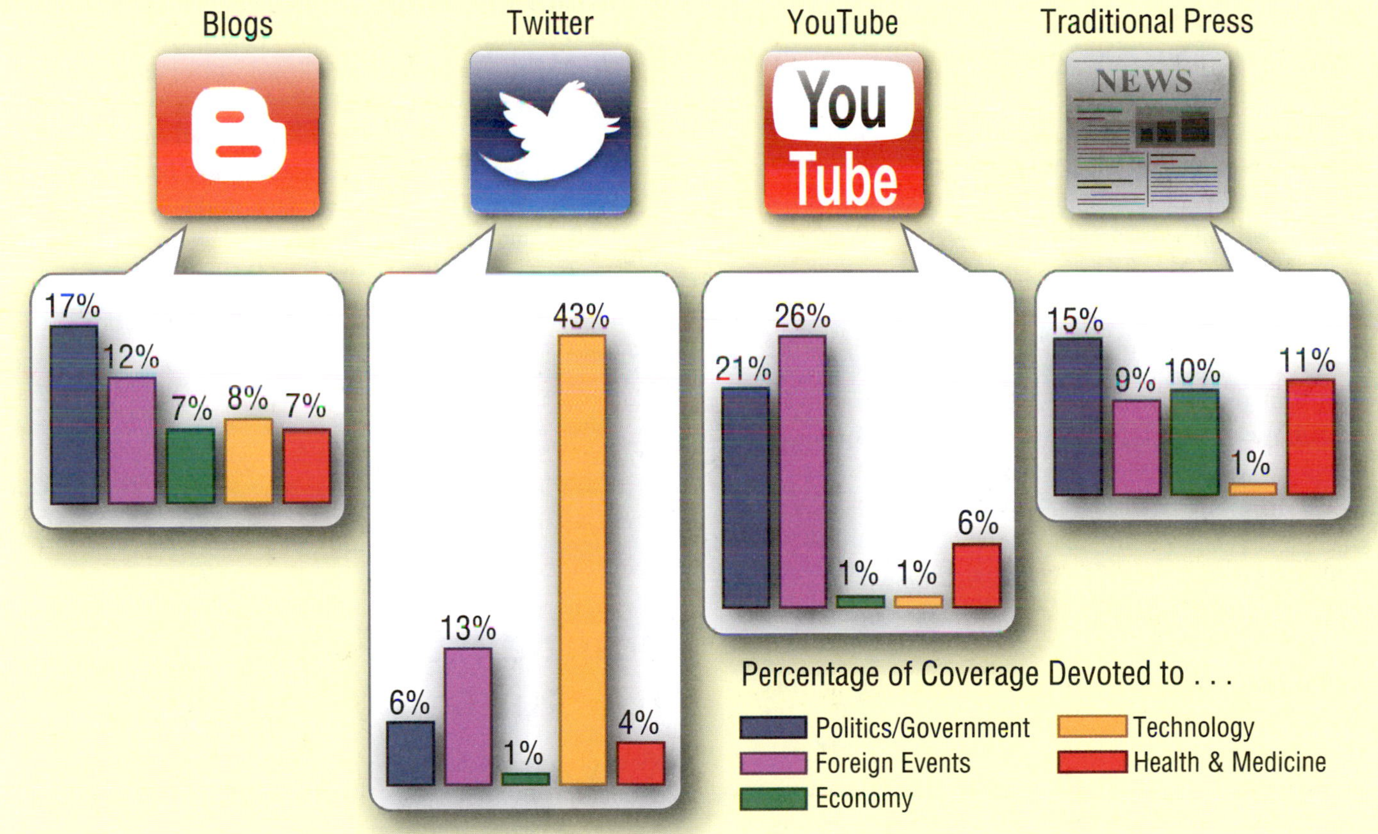

companies are again looking to outsiders for leadership. One reason is new owners. Seven of the top 25 newspapers in America are now owned by hedge funds, which had virtually no role a few years ago. The age of publicly traded newspaper companies is winding down. And some of the new executives are blunt in their assessments. John Paton, the new head of Journal Register newspapers told a trade group: "We have had nearly 15 years to figure out the Web and, as an industry, we newspaper people are no good at it." A question is how much time these private equity owners will give struggling news operations to turn around.

2. **Less progress has been made charging for news than predicted, but there are some signs of willingness to pay.** The leading study on the subject finds that so far only about three dozen newspapers have moved to some kind of paid content on their Web sites. Of those, only 1 percent of users opted to pay. And some papers that moved large portions of content to subscription gave up the effort. A new survey released for this report suggests that under certain circumstances the prospects for charging for content could improve. If their local newspaper would otherwise perish, 23 percent of Americans said they would pay $5 a month for an online version. To date, however, even among early adopters only 10 percent of those who have downloaded local news apps paid for them (this doesn't include apps for non-local news or other content). At the moment, the only news producers successfully charging for most of their content online are those selling financial information to elite audiences—the *Financial Times* is one, *The Wall Street Journal* is another, Bloomberg is a third—which means they are not a model that will likely work for general interest news.

3. **If anything, the metrics of online news have become more confused, not less.** Many believe that the economics of the Web, and particularly online news, cannot really progress until the industry settles on how to measure audience. There is no consensus on what is the most useful measure of online traffic. Different rating agencies do not even agree on how to define a "unique visitor." More audience research data exist about each user than ever before. Yet in addition to confusion about what it means, it is almost impossible get a full sense of consumer behavior—across sites, platforms, and devices. In March 2011, three advertising trade groups, supported by other media associations, announced an initiative to improve and standardize confusing digital media metrics called *Making Measurement Make Sense*, but the task will not be easy.

4. **Local news remains the vast untapped territory. Most traditional American media—and much of U.S. ad revenue–are local.** The dynamics of that market online are still largely undefined. The potential, though, is clear. Already 40 percent of all online ad spending is local, up from 30 percent just a year earlier. But the market at the local level is different than nationally and requires different strategies, both in content creation and economics. And the greatest local growth area last year was in highly targeted display ads that many innovators see as key to the future.

   The nature of local news content is also in many ways undefined. Yahoo's four-year old local news and advertising consortium has shown some success for certain participants but less for others. There are some prominent local news aggregators such as Topix and Examiner.com, and now AOL has entered the field with local reporting through Patch. Whether national networks will overtake small local startups or local app networks will mix news with a variety of other local information, the terrain here remains in flux.

5. **The new conventional wisdom is that the economic model for news will be made up of many smaller and more complex revenue sources than before.** The old news economic model was fairly simple. Broadcast television depended on advertising, newspapers on circulation revenue and a few basic advertising categories. Cable was split half from advertising and half from cable subscription fees. Online, most believe there will be many different kinds of revenue. This is because no one revenue source looks large enough and because money is divided among so many players.

6. **The bailout of the auto industry helped with the media's modest recovery in 2010.** One overlooked dimension in the year past: a key source of renewed revenue in news in 2010 was the recovery in the auto industry, aided by the decision to lend federal money to save U.S. carmakers. Auto advertising jumped 77 percent in local television, 22 percent in radio and 17 percent in magazines.

Agenda-Setting The belief that journalists don't tell you *what* to think but do tell you *what and whom to think about.*

Journalists Focus the Public's Attention

News organizations often are criticized for presenting a consistently slanted view of the news. Often news values are shaped by the way news organizations are structured and the routines they follow. The press in America, it is generally agreed, doesn't tell people what to think but does tell people what and whom to think *about*. This is called ***agenda-setting***. Agenda-setting works in two ways: the flow of information from one news organization to another and the flow of information from news organizations to their audiences.

In agenda-setting, the stories that appear in the nation's widely circulated print media provide ideas to the other media. For example, a widely circulated print media outlet, such as *The New York Times*, can identify specific stories as important by giving them in-depth attention, and this may set the news agenda on specific national issues.

Another type of agenda-setting occurs when a group of journalists, reporting the same story individually, presents a similar picture of the event they covered, rather than differing interpretations of events. This is called ***consensus journalism***.

The emergence of the Internet as a news source, however, means that people now have more places to look for news—even overseas—which means more viewpoints on stories are available. This puts a bigger burden on the news consumer to seek out and verify the most reliable sources of information.

David Sipress/Cartoonbank.com

"Let me answer your question by saying that you're being really aggressive, and it's totally freaking me out."

Are Journalists Biased?

It has not been shown in any comprehensive survey of news gathering that journalists with liberal or conservative values insert their personal ideology directly into their reporting or that the audience unquestioningly accepts one point of view. The belief in a causal relationship between the media and the audience's behavior is known as the ***magic bullet theory***. This belief was disproved long ago.

But the assumption that journalists' personal beliefs directly influence their professional performance is common. Although the reporting by some journalists and columnists certainly can be cited to support this idea, the majority of journalists, says media scholar Herbert J. Gans, view themselves as detached observers of events:

> Journalists, like everyone else, have values, [and] the two that matter most in the newsroom are getting the story and getting it better and faster than their prime competitors—both among their colleagues and at rival news media. Personal political beliefs are left at home, not only because journalists are trained to be objective and detached, but also because their credibility and their paychecks depend on their remaining detached. . . .
>
> The beliefs that actually make it into the news are professional values that are intrinsic to national journalism and that journalists learn on the job. However, the professional values that particularly antagonize conservatives (and liberals when they are in power) are neither liberal nor conservative but reformist, reflecting journalism's long adherence to good-government Progressivism.

Some press critics, in fact, argue that journalists most often present establishment viewpoints and are unlikely to challenge prevailing political and social values. The pressure to come up with instant analyses of news events also may lead to conformity in reporting—an unwillingness to think independently.

How the Public Perceives the Press

Although people tend to follow the news only when something important happens, they do have strong opinions about the news media. According to the latest study conducted by the Pew Research Center, "Ratings of large nationally influential newspapers such as *The New York Times* and the *Washington Post* . . . have dropped in recent years. . . . Local news outlets—local TV and papers that respondents are most familiar with—retain the highest favorability ratings among those who can rate them.

Consensus Journalism The tendency among many journalists covering the same event to report similar conclusions about the event.

Magic Bullet Theory The assertion that media messages directly and measurably affect people's behavior.

Chip Somodevilla/Getty Images News/Getty Images

Today, news organizations are rated more favorably than most public officials. On July 11, 2011, House Speaker John Boehner holds a press conference in Washington, D.C.

"Meanwhile, ratings of other political institutions have been falling at a comparable rate. The share giving a favorable rating to the Supreme Court stands at 66 percent today, down from 78 percent in 2001, while fewer (45 percent) give a favorable rating to Congress, down from 65 percent in 2001. As a result, news organizations continue to be seen more favorably by the American public than most governmental institutions, despite their declining ratings."

Credibility Attracts the Audience

Overall, the growing trust in Internet news sources and their growing popularity as information sources may be connected. If Internet news can maintain this believability standard, even more of the audience—which was leaving the broadcast networks even before online news began—may gravitate to the Internet.

This is a familiar pattern: In the nation's news history, newspaper audiences added radio and newsreels, then they moved to television for news. Now news audiences have moved to the Internet. The Internet combines all the news outlets anyone could want in one place—news and information on the news consumer's own timetable. The Pew Center calls this trend a "digital tide," and it's a tide that may be impossible to stop.

Review, Analyze, Investigate

REVIEWING CHAPTER 12

Early News Organizations Cooperate to Gather News

- ✓ The nation's first consecutively issued newspaper (published more than once) was the *Boston News-Letter*, which appeared in 1704.
- ✓ The invention of the telegraph in 1844 meant news that once took weeks to reach publication could be transmitted in minutes.
- ✓ In 1848, six newspapers in New York City formed the New York Associated Press, the first cooperative news gathering association.
- ✓ Today, most American newspapers and broadcast news operations subscribe to at least one news service, such as Associated Press (AP).
- ✓ Some U.S. newspaper organizations also run their own news services, which allow subscribers to publish each other's stories for a fee.

Civil War Brings Accreditation and Photojournalism

- ✓ In 1861, during the Civil War, President Lincoln introduced the practice of accreditation for journalists.
- ✓ During the Civil War, Mathew Brady introduced the concept of photojournalism—using images to help capture a story.

Tabloid News Takes Over

- ✓ The competition for newspaper readers spawned yellow journalism—stories about grisly crimes and illicit sex, often accompanied by large, startling photographs.
- ✓ In the 1930s, newspapers began to share the audience for news with radio.

Newsreels Bring Distant Events to American Moviegoers

- ✓ Produced by companies including British Pathé (from 1900 until 1970) and by Fox Movietone News (between

1919 and 1960), newsreels were shown in movie theaters to audiences hungry for the pictures that radio couldn't provide. Audiences also watched movie features such as *March of Time*.

✓ Newsreel footage usually took a week or more from the time it was shot to when audiences saw it.

Newspapers and Radio Personalize World War II

✓ In the 1930s, people began to turn to radio for instant news headlines and information.

✓ In the 1930s and 1940s, most radio stations maintained their own news departments until the advent of format radio.

✓ Journalist Ernie Pyle gave World War II the human touch because he wrote stories about the soldiers' lives, not troop movements.

✓ Very few radio stations today maintain full-time news departments, and radio stations with news formats tend to be concentrated in the nation's big cities.

TV News Enters Its Golden Age

✓ What has been called the Golden Age of Television News was the decade that began in 1961, with President John F. Kennedy's inauguration.

✓ In 1962, President Kennedy used live television to deliver his ultimatum to Soviet leader Nikita Khrushchev, urging him to stop sending ships to Cuba to help build missile sites in what was called the Cuban missile crisis. Faced with this ultimatum, the Soviet Union turned its ships around.

✓ Television became a window on the world with its coverage of events in the days following the assassination of President Kennedy.

TV News Changes the Nation's Identity

✓ Coverage of the war in Vietnam gave Americans an appetite for live television news.

✓ The Watergate hearings showed viewers the inner workings of national politics.

TV News Expands and Contracts

✓ Ted Turner founded CNN in 1980, offering round-the-clock news on cable.

✓ The 1980s brought broadcast deregulation and consolidation of the TV networks.

✓ In the 1990s, in general, the American public read fewer newspapers and watched less news on television.

Iraq War Produces "Embedded" Reporters

✓ Before the war in Iraq began in 2003, the U.S. military announced a plan to embed more than 600 reporters with American troops. Embedding offered the reporters access to the frontlines but also kept them within the military's control.

✓ In 2005, the Bush administration sought to influence coverage of the United States in Iraq by paying news outlets to publish stories written by American troops. Congress criticized the practice, saying the U.S. government should not attempt to manage the press.

Reality Shows and Advertising Supplements Blur the Line

✓ Reality TV shows tend to blur the line between entertainment and news.

✓ TV infomercials and advertising supplements called "advertorials" in newspapers and magazines make it harder for readers to differentiate between news content and advertising.

✓ The merging of news with entertainment and advertising makes it more difficult for viewers to separate facts from fiction.

The Internet Transforms News Delivery

✓ The Internet, unlike any other form of news and information delivery, is completely self-directed news and information—targeted to individual needs.

✓ Pew Research Center studies reveal that network and local news viewership has dropped substantially. People, instead, are turning to the Internet for news.

✓ Internet news sites rank higher in believability than either print or broadcast outlets as sources of news.

Information Access Creates a News Evolution

✓ The immediacy of news on the Internet means people can personalize the news.

✓ The Internet is replacing broadcast news because of its immediacy.

Journalists at Work

✓ The Pew Research Center's Project for Excellence in Journalism has described six major trends that are affecting the news media today.

1. The news industry is turning to executives from outside.
2. Less progress has been made charging for news than predicted, but there are some signs of willingness to pay.
3. If anything, the metrics of online news have become more confused, not less.
4. Local news remains the vast untapped territory.
5. The new conventional wisdom is that the economic model for news will be made up of many smaller and more complex revenue sources than before.

6. The bailout of the auto industry helped with the media's modest recovery in 2010.

✓ People today often use social media to share news.

✓ Half of Americans say they rely on the people around them to get at least some of their news.

Journalists Focus the Public's Attention

✓ The press in America doesn't tell you what to think. It does tell you what and whom to think about. This is called agenda-setting.

✓ Consensus journalism occurs when a group of journalists, reporting the same story individually, present a similar picture of the event rather than differing interpretations.

Are Journalists Biased?

✓ Contrary to the disproved magic bullet theory, most journalists see themselves as detached observers and reporters of events.

✓ Some press critics argue that journalists most often present establishment viewpoints and are unlikely to challenge prevailing political and social values.

How the Public Perceives the Press

✓ The public rates local news outlets—local TV and newspapers—higher than nationally influential newspapers.

✓ News organizations continue to rate higher with the public than most public officials.

Credibility Attracts the Audience

✓ The growing trust in Internet news sources may be related to the Internet's increasing popularity as a source of news.

✓ If Internet news can maintain its believability, even more of the TV news audience may gravitate to the Internet.

KEY TERMS

These terms are defined in the margins throughout this chapter and appear in alphabetical order with definitions in the Glossary, which begins on page 383.

CRITICAL QUESTIONS

1. List two specific ways in which news coverage changed during the Civil War.
2. List and explain three ways the Internet has changed consumers' news habits.
3. How is the decline in network TV news budgets likely to affect the delivery of news?
4. Discuss three important trends for news identified in the 2010 report of the Pew Research Center's Project for Excellence in Journalism.
5. What is the relationship between social media and news delivery? Explain.

WORKING THE WEB

This list includes both sites mentioned in the chapter and others to give you greater insight into news and information media.

Committee to Protect Journalists

http://www.cpj.org

This nonpartisan organization is dedicated to protecting freedom of the press around the world. It publishes stories about imprisoned and threatened journalists, organizes public protests and works through diplomatic channels to effect change. It also publishes Attacks on the Press, an annual survey of press freedom around the world. The Web site features links to news by country, special reports, and a multimedia section with video, audio and slideshows.

CyberJournalist.net
http://www.cyberjournalist.net

This news and resource site focuses on how the Internet, convergence and new technologies are changing the media. Included on the Web site are tips, news and commentary, examples of good online journalism and contributions from readers. Sections include Future of Media, Innovation, Social Media, Blog Scan and a job board.

Fox Movietone News
http://www.sc.edu/library/mirc

A portion of the Fox Movietone News film is housed in the University of South Carolina's Moving Image Research Collection. A sample of video clips—from Martin Luther King speaking on voting rights in May 1966 to a silent film of a suffrage rights group in New Orleans in September 1920—is available on the Web site.

Investigative Reporters and Editors (IRE)
http://www.ire.org

This organization, dedicated to improving the quality of investigative reporting, provides educational services to reporters and editors and works to maintain high professional standards. The Web site features news and publications, job and resource centers for members as well as a link to the National Institute for Computer-Assisted Reporting (NICAR).

The Online News Association (ONA)
http://www.journalist.org

ONA's members include news writers, producers, designers, editors, photographers and others who produce news for the Internet or other digital delivery systems. ONA partners with the Annenberg School of Communication at the University of Southern California to honor online journalistic excellence with their annual Online Journalism Awards.

Pew Research Center for People and the Press
http://people-press.org/reports

This is an independent, nonpartisan public opinion research organization that studies attitudes toward the press, politics and public policy issues. The Web site includes Survey Reports by the Center on a variety of current issues. Findings of polls sponsored by media organizations also are available.

Pew Research Center's Project for Excellence in Journalism
http://journalism.org

This research organization uses empirical methods to evaluate and study the performance of the press. Its goal is to help journalists and consumers develop a better understanding of what the press is delivering. Features of the site include Journalism Resources—with links to organizations, schools and career information—and the project's annual report the *State of the News Media*.

Talking Points Memo (TPM)
http://www.talkingpointsmemo.com

The flagship blog of TPM Media, LLC, Talking Points Memo is a collection of comments on political events from a liberal perspective, gathered by writer Josh Marshall. TPMCafé hosts online discussions about various political topics as well as readers' blogs. Streaming video accompanied by written commentary is available on TPMtv.

Unity: Journalists of Color, Inc.
http://www.unityjournalists.org

This alliance of four national associations—Asian American Journalists Association, National Association of Black Journalists, National Association of Hispanic Journalists and the Native American Journalists Association—advocates news coverage about people of color and challenges organizations at all levels to reflect the nation's diversity. Its goals include raising awareness and participation of the media industry in understanding diverse cultures, increasing and broadening news coverage focused on people of color, and dispelling racial and ethnic stereotypes and myths.

Vanderbilt University Television News Archive
http://tvnews.vanderbilt.edu

"The world's most extensive and complete archive of television news" holds network evening news broadcasts from ABC, CBS and NBC from 1968 to the present, as well as a daily news program from CNN (beginning in 1995) and Fox News Reports (beginning in 2004). DVD duplications of entire broadcasts as well as compilation videotapes of individual news stories may be borrowed for a fee.

Impact/Action Videos are concise news features on topics covered in this chapter, created exclusively for **Media/Impact**. They are available for students and instructors at CengageBrain.com, and include screen access for classroom viewing and discussion questions.

"It [the Internet] has rewritten the rules on how to reach voters, raise money, organize supporters, manage the news media, track and mold public opinion, and wage—and withstand—political attacks."

—Adam Nagourney, political writer, The New York Times

Society, Culture and Politics: Shaping the Issues

What's Ahead?

Early Mass Media Studies Assess Impact

Scholars Look for Patterns

How TV Affects Children's Behavior

Do the Mass Media Cause Violence?

National Political Campaigns Depend on Mass Media

Cost of Political Advertising Skyrockets

Voters and Campaigns Use the Internet and Social Media

Mass Media Reflect Cultural Values

Media Slow to Reflect Ethnic Diversity

Mass Media Face Gay and Lesbian Issues

How to Gauge Media Effects

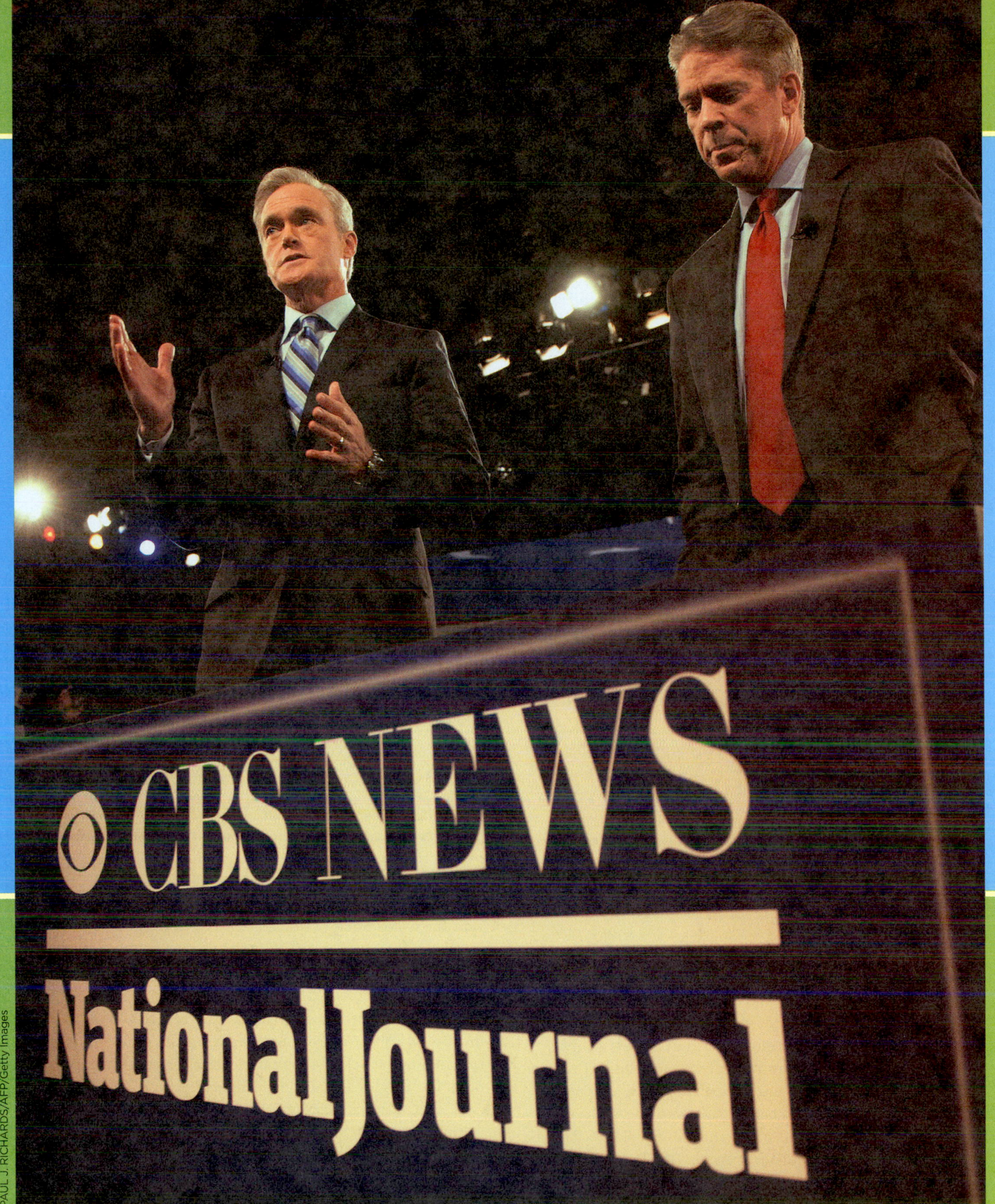

PAUL J. RICHARDS/AFP/Getty Images

On November 12, 2011 in Spartenburg, South Carolina, Scott Pelley (l) of CBS News and Major Garrett of the *National Journal* brief the audience before one of the nationally televised debates among Republican presidential hopefuls.

Researchers at the

Southern Illinois University School of Medicine have identified a new psychiatric condition they have dubbed "celebrity worship syndrome." This affliction is an unhealthy interest in the rich and famous. People who admire celebrities often want to be just like them, even though some celebrities set examples that aren't very positive. Celebrity worship is just one example of the effect of media on our lives.

Today, scholars understand that the media have different effects on different types of people with differing results, and generalizations about the media's effects are easy to make but difficult to prove. "We do not fully understand at present what the media system is doing to individual behavior, much less to American culture," according to media scholars William L. Rivers and Wilbur Schramm. "The media cannot simply be seen as stenciling images on a blank mind. That is too superficial a view of the communication process."

Early Mass Media Studies Assess Impact

The concept that the media have different effects on different types of people is relatively new. Early media observers were certain that a one-to-one relationship existed between what people read, heard and saw and what people did with that information. They also believed that the effects were the same for everyone.

The magic bullet theory, discussed later in the chapter (see "The Payne Fund Studies," p. 277) and sometimes called the hypodermic needle theory, alleged that ideas from the media were in direct causal relation to behavior. The theory held that the media could inject ideas into people the way liquids are injected through a needle. This early distrust of the media still pervades many people's thinking today, although the theory has been disproved.

Media research, like other social science research, is based on a continuum of thought, with each new study advancing slightly the knowledge from the studies that have come before. This is what has happened to the magic bullet theory. Eventually, the beliefs that audiences absorbed media messages uncritically and that all people reacted the same to each message were proven untrue. Research disclosed that analyzing media effects is a very complex task.

Media Effects Research An attempt to analyze how people use the information they receive from the media.

Some media research had been done before television use became widespread in the mid-1950s, but TV prompted scholars to take a closer look at media's effects. Two scholars made particularly provocative assertions about how the media influence people's lives: David M. Potter and Marshall McLuhan.

David Potter, a historian, arrived at just the right moment—when the public and the scholarly community were anxiously trying to analyze media's effects on society. In his book *People of Plenty*, published in 1954, Potter first articulated the idea that American society is a consumer society driven primarily by advertising.

Potter asserted that American advertising is rooted in American abundance: "Advertising is not badly needed in an economy of scarcity, because total demand is usually equal to or in excess of total supply, and every producer can normally sell as much as he produces. . . . It is when potential supply outstrips demand—that is, when abundance prevails—that advertising begins to fulfill a really essential economic function."

Potter also warned about the dangers of advertising: "Advertising has in its dynamics no motivation to seek the improvement of the individual or to impart qualities of social usefulness. . . . It has no social goals and no social responsibility for what it does with its influence." Potter's perspective was important in shaping the critical view of modern advertising. *People of Plenty* is still in print today.

Scholars Look for Patterns

Like Potter, Canadian author and educator Marshall McLuhan arrived at just the right moment. In the 1960s, McLuhan piqued the public's interest with his phrase "The medium is the message," which he later parodied in the title of his book *The Medium Is the Massage*. One of his conclusions was that the widespread use of television was a landmark in the history of the world, "retribalizing" society and creating a "global village" of people who use media to communicate.

McLuhan suggested that electronic media messages are inherently different from print messages—to watch information on TV is different from reading the same information in a newspaper. McLuhan never offered systematic proof for his ideas, and some people criticized him as a charlatan, but his concepts still are debated widely.

Scholars who analyze the media today look for patterns in media effects, predictable results and statistical evidence to document how the media affect us. Precisely because the media are ubiquitous, studies of their effects on American society are far from conclusive. In this chapter, you will learn about some of the major studies and some of the recent assertions about the role that the media play in our lives.

Media research today includes media effects research and media content analysis. ***Media effects research*** tries to analyze how people use the information they receive from the media—whether political advertising changes people's voting behavior, for example. ***Media content analysis*** examines what is presented by the media—how many children's programs portray violent behavior, for example. Sometimes these two types of analysis (effects research and content analysis) are combined in an attempt to evaluate the effect of some specific content on an audience.

The Payne Fund Studies

The prestigious Payne Fund sponsored the first major study of media in 1929. It contained 12 reports on media effects. One of these studies concentrated on the effects of movies on children. In his interviews, researcher Herbert Blumer simply asked teenagers what they remembered about the movies they had seen as children. Using this unsystematic approach, he reported that the teenagers had been greatly influenced by the movies because they *said* they had been greatly influenced.

Blumer's conclusion and other conclusions of the Payne Fund studies about the media's direct, one-to-one effect on people were accepted without question, mainly because these were the first major studies of media effects, and the results were widely reported. The Payne Fund studies were the source of the ***magic bullet theory***, the belief that media messages directly and measurably affect people's behavior.

The Payne Fund studies also contributed ammunition for the Motion Picture Producers and Distributors Association production code, adopted in 1930, which regulated movie content.

The Cantril Study

The Martians who landed in New Jersey in the Mercury Theater "War of the Worlds" broadcast of October 30, 1939 (see **Chapter 6**, "'War of the Worlds' Challenges Radio's Credibility," p. 117), sparked the next major study of media effects, conducted by Hadley Cantril at Princeton University. The results of the Cantril study contradicted the findings of the Payne Fund studies and disputed the magic bullet theory.

Cantril wanted to find out why certain people believed the Mercury Theater broadcast and others did not. After interviewing 135 people, Cantril concluded that high critical-thinking ability was the key. Better-educated people were much more likely to decide the broadcast was a fake. This finding might seem to be self-evident today, but the importance of the Cantril study is that it differentiated among listeners: People with different personality characteristics interpreted the broadcast differently.

The Lasswell Model

In 1948, political scientist Harold D. Lasswell designed a model to describe the process of communication that is still used today. Lasswell said the communication process could be analyzed by answering the five questions shown in **Illustration 13.1**.

Lasswell said you could analyze the process of communication by determining who the sender is and what the sender says. Next, you must identify which channel—or method—of communication the sender used. Then you must examine the audience and define the effect on that audience. Because Lasswell described the communication process so succinctly, most communications research still focuses on his five original questions.

How TV Affects Children's Behavior

The 1950s were a time of adjustment to the new medium of television, which at first was a novelty and then became a necessity. Since 1960, four of the major studies of the effects of television have focused on children.

Television in the Lives of Children

Published in 1961, by Wilbur Schramm, Jack Lyle and Edwin Parker, *Television in the Lives of Our Children* was the first major study of the effects of television on children. Researchers interviewed 6,000 children and 1,500 parents, as well as teachers and school officials.

Schramm and his associates reported that children were exposed to television more than to any other mass medium. On average, 5-year-old children watched television two hours every weekday. TV viewing time reached three hours by the time these children were 8 years old. In a finding that often was subsequently cited, Schramm said that from the ages of 3 to 16, children spent more time in front of the television set than they spent in school.

Children used television for fantasy, diversion and instruction, Schramm said. Children who had troubled relationships with their parents and children who were classified as aggressive were more likely to turn to television for fantasy, but Schramm could find no serious problems related to television viewing. Schramm also found, in support of Cantril, that different children showed different effects.

Media Content Analysis An attempt to analyze how mass media programming influences behavior.

Magic Bullet Theory The assertion that media messages directly and measurably affect people's behavior.

Media/Impact AUDIENCE

Illustration 13.1

Lasswell's Model

The Lasswell model analyzes the communication process by asking five questions: Who? Says what? On which channel? To whom? With what effect?

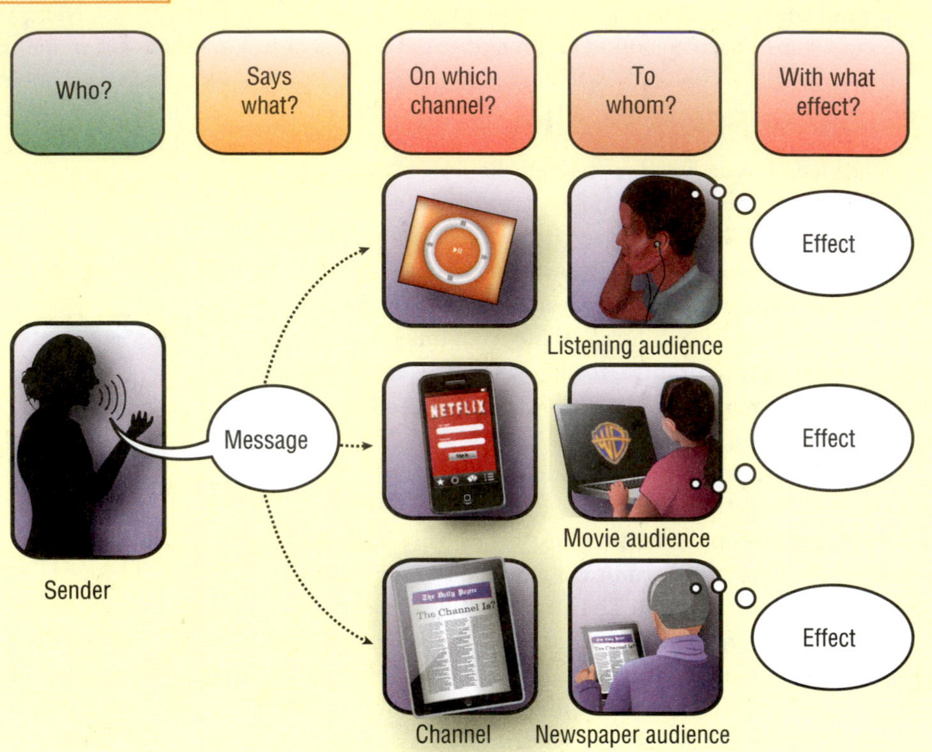

Television and Social Behavior

Television and Social Behavior, a study of the effects of television, was funded by $1 million appropriated by Congress in 1969, after the violent decade of the 1960s. The U.S. Department of Health, Education and Welfare, which sponsored the study, appointed a distinguished panel of social scientists to undertake the research.

The study's major findings, published in six volumes in 1971, concerned the effects of television violence on children. A content analysis of one week of prime-time programming, conducted by George Gerbner of the University of Pennsylvania, reported that eight out of 10 prime-time shows contained violence.

Television and Social Behavior did not make a direct connection between TV programming and violent behavior, however. The report said there was a "tentative" indication that television viewing caused aggressive behavior. According to the study, TV violence affected only *some* children who were already classified as aggressive children and *only* in some environments.

Even though the report avoided a direct statement about violent behavior in children as a result of television viewing, the U.S. surgeon general called for immediate action against violence on television. The television industry dismissed the results as inconclusive.

The Early Window

Several studies since 1971 have suggested that television violence causes aggression among children. In their 1988 book *The Early Window: Effects of Television on Children and Youth*, psychologists Robert M. Liebert and Joyce Sprafkin urged caution in drawing broad conclusions about the subject:

> Studies using various methods have supported the proposition that TV violence can induce aggressive and/or antisocial behavior in children. Whether the effect will hold only for the most susceptible individuals (e.g., boys from disadvantaged homes) or whether it will hold for a wider range of youngsters obviously depends in part upon the measure being used. . . . The occurrence of serious violent or criminal acts results from several forces at once. Researchers have said that TV violence is *a* cause of aggressiveness, not that it

is *the* cause of aggressiveness. There is no one, single cause of any social behavior.

Still, criticism of television's effects on children's behavior persists, especially the effects of advertising.

Television Advertising to Children

The effects of advertising on adults have been analyzed widely, but in 1979 the advertising of children's products became an object of serious government attention with Federal Trade Commission's release of the 340-page report *Television Advertising to Children*. The report, based on a two-year study, was designed to document the dangers of advertising sugar-based products to children, but embedded in the report was some provocative information about children's advertising.

Children are an especially vulnerable audience, said the FTC. The report concluded:

1. The average child sees 20,000 commercials a year, or about three hours of TV advertising a week.
2. Many children regard advertising as just another form of programming and do not distinguish between programs and ads.
3. Televised advertising for any product to children who do not understand the intent of the commercial is unfair and deceptive.

The report called for a ban on advertising to very young children, a ban on sugared products in advertising directed to children under age 12, and a requirement for counter-ads with dental and nutritional information to balance ads for sugared products.

The FTC report and subsequent research about children's advertising suggest that younger children pay more attention to television advertising than older children. But by sixth grade, children adopt what has been called a "global distrust" of advertising.

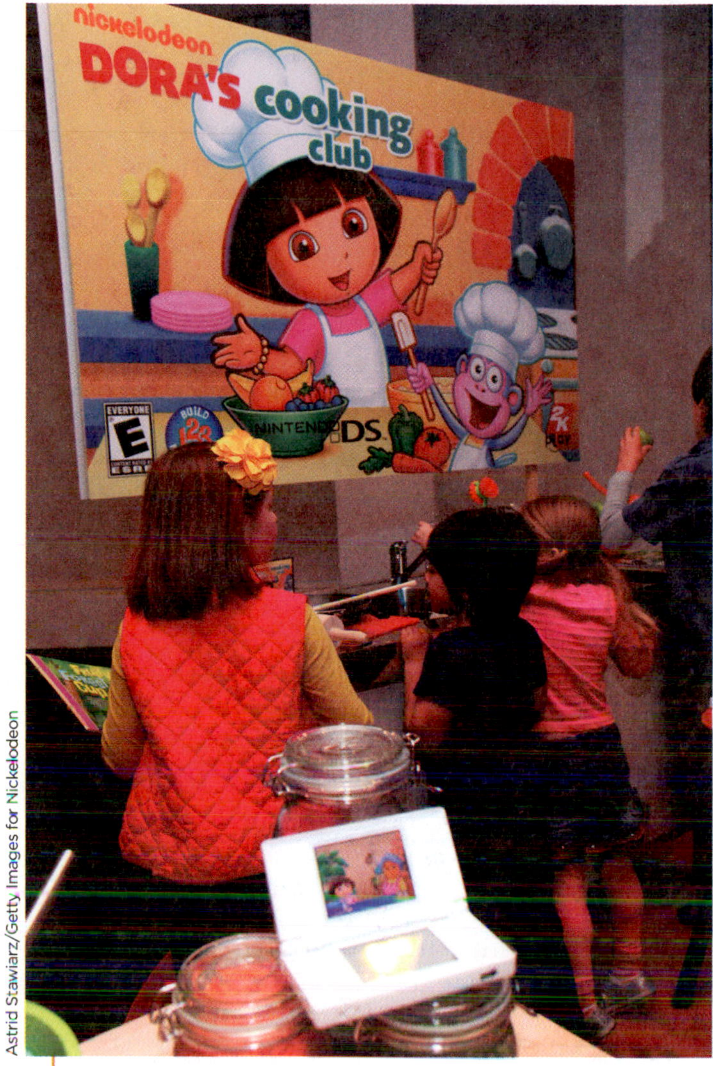

Astrid Stawiarz/Getty Images for Nickelodeon

Younger children are an especially vulnerable media audience because they tend to pay more attention to television advertising than older children do. On November 10, 2010, Nickelodeon promoted its popular TV character Dora the Explorer in connection with a new Nickelodeon Fit game, to encourage children to eat better and exercise.

Linking TV to School Performance

There have been many studies about children and television, such as the National Institute of Mental Health report. In 1981, a California study suggested a link between television viewing and poor school performance.

The California Assessment Program (CAP), which tests academic achievement, included a new question: "On a typical weekday, about how many hours do you watch TV?" The students were given a choice ranging from zero to six or more hours. An analysis of the answers to that question from more than 10,000 sixth graders was matched with the children's scores on the achievement test.

The results suggested a consistent relationship between viewing time and achievement. Students who said they watched a lot of television scored lower in reading, writing and mathematics than students who didn't watch any television. The average scores for students who said they viewed six or more hours of television a day were six to eight points lower than for those children who said they watched less than a half-hour of television a day.

Because the study didn't include information about the IQ scores or income levels of these students, the results cannot be considered conclusive. The study simply may show that children who watch a lot of television aren't studying.

Media/Impact AUDIENCE

Screen Time Higher Than Ever for Children

By Tamar Lewin

Jaden Lender, 3, sings along softly with the Five Little Monkeys app on the family iPad, and waggles his index finger along with the monkey doctor at the warning, "No more monkeys jumping on the bed!" He likes crushing the ants in Ant Smasher, and improving his swing in the golf app. But he is no app addict: when the one featuring Grover from *Sesame Street* does not work right, Jaden says, "Come on, iPad!'"—then wanders happily off to play with his train set.

"I'll lie to myself that these are skill builders," said his father, Keith Lender, who has downloaded dozens of tablet and smart phone apps for Jaden and his 1-year-old brother, Dylan. "No, I'm not lying," he said, correcting himself. "Jaden's really learning hand-eye coordination from the golf game, and it beats the hell out of sitting and watching television."

Despite the American Academy of Pediatrics' longstanding recommendations to the contrary, children under 8 are spending more time than ever in front of screens, according to a study [released October 30, 2011].

The report also documents for the first time an emerging "app gap" in which affluent children are likely to use mobile educational games while those in low-income families are the most likely to have televisions in their bedrooms.

The study, by Common Sense Media, a San Francisco nonprofit group, is the first of its kind since apps became widespread, and the first to look at screen time from birth. It found that almost half the families with incomes above $75,000 had downloaded apps specifically for their young children, compared with one in eight of the families earning less than $30,000.

Mascarucci/Corbis

A new 2011 study by Common Sense Media reports that children under 8 spend more time using media than ever, and more than half of these children have access to a mobile device like a Smartphone, but TV still accounts for the largest amount of screen time.

More than a third of those low-income parents said they did not know what an "app"—short for application—was.

"The app gap is a big deal and a harbinger of the future," said James Steyer, chief executive of Common Sense Media, which had 1,384 parents surveyed this spring for the study. "It's the beginning of an important shift, as parents increasingly are handing their iPhones to their 1½-year-old kid as a shut-up toy. And parents who check their e-mail three times on the way to the bus stop are constantly modeling that behavior, so it's only natural the kids want to use mobile devices too."

The study found that fully half of children under 8 had access to a mobile device like a smartphone, a video iPod, or an iPad or other tablet. Of course, television is still the elephant in the children's media room, accounting for the largest share of their screen time: about half of children under 2 watch TV or DVDs on a typical day, according to the study, and those who do spend an average of almost two hours in front of the screen.

But the results are particularly interesting because of the number of children who were included in the survey.

In 2010, new research further attempted to define whether children are poor students because they watch a lot of television or whether children who watch a lot of television are poor students for other reasons. Canadian researchers released a study in the May 2010 issue of the journal *Pediatrics and Adolescent Medicine* that linked a decline in classroom engagement with early television viewing. The study, "Prospective Associations Between Early Childhood Television Exposure and Academic, Psychosocial, and Physical Well-being by Middle Childhood," followed the TV viewing habits of 1,314 toddlers until they entered fourth grade.

From their analysis of the data, the researchers concluded that children who watched a lot of TV in their early years were less likely to perform well when they reached the fourth grade. The researchers noted that there were "long term risks associated with higher levels of [TV] exposure." (See **Media/Impact: Audience**, "Screen Time Higher Than Ever for Children," p. 280.)

Do the Mass Media Cause Violence?

Television and Behavior: Ten Years of Scientific Progress and Implications for the Eighties, published in 1982 by the National Institute of Mental Health (NIMH), compiled information from 2,500 individual studies of television. According to NIMH, three findings of these 2,500 studies, taken together, were that:

1. A direct correlation exists between televised violence and aggressive behavior, yet there is no way to predict who will be affected and why.
2. Heavy television viewers are more fearful, less trusting and more apprehensive than light viewers.
3. Children who watch what the report called "pro social" programs (programs that are socially constructive, such as *Sesame Street* and *SpongeBob*) are more likely to act responsibly.

Most of the latest studies of the mass media's role have continued to reinforce the concept that different people in different environments react to mass media differently.

In 1994, cable operators and network broadcasters agreed to use an independent monitor to review programming for violent content. The agreement came after Congress held hearings on the subject in 1993, and threatened to introduce regulations to curb violence if the industry didn't police itself. The agreement also called for the development of violence ratings for TV programming and endorsed a v-chip—*v* for "violence"—technology that would be built into a television set to allow parents to block programs rated as violent.

The monitoring is qualitative rather than quantitative, according to the agreement. This means that the programs are examined for content, not just for incidents of violence. The Telecommunications Act of 1996 established a television ratings code for content. This agreement continues a tradition of media self-regulation. That is, the broadcast, recording and movie media industries have responded—often reluctantly—to congressional pressure by offering to monitor themselves rather than invite the government to intrude on the content of their programs. (See **Media/Impact: Culture**, "Brutal Truths About Violence," p. 282.)

National Political Campaigns Depend on Mass Media

The mass media have transformed politics in ways that could never have been imagined when President Franklin D. Roosevelt introduced what were called Fireside Chats in 1933. Roosevelt was the first president to use the media effectively to stimulate public support.

The newest technology introduced during FDR's era—radio—gave him immediate access to a national audience. Roosevelt's media skill became an essential element in promoting his economic programs. Today, politics and the media seem irreversibly dependent on each other, one of the legacies of Roosevelt's presidency.

The Fireside Chats

In March 1933, just after he was inaugurated, FDR looked for a way to avoid a financial panic after he announced that he was closing the nation's banks. For a week, the country cooled off while Congress scrambled for a solution. On the Sunday night eight days after his inauguration, Roosevelt used radio to calm the nation's anxiety before the banks began to reopen on Monday. FDR went down to the basement of the White House to give his first Fireside Chat. There was a fireplace in the basement, but no fire was burning. The president could not find his script, so he borrowed a mimeographed copy from a reporter.

In his first address to the nation as president, FDR gave a banking lesson to his audience of 60 million people: "I want to talk for a few minutes with the people of the United States about banking. . . . First of all, let me state the simple fact that when you deposit money in a bank, the bank does not put the money into a safe deposit vault. It invests your money in many different forms." When he finished, he turned to people in the room and asked, "Was I all right?" America had its first media president, an

Media/Impact CULTURE

Brutal Truths About Violence

By A. O. Scott

Even before it opened in theaters on [April 16, 2010], *Kick-Ass* had achieved a degree of notoriety thanks to a scene in which Hit-Girl, a pint-size masked vigilante played by Chloë Grace Moretz, unleashes a barrage of obscenities against a room full of foes. Both the provocation and the published responses to it—more or less evenly split between shock and exhilaration—had a somewhat ritualized quality. We've been here before: A movie pointedly tests what seems to be an established boundary of propriety, and rhetorical battle lines are drawn. "How dare they!" faces off against "Oh, lighten up."

In the film, the latest comic-book-derived movie to defy the PG-13 norm and seek out an R rating, Hit-Girl is 11. Ms. Moretz, a charming and energetic performer, is 13. Anyone who has spent time around children that age knows that they say the darnedest things, including things not printable in this newspaper. Which is not to suggest that Hit-Girl's foulmouthed tirades are easy to shrug off. They aren't meant to be. But it's a little curious that what the character says should carry the queasy jolt of a taboo being smashed, as opposed to what she does.

What Hit-Girl does is attack her enemies with all kinds of weaponry: ultra-sharp blades; high-caliber firearms; her own feet and tiny fists. The results, while hardly realistic, are full of the sights and sounds of bodily harm. Bones crack, flesh bruises, blood gushes, limbs and extremities fly, and bodies hit the ground with a sickening thud.

This kind of grisly spectacle is nothing new, though there is some novelty in seeing a child, a girl in particular, mete out such mayhem. And in the climactic fight sequences, as Hit-Girl moves closer to exacting vengeance on the chief bad guy, she becomes a victim as well as an agent of the violence. After surviving a fusillade of machine-gun fire, she is punched, stomped on, thrown and threatened with a gun to her head. . . .

Lions Gate/Courtesy Everett Collection

The movie *Kick-Ass*, released in 2010, stars Hit-Girl, who wages different types of violent attacks against her enemies. In this article, *New York Times* movie critic A. O. Scott asks about movie violence, "When is enough enough?"

To criticize movie violence is the surest way to be branded a scold, a moralist, a worrywart who refuses to understand that movies are not real. As someone who often revels in the visceral thrills of cinematic action and the bloodthirsty satisfactions of dramatic vengeance, I'm not inclined to fit that stereotype. But I also think that the uncritical defense of brutality on film, especially of the unimaginative, half-jokey sadism that drives this latest superhero movie, can be evasive and irresponsible. It also disturbs me that, unlike naughty language or sexuality, violence is rarely seen as scandalous these days. . . .

Everybody can share in the bloodlust, and enjoy the kinetic choreography of flying bullets and spurting arteries. It's all in good fun, it's all kid's stuff, it doesn't mean anything. That's the conventional wisdom, in any case, which silences ethical objections to, let's say, the idea of showing a child's battered face as being in some way audacious. We will, I suppose, each find our own limits and draw our own boundaries, but it may also be time to articulate those and say when enough is enough.

elected leader talking directly to the people through the media.

Roosevelt's chats are cited as a legendary example of media politics, yet he gave only eight Fireside Chats in his first term of office. His other meetings with the press also enhanced his reputation for press access: In 13 years in office, he held more than 900 press conferences.

The People's Choice

The first major study of the influence of media on politics was *The People's Choice*, undertaken precisely because FDR seemed to be such a good media politician. This comprehensive examination of voter behavior in the 1940 presidential election was quite systematic.

Researchers Paul Lazarsfeld, Bernard Berelson and Hazel Gaudet followed 3,000 people in rural Erie County, Ohio, from May to November 1940 to determine what influenced the way these people voted for president. The researchers tracked how people's minds changed over the six-month period and then attempted to determine why. (It is important to remember this study was undertaken before television.) Radio had become the prevailing medium for political advertising beginning in 1932, when the two parties spent more money for radio time than for any other campaign item. What effect, the researchers wanted to know, did the media have on people's choosing one candidate over another? The results were provocative.

CBS Photo Archive/Getty Images

In 1932, Paul Lazarsfeld and his colleagues studied people's voting habits to attempt to document the media's effect on their decisions. In 1942, Lazarsfeld (left) worked with Dr. Frank Stanton (future president of the CBS network) on an audience analysis project. Viewers pressed a button on the Lazarsfeld-Stanton Program Analyzer when they saw a program they liked, and the machine printed out the results. The machine never gained widespread use.

Lazarsfeld and his colleagues found that only 8 percent of the voters in the study were actually *converted* by the media. The majority of voters (53 percent) were *reinforced* in their beliefs by the media, and 14 percent were *activated* to vote. Mixed effects or no effects were shown by the remaining 25 percent of the people.

Lazarsfeld said opinion leaders, who got their information from the media, shared this information with their friends. The study concluded that instead of changing people's beliefs, the media primarily activate people to vote and reinforce already held opinions. *The People's Choice* also made the following findings:

- Family and friends have more effect on people's decisions than the media.
- The media have different effects on different people, reinforcing Cantril's findings.
- A major source of information about candidates is other people.

The finding that opinion leaders often provide and shape information for the general population was a bonus—the researchers hadn't set out specifically to learn this. This transmission of information and ideas from mass media to opinion leaders and then to friends and acquaintances is called the ***two-step flow*** of communication.

The Unseeing Eye

In 1976, a second study of the media and presidential elections, called *The Unseeing Eye: The Myth of Television Power in National Elections*, revealed findings that paralleled those of *The People's Choice*.

With a grant from the National Science Foundation, Thomas E. Patterson and Robert D. McClure supervised interviews with 2,707 people from early September to just before Election Day in the November 1972 race between

Two-Step Flow The transmission of information and ideas from mass media to opinion leaders and then to friends.

Ed Clark/Time & Life Pictures/Getty Images

The series of debates in 1960 between Senator John F. Kennedy (left) and Vice President Richard Nixon were the first widely televised debates of presidential candidates. Kennedy's performance on the telecast often is credited for his narrow victory in the election. Shown is the second Kennedy-Nixon debate on October 8, 1960.

George McGovern and Richard Nixon. The study did not discuss political media events, but it did analyze television campaign news and political advertising.

The researchers concluded that although political advertising influenced 16 percent of the people they interviewed, only 7 percent were manipulated by political ads. The researchers defined people who were *influenced* as those who decided to vote for a candidate based mostly on what they knew and only slightly on what the ads told them. The 7 percent of the people in the survey who were *manipulated*, according to Patterson and McClure, were people who cited political advertising as a major factor in their choices. Patterson and McClure concluded that political advertising on TV has little effect on most people:

> By projecting their political biases . . . people see in candidates' commercials pretty much what they want to see. Ads sponsored by the candidate who shares their politics get a good response. They like what he has to say. And they like him. Ads sponsored by the opposing candidate are viewed negatively. They object to what he says. And they object to him.

Even though a minority of people are affected by political ads on TV, it is important to remember that in some elections the difference of a few percentage points can decide the outcome. Political advertising is designed to sway these swing voters. This is why political advertising continues to play such an important campaign role.

Election Campaigns on Television

So far, no convincing systematic evidence has shown that the mass media change the voting behavior of *large* groups of people. Yet, since John F. Kennedy debated Richard Nixon during the 1960 presidential campaign, many people deeply feel that the media—television in particular—have changed elections and electoral politics.

The series of debates between Kennedy and Nixon in 1960 were the first televised debates of presidential candidates in American history. Kennedy's performance in the debates often is credited for his narrow victory in the election. In his book *Presidents and the Press*, media scholar Joseph C. Spear wrote:

> As the panel began asking questions, Nixon tended to go on the defensive, answering Kennedy point by point and ignoring his huge audience beyond the camera. Kennedy, by contrast, appeared rested, calm, informed, cocksure. Whatever the question, he aimed his answer at the millions of Americans viewing the program in their living rooms.
>
> It was an unmitigated disaster for Nixon. In the second, third and fourth debates, he managed to recover somewhat from his initial poor performance, but it was too late. Surveys showed that an overwhelming percentage of the television audience had judged Kennedy the victor.

One legacy of Kennedy's television victory was that national political campaigns came to depend almost entirely on TV to promote presidential candidates, and televised presidential debates became a staple of every presidential election.

Television is a very efficient way to reach large numbers of people quickly, but campaigning on television also distances the candidates from direct public contact. Instead of meeting the public in person to promote and debate issues, candidates can isolate themselves from public scrutiny by using television ads to portray their views.

Cost of Political Advertising Skyrockets

Television advertising also is very expensive. The cost of national and statewide campaigns—especially since the year 2000—has skyrocketed. Presidential, gubernatorial, congressional and senatorial candidates typically devote 40 to 60 percent of their campaign budgets to advertising.

Many candidates run in metropolitan areas like Los Angeles, where the media markets are much larger than their districts. Television advertising in large markets reaches a bigger audience than candidates need, so they also use direct mail. But a candidate running for Congress in Des Moines, Iowa, might use mainly television because the entire district is included in the local TV station's coverage area. Historian James David Barber describes the public's role in politics:

> Particularly since television has brought national politics within arm's length of nearly every American, the great majority probably have at least some experience of the quadrennial passing parade. But millions vote their old memories and habits and interests, interpreting new perceptions that strike their senses to coincide with their prejudices and impulses.
>
> At the other end of the participation spectrum are those compulsive readers of *The New York Times* who delve into every twitch and turn of the contest. Floating in between are large numbers of Americans who pick up on the election's major events and personalities, following with mild but open interest the dominant developments.
>
> Insofar as the campaign makes a difference, it is this great central chunk of The People who swing the choice. They respond to what they see and hear. They are interested but not obsessed. They edit out the minor blips of change and wait for the campaign to gather force around a critical concern. They reach their conclusions on the basis of a widely shared common experience. It is through that middling throng of the population that the pulse of politics beats most powerfully, synchronizing to its insistent rhythm the varied vibrations of discrete events.

The rising cost of running for public office can exclude people without the means to raise huge sums of money. Since 1972, when political campaigns first began widespread use of television advertising, presidential campaign expenditures have skyrocketed from less than $2 million in 1972 to $2.4 billion in 2008. (See **Illustration 13.2**.) Most of this money went to pay for TV advertising.

Today the mass media are an essential part of American politics, changing the behavior of politicians as well as the electorate, which raises important questions about the role of the nation's mass media in governance and the conduct of elections.

Voters and Campaigns Use the Internet and Social Media

The year 2004 was the first presidential election year when the Internet began to play a role in national politics, as citizen blogs became an outlet for political debate, and bloggers covered the presidential campaigns along with members of the established press corps.

Bernard Schoenbaum/Cartoonbank.com

"Say, who the hell's been writing this stuff? It comes perilously close to the truth."

The New York Times noted in 2004, "Democrats and Republicans are sharply increasing their use of e-mail, interactive Web sites, candidate and party blogs and text messaging to raise money, organize get-out-the-vote efforts and assemble crowds for rallies. The Internet, they say, appears to be far more efficient, and less costly, than the traditional tools of politics, notably door knocking and telephone banks."

The Pew Research Center reported that 75 million Americans used the Internet for political news during the 2004 presidential election. "The effect of the Internet on politics will be every bit as transformational as television was," Republican national chairman Ken Mehlman told *The Times*. "If you want to get your message out, the old way of paying someone to make a TV ad is insufficient: You need your message out through the Internet, through e-mail, through talk radio."

Political consultants also experimented with political podcasts that featured daily downloaded messages from candidates and viral marketing videos supporting the candidates (see **Chapter 10**). Supporters passed along the video messages through e-mail to their friends—an online chain of free Internet political messaging that reached young voters more directly than traditional advertising.

By 2008, the Internet had become a central force in national politics. "The 2008 race for the White House fundamentally upended the way presidential campaigns are fought in the United States," wrote Adam Nagourney of *The New York Times*. "It has rewritten the rules on how to reach

Media/Impact
MONEY

Illustration 13.2

TV Political Campaign Spending in Presidential Elections, 1972–2008

The amount of money presidential candidates spend on advertising has soared since 1972. Of the $2.4 billion collected by all the candidates in the 2008 presidential campaign, most of the money went to pay for TV advertising.

Source: Center for Responsive Politics and http://www.opensecrets.org.

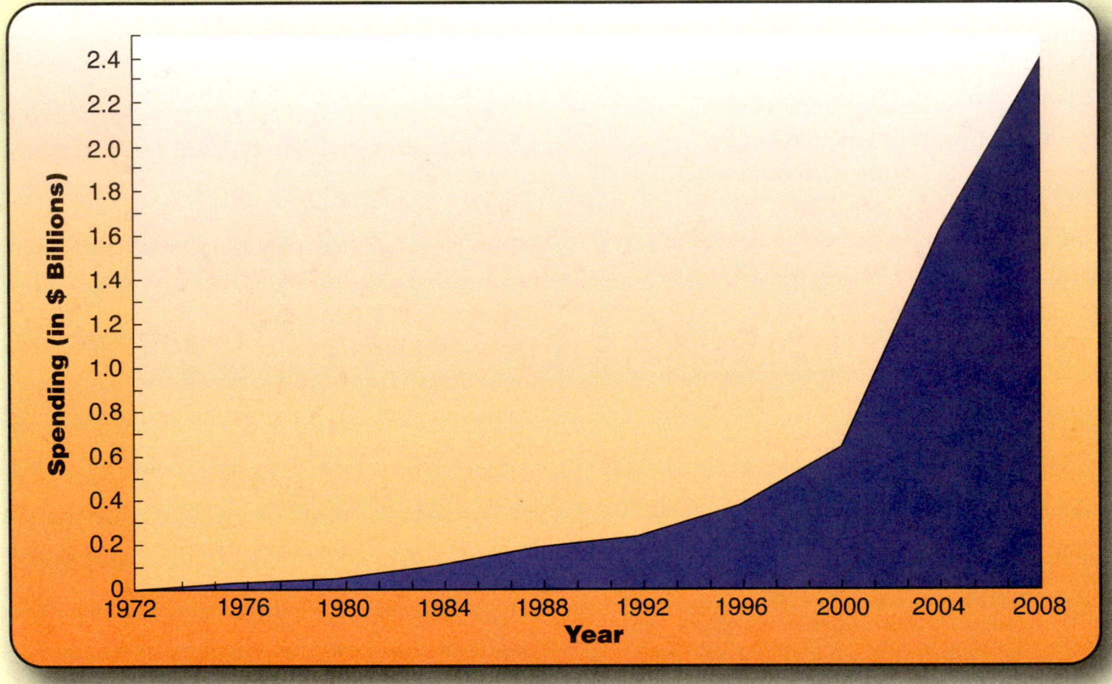

voters, raise money, organize supporters, manage the news media, track and mold public opinion, and wage—and withstand—political attacks, including many carried by blogs that did not exist four years ago. "

According to Mark McKinnon, a senior adviser to President George W. Bush's 2000 and 2004 campaigns, the year 2008 was when "campaigns leveraged the Internet in ways never imagined. The year we went to warp speed. The year the paradigm got turned upside down and truly became bottom up instead of top down." The Obama campaign especially used the Internet and social media, such as YouTube, as well as cell-phone text messaging. The Internet connection also helped the campaign raise record amounts of money.

Also in 2008, many younger voters sought alternative sources of information about the campaigns such as *The Daily Show* with Jon Stewart, and they shared blogs, video clips and online discussions through Facebook and YouTube, social media sites that were not a large factor in the 2004 election.

"According to interviews and recent surveys, younger voters tend to be not just consumers of news and current events but conduits as well—sending out e-mailed links and videos to friends and their social networks. And in turn, they rely on friends and online connections for news to come to them," reported political writer Brian Stelter. "In essence, they are replacing the professional filter—reading *The Washington Post,* clicking on CNN.com—with a social one." "Young people also identify online discussions with friends and videos as important sources of election information," wrote Stelter. "The habits suggest that younger readers find themselves going straight to the source, bypassing the context and analysis that seasoned journalists provide."

However, even though Internet political marketing may reach large groups of people quickly and efficiently, there is no clear understanding yet of how Internet political messages can be used to change people's minds. In the 2010 midterm election, most political campaigns used the Internet to spread their messages, but they still relied on television for the bulk of their advertising, and expenditures on Internet advertising remained very small.

Researchers estimated that the total amount expended for television advertising for the 2010 elections would reach between $3 billion and $4 billion, more than the two national presidential candidates spent together in 2008. Yet the campaigns reportedly spent only $50 million on the Internet, less than 2 percent of the total. (See **Media/Impact: Money**, "Political TV Ad Spending Sets Record," p. 288.)

"Advertising veterans say the stakes are too high to experiment with a medium that, despite its ability to monitor the browsing habits of consumers, might not be effective," reported the *Los Angeles Times*. So, for now, political campaigns are choosing to spend more money on the controlled messages that television advertising provides rather than the uncontrolled environment of the Internet.

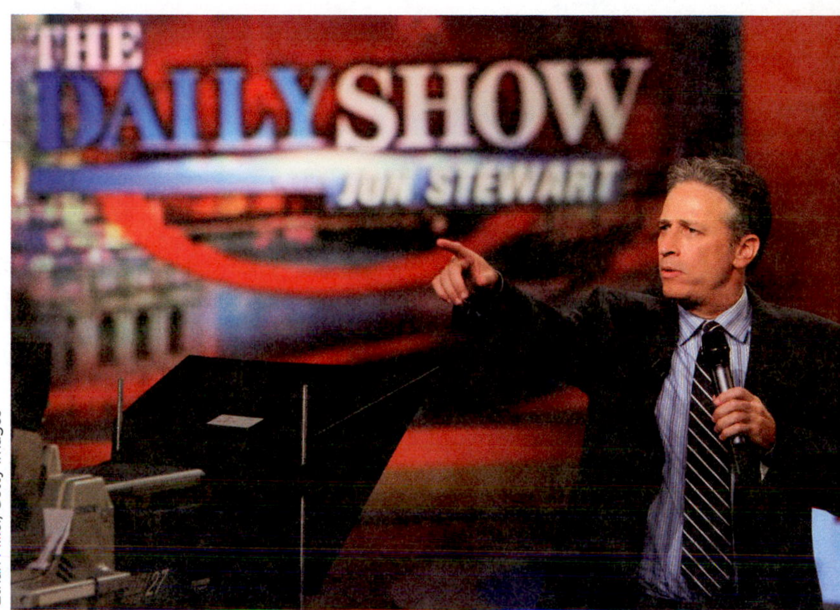

Ethan Miller/Getty Images

In 2008, younger voters sought alternative sources of information about the campaigns such as *The Daily Show* with Jon Stewart. On September 3, 2008, Stewart broadcast live from St. Paul, Minn., where the Republican Party was holding its national convention.

Mass Media Reflect Cultural Values

Because media research is a continuing process, new ideas will emerge in the next decade from today's ideas and studies. Several provocative recent analyses have extended the boundaries of media research.

Silencing Opposing Viewpoints

Political scientist Elisabeth Noelle-Neumann has asserted that because journalists in all media tend to concentrate on the same major news stories, the audience is assailed on many sides by similar information. Together, the media present the consensus; journalists reflect the prevailing climate of opinion.

As this consensus spreads, people with divergent views, says Noelle-Neumann, may be less likely to voice disagreement with the prevailing point of view. Thus, because of a "***spiral of silence***," the media gain more influence because opponents of the consensus tend to remain silent. The implication for future research will be to ask whether the media neutralize dissent and create a pattern of social and cultural conformity.

Losing a Sense of Place

In his book *No Sense of Place*, published in 1985, Joshua Meyrowitz provided new insight into television's possible effects on society. In the past, says Meyrowitz:

> Parents did not know what their children knew, and children did not know what their parents knew they knew. Similarly, a person of one sex could never be certain of what a member of the other sex knew. . . . Television undermines such behavioral distinctions because it encompasses children and adults, men and women and all other social groups in a single informational sphere or environment. Not only does it provide similar information to everyone but, even more significant, it provides it publicly and often simultaneously.

This sharing of information, says Meyrowitz, means that subjects that rarely were discussed between men and

Spiral of Silence The belief that people with divergent views may be reluctant to challenge the consensus of opinion offered by the media.

Media/Impact
MONEY

Political TV Ad Spending Sets Record: October 2010 Is the Busiest Month in History for Political Ads on TV

By Sherisse Pham

Politicians and outside political groups made their own contributions to the economic recovery—by purchasing billions of dollars in air time on local television in the run-up to the midterm elections. On Friday [November 5, 2010], the Nielsen Company released numbers which showed that October was the busiest month in history for political ads on TV.

William Thomas Cain/Getty Images

Candidates set a record for campaign spending in the 2010 mid-term elections, even without a presidential race. In most political contests, television advertising accounts for more than half of campaign spending, which means healthy earnings for local TV stations. A large crowd gathers for a get-out-the-vote rally in Philadelphia on October 10, 2010.

Television stations hit American viewers with 1.48 million political ads, said Nielsen, up from the 1.41 million political ads aired in October 2008.

In Ohio, where Democrats and Republicans went toe-to-toe in a tough election environment this year, viewers faced a deluge of political ads. Cleveland saw the brunt of it, with the state capital, Columbus, coming in a close second. Nielsen found about one of every four paid TV ads aired on local stations in October in both cities was from a political candidate or an outside political group.

Politicians and third party groups spent an estimated $564 million in Ohio, according to the non-partisan Campaign Finance Institute in this election, driving up the demand, and the prices, for local TV advertising.

Tony D'Angelo, director of sales at ABC 6 and Fox 28 in Columbus, Ohio, said politicians and outside groups are just like any other business trying to sell a product.

"Their Christmas is Election Day," said D'Angelo, "and someone either buys their toy or they don't."

Borrell Associates, a research firm, predicted TV ad spending nationwide will reach $4.2 billion in this [2010] election. And Kantar, a media consultant group, said spending will top $3 billion.

Peter Gusmano, a managing partner with media company GroupM Matrix, negotiates clients' advertising rates in local stations across the country. He said coveted ad slots, like those in the 11 p.m. newscast, were nearly impossible to buy because political ads were taking up three-quarters of the inventory. Moreover, Gusmano said, they gobbled up air time for as much as two months before the election.

Sherisse Pham, "Political TV Ad Spending Sets Record October is the Busiest Month in History for Political Ads on TV," November 8, 2010, ABCNews.com. Courtesy of ABC News.

women, for instance, or between children and adults, have become part of the public dialogue.

A second result of television viewing is the blurred distinction between childhood and adulthood, says Meyrowitz. When print dominated the society as a medium, children's access to adult information was limited. The only way to learn about "adult" concepts was to read about them, so typically children were not exposed to adult ideas or problems, and taboo topics remained hidden from children.

In a video world, however, any topic that can be portrayed in pictures on television challenges the boundaries that print places around information. This, says Meyrowitz, causes an early loss of the naïveté of childhood:

> Television removes barriers that once divided people of different ages and reading abilities into different social situations. The widespread use of television is equivalent to a broad social decision to allow young children to be present at wars and funerals, courtships and seductions, criminal plots and cocktail parties. . . . Television thrusts children into a complex adult world, and it provides the impetus for children to ask the meanings of actions and words they would not yet have heard or read about without television.

Meyrowitz concedes that movies offered similar information to children before television, but he says that the pervasiveness of television today makes its effects more widespread.

Television is blurring social distinctions—between children and adults, and between men and women. Complicating the current study of media effects is the increase in the variety and number of available media sources.

Stereotyping

Journalists often use shorthand labels to characterize ethnic and other groups. In his 1922 book *Public Opinion*, political journalist Walter Lippmann first identified the tendency of journalists to generalize about other people based on fixed ideas.

> When we speak of the mind of a group of people, of the French mind, the militarist mind, the bolshevik mind, we are liable to serious confusion unless we agree to separate the instinctive equipment from the stereotypes, the patterns, the formulae which play so decisive a part in building up the mental world to which the native character is adapted and responds. . . . Failure to make this distinction accounts for oceans of loose talk about collective minds, national souls and race psychology.

Joseph Farris/Cartoonbank.com

"Give up media."

The image of women portrayed by the media has been the subject of significant contemporary studies by many media researchers. Observers of the stereotyping of women point to past and current media portrayals showing very few women in professional roles or as strong, major characters.

The media's overall portrayal of women in mass culture is slowly improving, but in her book *Loving with a Vengeance: Mass-Produced Fantasies for Women*, Tania Modleski says that the portrayal in popular fiction of women in submissive roles goes back to 1740, with the British novel *Pamela*, which was published in America by Benjamin Franklin in 1744. Modleski analyzed the historical content of gothic novels, Harlequin romances and soap operas:

> In Harlequin Romances, the need of women to find meaning and pleasure in activities that are not wholly male-centered such as work or artistic creation is generally scoffed at.
>
> Soap operas also undercut, though in subtler fashion, the idea that a woman might obtain satisfaction from these activities [work or artistic creation]. . . . Indeed, patriarchal myths and institutions are . . . wholeheartedly embraced, although the anxieties and tensions they give rise to may be said to provoke the need for the texts in the first place.

The implication of Modleski's research is that women who read romance novels will believe they should act like the women in the novels they read. A stereotype that has existed since 1740 still shows up in today's mass media, often in advertising campaigns directed at women.

Media Begin to Reflect Racial Diversity

Beginning in the year 2000, the U.S. census allowed Americans to use more than one racial category to describe themselves, and the categories have been changed to reflect America's changing face. In the past, people were forced to choose one category from among the following: Black, White, Asian or Pacific Islander, American Indian or Alaskan Native, or "Other—specify in writing."

In the 2010 census, 9 million people chose more than one race, a change of about 32 percent since 2000. (See **Media/Impact: Audience**, "Census Data Tracks Rise in Multiracial Population of Youths," p. 291.) People who identify with more than one group also were able to check more than one description—African American and Asian, for example. All government forms are required to use the new categories.

This new census method allows people to identify themselves to the government and shows the evolving social landscape of the U.S. population. Yet the American media have been very slow to acknowledge America's changing population patterns. In fact, critics charge that the media have responded reluctantly to reflect accurately America's growing multicultural mix.

Specific media outlets, such as African American and Latino newspapers and magazines, have been able to cater to specific audiences. But the mainstream media, especially daily newspapers and the TV networks, traditionally have represented the interests of the mainstream culture. Scores of media studies have documented stereotypical representation and a lack of representation of people of color in all areas of the culture, even though the potential audience for ethnic media is very large.

Media scholar Carolyn Martindale, for example, in a content analysis of *The New York Times* from 1934 to 1994, found that most nonwhite groups were visible "only in glimpses." According to Martindale, "The mainstream press in the U.S. has presented minorities as outside, rather than a part of, American society."

After examining 374 episodes of 96 prime-time series on ABC, CBS, NBC, Fox, WB and UPN, the Center for Media and Public Affairs for the National Council of La Raza concluded that only 2 percent of prime-time characters during the 1994–1995 season were Latinos, and most of the roles played by those characters were minor. The study, *Don't Blink: Hispanics in Television Entertainment*, also revealed that although Latino characters were portrayed more positively than they had been in the past, they were most likely to be shown as poor or working class.

Based on a comprehensive analysis of the nation's newspapers, a 56-page *News Watch* report issued at a convention of the nation's African American, Asian, Latino and Native American journalists concluded that "the mainstream media's coverage of people of color is riddled with old stereotypes, offensive terminology, biased reporting and a myopic interpretation of American society."

To counteract stereotyping, the Center for Integration and Improvement of Journalism at San Francisco State University (which sponsored the study) offered the following Tips for Journalists:

- Apply consistent guidelines when identifying people of race. Are the terms considered offensive? Ask individual sources how they wish to be identified.
- Only refer to people's ethnic or racial background when it is relevant.
- When deciding whether to mention someone's race, ask yourself: Is ethnic/racial identification needed? Is it important to the context of the story?
- Consult a supervisor if you are unsure of the offensiveness or relevance of a racial or ethnic term.
- Use sensitivity when describing rites and cultural events. Avoid inappropriate comparisons. For example, Kwanzaa is not "African American Christmas."
- Be specific when using ethnic or racial identification of individuals. Referring to someone as Filipino American is preferred to calling that person Asian. The latter term is better applied to a group.

The issue of accurate reflection by mass media of a complex society invites analysis as the face of America grows more diverse every day.

Mass Media Face Gay and Lesbian Issues

In 1993, newspapers confronted an editorial dilemma when cartoonist Lynn Johnston, who draws the very popular syndicated strip *For Better or For Worse*, decided to reveal that Lawrence, one of the teenagers in the comic strip, was gay. Most newspapers published the strip, but 19 newspapers canceled their contracts for the comic, which was carried by Universal Press Syndicate of Kansas City.

Media/Impact AUDIENCE

Census Data Tracks Rise in Multiracial Population of Youths

By Susan Saulny

Among American children, the multiracial population has increased almost 50 percent, to 4.2 million, since 2000, making it the fastest growing youth group in the country. The number of people of all ages who identified themselves as both white and black soared by 134 percent since 2000 to 1.8 million people, according to census data released Thursday [March 24, 2011].

Census 2010 is the first comprehensive accounting of how the multiracial population has changed over 10 years, since statistics were first collected about it in 2000. It has allowed demographers, for the first time, to make comparisons using the mixed-race group—a segment of society whose precise contours and nuances were largely unknown for generations. The data shows that the multiracial population is overwhelmingly young, and that, among the races, American Indians and Native Hawaiians and Pacific Islanders are the most likely to report being of more than one race. Blacks and whites are the least likely.

In what experts view as a significant change from 2000, the most common racial combination is black and white. Ten years ago, it was white and "some other race"—a designation overwhelmingly used by people of Hispanic origin, which is considered by the government to be an ethnicity not a race.

"I think this marks a truly profound shift in the way Americans, particularly African-Americans, think about race and about their heritage," said C. Matthew Snipp, a professor in the sociology department at Stanford University.

Across the country, 9 million people—or 2.9 percent of the population—chose more than one race on the last census, a change of about 32 percent since 2000. But in the South and parts of the Midwest, the growth has been far greater than the national average. In North Carolina, for instance, the multiracial population grew by 99 percent. In Iowa, Indiana and Mississippi, the group grew by about 70 percent.

Orlando Sentinel/McClatchy-Tribune/Getty Images

According to the 2010 U.S. Census, the number of American children who are multiracial has increased nearly 50 percent in the last 10 years, to 4.2 million. Children at Wicklow Elementary in Sanford, Florida, eat lunch in the school cafeteria on October 14, 2011.

"The numbers, for mixed race families like my own, mean that the world must stop and recognize the changing face of today's family, the changing face of today's individual," said Suzy Richardson, founder of Mixed and Happy, a news and opinion Web site focused on issues of concern to multiracial families.

There are 57 racial combinations on the census. But of the population that chose more than one race, most chose one of the four most common combinations: 20.4 percent marked black and white; 19.3 percent chose white and "some other race." The third most common pairing was Asian and white, followed by American Indian and white. These four combinations account for three-fourths of the total mixed race population.

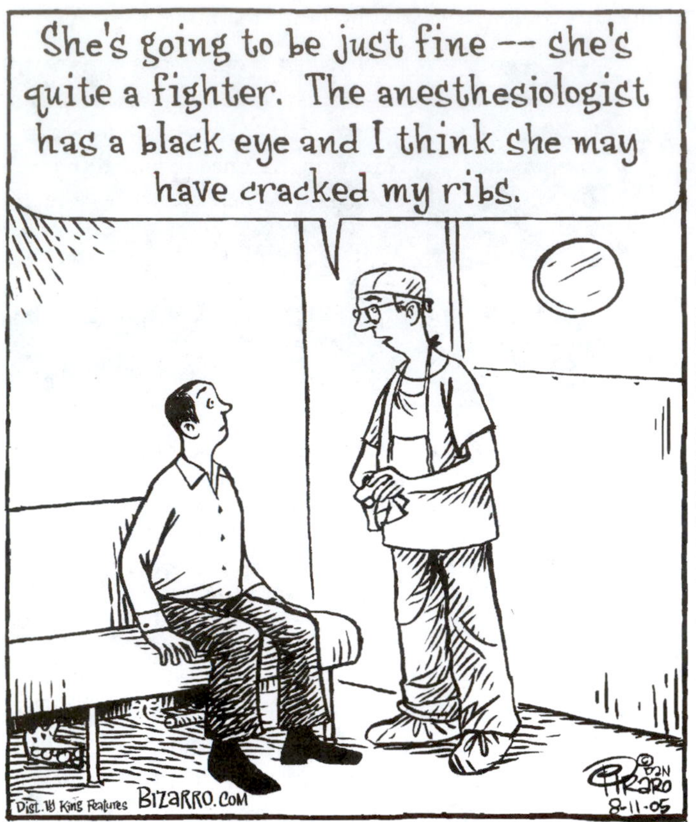
She's going to be just fine -- she's quite a fighter. The anesthesiologist has a black eye and I think she may have cracked my ribs.
BIZARRO.COM
8-11-05

At the request of his editor, cartoonist Dan Piraro supplied two different captions in 2005 for the same cartoon. Newspapers could choose which caption they wanted to use. Some newspaper editors objected to a caption on this cartoon that portrayed a same-sex male married couple.

One newspaper editor who refused to carry the strip explained, "We are a conservative newspaper in a conservative town." Another editor said he "felt the sequence condoned homosexuality 'almost to the point of advocacy.'" Responding to criticism that, by revealing Lawrence's sexual preference, she was advocating homosexuality, Johnston said, "You know, that's like advocating left-handedness. Gayness is simply something that exists. My strip is a reality strip, real situations, real crises, real people." One newspaper executive at a paper that carried the strip wrote, "It seems to me that what we're talking about here isn't the rightness or wrongness of homosexuality. It is about tolerance."

More than 10 years later, in 2005, a cartoon drawn by veteran cartoonist Dan Piraro appeared in two different versions. The first version showed a doctor outside a surgery room talking to a man, saying, "Your husband is in the recovery room. You could go back and see him if you like, but our government-sanctioned bigotry forbids it." Piraro's editor at King Features Syndicate, saying he had received complaints about Piraro's liberal bias, asked Piraro to draw a second version with the doctor talking to a man and saying, "She's going to be just fine—she's quite a fighter. The anesthesiologist has a black eye and I think she may have cracked my ribs."

Different papers chose which version to run, but some subscribers noticed the difference. "Not wishing to lose my voice entirely, I thought it was wise to send in a replacement caption for the same picture," Piraro said.

An understanding of the media portrayals of Americans' diverse lifestyles on television grabbed attention in 1997, when the program *Ellen* portrayed two women exchanging a romantic kiss. (Although promoted as the nation's first female television kiss, the first televised romantic lesbian relationship actually had been portrayed on the TV program *L.A. Law* in 1991.)

Same-sex issues remained primarily a subject for the nation's lesbian and gay newspapers and magazines, although in 1996, *The New Yorker* ran a controversial cover that portrayed two men kissing on a Manhattan sidewalk. Bringing the issue to a mainstream audience, as the *Ellen* television program did, presented a dilemma for the TV networks because, when notified beforehand about the content of the program, some local TV stations refused to show the episode. The reluctance of mainstream television to portray alternative relationships is as much a reflection of the networks trying to protect their economic interests as it is a reflection of the nation's social values.

By 2003, society's strong reactions to the portrayals of gay people on television seemed to have subsided when Bravo introduced its series *Queer Eye for the Straight Guy*. The title itself would have been shocking just a few years earlier, but audiences seemed ready for programming that featured gay men who advise a straight man about fashion, home decor, cuisine and culture. Television programming traditionally has been slow to adapt to changing social standards, trailing the culture's ability to accommodate its evolving diversity.

How to Gauge Media Effects

Scholars once thought the effects of media were easy to measure, as a direct relationship between media messages and media effects. Contemporary scholars now know that the relationship between media and their audiences is complex.

Communications scholar Neil Postman poses some questions to ask about mass media's relationship to cultural, political and social issues:

- What are the main psychic effects of each [media] form?
- What is the main relation between information and reason?

- What redefinitions of important cultural meanings do new sources, speeds, contexts and forms of information require?
- How do different forms of information persuade?
- Is a newspaper's "public" different from television's "public"?
- How do different information forms dictate the type of content that is expressed?

These questions should be discussed, says Postman, because "no medium is excessively dangerous if its users understand what its dangers are. . . . This is an instance in which the asking of the questions is sufficient. To ask is to break the spell."

Review, Analyze, Investigate

REVIEWING CHAPTER 13

Early Mass Media Studies Assess Impact

✓ Media scholars look for patterns in the effects of media rather than for anecdotal evidence.

✓ David Potter, in *People of Plenty*, described the United States as a consumer society driven by advertising.

Scholars Look for Patterns

✓ Canadian scholar Marshall McLuhan introduced the term *global village* to describe the way media bring people together through shared experience.

✓ The magic bullet theory, developed in the 1929 Payne Fund studies, asserted that media content has a direct causal relationship to behavior and that mass media affects everyone in the same way.

✓ Challenging the magic bullet theory, Hadley Cantril found that better-educated people listening to "War of the Worlds" were much more likely to detect that the radio broadcast was fiction. Today, scholars believe the media have different effects on different people.

✓ In 1948, political scientist Harold D. Lasswell described the process of analyzing communication as answering five questions: Who? Says what? On which channel? To whom? With what effect?

How TV Affects Children's Behavior

✓ In 1961, Wilbur Schramm and his associates revealed that children used TV for fantasy, diversion and instruction. Aggressive children were more likely to turn to TV for fantasy, said Schramm, but he could find no serious problems related to TV viewing.

✓ The 1971 report to Congress, *Television and Social Behavior*, made a faint causal connection between TV violence and children's violent behavior, but the report said that only some children were affected, and these children already had been classified as aggressive.

✓ Several recent studies have suggested that TV violence causes aggression among children. Researchers caution, however, that TV violence is not *the* cause of aggressiveness, but only *a* cause of aggressiveness.

✓ The Federal Trade Commission report *Television Advertising to Children* said that children see 20,000 commercials a year and that younger children are much more likely to pay attention to TV advertising than older ones.

✓ A study by the California Assessment Program of children's TV viewing habits seems to support the idea that children who watch a lot of TV do not perform as well in school as children who watch less television.

✓ A 2011 study by Common Sense Media reports that children under 8 spend more time than ever using media, and more than half of these children have access to a mobile device.

Do the Mass Media Cause Violence?

✓ The summary study by the National Institute of Mental Health in 1982 asserted that a direct connection exists between televised violence and aggressive behavior, but there is no way to predict who will be affected and why.

✓ Most of the latest studies of the media's role have continued to reinforce the concept that different people in different environments react to the media differently.

National Political Campaigns Depend on Mass Media

✓ Media politics began in 1933 with President Franklin Roosevelt's Fireside Chats. John F. Kennedy broadened the tradition when he and Richard Nixon appeared in the nation's first televised debate of presidential candidates, in 1960.

✓ The first major study of politics and the media, *The People's Choice*, concluded that only 8 percent of the voters in the study were actually converted by media coverage of the 1940 campaign.

✓ The 1976 study, *The Unseeing Eye*, revealed that only 7 percent of the people in the study were manipulated by TV ads. The researchers concluded that political advertising has little effect on most people.

- ✓ Television is a very efficient way to reach large numbers of people quickly, but campaigning through television also distances the candidates from direct public contact.

Cost of Political Advertising Skyrockets

- ✓ The rising cost of national political campaigns is directly connected to the expense of television advertising.
- ✓ Opinion leaders shape political views, a transmission of ideas that is called the *two-step flow* of communication.
- ✓ TV political advertising affects only a small percentage of people, but just a few percentage points decide many elections.
- ✓ Political spending by presidential candidates in 2008 totaled $2.4 billion.
- ✓ In most political contests, television advertising accounts for more than half of campaign spending, which means healthy earnings for local TV stations.
- ✓ Candidates spent record amounts, estimated at $3 billion to $4 billion for TV advertising in the 2010 mid-term elections, even without a presidential race.

Voters and Campaigns Use the Internet and Social Media

- ✓ The 2004 presidential election was the first election where the Internet began to play a role in national politics. In that election, 75 million people used the Internet to obtain political news.
- ✓ Candidates use Web sites, e-mail, blogs, podcasts and social-networking sites such as MySpace, Facebook and YouTube to reach the public.

Mass Media Reflect Cultural Values

- ✓ Elisabeth Noelle-Neumann has asserted that due to what she calls a "spiral of silence" supporting the consensus point of view, the media have more influence because opponents of the consensus tend to remain silent.
- ✓ Joshua Meyrowitz says that television viewing blurs the distinction between childhood and adulthood.
- ✓ Walter Lippmann first identified the tendency of journalists to generalize about groups of people and create stereotypes.
- ✓ Scholar Tania Modleski says the media's inaccurate portrayals of women are not new but began in 1740 with the publication of *Pamela*, the first novel.

Media Begin to Reflect Racial Diversity

- ✓ In the 2010 census 9 million people identified themselves as a member of more than one race.
- ✓ The mainstream media, especially daily newspapers and the TV networks, have traditionally represented the interests of the mainstream culture.
- ✓ A study of *The New York Times* from 1934 to 1994 found that most nonwhite groups were visible "only in glimpses."
- ✓ A study by the National Council of La Raza concluded that only 2 percent of prime-time characters during the 1994–1995 TV season were Latinos, and most of the roles played by those characters were minor.
- ✓ To avoid ethnic stereotyping, journalists should refer to people's ethnic or racial background only when it is relevant, use sensitivity when describing rites and cultural events and be specific when identifying someone's race or ethnicity, asking the person how he or she would like to be identified.

Mass Media Face Gay and Lesbian Issues

- ✓ The lesbian character on the TV program *Ellen* and the gay character Lawrence in the cartoon strip *For Better or For Worse* focused attention on media portrayals of gender issues in the 1990s.
- ✓ By 2003, the strong reactions to the portrayals of gay people on television seemed to have subsided when Fox Television introduced its series *Queer Eye for the Straight Guy*.
- ✓ The experience of the cartoonist Dan Piraro in 2005 is a reminder that same-sex issues still are a sensitive subject for media. At the insistence of his editor, Piraro provided two captions for the same cartoon, one that reflected a male-female couple and one that showed a male-male married couple.

How to Gauge Media Effects

- ✓ The relationship between media and their audiences is complex.
- ✓ Communications scholar Neil Postman says that scholars should continue to analyze the media's effects so people will not just accept what they see without question.

KEY TERMS

These terms are defined in the margins throughout this chapter and appear in alphabetical order with definitions in the Glossary, which begins on page 383.

CRITICAL QUESTIONS

1. How did each of the following people contribute to media effects research?
   a. David M. Potter
   b. Marshall McLuhan
   c. Harold D. Lasswell
   d. George Gerbner
2. Describe three studies involving children and TV and discuss the results. Why are children often the subject of television effects research?
3. Discuss your understanding of the role of American media, especially television, in political campaigns. Include reference to research about how political campaigns use media to try to influence voters.
4. Describe the nature and effects of the Internet on American politics.
5. How well and how fairly do you believe women, African Americans, Latinos and other ethnic groups are represented in American mass media? How well and fairly do you believe gay and lesbian issues are portrayed in American mass media? If you were an executive at a major media company, how would you address these issues?

WORKING THE WEB

This list includes both sites mentioned in the chapter and others to give you greater insight into social, cultural and political issues research.

Benton Foundation

http://www.benton.org

The foundation says that its mission is "to ensure that media and telecommunications serve the public interest and enhance our democracy." The foundation pursues this mission by "seeking policy solutions that support the values of access, diversity and equity, and by demonstrating the value of media and telecommunications for improving the quality of life for all." Its virtual library includes downloadable documents on issues ranging from the "digital divide" to telecommunications regulation and legislation to television/community media. The foundation was established by William Benton, whom pollster George Gallup called a father of advertising consumer research. Benton was also publisher of the Encyclopedia Britannica and a U.S. senator.

Center on Media and Child Health (CMCH)

http://www.cmch.tv

Dedicated to "understanding and responding to the effects of media on the physical, mental and social health of children through research, production and education," this center is located at Children's Hospital Boston along with Harvard Medical School and Harvard School of Public Health. Hot Topics in the site's section for parents and teachers include violence in video games, educational television and literacy, and obesity. The CMCH Database of Research catalogs current research on the relationship of media exposure to health-risk behaviors.

Joan Shorenstein Center on the Press, Politics and Public Policy (Harvard University)

http://www.hks.harvard.edu/presspol/

Dedicated to "exploring and illuminating the intersection of press, politics and public policy in theory and in practice," this research center is based at the John F. Kennedy School of Government at Harvard University. Downloadable Research & Publications documents include books written by Center faculty, staff and associates, newsletters from the Center and a variety of reports, papers and case studies. The center offers some internships and scholarships for students.

Media Awareness Network (MNet)

http://www.media-awareness.ca

This Canadian nonprofit organization promotes Internet and media education by producing online programs and resources, partnering with Canadian and international organizations, and speaking to audiences in Canada and around the world. MNet's focus is on providing educational information and materials empowering young people to develop the critical thinking skills needed to be "functionally literate" in media messages. The Web site deals with issues including media violence, online hate and media stereotyping (of ethnic minorities, girls and women, boys and men, and gays and lesbians).

Media Effects Research Lab at Penn State University

http://www.psu.edu/dept/medialab/

This research facility has conducted several experiments on hundreds of subjects testing the psychological effects of media content, form and technology. Research abstracts are available for viewing on a wide variety of subjects including Internet use and content credibility; cell phone usage and interaction with others; examinations of gender, racial and sexual minority stereotypes in the media; and fashion magazines' role in self-worth.

Media Research Hub (Social Science Research Council)

http://mediaresearchhub.ssrc.org

Part of the SSRC's Necessary Knowledge for a Democratic Public Sphere program, the Media Research Hub works to ensure that debates about media and communication technologies are shaped by "high-quality research and a rich understanding of the public interest." Its Resource Database is a community-maintained field mapping tool for work on the social dimensions of media, communications and technology. Research news, commentary and data are also available on the site. The program is run in partnership with the Center for International Media Action (CIMA) and the Donald McGannon Communication Research Center at Fordham University.

Moorland-Spingarn Research Center (MSRC) at Howard University

http://www.founders.howard.edu/moorland-spingarn

One of the largest repositories for "documentation of the history and culture of people of African descent in Africa, the Americas and other parts of the world," this site includes a link to the archives of the center's electronic journal (HUArchivesNet). Links to the Library Division and the Manuscript Division go to brief descriptions and samples of the center's holdings.

National Journal

http://www.nationaljournal.com

National Journal Group publishes nonpartisan magazines, newsletters, books and directories "for people who have a professional interest in politics, policy and government." Web site users can access online content from *National Journal Magazine*, *The Hotline* (daily news service for political insiders), and *CongressDaily*.

University of Iowa Department of Communication Studies: Political Communication and Campaigns

http://www.uiowa.edu/commstud/resources/polcomm.html

This resource site provides links to articles and a long list of Web sites relating to politics and to several political media consulting firms.

Wikipedia

http://www.wikipedia.org/

Wikipedia is a free online encyclopedia, written by volunteers who are mostly anonymous. Since its creation in 2001, Wikipedia has grown rapidly into a widely used Web site that is sometimes cited in news stories, although its contents often prove unreliable because of the way it is produced. Experts do not consistently review information on the site for accuracy.

Impact/Action Videos are concise news features on topics covered in this chapter, created exclusively for **Media/Impact**. They are available for students and instructors at CengageBrain.com, and include screen access for classroom viewing and discussion questions.

14

"As daunting as it is to publish such material over official objections, it would be presumptuous to conclude that Americans have no right to know what is being done in their name."

—The New York Times' *Note to Readers, November 28, 2010, explaining why* The Times *decided to publish stories based on information contained in classified documents posted on the Internet by* WikiLeaks.

Law and Regulation: Rewriting the Rules

What's Ahead?

U.S. Constitution Sets Free Press Precedent

Government Tries to Restrict Free Expression

Prior Restraint Rarely Used

Government Manages War Coverage

WikiLeaks Challenges Government Secrecy

Librarians Resist the PATRIOT Act

What Is the Standard for Obscenity?

Libel Law Outlines the Media's Public Responsibility

Invasion of Privacy Defined Four Ways

Debate Continues over Fair Trial, Courtroom Access and Shield Laws

FCC Regulates Broadcast and Cable

Telecommunications Act of 1996 Changes the Marketplace

Deregulation Unleashes the Media

Congress Attempts to Use Communications Decency Act

TV Industry Agrees to Ratings and the V-Chip

Government Monitors Broadcast Indecency

Intellectual Property Rights Affirmed

FCC Advocates Internet Regulation

Courts and Regulators Govern Advertising and PR

Law Must Balance Rights and Responsibilities

George Rose/Getty Images News/Getty Images

The U.S. Constitution establishes the right of free expression. Demonstrators carry signs in the Labor Day Parade on Fifth Avenue in New York City on Sept. 10, 2011.

According to the

precedent-setting *New York Times v. Sullivan* case, which helped define press freedom in 1964, the U.S. media's role is to encourage "uninhibited, robust and wide-open" debate. Arguments among the public, the government and the media about the best way for the media to maintain this public trusteeship form the core of challenges and rebuttals to legal and regulatory limits on the media.

New York Times columnist Tom Wicker wrote, for example, "Even though absolute press freedom may sometimes have to accommodate itself to other high constitutional values, the repeal or modification of the First Amendment seems unlikely. . . . If the true freedom of the press is to decide for itself what to publish and when to publish it, the true responsibility of the press must be to assert and defend that freedom."

The media are businesses operating to make a profit, but these businesses enjoy a special trust under the U.S. Constitution. The legal and regulatory issues the media face are attempts by the government to balance this special trust with the interests of individuals and the interests of government.

U.S. Constitution Sets Free Press Precedent

All legal interpretations of the press' responsibilities attempt to determine exactly what the framers of the U.S. Constitution meant when they included the First Amendment in the Bill of Rights in 1791. The First Amendment established the concept that the press should operate freely:

> Congress shall make no law respecting an establishment of religion, or prohibiting the free exercise thereof; or abridging the freedom of speech, or of the press; or the right of the people peaceably to assemble, and to petition the Government for a redress of grievances.

In his book *Emergence of a Free Press*, Leonard W. Levy explains his interpretation of the First Amendment:

> By freedom of the press the Framers meant a right to engage in rasping, corrosive and offensive discussions on all topics of public interest. . . . The press had become the tribune of the people by sitting in judgment on the conduct of public officials. A free press meant the press as the Fourth Estate, [as] . . . an informal or extra-constitutional fourth branch that functioned as part of the intricate system of checks and balances that exposed public mismanagement and kept power fragmented, manageable and accountable.

While efforts to interpret the Framers' meaning continue, as do challenges and rebuttals to subsequent laws and regulations, discussion of the restrictions and laws covering the press today can be divided into six categories: (1) federal government restrictions, (2) prior restraint, (3) censorship, (4) libel, (5) privacy and (6) the right of access.

Government Tries to Restrict Free Expression

At least four times in U.S. history before 1964, the federal government felt threatened enough by press freedom to attempt to restrict the press' access to information. These four notable attempts to restrict the way the media operate were the Alien and Sedition Laws of 1798, the Espionage Act of 1918, the Smith Act of 1940 and the Cold War congressional investigations of suspected Communists in the late 1940s and early 1950s. All four challenges were attempts by the government to control free speech.

The Alien and Sedition Laws of 1798

Under the provisions of the Alien and Sedition Laws of 1798, 15 people were indicted, 11 people were tried and 10 were found guilty. The Alien and Sedition Laws set a fine of up to $2,000 and a sentence of up to two years in jail for anyone who was found guilty of speaking, writing or publishing "false, scandalous and malicious writing or writings" against the government, Congress or the president. The laws expired in 1801, and when Thomas Jefferson became president that year, he pardoned everyone who had been found guilty under the laws.

The Espionage Act of 1918

Although Henry Raymond had challenged censorship of Civil War reporting (see **Chapter 12**), journalists and the general population during the Civil War had accepted government control of information. But during World War I, Congress passed the Espionage Act of 1918. Not all Americans supported U.S. entry into the war, and to stop criticism, the Espionage Act made it a crime to say or write anything that could be viewed as helping the enemy. Under the act, 877 people were convicted. Many, but not all, of them were pardoned when the war ended.

The most notable person cited under the Espionage Act of 1918 was labor organizer and Socialist Party presidential candidate Eugene V. Debs, who was sentenced to two concurrent 10-year terms for giving a public speech against the war. At his trial Debs said, "I have been accused of obstructing the war. I admit it. Gentlemen, I abhor war. I would oppose the war if I stood alone." Debs was released from prison by a presidential order in 1921.

The Smith Act of 1940

During World War II, Congress passed the Smith Act of 1940, which placed some restrictions on free speech. Only a few people were cited under it, but the members of the press were required to submit their stories for government censorship. President Franklin D. Roosevelt created the Office of Censorship, which worked out the voluntary Code of Wartime Practices with the press. The Code spelled out the kinds of information the press would not report about the war, such as troop and ship movements. The military retained power to censor all overseas war reporting.

The Office of Censorship also issued the Code of Wartime Practices for American Broadcasters, which were guidelines for news broadcasts and commentaries. (See **Media/Impact: Culture**, "Excerpts from the 1943 Code of Wartime Practices for American Broadcasters," p. 302.) The government exercised influence over broadcasters because it licensed broadcast outlets.

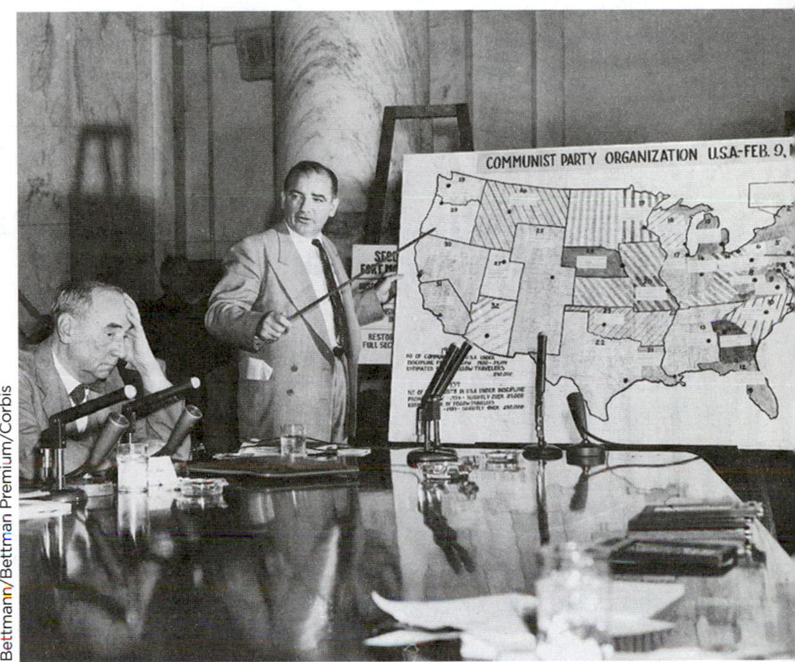

Bettmann/Bettman Premium/Corbis

Senator Joseph McCarthy (at the easel) explained his theory of Communism during the Army-McCarthy hearings in 1954. Army counsel Joseph N. Welch, who was defending people who had been declared subversive by McCarthy, is seated at the table. News reports and Edward R. Murrow's exposure of McCarthy's investigative excesses eventually triggered public criticism of McCarthy's tactics, and his Senate colleagues censured him.

HUAC and the Permanent Subcommittee on Investigations

The fourth major challenge to the First Amendment protection of free speech came in the late 1940s and early 1950s, culminating with the actions of the House Un-American Activities Committee (***HUAC***) against the Hollywood Ten (see **Chapter 7**) and the Senate's Permanent Subcommittee on Investigations presided over by Senator Joseph R. McCarthy.

These congressional committees set a tone of aggressive Communist-hunting. After television broadcasts of McCarthy's investigation of Communist influence in the Army and other reports eventually exposed his excesses, McCarthy's Senate colleagues censured him by a vote of 67 to 22. But while the hearings were being held, they established a restrictive atmosphere that challenged free expression.

Prior Restraint Rarely Used

Prior restraint means government censoring of information before the information is published or broadcast. The Framers of the Constitution clearly opposed prior restraint by law. However, in 1931, the U.S. Supreme Court established the circumstances under which prior restraint could be justified.

Near v. Minnesota

J. M. Near published the weekly *Saturday Press*, which printed the names of people who were violating the nation's Prohibition laws. Minnesota authorities obtained a court order forbidding publication of *Saturday Press*, but the U.S. Supreme Court overturned the state's action. In *Near v. Minnesota* in 1931, the Court condemned prior restraint, although it acknowledged that the government could limit information about troop movements during war and could control obscenity. The court also said that "the security of community life may be protected against incitements to acts of violence and the overthrow of orderly government."

Saturday Press had not violated any of these prohibitions, so the Minnesota court's order was lifted. But future attempts to stop other publications were based on the *Near v. Minnesota* decision, making it a landmark case.

In two important instances since *Near* (the Pentagon Papers and *United States v. The Progressive*), courts were

HUAC House Un-American Activities Committee.

Prior Restraint Government censorship of information before the information is published or broadcast.

Media/Impact CULTURE

Excerpts from the 1943 Code of Wartime Practices for American Broadcasters

Note: During World War II, the Office of War Information tried to control what was broadcast from the United States. Following are some of the rules radio broadcasters were expected to follow.

News Broadcasts and Commentaries

It is requested that news in any of the following classifications be kept off the air unless made available for broadcast by appropriate authority or specifically cleared by the Office of Censorship.

(a) Weather—Weather forecasts other than those officially released by the Weather Bureau.

(b) Armed forces—Types and movements of United States Army, Navy, and Marine Corps units, within or without continental United States.

Frederic Lewis/Getty Images

Under provisions of the 1943 Code of Wartime Practices for American Broadcasters, all live radio programs—including shows featuring performers such as Frank Sinatra (left) and comedian Fred Allen—were subject to on-air censorship.

Programs

(a) Request programs—No telephoned or telegraphed requests for musical selections should be accepted. No requests for musical selections made by word-of-mouth at the origin of broadcast, whether studio or remote, should be honored.

(b) Quiz programs—Any program which permits the public accessibility to an open microphone is dangerous and should be carefully supervised. Because of the nature of quiz programs, in which the public is not only permitted access to the microphone but encouraged to speak into it, the danger of usurpation by the enemy is enhanced.

Foreign Language Broadcasts

(a) Personnel—The Office of Censorship, by direction of the president, is charged with the responsibility of removing from the air all those engaged in foreign language broadcasting who, in the judgment of appointed authorities in the Office of Censorship, endanger the war effort of the United Nations by their connections, direct or indirect, with the medium.

(b) Scripts—Station managements are requested to require all persons who broadcast in a foreign language to submit to the management in advance of broadcast complete scripts or transcriptions of such material.

Excerpted from U.S. Government Office of Censorship, Code of Wartime Practices for American Broadcasters. *Washington, D.C.: Government Printing Office, 1943, pages 1–8.*

asked to bar publication of information to protect national security. In the military offensives in Grenada and the Persian Gulf, the federal government took action to prevent journalists from reporting on the government's activities.

The Pentagon Papers

On June 13, 1971, *The New York Times* published the first installment of what has become known as the Pentagon Papers, excerpts from what was properly titled *History of U.S. Decision-Making Process on Vietnam Policy*. The Pentagon Papers detailed decisions that were made about U.S. involvement in Vietnam starting in the 1940s.

The documents were labeled top secret, but they were given to *The Times* by one of the report's authors, Daniel Ellsberg, a consultant to the Defense Department and the White House. Ellsberg said he believed the papers had been improperly classified and that the public should have the information. After the first three installments were published in *The Times*, Justice Department attorneys obtained a restraining order against *The Times*, which stopped publication of the installments for two weeks while *The Times* appealed the case. While the case was being decided, *The Washington Post* began publishing the papers, and *The Post* was stopped, but only until the U.S. Supreme Court decided the *Times* case.

In *New York Times Co. v. United States*, the Court said the government did not prove that prior restraint was necessary. *The Times* and *The Post* then printed the papers, but the court action had delayed publication of the information for two weeks. This was the first time in the nation's history that the federal government had stopped a newspaper from publishing specific information. Legal fees cost *The Post* and *The Times* more than $270,000. (In 2009, Daniel Ellsberg's role in the Pentagon Papers case formed the basis for the Oscar-nominated movie, *The Most Dangerous Man in America*.) (See **Media/Impact: World**, "What Would Daniel Ellsberg Do with the Pentagon Papers Today?" p. 306.)

The Progressive Case

The next instance of prior restraint happened in 1979, when editors of *The Progressive* magazine announced that they planned to publish an article by Howard Morland about how to make a hydrogen bomb. The author said the article was based on information from public documents and interviews with government employees. The Department of Justice brought suit in Wisconsin, where the magazine was published, and received a restraining order to stop the information from being printed (*United States v. The Progressive*). *The Progressive* did not publish the article as planned.

Before the case could reach the U.S. Supreme Court, a Wisconsin newspaper published a letter from a man named Charles Hansen that contained much of the same information as the Morland article. Hansen sent eight copies of the letter to other newspapers, and the *Chicago Tribune* also published the letter, saying that none of the information was proprietary. Six months after the original restraining order, *The Progressive* published the article.

Government Manages War Coverage

The U.S. government historically has tried to control its image during wartime. Four recent examples of government press management are Grenada, the Gulf War, Afghanistan and Iraq. In 2009, the U.S. government eased previous restrictions on press access when, with the family's consent, it allowed reporters to photograph caskets of fallen soldiers that were being returned home.

Restricting Press Access in Grenada

In an incident in 1983 that never reached the courts but that was a type of prior restraint, the Reagan administration kept reporters away from the Caribbean island of Grenada, where the administration had launched a military offensive. A press blackout began at 11 p.m. on October 24, 1983. The administration didn't officially bar the press from covering the invasion on October 25, but the Pentagon refused to transport the press and turned back press yachts and airplanes that attempted to enter the war zone. About a dozen print journalists and photographers were able to get in, but no television crews were allowed.

More than 400 journalists from 170 news organizations around the world who couldn't get to Grenada were left on Barbados, waiting for the news to get to them. Charles Lachman of the *New York Post* flew to Barbados and then to St. Vincent. Then he and some other reporters paid $6,000 to charter a boat to Grenada. They arrived five days after the invasion and discovered that one of the casualties of the military's action had been a hospital.

News Blackouts and Press Pools During the Gulf War

In the 1990s, the Gulf War posed another tough battleground for the rights of reporters versus the rights of the military to restrict access. On Saturday, February 23, 1991, about three weeks into the Gulf War, when the ground assault began, the Defense Department announced the first total news blackout in U.S. military history.

For 24 hours, defense leaders were told to issue no statements about the actions of U.S. troops. Military officials said that instantaneous transmission of information from the battlefield meant that Iraq would be able to pick up live TV pictures. Press organizations protested the ban, but the

Win McNamee/Getty Images

U.S. Army Honor Guardsmen carry the flag-draped casket of Staff Sgt. Edward C. Kramer, who died in combat in Iraq. Because the ban on coverage of U.S. war casualties had been lifted and Kramer's family gave permission, the press was able to photograph this official transfer of his casket at Dover Air Force Base on July 1, 2009.

military argued that modern communications technology necessitated the blackout.

Pentagon rules for war coverage, reached in cooperation with journalists, imposed stricter limits on reporting in the Persian Gulf than in any previous U.S. war. Reporters had to travel in small "pools," escorted by public affairs officers. Every story produced by the pool was subject to military censorship. This system, called ***pool reporting***, had been created in response to reporters' complaints about news blackouts during the Grenada incident.

An unprecedented number of journalists—1,300 in Saudi Arabia alone—posed a challenge for military press officers. In a commentary protesting the restrictions, *The New Yorker* magazine said, "The rules, it is clear, enable the Pentagon to promote coverage of subjects and events that it wishes publicized and to prevent reporting that might cast it, or the war, in a bad light." Yet, in a *Los Angeles Times* poll of nearly 2,000 people two weeks after the fighting started, 79 percent approved of the Pentagon's restrictions, and 57 percent favored even further limits.

When the Persian Gulf War ended, many members of the U.S. press in the Middle East complained bitterly about their lack of access, but the military and the public seemed satisfied with the new rules for wartime coverage.

Pool Reporting An arrangement that places reporters in small, government-supervised groups to cover an event.

War in Afghanistan

During the early days of the war in Afghanistan, especially in the months immediately following the September 11, 2001, terrorist attacks in the United States, the military carefully controlled press access to information, citing security reasons. The military used press pools and also provided its own video footage of troop landings, produced by the military's combat film teams.

"In World War II, accredited journalists from leading news organizations were on the front lines to give the public an independent description of what was happening," said *The New York Times*. "In the new war on terrorism, journalists have had limited access to many of the United States forces that are carrying out the war. . . . The media's access to American military operations is far more limited than in recent conflicts."

"Embedded" Reporters During Iraq War

Beginning in 2003, during the Iraq War, the U.S. government adopted a system called *embedding*, which meant that members of the press traveled with the military, but the press' movements were restricted and managed by their military units.

Embedding was a reaction to the press' limited access in Afghanistan, but many journalists said they still had limited access to the real action in Iraq. However, the coverage left the impression with the public that the press was giving the whole story, when in fact the press had access to only a very limited view. (For more about embedded reporters, see **Chapter 12**.)

Photographs of War Fatalities

Twenty years ago during the Gulf War, the first Bush administration banned the media from covering the arrival of war fatalities as they were returned to the United States, saying the administration wanted to protect the families' privacy. Critics of the ban said that the government was trying to hide the consequences of war from public view.

In 2009, the Obama administration lifted the ban and allowed the press access to photograph the returning soldiers, with family permission.

WikiLeaks Challenges Government Secrecy

Founded in 2006 by Australian Julian Assange, WikiLeaks is a whistle-blowing organization devoted to uncovering government secrets and publishing them on its Web site, www.wikileaks.ch. Beginning in 2010, WikiLeaks began releasing classified U.S. diplomatic documents, including military information and State Department communications.

In late July 2010, WikiLeaks posted tens of thousands of confidential military documents about the wars in Iraq and Afghanistan. "The battlefield consequences of the release of these documents are potentially severe and dangerous for our troops, our allies and Afghan partners, and may well damage our relationships and reputation in that key part of world," Defense Secretary Robert M. Gates told Pentagon reporters.

On November 28, 2010, *The New York Times* began publishing a series of articles based on a new release of State Department documents. "Some 250,000 individual cables, the daily traffic between the State Department and more than 270 American diplomatic outposts around the world were made available to *The Times* by a source who insisted on anonymity," wrote *The Times* in an explanatory front page Note to Readers that accompanied the first article.

The Times acknowledged that WikiLeaks originally obtained the documents, but did not directly cite WikiLeaks as *The Times*' source. "As daunting as it is to publish such material over official objections, it would be presumptuous to conclude that Americans have no right to know what is being done in their name," *The Times* explained.

Outraged at the leaks, several countries called for Assange's arrest. For months, he eluded authorities by traveling to various European countries, including Sweden and England. In early December 2010, Swedish authorities charged Assange with sexual misconduct involving two women while he was in Sweden. Assange denied the charges and claimed they were driven by his role in the release of documents on WikiLeaks, but eventually turned himself in to British authorities on December 7, 2010. According to *The New York Times*, as of December 28, 2010, WikiLeaks had posted 391,832 secret documents on the Iraq war, 77,000 classified Pentagon documents on the Afghan conflict and 250,000 State Department cables.

In July 2010, the U.S. military charged Pfc. Bradley Manning, an intelligence analyst, with downloading large amounts of classified information from a computer at a military base in Iraq. Manning was imprisoned at Quantico Marine Corps Base in Virginia, on charges that could put him in prison for 52 years, according to the Army. On February 23, 2011, a British court ordered that Assange be extradited to Sweden. Assange appealed and the case is pending. The U.S. government did not file any charges against Assange for his role in publishing secret U.S. documents on the Internet.

WPA Pool/Getty Images

WikiLeaks founder Julian Assange leaves the High Court in London, England, on December 16, 2010. Despite U.S. government objections, WikiLeaks published about 2,000 confidential State Department documents on its Web site in November 2010.

When should the government be able to prevent military information from reaching the public? When should the press have access? The Supreme Court has never specifically addressed these questions, and the U.S. press and news organizations remain vulnerable to military restrictions.

Librarians Resist the PATRIOT Act

In 2001, a few weeks after the terrorist attacks on the World Trade Center in New York City, Congress passed the USA PATRIOT Act (which stands for Uniting and Strengthening America by Providing Appropriate Tools Required to Intercept and Obstruct Terrorism Act), designed to give the U.S. government broad powers to track, detain and interrogate people who are deemed a threat to the country. Among the provisions of the act is Section 215, which allows the Federal Bureau of Investigation to obtain "business records." These

Media/Impact
WORLD

What Would Daniel Ellsberg Do with the Pentagon Papers Today?

Before WikiLeaks, or Even the Internet, There Were Just Plain Leaks

By Noam Cohen

Daniel Ellsberg leaked the Pentagon Papers to *The New York Times*, which published them on June 13, 1971. Ellsberg commented on Julian Assange's WikiLeaks publication of classified documents on the Internet.

Two weeks ago [April 5, 2010], Wikileaks.org released a classified video showing a United States Apache helicopter killing 12 civilians in Baghdad. The reaction was so swift and powerful—an edited version has been viewed 6 million times on YouTube—that the episode provoked many questions about how such material is now released and digested.

Put another way: if someone today had the Pentagon Papers, or the modern equivalent, would he still go to the press, as Daniel Ellsberg did nearly 40 years ago, and wait for the documents to be analyzed and published? Or would that person simply post them online immediately?

Mr. Ellsberg knows his answer.

"As of today, I wouldn't have waited that long," he said in an interview last week. "I would have gotten a scanner and put them on the Internet."

In early 1971, Mr. Ellsberg, an analyst at the RAND Corporation, passed a *New York Times* reporter a copy of a top-secret report casting doubt on the war in Vietnam, the so-called Pentagon Papers. For months, he said, he waited, unsure if *The New York Times* would ever publish.

When the Nixon administration went to court and prevented *The Times* from publishing the full report, Mr. Ellsberg gave copies to *The Washington Post* and other newspapers. . . .

He does concede that something might have been lost had WikiLeaks been around in 1971. "I don't think it would have had the same impact, then or now, as having it in *The Times*," he said. The government's attempt to block publication—something ended by the Supreme Court—was the best publicity, he said.

But playing the government off newspapers, and newspapers against each other, still does not compare with the power of the World Wide Web. "Competition worked in a useful way," he said. "But the Internet has this viral aspect. It gets sent around and gets a broader audience."

In all his strategizing about getting attention for the material he leaked, Mr. Ellsberg can sound a lot like Julian Assange, the head of WikiLeaks, who is unabashed in saying that one of his group's principal obligations is "to get maximum political impact—to do justice to our material. . . ."

"Some people say that war is war and that we should expect these kinds of casualties to occur in war," Mr. Assange said. "But these kinds of war-is-war arguments are superfluous unless the public knows what war is."

Note: On June 13, 2011, the U.S. government publicly released the complete set of documents once known as the Pentagon Papers.

Excerpted from Noam Cohen, "What Would Daniel Ellsberg Do with the Pentagon Papers Today?" The New York Times, *April 18, 2010.*

could include public library records, including computer log-ins and lists of books people check out, although the act does not specifically mention libraries.

Librarians said they were ready to cooperate with an investigation if they received a search warrant. However, they claimed the PATRIOT Act would allow officials to seize anything they wished without a search warrant, which librarians said would inhibit the use of public libraries—a limit on free expression.

Some libraries posted signs to warn patrons that federal authorities might review their records; others systematically shredded patrons' sign-in sheets for using library computers. The American Library Association went on record opposing unwarranted government access to library records. The American Civil Liberties Union sued in several cities nationwide to keep library records private, and in 2004 a Los Angeles federal judge ruled that parts of the PATRIOT Act were unconstitutional violations of the First and Fifth amendments to the U.S. Constitution.

In 2005, the Federal Bureau of Investigation (FBI) demanded library records from Library Connection, a nonprofit library group in Bridgeport, Conn., saying the agency needed the information as part of a terrorism investigation under the PATRIOT Act. The American Civil Liberties Union challenged the request in court, saying the request was unconstitutional. Eventually the FBI withdrew its request.

The PATRIOT Act expired in late 2005, but in March 2006, Congress reauthorized the act for another four years, including Section 215. Opponents, including the American Library Association, vowed to renew their challenges to the most aggressive provisions of the act, especially Section 215, to stop what they said is an intrusion into important American civil liberties.

In 2007, a federal judge in New York struck down provisions of the PATRIOT Act that had authorized the government to issue so-called National Security Letters (***NSLs***), compelling businesses (such as Internet service providers, telephone companies and public libraries) to release customer information without a judge's order or grand jury subpoena. U.S. District Judge Victor Marrero said using the PATRIOT Act, even as rewritten and reauthorized in 2006, to obtain customer information without court authorization "offends the fundamental constitutional principles of checks and balances and separation of powers." President Obama signed a four-year extension of the PATRIOT Act on May 30, 2011.

What Is the Standard for Obscenity?

Different media industries historically have reacted differently to threats of ***censorship***, the practice of suppressing material that is considered morally, politically or otherwise objectionable. Most threats of censorship concern matters of morality.

According to the American Library Association, the top three reasons critics try to challenge content are

1. The material is considered "sexually explicit."
2. The material contains "offensive language."
3. The material is "unsuited to an age group."

In the United States, censorship almost always occurs after the fact. Once the material is printed or displayed, the courts can be asked to review the content for obscenity.

To try to avoid constant scrutiny, the motion picture and recording industries have accepted some form of self-regulation to avoid government intervention. The electronic media are governed by laws in the federal criminal code against broadcast obscenity, and the federal Cable Act of 1984 bars obscenity on cable TV.

Print media, including book publishers, have been the most vigorous defenders of the right to publish. The print media, of course, were the earliest media to be threatened with censorship, beginning with the philosopher Plato, who suggested in 387 B.C. that Homer's *Odyssey* be censored for immature readers.

Government efforts to block free expression happen on the local and federal levels.

Local Efforts

More than 2,000 years after Homer's *Odyssey* was threatened with censorship, Boston officials banned the sale of the April 1926 issue of H. L. Mencken's magazine *The American Mercury*. The local Watch and Ward Society had denounced a fictional story in the magazine as "salacious." The story featured "Hatrack," a prostitute whose clientele included members of various religious congregations who visited her after church.

In Boston, surrounded by his supporters, Mencken sold a copy of the magazine at a prearranged time to a member of the Watch and Ward. The chief of the Boston Vice Squad arrested Mencken and marched him to jail, where he spent the night before going to court the next morning. "Mencken passed an uneasy night," says Mencken's biographer Carl Bode, "knowing that he could be found guilty and perhaps even be imprisoned. . . . Returning to court he listened to

NSL National Security Letter.

Censorship The practice of suppressing material that is considered morally, politically or otherwise objectionable.

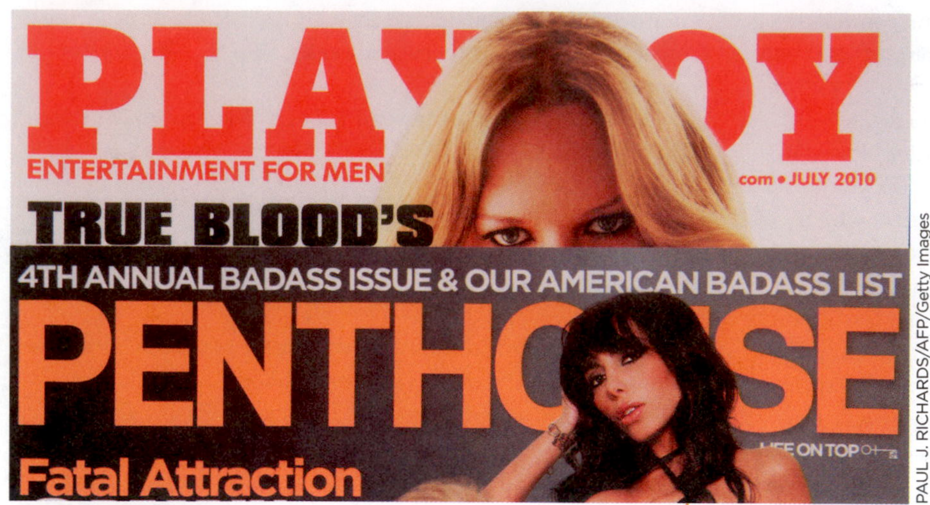

PAUL J. RICHARDS/AFP/Getty Images

Magazines often have been the objects of censorship. Because there is no national standard for obscenity, local juries and government regulators in each community are free to decide what they consider offensive. What is acceptable in one community may be censored in another. Bowing to community guidelines, some merchants display only the mastheads of magazines such as *Playboy* and *Penthouse* in their magazine racks and hide the rest of the cover.

Judge Parmenter's decision: 'I find that no offense has been committed and therefore dismiss the complaint.'"

Mencken spent $20,000 defending *The Mercury*, but according to Bode, "the net gain for both *The Mercury* and Mencken was great. *The Mercury* became the salient American magazine and Mencken the international symbol of freedom of speech."

Mencken was defending his magazine against local censorship. Until 1957, censorship in America remained a local issue because the U.S. Supreme Court had not considered a national censorship case.

U.S. Supreme Court Writes Obscenity Criteria

Today, censorship still is primarily a local issue, but two landmark Supreme Court cases—*Roth v. United States* and *Miller v. California*—established the major criteria for local censorship.

ROTH V. UNITED STATES. This decision in 1957 involved two separate cases. Samuel Roth was found guilty in New York of sending obscenity through the mail, and David S. Alberts was found guilty of selling obscene books in Beverly Hills. The case carries Roth's name because his name appeared first when the cases were combined for review. The U.S. Supreme Court upheld the guilty verdict and, according to legal scholar Ralph Holsinger, established several precedents:

- The First Amendment does not protect obscenity.
- Obscenity is defined as material "utterly without redeeming social importance."
- Sex and obscenity are not synonymous. Obscene material is material that appeals to "prurient [obsessively sexual] interest."
- A test of obscenity is "whether to the average person, applying contemporary community standards, the dominant theme of the material taken as a whole appeals to prurient interest." (This last description of obscenity has become known as the ***Roth test***.)

MILLER V. CALIFORNIA. In the late 1960s, a California court found Marvin Miller guilty of sending obscene, unsolicited advertising material through the mail. The case reached the U.S. Supreme Court in 1973. The decision described just which materials a state could censor and also set a three-part test for obscenity.

According to the Supreme Court, states may censor material that meets this three-part local test for obscenity. The local court, according to legal scholar Ralph Holsinger, must determine

1. Whether "the average person, applying contemporary community standards," would find that the work, taken as a whole, appeals to the prurient interest.
2. Whether the work depicts or describes, in a patently offensive way, sexual conduct specifically defined by the applicable state law.
3. Whether the work, taken as a whole, lacks serious *L*iterary, *A*rtistic, *P*olitical or *S*cientific value—often called the ***LAPS test***.

The *Roth* and *Miller* cases together established a standard for obscenity, leaving the decision in specific obscenity

Roth Test A standard court test for obscenity, named for one of the defendants in an obscenity case.

LAPS Test A yardstick for local obscenity judgments, which evaluates an artistic work's literary, artistic, political or scientific value.

challenges to local courts. The result is widely differing standards in different parts of the country because local juries and government regulators are free to decide what they consider offensive in their communities. Books and magazines that are available to young readers in some states may be unavailable in other states.

School Boards as Censors

Many censorship cases begin at schools and local-government boards, where parents' groups protest books, magazines and films that are available to students, such as these examples:

- Norwood High School in Colorado banned Rudolfo Anaya's award-winning book *Bless Me, Ultima* because of what the school considered "offensive language."
- A school board in New York removed 11 books from school libraries, including the novels *Slaughterhouse-Five* by Kurt Vonnegut and *Black Boy* by Richard Wright, plus a work of popular anthropology, *The Naked Ape* by Desmond Morris.
- A school district in Little Rock, Ark., removed Harry Potter books from its library because the school board claimed the tales of wizards and spells could harm schoolchildren.
- A school district in California required students to have parental permission to read *Ms.* magazine in the school library.
- A school board in Minnesota banned four books, including *Are You There, God? It's Me, Margaret* by Judy Blume, a writer well known for her young adult books.
- The state of Alabama ordered 45 textbooks pulled from the shelves after a federal judge said the books promoted "secular humanism."

The American Library Association (ALA) fiercely opposes any attempt to censor or restrict access to information. Since 1990, the ALA and several other organizations have sponsored Banned Books Week to bring public attention to the issue of censorship. "Censorship has no place in a free society," said ALA President Camila Alire during Banned Books Week in 2009. "Part of living in a democracy means respecting each other's differences and the right of all people to choose for themselves what they and their families read."

Most reported book challenges take place in schools and in public libraries, according to the ALA. These challenges usually are reversed when appealed, but while the specific issues are being decided, the books, magazines and films are unavailable, and censorship efforts have been increasing nationwide. The ALA reported 460 book challenges in 2009. (See **Media/Impact: Culture**, "Texas Board Adopts New Social Studies Curriculum," p. 310.)

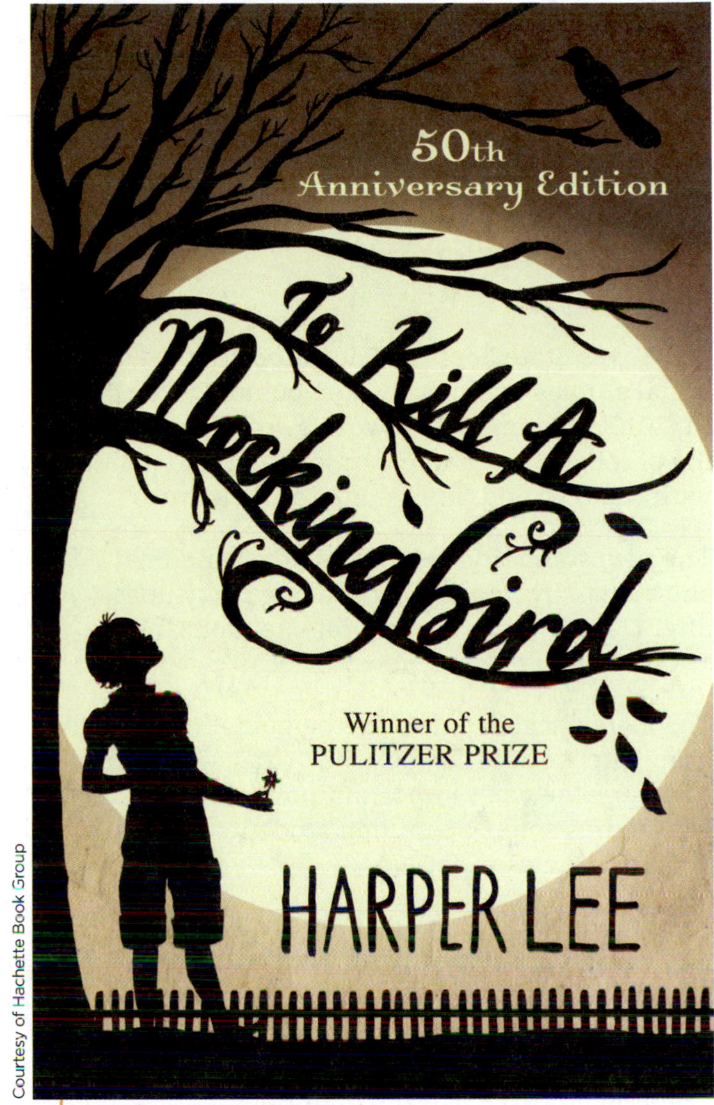

Courtesy of Hachette Book Group

Each year the American Library Association, along with several other organizations, sponsors Banned Books Week to bring public attention to the issue of censorship. Listed fourth on the 2009 Top Ten Most Frequently Challenged Books was the perennial classic *To Kill a Mockingbird* by Harper Lee, which celebrated its 50th anniversary in print in 2010.

The *Hazelwood* Case

In 1988, the U.S. Supreme Court for the first time gave public school officials considerable freedom to limit what appears in student publications. The case, *Hazelwood v. Kuhlmeier*, became known as the *Hazelwood* case because the issues originated at Hazelwood High School in Hazelwood, Mo.

Media/Impact
CULTURE

Texas Board Adopts New Social Studies Curriculum

By April Castro

The Texas State Board of Education adopted a social studies and history curriculum Friday [May 21, 2010] that amends or waters down the teaching of religious freedoms, America's relationship with the U.N. and hundreds of other items.

The new standards were adopted after a final showdown by two 9–5 votes along party lines, after Democrats' and moderate Republicans' efforts to delay a final vote failed.

The ideological debate over the guidelines, which drew intense scrutiny beyond Texas, will be used to determine what important political events and figures some 4.8 million students will learn about for the next decade.

The standards, which one Democrat called a "travesty," also will be used by textbook publishers who often develop materials for other states based on guidelines approved in Texas, although teachers in the Lone Star state have latitude in deciding how to teach the material. . . .

In one of the most significant changes leading up to the vote, the board watered down the rationale for the separation of church and state in a high school government class, pointing out that the words were not in the Constitution and requiring that students compare and contrast the judicial language with the wording in the First Amendment. . . .

Former board chairman Don McLeroy, one of the board's most outspoken conservatives, said the Texas history curriculum has been unfairly skewed to the left after years of Democrats controlling the board and he just wants to bring it back into balance. . . .

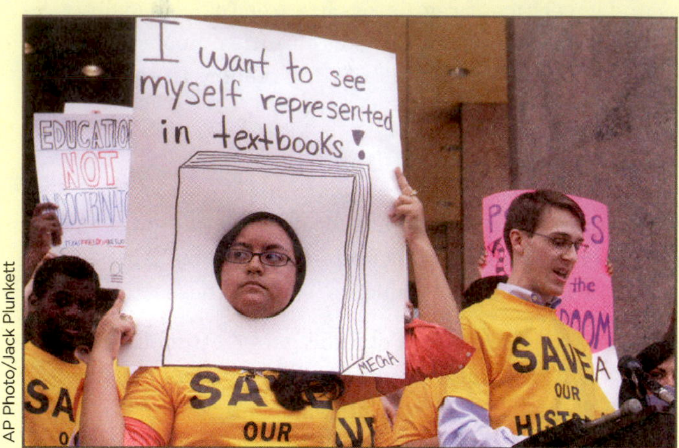

AP Photo/Jack Plunkett

On May 21, 2010, the Texas State Board of Education adopted new social studies and history curriculum guidelines and resisted efforts to include more Latino figures in the social studies curriculum. Diana Gomez (center) and Garrett Mize (right) speak at a March 2010 rally protesting the board's proposed changes.

During the months-long revision process, conservatives strengthened requirements on teaching the Judeo-Christian influences of the nation's Founding Fathers and required that the U.S. government be referred to as a "constitutional republic," rather than "democratic." Students will be required to study the decline in the value of the U.S. dollar, including the abandonment of the gold standard.

Educators have blasted the curriculum proposals for politicizing education. Teachers also have said the document is too long and will force students to memorize lists of names rather than thinking critically. . . .

At least one lawmaker vowed legislative action to "rein in" the board. "They have ignored historians and teachers, allowing ideological activists to push the culture war further into our classrooms," said Rep. Mike Villareal, a San Antonio Democrat. "They fail to understand that we don't want liberal textbooks or conservative textbooks. We want excellent textbooks, written by historians instead of activists."

April Castro, "Texas Board Adopts New Social Studies Curriculum," Associated Press, as published in the Austin American-Statesman, May 21, 2010. Retrieved from http://www.statesman.com. Used with permission of the Associated Press.

The high school paper, funded mostly from the school budget, was published as part of a journalism class. The principal at Hazelwood regularly reviewed the school paper before it was published, and in this case he deleted two articles the staff had written. One of the deleted articles was about student pregnancy and included interviews with three students who had become pregnant while attending school.

Although the article used pseudonyms instead of the students' names, the principal said he believed that the anonymity of the students was not sufficiently protected. He also believed that the girls' discussion of their use or nonuse of birth control was inappropriate for a school publication. By a vote of 5 to 3, the U.S. Supreme Court agreed.

"Even though the legal rights of children have gained broader recognition in recent years, it remains that children are not adults and that they have no explicit or implied right to behave with the full freedom granted to adults," wrote Jonathan Yardley, a *Washington Post* columnist. "Freedom entails the responsibility to exercise it with mature judgment, and this neither young children nor adolescents possess."

The same newspaper, however, carried an editorial that opposed the decision. "Even teenagers," the *Post* editorial said, "should be allowed to publish criticism, raise uncomfortable questions and spur debate on subjects such as pregnancy, AIDS and drug abuse that are too often a very real aspect of high school culture today."

The Hazelwood principal's action drew the attention of the *St. Louis Post-Dispatch*, which published the censored articles, bringing them a much wider audience than the students at Hazelwood High. Many states subsequently have adopted legislation to protect student newspapers from similar censorship. The Supreme Court decision is significant, however, because it may change the way local officials in some states monitor school publications.

Libel Law Outlines the Media's Public Responsibility

"Americans have increasingly begun to seek the refuge and vindication of litigation," writes legal scholar Rodney A. Smolla in his book *Suing the Press*. "Words published by the media no longer roll over us without penetrating; instead, they sink in through the skin and work inner damage, and a consensus appears to be emerging that this psychic damage is serious and must be paid for." Four cases show why the media become targets of litigation:

1. In 1983, actress Carol Burnett sued the *National Enquirer* for $10 million for implying in an article that she was drinking too much and acting rude in a Washington, D.C., restaurant.
2. In late 1984, General William C. Westmoreland filed a $120 million suit against CBS, charging that he was defamed in a 1982 CBS documentary, *The Uncounted Enemy: A Vietnam Deception*.
3. In 1989, entertainer Wayne Newton was awarded $6 million in damages after he sued NBC-TV for a story that linked him to organized crime figures.
4. In September 2010, Republican U.S. Senate candidate Jeff Greene, a Florida real estate developer who lost the Democratic primary sued the *St. Petersburg Times* and *The Miami Herald* for $500 million, saying the newspapers' stories were part of "a coordinated and agreed upon plan to assassinate Greene's character."

These four cases involve the law of ***libel***, which is one legal restraint on press freedom in the United States. (A libelous statement is one that unjustifiably exposes someone to ridicule or contempt.) These cases clearly indicate the media's legal vulnerability to charges of participating in and/or provoking irresponsible, damaging behavior. How can the country accommodate both the First Amendment concept of a free press and the right of the nation's citizens to keep their reputations from being unnecessarily damaged?

Sullivan Case Establishes a Libel Landmark

Modern interpretation of the free speech protections of the First Amendment began in 1964 with the landmark *New York Times v. Sullivan* case. With this case, the U.S. Supreme Court began a process that continues today to define how the press should operate in a free society. Many of today's arguments about the free press' role in a libel case derive from this decision.

The *Sullivan* case began in early 1960 in Alabama, where civil rights leader Dr. Martin Luther King, Jr., was arrested for perjury on his income tax form (a charge of which he was eventually acquitted). The Committee to Defend Martin Luther King bought a full-page ad in the March 29, 1960, *New York Times* that included statements about harassment of King by public officials and the police. The ad included a plea for money to support civil rights causes. Several notable people were listed in the ad as supporters, including singer

Libel A false statement that damages a person's character or reputation by exposing that person to public ridicule or contempt.

Bettmann/CORBIS

In the U.S., legal interpretation of free speech protections of the First Amendment began with the landmark *New York Times v. Sullivan* case. L. B. Sullivan (second from right) appears in November 1960 with his attorneys. Although Sullivan's libel suit was successful in Alabama, the Supreme Court decided in 1964 that he had failed to prove malice on the part of *The New York Times*.

Harry Belafonte, actor Sidney Poitier and former First Lady Eleanor Roosevelt.

L. B. Sullivan, who supervised the police and fire departments as commissioner of public affairs in Montgomery, Ala., demanded a retraction from *The Times* regarding the statements about King's harassment, even though he had not been named in the ad. *The Times* refused, and Sullivan sued *The Times* for libel in Montgomery County, where 35 copies of the March 29, 1960, *Times* had been distributed for sale. The trial in Montgomery County lasted three days, beginning on November 1, 1960. The jury found *The Times* guilty and awarded Sullivan $500,000.

Eventually, the case reached the U.S. Supreme Court. In deciding the suit, the Court said that although *The Times* might have been negligent because it did not spot some misstatements of fact that appeared in the ad, *The Times* did not deliberately lie—it did not act with what the court called *actual malice*.

To prove libel of a public official, the official must show that the defendant published information with *knowledge of its falsity* or out of *reckless disregard* for whether it was true or false, the court concluded. The *Sullivan* decision thus became the standard for subsequent libel suits: Public officials in a libel case must prove actual malice.

Redefining the *Sullivan* Decision

Three important cases further defined the *Sullivan* decision.

GERTZ V. ROBERT WELCH, INC. The 1974 decision in *Gertz v. Robert Welch Inc.* established the concept that the expression of opinions is a necessary part of public debate, and so an opinion—an editorial or a restaurant review, for example—cannot be considered libelous. The *Gertz* case also expanded the definition of *public official* to *public figure*. Today, the difference between public figures and private figures is very important in libel suits.

People who are defined as private citizens by a court must show only that the libelous information is false and that the journalist or news organization acted negligently in presenting the information. Public figures must show not only that the libelous information is false but also that the information was published with actual malice—that the journalist or the news organization knew that the information was untrue or deliberately overlooked facts that would have proved the published information was untrue.

HERBERT V. LANDO. The 1979 decision in *Herbert v. Lando* established the concept that because a public figure suing for libel must prove actual malice, the public figure can use the *discovery process* (the process by which potential witnesses are questioned under oath before the trial to help define the issues to be resolved at the trial) to determine a reporter's state of mind in preparing the story. Because of this decision, today reporters are sometimes asked in a libel suit to identify their sources and to give up their notes and the tapes of the interviews they conducted to write their stories.

MASSON V. NEW YORKER MAGAZINE. In 1991, the U.S. Supreme Court reinstated a $10 million libel suit brought against *The New Yorker* magazine by psychoanalyst Jeffrey M. Masson. Masson charged that author Janet Malcolm libeled him in two articles in *The New Yorker* and in a book when she deliberately misquoted him. Malcolm contended that the quotations she used were tape-recorded or were written in her notes.

Malcolm wrote, for example, that Mr. Masson said, "I was like an intellectual gigolo." However, this exact phrase was not in the transcript of her tape-recorded interview. Masson contended that he never used the phrase. Issues in the case include whether quoted material must be verbatim and whether a journalist can change grammar and syntax. When the case was heard again in 1994, the court found that Malcolm had changed Masson's words but that the changes did not libel Masson. The *Masson* case is an important example of the court's attempts to define the limits of libel.

Charges and Defenses for Libel

To prove libel under today's law, someone must show that

- The statement was communicated to a third party.
- People who read or saw the statement would be able to identify the person, even if that person was not actually named.
- The statement injured the person's reputation or income or caused mental anguish.
- The journalist or the print or broadcast organization is at fault.

Members of the press and press organizations that are faced with a libel suit can use three defenses: (1) truth, (2) privilege and (3) fair comment.

TRUTH. The first and best defense against libel, of course, is that the information is true. True information, although sometimes damaging, cannot be considered libelous. Publishing true information, however, can still be an invasion of privacy, as explained later in this chapter. Furthermore, truth is a successful defense only if truth is proved to the satisfaction of a judge or jury.

PRIVILEGE. The press is free to report what is discussed during legislative and court proceedings, even though the information presented in the proceedings by witnesses and others may be untrue or damaging. This is called ***qualified privilege***.

FAIR COMMENT. The courts also have carefully protected the press' freedom to present opinions. Because opinions cannot be proved true or false, the press is free to comment on public issues and to laud a play or pan a movie, for example.

Legal Outcomes Reflect Mixed Results

The outcomes of the four cases listed at the beginning of this discussion of libel law (on page 311) were the following:

1. The jury in the Carol Burnett case originally awarded her $1.6 million, but the amount was reduced to $150,000 on appeal.
2. The William Westmoreland case was settled before it went to the jury. CBS issued a statement acknowledging that General Westmoreland had acted faithfully in performing his duties, but the combined legal costs for both parties were more than $18 million.
3. The jury awarded Wayne Newton $19.2 million in 1986. NBC appealed the case, and in 1990 the courts overturned the award, ruling there was not enough evidence to prove actual malice, but NBC's legal costs were in the millions of dollars.
4. The Jeff Greene case is still pending. In responding to the charges, the editor of the *St. Petersburg Times* said, "It is our firm opinion that the allegations in this lawsuit are preposterous. We believe Jeff Greene is a sore loser and he's trying to blame the newspapers because he can't accept the verdict of the voters." The Greene case could be considered an example of a ***SLAPP*** suit—*s*trategic *l*awsuit *a*gainst *p*ublic *p*articipation. (See "Internet Comments Bring SLAPP Suits," below.)

In the three cases that have been resolved, the courts faulted members of the media for their reporting methods, even when members of the media and the media companies were not found legally responsible. All four cases show that journalists and media organizations must always be diligent about their responsibilities, and there are serious financial and professional consequences for news organizations that forget to act responsibly and heed the law.

Most successful libel judgments eventually are reversed or reduced when they are appealed. Often the major cost of a libel suit for the media is not the actual award but the defense lawyers' fees. Large media organizations carry libel insurance, but a small newspaper, magazine, book publisher, broadcast station or Internet site may not be able to afford the insurance or the legal costs.

"While most excessive trial awards are reduced in post-trial rulings or on appeal, the expense of litigating can be daunting. The danger is that excessive damage awards, and the cost of litigating and appealing them, may give editors and publishers pause when covering controversial people and topics," says Sandra S. Baron, executive director of the Libel Defense Resource Center.

Internet Comments Bring SLAPP Suits

Bloggers and other Internet users who post critical comments on a Web site like Facebook, Twitter and Yelp today may find themselves the target of what lawyers call a SLAPP. This is a common tactic of businesses and

Qualified Privilege The freedom of the press to report what is discussed during legislative and court proceedings.

SLAPP Strategic lawsuit against public participation.

MIKE SEGAR/Reuters/Corbis

In 1973, 10 years after her husband President John F. Kennedy was assassinated, a federal court established Jacqueline Kennedy Onassis' right to privacy in *Galella v. Onassis.* Photographer Ron Galella, pictured in New York City in 2008 with one of the images he took of Onassis, was placed under a restraining order to stay 25 feet away from Onassis and 30 feet away from her children.

government officials because suing someone for defamation can intimidate the person with the prospect of an expensive court battle against a well-financed opponent.

Today, the Internet makes a person's critical comments available instantly, and some companies and public officials are threatening libel suits against their critics. There are 27 states with anti-SLAPP laws, which may require that the person who brings the suit pay the combined legal costs if the suit is dismissed. Federal anti-SLAPP legislation, which would make protections uniform across the country, is being debated in Congress. "Just as petition and free speech rights are so important that they require specific constitutional protections, they are also important enough to justify uniform national protections against SLAPPs," said Mark Goldowitz, director of the California Anti-SLAPP Project.

Invasion of Privacy Defined Four Ways

The public seems to think invasion of privacy is one of the media's worst faults. However, libel suits are much more common in the United States than suits about invasion of privacy. Because there is no U.S. Supreme Court decision covering privacy like *The New York Times v. Sullivan* covers libel, each of the states has its own privacy protections for citizens and its own restrictions on how reporters can get the news and what can be published.

Privacy is an ethical issue as well as a legal one. (See **Chapter 15** for a discussion of the ethics of privacy.) Generally, the law says the media can be guilty of invasion of privacy in four ways:

1. By intruding on a person's physical or mental solitude.
2. By publishing or disclosing embarrassing personal facts.
3. By giving someone publicity that places the person in a false light.
4. By using someone's name or likeness for commercial benefit.

If they are successful, people who initiate privacy cases can be awarded monetary damages to compensate them for the wrongdoing. However, very few invasion of privacy cases succeed.

Physical or Mental Solitude

The courts in most states have recognized that a person has a right not to be pursued by the news media unnecessarily. A reporter can photograph or question someone on a public street or at a public event, but a person's home and office are private. For this reason, many photographers request that someone who is photographed in a private situation sign a release form, designating how the photograph can be used.

One notable case establishing this right of privacy is *Galella v. Onassis*. Jacqueline Onassis, widow of President John F. Kennedy, charged that Ron Galella, a freelance photographer, was pursuing her unnecessarily. He had used a telephoto lens to photograph her on private property, and he had pursued her children at private schools. In 1973, Galella was ordered to stay 25 feet away from Onassis and 30 feet away from her children.

Embarrassing Personal Facts

The personal facts the media use to report a story should be newsworthy, according to the courts. If a public official is caught traveling with her boyfriend on taxpayers' money while her husband stays at home, information about the boyfriend is essential to the story. If the public official is reported to have contracted AIDS from her boyfriend, the information probably is not relevant to the story and could be protected under this provision of privacy law.

In reality, however, public officials enjoy few legal protections from reporting about their private lives. Information available from public records, such as court proceedings, is not considered private. If the public official's husband testifies in court about his wife's disease, this information could be reported.

Bartnicki v. Vopper

In an important case for the press, *Bartnicki v. Vopper*, the U.S. Supreme Court in 2001 reaffirmed the media's right to broadcast information and to comment on that information, no matter how the information was obtained.

The case resulted from a cell phone conversation between Pennsylvania teachers' union negotiator Gloria Bartnicki and Anthony Kane, the union's president. The union was in the middle of negotiating a teachers' contract. During the conversation (which was intercepted and taped without Bartnicki's or Kane's knowledge), Kane is heard to say that if the school board didn't increase its offer, "We're going to have to go to their homes . . . to blow off their front porches."

A local activist gave the tape to radio station WILK-AM, and talk-show host Fred Vopper (who uses the on-air name Fred Williams) aired the tape. Bartnicki and Kane sued Vopper under the federal wiretap law, which provides civil damages and criminal prosecution for someone who disseminates information that is illegally intercepted. The case pitted the public's right to know versus the erosion of personal privacy by new technologies.

U.S. Supreme Court Justice John Paul Stevens wrote the opinion for the 6–3 majority that "a stranger's illegal conduct does not suffice to remove the First Amendment shield from speech about a matter of public concern." In this decision, the court again reaffirmed the press' right to report information in the public interest.

False Light

A writer who portrays someone in a fictional version of actual events should be especially conscious of ***false light*** litigation. People who believe that what a writer or photographer *implies* about them is incorrect (even if the portrayal is flattering) can bring a false-light suit.

The best-known false-light suit is the first, *Time Inc. v. Hill*. In 1955, *Life* magazine published a story about a Broadway play, *The Desperate Hours*, which portrayed someone taking a hostage. The author of the play said he based it on several real-life incidents. One of these involved the Hill family, a husband and wife and their five children who had been taken hostage in their Philadelphia home by three escaped convicts. The Hills told police the convicts had treated them courteously, but the Hills were frightened by the events and eventually moved to Connecticut.

When *Life* decided to do the story about the play, the cast went to the Hills' old home, where *Life* photographed the actors in scenes from the play—one son being roughed up by the convicts and a daughter biting a convict's hand. None of these incidents had happened to the Hills, but *Life* published the photographs along with a review of the play.

The Hills sued Time Inc., which owned *Life* magazine, for false-light invasion of privacy and won $75,000, which eventually was reduced to $30,000. When the case went to the U.S. Supreme Court, the Court refused to uphold the decision, saying the Hills must prove *actual malice*. The Hills dropped the case, but the establishment of actual malice as a requirement in false-light cases was important.

In 1974, in *Cantrell v. Forest City Publishing Co.*, the U.S. Supreme Court held that a reporter for the Cleveland *Plain Dealer* had wrongly portrayed the widow of an Ohio man who was killed when a bridge collapsed. The story talked about the woman as if the reporter had interviewed her, although he had only interviewed her children. She was awarded $60,000 in her false-light suit, and the Supreme Court upheld the verdict.

"Eight justices held that a properly instructed jury had come to the correct conclusion in finding actual malice," writes legal scholar Ralph L. Holsinger. "There was enough evidence within the story to prove that the reporter's word portrait of Mrs. Cantrell was false. The story indicated that he had seen her and perhaps had talked with her. He had done neither." Only a few false-light cases have been successful, but the lesson for the press is that portraying events and people truthfully avoids the problem altogether.

Right of Publicity

This facet of privacy law is especially important in the advertising and public relations industries. A portable toilet seems a strange fixture to use to establish a point of law, but a case brought by former *Tonight Show* host Johnny Carson demonstrates how the right of publicity protects someone's name from being used to make money without that person's permission.

In *Carson v. Here's Johnny Portable Toilets*, Carson charged, in 1983, that a Michigan manufacturer of portable toilets misappropriated Carson's name to sell the toilets. The manufacturer named his new line Here's Johnny Portable Toilets and advertised them with the phrase "The World's Foremost Commodian." Carson said he did not want to be associated with the product although he would be. Since he began hosting *The Tonight Show* in 1957, he said, he had been

False Light The charge that what was implied in a story about someone is incorrect.

introduced by the phrase "Here's Johnny." The court agreed that "Here's Johnny" violated Carson's right of publicity.

The right of publicity can apply to a person's picture on a poster or name in an advertisement. In some cases, this right is covered even after the person dies, so that the members of the immediate family of a well-known entertainer, for example, are the only people who can authorize the use of the entertainer's name or likeness.

Debate Continues over Fair Trial, Courtroom Access and Shield Laws

The answers to three other questions that bear on press freedoms and individual rights remain discretionary for the courts:

1. When does media coverage influence a jury so much that a defendant's right to a fair trial is jeopardized?
2. How much access should the media be granted during a trial?
3. Should journalists be required to reveal information they obtained in confidence while reporting a story if a court decides that information is necessary to the judicial process?

Stefan Zaklin/epa/Corbis

In 2005, *New York Times* reporter Judith Miller spent 85 days in jail because she refused to reveal a confidential source to a Washington, D.C., grand jury. Eventually she revealed the source as I. Lewis Libby (in center of photo, leaving a federal court hearing in 2007), Vice President Dick Cheney's chief of staff. Libby was found guilty of perjury and obstruction of justice, but in July 2007 President Bush commuted Libby's sentence.

Fair Trial

The best-known decision affecting prejudicial press coverage of criminal cases is *Sheppard v. Maxwell*. In 1954, Dr. Samuel Sheppard of Cleveland was sentenced to life imprisonment for murdering his wife. His conviction followed reams of newspaper stories, many of which proclaimed his guilt before the jury had decided the case. The jurors, who went home each evening, were told by the judge not to read newspapers or pay attention to broadcast reports, but no one monitored what the jurors did.

Twelve years later, lawyer F. Lee Bailey took Sheppard's trial to the U.S. Supreme Court, where the conviction was overturned on the premise that Sheppard had been a victim of a biased jury. In writing the decision, Justice Tom C. Clark prescribed several remedies. He said that the reporters should have been limited to certain areas in the courtroom, that the news media should not have been allowed to interview the witnesses and that the court should have forbidden statements outside of the courtroom.

Courtroom Access

The outcome of the *Sheppard* case led to many courtroom experiments with restrictions on the press. The most widespread practices were restraining (gag) orders and closed proceedings. With a gag order, the judge limited what the press could report. Closed proceedings excluded the press from the courtroom. But since 1980, several court cases have overturned most of these limitations. Today the press is rarely excluded from courtroom proceedings, and the exclusion lasts only as long as it takes the news organization to appeal to a higher court for access.

The presence of cameras in the courtroom is a sticky issue between judges, who want to avoid the disruption of cameras, and broadcast news people, who want to photograph what is going on. In selected cases, however, cameras have been allowed to record complete trials. In 1994, for example, Court TV broadcast the entire murder trial of O. J. Simpson. Allowing cameras in the courtroom is a state-by-state decision. (See **Illustration 14.1**.) Some states allow cameras during civil but not criminal trials. Other states try to completely limit access. The U.S. courts and the press are not yet completely comfortable partners.

Shield Laws

Traditionally, U.S. courts have been reluctant to ask journalists to reveal information they gather from confidential

Media/Impact AUDIENCE

Illustration 14.1

Cameras in the Courtroom: A State-by-State Guide

Most states allow at least some camera access to courtroom proceedings.

Radio-Television Digital News Association, http://www.rtnda.org/pages/media_items/cameras-in-the-court-a-state-by-state-guide55.php.

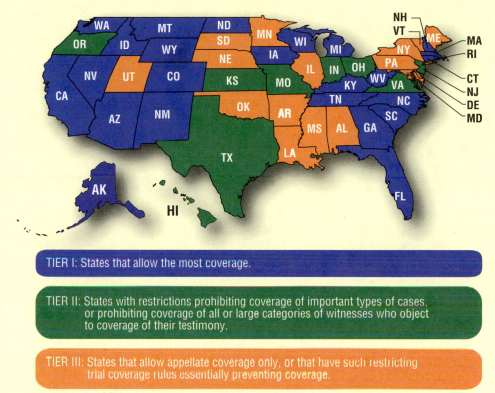

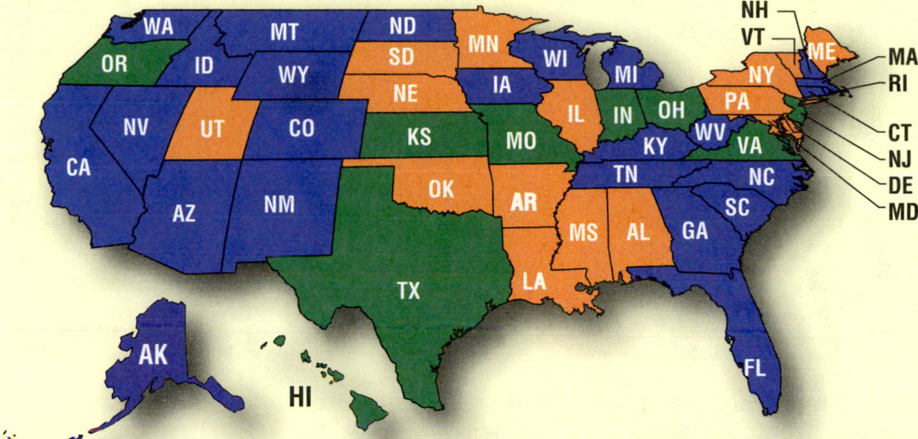

MT

FL
TIER I: States that allow the most coverage.
TIER II: States with restrictions prohibiting coverage of important types of cases, or prohibiting coverage of all or large categories of witnesses who object to coverage of their testimony.
TIER III: States that allow appellate coverage only, or that have such restricting trial coverage rules essentially preventing coverage.
The District of Columbia is the only jurisdiction that prohibits trial and appellate coverage entirely.

sources as part of their reporting on stories. In 1972, in *Branzburg v. Hayes*, the U.S. Supreme Court ruled for the first time that journalists do not have a constitutional privilege to refuse to testify but that there was "merit in leaving state legislatures free, within First Amendment limits, to fashion their own standards."

According to the Congressional Research Service, "31 states and the District of Columbia have recognized a journalist's privilege through enactment of press '***shield laws***,' which protect the relationship between reporters, their source, and sometimes, the information that may be communicated in that relationship." This means, for example, that reporters in California, Alaska and Colorado have state shield law protection, but reporters in Texas, South Dakota and Connecticut do not. There is no federal shield law that protects all U.S. journalists equally.

The role of shield laws in protecting journalists became particularly important in 2004–2005, when *New York Times* reporter Judith Miller refused to testify before a federal grand jury that was investigating whether Bush administration officials leaked the identity of a Central Intelligence Agency operative, Valerie Plame. In the summer of 2004, Miller was called before a Washington, D.C., grand jury that was investigating the leak of Plame's name; in the fall of 2004, she was held in contempt and served 85 days in jail the summer of 2005. In October 2005, Miller revealed to the grand jury that her source was I. Lewis Libby, Vice President Dick Cheney's chief of staff.

Even though Miller said she had received Libby's permission to reveal his name, which released her from her confidentiality agreement, some lawyers and journalists expressed concern that Miller's actions had weakened journalists' lengthy legal history of protecting their sources.

MN

VT

NY

KS

WV

MD

KY

OK

AZ
NM

TX

Shield Laws Laws that protect journalists from revealing their sources and the information that is communicated between journalists and their sources in a journalistic relationship.

Mario Tama/Getty Images

After several court challenges to reporters' ability to keep their sources confidential, journalists lobbied for a national shield law in front of *The New York Times* building in 2005. Although many states have shield laws to protect journalists' sources, there is no federal shield law.

Eventually Libby, who had testified to a grand jury about the case, was found guilty of perjury and obstruction of justice, but President Bush commuted his sentence in 2007.

After the Miller case, some members of Congress introduced legislation to create a federal shield law to protect journalists on a national level, but Congress never seriously considered the issue. This leaves journalists still at the mercy of individual state shield laws. (Valerie Plame's experiences formed the basis for the 2010 movie *Fair Game*, starring Naomi Watts and Sean Penn.)

FCC Regulates Broadcast and Cable

All the American media are expected to abide by the country's laws. Regulation of the media comes from government agencies that oversee aspects of the media business. The print industry is not regulated specifically by any government agency. The largest single area of regulation comes from the Federal Communications Commission (FCC), which oversees broadcasting. Other regulating agencies, such as the Federal Trade Commission, scrutinize specific areas that relate to the media, such as advertising.

Since 1927, the rationale for broadcast regulation has been that the airwaves belong to the public and that broadcasters are trustees operating in the public interest. The history of U.S. broadcast regulation can be traced to government's early attempt to organize the airwaves. The FCC, based in Washington, D.C., now has five commissioners who are appointed by the president and are approved by the Senate. Each commissioner serves a five-year term, and the president appoints the chairperson.

Today FCC regulation touches almost every aspect of station operations. Most important, U.S. broadcast stations must be licensed by the FCC to operate. Because the print media are unregulated by any government agency, the government exercises more direct control over the broadcast media than over the print media. Like the print media, broadcasters must also follow court rulings on issues such as libel, obscenity and the right of privacy.

Telecommunications Act of 1996 Changes the Marketplace

On February 8, 1996, President Clinton signed the Telecommunications Act of 1996, the most far-reaching reform in U.S. government regulation of mass media since the creation of the FCC. The act affects all aspects of the media industries, especially broadcast, cable, telephone and computer networks. The act is transforming the nation's media industries.

The last time the government intervened in a similar way to affect the development of the media business was in 1934, when Congress created the FCC to regulate broadcasting in the "public interest, convenience and necessity." The Telecommunications Act, however, is an extension of the philosophy of deregulation—that free competition, with less government regulation, eventually will improve consumers' choices, lower costs and encourage investment in new technologies. Critics, however, say the act helps large media companies get bigger because only the large companies can afford to upgrade their equipment and delivery systems to take advantage of new markets.

This philosophy of open competition, as established in the Telecommunications Act of 1996, governs the media industries in the 21st century. The strategies of providing multiple services and targeting select users are two examples of the effects of the act today.

Angela Weiss/Getty Images

The Telecommunications Act of 1996 affects telecommunications, broadcast and cable. It eliminated many of the restrictions on the services a cable company like Comcast can offer and how much it charges for those services. On May 11, 2010, Comcast Chairman and CEO Brian Roberts appears in Los Angeles at a cable industry luncheon.

Goal: To Sell Consumers "The Bundle"

"It's War!" declared *The Wall Street Journal* on September 16, 1996. The battlefield was telecommunications, and the goal was ***The Bundle***. In telecommunications this term describes the combination of services the media industries can now offer. Following passage of the 1996 Telecommunications Act, large companies began positioning themselves to deliver the combination of telecommunications services that they think consumers want. The *Journal* reported:

> Thanks to a combination of deregulation and new technologies, war has broken out in the communications market. Everybody has joined the fray—long-distance telephone giants, the regional [local telephone] Bell companies and the cable-TV operators, the satellite outfits, the fledgling digital wireless phone firms and the Internet service providers. Even your old-fashioned power company.
>
> And they all want the same thing: to invade one another's markets and sell you one another's products and services. In short, they want to sell you The Bundle.

Your long-distance telephone company, such as AT&T or Sprint, would like to become your local telephone company, as well as your Internet service provider. This same long-distance company also wants to provide your TV programs, replacing the local cable system, adding these charges to your monthly telephone bill. Local telephone companies, the Regional Bell Operating Companies (***RBOC***), want their slice of revenue, too.

"The act so completely dismantles the existing regulatory structure that the telecommunications industry begins to look like a free-for-all," says Howard Anderson, founder and manager of Yankee Group, a Boston-based consulting firm. "Everyone is already trying to build multimedia networks to deliver everything from telephone and mobile services to Internet access and video-on-demand."

Targeting the "Power User"

This bundling of services means that you can pay one monthly bill for several types of media services to a single company, which, of course, dramatically increases that company's portion of media revenue. "The goal for these companies is twofold," says Richard Siber, a wireless analyst for Andersen Consulting in Boston. "One is locking in a customer for life and providing one-stop shopping. And the other is revenue maximization, getting you to use their products more and more."

BusinessWeek magazine called this intense competition for customers a "telescramble." The primary target is the so-called "power user," someone who uses a lot of media at home or in business. While the average consumer spends about $100 a month on media services, an upscale customer averages $300 a month, or $3,000 to $3,500 a year.

The Telecommunications Act of 1996 created this battlefield for consumers' attention with huge financial incentives for the winners. The economic future of every media company in the country is, in some way, being affected by this battle. That is why it is so important to understand this single piece of legislation.

The Bundle The combination of telecommunications services that the media industries can offer consumers.

RBOC Regional Bell Operating Companies.

Deregulation Unleashes the Media

The major provisions of the Telecommunications Act affect telecommunications, broadcast and cable. The Communications Decency Act, which is part of the Telecommunications Act, attempts to regulate access to cable and television programming and monitor the content of computer networks, including the Internet.

Creates a Goal of Universal Service

The Telecommunications Act of 1996 established, for the first time in federal legislation, a goal of universal service—meaning that, as a matter of public policy, everyone in the United States should have access to affordable telecommunications services. The intent of the act is to make telecommunications available to everyone.

The FCC, of course, defines which type of access is offered in the "universal service" package. Does "universal service" mean only a telephone, or should "universal service" include access to the Internet? The FCC decides what exactly constitutes "universal service" and whether access to the Internet will be part of that service guarantee, in an effort to use telecommunications to improve the economies of rural areas and central cities, as well as the rest of the nation.

Deregulates Free Media

The Telecommunications Act of 1996 continued a policy of deregulation of commercial radio and television ownership that began in the 1980s. Radio and over-the-air broadcast television are viewed as "free media." Unlike cable stations and satellite companies, which require extra equipment and charge consumers for their services, over-the-air broadcasting is available to anyone with a radio or television—and 99 percent of U.S. households have a TV set. Over-the-air broadcasting offers the largest potential audience for free media.

Relaxes Ownership and Licensing Rules

Previously, broadcast companies were allowed to own only 12 television stations. The act eliminated limits on the number of television stations one company could own and instead used a station's potential audience to measure ownership limits. The act said existing television networks (such as NBC and ABC) can begin new networks, but they cannot buy an existing network. NBC cannot buy ABC, for example, but NBC could begin a second network of its own, such as NBC2.

Before the act passed, radio broadcasters were allowed to own 20 AM or 20 FM radio stations nationwide. The act removed the limit on the number of radio stations a company can own, and in each market, the number of stations that one owner can hold depends on the size of the market. In a large market with 45 or more commercial radio stations, for example, a broadcaster may own eight stations; in a market with 14 stations, a broadcaster may own up to five stations.

The act also allows ***cross-ownership***. This means that companies can own television and radio stations in the same broadcast market. Companies also can own broadcast and cable outlets in the same market.

In 1999, the FCC further relaxed TV station ownership rules by allowing one broadcast company to own two TV stations in the same market, as long as eight other stations with different owners are still operating in the market after the deal. In 2002, the FCC began considering further relaxation of the ownership rules that, for example, would allow broadcasters to own newspapers. In 2010, a federal court lifted the ban on media cross-ownership altogether. The FCC is expected to revisit the cross-ownership rules in 2011.

In 2003, the FCC removed even more restrictions on broadcast ownership, making it easier for media companies to expand the number of stations they own, and included the provision that allows one company to own TV stations that reach 35 percent of the U.S. population. Today, the 35 percent limit still applies, although the industry continues to lobby to reduce the limitation or remove it completely.

The FCC licenses every broadcast station in the country—television and radio. In the past, renewal was a very complicated, rigorous process. Television stations were required to renew their licenses every five years and radio stations every seven. The Telecommunications Act extended the renewal period for both radio and television to every eight years.

Cross-Ownership The practice of one company owning TV and radio stations in the same broadcast market.

Creates Local Phone Competition

Due to deregulation, cable, satellite and telephone companies today are competing to deliver telecommunications services to home customers.

To encourage competition for delivery of video services, the Telecommunications Act of 1996 allowed local telephone companies to get into the video delivery business. The act repealed the FCC's "telco-cable cross-ownership" restrictions (***telco*** is an abbreviation for "telephone company"). Local telephone companies can deliver video services either by an agreement with a cable operator or by creating their own delivery system. In turn, the cable companies were allowed to enter the local telephone business. Large cable companies also may deliver new types of telephone services, such as carrying messages to and from wireless cell phones.

To add to competition in the local telephone business, the act also allowed long-distance carriers to offer local telephone service. Within two months of the act's passage, the long-distance carrier AT&T filed to be allowed to offer local telephone service in all 50 states. "If we get this right," said former FCC Chairman Reed Hundt, "you'll be buying communications services like shoes. Different styles, different vendors."

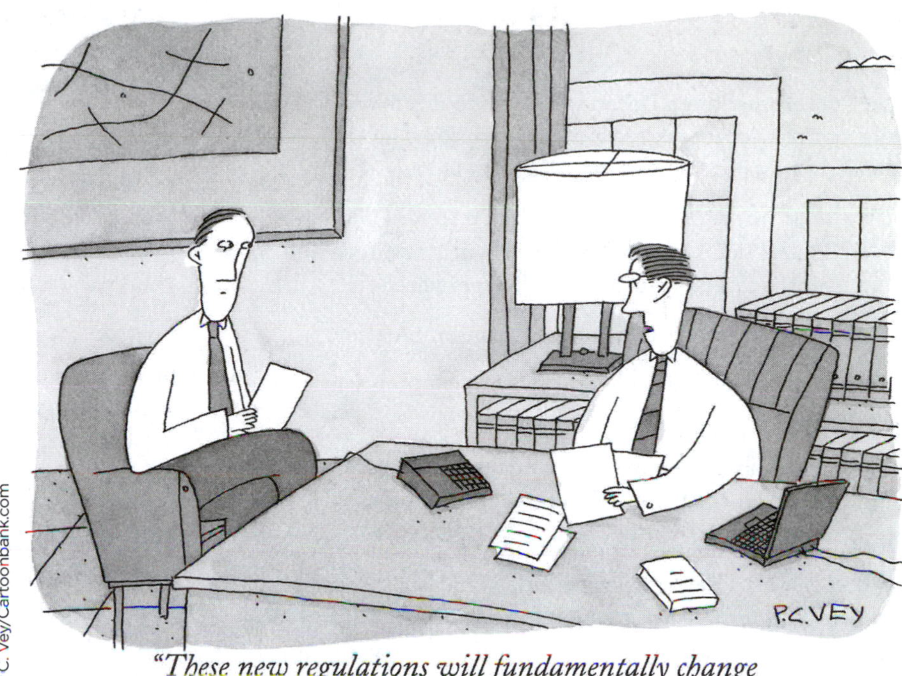

Peter C. Vey/Cartoonbank.com

"These new regulations will fundamentally change the way we get around them."

Until the market for telecommunications stabilizes, however, the choices are confusing for consumers and frustrating for people in the media industries who are trying to position themselves for a new future that isn't yet completely defined.

Ends Cable Rate Regulation

In an attempt to control spiraling cable charges to consumers, Congress passed the 1992 Cable Act to regulate rates. The cable companies, facing competition from the local telephone companies, argued that Congress should remove rate regulation to allow them to compete and to help raise cable income.

The Telecommunications Act of 1996 removed most rate regulation for all cable companies. All that remains is regulation to monitor the "basic tier" of cable service, often called "basic cable."

Congress Attempts to Use Communications Decency Act

Along with the major provisions of the Telecommunications Act to increase competition, Congress added several provisions to control content. These provisions, together called the Communications Decency Act (CDA), attempted to define and control users' access to specific types of programs and content. However, most provisions of the act subsequently were overruled by the Supreme Court as violations of the First Amendment.

Adds Program Blocking

One provision of the Telecommunications Act required cable owners to take steps within 30 days after the bill was signed to ensure that cable shows "primarily dedicated to sexually oriented programming or other programming that is indecent" did not accidentally become available to people who did not subscribe to the programs. This meant that every cable operator would have to provide a free "lock box" to every cable subscriber's home to block programs, whether or not the customer requested it.

On March 9, 1996, the day the program-blocking provision of the act was scheduled to go into effect, Playboy Enterprises successfully won a temporary restraining order, which prevented the application of the law. "Attorneys for Chicago-based Playboy argued that the provision violated constitutional protections of free speech and equal protection. Justice Department attorneys argued that the government has the right and duty to regulate the distribution of indecent material if it can be viewed or heard by children," reported *Bloomberg Business News*.

Telco An abbreviation for "telephone company."

Addresses Indecent Material on the Internet

The Communications Decency Act made it a felony to send indecent material over computer networks. The CDA also prohibited using a telecommunications device to

- Make or initiate any communication that is obscene, lewd, lascivious, filthy or indecent with intent to annoy, abuse, threaten or harass another person.
- Make or make available obscene communication.
- Make or make available an indecent communication to minors.
- Transmit obscene material—including material concerning abortion—for any indecent or immoral use.

The act relied on a very broad definition of the word *indecent*, and courts have generally ruled that such speech is protected under the First Amendment. Under the act's provisions, violators could be charged with a felony and fined up to $250,000. More than 50 opponents of the act's indecency provision, including the American Library Association and the American Civil Liberties Union, went to court in Philadelphia to challenge the law.

On June 12, 1996, the three-judge panel unanimously declared that the Internet indecency provision was unconstitutional, and the judges blocked enforcement of the law. They issued a restraining order, which meant that the Internet indecency provision could not be enforced and violations could not even be investigated.

The federal government had argued the Internet should be regulated like radio and television, but the judges said material on the Internet deserves the same protection as printed material. In presenting the court's opinion, Judge Stewart R. Dalzell made very strong arguments defending access to the Internet. "Just as the strength of the Internet is chaos," Judge Dalzell wrote, "so the strength of our liberty depends upon the chaos and cacophony of the unfettered speech the First Amendment protects."

In 1997, the U.S. Supreme Court struck down the indecency provision of the Communications Decency Act, making it much harder for Congress to limit Internet access in the future. What is interesting is that the courts are defining and protecting an electronic delivery system—the Internet—as if it were a print medium.

COPA Child Online Protection Act. A law aimed at preventing minors from getting access to sexually explicit online material.

This effort is important because Congress and the president, through the FCC, historically have regulated the broadcast industries, but none of the regulations that apply to the broadcast media also apply to print. The content of the print media, by law and by practice, has historically remained unregulated because of the First Amendment's protection of free expression.

Child Online Protection Act Fails

In 1998, after the U.S. Supreme Court found the indecency provision of the Communications Decency Act unconstitutional, Congress passed the Child Online Protection Act (***COPA***), aimed at preventing minors from getting access to sexually explicit online material, even though the material is legal for adults. Congress based the legislation on the idea that the government has a responsibility to protect children from content that is legal for adults but could be considered harmful to minors.

Congress wanted to fine offenders $150,000 for each day they violated the law and face up to six months in prison. Among the law's provisions was the requirement that libraries and schools that receive federal funding must install filtering software on public computers. Several organizations, including the American Library Association and the American Civil Liberties Union (ACLU), immediately challenged the law in court on First Amendment grounds, saying the law was too restrictive. In 2002, the U.S. Supreme Court agreed that Congress had no authority to limit Internet access.

Supreme Court Upholds Internet Filters for Public Libraries

One year later, however, the Supreme Court upheld another law that said that libraries that take federal funds must equip their computers with anti-pornography filters. The case was defended in court on behalf of 13-year-old Emalyn Rood, who logged onto the Internet in an Oregon library to research information on lesbianism, and Mark Brown, who found information about his mother's breast cancer on a Philadelphia library computer—information that might have been blocked by a commonly used Internet filter.

In a close 5–4 decision in *United States v. American Library Association*, the U.S. Supreme Court said the requirement for Internet filters is "a valid exercise of Congress' spending power." This decision allows the U.S. government to require Internet filters at libraries that receive federal funding. Librarians argued that Internet filters are a form of censorship that blocks valuable information from people who need it.

TV Industry Agrees to Ratings and the V-Chip

Under pressure from Congress, television executives agreed to implement a voluntary ratings system for television programs by January 1997. The new ratings system *applies to all programming except sports, news magazines and news shows.*

The ratings divide programming into six categories, ranging from TVY (appropriate for all children but specifically designed for a very young audience, including children ages two to six) to TVMA (specifically designed to be viewed by adults and therefore possibly unsuitable for children younger than 17).

Unlike movies (which are rated by an independent board), TV shows are rated by producers, networks, cable channels, syndicators and other people who originate the programs. These ratings evaluate violence and sexual content, and the results are displayed on the screen at the beginning of each program and coded into each TV program. The codes are read by a v-chip, a microchip device required to be included with all new television sets. The v-chip allows parents to program the TV set to eliminate shows the parents find objectionable, although follow-up studies have shown that few parents use this option.

Six months after this rating system was adopted, the TV networks added a more specific rating for violent or sexual content. Today, the broadcast networks and program services post content ratings on most of their progams.

David Sipress/Cartoonbank.com

"Welcome to 'All About the Media,' where members of the media discuss the role of the media in media coverage of the media."

Government Monitors Broadcast Indecency

In early 2004, responding to congressional pressure for more government control over the airwaves, the Federal Communications Commission proposed a $775,000 fine against Clear Channel Communications for a Florida radio broadcast of various episodes of "Bubba the Love Sponge." The FCC fined Clear Channel the maximum amount then allowed—$27,500 for each time the episode ran (a total of $715,000) plus $40,000 for record-keeping violations at the station. Clear Channel said the programs were meant to entertain, not to offend its listeners.

FCC Chairman Michael Powell also urged Congress to increase the maximum fine for indecency to $275,000 per incident, saying the maximum fine of $27,500 per episode wasn't large enough to discourage objectionable programming.

Just a few days later, singers Janet Jackson and Justin Timberlake, performing on CBS-TV during halftime at the Super Bowl, caused another controversy when Timberlake reached over to Jackson and ripped off part of her costume, exposing her breast to an estimated 90 million Americans and a much bigger worldwide audience.

Jackson and Timberlake apologized for the incident, but FCC Chairman Powell launched an investigation. FCC rules say that radio and over-the-air TV stations may not air obscene material at any time. The rules also bar stations from broadcasting indecent material—references to sex or excretions—between 6 a.m. and 10 p.m., when the FCC says children are more likely to be listening or watching. Cable and satellite programming is not covered by the restrictions. The FCC fined CBS $550,000 for the Janet Jackson incident.

CBS appealed the Jackson fine in 2007 before the 3rd U.S. Circuit Court of Appeals in Philadelphia, saying the network had taken precautions beforehand to avoid any incidents, including a five-second audio delay. In 2008 a federal appeals court overturned the decision, saying, "The FCC cannot impose liability on CBS for the acts of Janet Jackson and Justin Timberlake, independent contractors hired for the limited purposes of the Halftime Show."

Michael Caulfield Archive/WireImage/Getty Images

In 2002, when the singer Cher appeared on the Billboard Music Awards, she made some impromptu comments that included a profanity. The FCC fined the Fox television network, which broadcast the awards, for indecency. In July 2010, a three-judge panel in New York, hearing the Billboard Music Awards case and several others dealing with the issue of fleeting expletives, struck down the indecency rule, saying it had a "chilling effect" that interfered with freedom of expression.

Then in a July 2010 ruling on a group of indecency cases, a federal appeals court in New York found that the FCC's indecency policy violated the First Amendment. The cases involved ***fleeting expletives***, profanity uttered without warning on live television. In the instances cited, celebrities including Cher and Bono made impromptu remarks during awards shows on live television, and the FCC fined the networks that aired the shows.

The court said that the FCC's policy against indecency had a chilling effect on free speech "because broadcasters have no way of knowing what the FCC will find offensive." A month later, the FCC appealed the decision, saying the ruling raised "serious concerns about the commission's ability to protect children and families from indecent broadcast programming." The appeal is still pending.

These controversies highlight the difficulties that arise when a federal government agency attempts to monitor free expression and no clear national standards of broadcast obscenity have been established. The definition of broadcast indecency often is based on politics and public pressure at the FCC, which shifts emphasis from one presidential administration to another.

The main issues are these: How much power should a government entity have to decide what's obscene or indecent and then to enforce those restrictions? And what effect, if any, will these decisions have on broadcast programming in a media environment with so many alternative, unregulated outlets available to consumers?

Fleeting Expletives Profanity uttered without warning on live television.

Intellectual Property Rights The legal right of ownership of ideas and content published in any medium.

DMCA Digital Millennium Copyright Act.

WIPO World Intellectual Property Organization.

Intellectual Property Rights Affirmed

The right of ownership for creative ideas in the United States is legally governed by what are called ***intellectual property rights***. Four recent developments—the Digital Millennium Copyright Act, the U.S. Supreme Court decision in *New York Times Co. v. Tasini* and decisions in *MGM v. Grokster* and *Arista Records v. Lime Group*—are beginning to define the issues of electronic copyright in the digital era. Additionally, independent progressive organizations have been working to give copyright holders greater flexibility in handling their intellectual property.

Digital Millennium Copyright Act

Passed in 1998, the Digital Millennium Copyright Act (***DMCA***) is comprehensive legislation that begins to address the copyright issues provoked by the Internet. The law makes several changes in U.S. copyright law to bring it into compliance with two World Intellectual Property Organization (***WIPO***) treaties about digitally transmitted copyrighted and stored material. The WIPO is responsible for promoting the protection of intellectual property throughout the world.

The DMCA is designed to prevent illegal copying of material that is published and distributed on the Internet. The

DMCA makes it illegal to circumvent technology that protects or controls access to copyrighted materials, such as the recordings shared on the Internet. The DMCA also makes it illegal to manufacture materials that will help people gain access to copyrighted materials. Congress allowed a two-year period before the act was implemented so that Congress could study its ramifications. The DMCA became effective on October 28, 2000.

Supporters of the DMCA—which includes most of the media industries that hold copyrights on creative works, such as movies, books and recordings—say the DMCA is an important law that must be enforced to protect intellectual property. Opponents say the law goes too far and limits technological development.

In March 2007, media conglomerate Viacom, whose media properties include MTV, Comedy Central and Nickelodeon, sued Google and YouTube, saying the companies deliberately gathered a library of copyrighted video clips without permission. Earlier in 2007, Viacom asked YouTube to remove 100,000 clips that it said infringed on Viacom copyrights.

Google said the "safe harbor" provisions of the DMCA covered the company. Generally these provisions say that Web site owners are not liable for copyrighted material that others upload to their site if the Web site owners promptly remove the material when the copyright owner asks them to do so.

According to *The New York Times*, Google argued that the DMCA "balances the rights of copyright holders and the need to protect the Internet as an important new form of communication. By seeking to make carriers and hosting providers liable for Internet communications, Viacom's complaint threatens the way hundreds of millions of people legitimately exchange information, news, entertainment, and political and artistic expression." However, Google announced four months later that it was developing video recognition technology that could detect and remove copyrighted material from its site before it was posted.

New York Times Co. v. Tasini

In 2001, a U.S. Supreme Court decision in *New York Times Co. v. Tasini* affirmed that freelance writers separately own the electronic rights to material they have written, even though a publisher has first published their writing in printed form. In 1993, freelance writer Jonathan Tasini, president of the National Writers Union, discovered that an article he had written for *The New York Times* was available on a database for Mead Data Center Corporation, which was paying royalties for the material to *The Times*. Tasini hadn't been paid for this use, so Tasini sued *The New York Times* and several other publishing companies (including Newsday Inc., the Atlantic Monthly Co. and Time Inc.).

The suit claimed the publishers had violated copyright law by using writers' work on electronic databases without their permission and that this limited the rights of freelance authors to have their articles published and receive compensation for their work. Several writers' organizations, including the Authors Guild, joined Tasini in the suit. *The Times* claimed the digital versions of written works were simply "revisions" of paper copies, which meant the rights belonged to the publisher so the writers deserved no further compensation.

On June 25, 2001, by a vote of 7–2, the U.S. Supreme Court agreed with Tasini. Writing the majority opinion, Justices Breyer and Stevens said that upholding the freelance authors' copyright would encourage the development of new technologies and the creation of new artistic work. The court said *The Times* must delete thousands of articles from its database for which it had not obtained the rights. "Once again, the legal system has come down in favor of the individual creator's rights in the digital age," Tasini told *Publishers Weekly*. "Everywhere you look, the law supports creators."

This case is very important—not only for freelancers but also for anyone who creates intellectual property. The court established the legal concept that the right to reproduce creative material electronically is very distinct from the right to reproduce creative material in print and that writers and other creative artists should be compensated separately for electronic and print rights to their work.

Metro-Goldwyn-Mayer Studios Inc. v. Grokster Ltd. and Arista Records LLC v. Lime Group LLC

In 2005, the U.S. Supreme Court ruled in a unanimous decision in the *Grokster* case that a software company can be held liable for copyright infringement if someone uses the company's software to illegally download songs and movies, known as illegal file sharing. The decision effectively shut down the Internet sites Grokster and StreamCast, also named in the suit. The companies provided free software that allowed users to download Internet content for free.

In 2010, a New York district court ordered that the major remaining file-sharing Web site, LimeWire, shut down in response to a suit by 14 recording companies, including Arista Records, Capitol Records and Virgin Records, who alleged that LimeWire was guilty of copyright infringement. (Lime Group LLC is the parent company of the Web site LimeWire.) The court required LimeWire to disable "searching, downloading, uploading, file trading and/or file distribution functionality." The same day, LimeWire removed its file-sharing function and closed the site.

The Grokster and LimeWire cases are two more examples of the strong legal tradition in the U.S. of guaranteeing intellectual copyright protection for creative content and the aggressiveness with which mass media companies pursue people who try to use intellectual property without permission or payment.

FCC Advocates Internet Regulation

In December 2010, FCC Chairman Julius Genachowski proposed a regulatory plan that would guarantee open access to the Internet and forbid Internet service providers from blocking any content that is considered lawful. This policy, called *Net neutrality* (also discussed in **Chapter 9**), requires Internet service providers to explain any restrictions they place on the content they carry. Under the proposed plan, companies also could charge more for premium services, such as streaming movies, but the FCC would require those companies to justify their rates.

The discussion about Net neutrality, and whether the FCC should even play a role in regulating the Internet, is based on whether Internet access services are classified as "information services" or "telecommunications services." The FCC has little power to regulate an information service company. But if Internet access is classified as a telecommunications service, the FCC could have a much larger role in its regulation, as it now does for traditional telephone companies. The FCC could, for example, monitor rates or investigate interruptions in service and restrictions on content. The new FCC open access rules took effect in November 2011.

Courts and Regulators Govern Advertising and PR

Advertising and public relations are governed by legal constraints and by regulation. *New York Times v. Sullivan* (see p. 311) was a crucial case for advertisers as well as for journalists. Since that decision, two other important court cases have defined the advertising and public relations businesses—the *Central Hudson* case for advertising (which is defined as "commercial speech" under the law) and the *Texas Gulf Sulphur* case for public relations.

Hudson Test A legal test that establishes a standard for commercial speech protection.

Central Hudson Case

In 1980, in *Central Hudson Gas & Electric Corp. v. Public Service Commission*, the U.S. Supreme Court issued the most definitive opinion yet on commercial speech. During the energy crisis atmosphere of the 1970s, the New York Public Utilities Commission had banned all advertising by public utilities that promoted the use of electricity. Central Hudson Gas & Electric wanted the ban lifted, so the company sued the commission.

The commission said the ban promoted energy conservation; the Supreme Court disagreed, and the decision in the case forms the basis for commercial speech protection today. "If the commercial speech does not mislead, and it concerns lawful activity," explains legal scholar Ralph Holsinger, "the government's power to regulate it is limited. . . . The state cannot impose regulations that only indirectly advance its interests. Nor can it regulate commercial speech that poses no danger to a state interest." The decision prescribed standards that commercial speech must meet to be protected by the First Amendment.

The main provisions of the standards are that (1) the advertisement must be for a lawful product and (2) the advertisement must not be misleading. This has become known as the ***Hudson test***. To be protected, then, an advertisement must promote a legal product and must not lie. This would seem to have settled the issue, but controversy continues.

Should alcohol advertising be banned? What about advertisements for condoms or birth control pills? Courts in different states have disagreed on these questions, and no Supreme Court decision on these specific issues exists, leaving many complex questions undecided. The Hudson test remains the primary criteria for determining what is protected commercial speech.

Texas Gulf Sulphur Case

The most important civil suit involving the issue of public relations occurred in the 1960s in *Securities and Exchange Commission v. Texas Gulf Sulphur Company*. Texas Gulf Sulphur (TGS) discovered ore deposits in Canada in late 1963 but did not announce the discovery publicly. TGS quietly purchased hundreds of acres surrounding the ore deposits, and TGS officers began to accumulate more shares of the company's stock. Meanwhile, the company issued a press release that said that the rumors about a discovery were "unreliable." When TGS announced that it had made a "major strike," which boosted the price of the company's stock, the Securities and Exchange Commission took the company to court.

The U.S. Court of Appeals, Tenth Circuit, ruled that TGS officers had violated the disclosure laws of the Securities and Exchange Commission. The court also ruled that TGS had issued "a false and misleading press release." Company officers and their friends were punished for withholding the information. According to *The Practice of Public Relations*, "the case proved conclusively that a company's failure to make known material information (information likely to be considered important by reasonable investors in determining whether to buy, sell or hold securities) may be in violation of the antifraud provision of the Securities and Exchange Acts."

The *Texas Gulf Sulphur* case remains a landmark in the history of public relations law. The decision in the case means public relations people can be held legally responsible for information that they do not disclose about their companies. This decision means that public relations people at publicly held corporations (businesses with stockholders) are responsible not only to their companies but also to the public.

Andrew Harrer/Bloomberg via Getty Images

The Federal Trade Commission, based in Washington, D.C., enforces federal policies that cover deceptive advertising. The FTC can fine an advertiser who doesn't comply with an FTC order.

Government Regulates Advertisers

The main regulatory agency for advertising and public relations issues is the Federal Trade Commission (FTC), although other agencies such as the Securities and Exchange Commission and the Food and Drug Administration sometimes intervene to question advertising practices.

In 1914, the Federal Trade Commission assumed the power to oversee deceptive interstate advertising practices under the Federal Trade Commission Act. Today, the FTC's policy covering deceptive advertising says, "The Commission will find an act or practice deceptive if there is a misrepresentation, omission or other practice that misleads the consumer acting reasonably in the circumstances, to the consumer's detriment."

The commission acts when it receives a complaint the staff feels is worth investigating. The staff can request a *letter of compliance* from the advertiser, with the advertiser promising to change the alleged deception without admitting guilt. Next, the advertiser can argue the case before an administrative law judge, who can write a consent agreement to outline what the advertiser must do to comply with the law. A cease-and-desist order can be issued against the advertiser, although this is rare. The FTC can fine an advertiser who doesn't comply with an FTC order.

The Federal Trade Commission's five members serve seven-year terms. They are appointed by the president and confirmed by the U.S. Senate, and no more than three of the members can be from one political party. Because the FTC's members are presidential appointees, the commission's actions often reflect the political climate under which they operate. In the 1970s, the FTC became a very active consumer advocacy agency. This was challenged in the 1980s, when presidential policy favored easing regulations on business practices. Under President Clinton in the 1990s, the FTC moved aggressively to cite companies for wrongdoing. For example, in 1997, the FTC conducted hearings to determine whether the government should impose safeguards on information access on the Internet to protect consumers' privacy. The George W. Bush administration was less aggressive in monitoring advertising claims. The Obama administration has shown a willingness to once again use the government's enforcement authority.

Law Must Balance Rights and Responsibilities

Legal and regulatory issues governing advertising and public relations, then, are stitched with the same conflicting values that govern all aspects of media. The courts, the FCC, the FTC and other government agencies that monitor the media industries are the major arbiters of ongoing constitutional clashes.

Important legal decisions make lasting and influential statements about the role of law in protecting the constitutional guarantee of free expression in a country with constantly shifting public values. Through the courts and regulation, the government also must balance the business needs of the media industries with the government's role as a public interest representative.

Review, Analyze, Investigate

REVIEWING CHAPTER 14

U.S. Constitution Sets Free Press Precedent

- ✓ The U.S. media's role is to encourage "uninhibited, robust and wide-open" debate.
- ✓ The legal and regulatory issues that media face are attempts to balance the media's rights and responsibilities.

Government Tries to Restrict Free Expression

- ✓ Before 1964, the First Amendment faced only four notable government challenges: the Alien and Sedition Laws of 1798, the Espionage Act of 1918, the Smith Act of 1940 and the Cold War congressional investigations of suspected communists in the late 1940s and early 1950s.
- ✓ All of these challenges were attempts to limit free expression.

Prior Restraint Rarely Used

- ✓ American courts rarely have invoked prior restraint. The two most recent cases involved the publication of the Pentagon Papers by *The New York Times* and the publication of directions to build a hydrogen bomb in *The Progressive* magazine.
- ✓ In both cases, the information eventually was printed, but the intervention of the government delayed publication.

Government Manages War Coverage

- ✓ Attempts by the Reagan administration to limit reporters' access to Grenada during the U.S. invasion in October 1983 were a subtle form of prior restraint.
- ✓ Pentagon rules for Gulf War coverage in 1991, reached in cooperation with journalists, imposed stricter restrictions on reporting than in any previous U.S. war.
- ✓ In 2001, the U.S. government controlled release of information to the American public about the war in Afghanistan even more than in the Gulf War.
- ✓ During the early months of the war in Afghanistan, the military used press pools and provided its own video footage of troop landings, produced by the military's combat film teams.
- ✓ During the Iraq War in 2003, the U.S. government used a system called embedding, which meant that members of the press traveled with the military, but the press' movements were restricted and managed by their military units.
- ✓ Twenty years ago during the Gulf War, the Bush administration banned the media from covering the return of war fatalities to the United States, saying they wanted to protect the families' privacy. Critics of the ban said the government was trying to hide the consequences of war from public view. In 2009, the Obama administration lifted the ban and now allows press coverage of the arrival of fallen soldiers, with family permission.

WikiLeaks Challenges Government Secrecy

- ✓ In 2010, WikiLeaks began releasing classified U.S. diplomatic documents about the Iraq and Afghanistan wars on its Web site.
- ✓ The U.S. government warned that the WikiLeaks postings could endanger military personnel and civilians.
- ✓ On November 28, 2010, *The New York Times* began publishing a series of articles based on a new release of U.S. State Department documents posted on WikiLeaks.
- ✓ On February 23, 2011, WikiLeaks founder Julian Assange was ordered extradited to Sweden, but he planned to appeal. The U.S. government did not file any charges against Assange for publishing secret U.S. documents on the Internet.
- ✓ The U.S. military charged Pfc. Bradley Manning with downloading large amounts of classified information from a military database.

Librarians Resist the PATRIOT Act

- ✓ Among the provisions of the PATRIOT Act is Section 215, which allows the Federal Bureau of Investigation to monitor business records, including computer log-ins and the lists of books people check out of public libraries.
- ✓ The American Library Association and the American Civil Liberties Union challenged Section 215 in court.
- ✓ In 2007, a federal district court agreed that some provisions of the PATRIOT Act go against constitutional principles of checks and balances and separation of powers.
- ✓ President Obama signed a four-year extension of the PATRIOT Act on May 30, 2011.

What Is the Standard for Obscenity?

- ✓ *Roth v. United States* defined obscenity as material that is "utterly without redeeming social importance."
- ✓ *Miller v. California* established a three-part local test for obscenity: whether "the average person, applying contemporary community standards," would find that the work, taken as a whole, appeals to the prurient interest; whether the work depicts or describes, in a patently offensive way, sexual conduct specifically defined by the applicable state law; and whether the work, taken as a

whole, lacks serious literary, artistic, political or scientific value (often called the LAPS test).

- ✓ In the 1988 *Hazelwood* case, the U.S. Supreme Court gave public school officials considerable freedom to limit what appears in student publications.

Libel Law Outlines the Media's Public Responsibility

- ✓ In 1964, the *New York Times v. Sullivan* case set a precedent, establishing that to be successful in a libel suit, a public official must prove actual malice.
- ✓ The press can use three defenses against a libel suit: truth, privilege and fair comment.
- ✓ Most successful libel judgments eventually are reversed or reduced when they are appealed. Often the major cost of a libel suit is not the actual award but the defense lawyers' fees.
- ✓ *Gertz v. Robert Welch, Inc.* established the concept that the expression of opinions is a necessary part of public debate.
- ✓ Because of the *Herbert v. Lando* decision, today reporters can be asked in a libel suit to identify their sources and to surrender their notes.
- ✓ The *Masson v. New Yorker Magazine* case addressed the journalist's responsibility for direct quotations.
- ✓ Businesses and public officials have used SLAPP suits to try to intimidate individuals and news organizations that write unfavorable stories or post critical comments on the Internet.

Invasion of Privacy Defined Four Ways

- ✓ Invasion-of-privacy lawsuits are much less common than libel suits.
- ✓ There is no U.S. Supreme Court decision that governs invasion of privacy, so each state has its own interpretation of the issue.
- ✓ Generally, the media can be guilty of invading someone's privacy by intruding on a person's physical or mental solitude, publishing or disclosing embarrassing personal facts, giving someone publicity that places the person in a false light or using someone's name or likeness for commercial benefit.
- ✓ In an important case for the press, *Bartnicki v. Vopper*, in 2001, the U.S. Supreme Court reaffirmed the media's right to broadcast information and to comment on that information, no matter how the information was obtained.

Debate Continues over Fair Trial, Courtroom Access and Shield Laws

- ✓ *Sheppard v. Maxwell* established the legal precedent for limiting press access to courtrooms and juries.
- ✓ In 2005, *New York Times* reporter Judith Miller spent 85 days in jail because she refused to reveal a confidential source to a Washington, D.C., grand jury. Eventually she revealed her source's name (I. Lewis Libby, Vice President Dick Cheney's chief of staff) after he released her from their confidentiality agreement. Libby was convicted of perjury and obstruction of justice, but President Bush commuted his sentence in 2007.
- ✓ Individual state shield laws protect journalists from being compelled to reveal their sources, but no federal shield law guarantees these rights to every journalist nationwide.

FCC Regulates Broadcast and Cable

- ✓ Unlike print, the broadcast media are regulated by a federal agency, the Federal Communications Commission.
- ✓ Since 1972, the concept behind broadcast regulation has been based on the belief that broadcasters are trustees operating in the public interest.

Telecommunications Act of 1996 Changes the Marketplace

- ✓ The Telecommunications Act of 1996 was the most far-reaching reform in the way the U.S. government regulates mass media in more than 60 years.
- ✓ Following passage of the Telecommunications Act, large companies began positioning themselves to deliver the combination of telecommunications services they think consumers want.
- ✓ The major provisions of the Telecommunications Act of 1996 affect telecommunications, broadcast, satellite and cable.

Deregulation Unleashes the Media

- ✓ The FCC under President Clinton moved to a policy of deregulation of station ownership and regulation of broadcast programming.
- ✓ In 2003, the FCC adopted regulations that allow one company to control 35 percent of the broadcast audience. Those regulations are still in place today.
- ✓ In 2010, a federal court lifted the ban on media cross-ownership. The FCC is expected to revisit the cross-ownership rules in 2011.

Congress Attempts to Use Communications Decency Act

- ✓ The Communications Decency Act (CDA), which was part of the Telecommunications Act, attempted to regulate access to cable and TV programming and monitoring of computer networks, including the Internet.
- ✓ In 1997, the U.S. Supreme Court blocked enforcement of the Internet indecency provisions of the CDA.
- ✓ In 1998, Congress passed the Child Online Protection Act (COPA), aimed at preventing minors from getting access to sexually explicit material, even though the material is legal for adults. Several organizations, including the American Library Association and the American

Civil Liberties Union, immediately challenged the law in court on First Amendment grounds. In 2002, the U.S. Supreme Court agreed that Congress has no authority to restrict Internet access.

- ✓ In 2003, the U.S. Supreme Court ruled that the federal government may withhold funding from schools and libraries that refuse to install Internet filters for pornography on their computers.

TV Industry Agrees to Ratings and the V-Chip

- ✓ Under pressure from Congress, television executives devised a voluntary system of ratings for TV programming.
- ✓ The new programming codes can be read by a v-chip, which allows parents to program a TV set to eliminate objectionable programs.

Government Monitors Broadcast Indecency

- ✓ In 2004, the FCC increased fines for broadcast programs the FCC determines are indecent.
- ✓ The FCC fined CBS-TV for Janet Jackson's "wardrobe malfunction" during the 2004 Super Bowl.
- ✓ In a July 2010 ruling on a group of indecency cases concerning fleeting expletives, a federal appeals court in New York found that the FCC's indecency policy violated the First Amendment. The FCC said it would appeal.

Intellectual Property Rights Affirmed

- ✓ The right of ownership of creative ideas in the United States is legally governed by what are called intellectual property rights. The Digital Millennium Copyright Act (DMCA), the U.S. Supreme Court decision in *New York Times Co. v. Tasini*, and the U.S. Supreme Court decision in *Metro-Goldwyn Mayer Studios Inc. et al. v. Grokster Ltd. et al.* have begun to define the issues of electronic copyright in the digital era.
- ✓ In 2010, a New York district court required LimeWire to shut down because of copyright infringement in response to a suit by 14 recording companies.
- ✓ All four cases affirm the strong legal tradition in the United States of guaranteeing intellectual copyright for creative content.

FCC Advocates Internet Regulation

- ✓ In December 2010, FCC Chairman Julius Genachowski proposed a regulatory plan to guarantee open access to the Internet and forbid Internet service providers from blocking any content that is considered lawful.
- ✓ The issue of Net neutrality, and whether the FCC should play a role in regulating the Internet, is based on whether Internet access services are classified as "information services" or "telecommunications services."
- ✓ The FCC's power to regulate an information service is limited, but the FCC has wider authority to regulate telecommunications services.
- ✓ New net neutrality rules took effect in November 2011.

Courts and Regulators Govern Advertising and PR

- ✓ The Hudson test for advertising means that to be protected by the First Amendment, an advertisement must promote a legal product and must not lie.
- ✓ The *Texas Gulf Sulphur* case established the concept that a publicly held company is responsible for any information it withholds from the public.
- ✓ The main government agency regulating advertising is the Federal Trade Commission (FTC). The agency today is becoming more aggressive about policing advertisers than it was during the previous 20 years.

Law Must Balance Rights and Responsibilities

- ✓ The courts, the FCC and the FTC arbitrate the media's rights and responsibilities.
- ✓ Government must balance the media's business needs with the government's role to protect the interests of the public.

KEY TERMS

These terms are defined in the margins throughout this chapter and appear in alphabetical order with definitions in the Glossary, which begins on page 383.

CRITICAL QUESTIONS

1. Cite five major events/legal decisions in the evolution of the interpretation of the First Amendment in America from its beginnings to today.
2. Why is *New York Times v. Sullivan* a precedent-setting case for the American media?
3. List and describe the four elements necessary to prove libel.
4. Why are the courts generally so reluctant to use prior restraint to stop publication? List two cases in which the courts did invoke prior restraint.
5. List and explain three specific cases that demonstrate how the U.S. legal system is responding to challenges created by the relationship between mass media and the Internet.

WORKING THE WEB

This list includes both sites mentioned in the chapter and others to give you greater insight into media law and regulation.

American Booksellers Foundation for Free Expression (ABFFE)

http://www.abffe.org

The self-described "bookseller's voice in the fight against censorship," this foundation participates in legal cases about First Amendment rights and provides education about the importance of free expression. Archived articles from the *ABFFE Update* and the downloadable Banned Books Week Handbook are available on the Web site.

American Library Association (ALA)

http://www.ala.org

This association's mission is to provide leadership for the development, promotion and improvement of library and information services and the profession of librarianship in order to enhance learning and ensure access to information for all. However, the ALA is open to any interested person or organization. Among the professional tools available on the Web site of this 130-year-old organization are articles, guidelines and other resources about such issues as censorship, copyright, diversity and equal access. ALA also sponsors a number of electronic discussion lists for participation by members and others with shared interests.

Federal Communications Commission (FCC)

http://www.fcc.gov

This U.S. government agency, established by the Communications Act of 1934, regulates interstate and international communications by radio, television, wire, satellite and cable. Its jurisdiction covers the 50 states, the District of Columbia and U.S. possessions. The site holds FCC news headlines—daily and archived—as well as links to media rules and regulations, strategic goals of the commission, bureaus and offices, advisory committees, and even a kids' zone. The Consumer and Governmental Affairs Bureau section allows consumers to file or research individual informal complaints relating to FCC regulations.

FindLaw

http://www.findlaw.com

FindLaw provides legal information for the public on a host of topics, including intellectual property, copyright and the Internet as well as civil rights, education law, employees' rights and criminal law. Users can find and share legal information on FindLaw Q&A.

Freedom of Information Center (University of Missouri School of Journalism, Columbia)

http://www.nfoic.org/foi-center/

Founded in 1958, the Center provides information to the general public and the media through a collection of more than 1 million articles and documents about access to government information at local, state and federal levels. The Web site features links to state and international FOI laws, a media law guide, and an index to research files that have been compiled since the Center's inception.

Index on Censorship

http://www.indexoncensorship.org

This Web site of a periodical founded in 1972 by a group of writers, journalists and artists describes itself as "one of the world's leading repositories of original, challenging, controversial and intelligent writing on free expression issues." Users can explore censorship issues from around the world as well as news, sponsored events, projects and awards through its Free Speech Blog and its Uncut blog.

Media Center at New York Law School

http://www.nyls.edu/centers/projects/media_center

The Media Center sponsors pedagogy, scholarship and projects relating to evolving communication and information technologies and the laws that regulate them. Its goals are to promote scholarship, to preserve democratic values through effective media policy and to train lawyers to understand the law of media and the role of media in the law. The Center's Library holds comprehensive indexes of U.S. laws and cases, as well as articles and papers on various media law issues.

Media Law Resource Center (MLRC)

http://www.medialaw.org

This nonprofit information clearinghouse is a membership organization for media companies (publishers, broadcasters and web content providers), insurers, and professional and public interest organizations. Available to the general public on the Web site is Libel FAQs, a basic introduction to libel, privacy and related law in the media, in addition to selected articles and reports from MLRC.

Silha Center for the Study of Media Ethics and Law (University of Minnesota)

http://www.silha.umn.edu/

The Silha Center examines the theoretical and practical applications of freedom and fairness in journalism. Major projects include media accountability, points of convergence of media ethics and law, and libel and privacy. The Web site includes articles from the quarterly *Silha Center Bulletin* and links to law-related and media-ethics-related Web sites as well as legislative testimony and briefs on a number of issues.

Student Press Law Center (SPLC)

http://www.splc.org

This advocate for student free press rights provides information, advice and legal assistance to students and educators. News Flashes link to current and archived articles about high school and college journalism controversies. The Web site also offers articles from the SPLC Blog. The Resource Center includes information about obtaining legal help, browsing through the online law library and testing your knowledge of student press law (30-minute quiz) and the First Amendment (10-minute quiz).

WikiLeaks

http://www.wikileaks.ch/

Funded as part of a "project of the sunshine press" and based in Melbourne, Australia, WikiLeaks publishes and comments on leaked documents alleging government and corporate misconduct. Unlike Wikipedia, source documents published on WikiLeaks cannot be edited or changed by the public. WikiLeaks claims that "transparency in government activities leads to reduced corruption, better government and stronger democracies." The site provides separate discussion and source pages for all of the content published on the site. In addition, WikiLeaks says that, as far as they are aware, "none of the thousands of WikiLeaks sources have been exposed, via WikiLeaks or any other method."

Impact/Action Videos are concise news features on topics covered in this chapter, created exclusively for **Media/Impact**. They are available for students and instructors at CengageBrain.com, and include screen access for classroom viewing and discussion questions.

"The real issue is: by paying for interviews, are you changing the news?"

—David Westin, former president, ABC News

Ethics: Placing Responsibility

What's Ahead?

Ethics Define Responsibilities

Truthfulness Affects Credibility

Fairness Means Evenhandedness

Privacy Involves Respect

Responsibility Brings Trust

Five Philosophical Principles Govern Media Ethics

Media's Ethical Decisions Carry Consequences

Professional Associations Proscribe Behavior

Media Organizations Respond to Criticism

Professional Ethics Preserve Media Credibility

Fred Vuich/*Sports Illustrated*/Getty Images

Reporters and photographers surround Penn State trustee Kenneth Frazier on November 11, 2011. Frazier was selected to chair a committee to investigate the charges against former Penn State coach Jerry Sandusky for alleged child sexual abuse and the alleged subsequent coverup.

"Most of us would rather publish a story than not," explains journalist Anthony Brandt in an *Esquire* magazine article about ethics. "We're in the business of reporting, after all; most of us believe the public should know what's going on, has a right to know, has, indeed, a responsibility to know, and that this right, this responsibility, transcends the right to privacy, excuses our own pushiness, our arrogance, and therefore ought to protect us from lawsuits even when we are wrong.

"But most reporters also know there are times when publishing can harm or ruin people's lives. Members of the press sometimes print gossip as truth, disregard the impact they have on people's lives, and are ready to believe the worst about people because the worst sells. . . . We in the media have much to answer for."

Ethics Define Responsibilities

Discussions about how journalists answer for what they do center on ***ethics***. The word derives from the Greek word *ethos*, meaning the guiding spirit or traditions that govern a culture. Part of America's culture is the unique protection offered to journalists by the First Amendment of the U.S. Constitution, so any discussion of ethics and the American media acknowledges the cultural belief that the First Amendment privilege carries with it special obligations. Among these obligations are ***professional ethics***, the rules or standards governing the conduct of the members of a profession.

Journalists are no more likely to exploit their positions than people in other professions, but when journalists make the wrong ethical choices, the consequences can be very damaging and very public. "It may well be that if journalism loses touch with ethical values, it will then cease to be of use to society, and cease to have any real reason for being," writes media ethics scholar John Hulteng. "But that, for the sake of all of us, must never be allowed to happen."

Journalists sometimes make poor ethical judgments because they work quickly and their actions can be haphazard because the lust to be first with a story can override the desire to be right, because they sometimes don't know enough to question the truthfulness of what they're told, because they may win attention and professional success quickly by ignoring ethical standards, and because journalists sometimes are insensitive to the consequences of their stories for the people they cover.

The media face four types of ethical issues:

1. Truthfulness
2. Fairness
3. Privacy
4. Responsibility

Consider these actual situations:

1. **Truthfulness.** A public relations agency hired by the U.S. government paid a commentator to promote a new federal education initiative. The contract also required the commentator to gain access for government officials to other journalists to convince the journalists about the new law's merits. By not disclosing the payment, did the commentator mislead his readers, or was he simply doing the job he was paid to do? Were the opinions he promoted truly his positions on the issues, or did he take the positions because he'd been paid to publicly promote a specific agenda?

2. **Fairness.** Two television commentators each admitted separately that they gave political donations to candidates. One commentator gave a donation to a Democratic candidate for national office and then questioned the candidate's opponent on the air. The second commentator gave money to friends who were running in local races and never covered these candidates. The TV network employers suspended each commentator for two days. The network said that company policy forbid the donations. Should commentators, who are expected to be partisan, be subject to the same ethical standards as news employees? Is their fairness on the job compromised if they make political donations?

3. **Privacy.** Reporters at a tabloid newspaper hacked into personal email accounts and illegally obtained access to personal voicemails of celebrities and public officials. Did the reporters infringe on the person's privacy, or should public figures just except this type of reporting?

4. **Responsibility.** A family that was hoping to be hired by a reality TV show concocted a story that their son had been swept away in a balloon-like object that resembled a flying saucer. This object had been built by the father, who told authorities that his son had crawled inside it without his knowledge. When the flying saucer was launched, the father said, he couldn't find his son, who was dubbed "Balloon Boy." The father told the journalists who arrived at the scene that he assumed the boy was inside the saucer.

Ethics The rules or standards that govern someone's conduct.

Professional Ethics The rules or standards governing the conduct of the members of a profession.

Truth versus falsehood is the issue for the journalist who accepted payment to write stories in example 1. Fairness versus bias is the question for the commentators who gave the political donations in example 2. Personal privacy versus invasion of privacy is the debate facing the reporters who hacked emails and voicemails in example 3. Responsibility versus irresponsibility is the issue for the journalists who covered the Balloon Boy in example 4.

Some ethical debates are easier to resolve than others. These four incidents and several other examples described in this chapter demonstrate the amazing range of situations covered by media ethics and the different ways that media organizations get their jobs done.

"No comment for now, but there'll be a press leak at five."

Truthfulness Affects Credibility

Truthfulness in reporting means more than accuracy and telling the truth to get a story. Truthfulness also means not misrepresenting the people or the underlying motives of a story to readers and viewers, as well as not reporting disinformation. Another aspect of truthfulness is the belief that government officials should not use the media for their own ends by planting stories that aren't true.

Hidden Motives or Sponsors

The journalist described in example 1 (on p. 336) is syndicated columnist Armstrong Williams, who received $250,000 from a public relations firm to promote President George W. Bush's No Child Left Behind initiative to African Americans. In 2005, *USA Today* revealed that Williams' contract with the PR firm said he would "utilize his long-term working relationships with *America's Black Forum* [an African American news program] to encourage the producers to periodically address the No Child Left Behind Act."

When Williams' payment arrangement became public, Williams attributed the lapse to the fact that he was not trained as a journalist. He apologized for "blurring his roles as an independent conservative commentator and a paid promoter."

Misrepresentation

In 2010, *The New York Times* suspended reporter Zachery Kouwe after editors said Kouwe had plagiarized portions of an article he had written for *The Times* from an article by another reporter that had appeared earlier online in *The Wall Street Journal*. When editors of *The Journal* contacted *The Times* about the similarity, *Times* editors investigated some of Kouwe's other stories and found more examples of plagiarism.

"In a number of business articles in *The Times* over the past year, and in posts on the DealBook blog on NYTimes.com, a *Times* reporter appears to have improperly appropriated wording and passages published by other news organizations," wrote *The Times* on its Corrections page. "A subsequent search by *The Times* found other cases of extensive overlap between passages in Mr. Kouwe's articles and other news organizations'. . . . Copying language directly from other news organizations without providing attribution—even if the facts are independently verified—is a serious violation of *Times* policy and basic journalistic standards. It should not have occurred." Kouwe resigned.

In another case of misrepresentation that involved a movie studio and several newspapers, Universal Pictures created a series of newspaper stories in 2009 purportedly taken from real Alaska news publications to promote its movie *The Fourth Kind*. The movie claimed to be a true story about alien abductions that allegedly occurred in Nome, Alaska, and the false news articles were used in movie ads to give the subject legitimacy. The *Fairbanks Daily News-Miner* explained what Universal did:

> To bolster that claim [that the story about the aliens was true], articles were posted that professed to be from real Alaska publications, but were actually created to bolster the movie's storyline. The articles included an obituary and news story about the death of a character in the movie, Dr. William Tyler, that

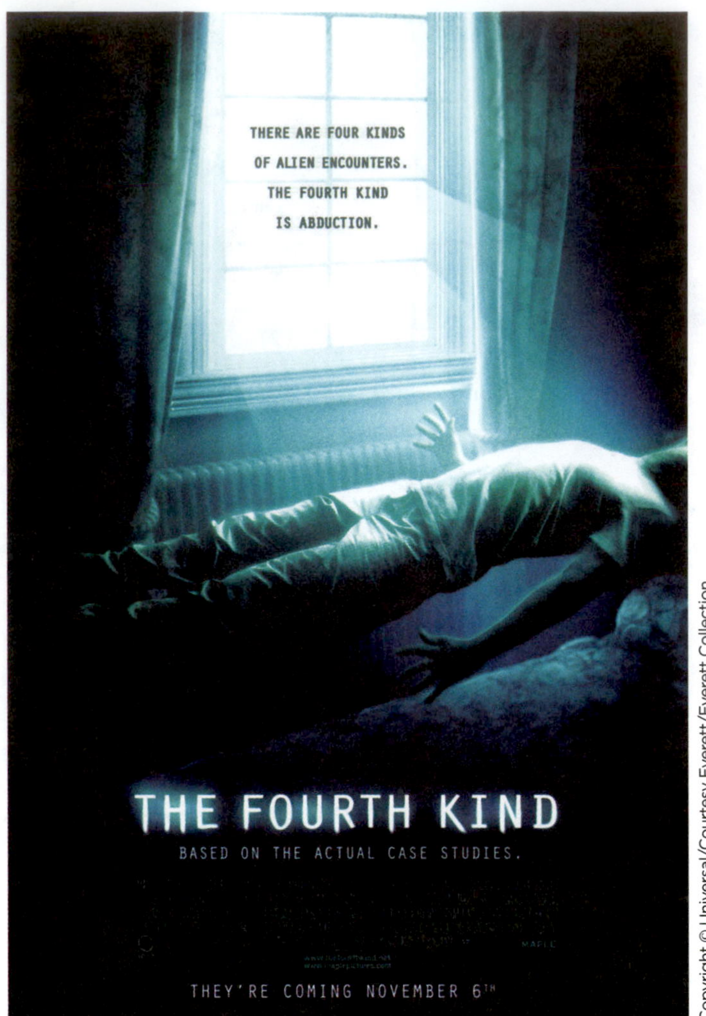

THERE ARE FOUR KINDS
OF ALIEN ENCOUNTERS.
THE FOURTH KIND
IS ABDUCTION.
THE FOURTH KIND
BASED ON THE ACTUAL CASE STUDIES.
THEY'RE COMING NOVEMBER 6TH

In 2009, Universal Pictures posted fake stories purported to be from Alaska news publications to promote its movie *The Fourth Kind*. When the fabrications were discovered, Universal paid the Alaska Press Club a $20,000 settlement.

> supposedly were from the *Daily News-Miner*. Neither the story nor the obituary ever appeared in the newspaper. Fake articles were listed from other newspapers in Alaska, including the *Nome Nugget*, alongside authentic new stories.

Universal paid $20,000 to the Alaska Press Club as part of a settlement with several Alaska newspapers once the deception was discovered. An attorney for the newspapers told the *Los Angeles Times*, "If people can't rely on the fact that when they look at a news article on the Web that it's from the newspaper it appears to be. . .it erodes confidence in the world of journalism."

Another celebrated case of misrepresentation happened in 2006 when author James Frey admitted that his personal memoir, *A Million Little Pieces*, contained many fabrications. In the book, selected by Oprah Winfrey in September 2005 for her book club, Frey detailed his battle with drug addiction and his ultimate recovery. The book quickly became a best seller.

In January 2006, The Smoking Gun Web site posted information that disputed the truthfulness of many of the incidents Frey described. Frey's publisher, Doubleday, initially defended the book, but then Winfrey invited Frey to appear on her show, where Frey admitted he'd falsified many parts of *A Million Little Pieces*, including descriptions of time he spent in police custody and in jail.

He also admitted to Winfrey that the first pages of his just-published sequel, *My Friend Leonard*, were a fabrication, since *Leonard* started with Frey's 87th day in jail, which never occurred. Frey told Winfrey the invented stories "portrayed me in ways that made me tougher and more daring and more aggressive than in reality I was, or I am." He then publicly apologized to his readers.

Doubleday said it would include a detailed list of Frey's fabrications, compiled by the author, in all future copies of *A Million Little Pieces*. *The New York Times Book Review* continued to categorize the book in its nonfiction best-seller list, but the editors added a note saying, "Both author and publisher acknowledge that this memoir contains numerous fabrications."

A month after Frey admitted his mistakes on television, Riverhead Books, which published *Leonard* and had signed Frey to write two more books, cancelled the contract, and his agent dropped him. Sales of *A Million Little Pieces* dropped quickly after the *Oprah* confrontation; however, *The New York Times* reported in March 2006 that Frey's royalties for 2005 totaled more than $5 million.

The most well-known case of serious journalistic misrepresentation involved Jayson Blair, another *New York Times* reporter, six years before the Zachery Kouwe incident. On May 1, 2003, *The Times* published a front-page story, "*Times* Reporter Who Resigned Leaves Long Trail of Deception," which began: "A staff reporter for *The New York Times* committed frequent acts of journalistic fraud while covering significant news events in recent months, an investigation by *Times* journalists has found. The widespread fabrication and plagiarism represent a profound betrayal of trust and a low point in the 152-year history of the newspaper." *The Times* said that as a reporter for *The Times*, 27-year-old Blair had:

- Written stories purported to be filed in Maryland, Texas and other states, when often he was still in New York.
- Fabricated comments.
- Concocted scenes.
- Stolen material from other newspapers and wire services.

- Selected details from photographs to create the impression he had been somewhere or seen someone, when he hadn't.

The Times then published an exhaustive, unprecedented eight-page accounting of 73 significant falsehoods in Blair's stories *The Times* had published, detailing every traceable error, based on an internal investigation by its own reporters. In one story, for example, Blair had reported details from inside the National Naval Medical Center in Bethesda, Md., but the hospital said Blair had never been there. In another story about a stricter National Collegiate Athletic Association standard for class attendance, Blair quoted someone who said he had never talked to Blair and used quotes from another newspaper as his own.

When discussing Blair's case, Alex S. Jones, a former *Times* reporter and co-author of *The Trust: The Private and Powerful Family Behind The New York Times*, told the *Times*: "To the best of my knowledge, there has never been anything like this at *The New York Times*. . . . There has never been a systematic effort to lie and cheat as a reporter at *The New York Times* comparable to what Jayson Blair seems to have done."

Less than two months later, *The Times*' two top editors, who were responsible for hiring and supervising Blair, resigned.

Misrepresenting the facts or creating false stories and attributing them to others can cause readers to question all information published by similar sources. Which are actual people and which are not? Is the story fiction or fact? Misrepresentation directly affects the credibility of the company that publishes the books, stories, even the ads and indirectly affects the credibility of all authors, all journalists and all publishers.

Disinformation

In October 1986, the press learned that two months earlier the Reagan administration had launched a ***disinformation*** campaign to scare Libyan leader Muammar Qaddafi. Selected U.S. government sources had planted stories with reporters that U.S. forces were preparing to strike Libya.

The first report about the bogus preparations appeared in the August 25, 1986, issue of *The Wall Street Journal*, which first used the word *disinformation* to describe the practice of government officials intentionally planting false information with reporters.

On the basis of a statement by White House spokesman Larry Speakes that the *Journal*'s article about an impending strike on Libya was "authoritative," other newspapers, including *The Washington Post*, carried the story. This example brings up the ethical question of the government's responsibility to tell the truth and not to use the news media for its own ends. State Department spokesman and former television reporter Bernard Kalb resigned when he

Ulf Andersen/Getty Images

In 2006, author James Frey admitted to Oprah Winfrey that his memoir, *A Million Little Pieces*, contained fabrications. Frey's book had been chosen as an Oprah Book Club selection, and he previously had promoted the book on her show.

AP Photo/Jennifer Szymaszek

In May 2003, *The New York Times* admitted in a front-page story that Times reporter Jayson Blair had fabricated comments, concocted scenes, stolen material from other news services and selected details from photos to create an impression he had been in certain places and interviewed people when he hadn't.

Disinformation The intentional planting of false information by government sources.

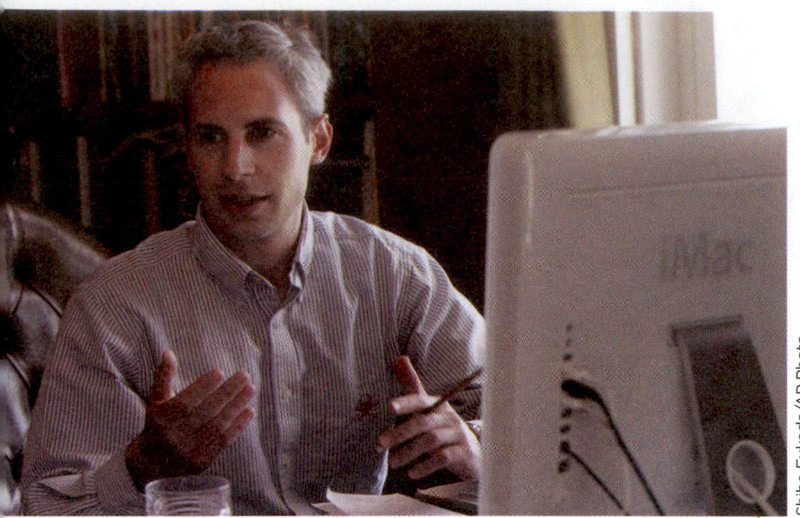

Shiho Fukada/AP Photo

In April 2006, federal investigators charged *New York Post* contributor Jared Paul Stern with attempting to extort money from a wealthy businessman in exchange for keeping unfavorable information out of the paper. Stern denied the charges but was suspended from the paper and has not worked there since. Federal prosecutors eventually dropped the case.

learned about the disinformation campaign, saying, "Faith in the word of America is the pulse beat of our democracy."

Disinformation also was at the center of the 2007 trial of presidential adviser I. Lewis Libby, in which Libby was found guilty of perjury and obstruction of justice for leaking the name of CIA operative Valerie Plame to journalists and then denying before a Washington, D.C., grand jury that he had done so. (See **Chapter 14**.) President Bush commuted Libby's sentence. Former *New York Times* Executive Editor Max Frankel said the case showed "the shameless ease with which top-secret information is bartered in Washington for political advantage."

Fairness Means Evenhandedness

Fairness implies impartiality—that the journalist has nothing personal to gain from a report, that there are no hidden benefits to the reporter or to the source from the story being presented or being withheld. Criticism of the press for unfairness results from

- Close ties that develop between reporters and the stories they cover—called *insider friendships*.
- Reporters who accept personal or financial benefits from sources, sponsors or advertisers—called *conflicts of interest*.
- Reporters who pay their sources for stories—called *checkbook journalism*.

Insider Friendships

The TV commentators in example 2 (on p. 336) are Keith Olbermann and Joe Scarborough, who both work for MSNBC. On November 5, 2010, MSNBC announced that it was suspending Olbermann without pay after MSNBC TV President Phil Griffin learned that Olbermann had violated newsroom policies by contributing to three Democratic congressional candidates.

Olbermann admitted he made three donations of $2,400 but issued a statement that said he did not use his influence in any other way. "I did not privately or publicly encourage anyone else to donate to these campaigns, nor to any others in this election or any previous ones, nor have I previously donated to any political campaign at any level," he said. MSNBC, which originally suspended him indefinitely, announced a two-day suspension.

Less than a month later, MSNBC announced another two-day suspension of the co-host of its morning program after the online site Politico reported that Joe Scarborough had donated $4,000 in recent years to three Republican candidates in Florida. The contributions, Scarborough said, "were not relevant to my work at MSNBC." He had not reported on any of the races to which he gave money, he said. (See **Media/Impact: People**, "Keith Olbermann and Joe Scarborough Suspended Over Campaign Donations," p. 341.)

Scarborough's suspension "underscored the idiosyncrasy of a policy that seeks to protect NBC's journalistic integrity, but does not differentiate between news reporters and political commentators," wrote *The New York Times* (NBC owns MSNBC.). MSNBC President Phil Griffin said, "As Joe recognizes, it is critical that we enforce our standards and politics." Scarborough said, in a statement, "There is nothing more important than maintaining the integrity" of the news.

In the Olbermann and Scarborough examples, MSNBC was dealing with the potential public perception that insider contacts could affect its news coverage, even though Olbermann and Scarborough are commentators, not news reporters. The network believed that political donations could interfere with the public's trust in the rest of its news organization. Even the appearance of insider friendships removes the very important element of a news organization's independence from the people and events it covers.

In an example of someone using insider friendships to keep a story out of the news, federal investigators in 2006 charged Jared Paul Stern, a contributor to the *New York Post*'s celebrity column Page Six, with trying to extort money from wealthy businessman Ronald W. Burkle. Burkle accused Stern of demanding money in exchange for keeping negative information about Burkle out of the *Post*'s gossip column.

Media/Impact

PEOPLE

Keith Olbermann and Joe Scarborough Suspended Over Campaign Donations

By Brian Stelter

Jeffrey Ufberg/WireImage/Getty Images

Jamie McCarthy/WireImage/Getty Images

In November 2010, MSNBC commentators Keith Olbermann (left) and Joe Scarborough each were suspended for two days in separate incidents after it was discovered that they had made campaign contributions to political candidates. Both said they had not used their influence to promote the candidates to whom they had given money. Olbermann resigned from MSNBC in January 2011.

In a mirror image of Keith Olbermann's suspension two weeks ago, MSNBC suspended its morning host Joe Scarborough on Friday [November 19, 2010] after *Politico* uncovered $4,000 in donations he had made to political candidates.

MSNBC said Mr. Scarborough, the co-host of *Morning Joe*, would sit out for two days, the same short period of time that Mr. Olbermann was suspended after donating $7,200 to candidates.

The donations in both cases were violations of a policy at MSNBC and its parent, NBC News, which prohibits political contributions without advance approval.

In a contrite statement Friday afternoon, Mr. Scarborough apologized to his employer and said, "This will not happen again."

The contributions, he said, were "not relevant to my work at MSNBC" because they were made "to close personal friends and family members and were limited to local races." For those reasons, he said, he thought he did not need permission from NBC. News of his suspension revived the widespread criticism of the network that started after Mr. Olbermann was sidelined on Nov. 5. The suspension also underscored the idiosyncrasy of a policy that seeks to protect NBC's journalistic integrity, but does not differentiate between news reporters and political commentators. Mr. Scarborough is the latter, as *Morning Joe* viewers well know. But Phil Griffin, the president of MSNBC, said in a statement Friday, "As Joe recognizes, it is critical that we enforce our standards and policies."

Politico found evidence that Mr. Scarborough had given money in recent years to three Republican candidates in Florida, the state where he was a Republican congressman between 1994 and 2001. *Politico* said Mr. Scarborough's wife matched each of the donations.

There was no indication that Mr. Scarborough had talked on television about any of the candidates he supported. "To be blunt," he said in his statement, "I had no interest in their campaigns other than being kind to longtime friends."

Mr. Olbermann came under fire in part because he had publicly criticized the opponent of one of the three Democratic candidates he donated to. Mr. Olbermann later said he had done so unknowingly.

The policy toward political contributions "needs debate," Mr. Olbermann said on *Countdown* on the day he returned from his two-day suspension. It is unclear whether Mr. Scarborough agrees.

In his statement, Mr. Scarborough said "there is nothing more important than maintaining the integrity" of the NBC News brand.

From Brian Stelter, "2nd MSNBC Host Suspended Over Campaign Donations," The New York Times, *November 20, 2010, page B1.*

Stern denied the charges, but *The New York Times* reported that private investigators recorded several conversations between Burkle and Stern, which included a discussion about "protection" against negative coverage in exchange for $100,000 plus a $10,000 monthly stipend. When the payment didn't arrive as scheduled, according to the *New York Daily News*, Stern also reportedly sent e-mails asking where the money was.

The criminal charges against Stern, if true, added an unusual twist to the issue of insider friendships because they involved a request for direct payment to Stern. "Taking money in exchange for treatment is . . . what is different here," reported *The New York Times*. "But given the murky world in which gossip is reported, the prospect of a cash for coverage deal is not an unimaginable one." Stern was suspended from the *Post* and has not worked there since. Federal prosecutors eventually dropped the case.

Conflicts of Interest

Reporters with conflicts of interest are divided between at least two loyalties, and the ethical question is, how will the stories the reporters write and the integrity of the organizations for which they work be affected?

One type of conflict of interest happens when reporters accept free meals and passes to entertainment events (freebies) and free trips (junkets). In one survey of newspapers, nearly half said they accepted free tickets to athletic events, and nearly two-thirds accepted free tickets to artistic events. In an editorial about junkets, *The New York Times* said, "Accepting junkets and boondoggles does not necessarily mean that a reporter is being bought—but it inescapably creates the appearance of being bought."

Accepting junkets and freebies creates an appearance of conflict of interest—even if the reporters don't write favorably about the places they visit. In 2010, however, a newspaper took the unusual step of taking money from an advertiser to help pay for its coverage of the war in Afghanistan.

On September 27, 2010, the *New Hampshire Union Leader* (*UL*), the state's largest newspaper, announced that the paper had accepted underwriting from three major New Hampshire businesses so its publisher and a staff photographer could travel to Afghanistan to report on a New Hampshire National Guard unit serving there. One of the underwriters, BAE Systems, is the state's largest manufacturing firm and works mainly in the defense industry, according to a story about the incident published by The Newspaper Guild.

Checkbook Journalism The practice of a news organization paying for an interview or a photograph.

Citing declining revenue because of the recession, the newspaper's publisher wrote, "I had a hunch that I knew some companies that would feel the same way as the *Union Leader*, that the story of Charlie Company ought to be told and that, with their assistance, New Hampshire's newspaper and UnionLeader.com could and should tell it."

Many readers didn't agree. "The *UL* takes money from BAE and other companies? That is obvious conflict of interest," wrote one reader. "How can we trust the *UL* to report on these companies in an objective way when they are taking money from them? We can't. These stories will be nothing more than propaganda."

In a similar type of conflict of interest, *The Washington Post* in 2009 issued invitations to lobbyists, members of Congress and other influential people in Washington to attend a *Washington Post* "salon" at publisher Katharine Weymouth's home. Guests were invited to buy sponsorships ($25,000 for one or $250,000 for the entire series) to attend off-the-record dinners hosted by the newspaper's editor, Marcus Brauchli.

After a story on *Politico* (an online competitor) made the event public, *The Post* cancelled it, and Weymouth apologized to *The Post*'s readers, although she said *Politico* had characterized the invitation incorrectly. The planned event highlights the conflicts of interest that can develop when the business side of a media organization overlaps the news side.

Checkbook Journalism

In 2009, some journalists who were covering the kidnapping story of Jaycee Lee Dugard—a young girl who said she had been held in captivity for 18 years in Antioch, Calif.—offered payments to several neighbors near the place where she lived with her alleged kidnappers, Phillip and Nancy Garrido. Interview payments to witnesses are quite common in Europe, but they present serious ethical problems for reporters who cannot pay for information about the story they are covering.

According to the *Los Angeles Times*, one Garrido neighbor, Damon Robinson, was talking to reporters from CNN, the Associated Press and the *Times* when a British journalist offered Robinson $2,000 if he would stop talking with other reporters and give the British journalist an exclusive. According to the *Times*, "Robinson complied."

Two years later, when Jaycee Lee Dugard was ready to talk with the press, ABC News paid for exclusive rights to the interview. (See **Media/Impact: Money**, "For Instant Ratings, Interviews with a Checkbook," p. 344.)

A news organization paying someone for an interview or information is using ***checkbook journalism***. Besides the ethical questions about whether participants, witnesses and even criminals should profit financially from manufactured publicity, there are other hazards in any type of checkbook journalism. One danger is that a paid interviewee will sensationalize the information to bring a higher price, so the interviewee's truthfulness cannot always be trusted. A second hazard is that such interviews often become the exclusive property of the highest bidder, shutting out smaller news organizations and independent journalists from the information. A third possibility is that the person who is paid by the news organization to comment could possibly carry a hidden agenda.

Justin Sullivan/Getty Images

In September 2009, members of the press swarmed the Antioch, Calif., neighborhood of Jaycee Lee Dugard—who said she was kidnapped and held against her will for 18 years by Phillip and Nancy Garrido at this house. In 2011, ABC News paid Dugard for an exclusive interview, an example of checkbook journalism.

Privacy Involves Respect

Privacy for Personal Communications

Privacy for email and voicemail communications is a very important ethical and legal issue (see also Chapter 14). In July 2011, the British newspaper *The Guardian* reported that journalists at the competing British tabloid *News of the World* (owned by a subsidiary of Rupert Murdoch's News Corp.), repeatedly had hacked emails and voicemails belonging to British and U.S. celebrities and government officials. This is the case listed as example 3 on p. 336. There were at least 800 documented hacking victims, allegedly including Queen Elizabeth II, former Prime Minister Gordon Brown as well as actor Jude Law.

Murdoch printed a public apology and then shut down the 168-year-old newspaper. Parliament convened an investigatory commission, and the FBI opened an investigation into possible U.S. hacking victims. In January 2012, News Corp. agreed to pay substantial damages to 37 victims, including Jude Law, and more than two dozen suits are still pending. (See **Media/Impact: Culture**, "Fresh Hacking Emails Released," p. 346.)

Reporting on illnesses and on rape are other examples of a complex ethical dilemma of privacy: How does the press balance the goal of truthfulness and fact-finding with the need for personal privacy? Is the private grief that such a report may cause worth the public good that can result from publishing the information?

Reporting an Illness

Because some people with AIDS are homosexual, announcing that a person is ill with AIDS can reflect on the person's private sexual behavior. One argument in favor of the press reporting the nature of the illness is that covering up the information means the public won't understand the widespread extent of the public health problem that AIDS represents.

"Covering up the truth, by doctors or journalists, stigmatizes other sufferers—the less widely the disease is acknowledged, the less easily they can be accepted. And it shields communities and industries from understanding the full, devastating effect of AIDS," argued *Newsweek* in a story called "AIDS and the Right to Know." The counterargument is that a person's illness and death are strictly private matters and that publishing the information is a violation of that person's privacy.

Roy Cohn became a public figure in the 1950s during the McCarthy hearings, as counsel for the Senate committee investigating Communist activity. As a lawyer in the 1980s, he defended many organized crime figures, and he lived a high-profile existence in New York City. A week before Cohn died, columnists Jack Anderson and Dale Van Atta published a story saying that Cohn was being treated with azidothymidine (AZT), then used exclusively for AIDS patients. It was the first time that a major public figure had been exposed as an AIDS victim. After Cohn's death, *Harper's* magazine published copies of the hospital records on which Van Atta had based his column, which showed that Cohn had been a victim of AIDS.

A second example of a story about someone dying of AIDS represents one journalist's answer to the debate. *Honolulu*

Media/Impact
MONEY

For Instant Ratings, Interviews with a Checkbook

By Brian Stelter and Bill Carter

Before the subjects of headlining news stories agree to a television interview these days, some have one question: how much money can I make?

ABC and NBC, embroiled in a fight for viewers in the mornings, are increasingly in the news for their willingness to pay thousands of dollars to gain exclusive access to news subjects.

The practice was especially visible last week when ABC News ran an exclusive interview with Meagan Broussard, one of the women who was sent lewd photos by [New York Congressman] Anthony Weiner, after the network paid her about $15,000 for photos. ABC said its extensive reporting, including the interview, led to Mr. Weiner's admissions about his online behavior.

Also last week, ABC announced that Diane Sawyer had secured the first-ever interview with Jaycee Lee Dugard, the young woman held captive for 18 years in California. ABC declared that it had not paid any fee for the interview, but last year, according to a longtime ABC News executive aware of the deal, the network paid a six-figure sum for rights to home movies of Ms. Dugard.

The networks provide perks besides paychecks, too: When David Goldman, a subject in a custody battle over his son, brought his son back to the United States from Brazil last year, he was provided both a ride on a private jet by NBC and accommodations at Universal Studios, an amusement park partly owned by NBC's parent company.

Network representatives say their only payments are licensing fees for photographs and videos, not for interviews.

James Goldston, the executive producer of ABC's morning show, "Good Morning America," said the fees paid were relatively small and called the licensing "a very small part of the work that we do."

VANDERLEI ALMEIDA/AFP/Getty Images

NBC News provided a private jet for David Goldman to bring his son to the U.S. from Rio de Janeiro, Brazil, as well as accommodations at Universal Studios, an amusement park partly owned by NBC's parent company. Goldman, who was involved in a custody battle, gave NBC the first interviews about his son, an example of checkbook journalism.

In other interviews last week, the licensing distinction was glossed over—and even laughed at—by current and former network employees and executives, some of whom said the practice was at best a questionable breach of ethics.

"The real issue is: by paying for interviews, are you changing the news?" said David Westin, who was the president of ABC News until last winter, when many licensing deals were done. The economic tradeoff rarely makes sense, Mr. Westin said, in a time of budget and staff cuts at network news divisions.

"If you could prove that by spending $20,000 you would make $70,000, O.K., I can justify that," Mr. Westin said. "But I'll be doggone if you could go through any of those payments, trace them through and see if it made any sense."

The Poynter Institute, the journalism ethics group, said last week that the payments corrupted journalism. The group suggested that the trend could be reversed if networks would agree to pay license fees only to people not involved in the story, like eyewitnesses who happen to record a news event.

Star-Bulletin managing editor Bill Cox announced in a column published September 1, 1986, that he was going on disability leave because he had AIDS. "As a journalist," he wrote, "I have spent my career trying to shed light in dark corners. AIDS is surely one of our darkest corners. It can use some light." (For more information about privacy law and the media, see **Chapter 14**.)

Reporting on Rape

Privacy is an important issue in reporting on rape cases. Common newsroom practice forbids the naming of rape victims in stories. In 1989, editor Geneva Overholser of *The Des Moines Register* startled the press community when she wrote an editorial arguing that newspapers contribute to the public's misunderstanding of the crime by withholding not only the woman's name but an explicit description of what happened.

In 1990, *The Register* published a five-part series about the rape of Nancy Ziegenmeyer, with Ziegenmeyer's full cooperation. Ziegenmeyer had contacted *The Register* after Overholser's column appeared, volunteering to tell her story. The Ziegenmeyer series provoked wide-ranging debate among editors about this aspect of privacy. Is there more benefit to society by printing the victim's name, with the victim's permission, than by withholding it? Should the press explicitly describe sexual crimes, or is that merely sensationalism, preying on the public's salacious curiosity?

The Cohn, Liberace and Ziegenmeyer cases demonstrate how complex privacy issues in today's society have become. When is it in the public interest to divulge personal information about individuals? Who should decide?

David Peterson, 1990/*The Des Moines Register and Tribune Company*. Reprinted with permission.

In 1990, *The Des Moines Register* published Nancy Ziegenmeyer's name in a story about her rape, with Ziegenmeyer's cooperation. Publication of the victim's name sparked an ethical debate among news organizations about whether it is an invasion of privacy to use the victim's name in a rape story. While the names of adult victims of other crimes are used routinely in news stories, the names of rape victims commonly are not.

Responsibility Brings Trust

The events journalists choose to report and the way they use the information they gather reflect on the profession's sense of public responsibility. Most reporters realize that they often change the character of an event by covering that event. The mere presence of the media magnifies the importance of what happens.

A Staged Event

In October 2009, Richard and Mayumi Heene told authorities in Fort Collins, Colo., that they believed their young son Falcon was inside a runaway flying object that Richard Heene had designed. Reporters from all over the country rushed to cover the story. TV networks offered live coverage that showed video of the flying object (which resembled a small flying saucer). Soon, however, it was discovered that Falcon, who became known as "Balloon Boy," had never been in the flying object. Eventually the Heenes admitted the story was a hoax, designed to attract attention to the family in hopes of landing a reality TV show. This is example number 4 (on p. 337).

Two months later, the Heenes were sentenced to some jail time and community service work and ordered to pay for the expense of police chasing the balloon and investigating the hoax. The willingness of reporters to perpetuate the false story through their coverage pointed out how easily reporters can be fooled and how important it is for journalists to verify the information they report.

The media can be exploited by people in trouble or by people who covet the notoriety that media coverage brings. The media can exploit an event for its shock value to try to attract an audience, without adequately verifying the information in the story.

The staged event especially demonstrates the important responsibility that all members of the media share for what some of them do. The credibility of any news organization rests on the way the reporters get the story as much as on the story that's reported. Portraying inaccurate or staged information, even in just one story, ultimately causes readers and viewers to doubt the believability of all stories.

Sometimes reporters' rush to get a story or bad judgment causes serious mistakes to be aired or printed. During the

Media/Impact CULTURE

Bloomberg/Getty Images

News Corp. owner Rupert Murdoch (right) and James Murdoch, News Corp.'s Deputy Chief Operating Officer and Rupert Murdoch's son, testify before the British Parliament's Culture, Media and Sports Committee on July 19, 2011 about their role in a phone hacking scandal at News Corp.'s *News of the World*. This is an example of the legal and ethical consequences of invasion of privacy.

Murdoch Settles Suits by Dozens of Victims of Hacking

By Sarah Lyall and Ravi Somaiya

Note: In August 2011, the British Parliament's Committee on Culture, Media and Sport began an investigation into charges that reporters at the British newspaper News of the World *hacked into hudreds of private voicemail and email accounts of celebrities, government officials and citizens—a classic example of invasion of privacy. The company shut down the newspaper and in January 2012, News Corp. agreed to pay damages to 37 victims, and more than two dozen cases are still pending.*

LONDON—Rupert Murdoch's media empire has agreed to pay substantial damages to several dozen high-profile victims of phone and e-mail hacking, and lawyers for those victims said that they had seen documents showing that senior managers not only knew about the hacking but also lied about it and destroyed evidence as part of a cover-up.

The High Court hearing at which the settlements were detailed was a humiliating occasion for Mr. Murdoch's News Group Newspapers, which published the now-defunct tabloid at the heart of the hacking scandal, *The News of the World*. In a courtroom so jammed with lawyers, victims and members of the news media that some people had to sit on the floor, News Group's lawyer, Michael Silverleaf, repeatedly expressed the company's "sincere apologies" for "the damage, as well as the distress" caused to victim after victim.

The list of 37 victims settling with the company included politicians, celebrities, actors and sports figures, as well as people in their inner circles—employees, spouses, lovers. It is unclear how much News Group will end up having to pay after all the cases are finally settled, but the total bill for the 18 victims whose settlement details were disclosed Thursday reaches well above $1 million.

According to the police, there may be as many as 800 victims.

The settlements disclosed include those of the actor Jude Law, who received £130,000, about $200,000; Sadie Frost, his ex-wife, who received $77,000; Ben Jackson, his assistant, who received $61,000; Gavin Henson, a Welsh rugby star, who also received $61,000; and Denis MacShane, a member of Parliament, who received $50,000.

In each case, News Group also agreed to pay the complainant's legal costs, any of which could easily have run into six figures. One complainant, speaking on the condition on anonymity, said that his came to more than $300,000—an amount that does not include News International's fees.

Even for some of those who had settled, the matter was not over. "This is still only Act Four, Scene Four, of a five-act play," said Chris Bryant, a member of Parliament, who was awarded about $46,000 after his phone was hacked.

Tamsin Allen, a lawyer representing a number of the victims, said that it was their perseverance, even when News Group was aggressively denying that it had ever hacked anyone, that had led to the settlement.

"It is a credit to them, the claimants, that they kept on," she said, "because we have now discovered a massive conspiracy involving criminal activity and a cover-up."

From Sarah Lyall & Ravi Somaiya, "Murdoch Settles Suits by Dozens of Victims of Hacking," The New York Times, January 19, 2012.

2004 presidential election campaign, two incidents proved that even large news organizations aren't immune to serious journalistic lapses.

Fabricated Documents

On September 8, 2004, CBS News correspondent Dan Rather presented documents on the CBS program *60 Minutes* that purported to show there were gaps in President Bush's Vietnam-era Texas Air National Guard service. Almost immediately after the broadcast, questions arose about whether the documents were authentic, but for several days CBS and Rather stood by the report.

The documents were supposed to have come from the files of Bush's squadron commander, but then the man who gave the files to CBS admitted that he lied about where the documents came from. A week later, Rather, who also anchored the *CBS Evening News* at the time, apologized during the evening newscast. "I want to say personally and directly I'm sorry," he said. "This was an error made in good faith." CBS appointed a fact-finding panel, which launched a three-month investigation into why Rather's *60 Minutes* producers did not substantiate the information before airing the story.

In January 2005, the panel issued its report, which found, among other things, that the program's primary producer, Mary Mapes, did not scrutinize the background of the person who had provided the documents and that the segment's producers did not report that four experts who looked at the documents could not guarantee their authenticity. CBS fired Mapes and asked three other producers who had been involved in the report to resign.

Rather, who said he previously had considered stepping down as *CBS Evening News* anchor, was replaced, but stayed on as a correspondent. CBS then instituted new procedures that required independent review for investigative stories and appointed a new vice president for Standards and Practices, Linda Mason. "Standards are not an end in themselves," Mason told *The New York Times*. "Standards are a way we can achieve fairness and accuracy."

Phony Web Story

In October 2004, less than a month after the CBS incident, Fox News was forced to apologize to visitors to the Fox News Web site after Fox's chief political correspondent Carl Cameron posted a story that quoted presidential candidate John Kerry saying, "Didn't my nails and cuticles look great? What a good debate!" after his October televised debate with President Bush. "Women should like me! I do manicures," the story also quoted Kerry as saying.

Fox quickly retracted the article, and Paul Schur, a network spokesman, said, "This was a stupid mistake and a lapse in judgment, and Carl regrets it." Schur said Cameron had been reprimanded, but Schur did not explain how such an irresponsible story managed to escape review before it appeared on the Fox site.

All news organizations must accept responsibility for a lack of editorial review and oversight of stories that should have been stopped before they reach the public. In the CBS case, producers hurried to get the story on the air before checking it thoroughly. At Fox News, an errant reporter called the credibility of the entire news organization into question, but the news organization itself ultimately is at fault for its lack of safeguards. Responsible news organizations encourage ethical behavior as well as constantly remind reporters about their special responsibility to the public and to their profession.

Five Philosophical Principles Govern Media Ethics

Scholars can prescribe only general guidelines for moral decisions because each situation presents its own special dilemmas. First it is important to understand the basic principles that underlie these philosophical discussions. In their book *Media Ethics*, Clifford G. Christians, Kim B. Rotzoll and Mark Fackler identify five major philosophical principles underlying today's ethical decisions: (1) Aristotle's golden mean, (2) Kant's categorical imperative, (3) Mill's principle of utility, (4) Rawls' veil of ignorance and (5) the Judeo-Christian view of persons as ends in themselves.

1. *Aristotle's golden mean*: According to Aristotle, virtue is "the mean between two extremes." This is a philosophy of moderation and compromise, often called the *golden mean*. The journalistic concept of fairness reflects this idea.

2. *Kant's categorical imperative*: "Act on that maxim which you will to become a universal law." Eighteenth-century philosopher Immanuel Kant developed this idea, an extension of Aristotle's golden mean. Kant's test—that you make decisions based on principles that you want to be universally applied—is called the *categorical imperative*. This means you choose an action by asking yourself the question, What would happen if everyone acted this way?

3. *Mill's principle of utility*: "Seek the greatest happiness for the greatest number." In the 19th century, John Stuart Mill taught that the best decision is one with the biggest overall benefit for the most human beings.

4. *Rawls' veil of ignorance*: "Justice emerges when negotiating without social differentiations." John Rawls' 20th-century theory supports an egalitarian society that asks everyone to work from a sense of liberty and basic respect for everyone, regardless of social position.

GET ALL THE INFORMATION YOU CAN, WE'LL THINK OF A USE FOR IT LATER.
CHRIS
SLANE

CSL, CartoonStock Ltd

5. *Judeo-Christian view of persons as ends in themselves*: "Love your neighbor as yourself." Under this longstanding ethic of religious heritage, people should care for one another—friends as well as enemies—equally and without favor. Trust in people and they will trust in you.

In American society, none of these five philosophies operates independently. Ethical choices in many journalistic situations are not exquisitely simple. What is predictable about journalistic ethics is their unpredictability. Therefore, journalists generally adopt a philosophy of situational ethics: Because each circumstance is different, a journalist must decide the best action to take in each situation.

Should the press adopt Rawls' idea of social equality and cover each person equally, or should public officials receive more scrutiny than others because they maintain a public trust? Is it a loving act in the Judeo-Christian tradition to allow bereaved parents privacy to grieve for their child's death by drowning, or is the journalist contributing to society's greater good by warning others about the dangers of leaving a child unattended? Questions like these leave the press in a continually bubbling cauldron of ethical quandaries.

Media's Ethical Decisions Carry Consequences

Ethical dilemmas might seem easier to solve with a rule book nearby, and several professional media organizations have tried to codify ethical judgments to ensure the outcomes in difficult situations. Codes of ethics can be very general ("Truth is our ultimate goal"—Society of Professional Journalists); some are very specific ("We will no longer accept any complimentary tickets, dinners, junkets, gifts or favors of any kind"—*The San Bernardino* [Calif.] *Sun*); and some are very personal ("I will try to tell people what they ought to know and avoid telling them what they want to hear, except when the two coincide, which isn't often"—CBS commentator Andy Rooney).

Some ethical decisions carry legal consequences—for example, when a journalist reports embarrassing facts and invades someone's privacy. First Amendment protections shield the media from government enforcement of specific codes of conduct, except when ethical mistakes also are judged by the courts to be legal mistakes. In most cases, however, a reporter or a news organization that makes an ethical mistake will not face a lawsuit.

The consequences of bad ethical judgments usually involve damage to the newsmakers and to the individual journalist, damage to the reputation of the news organization where the journalist works, and damage to the profession in general.

NAB National Association of Broadcasters, the lobbying organization that represents broadcasters' interests.

Professional Associations Proscribe Behavior

Professional codes of ethics set a leadership tone for a profession, an organization or an individual. Several groups have attempted to write rules governing how the media should operate.

Television stations that belonged to the National Association of Broadcasters (***NAB***), for example, once subscribed to a code of conduct the NAB developed. This code covered news reporting and entertainment programming. One provision of the NAB code said, "Violence, physical or psychological, may only be projected in responsibly handled contexts, not used exploitatively. Programs involving violence should present the consequences of it to its victims and perpetrators." Members displayed the NAB Seal of Approval before broadcasts to exhibit their compliance with the code.

In 1976, a decision by a federal-court judge in Los Angeles abolished the broadcast codes, claiming the provisions violated the First Amendment. Today, codes of ethics for both print and broadcast are voluntary, with no absolute penalties for people who violate the rules. These codes are meant as guidelines. Many media organizations, such as CBS News, the *Los Angeles Times*, and *The New York Times*, maintain their own detailed standards and hire people specifically to monitor ethical conduct. Other organizations use guidelines from professional groups as a basis to develop their own philosophies. Advertising and public relations organizations also have issued ethics codes.

Three widely used codes of ethics are the guidelines adopted by the Society of Professional Journalists, the Radio Television Digital News Association and the Public Relations Society of America.

Society of Professional Journalists Outlines Conduct

This code lists specific canons for journalists. The code's major points follow.

Seek Truth and Report It. Journalists should be honest, fair and courageous in gathering, reporting and interpreting information. Journalists should:

- Test the accuracy of information from all sources and exercise care to avoid inadvertent error. Deliberate distortion is never permissible. . . .
- Identify sources whenever feasible. The public is entitled to as much information as possible on sources' reliability. . . .
- Make certain that headlines, news teases and promotional material, photos, video, audio, graphics, sound bites and quotations do not misrepresent. They should not oversimplify or highlight incidents out of context.
- Never distort the content of news photos or video. Image enhancement for technical clarity is always permissible. Label montages and photo illustrations.
- Avoid misleading reenactments or staged news events. . . .
- Never plagiarize. . . .
- Avoid stereotyping by race, gender, age, religion, ethnicity, geography, sexual orientation, disability, physical appearance or social status. . . .
- Distinguish between advocacy and news reporting. Analysis and commentary should be labeled and not misrepresent fact or context.
- Distinguish news from advertising and shun hybrids that blur the lines between the two.
- Recognize a special obligation to ensure that the public's business is conducted in the open and that government records are open to inspection.

Minimize Harm. Ethical journalists treat sources, subjects and colleagues as human beings deserving of respect. Journalists should:

- Show compassion for those who may be affected adversely by news coverage. Use special sensitivity when dealing with children and inexperienced sources or subjects.
- Be sensitive when seeking or using interviews or photographs of those affected by tragedy or grief.
- Recognize that gathering and reporting information may cause harm or discomfort. Pursuit of the news is not a license for arrogance. . . .
- Show good taste. Avoid pandering to lurid curiosity. . . .
- Balance a criminal suspect's fair trial rights with the public's right to be informed.

Act Independently. Journalists should be free of obligation to any interest other than the public's right to know. Journalists should:

- Avoid conflicts of interest, real or perceived.
- Remain free of associations and activities that may compromise integrity or damage credibility.
- Refuse gifts, favors, fees, free travel and special treatment, and shun secondary employment, political involvement, public office and service in community organizations if they compromise journalistic integrity. . . .

Be Accountable. Journalists are accountable to their readers, listeners, viewers and each other. Journalists should:

- Clarify and explain news coverage and invite dialogue with the public over journalistic conduct.
- Encourage the public to voice grievances against the news media.
- Admit mistakes and correct them promptly.
- Expose unethical practices of journalists and the news media.
- Abide by the same high standards to which they hold others.

Radio Television Digital News Association (RTDNA) Code Covers Electronic News

The RTDNA Code of Ethics and Professional Conduct, last updated in September 2000, offers general principles for electronic news reporters ("Professional electronic journalists should recognize that their first obligation is to the

Kevin C. Cox/Getty Images

Professional codes of ethics provide guidelines for how journalists should do their jobs. On January 9, 2011, reporters interview witness Joe Zamudio across the street from a Tucson, Ariz., shopping center where a gunman opened fire at a "Congress on Your Corner" event organized by U.S. Representative Gabrielle Giffords. Six people were killed and 14 others, including Giffords, were injured.

public"), as well as specific guidelines ("Professional electronic journalists should not manipulate images or sounds in any way that is misleading"). Following is the RTDNA ethics code, reprinted in its entirety.

PREAMBLE

Professional electronic journalists should operate as trustees of the public, seek the truth, report it fairly and with integrity and independence, and stand accountable for their actions.

PUBLIC TRUST: Professional electronic journalists should recognize that their first obligation is to the public.

Professional electronic journalists should:

- Understand that any commitment other than service to the public undermines trust and credibility.
- Recognize that service in the public interest creates an obligation to reflect the diversity of the community and guard against oversimplification of issues or events.
- Provide a full range of information to enable the public to make enlightened decisions.
- Fight to ensure that the public's business is conducted in public.

TRUTH: Professional electronic journalists should pursue truth aggressively and present the news accurately, in context, and as completely as possible.

Professional electronic journalists should:

- Continuously seek the truth.
- Resist distortions that obscure the importance of events.
- Clearly disclose the origin of information and label all material provided by outsiders.

Professional electronic journalists should not:

- Report anything known to be false.
- Manipulate images or sounds in any way that is misleading.
- Plagiarize.
- Present images or sounds that are reenacted without informing the public.

FAIRNESS: Professional electronic journalists should present the news fairly and impartially, placing primary value on significance and relevance.

Professional electronic journalists should:

- Treat all subjects of news coverage with respect and dignity, showing particular compassion to victims of crime or tragedy.
- Exercise special care when children are involved in a story and give children greater privacy protection than adults.
- Seek to understand the diversity of their community and inform the public without bias or stereotype.
- Present a diversity of expressions, opinions, and ideas in context.
- Present analytical reporting based on professional perspective, not personal bias.
- Respect the right to a fair trial.

INTEGRITY: Professional electronic journalists should present the news with integrity and decency, avoiding real or perceived conflicts of interest, and respect the dignity and intelligence of the audience as well as the subjects of news.

Professional electronic journalists should:

- Identify sources whenever possible. Confidential sources should be used only when it is clearly in the public interest to gather or convey important information or when a person providing information might be harmed. Journalists should keep all commitments to protect a confidential source.
- Clearly label opinion and commentary.
- Guard against extended coverage of events or individuals that fails to significantly advance a story, place the event in context, or add to the public knowledge.
- Refrain from contacting participants in violent situations while the situation is in progress.
- Use technological tools with skill and thoughtfulness, avoiding techniques that skew facts, distort reality, or sensationalize events.
- Use surreptitious newsgathering techniques, including hidden cameras or microphones, only if there is no other way to obtain stories of significant public importance and only if the technique is explained to the audience.
- Disseminate the private transmissions of other news organizations only with permission.

Professional electronic journalists should not:

- Pay news sources who have a vested interest in a story.
- Accept gifts, favors, or compensation from those who might seek to influence coverage.
- Engage in activities that may compromise their integrity or independence.

INDEPENDENCE: Professional electronic journalists should defend the independence of all journalists from those seeking influence or control over news content.

Professional electronic journalists should:

- Gather and report news without fear or favor, and vigorously resist undue influence from any outside forces, including advertisers, sources, story subjects, powerful individuals, and special interest groups.
- Resist those who would seek to buy or politically influence news content or who would seek to intimidate those who gather and disseminate the news.
- Determine news content solely through editorial judgment and not as the result of outside influence.
- Resist any self-interest or peer pressure that might erode journalistic duty and service to the public.
- Recognize that sponsorship of the news will not be used in any way to determine, restrict, or manipulate content.
- Refuse to allow the interests of ownership or management to influence news judgment and content inappropriately.
- Defend the rights of the free press for all journalists, recognizing that any professional or government licensing of journalists is a violation of that freedom.

ACCOUNTABILITY: Professional electronic journalists should recognize that they are accountable for their actions to the public, the profession, and themselves.

Professional electronic journalists should:

- Actively encourage adherence to these standards by all journalists and their employers.
- Respond to public concerns. Investigate complaints and correct errors promptly and with as much prominence as the original report.
- Explain journalistic processes to the public, especially when practices spark questions or controversy.
- Recognize that professional electronic journalists are duty-bound to conduct themselves ethically.
- Refrain from ordering or encouraging courses of action that would force employees to commit an unethical act.
- Carefully listen to employees who raise ethical objections and create environments in which such objections and discussions are encouraged.
- Seek support for and provide opportunities to train employees in ethical decision-making.

Public Relations Society of America Sets Standards

The Code of Professional Standards, first adopted in 1950 by the Public Relations Society of America, has been revised several times. Here are some excerpts:

- A member shall deal fairly with clients or employers, past, present, or potential, with fellow practitioners and with the general public.
- A member shall adhere to truth and accuracy and to generally accepted standards of good taste.
- A member shall not intentionally communicate false or misleading information, and is obligated to use care to avoid communication of false or misleading information.

- A member shall be prepared to identify publicly the name of the client or employer on whose behalf any public communication is made.
- A member shall not guarantee the achievement of specified results beyond the member's direct control.

Media Organizations Respond to Criticism

Prescriptive codes of ethics are helpful in describing what journalists should do, and informal guidelines can supplement professional codes. Many journalists use good judgment, but what happens when they don't? People with serious complaints against broadcasters sometimes appeal to the Federal Communications Commission, but what about complaints that must be handled more quickly? The press has offered three solutions: news councils, readers' representatives and correction boxes.

News Councils

News councils originated in Great Britain. They are composed of people who formerly worked or currently work in the news business, as well as some laypeople. The council reviews complaints from the public, and when the members determine that a mistake has been made, the council reports its findings to the offending news organization.

In 1973, the Twentieth-Century Fund established a National News Council in the United States, which eventually was funded through contributions from various news organizations. The council was composed of 18 members from the press and the public. The council was disbanded in 1984, largely because some major news organizations stopped giving money to support it but also because several news managers opposed the council, arguing that the profession should police itself.

Today, only two news councils exist in the United States, the Minnesota News Council and the Honolulu Community Media Council. The Minnesota council is older. Since 1970, the council's 24 members, half of them journalists and half of them public members such as lawyers and teachers, have reviewed complaints about the state's media. Half of the complaints have been ruled in favor of the journalists. The council has no enforcement power, only the power of public scrutiny.

Media ethics scholar John Hulteng offers this evaluation of news councils:

> It would seem that—as with the [ethics] codes—the great impact of the press councils is likely to be on the responsible editors, publishers and broadcasters who for the most part were already attempting to behave ethically. . . . An additional value of the councils may be the mutual understanding that grows out of the exchange across the council table between the members of the public and the managers of the media. These values should not be dismissed as insignificant, of course. But neither should too much be expected of them.

Readers' Representatives

The *readers' representative* (also called an ombudsperson or public reporter) is a go-between at a newspaper who responds to complaints from the public and regularly publishes answers to criticism in the newspaper.

About two dozen newspapers throughout the country, including *The Washington Post*, *The New York* Times, *The Kansas City Star* and the Louisville *Courier-Journal*, have tried the idea, but most newspapers still funnel complaints directly to the editor.

The *Los Angeles Times* publishes a regular blog called *Readers' Representative Journal*, which the newspaper says is designed to "help readers understand the thinking behind what appears in the *Times*, and to provide insight for the newsroom into how readers respond to their reporting."

Correction Boxes

The *correction box* is a device that often is handled by a readers' representative but also has been adopted by many papers without a readers' representative. The box is published in the same place, usually a prominent one, in the newspaper every day and on the newspaper's Web site with the corrected story and a note about the correction.

As a permanent feature of the newspaper, the correction box leads readers to notice when the newspaper retracts or modifies a statement. It is used to counter criticism that corrections sometimes receive less attention from readers than the original stories.

The New York Times, for example, regularly publishes a small correction box to fix small errors in its stories. But when *The Times* discovered in 2010 that its reporter Zachery Kouwe had plagiarized stories from *The Wall Street Journal* (see p. 337), *The Times* published a specific explanation as a lengthy Editor's Note, which gave the incident more prominent attention.

Professional Ethics Preserve Media Credibility

News councils, readers' representatives and correction boxes help newspapers handle criticism and avert possible legal problems that some stories foster, but these solutions address only a small percentage of issues and only for print journalism. In newsrooms every day, reporters face the same ethical decisions all people face in their daily lives—whether to be honest, how to be fair, how to be sensitive and how to be responsible.

The difference is that, unlike personal ethical dilemmas that people can debate privately, reporters and editors publish and broadcast the results of their ethical judgments, and those judgments become public knowledge—in newspapers, magazines and books and on radio, television and the Internet. So the media's ethical decisions have the potential to affect society.

A profession that accepts ethical behavior as a standard helps guarantee its future. The major commodity the press in America has to offer is information, and when the presentation of that information is weakened by untruth, bias, intrusiveness or irresponsibility, the press gains few advocates and acquires more enemies. Writes John Hulteng:

> The primary objective of the press and those who work with it is to bring readers, listeners and viewers as honest, accurate and complete an account of the day's events as possible. . . . The need to be informed is so great that the Constitution provides the press with a First Amendment standing that is unique among business enterprises. But as with most grants of power, there is an accompanying responsibility, not constitutionally mandated but nonetheless well understood: that the power of the press must be used responsibly and compassionately.

Review, Analyze, Investigate

REVIEWING CHAPTER 15

Ethics Define Responsibilities

- ✓ The word *ethics* derives from the Greek word *ethos*, which means the guiding spirit or traditions that govern a culture.
- ✓ When journalists make the wrong ethical choices, the consequences are very public.
- ✓ Journalists' ethical dilemmas can be discussed using four categories: truthfulness, fairness, privacy and responsibility.

Truthfulness Affects Credibility

- ✓ Truthfulness means more than telling the truth to get a story. Truthfulness also means not misrepresenting the people or the situations in the story for readers or viewers.
- ✓ Syndicated columnist Armstrong Williams received $250,000 from a public relations firm to promote President Bush's No Child Left Behind initiative to African Americans. In 2005, after *USA Today* revealed the arrangement, Williams attributed his lapse to the fact that he was not trained as a journalist.
- ✓ Truthfulness means that government agencies should not knowingly provide disinformation to the press.
- ✓ Disinformation was the issue at the 2007 trial of presidential advisor I. Lewis Libby.
- ✓ In 2010, *The New York Times* suspended reporter Zachery Kouwe after editors said Kouwe had plagiarized portions of an article he had written for *The Times* from an article by another reporter that had appeared online in *The Wall Street Journal*. Kouwe resigned.
- ✓ In 2009, Universal Pictures posted fake stories purported to be from Alaska news publications to promote its movie *The Fourth Kind*. When the fabrications were discovered, Universal paid the Alaska Press Club a $20,000 settlement.
- ✓ In 2006, author James Frey admitted he had fabricated many incidents in his memoir *A Million Little Pieces*. Frey apologized.
- ✓ A classic example of a journalistic misrepresentation is Jayson Blair, a reporter for *The New York Times*, who admitted in May 2003 that he had fabricated comments, concocted scenes, stolen material from other newspapers and news services and selected details from photos to create an impression he had been in certain places and interviewed people when he hadn't.

Fairness Means Evenhandedness

- ✓ Fairness implies impartiality—that the journalist has nothing personal to gain from a report and that there are no hidden benefits to the reporter or to the source from the story being presented.
- ✓ Criticism of the press for unfairness results from insider friendships, conflicts of interest and checkbook journalism.
- ✓ As examples of insider friendships, in 2010, MSNBC commentators Keith Olbermann and Joe Scarborough each were suspended for two days after it was discovered that they had made campaign contributions to political candidates.
- ✓ In another example of insider friendship, in 2010, the *New Hampshire Union Leader* accepted underwriting from three major New Hampshire businesses including

BAE Systems, a defense contractor, so the newspaper's publisher and a staff photographer could travel to Afghanistan to report on a New Hampshire National Guard unit serving there.

✓ In 2009, *The Washington Post* lost credibility when its publisher invited sponsorships in exchange for attendance at an exclusive "salon" at her home. *The Post* eventually cancelled the event and printed an apology.

✓ In 2011, ABC News paid kidnapping victim Jaycee Lee Dugard for exclusive rights to an interview, an example of checkbook journalism.

Privacy Involves Respect

✓ Privacy for personal communications such as emails and voicemails became a big issue in 2011 when reporters at Rupert Murdoch's *News of the World* hacked celebrity emails and voicemails.

✓ An important invasion-of-privacy issue is the publication of names of AIDS victims and rape victims.

✓ Reporters must decide whether the public interest will be served by revealing these names.

Responsibility Brings Trust

✓ Responsibility means that reporters and editors must be careful about the way they use the information they gather.

✓ Live events, such as the "Balloon Boy" hoax, offer especially perilous ethical situations for reporters because they must verify information quickly and are vulnerable to mistakes.

✓ During the 2004 presidential campaign, CBS's *60 Minutes*' undocumented report of President Bush's Air National Guard service and Fox News's phony report about presidential candidate Senator John Kerry are two examples of news organizations forgetting their responsibilities to the public.

Five Philosophical Principles Govern Media Ethics

✓ Five philosophical principles underlying the practical application of ethical decisions are (1) Aristotle's golden mean, (2) Immanuel Kant's categorical imperative, (3) John Stuart Mill's principle of utility, (4) John Rawls' veil of ignorance and (5) the Judeo-Christian view of persons as ends in themselves.

✓ Journalists adopt a philosophy of situational ethics.

Media's Ethical Decisions Carry Consequences

✓ Some ethical decisions carry legal consequences, such as when a journalist reports embarrassing facts and invades someone's privacy.

✓ In most cases, a reporter or a news organization that makes an ethical mistake will not face a lawsuit.

Professional Associations Proscribe Behavior

✓ Several media professions have adopted ethics codes to guide their conduct.

✓ Three of these ethics codes are the guidelines adopted by the Society of Professional Journalists, the Radio Television Digital News Association and the Public Relations Society of America.

Media Organizations Respond to Criticism

✓ The three responses of the U.S. press to criticism have been to create news councils, to employ readers' representatives and to publish correction boxes in the printed newspaper and online.

✓ The National Press Council, created to hear consumer complaints about the press, was created in 1973 but disbanded in 1984. Today only two news councils still exist in the United States—the Minnesota News Council and the Honolulu Community Media Council.

Professional Ethics Preserve Media Credibility

✓ The media's ethical decisions can broadly affect society.

✓ The major commodity the American press has to offer is credibility, and when the presentation of information is weakened by untruth, bias, intrusiveness or irresponsibility, the press gains few advocates and acquires more enemies.

KEY TERMS

These terms are defined in the margins throughout this chapter and appear in alphabetical order with definitions in the Glossary, which begins on page 383.

Checkbook Journalism 342
Disinformation 339
Ethics 336
NAB 348
Professional Ethics 336

CRITICAL QUESTIONS

1. When you read about high-profile media ethics cases like the ones in this chapter, do you ever think about the possibility that what you're reading, hearing or seeing in the mass media may not be true, or at least not what you understand it to be? How does this affect the way you obtain or use information?

2. How does checkbook journalism affect the quality of reporting?

3. Pick any of the ethical situations specified in this chapter and describe how each of the following philosophical principles would define your decision.
   a. Aristotle's golden mean
   b. Kant's categorical imperative
   c. Mill's principle of utility
   d. Rawls' veil of ignorance

4. What is your opinion about the question in the Ziegenmeyer case of releasing the name of a victim of rape with the victim's consent? How would you balance the protection of victims with the public's interest in the non-anonymous comments of the victim? Should rape victims be more deserving of anonymity than victims of other crimes? Explain.

5. What effect do you believe ethics codes, such as those described in this chapter, have on the professionals for whom they have been developed?

WORKING THE WEB

This list includes both sites mentioned in the chapter and others to give you greater insight into media ethics.

Columbia Journalism Review (CJR)

http://www.cjr.org

The mission of this publication from Columbia University Graduate School of Journalism is "to encourage and stimulate excellence in journalism in the service of a free society." The Web site's search capabilities allow users to access all past posts from *CJRDaily.org* and Campaign Desk (political journalism coverage), as well as back issues (http://backissues.cjrarchives.org). Its resources include "Who Owns What," a guide to what the major media companies own; "Language Corner," a guide to writing in English; and CJR study guides for journalism students. The site promises fresh media analysis and criticism every day as well as specials and interactive features about the performance and problems of the press.

EthicNet, European Ethics Codes

http://ethicnet.uta.fi/

This databank holds links to English translations of journalism codes of ethics from most European countries (maintained by the Department of Journalism and Mass Communication, University of Tampere, Finland). There are also links to press councils' Web sites, Ethics on the World Wide Web from California State University at Fullerton (http://ethicnet.uta.fi/links).

Fairness & Accuracy in Reporting (FAIR)

http://www.fair.org/index.php

This national media watch group offers "well-documented criticism of media bias and censorship." An anticensorship organization, FAIR is a progressive group that believes structural reform is needed to promote strong nonprofit sources of information. FAIR's critique of the current state of the media is explained in its overview, "What's Wrong with the News?" Viewers can browse archived articles on issues from Abortion to Youth.

Freedom Forum

http://www.freedomforum.org

This nonpartisan foundation is dedicated to "free press, free speech and free spirit for all people." The Freedom Forum is the main funder of the Newseum, an interactive museum of news in Washington, D.C. (http://www.newseum.org); the First Amendment Center, which features current news and commentary as well as a First Amendment glossary and lesson plans (http://www.firstamendmentcenter.org); and the Diversity Institute, based at the John Seigenthaler Center at Vanderbilt University in Nashville, Tenn., dedicated to developing and retaining a diverse workforce in U.S. newsrooms (http://freedomforumdiversity.org).

Indiana University Index of Journalism Ethics Cases

http://journalism.indiana.edu/resources/ethics/

This set of cases was created to help teachers, researchers, professional journalists and consumers of news explore ethical issues of journalism. The issues include sensitive news topics, covering politics, invading privacy and being first.

Minnesota News Council

http://news-council.org

Based on the British Press Council (now the Press Complaints Commission), the News Council has 24 members, half journalists and half laypeople who hear complaints against news organizations. The Web site contains past articles from the Council's *Newsworthy* magazine, a monthly electronic newsletter—*Newsworthy Online*—and a long list of links to various ethics resources.

Poynter Online

http://www.poynter.org

This Web site of the St. Petersburg, Fla., center for journalists, future journalists and journalism teachers features news and tips for students about reporting and writing, ethics and diversity, journalism education and more. The training section includes information on seminars and webinars, career coaching and Poynter publications. Users can connect with an online community of groups based on various journalism topics.

Project for Excellence in Journalism: Ethics Codes

http://www.journalism.org/resources/ethics_codes

This is a direct Web link to a list of professional ethics codes used throughout various media industries in the U.S. and Europe. Includes sites for specific U.S. news organizations (such as the *Los Angeles Times*, *The New York Times*, the *Detroit Free Press*, and the Corporation for Public Broadcasting) as well as international ethics codes, such as the BBC Editorial Guidelines and the International Federation of Journalists' Declaration of Principles on the Conduct of Journalists.

Radio Television Digital News Association (RTDNA; formerly Radio-Television News Directors Association)

http://www.rtdna.org

RTDNA is a professional organization that serves the electronic news profession. Its membership consists of more than 3,000 news directors, associates, educators and students. The association's educational arm, RTDNF, was created to help members uphold ethical journalism standards in the newsroom. Ethics information—including the association's Code of Ethics and Professional Conduct, details on the Journalism Ethics Project, and coverage guidelines—is available in the Web site's Best Practices section.

Society of Professional Journalists (SPJ)

http://www.spj.org

The nation's most broad-based journalism organization, SPJ is dedicated to "encouraging the free practice of journalism and stimulating high standards of ethical behavior." Features include freedom of information; ethics (including the SPJ Code of Ethics); *Rainbow Diversity Sourcebook*, *Journalists Toolbox*, SPJ blogs and other publications including the current issue of the association's online magazine *Quill*.

Impact/Action Videos are concise news features on topics covered in this chapter, created exclusively for **Media/Impact**. They are available for students and instructors at CengageBrain.com, and include screen access for classroom viewing and discussion questions.

16

"Policy and regulatory frameworks [for communications] should allow new technologies to contribute everything they have to offer."

—The World Bank, 2010

Global Media: Discovering New Markets

What's Ahead?

- World Media Systems Vary
- Five Political Theories Describe How World Media Operate
- Western Europe and Canada Are Similar to the United States
- Eastern Europe Is in Transition
- Middle Eastern and North African Media Work Under Government Controls
- African Media Find a New Voice
- Media Explode in Asia and the Pacific
- Government, Large Corporations and Family Dynasties Control Latin American and Caribbean Media
- *International Herald Tribune* Seeks a Global Audience
- Critics Cite Western Communications Bias
- Internet Expands Media's Global Reach
- Cell Phones Open Communications Channels
- Reporters Risk Their Lives to Report World Events
- Global Media Chase International Consumers
- Ideas Transcend Borders

Photo by Shirley Biagi

American mass media, especially movies, are very popular in Europe and usually are released simultaneously in the U.S. and overseas. In August 2011, an ad on the side of a double-decker bus for the American movie *Cowboys and Aliens* promotes the film in front of London's Paddington Station.

Dan Kitwood/Getty Images

In Britain, people pay an annual license fee to support the British Broadcasting Corporation (BBC). In Birmingham, England, on October 2010, Foreign Secretary William Hague is interviewed on BBC Radio.

In the United States,

many students assume that mass media in most countries operate like the U.S. media, but media industries in different countries are as varied as the countries they serve. Can you identify the countries in the following media situations?

1. People in this country have access to more wireless Internet ***hot spots*** than anywhere else in the world. (A hot spot is a public area like a restaurant or hotel where a wireless Internet router allows people with laptops and hand-held Internet devices, such as smartphones, to use the Internet without a wired connection.)
2. In this country, a weekly TV game show features people eating overly spicy foods. The champion is dubbed Super Spiciness King.
3. This country's president shut down the nation's oldest broadcast station in 2010 because the station did not televise his long speeches in their entirety.
4. This country's TV license police can knock on people's doors, fine them approximately $250 and threaten them with jail if they don't pay the annual TV license fee.

Hot Spot A public area like a restaurant or hotel where people with laptops and hand-held Internet devices can connect to the Internet without a wire.

World Media Systems Vary

The country in the world with the largest number of wireless locations is the United States, according to JiWire, a leading hot spot directory. (See **Illustration 16.1**, p. 375.) In the U.S., the city with the most wireless locations (hot spots) is Brooklyn, New York, with 1,517—about three times the number of hot spots that are available in Los Angeles (551).

The TV game show with the spicy foods (example 2) is very popular in Japan, where *TV Champion* is one of several shows in which contestants vie for modest prizes and national attention by showing *gaman*, or endurance.

The station that was forced off the air is Venezuela's RCTV, shut down by President Hugo Chávez in January 2010. Cable providers took the station off the air shortly past midnight on January 24, 2010, after RCTV did not broadcast a long speech by Chávez at a pro-government rally. "There are some that take pleasure in challenging the government," Chávez said. "If they do not follow the law, they have to go. But it's their decision, not ours."

People who live in the United Kingdom are responsible for paying a yearly TV license fee (example 4). The fee is due at the post office each year, so the collectors who fine people who haven't paid the fee are actually members of the post office. The government collects more than $2 billion a year from the fees, which allows the British Broadcasting Corporation to operate several radio and TV stations without advertising.

These examples help demonstrate the complexity of defining today's international media marketplace, which clearly is a marketplace in rapid transition. This chapter examines various aspects of global media, including political theories and the media, world media systems, news and information flow, and global media markets.

Five Political Theories Describe How World Media Operate

No institution as sizable and influential as the mass media can escape involvement with government and politics.

The media are not only channels for the transmission of political information and debate but also significant players with a direct stake in government's regulatory and economic policies, as well as government's attitude toward free speech and dissent.

Remember that *the way a country's political system is organized affects the way the mass media within that country operate.* Media systems can be divided broadly into those systems that allow dissent and those that do not.

To categorize the political organization of media systems, scholars often begin with the 1956 book *Four Theories of the Press*, by Fred S. Siebert, Theodore Peterson and Wilbur Schramm. These four theories, which originally were used to describe the political systems under which media operated in different countries, were (1) the Soviet theory, (2) the authoritarian theory, (3) the libertarian theory and (4) the social responsibility theory. Scholars recently added a fifth description, the more modern (5) developmental theory, to update the original categories used to help describe the world's mass media systems.

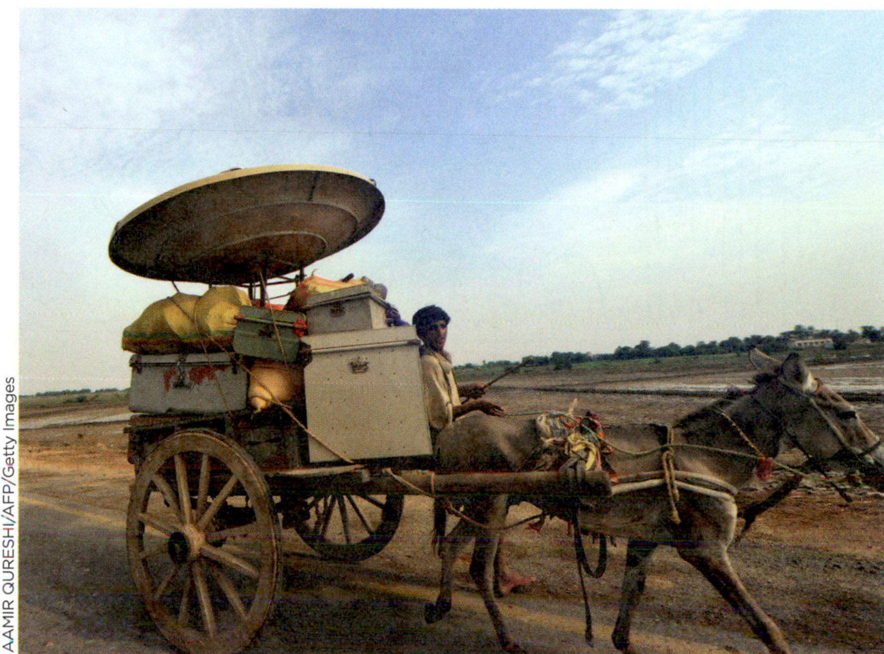

AAMIR QURESHI/AFP/Getty Images

The political theory that best describes the way the media in Pakistan operate is the developmental theory. On August 15, 2010, a Pakistani flood victim has loaded his possessions, including a satellite dish, on a cart.

The Soviet Theory

Historically in the Soviet Union (which dissolved in 1991 into several independent nations and states), the government owned and operated the mass media. All media employees were government employees, expected to serve the government's interests.

Top media executives also served as leaders in the Communist Party. Even when the press controls loosened in the 1980s, the mass media were part of the government's policy. Government control came *before* the media published or broadcast; people who controlled the media could exercise *prior restraint*. They could review copy and look at programs before they appeared.

This description of the Soviet press system was conceived before the events of the 1990s challenged the basic assumptions of Soviet government. Many Eastern bloc countries, such as Romania, Slovakia and the Czech Republic, which once operated under Soviet influence, based their media systems on the Communist model. Today, the media systems in these countries are in transition.

The Authoritarian Theory

Media that operate under the authoritarian theory can be either publicly or privately owned. This concept of the press developed in Europe after Gutenberg. Until the 1850s, presses in Europe were privately owned, and the aristocracy (which governed the countries) wanted some sort of control over what was printed about them. The aristocracy had the financial and political power necessary to make the rules about what would be printed.

The first idea was to license everyone who owned a printing press so the license could be revoked if someone published something unfavorable about the government. The British crown licensed the first colonial newspapers in America. Licensing wasn't very successful in the United States, however, because many people who owned presses didn't apply for licenses.

The next authoritarian attempt to control the press was to review material after it was published. A printer who was discovered publishing material that strongly challenged the government could be heavily fined or even put to death. Today, many governments still maintain this type of rigid control over the media. Most monarchies, for example, operate in an authoritarian tradition, which tolerates very little dissent. Media systems that serve at the government's pleasure and with the government's approval are common.

The Libertarian Theory

The concept of a libertarian press evolved from the idea that people who are given all the information on an issue will be able to discern what is true and what is false and will make

"Responding to viewer sentiment, we have eliminated world news and expanded our entertainment and sports news."

CSL, CartoonStock Ltd

good choices. This is an idea embraced by the writers of the U.S. Constitution and by other democratic governments.

This theory assumes, of course, that the media's main goal is to convey the truth and that the media will not cave in to outside pressures, such as from advertisers or corporate owners. This theory also assumes that people with opposing viewpoints will be heard—that the media will present all points of view, in what is commonly called the free marketplace of ideas.

The First Amendment to the U.S. Constitution concisely advocates the idea of freedom of the press. Theoretically, America today operates under the libertarian theory, although this ideal has been challenged often by changes in the media industries since the Constitution was adopted.

The Social Responsibility Theory

This theory accepts the concept of a libertarian press but prescribes what the media should do. Someone who believes in the social responsibility theory believes that members of the press will do their jobs well only if periodically reminded about their duties. The theory grew out of the 1947 Hutchins Commission Report on the Free and Responsible Press. The commission listed five goals for the press, including the need for truthful and complete reporting of all sides of an issue.

The commission concluded that the American press's privileged position in the Constitution means that the press must always work to be responsible to society.

If the media fail to meet their responsibilities to society, the social responsibility theory holds that the government should encourage the media to comply. In this way, the libertarian and the social responsibility theories differ. The libertarian theory assumes the media will work well without government interference; the social responsibility theory advocates government oversight for media that don't act in society's best interest.

The Developmental Theory

The most recent description for media systems is the developmental or Third World theory. Under this theory, named for the developing nations where it is most often found, the media *can* be privately owned but usually are owned by the government.

The mass media in the developmental category are used to promote the country's social and economic goals and to direct a sense of national purpose. For example, a developmental media system might be used to promote birth control or to encourage children to attend school. The media are an outlet for some types of government propaganda, then, but in the name of economic and social progress, as defined by the government.

Although the theory that best describes the American media is the libertarian theory, throughout their history the American media have struggled with both authoritarian and social responsibility debates: Should the press be free to print secret government documents, for example? What responsibility do television networks have to provide worthwhile programming to their audiences? The media, the government and the public continually modify and adjust their interpretations of just how the media should operate.

It has been nearly six decades since scholars began using the political theories of the press to define the world's media systems. With today's transitional period in global history, even the recent addition of the developmental theory still leaves many media systems beyond convenient categorization.

Media systems vary throughout the world. The print media form the basis for press systems that developed in North America, Australia, Western Europe and Eastern Europe—where two-thirds of the world's newspapers are published. Many developing countries matured after broadcast media were introduced in the 1920s, and newsprint in these countries often is scarce or government-controlled, making radio their dominant communications medium. Radio receivers are inexpensive, and many people can share one radio.

Television, which relies on expensive equipment, is widely used in prosperous nations and in developing countries' urban areas. Yet many countries still have only one television service, usually run by the government. In many developing countries, all broadcasting—television and radio—is owned and controlled by the government.

The Internet is blurring international media borders because it is very difficult to control the flow of digital information across geographical and ideological boundaries, although some countries try.

What follows is a description of today's media systems by geographic region: Western Europe and Canada; Eastern Europe; the Middle East and North Africa; Africa; Asia and the Pacific; and Latin America and the Caribbean.

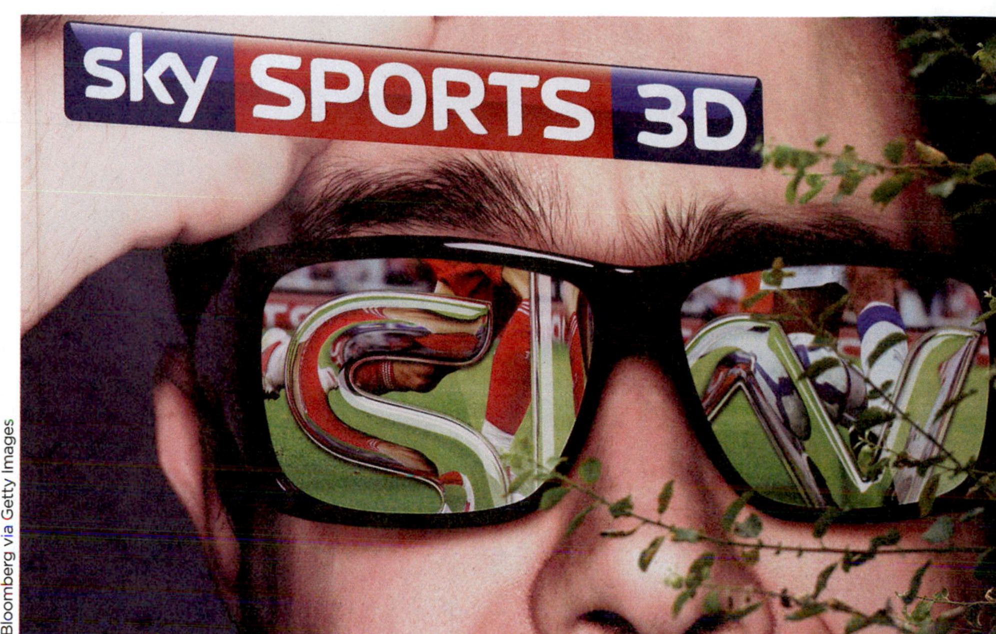

Bloomberg via Getty Images

In Western Europe—where the print media, including newspapers, are more popular than broadcasts—people watch half as much television as people in the United States. Like the United States, however, sports programming is very popular TV entertainment. An ad for British Sky Broadcasting promotes 3-D sports on television.

Western Europe and Canada Are Similar to the United States

Western European and Canadian media prosper under guarantees of freedom of expression similar to the First Amendment, but each nation has modified the idea to reflect its values. For example, in Great Britain the media are prohibited from commenting on a trial until the trial is finished, and in 2003, Britain banned all tobacco advertising in newspapers, on billboards and on the Internet.

France and Greece, unlike the United States, give more libel protection to public figures than to private citizens. Scandinavian journalists enjoy the widest press freedoms of all of Western Europe, including almost unlimited access to public documents.

Of the Western nations, Canada is the most recent country to issue an official decree supporting the philosophy of press freedom. In 1982, Canada adopted the Canadian Charter of Rights and Freedoms. Before 1982, Canada did not have its own constitution and instead operated under the 1867 British North America Act, sharing the British free press philosophy. In 2010, however, Canada's Supreme Court ruled that Canadian reporters do not have a constitutional right to offer their sources blanket confidentiality. Like the U.S., Canada does not have a national shield law. (See p. 317, **Chapter 14**.)

Print Media

Johannes Gutenberg's invention of movable type rooted the print media in Western Europe. Today, Western European and Canadian media companies produce many fine newspapers. *The Globe and Mail* of Toronto, *The Times* of London, *Frankfurter Allgemeine* of Germany, *Le Monde* of France and Milan's *Corriere della Sera* enjoy healthy circulations.

Whereas Canadian journalists have adopted the U.S. values of fairness and balance as a journalistic ethic, Western European newspapers tend to be much more partisan than the U.S. or Canadian press, and newspapers (and journalists) are expected to reflect strong points of view.

Broadcast Media

As in the United States, the print media in Western Europe are losing audiences to broadcast and cable. Government originally controlled most of Western Europe's broadcast stations. A board of governors, appointed by the queen, supervises the British Broadcasting Corporation (***BBC***), for example.

BBC British Broadcasting Corporation, the government-funded British broadcast network.

MANDEL NGAN/AFP/Getty Images

In Eastern Europe, mass media have begun to cover Western leaders when they visit. In Kosovo on October 13, 2010, Nebi Qena of Associated Press (middle) and Anamari Repic of Radio Television Kosovo interview U.S. Secretary of State Hillary Clinton in Pristina, Kosovo, during a diplomatic visit.

To finance the government-run broadcast media, countries like the United Kingdom tax the sale of radios and TVs or charge users an annual license fee, which funds the broadcasts. The BBC collects 3.6 billion pounds annually in license fees, but in 2010, because of government budget cuts, the BBC governing board reduced staff positions and proposed cuts to employee pensions. The BBC's 4,100 reporters, who are members of the National Union of Journalists, announced a series of 48-hour strikes in protest, and BBC management was forced to replace scheduled live shows with pre-recorded programs during the strikes.

ITV is the largest commercial network in the United Kingdom, with four separate channels. ITV is a "public service broadcaster," which means the network is required to offer public service programming and is regulated by the government, but the channels are very similar to commercial networks in the U.S.

Western Europeans watch about half as much television as people in the United States—an average of three hours a day per household in Europe, compared with seven hours a day per household in the United States. One reason for the difference in viewing time may be that some Western European TV stations don't go on the air until late afternoon. In the majority of countries, commercials are shown back to back at the beginning or the end of a program.

Europe gets much of its programming from the United States. Of the 125,000 hours of TV broadcast in Western Europe each year, less than half are produced in Europe. Many of the programs come from America, with a few shows imported from Australia and Japan. U.S. imports are attractive because buying U.S. programs is cheaper than producing new programming within the country.

The European Union (EU) constitutes a single, unified European market. The policy adopted by the EU is Television Without Frontiers, which promotes an open marketplace for television programs among countries in the EU and between EU countries and the United States.

Some members of the EU (especially France) have proposed quotas to limit imported TV programs, charging that U.S. imports are an example of "cultural imperialism." Countries that favor quotas fear that the importation of U.S. programs imposes a concentration of U.S. values on their viewers.

The United States opposes such quotas, of course, because Western European commercial broadcasting offers a seemingly insatiable market for recycled U.S. programs. Broadcasting in Western Europe is slowly evolving to private ownership and commercial sponsorship.

Eastern Europe Is in Transition

The democratization of Eastern Europe is transforming the print and broadcast media in these countries at an unprecedented pace. Everette E. Dennis, executive director of the Gannett Center for Media Studies, and Jon Vanden Heuvel described the Eastern European challenges in a report issued after a Gannett-sponsored fact-finding trip: "Mass communication in the several countries of the region was reinventing itself. While grassroots newspapers and magazines struggled for survival, new press laws were being debated and enacted; elements of a market economy were coming into view; the media system itself and its role in the state and society were being redefined, as was the very nature of journalism and the job description of the journalist, who was no longer a propagandist for the state."

Eastern Europe today is in transition, defining a new balance between a desire for free expression and the indigenous remnants of government-controlled systems. In many of these countries, mass media played a central role in upsetting the established power structure. Often one of the first targets of the revolutionary movements is a nation's broadcast facilities.

For example, in Romania in 1989, opposition leaders of the National Salvation Committee and sympathetic employees barricaded themselves in a Bucharest TV station, rallying the audience to action. "Romania was governed from a hectic studio littered with empty bottles, cracked coffee mugs and half-eaten sandwiches, and run by people who had not slept in days," the Associated Press reported.

Print Media

Print media were strictly controlled under Communism, with high-ranking party officials forming the core of media management. Because paper supplies were limited, newspapers rarely exceeded 12 pages. Revolutionary leader Vladimir Lenin, who said a newspaper should be a "collective propagandist," a "collective agitator" and a "collective organizer," founded *Pravda*, the Soviet Union's oldest newspaper, in 1912. The Eastern European nations developed their press policies following the Soviet model.

In the late 1980s, Soviet President Mikhail Gorbachev relaxed media controls as part of his policy of *glasnost*. In 1988, the first paid commercials (for Pepsi-Cola, Sony and Visa credit cards) appeared on Soviet TV, and in 1989, the Soviet daily newspaper *Izvestia* published its first Western ads (including ads for perfume and wines from the French firm Pechiney and for Dresdner, a German bank).

In 1990, the Supreme Soviet, the legislative body, outlawed media censorship and gave every citizen the right to publish a newspaper. Within five months, more than 100 newspapers began publication. Then, showing how quickly government positions can change, in early 1991, Gorbachev asked the Supreme Soviet to suspend these press freedoms, but they refused. Less than a year later, Gorbachev's successor, President Boris Yeltsin, again began to relax government control of the press. In 1996, facing bankruptcy, *Pravda* ceased publication.

Today Russian officials, such as Prime Minister Vladimir Putin, maintain a tight rein on the press, and several reporters who have written critically about the government have been brutally injured or killed, although the government disavows any connection to the attacks. (See **Media/Impact: People**, "Beaten Russian Reporter Mikhail Beketov Convicted of Slander," p. 366.) Putin "thinks that democracy stands in his way," former Soviet leader Mikhail S. Gorbachev told *The New York Times* in an interview published on October 26, 2010. "I am afraid that they [Prime Minister Putin and President Dmitri A. Medvedev] have been saddled with this idea that this unmanageable country needs authoritarianism. They think they cannot do without it."

Broadcast Media

Television in the Eastern bloc countries developed under Communist direction because the Communist governments were in power before TV use was widespread. Radio broadcasting also was tightly controlled, although foreign broadcasts directed across Eastern European borders, such as Voice of America and Radio Free Europe, usually evaded jamming attempts by Radio Moscow. Today Eastern Europe is creating a new media environment.

As Eastern European governments change and realign themselves, the adjustments facing Eastern European media are unprecedented. According to Everette E. Dennis and Jon Vanden Heuvel: "Once the revolution came, among the first acts of new government was to take (they would say liberate) electronic media and open up the print press. Permitting free and eventually independent media was a vital beginning for democracy in several countries and a clear break with the past. The freeing up of the media system, speedily in some countries and incrementally in others, was the lifting of an ideological veil without saying just what would replace it."

Middle Eastern and North African Media Work Under Government Controls

Press history in the Middle East and North Africa begins with the newspaper *Al-Iraq*, first published in 1817, although the first *daily* newspaper didn't begin publishing until 1873. With one exception, development of the press throughout this region follows the same pattern as in most developing countries: More newspapers and magazines are published in regions with high literacy rates than in regions with low literacy rates.

The exception is Egypt, where less than half the people are literate. Yet Cairo is the Arab world's publishing center. *Al Ahram* and *Al Akhbar* are Egypt's leading government-controlled daily newspapers.

Print Media

The Middle Eastern press is tightly controlled by government restrictions, through ownership and licensing, and it is not uncommon for opposition newspapers to disappear and for journalists to be jailed or to leave the country following political upheaval.

According to global media scholar Christine Ogan, "Following the revolution in Iran, all opposition and some moderate newspapers were closed, and according to the National Union of Iranian Journalists (now an illegal organization), more than 75 percent of all journalists left the country, were jailed, or no longer work in journalism." The Palestinian

Media/Impact
PEOPLE

Beaten Russian Reporter Mikhail Beketov Convicted of Slander

By Nataliya Vasilyeva

STARBEYEVO, Russia—A muckraking Russian reporter left handicapped by a 2008 beating was convicted Wednesday [November 10, 2010] of defaming an official he criticized when writing about highway corruption and the destruction of the Khimki forest near Moscow.

Mikhail Beketov's supporters said the verdict was just another sign of the degradation of media freedom in Russia. Another journalist covering the same story was beaten so badly over the weekend that doctors placed him into an artificial coma to protect his brain.

Beketov, a reporter for the *Khimkinskaya Pravda* newspaper, irked authorities with his articles about corruption involving the Khimki forest, part of which officials have torn down to make way for a highway to St. Petersburg that may or may not be built.

Beketov now uses a wheelchair and is unable to speak after a vicious beating by two unidentified assailants near his home left him unconscious in the snow and forced doctors to amputate his leg. His supporters claim the attack was retaliation for articles criticizing local authorities.

One of the officials Beketov criticized was Vladimir Strelchenko, the mayor of Khimki, a town just outside Moscow that is home to the forest. Beketov gave a 2007 television interview in which he accused Strelchenko of being involved in blowing up his car.

Strelchenko sued for slander, and the court in Khimki issued a 5,000-ruble ($160) fine Wednesday, but said Beketov didn't have to pay because of a technicality.

Misha Japaridze/AP Photos

Mikhail Beketov arrives at a court hearing in Khimki, near Moscow, on November 9, 2010. A reporter who wrote stories critical of plans to cut down a local forest to build a highway, Beketov was brutally beaten in 2008 and left brain damaged. He was found guilty of slandering the public official he named in his story.

Beketov's assistant said he would appeal.

The scandal over the highway was also a chief topic in the writings of Oleg Kashin, a reporter for the respected *Kommersant* newspaper who was brutally attacked Saturday in Moscow. . . .

Russia has seen a wave of assaults on journalists and activists, and in most cases the perpetrators are never found.

press was subject to censorship by the Israeli government, and all Palestinian newspapers and magazines once required permission from the Israeli government to be published.

Broadcast Media

The foreign-language press is especially strong in the Middle East because of the large number of immigrants in the area, and foreign radio is very popular. Governments within each country control radio and television almost completely, and television stations in Sudan and Yemen, for example, broadcast for only a few hours a day beginning in mid-afternoon.

In the larger Arab states (Jordan, Lebanon, Saudi Arabia and Egypt), TV stations typically broadcast from early morning until midnight. Radio signals beamed from Europe have become one of the region's alternative, affordable sources of news. According to the *Los Angeles Times*, "Because of tight censorship, newspapers and television stations in the Arab world frequently reflect the biases or outright propaganda of their governments. But radio broadcasts from outside the region travel easily across borders and long distances, and many Arabs regard those stations as the most reliable sources of unbiased news." The BBC (based in London) and Radio Monte Carlo Middle East (based in Paris) are the main across-the-border program sources.

KARIM JAAFAR/AFP/Getty Images

The Middle Eastern TV network Al Jazeera, launched in 1996, continues to be a focus of global attention because of its promise to offer independent coverage of events in the Middle East. Al Jazeera figured prominently in coverage of the protest demonstrations in Cairo, Egypt, in January 2011. An English-language version of Al Jazeera, launched in 2006, is available on the Internet at http://english.aljazeera.net.

Also, because of careful government control of television programming, another alternative medium has emerged—DVDs. Says global media scholar Christine Ogan, "Since only Egypt, Turkey, Lebanon and Israel [of the Gulf countries] have copyright laws, pirated films from Europe, the United States, India and Egypt circulate widely in most countries. . . . The widespread availability of content that cannot be viewed on television or at the cinema (Saudi Arabia even forbids the construction of cinemas) has reduced the popularity of broadcast programming."

In the Middle East, as in other developing regions, the government-owned media are perceived as instruments of each country's social and political structure. When demonstrators calling for the ouster of President Hosni Mubarak filled Tahrir Square in Cairo, Egypt, in late January 2011, the government quickly shut down access to the Internet. Officials blamed social media, such as Twitter and Facebook, for mobilizing the demonstrators. This marked the first time that a government had deliberately denied Internet communications access to an entire country. (See **Media/Impact: World**, "How the Egyptian Government Killed the Internet in January 2011," p. 368.)

Within 24 hours of the Internet shutdown, a new voice-based social media platform, Saynow, joined with Google and Twitter to create an alternative way to communicate. Saynow distributed three phone numbers Egyptians could call to record messages that were then distributed using cell phone access.

The Arabic-language channel Al Jazeera, founded in 1996 as an independent satellite TV channel based in Doha, Qatar, is the Middle East's most-watched TV network. Al Jazeera, available since 2006 in an English-language version at http://english.aljazeera.net, has made its reputation through comparatively independent news reporting and coverage of events in the region. Al Jazeera was widely credited with extensive video coverage of the January 2011 Cairo protests, although the network reported continued disruptions in transmission of its signal during its live coverage of the demonstrations.

Al Jazeera blamed the interruptions on "powers that do not want our important images pushing for democracy and reform to be seen by the public," but did not specify who the "powers" were. Al Jazeera did tell *The New York Times* that

Media/Impact
WORLD

Ben Curtis/AP Photos

On January 27, 2011, thousands of demonstrators filled the streets of Cairo, Egypt, demanding that President Hosni Mubarak step down. The government quickly shut off Internet access, blaming social media outlets like Facebook and Twitter for creating momentum for the demonstrations. Mubarak eventually resigned.

How the Egyptian Government Killed the Internet in January 2011

How Do You Turn Off the Internet in an Entire Country?

By Jennifer Valentino-DeVries

In the case of Egypt, it was probably done with a few phone calls, says Jim Cowie, the co-founder and chief technology officer of Renesys Corp., a company that analyzes how the Internet is performing around the world.

Egypt severed mobile and Web communications late Thursday [January 27, 2011], *The Journal* reported.

Mr. Cowie said in an interview. . .that he isn't privy to how Egypt actually shut down the Web but outlined a scenario based on his "knowledge of how the Internet is structured."

"People have talked about a 'kill switch'" that would link to every router and be able to shut each one off from a central location, "but that is not realistic," he said. "What is most likely is that somebody in the government gives a phone call to a small number of people and says, 'Turn it off.' And then one engineer at each service provider logs into the equipment and changes the configuration of how traffic should flow."

Mr. Cowie said a detailed look at the traffic shows that Egypt's Internet providers started shutting down their networks at about midnight Cairo time. Rather than turning off all at once, they each initiated the process separately, starting with Telecom Egypt at 12 minutes and 43 seconds after midnight. Raya started the process about a minute later, and the other networks followed at intervals of two to six minutes. This could lend credence to the theory that a decision to shut down was made around midnight and each operator was notified in succession and began the process shortly thereafter.

In many countries, including Egypt, the Internet involves a few large providers that sell service to smaller providers. The large providers—of which there are a handful in Egypt—pay money to international carriers to transmit Internet data over undersea cables. Ordinarily, the large providers announce via computer code that they will accept and send transmissions. But late Thursday [January 27, 2011], the code at most providers simply switched to stop allowing that—thus blocking communications altogether.

About 3,500 of these "border gateway protocol" routes were withdrawn, Renesys reported. BGPmon, which also monitors such traffic, said more than 88 percent of Egyptian networks were unreachable as of early Friday morning, Egyptian time. As of Friday evening, Renesys reported that 93 percent were offline. . . .

So could this sort of shutdown happen in the U.S.? Mr. Cowie said it's unlikely, and not just because of the legal issues involved. Egypt's Internet ecosystem is small enough that a few phone calls could shut it down, but that's not the case in the U.S. "To say the least it would be very implausible," Mr. Cowie said. "You'd have to make far too many phone calls, and most of those people would ignore you."

"signals on the Nilesat platform were cut, and frequencies on the Arbsat and Hotbird platforms were disrupted continually forcing millions of viewers across the Arab world to change satellite frequencies throughout the day."

In an unprecedented show of solidarity with Al Jazeera, 10 other channels in the region interrupted their own programming to simulcast Al Jazeera coverage of the demonstrations live to their viewers. The government efforts failed to stop the demonstrations and eventually President Mubarak resigned.

The rapid spread of technological developments, such as the growing availability of DVDs, wider access to the Internet, and the ongoing influence of new media outlets such as the satellite network Al Jazeera, demonstrate serious challenges to traditional government authority over mass media in the Middle East.

Per-Anders Pettersson/Getty Images

Less than 5 percent of Africa's population has access to the Web, and Internet access is concentrated in urban areas. In South Africa in January 2010, two women use a laptop at a café in Johannesburg's exclusive shopping mall, Nelson Mandela Square.

African Media Find a New Voice

Most of the new nations of Africa were born after 1960. African history is a record of colonialism, primarily by the British, French, Dutch and Portuguese, and the early print media were created to serve the colonists, not the native population.

Print Media

The first English-language newspaper in sub-Saharan Africa, the *Capetown Gazette and African Advertiser*, appeared in South Africa in 1800. A year later, the first black newspaper, the *Royal Gazette and Sierra Leone Advertiser*, appeared in Sierra Leone.

French settlement in Africa is reflected in the pages of more than 60 newspapers, including *Fraternité-Matin*, French Africa's major daily. A Portuguese settler founded *Noticias*, published in Mozambique. In Kenya, three tabloid newspapers enjoy wide circulations with relative independence: the English-language *Daily Nation* and *The Standard* and the Swahili daily *Taifa Leo*.

According to media scholar L. John Martin, Africans have never had an information press. Theirs has always been an opinion press. Advocacy journalism comes naturally to them. To the extent that they feel a need for hard news, that need is satisfied by the minimal coverage of the mass media, especially radio.

African culture is very diverse, with an estimated 800 to 2,000 language dialects, making it impossible to create a mass circulation newspaper that can appeal to a wide readership. One publication with a wide circulation in the continent is a magazine called *Drum*, published in South Africa but also distributed throughout Africa.

Today, most newspapers in South Africa, for example, are published either in English or in Afrikaans, a language that evolved from South Africa's 17th-century Dutch settlers. South Africa's first Afrikaans newspaper, *Di Patriot*, began in 1875. South Africa's highest circulation newspaper is *The Star*. Avusa Limited publishes the *Sowetan*, a handsome newspaper based in Johannesburg, with color graphics, an appealing design and a healthy circulation. Many of the *Sowetan*'s original editors spent time in jail for speaking out against apartheid. Avusa also owns South Africa's biggest-selling weekly newspaper, the *Sunday Times*, and a daily print and Internet newspaper, *The Times*.

From 1985 to 1990, the South African government demonstrated its distaste for dissident speech when it instituted strict limits on domestic and international news coverage in the region. Because of violent demonstrations supporting the opposition African National Congress, President P. W. Botha declared a state of emergency in the country in 1985. In 1988, the government suspended the *New Nation* and four other alternative publications.

The suspensions and regulations that prevented journalists from covering unrest show the power of government to limit reporting on dissent.

Broadcast Media

Radio is a very important medium in Africa. One reason for radio's dominance over print is that literacy rates are lower in Africa than in many other regions of the world. Radio is also very accessible and the cheapest way for people to follow the news. Some governments charge license fees for radio sets, which are supposed to be registered, but many sets go unregistered. Most stations accept advertising, but the majority of funding for radio comes from government subsidies.

A relatively small percentage of the African public own a TV set, and less than 5 percent of Africa's population has access to the Internet. "Attempts to bring affordable high-speed Internet service to the masses have made little headway on the [African] continent," according to journalist Ron Nixon. "A lack of infrastructure is the biggest problem. In many countries, communications networks were destroyed during years of civil conflict, and continuing political instability deters governments or companies from investing in new systems." Media in the region are concentrated in urban areas, although the growing availability of cell phone signals throughout Africa has the potential to expand communications rapidly, once the political unrest subsides.

Media Explode in Asia and the Pacific

The development of media in this region centers primarily in four countries: Japan, with its prosperous mix of public and private ownership; Australia, where media barons contributed their entrepreneurial fervor; India, which has seen phenomenal media growth; and the People's Republic of China, with its sustained government-controlled media monopoly.

Japan

Japan boasts more newspaper readers than any other nation in the world. Japan's three national daily newspapers—*Asahi Shimbun, Yomiuri Shimbun* and *Mainichi Shimbun*—are based in Tokyo. These three papers, each of them more than 100 years old, account for almost half the nation's newspaper circulation. Broadcast media in Japan developed as a public corporation called the Japanese Broadcasting Corporation (NHK). During World War II, NHK became a propaganda arm of the government, but after the Japanese surrender, the United States established the direction for Japanese broadcasting.

ABC Australian Broadcasting Corporation.

Japan created a licensing board similar to the Federal Communications Commission, but an operating board similar to that of Great Britain's BBC. Japan also decided to allow private broadcast ownership. As a result, Japan today has a mixed system of privately owned and publicly held broadcast media. NHK continues to prosper and, according to broadcast scholar Sydney W. Head, "NHK enjoys more autonomy than any other major public broadcasting corporation. In a rather literal sense, the general public 'owns' it by virtue of paying receiver fees.

"The government cannot veto any program or demand that any program be aired. It leaves the NHK free to set the level of license fees and to do its own fee collecting (which may be why it rates as the richest of the world's fee-supported broadcasting organizations)."

Private ownership is an important element in the Japanese media, and newspaper publishers own many broadcasting operations. NHK owns many more radio properties than private broadcasters do; NHK shares television ownership about equally with private investors. Japan has very few cable systems, which may hinder access to global communications networks, but its cellular and Internet networks are growing rapidly. Japan is ranked eighth in the world in the number of wireless hot spots available to the public (see p. 375). Tokyo also is the home of Sony Corp., which owns Sony Music and Sony Pictures and is one of the world's largest manufacturers of electronic products, including television sets and PlayStation 3. Sony has 167,000 employees worldwide.

Australia

In Australia, acquisitions by media moguls such as Rupert Murdoch skyrocketed in the 1980s. The Murdoch empire controls 60 percent of Australia's newspaper circulation, which includes the *Daily Telegraph* in Sydney and *The Herald-Sun* in Melbourne. Murdoch, although somewhat burdened with debt because of his acquisitions binge in the 1980s, emerged in the 1990s as Australia's uncontested print media baron.

Australian Broadcasting Corporation (***ABC***), modeled after the BBC, dominates broadcasting in Australia. Three nationwide commercial networks operate in the country. All three were suffering financial difficulty in the 1990s, a legacy "of the heydays of the 1980s, when aspiring buyers, backed by eager bank lenders, paid heady prices for broadcast and print assets," reported *The Wall Street Journal*. But they have recovered and today are very prosperous.

India

Entrepreneurship is an important element in the print media of India, which gained independence from Britain in 1947. Forty years after independence, in 1987, Indian print media had multiplied 1,000 times—from 200 publications in 1947 to nearly 25,000 publications.

Broadcasting in India follows its British colonial beginnings, with radio operating under the name All India Radio (AIR) and TV as Doordarshan ("distance view"). Doordarshan uses satellite service to reach remote locations, bringing network TV to four out of five people in the country. As in most developing countries, the network regularly broadcasts programs aimed at improving public life and about subjects such as family planning, health and hygiene.

One of the most prosperous industries in India today is filmmaking. The film industry, which produces 800 films a year (almost twice as many as Hollywood), is centered around a place called Film City near Mumbai, where 16 film studios employ thousands of people who work at dozens of sprawling sets. The industry is known as Bollywood, a mix of *Bombay*, the former name of Mumbai, and *Hollywood*.

People's Republic of China

Social responsibility is a very important element of media development in the People's Republic of China, where a media monopoly gives government the power to influence change. At the center of Chinese media are the two Communist Party information sources, the newspaper *People's Daily* and Xinhua, the Chinese news agency. These two sources set the tone for the print media throughout China, where self-censorship maintains the government's direction.

Broadcasting in China, as in India, offers important potential for social change in a vast land of rural villages. China's three-tier system for radio includes a central national station; 100 regional, provincial and municipal networks; and grassroots stations that send local announcements and bulletins by wire to loudspeakers in outdoor markets and other public gathering places.

A television set is a prized possession in China. The Chinese have bought some U.S. TV programs and accepted some U.S. commercials, but they produce most of the programming themselves. Chinese media today sometimes use information and entertainment programming from the West to show the dangers of Western influence, proving the power and the reach of a government media monopoly. In the new market economy in China, there are 10 times as many newspapers and magazines today as there were in 1978.

With the increased competition for readers, some of the print media are beginning to look like Western tabloids, running some sensationalist stories. This sensationalism has angered Communist Party officials, who are trying to maintain control over what is published. In 1996, the president of the popular newspaper *Beijing Youth Daily* was disciplined after the paper ran a story about a poisoning case involving a state-run business.

"The leadership of the news media must be tightly held in the hands of those who are loyal to Marxism, the party and the people," said President Jiang Zemin. With the inevitable influx of Western media during the 2008 Beijing Olympics, the Chinese government originally pledged to open up media outlets completely but still restricted journalists' access to many Western news outlets.

China has 384 million Internet users, and the government has placed various controls on Web site access, especially for social networking sites, such as Facebook and Twitter, but technology-savvy people in the country often manage to find ways around the government's limits. (See **Media/Impact: Audience**: "Despite Censorship, Cracks Widen in China's Great Firewall," p. 372.)

Government, Large Corporations and Family Dynasties Control Latin American and Caribbean Media

In Latin America, where hectic political change is the norm, media have been as volatile as the region. Media are part of the same power structure that controls politics, business and industry. In some Latin American countries, such as Brazil, a family dynasty dominates the media, and in many countries one corporation is allowed to control different types of media outlets.

For example, Televisa, based in Mexico, owns more than 258 affiliated TV stations, 31 pay TV channels, and 158 publications. Organization Editorial Mexicana owns 70 newspapers, 24 radio stations and 43 Internet sites.

Print Media

In Santiago, Chile, the newspaper *El Mercurio* was founded in 1827. Today the El Mercurio company owns nine newspapers and 32 radio stations. *O Estado de São Paulo* in Brazil, owned by the Mesquita family, has represented editorial independence in the region for more than 100 years and often is mentioned as one of the country's best newspapers. Argentina's *La Prensa* refuses government subsidies and has survived great conflicts with people like dictator Juan Perón, who shut down the newspaper from 1951 to 1955.

Home delivery for newspapers and magazines is uncommon in Latin America; the centers of print media merchandising are street-corner kiosks, where vendors offer a

Media/Impact AUDIENCE

Despite Censorship, Cracks Widen in China's Great Firewall

By David Pierson

Reporting from Beijing—Zhang Shan never paid much attention to Internet censorship in China. The stylish art gallery clerk said it didn't really matter in her everyday life.

Then last year, she lost access to some of her favorite Web sites. First YouTube. Then Twitter. Then Facebook.

It was her first memorable brush with the so-called Great Firewall of China—one of many powerful mechanisms the Chinese government uses to block content too sensitive for the eyes of its 384 million Internet users.

"I really didn't like it," said Zhang, standing outside a popular Beijing shopping mall.

Then she cautiously lowered her voice and said, "But a friend of mine gave me a program where I can log in and I can visit all those Web sites again. Many of my friends are also using the same program. . . ."

If cyber censorship in China is a never-ending game of cat and mouse, the mice are multiplying fast. Despite increasingly aggressive government measures to tighten the flow of information and to snoop on suspected dissidents, China's resourceful netizens are finding ways to evade the country's Internet restrictions.

Known as *fanqiang*, or "scaling the wall," these work-arounds typically involve tapping into remote servers located outside China that aren't subject to Chinese government control. Although these skills are largely the province of tech-savvy Chinese bloggers and students, word is spreading fast about how to gain access to taboo sites. . . .

LIU JIN/AFP/Getty Images

With 384 million people online, China is home to the world's largest Web population. The Chinese government has blocked Internet users from accessing sites the government finds offensive, especially social networking sites such as Facebook and Twitter, but Chinese users have found technological "workarounds" to maintain access. On March 4, 2010, Chinese journalists report on the Third Session of the 11th National People's Congress in Beijing.

Recent crackdowns on social networking sites appear to be alienating some ordinary Chinese who previously showed little concern about the government's efforts to limit their access to pornography or politically sensitive material.

"The best censorship is the censorship you don't know about. But with all the recent troubles, it's becoming more public," said Xizo Qiang, director of the China Internet Project at UC Berkeley. "That undermines the goal of censorship itself. It's converting more and more people."

Excerpted from David Pierson, "Despite Censorship, Cracks Widen in China's Great Firewall," latimes.com, January 16, 2010.

variety of publications. *Manchete*, published in Brazil, is one of the most widely circulated national magazines, similar in size and content to *Life* magazine.

Broadcast Media

Broadcasting operates in a mix of government and private control, with government often owning a few key stations and regulating stations that are privately owned, but the pattern varies.

Cuba's broadcast media are controlled totally by the government, for example. In Costa Rica and Ecuador, almost all the broadcast media are privately owned. In Brazil, private owners hold most of the radio stations and television networks, including TV Globo Network, which claims to be the world's fourth largest television network (after the United States' original three TV networks).

International Herald Tribune Seeks a Global Audience

One of the largest global media presences is the *International Herald Tribune* (***IHT***), based in Paris and published in English. Called "the world's daily newspaper," the *International Herald Tribune* was founded in 1887 by American entrepreneur J. Gordon Bennett, Jr., and today is the world's largest English-language newspaper. (See **Media/Impact: World**, "*International Herald Tribune* Timeline 1887–Today," p. 374.) Known for its independence, the newspaper was co-owned by *The Washington Post* and *The New York Times* until 2003, when *The New York Times* became the paper's sole owner.

The *IHT* is the first truly global newspaper, published at 35 sites around the world and covering international news every day. With a global outlook and available by subscription in an electronic edition, the *IHT* counts most of the world's opinion leaders and decision makers among its subscribers.

The paper has a circulation of 241,000 and an international readership in 180 countries throughout Europe, Asia, the Middle East, Russia, Africa and the Americas. The biggest regular audience for the print edition is American tourists traveling abroad, and the Internet edition receives 7 million visitors a month.

Critics Cite Western Communications Bias

Countries in many developing nations, such as Cuba, historically have criticized what they believe is a Western bias to the flow of information throughout the world. These countries charge that this practice impos
rialism, centered in Western ideology. In fact,
major international news services are based in the

The Associated Press, Reuters (Great Britain), Agen
France-Presse (France), Deutsche Presse-Agentur (Germany) and Agencia Efe (Spain) supply news to the print and broadcast media. Visnews, based in Great Britain, the U.S.-based Cable News Network and World International Network (WIN) offer international video services. Sky TV in Europe and Star TV in Asia deliver programs by satellite. The Internet, of course, ignores all national borders.

Despite Western dominance of global news organizations, many regions of the world support information services within their own countries and even within their regions. Middle East News Agency (MENA), based in Egypt, serves all the countries of the Middle East, while News Agency of Nigeria (NAN) limits services to Nigeria, for example.

Within the past 50 years, news services outside the Western orbit have been created—Russian Information Agency (RIA); Asian-Pacific News Network in Japan; Caribbean News Agency (CANA); Pan-African News Agency (PANA); Non-Aligned News Agency (NANA), linking the nonaligned nations with the national news agencies, based in Yugoslavia; and Inter Press Service (IPS), based in Rome as an "information bridge" between Europe and Latin America.

Even with the creation of these added sources of information and the Internet, Western news services dominate. Critics of the system of news and information flow have called for a New World Information and Communications Order (***NWICO***), saying that the existing system is ***ethnocentric***, or promotes the superiority of one ethnic group (in this case, the Western world) over another.

According to Robert G. Picard in *Global Journalism: Survey of International Communication*, "Developing world media and governments have argued that Western ethnocentrism creates an unequal flow of information by providing a large stream of information about events in the developed world but only a very small flow from the developing world." Internet access to news outlets like the *International Herald Tribune* and the availability of original Internet news reports from throughout the world could potentially change the balance.

IHT International Herald Tribune, the world's largest English-language newspaper.

Ethnocentric Promoting the superiority of one ethnic group over another.

NWICO New World Information and Communications Order. The concept that mass media should include all areas of the world, not just the West.

ct

... Tribune ... Today

1887 On Oc... er 4, American entrepreneur J. Gordon Bennett, Jr., publishes the first issue of the *New York Herald*'s European edition in Paris.

1928 The *Herald* becomes the first newspaper distributed by airplane, with copies flown to London from Paris in time for breakfast.

1940 The occupation of Paris interrupts publishing.

1944 Publishing resumes.

1959 The *New York Herald Tribune* and its European edition are sold to John Hay Whitney, the U.S. ambassador to Britain.

1966 The New York paper closes. The Whitney family keeps the Paris paper going through partnerships. In December *The Washington Post* becomes a joint owner.

1967 In May *The New York Times* becomes a joint owner, and the newspaper becomes the *International Herald Tribune*, emphasizing its global perspective.

1974 The *IHT* pioneers the electronic transmission of facsimile pages across countries with the opening of a printing site near London. A second site is opened in Zurich in 1977.

1980 The *IHT* begins sending page images via satellite from Paris to Hong Kong, making it the first daily newspaper to be electronically sent across continents and simultaneously available to readers on opposite sides of the world.

Samir Hussein/Getty Images

The *International Herald Tribune* (*IHT*), published in Paris and owned by *The New York Times*, is the largest general circulation, English-language daily in the world. In November 2010 the *IHT* sponsored a fashion forum in London, England.

1991 *The Washington Post* and *The New York Times* become sole and equal shareholders of the newspaper.

2003 *The New York Times* acquires full ownership of the *International Herald Tribune*.

2005 The 25th anniversary of the *International Herald Tribune* publishing activities in Asia is marked by the opening of *IHT*'s Hong Kong newsroom, allowing *IHT* to be published in both Paris and Hong Kong.

2006 *IHT* becomes the first international daily newspaper to be printed in Russia, ensuring early morning distribution with the *Moscow Times*.

2008 *IHT* and Reuters join forces to launch Business with Reuters and Business Asia with Reuters. Seven million users visit iht.com each month.

2009 IHT launches the global edition online, in coordination with *The New York Times*. The paper is edited in New York, Paris and Hong Kong.

Today The IHT is available in 180 countries and on the Web.

Media/Impact WORLD

Illustration 16.1

Top 10 Countries with Public Wireless Locations (Hot Spots)

The United Kingdom has more public wireless locations than any other country, and China (ranked third) has almost as many hot spots as the U.S. The UK has 20 times more hot spots than Sweden, which is ranked tenth.

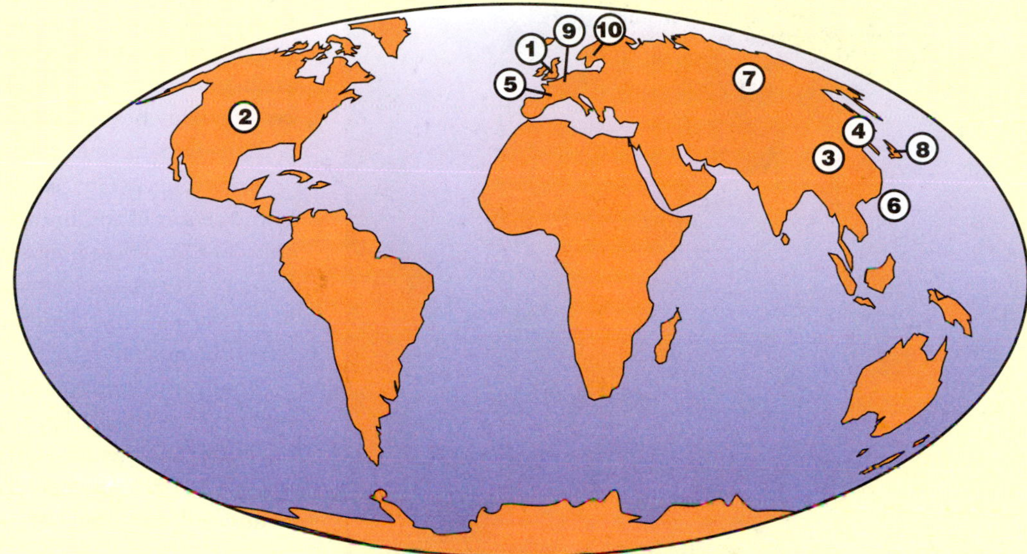

JiWire.com, JiWire Mobile Audience Insights Report, December 12, 2011.

1 United Kingdom, 181,719 wireless locations
2 United States, 110,559
3 China, 103,770
4 South Korea, 83,639
5 France, 35,912
6 Taiwan, 19,311
7 Russian Federation, 16,678
8 Japan, 15,662
9 Germany, 14,874
10 Sweden, 9,052

Internet Expands Media's Global Reach

When communication stays within borders, it is easier for governments to control information. The Internet makes it possible for information and entertainment to travel effortlessly across borders.

Until recently, most developing countries were limited to traditional mass media delivery systems—print and broadcast. These systems were regional by nature because they were confined by geography and economics. Print media could travel only through the mail and by carrier. Radio and television were limited by the reach of their towers and depended on people having enough money to purchase receivers. Information from outside the country was limited to reports filtered through each nation's print and broadcast outlets; similarly, news and information about other countries reached the U.S. only through traditional print and broadcast organizations.

A country with government controls on the mass media can use those controls to combat dissent and limit awareness. But digital signals carried on the Internet break down international barriers because the delivery system knows no limits. Information on the Internet is controlled by individuals rather than by institutions, which is precisely why many governments are afraid of the influence that access to the Internet will have if allowed to operate unchecked within their countries.

Governments that are accustomed to controlling information, especially in developing countries, have tried to stop the information flow by pricing Internet access beyond what most people can afford. According to the World Bank, the average consumer pays about $22 a month for Internet access, but in Tanzania, for example, the price is $95 a month, and in South Africa the cost is $60 a month.

Also, many countries simply don't have reliable telecommunications technology in place—telephone, broadband, cellular or satellite connections—to handle Internet traffic. None of the countries in South America or Africa is listed among the countries with the highest number of wireless hot spots available to the public, for example. (See **Illustration 16.1**.)

This often means that in poorer countries, only the wealthy and powerful have access to the international flow of information that the Internet offers. As digital technology

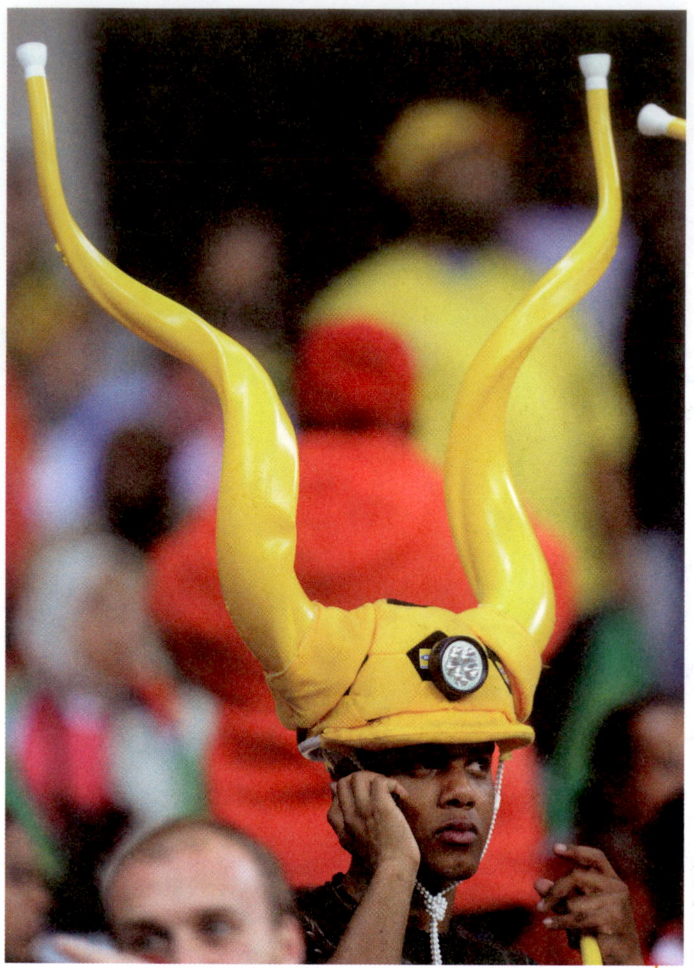

LIU JIN/AFP/Getty Images

Digital technology has blurred the territorial boundaries between nations. Today cell phones are the fastest growing communications technology in developing countries, such as Africa. In Cape Town a fan wearing a horn hat uses his cell phone at the World Cup football match on June 24, 2010.

grows more affordable, however, it will be difficult even for developing countries to stop information from seeping across their borders. The most promising new and simplest technology today is the cell phone.

Cell Phones Open Communications Channels

In 2002, for the first time, the number of cell phones in the world exceeded the number of landline phones, according to the World Bank. Wireless networks offer the easiest way for developing countries to modernize their communications systems because these countries have never had extensive wired networks. "The mobility, ease of use, flexible deployment, and relatively low and declining rollout costs of wireless technologies enable them to reach rural populations with low levels of income and literacy," reports the World Bank.

"From Kenya to Colombia to South Africa . . . cell phones are becoming the truly universal technology," according to Anand Giridharadas, reporting for *The New York Times*. "The number of mobile subscriptions in the world is expected to pass five billion this year [2010], according to the International Telecommunication Union, an intergovernmental organization. That would mean more human beings today have access to a cell phone than the United Nations says have access to a clean toilet."

According to Giridharadas, "The phone has also moved to the center of community life in many places. In Africa, churches record sermons with cell phones, then transmit them to villages to be replayed. In Iran and Moldova, phones helped to organize popular uprisings against authoritarian governments."

The World Bank points out the interrelationship between reliable communications systems and economic development. Farmers can price and sell goods to markets they could never reach otherwise; city dwellers can transfer money to rural relatives through an online banking network; and smart wireless phones give users access to the Internet, music downloads, movies, radio, games and information services.

While access to information from outside the country is a major benefit of wireless networks, many governments consider outsiders—and the information they offer—a threat. Digital technology is much more difficult for governments to restrict. Governments can try to limit which messages pass the country's borders, often with little success. Information can travel from anywhere in the world to any destination in the world and back again.

The Internet is as near as a cell phone, which is becoming an indispensable tool in the developing world for individuals, businesses and governments. For developing countries especially, today's digital technology offers a faster path to economic growth, increased literacy and freedom of expression.

Reporters Risk Their Lives To Report World Events

Journalists in many developing countries are often targets for political and terrorist threats, where a reporter's life can be very hazardous.

According to *Global Journalism: Survey of International Communication*, "Threats to journalists come not only from governments but from terrorist groups, drug lords and quasi-government hit squads as well. Numerous news organizations have been bombed, ransacked and destroyed by opponents. Dozens of Latin American journalists have been murdered for their beliefs or for writing articles that contain those beliefs."

Media/Impact CULTURE

Committee to Protect Journalists Monitors Reporters Killed in 2011

The Committee to Protect Journalists (CPJ) reports the number of journalists killed each year while on assignment. In 2011, photographer Chris Hondros (photo right) was among the journalists who died, caught in crossfire in Libya.

CPJ statistics are divided into "motive confirmed" and "motive unconfirmed." A *motive confirmed* death is one where CPJ finds that the reporter was killed "in direct reprisal for his/her work; was killed in crossfire during a combat situation; or was killed on a dangerous assignment." If the motive is unclear, but it is possible that the journalist was killed because of his/her work, the case is classified as *motive unconfirmed*. A *media worker* is someone who supports reporters, such as a translator or driver.

46 Journalists Killed, Motive Confirmed
35 Journalists Killed, Motive Unconfirmed
5 Media Workers Killed

86 Total Number of Journalists and Media Workers Killed in 2011

Source: Adapted from Committee to Protect Journalists, http://cpj.org/2011/.

Getty Images

Getty Images photographer Chris Hondros, 41, was caught in crossfire and killed by a rocket-propelled grenade in Libya on April 21, 2011. This tribute to Hondros was posted outside Getty Image's London office.

According to Reporters Without Borders, which tracks deaths and injuries suffered by journalists throughout the world, 76 journalists and media assistants were killed, 33 journalists were kidnapped and 573 journalists were arrested in 2009 while they were on the job. (See **Media/Impact: Culture**, "Committee to Protect Journalists Monitors Reporters Killed in 2011.")

Journalists face danger because the mass media often represent potential opposition to the political power of a country's leadership. In all parts of the world, the dangers that journalists face to report unraveling news events form a central part of each nation's political history.

Global Media Chase International Consumers

International communication on the Internet is just the beginning of an easy, affordable and accessible transfer of information and entertainment back and forth between other countries and the United States. Media companies in the United States also are looking longingly at the large populations in other countries that are just beginning to acquire the tools of communication, making millions of people instantly available for all types of products.

Today's media markets are increasingly global. U.S. media companies are searching for new markets overseas at the same time that overseas media companies are purchasing pieces of media industries in the United States and other countries. Here are some recent examples:

- In 2010, IBM announced that it will supply computing technology and services to upgrade the cell phone network across 16 nations in sub-Saharan Africa.
- The Russian government launched a news cable channel called Russia Today, financed by the Russian government and available to viewers in the U.S., which reports news in America from a Russian perspective.
- In 2007, a nonprofit group called One Laptop Per Child, based in Cambridge, Mass., launched an effort to provide each of the 2 billion children in the developing world with a laptop computer. The organization had distributed 1.6 million laptops as of 2010.
- Rupert Murdoch expanded his Hong Kong–based satellite TV network, British Sky Network, into India. Murdoch said he planned to offer more than just TV coverage in India. "Our plan is not just to beam signals into India but also to take part in Indian films, make television programs and broadcast them."

- Jun Murai, who has been called the father of Japan's Internet, created a nonprofit network to connect all of Japan's universities to the Internet, without government approval. Ultimately, he says, he "wants to connect all the computers in this world."
- U.S.–British advertising and public relations partnerships are growing. The British firm Shandwick is the largest agency in the United Kingdom. More than half of Shandwick's business comes from the United States.

CSL, CartoonStock Ltd

"Okay, you can have freedom of speech, but watch your language!"

All these companies have positioned themselves to take advantage of the emerging global media marketplace. This media marketplace includes news and information services, print, broadcast programming, movies and music, as well as products and the advertising to sell those products.

Fueling the move to global marketing is the decision by the European countries to eliminate all trade barriers. A further sign of the times is the shrinking proportion of worldwide advertising expenditures generated by the United States, which has long been the world's advertising colossus. In recent years, advertising spending by companies *outside* the United States has overtaken the amount spent by companies *in* the United States.

Ideas Transcend Borders

Along with the transfer of information in the new global communications future, however, comes the transfer of ideas. Says the *Los Angeles Times*:

> Historically, the empowered elite have always sought to suppress the wider distribution of ideas, wealth, rights and, most of all, knowledge. This is as true today as it was . . . when the German printer Gutenberg invented movable type to print the Bible. For two centuries afterward, government tightly controlled what people could read through the widespread use of "prior restraint." . . .
>
> Just as censorship of the printed word could not continue with the emergence of democracy in 17th century Britain and 18th century America, so today suppression of the electronic media is thwarted by technology and rapidly growing economies around the world.

Governments that are accustomed to controlling the information that crosses their borders face unprecedented access within their countries to global information sources. According to media theorist Ithiel de Sola Pool, "International communications is often considered a mixed blessing by rulers. Usually they want technical progress. They want computers. They want satellites. They want efficient telephones. They want television. But at the same time they do not want the ideas that come with them."

Many governments that control the media, especially broadcast media and the Internet, will continue to control access to the messages as long as they can regulate newsprint and satellites, but this is becoming increasingly difficult. As more national media boundaries disappear throughout the world, news, information and entertainment will be able to move instantly from each home country to become part of the global media dialogue. Today the mass media industries operate in a media marketplace without boundaries, using a global delivery system that is truly "transnational." According to *The Economist*,

> Optimists declare that the world is headed unstoppably for an electronic Renaissance. How arrogant; how naive. The essence of a technology of freedom is that it endows its users with the freedom to fail. But pessimists are equally wrong to think that failure is inevitable. Nothing is inevitable about this technology except its advance. . . . As the universe behind the screen expands, it will be the people in front who shape the soul of the new machine.

Review, Analyze, Investigate

REVIEWING CHAPTER 16

World Media Systems Vary

- ✓ Media industries in different countries are as varied as the countries they serve.
- ✓ The U.S. isn't necessarily always the leader in adopting innovative technologies.

Five Political Theories Describe How World Media Operate

- ✓ The original four theories on the press (the Soviet theory, the authoritarian theory, the libertarian theory and the social responsibility theory) plus the developmental theory still leave many press systems beyond specific categorization.
- ✓ The global media theory that best describes the American media is the libertarian theory, although American media also have struggled with authoritarian and social responsibility debates.

Western Europe and Canada Are Similar to the United States

- ✓ Until the 1850s, presses in Europe were privately owned.
- ✓ The print media form the basis for press development in North America, Australia, Western Europe and Eastern Europe.
- ✓ Today Western European and Canadian media prosper under guarantees of freedom of expression similar to the First Amendment of the U.S. Constitution, although each nation has modified the idea to reflect differing values.
- ✓ In 1982, Canada adopted the Canadian Charter of Rights and Freedom, becoming the most recent Western country to issue an official decree supporting the philosophy of press freedom.
- ✓ Scandinavian journalists enjoy the widest press freedoms of all of Western Europe, including almost unlimited access to public documents.
- ✓ Western European newspapers tend to be much more partisan than U.S. or Canadian newspapers.
- ✓ To finance the government-run broadcast media, countries like the United Kingdom may tax the sale of radios and TVs or charge users an annual license fee, which funds the broadcasts.
- ✓ ITV, a "public service broadcaster," is the largest commercial network in the United Kingdom, with four separate channels.
- ✓ Western Europeans watch about half as much TV as people in the United States.
- ✓ Many TV stations in Europe don't go on the air until late afternoon.
- ✓ Most Western European programming comes from the United States.
- ✓ U.S. programs are attractive to European broadcasters because buying U.S. programs is cheaper than producing their own.
- ✓ Some members of the European community have proposed quotas on the importation of U.S. programs.

Eastern Europe Is in Transition

- ✓ Many Eastern European nations developed their press policies following the Soviet model.
- ✓ Eastern Europe, which is in transition, is defining a new balance between the desire for free expression and the remnants of government control.
- ✓ In many Eastern European countries, the media play a central role in upsetting the established power structure.
- ✓ Television in the Eastern bloc countries developed under Communist direction because the Communist governments were in power before TV use was widespread; radio broadcasting also was tightly controlled.
- ✓ Pravda, the Soviet Union's oldest newspaper, was founded in 1912. In 1996, facing bankruptcy, *Pravda* ceased publication.
- ✓ Media freedom groups say Russia is one of the world's most dangerous countries for journalists.

Middle Eastern and North African Media Work Under Government Controls

- ✓ Press history in the Middle East and North Africa begins with the newspaper *Al-Iraq*, first published in 1817, although the first daily newspaper didn't begin publishing until 1873.
- ✓ In the Middle East and North Africa, more newspapers and magazines are published in regions with high literacy rates than in regions with low literacy rates; the one exception is Cairo, Egypt, which is the Arab world's publishing center.
- ✓ Radio often is the dominant medium in developing countries; television is in widespread use in prosperous nations and in urban areas of developing countries. Yet

most countries still have only one TV service, usually run by the government.

- ✓ Radio Monte Carlo and the BBC offer alternative radio programming across Middle Eastern borders.
- ✓ The Middle Eastern press is tightly controlled by government restrictions, through ownership and licensing.
- ✓ Al Jazeera is the Middle East's most-watched TV network and has made its controversial reputation by promising independent news reporting and coverage.
- ✓ In the Middle East, as in other developing regions, the mass media are perceived as instruments of each country's social and political agendas.

African Media Find a New Voice

- ✓ The first English-language newspaper in sub-Saharan Africa appeared in Capetown, South Africa, in 1800; a year later, the first black newspaper appeared in Sierra Leone.
- ✓ African culture is very diverse, making it impossible to create a mass circulation newspaper that can appeal to a wide readership.
- ✓ In Africa, radio is a much more important medium than print because it is an inexpensive way for people to follow the news.
- ✓ Suspension of five publications in South Africa throughout the state of emergency during 1985–1990 demonstrates the power of government to limit reporting on dissent.
- ✓ People in Africa have limited access to the Internet. Internet access is mostly available in urban areas.

Media Explode in Asia and the Pacific

- ✓ Japan's three major newspapers are each more than 100 years old.
- ✓ The three major Japanese national dailies account for almost half the nation's newspaper circulation.
- ✓ Japan today has a mixed system of privately owned and publicly held broadcast media.
- ✓ Entrepreneurs, including Rupert Murdoch, control large segments of Australia's media.
- ✓ The Australian Broadcasting Corporation (ABC) dominates broadcasting in Australia.
- ✓ Since India's independence in 1947, the number of publications has increased 1,000 times.
- ✓ Broadcasting in India follows its British colonial beginnings.
- ✓ The most successful media business in India is filmmaking, an industry nicknamed Bollywood. The industry is based in Film City, a settlement near Mumbai.
- ✓ Chinese media operate under a government monopoly, supported by a belief in the media's social responsibility.

Government, Large Corporations and Family Dynasties Control Latin American and Caribbean Media

- ✓ Media in Latin America are part of the power structure, and media often are owned by family dynasties.
- ✓ In Santiago, Chile, the Edwards family has owned *El Mercurio* since 1880.
- ✓ Dictator Juan Peron shut down Argentina's independent newspaper *La Prensa* from 1951 to 1955.

International Herald Tribune Seeks a Global Audience

- ✓ The *International Herald Tribune* was founded in 1887 by American entrepreneur J. Gordon Bennett, Jr., and today is the world's largest English-language newspaper.
- ✓ The newspaper was co-owned by the *Washington Post* and *The New York Times* until 2003, when *The New York Times* became the paper's sole owner.
- ✓ The *IHT* is the first truly global newspaper, published at 35 sites around the world and covering world news every day.

Critics Cite Western Communications Bias

- ✓ Many developing nations criticize the news media for their Western slant.
- ✓ Despite Western dominance of global news organizations, many regions of the world have their own news services.
- ✓ The New World Information and Communications Order (NWICO) advocates parity for the media in all countries.

Internet Expands Media's Global Reach

- ✓ Governments that are used to controlling information, especially in developing countries, have tried to stop the information flow by pricing Internet access out of the reach of the average consumer.
- ✓ Many countries simply don't have reliable telecommunications technology in place—telephone, broadband, cellular or satellite connections—to handle Internet traffic.
- ✓ More than any other factor, the economic uses of the Internet guarantee its future as a global communications medium.

Cell Phones Open Communications Channels

- ✓ In 2002, for the first time, the number of cell phones in the world exceeded the number of landline pones.
- ✓ Wireless networks offer the easiest way for developing countries to modernize their communications systems because these countries have never had extensive wired networks.

Reporters Risk Their Lives to Report World Events

- ✓ Journalists in Latin America and many other developing countries face danger because the media represent a challenge to political power.
- ✓ In 2011, 86 journalists and media workers were killed on the job.

Global Media Chase International Consumers

- ✓ U.S. media companies are looking for markets overseas at the same time that overseas media companies are purchasing pieces of media industries in the United States and other countries.
- ✓ Fueling the move to global marketing is the decision by the European countries to eliminate all trade barriers.

Ideas Transcend Borders

- ✓ Along with the transfer of information in the new global communications future comes the transfer of ideas.
- ✓ Governments that are accustomed to controlling the information that crosses their borders face unprecedented access within their borders to global information sources.
- ✓ Today the media industries operate in a marketplace that is "transnational."

KEY TERMS

These terms are defined in the margins throughout this chapter and appear in alphabetical order with definitions in the Glossary, which begins on page 383.

CRITICAL QUESTIONS

1. In what ways might a nation's media system be shaped by its government's political philosophy? Cite three specific examples.
2. Compare the evolution of mass media in the various regions of the world. Give three specific examples.
3. Discuss the role of radio in developed and less-developed countries. Cite three specific examples.
4. Explain how the *International Herald Tribune* became one of the largest global media presences. What will the *IHT* have to do to stay competitive in the growing global media market?
5. Discuss the global consequences of international access to the Internet, including the impact of the Internet on government control of information and ways that developing countries attempt to deal with the loss of control.

WORKING THE WEB

This list includes both sites mentioned in the chapter and others to give you greater insight into global media.

BBC News

http://www.bbc.co.uk

The British Broadcasting Company's Web site with a UK and an international version is customizable with content choices including news, sports, weather, radio, TV, entertainment, history and blogs. The international version, which offers news and audio in 32 languages, has links to BBC TV and radio channels around the world. Its Country Profiles (located in the News section) provide background on every nation in the world. A complete A–Z directory of BBC sites is also available.

Foreign Policy Magazine

http://www.foreignpolicy.com

A bimonthly magazine about global politics and economics, *Foreign Policy*'s mission is to explain "how the process of globalization is reshaping nations, institutions, cultures, and, more fundamentally, our daily lives." Articles from current issues are available for free as well as Special Reports, which combine *Foreign Policy* articles and links to other sources, and Breaking Global News, stories from international and regional news hubs updated every minute.

Global Media Journal (GMJ)

http://lass.calumet.purdue.edu/cca/gmj

A journal published by Purdue University Calumet since 2002, *GMJ* aims to publish works that assess global media concentration, global media and consumer culture, media regulations, alternative media and other timely issues. *GMJ* has established African, American, Arabic, Australian, Canadian, Chinese, Indian, Pakistan, Persian, Polish, Spanish, Mexican, Mediterranean and Turkish editions.

Global Media Monitor (GMM)

http://lass.calumet.purdue.edu/cca/gmm

Serving as a "clearinghouse for numerous issues related to global communication and mass media studies," the GMM Web site was founded by editor Yahya R. Kamalipour of Purdue University Calumet while working on his e-journal *Global Media Journal*. The Web site houses numerous reference links to a variety of mass media subjects including international news and programs, news agencies, organizations, scholars and experts.

International Center for Journalists

http://www.icfj.org

This nonprofit professional organization promotes quality journalism around the world, and believes that "independent, vigorous media are crucial in improving the human condition." It offers programs, seminars and fellowships for journalists in the United States and abroad, as well as online resources, instructor-led and distance courses in English, Arabic and Persian.

International Herald Tribune

http://www.iht.com

The "global edition of *The New York Times*," the *International Herald Tribune* is the world's daily newspaper for global readers with articles from its own correspondents and *New York Times* reporters. Its sections are those of any local paper (Business, Tech/Media, Travel, Style, Culture, Health, Sports and Opinion), but the content is international (including a currency converter in the Business Market Tools section). The Web site includes four regional versions: Europe, the Americas, Asia-Pacific and Africa and Middle East.

International Women's Media Foundation (IWMF)

http://www.iwmf.org

This organization raises awareness about, creates opportunities for and builds networks of female journalists around the world. "No press is truly free unless women share an equal voice" is its motto. Online resources include links to online training, tips and guides, statistics and studies, links to Web sites of interest to women in the media, and publications and newsletter articles.

Internews

http://www.internews.org

An international media development organization based in California, Internews has offices in 23 countries in Africa, Asia, Europe, the Middle East and North America. Its goal is to "empower local media worldwide to give people access to information they need Current Internews activities include providing training for media professionals in journalism, production and management; supporting media infrastructure; and adopting and implementing fair media laws and policies.

Funders of projects have included the Bill and Melinda Gates Foundation, the National Science Foundation, UNICEF, the World Bank, and many others. A long list of related organizations is available on the Web site.

Reporters Without Borders

http://www.rsf.org

An international organization that works for freedom of the press around the world, Reporters Without Borders defends journalists who are threatened, imprisoned or persecuted; works to improve the safety of journalists in war zones; and opposes censorship. The Web site provides news and online petitions in five languages about attacks on press freedom and journalists in Africa, the Americas, Asia, Europe and the former USSR, the Middle East and Northern Africa, within the United Nations and on the Internet.

Worldpress.org

http://www.worldpress.org

Worldpress.org is a digest of world news from the world's newspapers. The site contains originally written material and articles reprinted from the press outside the United States. Besides the latest news stories, resources include world headlines (updated every 15 minutes), a directory of world newspapers, World Press and other RSS news feeds, country maps and profiles (from the CIA World Factbook), the texts of documents in the news and links to think tanks and nongovernmental organizations. The homepage also has a link to world cartoons, a currency converter and Worldtimeserver.com. The site's most recent feature is World Blogs.

Impact/Action Videos are concise news features on topics covered in this chapter, created exclusively for **Media/Impact**. They are available for students and instructors at CengageBrain.com, and include screen access for classroom viewing and discussion questions.

Glossary

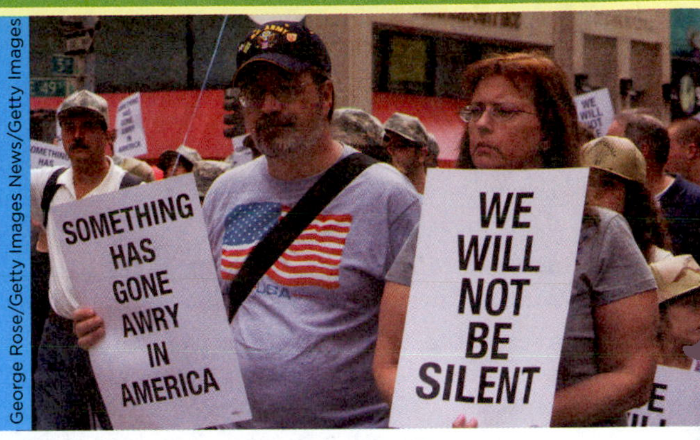

George Rose/Getty Images News/Getty Images

ABC Audit Bureau of Circulations.

ABC Australian Broadcasting Corporation.

Accreditation The process by which the government certifies members of the press to cover government-related news events.

Advance An amount the publisher pays the author before the book is published.

Advertising Campaign A planned advertising effort, coordinated for a specific time period.

Advertorial Paid advertising supplements in newspapers and magazines that often look similar to the regular news pages.

Affiliates Stations that use network programming but are owned by companies other than the networks.

Agenda-Setting The belief that journalists don't tell you *what* to think but do tell you *what and whom to think about*.

All-Platform Journalists Broadcast journalists who act as their own producer, cameraperson and editor, and sometimes even transmit live video.

Alternative, or Dissident, Press Media that present alternative viewpoints that challenge the mainstream press.

Analog In mass communications, a type of technology used in broadcasting, whereby video or audio information is sent as continuous signals through the air on specific airwave frequencies.

Ancillary Rights Marketing opportunities related to a movie, in addition to direct income from the movie itself.

ASCAP American Society of Composers, Authors and Publishers.

Audiobooks Abridged or complete versions of classic books and popular new titles on CDs.

Avatar An icon or a representation of a user—a digital stand-in—that people create to represent their online identity.

BBC British Broadcasting Corporation, the government-funded British broadcast network.

Blacklisting Studio owners' refusal to hire someone who was suspected of taking part in subversive activities.

Blanket Licensing Agreement An arrangement whereby radio stations become authorized to use recorded music for broadcast by paying a fee.

Blind Booking The practice of renting films to exhibitors without letting them see the films first.

Block Booking The practice of requiring theaters to take a package of movies instead of showing the movies individually.

Blockbuster A book that achieves enormous financial success.

Blog Short for Web log. A running Internet discussion group, where items are posted in reverse chronological order. Blogs usually focus on a specific topic.

BMI Broadcast Music, Inc., a cooperative music licensing organization.

Browser Software that allows people to display and interact with information on Web pages.

Bundles/The Bundle A collection of programs and/or media services offered together for a set fee. In telecommunications, the combination of telecommunications services that the media industries can offer consumers.

CATV Community antenna television or cable television.

CDA Communications Decency Act.

CD-RW Drives Computer drives that are used to read data and music encoded in digital form and can be used to record more than once.

Censorship The practice of suppressing material that is considered morally, politically or otherwise objectionable.

Checkbook Journalism The practice of a news organization paying for an interview or a photograph.

Click-Through Rate The rate at which people who see an ad on an Internet site click through to learn more.

Cloud Computing The remote use by one business of another company's computer space, operating "in the cloud."

Company Magazines Magazines produced by businesses for their employees, customers and stockholders.

Compatible Media that can function well with one another to exchange and integrate text, pictures, sound and video.

Concentration of Ownership The current trend of large companies buying smaller companies so that fewer companies own more types of media businesses.

Conglomerates Companies that own media companies as well as businesses that are unrelated to the media business.

Consensus Journalism The tendency among many journalists covering the same event to report similar conclusions about the event.

Consumer Magazines All magazines sold by subscription or at newsstands, supermarkets and bookstores.

Convergence The melding of the communications, computer and electronics industries. Also used to describe the economic alignment of the various media companies with each other to take advantage of technological advancements.

Cooperative News Gathering Member news organizations that share the expense of getting the news.

COPA Child Online Protection Act. A law aimed at preventing minors from getting access to sexually explicit online material.

CPM Cost-per-thousand, the cost of an ad per 1,000 people reached. (M is the Roman numeral for 1,000.)

Crisis Communication A timely public relations response to a critical situation that could cause damage to a company's reputation.

Cross-Ownership The practice of one company owning radio and TV stations in the same broadcast market.

Cybersmears Negative information organized and presented on the Internet as continuing attacks against a corporation.

Data Compression The process of squeezing digital content into a smaller electronic space.

DBS Direct broadcast satellite.

Demographics Data about consumers' characteristics, such as age, gender, income level, marital status, geographic location and occupation.

Deregulation Government action that reduces government restrictions on the business operations of an industry.

Digital Audio Broadcast A new form of audio transmission that eliminates all static and makes more program choices possible.

Digital Communication Data in a form that can be transmitted and received electronically.

Digital Divide The lack of access to digital technology among low-income, rural and minority groups.

Digital Media All emerging communications media that combine text, graphics, sound and video using computer technology.

Direct Sponsorship A program that carries an advertiser's name in the program title.

Disinformation The intentional planting of false information by government sources.

DMCA Digital Millennium Copyright Act.

Drive-Time Audiences People who listen to the radio in their cars during 6 to 9 a.m. and 4 to 7 p.m.

DVR Digital video recorders.

E-books Electronic books.

E-mail Mail that is delivered electronically over the Internet.

Embedded During the Iraq War, a term used to describe journalists who were allowed to cover the war on the frontlines, supervised by the U.S. military.

Ethics The rules or standards that govern someone's conduct.

Ethnocentric Promoting the superiority of one ethnic group over another.

False Light The charge that what was implied in a story about someone is incorrect.

FCC Federal Communications Commission.

Feedback A response sent back to the sender from the person who receives the communication.

File Sharing The peer-to-peer distribution of copyrighted material on the Internet without the copyright owner's permission.

Fleeting Expletives Profanity uttered without warning on live television

Freelancers Writers who are not on the staff of a magazine but who are paid for each individual article published.

HD Radio Hybrid digital technology that improves sound quality and makes it possible for radio stations to transmit real-time text messaging along with their programming.

High-Definition Television (HDTV) The industry standard for digital television transmission as of 2009; it provides a picture with a clearer resolution than earlier TV sets.

Home Page The first page of a Web site, which welcomes the user.

Hot Spot A public area like a restaurant or hotel where people with laptops and hand-held Internet devices can connect to the Internet without a wire.

HTML Hypertext markup language.

HTTP Hypertext transfer protocol.

HUAC House Un-American Activities Committee.

Hudson Test A legal test that establishes a standard for commercial speech protection.

IHT International Herald Tribune, the world's largest English-language newspaper.

Intellectual Property Rights The legal right of ownership of ideas and content published in any medium.

Interactive A message system that allows senders and receivers to communicate simultaneously.

Internet An international web of computer networks.

ISP Internet service provider, also called an Internet access provider.

LAPS Test A yardstick for local obscenity judgments, which evaluates an artistic work's literary, artistic, political or scientific value.

Libel A false statement that damages a person's character or reputation by exposing that person to public ridicule or contempt.

Links Electronic connections from one source of information to another.

LP Long-playing record.

Magic Bullet Theory The assertion that media messages directly and measurably affect people's behavior.

Mass Communication Communication from one person or group of persons through a transmitting device (a medium) to large audiences or markets.

Mass Market Books Books distributed through "mass" channels—newsstands, chain stores, drugstores and supermarkets.

Mass Media Industries Eight types of media businesses: books, newspapers, magazines, recordings, radio, movies, television and the Internet.

Media Content Analysis An attempt to analyze how mass media programming influences behavior.

Media Effects Research An attempt to analyze how people use the information they receive from the media.

Media Plural of the word *medium*.

Medium The means by which a message reaches the audience. The singular form of the word *media*.

Message Pluralism The availability to an audience of a variety of information and entertainment sources.

MPA The Association of Magazine Media, originally the Magazine Publisher's Association.

MPAA Motion Picture Association of America.

Muckrakers Investigative magazine journalists who targeted abuses by government and big business.

NAB National Association of Broadcasters, the lobbying organization that represents broadcasters' interests.

Narrowcasting Segmenting the radio audience.

Net Neutrality Rules for Internet service providers that require them to keep their networks open and available to carry all legal content. Under these rules, providers cannot restrict access to their network by other providers nor can they limit the type or delivery of content they carry.

Network A collection of radio or TV stations that offers programs, usually simultaneously, throughout the country, during designated program times.

NII National Information Infrastructure.

Noise Distortion (such as static) that interferes with clear communication.

NSL National Security Letter.

NWICO New World Information and Communications Order. The concept that mass media should include all areas of the world, not just the West.

O & Os TV stations that are owned and operated by the networks.

Pass-Along Readership People who share a magazine with the original recipient.

Payola The practice of accepting payment to play specific recordings on the air.

Penny Press or Penny Paper A newspaper produced by dropping the price of each copy to a penny and supporting the production cost through advertising.

Persuasion The act of using argument or reasoning to induce someone to do something.

Phonetic Writing The use of symbols to represent sounds.

Photojournalism Using photographs to accompany text to capture a news story.

Pictograph A symbol of an object that is used to convey an idea.

Podcast An audio or video file made available on the Internet for anyone to download, often available by subscription.

Point-of-Purchase Magazines Magazines that consumers buy directly, not by subscription. They are sold mainly at checkout stands in supermarkets.

Pool Reporting An arrangement that places reporters in small, government-supervised groups to cover an event.

Pop-Up An advertisement on a Web site that appears on the screen either behind a Web page when someone leaves the site or on top of the Web site home page when someone first visits.

Prime Time The TV time period from 7 to 11 p.m. when more people watch TV than at any other time.

Prior Restraint Government censorship of information before the information is published or broadcast.

Professional Ethics The rules or standards governing the conduct of the members of a profession.

Public Domain Publications, products and processes that are not protected by copyright and thus are available free to the public.

Publicity Uncontrolled free use of media by a public relations firm to create events and present information to capture press and public attention.

Public Relations Creating understanding for, or goodwill toward, a company, a person or a product.

Publishing Placing items on the Web.

Qualified Privilege The freedom of the press to report what is discussed during legislative and court proceedings.

Rating The percentage of the total number of households *with TV sets* tuned to a particular program.

RBOC Regional Bell Operating Companies.

Rep Firm A company of advertising sales representatives who sell advertising time and space in their market to companies outside their geographic area.

RIAA (Recording Industry Association of America) Industry association that lobbies for the interests of the nation's major recording companies. Member companies account for 95 percent of all U.S. recording company sales.

Roth Test A standard court test for obscenity, named for one of the defendants in an obscenity case.

Royalty An amount the publisher pays an author, based on an established percentage of the book's price; royalties run anywhere from 6 to 15 percent.

RPM Revolutions per minute.

RSS Really Simple Syndication. Allows a person to create a personal set of Internet programs and services to be delivered to a single Web site.

Satellite Radio Radio transmission by satellite, with limited or no advertising, available by subscription.

Search Advertising Advertising in the form of a list and/or link to a company's site domain name through a specific online search word or phrase.

Search Engine The tool used to locate information in a computer database.

Search Marketing Positioning Internet advertising prominently next to consumers' related online search results.

Seditious Language Language that authorities believe could incite rebellion against the government.

Selective Perception The concept that each person processes messages differently.

Server The equipment that delivers programs from their source to the programs' subscribers.

Share The percentage of the audience *with TV sets turned on* that is watching a particular program.

Shield Laws Laws that protect journalists from revealing their sources and the information that is communicated between journalists and their sources in a journalistic relationship.

Situation Comedy A TV program that establishes a regular cast of characters typically in a home or work situation. Also called a sitcom.

SLAPP Strategic lawsuit against public participation.

Spam Unsolicited bulk e-mail.

Spiral of Silence The belief that people with divergent views may be reluctant to challenge the consensus of opinion offered by the media.

Star System Promoting popular movie personalities to lure audiences.

Studio System An early method of hiring a stable of salaried stars and production people under exclusive contracts to a specific studio.

Subscription Television A new term used to describe consumer services delivered by cable and satellite program delivery.

Subsidiary Rights The rights to market a book for other uses—to make a movie or to print a character from the book on T-shirts, for example.

Sweeps The months when TV ratings services gather their most important ratings—February, May and November.

Syndicates News agencies that sell articles for publication to a number of newspapers simultaneously.

Syndicators Services that sell programming to broadcast stations and cable.

Tabloid A small-format newspaper that features large photographs and illustrations along with sensational stories.

Telcos An abbreviation for telephone companies.

30-Year Rule Developed by Paul Saffo, the theory that it takes about 30 years for a new technology to be completely adopted within a culture.

Time-Shifting Recording a television program on a DVR to watch at a more convenient time.

Trade, Technical and Professional Magazines Magazines dedicated to a particular business or profession.

Two-Step Flow The transmission of information and ideas from mass media to opinion leaders and then to friends.

Vertical Integration An attempt by one company to simultaneously control several related aspects of the media business.

Viral Marketing Creating an online message that is entertaining enough to get consumers to pass it on over the Internet like a virus.

Webzine (also called **zines**) Online magazine available on the Internet.

Wi-Fi An abbreviation for *Wi*reless *Fi*delity.

Wiki Technology that allows many users to collaborate to create and update Internet pages.

WIPO World Intellectual Property Organization.

Yellow Journalism News that emphasizes crime, sex and violence; also called jazz journalism and tabloid journalism.

Media Information Resource Guide

Photo by Vic Biondi

This directory offers a selection of current information sources to help research mass media topics. Many of these are print publications, and some are available as e-books or online journals. Also included is a list of associations that can provide information, including job listings, for specific media industries.

The study of mass media covers many areas of scholarship besides journalism and mass communication. Historians, psychologists, economists, political scientists and sociologists, for example, often contribute ideas to media studies. This directory therefore includes a variety of information sources from academic and industry publications as well as from popular periodicals.

These Research Sources Will Give You a Good Overview

The New York Times is the best daily source of information about the media industries, especially the paper's Business section, where you will find regular reports on earnings, acquisitions and leaders in the media industries. *The New York Times* archive online helps locate the articles you need.

The *Los Angeles Times'* daily Calendar section follows the media business very closely, especially television and movies, because many of the media production companies are based in Los Angeles.

The Wall Street Journal and *The Washington Post* also carry media information and both archives are indexed online. *The Wall Street Journal* charges users for access to some of its articles.

Advertising Age publishes special issues throughout the year focusing on newspapers, magazines, broadcasting and the Internet, as well as periodic estimates of total advertising revenue in each industry throughout the year. *Advertising Age* has an online index at *adage.com* but charges a fee and requires user registration for some articles and most statistical tables.

Columbia Journalism Review and *American Journalism Review* regularly critique developments in the print, broadcast and Internet industries. *Columbia Journalism Review* is published by New York's Columbia University Graduate School of Journalism. *American Journalism* is published by the University of Maryland Foundation at the Philip Merrill College of Journalism.

Communication Abstracts, *Communication Research*, *Journal of Communication* and *Journalism Quarterly* offer scholarly articles and article summaries about media issues. Journals that cover specific media topics include *Journal of Advertising Research*, *Newspaper Research Journal* and *Public Relations Review*.

The Veronis Suhler Stevenson Communications Industry Forecast, published exclusively online at *vss.com*, follows all the media industries. The *Forecast* offers historical media tables that track past performance, as well as projections for media industry growth. Check to see if your library offers free access to the *Forecast*.

Questia is an online library of books, journals and magazine and newspaper articles. The communication section features categories such as media studies on film; TV, Internet and print media; journalism history and ethics; and advertising and public relations.

These Resources Offer Specific Media Industry Information

Editor & Publisher, issued monthly and updated regularly online, follows the newspaper industry, including information about industry revenue.

Broadcasting & Cable Yearbook is an annual compilation of material about the broadcast industry. Also listed are syndicators, brokers, advertising agencies and associations.

Encyclopedia of American Journalism, edited by Stephen Vaughn (Routledge, 2009) is the only single-volume reference work covering the history of journalism in the United States. The *Encyclopedia* documents the historical distinctions between print media, radio, television and the Internet and their roles in the formation of a variety of social movements in the United States, including peace and protest, civil and consumer rights, environmentalism and globalization.

Ulrich's Periodicals Directory lists journals, magazines and newspapers alphabetically and by subject. Its online counterpart, *Ulrichsweb.com*, is continually updated with new information and includes an archive.

ASCAP (The American Society of Composers, Authors and Publishers) lists a number of reference books, periodicals, directories and professional organizations pertaining to the recording industry in its online resource guide.

Hollywood Creative Directory, produced by *The Hollywood Reporter*, is a comprehensive list that includes names, numbers and Web site listings of producers and executives in film and television, production companies, studios and networks.

For annual compilations of movie listings and reviews, check *Roger Ebert's Movie Yearbook* (Andrews McMeel, 2010) and *Leonard Maltin's 2011 Movie Guide* (Signet, 2010).

The National Association of Broadcasters (NAB) produces a variety of publications that cover the radio and television industries, including an annual overview of TV called *The Television Industry: A Market-by-Market Review*.

Standard Directory of Advertising Agencies is an annual publication that lists advertising agencies alphabetically, as well as the accounts they manage.

Digital Media Wire publishes daily online newsletters and updated directories covering the business of digital media (including music, videos, gaming and mobile media). Its *Digital Entertainment & Media Directory* is available in hard copy and electronic versions.

These Resources Will Help You Uncover U.S. Media History

John P. Dessauer's *Book Publishing: What It Is, What It Does* (R. R. Bowker, 1981) succinctly explains the history of the book publishing business. Another historical perspective and overview is available in *Books: The Culture & Commerce of Publishing* by Lewis A. Coser et al. (Basic Books, 1982). *Book Business: Publishing Past, Present and Future* by Jason Epstein (Norton, 2002) assesses the past and present book business. *The Book Publishing Industry* by Albert N. Greco, 2nd edition (Erlbaum, 2004) discusses marketing, production and changing technology.

The Journalist's Bookshelf by Roland E. Wolseley and Isabel Wolseley (Berg, 1986) is a comprehensive listing of resources about American print journalism.

The classic early history of American magazines is Frank Luther Mott's *History of American Magazines* (Appleton, 1930). *Pages from the Past: History and Memory in American Magazines* by Carolyn Kitch (University of North Carolina Press, 2008) examines the role of magazines in creating collective memory and identity for Americans.

The Music Business and Recording Industry by Geoffrey Hull, Thomas Hutchinson and Richard Strasser (Routledge, 2010) is a textbook that examines the economics of today's recording industry. *Appetite for Self-Destruction: The Spectacular Crash of the Record Industry in the Digital Age* by Steve Kopper (Soft Skull Press, 2009) offers a critical look at the last 30 years of the music business. *This Business of Music* by M. William Krasilovsky, Sidney Shemel, John M. Gross and Jonathan Feinstein (Billboard Publications, 2007) explains how the recording industry works.

Listening In: Radio and American Imagination by Susan J. Douglas (University of Minnesota Press, 2004) and *Radio Reader: Essays in the Cultural History of Radio* by Michele Hilmes (Routledge, 2001) specifically discuss the cultural impact of radio in the 20th century.

A History of Films by John L. Fell (Holt, Rinehart & Winston, 1979) and *Movie-Made America: A Cultural History of American Movies,* revised edition, Vintage, 1994) by Robert Sklar provide a good introduction to the history of movies. Works examining the cultural, social and economic impacts on American society include *Movies and American Society* edited by Steven J. Ross (Wiley-Blackwell, 2002) and *American Film: A History* by Jon Lewis (Norton, 2007).

Halliwell's Film Guide (HarperCollinsUK, 2008) is a great 1400-page encyclopedic source for movie information. Another good movie information resource is *The Film Encyclopedia* (Collins, 2008), currently in its 6th edition, by Ephraim Katz.

The Columbia History of American Television by Gary Edgerton (Columbia University Press, 2007) follows the technological developments and cultural relevance of TV from its pre-history to the present. *From Daytime to Primetime: The History of American Television Programs* by James W. Roman (Greenwood, 2008) offers up-to-date, comprehensive coverage of TV history. The classic television history is Eric Barnouw's *Tube of Plenty* (Oxford University Press, 1975). Christopher H. Sterling and John M. Kittross provide another overview of radio and television history in *Stay Tuned: A History of American Broadcasting*, 3rd edition (Routledge, 2001).

Confessions of an Advertising Man by David Ogilvy (Southbank, 2004) is the classic insider's view of the business. Three other histories of American advertising are *The Making of Modern Advertising* by Daniel Pope (Basic Books, 1983), *Advertising the American Dream* by Roland Marchand (University of California Press, 1986) and *The Mirror Makers: A History of American Advertising and Its Creators* by Stephen Fox (University of Illinois Press, 1997).

In 1923, Edward L. Bernays wrote the first book specifically about public relations, *The Engineering of Consent* (University of Oklahoma Press, reprinted in 1955). For an understanding of today's public relations business, you can read *This Is PR: The Realities of Public Relations* by Doug Newsom, Judy VanSlyke Turk and Dean Kruckeberg (Cengage, 2009).

A Social History of the Media: From Gutenberg to the Internet by Peter Burke and Asa Briggs, 2nd edition (Polity, 2005) and *Convergence Culture: Where Old and New Media Collide* by Henry Jenkins (NYU Press, 2008) discuss the emergence and evolution of communications media, their social impact and the relationship between the media producers and consumers.

To learn more about newsreels and to view the actual films, visit the University of South Carolina Web site, *www.sc.edu/library/newsfilm*. Other major newsreel collections exist at the National Archives and Records Administration Web site at *www.archives.gov* and at the Library of Congress, *www.loc.gov/library/libarch-digital.html*. British Pathé newsreels are located at *www.britishpathe.com*.

The most comprehensive academic journals specifically devoted to media history are *American Journalism*, published by the American Journalism Historians Association, and *Journalism History*, published by the E. W. Scripps School of Journalism at Ohio University, with support from the History Division of the Association for Education in Journalism and Mass Communication.

For information about historical events and people in the media who often are omitted from traditional histories, you can refer to *Up from the Footnote: A History of Women Journalists* by Marion Marzolf (Hastings House, 1977); *Great Women of the Press* by Madelon Golden Schilpp and Sharon M. Murphy (Southern Illinois University Press, 1983); *Taking Their Place: A Documentary History of Women and Journalism* by Maurine Hoffman Beasley and Sheila Jean Gibbons, 2nd edition (Strata Publishing, 2002); *Journalistas: 100 Years of the Best Writing and Reporting by Women Journalists*, edited by Eleanor Mills (Seal Press, 2005); *Black Journalists: The NABJ Story* by Wayne Dawkins, updated edition (August Press, 1997); *Ladies' Pages: African American Women's Magazines and the Culture that Made Them* by Noliwe M. Rooks (Rutgers University Press, 2004); *Minorities and Media: Diversity and the End of Mass Communication* by Clint C. Wilson and Felix Gutiérrez (Sage, 1985); *Gender, Race and Class in Media* by Gail Dines and Jean M. Humez (Sage, 2002); and *Facing Difference: Race, Gender and Mass Media* by Shirley Biagi and Marilyn Kern-Foxworth (Pine Forge Press, 1997).

These Web Sites Help You Locate Current Media Industry News

Thousands of Web sites on the Internet offer useful material about the mass media. What follows is an alphabetical list of the specific sites that also appear at the end of each chapter. If you can't reach the Web site at the address listed, search using the site's name, listed in **bold type**.

To find Web sites on a specific media topic, check **Working the Web** at the end of each chapter.

Academy of Motion Picture Arts and Sciences
http://www.oscars.org

Adrants
http://www.adrants.com

Advertising Age
http://www.adage.com

Advertising Council
http://www.adcouncil.org

All About Public Relations
http://www.aboutpublicrelations.net

AllYouCanRead.com
http://www.allyoucanread.com

Amazon
http://www.amazon.com

American Advertising Federation
http://www.aaf.org

American Association of Advertising Agencies
http://www.aaaa.org

American Booksellers Association
http://www.bookweb.org

American Booksellers Foundation for Free Expression (ABFFE)
http://www.abffe.org

American Library Association (ALA)
http://www.ala.org

American Marketing Association
http://www.marketingpower.com

American Society of Journalists and Authors (ASJA)
http://www.asja.org

American Society of Newspaper Editors (ASNE)
http://www.asne.org

American Top 40 with Ryan Seacrest
http://www.at40.com

AOL Music
http://music.aol.com

Apple.com/iTunes
http://www.apple.com/itunes

Apple Inc.
http://www.apple.com

Association of American Publishers
http://www.publishers.org

Association of Hispanic Advertising Agencies
http://www.ahaa.org

Barnes & Noble
http://www.barnesandnoble.com

BBC News
http://www.bbc.co.uk

Benton Foundation
http://www.benton.org

Biblio
http://www.biblio.com

Billboard
http://billboard.biz and http://billboard.com

BookFinder
http://www.bookfinder.com

The Broadcast Archive
http://www.oldradio.com

Canadian Broadcasting Corporation (CBC) Radio-Canada
http://www.cbc.ca/radio

CBS Corporation
http://www.cbscorporation.com

CBS Radio
http://www.cbsradio.com

Center for Media and Democracy: PRWatch
http://www.prwatch.org

Center on Media and Child Health (CMCH)
http://www.cmch.tv

Chartered Institute of Public Relations
http://www.cipr.co.uk

Clio Awards
http://www.clioawards.com

CNET
http://www.cnet.com

***Columbia Journalism Review* (*CJR*)**
http://www.cjr.org

Committee to Protect Journalists
http://www.cpj.org

CondèNet—Web site for Condè Nast Publications
http://www.condenet.com

CyberJournalist.net
http://www.cyberjournalist.net

The Dallas Morning News
http://www.dallasnews.com

DEG Digital Entertainment Group
http://www.dvdinformation.com

Disney-ABC Television Group
http://www.disneyabctv.com

Electronic Frontier Foundation (EFF)
http://www.eff.org

EthicNet, European Ethics Codes
http://ethicnet.uta.fi/

Facebook
http://facebook.com

Fairness & Accuracy in Reporting (FAIR)
http://www.fair.org/index.php

Federal Communications Commission (FCC)
http://www.fcc.gov

Federal Trade Commission (FTC)
http://www.ftc.gov

FindLaw
http://www.findlaw.com

Folio: The Magazine for Magazine Management
http://www.foliomag.com

***Foreign Policy* Magazine**
http://www.foreignpolicy.com

Fox Movietone News
http://www.sc.edu/library/mirc

Freedom Forum
http://www.freedomforum.org

Freedom of Information Center (University of Missouri School of Journalism, Columbia)
http://www.nfoic.org/foi-center/

Friday Morning Quarterback (FMQB)
http://www.fmqb.com

Gannett Company, Inc. (owner of *USA Today*)
http://www.gannett.com

General Electric
http://www.ge.com

***Global Media Journal* (*GMJ*)**
http://lass.calumet.purdue.edu/cca/gmj

Global Media Monitor (GMM)
http://lass.calumet.purdue.edu/cca/gmm

Google Book Search
http://books.google.com

Honolulu Star-Advertiser
http://www.staradvertiser.com

Index on Censorship
http://www.indexoncensorship.org

Indiana University Index of Journalism Ethics Cases
http://journalism.indiana.edu/resources/ethics/

IndieBound
http://www.indiebound.org

Inside Radio
http://www.insideradio.com

Insound
http://www.insound.com

Institute for Public Relations
http://www.instituteforpr.com

International Center for Journalists
http://www.icfj.org

International Herald Tribune
http://www.iht.com

International Women's Media Foundation (IWMF)
http://www.iwmf.org

The Internet Movie Database (IMDB)
http://www.imdb.com

Internews
http://www.internews.org

Investigative Reporters and Editors (IRE)
http://www.ire.org

iVillage
http://www.ivillage.com

Joan Shorenstein Center on the Press, Politics and Public Policy (Harvard University)
http://www.hks.harvard.edu/presspol/

Journal of Electronic Publishing (JEP)
http://www.journalofelectronicpublishing.org

Los Angeles Times
http://www.latimes.com

Lucasfilm
http://www.lucasfilm.com

Media Awareness Network (MNet)
http://www.media-awareness.ca

Media Center at New York Law School
http://www.nyls.edu/centers/projects/media_center

Media Effects Research Lab at Penn State University
http://www.psu.edu/dept/medialab/

Media Law Resource Center (MLRC)
http://www.medialaw.org

MediaPost Communications
http://www.mediapost.com

Media Research Hub (Social Science Research Council)
http://mediaresearchhub.ssrc.org

The Miami Herald
http://www.miamiherald.com

Minnesota News Council
http://news-council.org

MIT Media Lab Project
http://www.media.mit.edu

Moorland-Spingarn Research Center (MSRC) at Howard University
http://www.founders.howard.edu/moorland-spingarn

Motion Picture Association of America (MPAA) and Motion Picture Association (MPA)
http://www.mpaa.org

MPA—The Association of Magazine Media and the American Society of Magazine Editors (ASME)
http://www.magazine.org

Napster
http://www.napster.com

National Association of Broadcasters (NAB)
http://www.nab.org

National Cable & Telecommunications Association
http://www.ncta.com

National Journal
http://www.nationaljournal.com

National Public Radio
http://www.npr.org

Netflix
http://www.netflix.com

News Corporation
http://www.newscorp.com

Newspaper Association of America (NAA)
http://www.naa.org

Newsweek
http://www.newsweek.com

The New York Times
http://www.nytimes.com

Nielsen Media Research
http://www.nielsenmedia.com

Northwestern University Library: Broadcast, Cable and Satellite Resources on the Internet
http://www.library.northwestern.edu/media/resources/broadcast.html

The Online News Association (ONA)
http://www.journalist.org

Online Public Relations
http://www.online-pr.com

Online Publishers Association (OPA)
http://www.online-publishers.org

O, The Oprah Magazine
http://www.oprah.com/omagazine.html

Pandora: Radio from the Music Genome Project
http://pandora.com

Parental Media Guide
http://parentalguide.org/movies.html

Pew Internet & American Life Project
http://www.pewinternet.org

Pew Research Center for People and the Press
http://people-press.org/reports

Pew Research Center's Project for Excellence in Journalism
http://journalism.org

Poynter Online
http://www.poynter.org

PR Newswire
http://prnewswire.com

Project for Excellence in Journalism: Ethics Codes
http://www.journalism.org/resources/ethics_codes

PRWeb
http://www.prweb.com

PRWeek
http://www.prweekus.com

Public Broadcasting (PBS)
http://www.pbs.org

Public Relations Society of America (PRSA)
http://www.prsa.org

Public Relations Student Society of America (PRSSA)
http://www.prssa.org

Radio Advertising Bureau
http://www.rab.com

Radio Lovers
http://www.radiolovers.com

Radio Television Digital News Association (RTDNA; formerly Radio-Television News Directors Association)
http://www.rtdna.org

Radio Time
http://radiotime.com

Recording Industry Association of America (RIAA)
http://www.riaa.com

Reporters Without Borders
http://www.rsf.org

Salon
http://www.salon.com

Scholastic Corporation
http://www.scholastic.com

Screenwriters Federation of America (SFA)
http://www.screenwritersfederation.org

Silha Center for the Study of Media Ethics and Law (University of Minnesota)
http://www.silha.umn.edu/

Sirius XM
http://www.siriusxm.com

Slate
http://www.slate.com

Society of Professional Journalists (SPJ)
http://www.spj.org

Sony Corporation of America
http://www.sony.com

Sports Illustrated
http://sportsillustrated.cnn.com

Student Press Law Center (SPLC)
http://www.splc.org

Sundance Institute
http://www.sundance.org

Talking Points Memo (TPM)
http://www.talkingpointsmemo.com

Television Bureau of Advertising (TVB)
http://www.tvb.org

Time Warner Inc.
http://www.timewarner.com

Topix
http://www.topix.net

Tribune Company
http://www.tribune.com

TV.com
http://www.tv.com

Twitter
http://twitter.com

United Artists
http://www.unitedartists.com

Unity: Journalists of Color, Inc.
http://www.unityjournalists.org

Universal Music Group (UMG)
http://www.universalmusic.com

University of Iowa Department of Communication Studies: Political Communication and Campaigns
http://www.uiowa.edu/commstud/resources/polcomm.html

U.S. Census Bureau Statistical Abstract: Information and Communications
http://www.census.gov/compendia/statab/cats/information_communications.html

Vanderbilt University Television News Archive
http://tvnews.vanderbilt.edu

Viacom Inc. (owner of Nickelodeon, Comedy Central and Nick at Nite)
http://viacom.com

Walt Disney Company (owner of ABC)
http://disney.go.com

Warner Bros.
http://www.warnerbros.com

The Washington Post
http://www.washingtonpost.com

Whatis.com
http://whatis.techtarget.com

WikiLeaks
http://www.wikileaks.ch/

Wikipedia
http://www.wikipedia.org/

Worldpress.org
http://www.worldpress.org

YouTube
http://www.youtube.com

More Media Research Sources You Can Use

Many magazines publish information about the mass media industries. The following is a listing of the major magazine titles in each subject area. Many of these magazines offer companion Web sites.

ADVERTISING

Advertising Age

Adweek and *Adweek: National Marketing Edition*

Journal of Advertising

Journal of Advertising Research

BROADCASTING

Broadcasting & Cable

Emmy, published by the Academy of Television Arts and Sciences

Federal Communications Law Journal

Journal of Broadcasting and Electronic Media, published by Broadcast Education Association

RTDNA Communicator, published by the Radio-Television Digital News Association

TV Guide

MAGAZINE AND BOOK PUBLISHING

Bookwoman, published by the Women's National Book Association

Folio, the magazine for magazine management

Publishers Weekly, the journal of the book industry

MOVIES

Film Comment, published by the Film Society of Lincoln Center

Hollywood Reporter

Variety

Video Age

NEWSPAPERS

Editor & Publisher

Journalism & Communication Monographs, published by the Association for Education in Journalism and Mass Communication

Newspaper Research Journal, published by the Association for Education in Journalism and Mass Communication

Presstime, published by the Newspaper Association of America

Quill, published by the Society of Professional Journalists

PUBLIC RELATIONS

Public Relations Journal

PR Week

RECORDINGS

Billboard

Cash Box

Down Beat

Music Index, a specialized index of articles on the music industry

Rolling Stone

DIGITAL MEDIA AND THE WEB

AI Magazine

Communications Daily

Computer Gaming World

Information Today

MacWorld

PC Magazine

PC World

Technical Communication

Wired

Global Media

ADVERTISING

International Journal of Advertising, England

BROADCASTING

Broadcast, England

Cable and Satellite Europe, England

MOVIES

Cineaction, Canada

Empire, England

Film Ireland

Film Ink, Australia

RECORDINGS

Musical America International Directory of the Performing Arts

OTHER

OPMA Overseas Media Guide, England

Media-Related Topics

Censorship News, published by the National Coalition Against Censorship

Communication Research

Entertainment Law Reporter covers legal issues related to motion pictures, radio, TV and music

News Media and the Law, published by Reporters Committee for Freedom of the Press

Nieman Reports, published by the Nieman Foundation for Journalism at Harvard University

CASEY KELBAUGH/The New York Times/Redux Pictures

References

Chapter 1 Mass Media and Everyday Life

Associated Press (2007, April 18). Clear Channel accepts $19.4 billion offer. Money.AOL.com.

Association of American Publishers (2010, April 7). AAP reports book sales estimated at 23.9 billion in 2009. Publishers.org.

Bagdikian, B. (1980, Spring). Conglomeration, concentration, and the media. *Journal of Communication*, 60.

Bagdikian, B. (1983). *The media monopoly*. Boston: Beacon Press.

Carr, D. (2007, January 15). 24-hour newspaper people. *The New York Times*, C1.

Carr, D. (2011, January 2). The great mashup of 2011. NYTimes.com.

eMarketer (2011, January 4). Online ad spending set to break records. eMarketer.com.

Gilder, G. (1994, February 28). Life after television, updated. *Forbes*, 17.

Graham, J. (2005, May 20). Google gets personal. *USA Today*, 6B.

Greene, J. (2003, April 28). The year of living wirelessly. BusinessWeek.com.

Gustin, S. (2010, February 23). One-third of Americans lack high-speed Internet access. DailyFinance.com.

Hernandez, D. (2011, August 6). Too much Facebook time may be unhealthy for kids. LATimes.com.

Jenkins, H. (2000, March). Digital land grab. *Technology Review*, 103.

Kharif, O. (2005, June 21). Nearly everything gets unplugged. BusinessWeek.com.

Kim, R. (2005, May 28). Sales of cell phones totally off the hook. *San Francisco Chronicle*, C1.

Kirkpatrick, D. D. (2003, April 14). Murdoch's first step: Make the sports fan pay. *The New York Times*, C1.

Ives, N. (2010, June 28). Mounting web woes pummel newspapers. *Advertising Age*, 6.

Lang, B. (2010, September 20). Ipsos OTX study: People spend more than half their day consuming media. TheWrap.com.

Liebling, A. J. (1961). *The press*. New York: Ballantine.

Lohr, S. (2010, March 16). How privacy vanishes online. NYTimes.com.

Lohr, S. (2011, October 23). More jobs predicted for machines, not people. NYTimes.com.

Los Angeles Times (2011, January 26). Mobile app revenue will triple to $15 billion this year, Gartner says. LATimes.com.

Nielsenwire (2009, December 21). Study: More cellular-only homes as Americans expand mobile media usage. Nielsenwire.com.

Plato (1961). *Collected works*. Princeton, N.J.: Phaedrus.

Raine, G. (2005, September 27). Net ad revenues grow steadily. *San Francisco Chronicle*, D1.

Rose, L. (2007, February 7). The best-paid talking heads. Forbes.com.

Rosenbloom, S. (2010, February 27). Cell phone applications let shoppers point, click and purchase. *The New York Times*, A1.

Scott, A. O. (2008, November 23). The screening of America. *The New York Times Magazine*, 21.

Siebert, T. (2007, February). World wide web: Hearing is believing. MediaPost.com.

Siklos, R. (2005, August 1). Behind Murdoch rift, a media dynasty unhappy in its own way. *The New York Times*, C1.

Siklos, R. (2007, May 13). Tilting at a digital future. *The New York Times*, 3-1.

Siklos, R., & Holson, L. (2005, August 8). NBC Universal aims to be prettiest feather in G.E.'s cap. *The New York Times*, C1.

Smith, A. (1980). *Goodbye Gutenberg*. New York: Oxford University Press.

Soto, M. (2000, May 4). Microsoft executive Nathan Myhrvold resigns. SeattleTimes.nwsource.com.

Story, L. (2007, January 15). Anywhere the eye can see, it's now likely to see an ad. *The New York Times*, A1.

Stout, H. (2010, May 2). Antisocial networking? *The New York Times*, ST2.

Sutel, S. (2005, September 20). *New York Times* to cut 4 percent of work force. Associated Press, AOL Business News. AOL.com.

Veronis Suhler Stevenson (2010, August 10). New VSS forecast: Predicts pick-up in total communications spending 2010–2014 driven by gradual economic recovery, advances in digital technology and secular shifts in business and consumer spending and consumption. VSS.com.

Verrier, R. (2011, January 28). Movie ticket prices reach new milestone. LATimes.com.

Chapter 2 Books: Rearranging the Page

Andriani, L. (2009, August 14). Cengage Learning to rent print textbooks. PublishersWeekly.com.

Associated Press (2009, August 20). Microsoft, Yahoo, Amazon to fight Google book deal. SFGate.com.

Associated Press (2010, November 9). Publishers to get 70 percent of sales on Kindle. WSJ.com.

Associated Press. (2011, August 30). Books-A-Million will assume 14 Borders leases. SFGate.com.

Auletta, K. (2010, April 26). Publish or perish. NewYorker .com.

Bosman, J. (2010, August 3). Biggest U.S. book chain up for sale. NYTimes.com.

Bosman, J. (2010, August 14). Quick change in strategy for a bookseller. NYTimes.com.

Bosman, J. (2010, December 8). Lusty tales and hot sales: Romance e-books thrive. NYTimes.com.

Bosman, J. (2011, June 23). Rowling releases 'Harry Potter' into the ether on Pottermore. NYTimes.com.

Boss, S. (2007, May 13). The great mystery: Making a bestseller. *The New York Times*, 3-1.

Bradley, T. (2009, September 21). Opposition mounting against Google books settlement. SFGate.com.

Clifford, S. & Bosman, J. (2011, February 27). Publishers look beyond bookstores. NYTimes.com.

Coser, L. A., Kadushin, C., & Powell, W. F. (1982). *Books: The culture and commerce of publishing*. New York: Basic Books.

Davis, K. C. (1984). *Two-bit culture: The paperbacking of America*. Boston: Houghton Mifflin.

Dessauer, J. P. (1974). *Book publishing: What it is, what it does*. New York: R. R. Bowker.

Donadio, R. (2008, April 27). You're an author? Me too! *The New York Times Book Review*, 27.

Flood, A. (2011, August 18). James Patterson brand makes him world's best-paid writer. Guardian.co.uk.

Galassi, J. (2010, January 3). There's more to publishing than meets the screen. NYTimes.com.

Hart, J. D. (1950). *The popular book*. Berkeley: University of California Press.

Helft, M. (2009, April 29). U.S. opens inquiry into Google books deal. *The New York Times*, B5.

Helft, M. (2009, September 24). Google books settlement delayed indefinitely. NYTimes.com.

Helft, M. (2011, March 22). Judge reject's Google's deal to digitize books. NYTimes.com.

Hoffman, J. (2007, April 15). Comparative literature. *The New York Times Book Review*, 27.

Hyde, C. R. (2010, November 2). The (paltry) economics of being a novelist. DailyFinance.com.

Itzkoff, D. (2009, September 8). Not a typo: James Patterson signs 17-book deal. NYTimes.com.

Kelly, K. (2006, May 14). What will happen to books? *The New York Times Magazine*, 43–71.

Kennedy, R. (2005, June 5). Cash up front. *The New York Times Book Review*, 14.

Mackay, R. (2010, December 27). Julian Assange's 1.3 million reasons to write. NYTimes.com.

Mahler, J. (2010, January 24). James Patterson Inc. NYTimes.com.

McMurtrie, H. (2009, March 15). The Kindle 2: A thin read. SFGate.com.

Miller, C. C. (2010, July 19). E-books top hardcovers at Amazon. NYTimes.com.

Miller, C. C. & Bosman, J. (2011, May 19). E-books outsell print books at Amazon. NYTimes.com.

Randolph, E. (2008, June 18). Reading into the future. NYTimes.com.

Reuters (2010, August 24). Book chain reports loss as it fights with investor. NYTimes.com.

Rich, M. (2007, June 1). Sales barely up, book trade yearns for next blockbuster. *The New York Times*, C3.

Rich, M. (2008, July 27). Literacy debate: Online, r u really reading? *The New York Times*, A1.

Rich, M. (2009, May 17). Steal this book (for $9.99). *The New York Times*, WK3.

Rich, M. (2009, May 29). Declining book sales cast gloom at an Expo. *The New York Times*, B4.

Rich, M. (2010, February 11). E-book's cost is going up. *The New York Times*, B1.

Rich, M. (2010, February 19). Judge hears arguments on Google book settlement. *The New York Times*, B4.

Rich, M. (2010, February 22). Textbooks that professors can rewrite digitally. *The New York Times*, B4.

Rich, M. (2010, March 1). Math of publishing meets the e-book. *The New York Times*, B1.

Richtel, M., & Miller, C. C. (2010, September 1). Of two minds about books. NYTimes.com.

Rothstein, E. (2007, April 9). Sampling, if not digesting, the digital library. *The New York Times*, B3.

Stelter, B. (2010, December 27). WikiLeaks founder signs book deal. NYTimes.com.

Stone, B. (2009, October 7). New Kindle to download books beyond U.S. NYTimes.com

Stone, B., & Wortham, J. (2010, January 27). Apple reveals the iPad tablet. NYTimes.com.

Streitfield, D. (2005, July 17). Publisher loses ruling on e-books. LATimes.com.

Stross, R. (2009, October 4). Will books be Napsterized? NYTimes.com

Tedeschi, B. (2010, May 13). E-reader applications for today, and beyond. *The New York Times*, B10.

Trachtenberg, J. A. (2010, May 21). E-books rewrite bookselling. WSJ.com.

Trachtenberg, J. A. (2010, September 28). Authors feel pinch in age of e-books. WSJ.com.

Trachtenberg, J. A. (2010, December 6). Google opens online bookstore. WSJ.com.

Weinberg, S. (2010, March 16). Enhanced e-books: A boon for readers, a headache for agents. DailyFinance.com.

Weinberg, S. (2010, August 2). Amazon's new Kindles sell out in just five days. DailyFinance.com.

White, E. B. (1976). *Letters of E. B. White*. New York: Harper & Row.

Chapter 3 Newspapers: Expanding Delivery

Ahrens, F. (2009, March 26). *Washington Post* to offer new buyouts to employees. WashingtonPost.com.

Associated Press (2010, January 16). MediaNews holding company filing Chapter 11. SFGate.com.

Associated Press (2010, February 12). *USA Today* mandates staff furloughs to save money. NYTimes.com.

Associated Press (2010, August 27). *USA Today* plans overhaul to emphasize mobile devices. NYTimes.com.

Associated Press (2010, November 1). *National Enquirer's* owner to file for bankruptcy. LATimes.com.

Associated Press (2011, November 10). *National Enquirer's* owner to file for bankruptcy. LATimes.com.

Auletta, K. (2005, October 10). Fault line. *The New Yorker*, 51.

Avriel, E. (2007, July 2). *N.Y. Times* publisher: Our goal is to manage the transition from print to Internet. Haaretz.com.

Carr, D. (2010, October 5). At flagging Tribune, tales of a bankrupt culture. NYTimes.com.

Carr, D. (2011, April 11). At Gannett, furloughs but nice paydays for brass. NYTimes.com.

De Falco, B. (2011, January 11). Gannett to cut staff at 3 N.J. papers by nearly half. SFGate.com.

De La Merced, M. (2009, December 8). Tribune files for bankruptcy. NYTimes.com.

Dertouzos, J., & Quinn, T. (1985, September). Bargaining responses to the technology revolution: The case of the newspaper industry. *Labor management cooperation brief.* Washington, D.C.: U.S. Department of Labor.

Johnson, K. (2009, February 27). Part of Denver's past, the Rocky says goodbye. NYTimes.com.

Kessler, K. (1984). *The dissident press*. Beverly Hills, Calif.: Sage.

Marzolf, M. (1977). *Up from the footnote*. New York: Hastings House.

Perez-Peña, R. (2007, May 1). Newspaper circulation in steep slide across nation. *The New York Times*, C10.

Perez-Peña, R. (2008, April 7). Tough guy in a mean business. *The New York Times*, C1.

Perez-Peña, R. (2009, March 12). As cities go from two newspapers to one, some talk of zero. *The New York Times*. A1.

Perez-Peña, R. (2010, January 21). *The Times* to charge for frequent access to its web site. NYTimes.com.

Peters, J. W. (2010, September 5). Some newspapers, tracking readers online, shift coverage. NYTimes.com.

Peters, J. W. (2010, October 25). Newspaper circulation falls broadly but at slower pace. NYTimes.com.

Pew Research Center's Project for Excellence in Journalism, *The State of the News Media* 2011. Stateofthemedia .org/2011.

Plambeck, J. (2010, April 27). Newspaper circulation falls nearly 9 percent. *The New York Times*, B3.

Rainey, J. (2011, February 5). Consolidation seen as inevitable for Southern California newspapers. LATimes.com.

Reuters (2010, May 21). Tribune facing legal battle with creditors. *The New York Times*, B4.

Reuters (2011, December 12). To reorganize debt, publisher of papers files for bankruptcy. NYTimes.com.

Richman, D., & James, A. (2009, March 16). *Seattle P-I* to publish last edition Tuesday. SeattlePI.com.

Rutherford, L. (1963). *John Peter Zenger*. Gloucester, Mass.: Peter Smith.

Saltmarsh, M. (2010, March 26). Murdoch finalizes paywall for two British papers. NYTimes.com.

Schilpp, M. G., & Murphy, S. M. (1983). *Great women of the press*. Carbondale: Southern Illinois University Press.

Seelye, K. Q. (2005, September 21). Times company announces 500 job cuts. *The New York Times*, C5.

Seelye, K. Q., & Sorkin, A. R. (2007, April 2). Tribune accepts real estate magnate's bid. NYTimes.com.

Smith, A. (1980). *Goodbye Gutenberg*. New York: Oxford University Press.

Sorkin, A. R. (2007, May 2). First the bid, now the jockeying. *The New York Times*, C1.

Stelter, B. (2011, October 13). *New York Times* plans staff reductions. NYTimes.com.

Swanberg, W. A. (1971). *Citizen Hearst*. New York: Bantam Books.

Wells, I. B. (1970). *The crusade for justice: The autobiography of Ida B. Wells*. Chicago: University of Chicago Press.

Yardley, W., & Perez-Peña, R. (2009, March 17). In Seattle, a newspaper loses its paper routes. *The New York Times*, A1.

Zezima, K. (2005, August 8). Abolitionist's family celebrates a legacy of nonconformity. *The New York Times*, A10.

Chapter 4 Magazines: Targeting the Audience

Bercovici, J. (2009, October 5). Condé Nast closes beloved *Gourmet* magazine and three others. DailyFinance.com.

Bercovici, J. (2010, August 2). *Newsweek* gets sold to Sidney Harman. So long, *Newsweek*. DailyFinance.com.

Biagi, S. (1987). *NewsTalk I*. Belmont, Calif.: Wadsworth.

Carr, D. (2011, May 9). *The New Yorker* begins to offer iPad subscriptions. NYTimes.com.

Clifford, S. (2010, February 9). Newsstand sales and circulation fall for magazines. *The New York Times*, B3.

Clifford, S. (2010, May 6). As *Newsweek* goes on block, an era fades. *The New York Times*, A1.

Clifford, S. (2010, May 16). Fans of *Gourmet Magazine* accept no stand-ins. NYTimes.com.

Holson, E. (2007, May 25). OMG! Cute boys, kissing lips and lots of pics as magazines find a niche. *The New York Times*, C1.

Kobak, J. B. (1985, April). 1984: A billion-dollar year for acquisitions. *Folio*, 14, 82–95.

Lee, F. R. (2005, August 10). He created a mirror for black America. *The New York Times*, B1.

Mechanic, M. (2001, March 19). Doing the bare minimum media: Magazines are rethinking the Internet. *Newsweek*, 62F.

O'Brien, K. J. (2007, March 18). Magazine publishers see future, but no profit in shift to Internet. IHT.com.

Olivarez-Giles, N. (2010, November 30). *Project*, Richard Branson's iPad-only magazine, now available in Apple's app store. LATimes.com.

Paneth, D. (1983). *Encyclopedia of American journalism*. New York: Facts on File.

Perez-Peña, R. (2008, July 20). Undercover publisher. *The New York Times*, BU1.

Peters, J. W. (2010, November 29). Magazines take a shot at the net. *The New York Times*, B6.

Peters, J. W. (2011, January 16). For magazines, a bitter pill in iPad. NYTimes.com.

Peters, J. W. (2011, November 13). *Newsweek*, mired in red ink, cancels longtime political series. NYTimes.com.

Peters, J. W. (2011, November 20). At 154, a digital milestone. NYTimes.com.

Rose, M. (2000, November 6). Problems for magazines come into view. *The Wall Street Journal*, B18.

Schilpp, M. G., & Murphy, S. M. (1983). *Great women of the press*. Carbondale: Southern Illinois University Press.

Seelye, K. Q. (2007, January 19). Time Inc. cutting almost 300 magazine jobs to focus more on Web sites. NYTimes.com.

Seelye, K. Q. (2007, February 23). New Republic to cut back publication schedule. NYTimes.com.

Seelye, K. Q. (2007, March 27). *Life* magazine, its pages dwindling, will cease publication. NYTimes.com.

Seelye, K. Q., & Siklos, R. (2007, January 15). As Time Inc. cuts jobs, one writer on Britney may have to do. NYTimes.com.

Smith, S. (2010, December 14). Has the age of uber-cocooning begun? Digital media October boxscores. MinOnline.com.

Swanberg, W. A. (1972). *Luce and his empire*. New York: Scribner's.

Tarbell, I. (1939). *All in the day's work*. New York: MacMillan.

Wyatt, E. (2005, June 2). 80 years of *The New Yorker* to be offered in disc form. *The New York Times*, B3.

Chapter 5 Recordings: Demanding Choices

Associated Press (2008, July 26). Merger of Sirius and XM approved by FCC. NYTimes.com.

Chmielewski, D. C. (2004, October 27). iPod's rock and rollout. MercuryNews.com.

Denisoff, R. S. (1975). *Solid gold*. New Brunswick, N.J.: Transaction Books.

Evangelista, B. (2003, April 25). Apple kicks off online music store. *San Francisco Chronicle*, B1.

Evangelista, B. (2003, April 30). New tactic by record industry. *San Francisco Chronicle*, B1.

Evangelista, B. (2003, September 3). RIAA decries drop in CD sales. *San Francisco Chronicle*, B1.

Frost, L. (2007, January 26). Music industry pauses over ad-funded downloads. Money.aol.com.

Gomes, L. (2001, February 13). Napster suffers a rout in appeals court. *The Wall Street Journal*, A3.

Gomes, L. (2001, March 5). Judge starts process of silencing Napster. *The Wall Street Journal*, B6.

Holloway, L. (2003, June 26). Recording industry to sue Internet music swappers. *The New York Times*, C4.

Karnowski, S. (2009, June 18). Jury rules against Minn. woman in download case. SFGate.com.

Kopytoff, V. (2003, September 4). Music lawsuits snare 18 in Bay Area. *San Francisco Chronicle*, A1.

Lee, E. (2007, March 22). Music industry threatens student downloaders at UC. SFGate.com.

Leeds, J. (2005, November 8). Grokster calls it quits on sharing music files. *The New York Times*, C1.

Leeds, J. (2007, February 19). Music labels offer teasers to download. *The New York Times*, C1.

Leeds, J. (2007, May 28). Plunge in CD sales shakes up big labels. *The New York Times*, B1.

Leeds, J. (2007, October 5). Labels win suit against song sharer. NYTimes.com.

McBride, S., & Smith, E. (2008, December 19). Music industry to abandon mass suits. WSJ.com.

Metz, R. (1975). *CBS: Reflections in a bloodshot eye*. Chicago: Playboy Press.

Mostrous, A. (2010, March 1). Music industry needs clear strategy and control over illegal downloads. Business .TimesOnline.co.uk.

Pareles, J. (2005, August 23). Swaggering past 60, unrepentant. *The New York Times*, B1.

Pfanner, E. (2009, April 18). File-sharing site violated copyright, court says. NYTimes.com.

Pfanner, E. (2009, July 20). Music industry lures "casual" pirates to legal sites. NYTimes.com.

Pham, A. (2011, May 10). Warner Music Group debt is downgraded. LATimes.com.

Plambeck, J. (2010, February 26). 10 billionth download for iTunes. *The New York Times*, C5.

Plambeck, J. (2010, May 31). As CD sales wane, music retailers diversify. *The New York Times*, B5.

Pogue, D. (2005, August 7). Britney to rent, lease or buy. *The New York Times*, 2-1.

Recording Industry Association of America (2010, May 12). Federal court issues landmark ruling against LimeWire. RIAA.com.

Rendon, J. (2003, July 20). From a store with 300,000 titles, a big music lesson. *The New York Times*, BU5.

Sabbagh, D. (2008, June 18). Music sales fall to their lowest level in over 20 years. Timesonline.com.

Sachs, T., & Nunziato, S. (2007, April 5). Spinning into oblivion. NYTimes.com.

Sandoval, G. RIAA in pickle over Jammie Thomas. News. CNET.com.

Satter, R. G. (2011, January 21). IFPI: growth in digital music sales is slowing. SFGate.com.

Segal, D. (2010, April 25). They're calling almost everyone's tune. *The New York Times*, BU1.

Sisario, B. (2011, November 17). Google opens a digital music store. NYTimes.com.

Smart, J. R. (1977). *A wonderful invention: A brief history of the phonograph from tinfoil to the LP*. Washington, D.C.: Library of Congress.

Smith, E. (2004, October 11). Concert industry blames creeping prices for slow summer. *The Wall Street Journal*, B1.

Smith, E. (2011, December 15). Sony, Warner join suit against Grooveshark music service. WSJ.com.

Spiegel, B. (2011, December 1). Fukadelic sold here, on vinyl. NYTimes.com.

Sweeney, M. & Sabbagh, D. (2011, November 11). Universal and Sony reach deal to buy EMI for 2.5 billion British pounds. Guardian.co.uk.

Trachtenberg, J. A. (1994, August 2). Music industry fears bandits on the information highway. *The Wall Street Journal*, B21.

Veiga, A. (2003, May 2). Students settle music suit. *San Francisco Chronicle*, B1.

Veiga, A. (2003, October 9). New version of Napster service debuts. AOL Business News. AOL.com.

Wood, M. (2009, October 25). Making the U2 set so big that it's invisible. LATimes.com.

Chapter 6 Radio: Riding the Wave

Associated Press (2007, April 14). $12.5 million "payola" fine. *San Francisco Chronicle*, C2.

Barnouw, E. (1978). *Tube of plenty*. New York: Oxford University Press.

Bittner, J. (1982). *Broadcast law and regulation*. Englewood Cliffs, N.J.: Prentice Hall.

Dow Jones Newswire (2005, May 16). XM satellite radio surpasses 4 million subscribers; nears target. AOL Business News. AOL.com.

Fabrikant, G. (2009, April 30). Radio giant faces crisis in cash flow. NYTimes.com.

Farhi, P. (2011, November 16). CBS Radio to start all-news station in D.C. area. Washingtonpost.com.

Feder, B. J. (2002, October 11). FCC approves a digital radio technology. *The New York Times*, B1.

Fleishman, G. (2005, July 28). Revolution on the radio. *The New York Times*, C11.

Fornatale, P., & Mills, J. E. (1980). *Radio in the television age*. New York: Overlook Press.

Frere-Jones, S. (2010, June 14 & 21). You, the D. J. *The New Yorker*, 138.

Jensen, E. (2010, April 26). Classical music's comeback, on public radio. *The New York Times*, B7.

Labaton, S. (2007, March 7). FCC chief questioning radio deal. *The New York Times*, C1.

Leeds, J. (2005, July 28). Payola or no, edge still to the big. *The New York Times*, B1.

Leeds, J. (2007, March 6). Broadcasters agree to fine over payoffs. *The New York Times*, C1.

Leeds, J. (2007, April 16). Amid turbulence at CBS Radio, an old hand is back. *The New York Times*, C4.

Leeds, J., & Story, L. (2005, July 26). Radio payoffs are described as Sony settles. *The New York Times*, A1.

Levine, R. (2007, March 19). A fee per song can ruin us, Internet radio companies say. *The New York Times*, C4.

McMahan, T. (2009, July 14). Pandora sings new tune with royalty agreement, funding. Blogs.WSJ.com.

McMahan, T. (2009, October 2) A venture firm's gift to Pandora. Blogs.WSJ.com.

MacFarland, D. R. (1979). *The development of the top 40 radio format*. New York: Arno Press.

Manly, L. (2005, July 31). Spin control: How payola went corporate. *The New York Times*, 4-1.

Miller, C. (2009, September 10). Listening to radio on the web? That's so last year. *Bits*. Bits.blogs.NYTimes.com.

Miller, C. (2010, March 8). How Pandora slipped past the junkyard. *The New York Times*, B1.

Mindlin, A. (2007, May 7). Counting radio listeners stirs controversy. *The New York Times*, C4.

Norris, F. (2007, February 23). Satellite radio: Good music, bad investment. *The New York Times*, C1.

Plambeck, J. (2010, April 19). Saving the neglected history of FM radio's unsung pioneer. *The New York Times*, B7.

Pickler, N. (2001, September 26). First satellite radio service begins. *San Francisco Chronicle*, B3.

Rainey, J. (2010, October 20). Public radio is enjoying boom times. LATimes.com.

Settel, L. (1960). *A pictorial history of radio*. New York: Citadel Press.

Shenon P. (2008, March 25). Justice Dept. approves XM merger with Sirius. *The New York Times*, C1.

Siklos, R. (2007, February 14). Is radio still radio if there's video? *The New York Times*, C1.

Spencer, K. (2011, November 4). College radio heads: off the dial. NYTimes.com.

Sperber, A. M. (1986). *Murrow: His life and times*. New York: Freundlich.

Stimson, L. (2010, September 1). AM HD radio has stalled; now what? *Radio World*. RWOnline.com.

Sutel, S. (2007, March 20). Online broadcast ruling is opposed. *The Sacramento Bee*, D3.

Chapter 7 Movies: Picturing the Future

Arango, T., & Carr, D. (2010, November 25). Netflix's move onto the web stirs rivalries. *The New York Times*, A1.

Associated Press (2011, July 16). *Harry Potter* conjures first-day record of $92.1 million. Sacbee.com.

Balio, T. (1976). *The American film industry*. Madison: University of Wisconsin Press.

Barnes, B. (2010, July 24). In Hollywood, everybody's a digital revolutionary. NYTimes.com.

Barnes, B. (2011, September 4). Neither Smurf nor wizard could save summer movie attendance. NYTimes.com.

Burrows, P. (2010, December 5). Will Netflix kill the Internet? *Bloomberg Businessweek*. SFGate.com.

Carr, D. (2008, February 26). In Los Angeles, Oscar statues become a popular export. NYTimes.com.

Chinnock, C. (1999, August 9). Lights! Camera! Action! It's the dawn of digital cinema. *Electronic Design*, 32F.

Chmielewksi, D. C. (2011, June 6). Disney film studio layoffs expected soon. LATimes.com.

Cieply, M. (2010, March 3). 3-D films fuel a rise in box office revenues. *The New York Times*, C2.

Cieply, M., & Barnes, B. (2009, March 23). No more easy money. *The New York Times*, B1.

Cieply, M. (2011, July 31). Charging a premium for movies, at a cost. NYTimes.com.

Dargis, M. (2007, March 18). The revolution will be downloaded (if you're patient). *The New York Times*, C1.

Denby, D. (2007, January 8). Big pictures. *The New Yorker*, 54.

Ellis, J. C. (1985). *A history of American film*, 2nd ed. Englewood Cliffs, N.J.: Prentice Hall.

Evangelista, B. (2003, April 28). Heading off film piracy. *San Francisco Chronicle*, E1.

Fabrikant, G., & Waxman, S. (2005, December 9). Viacom's Paramount to buy DreamWorks for $1.6 billion. NYTimes.com.

Fritz, B. (2010, May 31). Summer box office sees its worst Memorial Day weekend in 17 years. LATimes.com.

Fritz, B. (2011, July 9). Not much demand yet for premium video on demand. LATimes.com.

Gentile, G. (2003, May 20). Disney to test options for movie viewing. *San Francisco Chronicle*, B3.

Goldberg, B. (2001, September). DMCA nets a criminal prosecution and prompts a protest. *American Libraries*, 18.

Goldstein, P. (2010, January 30). Is this a box-office record with an *? LATimes.com.

Guthman, E. (2003, January 20). Sundance grows up. *San Francisco Chronicle*, D1.

Halbfinger. D. M. (2008, March 13). With theaters barely digital, studios push 3-D. *The New York Times*, B1.

Helft, M. (2007, January 16). The shifting business of renting movies, by the disc or the click. *The New York Times*, C1.

Holson, L. M. (2005, July 22). Film studios said to agree on digital standards. *The New York Times*, C9.

Keegan, R. (2011, September 25). 3-D makeover coming to aging Hollywood blockbusters. LATimes.com.

Kehr, D. (2011, March 6). It's delivery, stupid: Goodbye, DVD. Hello, future. *The New York Times,* AR14.

King, S. (2011, November 28). 'Hugo' revives interest in Georges Melies. LATimes.com.

Kopytoff, V. G. (2010, September 26). Shifting online, Netflix faces new competition. NYTimes.com.

LaSalle, M. (2005, July 13). Blame the economy, the product, the theaters—we're just not going to movies the way we used to. SFGate.com.

Leeds, J. (2007, March 1). A comeback in 3-D, but without those flimsy glasses. *The New York Times*, B9.

Leonhart, D. (2010, March 1). Why "Avatar" is not the top-grossing film. NYTimes.com.

McGrath, C. (2010, May 23). A gamer's world, but a dramatist's sensibility. *The New York Times*, AR18.

Motion Picture Association of America (1954). *Motion picture production code.*

Nakashima, R. (2009, March 10). Sony Pictures to cut nearly 350 jobs. SFGate.com.

Schuker, L. A. E., & Smith, E. (2010, May 22). Hollywood eyes shortcut to TV. WSJ.com.

Scott, A. O. (2007, March 18). The shape of cinema, transformed at the click of a mouse. *The New York Times*, 2-1.

Sklar, R. (1975). *Movie-made America*. New York: Random House.

Smith, D. (2010, April 23). *Streaming putting video stores out of business*. Sacbee.com.

Solomon, C. (2011, August 16). A little lamp lights the way for Pixar's success. LATimes.com.

Squire, J. E. (ed.). (1983). *The movie business book*. New York: Simon & Schuster.

Stelter, B. (2010, August 10). Netflix to stream films from Paramount, Lions Gate, MGM. NYTimes.com.

Thompson, N. (2003, June 26). Netflix's patent may reshape DVD rental market. *The New York Times*, C4.

Trumbo, D. (1962). *Additional dialogue: Letters of Dalton Trumbo, 1942–1962*. New York: M. Evans.

Verrier, R. (2010, May 7). FCC paves way for studios to push movies into the home, rattling theaters. LATimes.com.

Waxman, S. (2005, December 12). DreamWorks deal played like a drama. *The New York Times*, C1.

Waxman, S. (2007, April 26). Hollywood's shortage of female power. *The New York Times*, B1.

Chapter 8 Television: Changing Channels

Arango, T. (2009, February 28). Broadcast TV faces struggle to stay viable. *The New York Times*, A1.

Associated Press (2010, July 10). Mariners-Yankees will be in 3D. Sports.ESPN.go.com.

Associated Press (2010, August 24). Toshiba developing no-glasses 3-D televisions. SFGate.com.

Associated Press (2011, April 6). Hit show 'Mad Men' will be streamed on Netflix. SFGate.com.

Barnes, B., & Jordan, M. (2005, May 2). Big four TV networks get a wake-up call—in Spanish. WSJ.com.

Barnouw, E. (1975). *Tube of plenty*. New York: Oxford University Press.

Bauder, D. (2007, May 9). 2.7 million TV viewers missing this spring. *San Francisco Chronicle*, A2.

Bauder, D. (2009, November 30). Jay Leno losing his audience to DVR machines. WashingtonPost.com.

Biagi, S. (1987). *NewsTalk II*. Belmont, Calif.: Wadsworth.

Brooks, T. (2011, April 18). Is TV still a 'vast wasteland'? *Advertising Age.*

Brown, L. (1971). *Television: The business behind the box.* New York: Harcourt Brace Jovanovich.

Carr, D. (2011, December 24). New rules for the ways we watch. NYTimes.com.

Carter, B. (2011, February 21). Networks have lost key viewers at 10 p.m. *The New York Times*, B1.

Carter, B. (2011, October 23). In a gloomy economy, TV sitcoms are making a comeback. NYTimes.com.

Chen, K., & Peers, M. (1999, August 6). FCC relaxes its rules on TV station ownership. *The Wall Street Journal*, A3.

Chmielewski, D., & Guynn, J. (2010, August 18). Google TV plan is causing jitters in Hollywood. LATimes.com.

Dvorak, P. (2005, April 21). Advanced TV will be a test of Sony revival. WSJ.com.

FitzGerald, T. (May 4, 2011). Pac-12 gets richest TV deal. SFGate.com.

Fritz, B. & Verrier, R. (2011, March 2). DirecTV prepares to launch premium video on demand; theater executives alarmed. LATimes.com.

Greenfield, J. (1977). *Television: The first fifty years*. New York: Abrams.

Hart, K. (2009, June 7). Your antenna's big day. WashingtonPost.com.

Helft, M. (2010, September 5). Apple faces many rivals for streaming to TVs. NYTimes.com.

James, M., & Flint, J. (2009, December 3). Comcast strikes deal to buy NBC Universal from GE. LATimes.com.

Jensen, E. (2011, February 28). Public broadcasters start to sweat, as a budget threat looks serious. *The New York Times*, B4.

Jensen, E. (2011, May 30). PBS plans promotional breaks within programs. NYTimes.com.

Kantor, J. (2005, October 30). The extra-large, ultra-small medium: What happens when television becomes a matter of extremes. *The New York Times*, 2-1.

Manly, L., & Hernandez, R. (2005, August 8). Nielsen, long a gauge of popularity, fights to preserve its own. *The New York Times*, C1.

McGrath, C. (2008, February 17). Is PBS still necessary? *The New York Times*, AR1.

Minow, N. (1964). *Equal time: The private broadcaster and the public interest*. New York: Atheneum.

Newman, J. (2010, August 23). TV makers predicting a bright future for 3-D sets. NYTimes.com.

Richtel, M., & Stelter, B. (2010, August 23). In the living room, hooked on pay TV. NYTimes.com.

Sandomir, R. (2011, June 7). NBC wins TV rights to four more Olympics. NYTimes.com.

Severo, R. (2003, June 13). David Brinkley, 82, newsman model, dies. *The New York Times*, A26.

Sherr, I. (2010, September 1). Apple makes Internet-TV push. WSJ.com.

Sorkin, A. R. (2003, April 10). Murdoch adds to his empire by agreeing to buy DirecTV. *The New York Times*, C1.

Stelter, B. (2009, May 8). PBS to shorten time commitments for sponsorships. *The New York Times*, B3.

Stelter, B. (2009, June 14). Changeover to digital TV off to a smooth start. NYTimes.com.

Stelter, B. (2010, January 5). Discovery, Imax and Sony form 3-D television channel. NYTimes.com.

Stelter, B. (2010, March 8). Disney-Cablevision fight signifies more to come. *The New York Times*, B1.

Stelter, B. (2011, January 2). TV viewing continues to edge up. NYTimes.com.

Stelter, B. (2011, February 4). CBS and DirecTV results attest to media strength. *The New York Times*, B2.

Stelter, B. & Chozick, A. (2011, December 15). Paying a 'sports tax,' even if you don't watch. NYTimes.com.

Stelter, B., & Stone, B. (2010, January 6). Television begins a push into the 3rd dimension. NYTimes.com.

Sterling, C., & Kittross, J. (1990). *Stay tuned: A concise history of American broadcasting*, 2nd ed. Belmont, Calif.: Wadsworth.

Story, L. (2007, January 29). At last, television ratings go to college. *The New York Times*, C1.

Story, L. (2007, June 1). Agencies and networks ponder Nielsen ad ratings. *The New York Times*, C6.

Taub, E. A. (2007, January 11). On display, the video frontier. *The New York Times*, C11.

Tsukayama, H. (2011, October 5). TV on your Xbox, coming soon. Washingtonpost.com.

Wakabayahi, D. (2009, November 27). Sony bets on 3-D to drive TV sales. WSJ.com.

Chapter 9 Digital Media: Widening the Web

Arango, T. (2009, March 23). Rights clash on YouTube, and videos disappear. *The New York Times*, B1.

Arango, T. (2010, October 28). Judge tells LimeWire, the file-trading service, to disable its software. NYTimes.com.

Associated Press (2009, May 6). A fifth of U.S. homes have cell phones, no landlines. NYTimes.com.

Associated Press (2011, December 4). Study confirms many of us go online for no reason. SFGate.com.

Barnes, R. (2011, June 28). Court strikes down law on violent video games. Washingtonpost.com.

Batteiger, J. (2009, February 18). Landlines losing to cellular. SFGate.com.

Chmielewski, D. C. (2011, June 8). Online advertising to reach $31 billion in 2011. LATimes.com

Cohen, N. (2007, March 12). After false claim, Wikipedia to check degrees. *The New York Times*, C6.

Cohen, N. (2009, August 25). Wikipedia to limit changes to articles on people. NYTimes.com.

Cruz, N. (2009, December 16). Americans have gone text-crazy. LATimes.com.

Fidler, R. (1997). *Mediamorphosis*. Thousand Oaks, Calif.: Pine Forge Press.

Fitzhugh, M. (2010, April 16). Seas of spam keep rising, despite efforts to hold back the flood. DailyFinance.com.

Gnatek, T. (2005, October 5). Darknets: Virtual parties with a select group of invitees. *The New York Times*, E2.

Hansell, S. (2009, May 22). Counting down to the end of Moore's Law. NYTimes.com.

Hardy, Q. (2011, November 14). Will cloud computing make everything (and everyone) work harder? NYTimes.com.

Helft, M. (2010, May 27). Apple is no. 1 in tech, overtaking Microsoft. *The New York Times*, B1.

Isaacson, W. (2011, October 29). The genius of Jobs. NYTimes.com.

Johnson, F. (2009, September 21). FCC Chairman proposes "net neutrality" rules. WSJ.com.

Johnson, F. (2009, October 22). FCC adopts open net rules. WSJ.com.

Kang, C. (2011, October 11). U.S. has more cell phones than people. Washingtonpost.com.

Kim, R. (2010, June 17). Keeping core gamers while expanding audience. SFGate.com.

Liptak, A., & Stone, B. (2008, February 19). Web site that posts leaked material ordered shut. NYTimes.com.

Liptak, A. (2010, November 2). Justices debate video game ban. NYTimes.com.

Lopez, S. (2009, May 6). The rigors of life unplugged. LATimes.com.

Markoff, J., & Holson, L. M. (2005, October 13). With New iPod, Apple aims to be a video star. *The New York Times*, C1.

Markoff, J. (2010, March 2). U.S. to reveal some rules on security for Internet. *The New York Times*, A14.

Markoff, J. (2011, October 5). Steve Jobs, Apple visionary, dies at 56. NYTimes.com.

Milian, M. (2010, June 17). E3: Nintendo booth tour, 3Ds wow crowds. LATimes.com.

Mintz, J. (2007, January 18). MySpace hit with online predator suit. Associated Press on AOL Money & Finance News. AOL.com.

Perez-Peña, R. (2009, May 29). Time Warner plans to spin off AOL, ending huge deal that failed. *The New York Times*, B4.

Sanger, D. E. (2010, January 26). In digital combat, U.S. finds no easy deterrent. *The New York Times*, A1.

Stone, B. (2009, March 29). Is Facebook growing up too fast? *The New York Times*, BU1.

Stone, B. (2010, January 28). With its tablet, Apple blurs line between devices. *The New York Times*, A1.

Stone, B. (2010, May 23). Google: Sure it's big, but is that bad? *The New York Times*, B1.

Stone, B., & Vance, A. (2010, April 19). "Cloud" computing casts a spell. *The New York Times*, B1.

Swartz, J. (2005, August 22). Anti-porn spam laws to shield kids backfire. USAToday.com on AOL News.

Wachter, S. (2010, October 24). Beaming to the cloud all the mess that is our digital life. NYTimes.com.

Wollman, D. (2010, October 20). UN report: Internet users to surpass 2B in 2010. WashingtonPost.com.

Wright, R. (1997, May 19). The man who invented the Web. *Time*, 68.

Wyatt, E. (2005, November 4). Want *War and Peace* online? How about 20 pages at a time? NYTimes.com.

Zickuhr, K. (2010, December 16). Generations online in 2010. Pewresearch.org.

Chapter 10 Advertising: Motivating Consumers

Associated Press (2010, November 15). Facebook enters e-mail, messaging arena. LATimes.com.

Atwan, R. (1979). Newspapers and the foundations of modern advertising. In *The commercial connection*, ed. J. W. Wright. New York: Doubleday.

Beatty, S. G. (1996, June 11). Seagram flouts ban on TV ads pitching liquor. *The Wall Street Journal*, B1.

Boorstin, D. J. (1986). The rhetoric of democracy. In *American mass media: Industries and issues*, 3rd ed., ed. R. Atwan, B. Orton, & W. Vesterman. New York: Random House.

Cardwell, A. (2001, February 1). The new ad game: Online games are more than just a good time; they're the hottest new ad space on the web. *Ziff Davis Smart Business for the New Economy*, 53.

Carter, B. & Vega, T. (2011, May 13). In shift, ads try to entice over-55 set. NYTimes.com.

Clifford, S. (2009, March 4). Your ad here, not there. *The New York Times*, B1.

Clifford, S. (2009, March 11). Advertisers get a trove of clues in Smartphones. *The New York Times*, A1.

Clifford, S. (2010, March 12). Instant ads set the pace on the web. *The New York Times*, B1.

Elliott, S. (2002, March 31). Advertising's big four: It's their world now. *The New York Times*, 3-1.

Elliott, S. (2005, November 3). Liquor ads move to satellite radio. *The New York Times*, C6.

Elliott, S. (2009, May 29). Campaigns address today's anxieties by looking back. *The New York Times*, B4.

Elliott, S. (2010, October 29). Super Bowl ad slots sell out early. NYTimes.com.

Feder, B. (2007, January 29). Billboards that know you by name. *The New York Times*, C4.

Flint, J., Branch, S., & O'Connell, V. (2001, December 14). Breaking longtime taboo, NBC network plans to accept liquor ads. *The Wall Street Journal*, B1.

Fowles, J. (1985). Advertising's fifteen basic appeals. In *American mass media: Industries and issues*, 3rd ed., ed. R. Atwan, B. Orton, & W. Vesterman. New York: Random House.

Fox, S. (1984). *The mirror makers: A history of American advertising and its creators*. New York: Morrow.

Georgiadis, A. (2010, November 1). Why marathons are hot spot to chase consumers. *Advertising Age*, 1.

Guynn, J., & Sarno, D. (2010, April 8). Apple launches ad system for mobile devices in race with Google. LATimes.com.

Internet Advertising Bureau. (2010, October 12). Internet ad revenues break records, climb to more than $12 billion for first half of '10. IAB.com.

Jones, E. R. (1979). *Those were the good old days*. New York: Simon & Schuster.

Kaufman, L. (1987). *Essentials of advertising*, 2nd ed. New York: Harcourt Brace Jovanovich.

Kiley, D. (2005, March 7). A green flag for booze. *BusinessWeek*, 95.

Li, S. & Sarno, D. (2011, August 21). Advertisers start using facial recognition to tailor pitches. LATimes.com.

Nielsenwire (2010, January 20). Survey: Most Super Bowl viewers tune in for the commercials. Blog.Nielsen.com.

Pfanner, E. (2009, July 4). Internet companies and ad agencies go from old enemies to new friends. *The New York Times*, B7.

Pfanner, E. (2011, March 9). British television opens a door for product placement in shows. *The New York Times*, B3.

Price, J. (1986). Now a few words about commercials. In *American mass media: Industries and issues*, 3rd ed., ed. R. Atwan, B. Orton, & W. Vesterman. New York: Random House.

Schudson, M. (1984). *Advertising: The uneasy persuasion*. New York: Basic Books.

Singer, N. (2011, September 10). On campus, it's one big commercial. NYTimes.com.

Stelter, B. (2010, January 25). Court ruling invites a boom in political ads. *The New York Times*, B1.

Story, L. (2007, April 28). Overture to an untapped market. *The New York Times*, B1.

Story, L. (2008, March 10). To aim ads, web is keeping closer eye on what you click. *The New York Times*, A1.

Stross, R. (2009, February 8). Why television still shines in a world of screens. *The New York Times*, BU3.

Sweney, M. (2011, July 27). Advertising watchdog orders L'Oreal to drop airbrushed ads. *The Guardian*, National–13.

Sylvers, E. (2007, February 14). The ad-free cell phone may soon be extinct. *The New York Times*, C5.

Vega, T. (2011, November 6). A site to help marketers appeal to African-Americans. NYTimes.com.

Whitaker, L. (2001, July 21). Converting Web surfers to buyers: Online promotion. *Time*, 46+.

Chapter 11 Public Relations: Promoting Ideas

Acohido, B. & Swartz, J. (2011, May 10). PR firm's Google attack fails. *USA Today*, B1.

Ambrosio, J. (1980, March/April). It's in the *Journal*, but this is reporting? *Columbia Journalism Review*, 18, 35.

Berr, J. (2010, January 28). Facing its "Tylenol Moment," Toyota needs to move fast. DailyFinance.com.

Bernays, E. L. (1955). *The engineering of consent*. Norman: University of Oklahoma Press.

Blyskal, B., & Blyskal, M. (1985). *PR: How the public relations industry writes the news*. New York: Morrow.

Bumiller, E. (2003, February 9). War public relations machine is put on full throttle. *The New York Times*, A1.

Bumiller, E. (2003, April 20). Even critics of war say the White House spun it with skill. *The New York Times*, B14.

Bush, M. (2010, March 1). The cult of Toyota. *Advertising Age*, 1.

Bush, M. (2010, March 1). Internal communication is key to repairing Toyota reputation. *Advertising Age*, 1.

Clifford, S. (2010, January 25). Corporate antagonism goes public. *The New York Times*, B1.

Cutlip, S., Center, A., & Broom, A. (1985). *Effective public relations*, 6th ed. Englewood Cliffs, N.J.: Prentice Hall.

Fleischman, D. E. (1931, February). Public relations—A new field for women. *Independent woman*. As quoted in S. Henry, *In her own name: Public relations pioneer Doris Fleischman Bernays*. Paper presented to the Committee on the Status of Women Research Session, Association for Education in Journalism and Mass Communication, Portland, Ore., July 1988.

Foster, L. G. (1983, March). The role of public relations in the Tylenol crisis. *Public Relations Journal*, 13.

Glover, M. (1996, March 6). Juice maker in PR mode: Odwalla's ads explain status. *The Sacramento Bee*, B6.

Goldsborough, R. (2001, June). Dealing with Internet smears. *Campaigns & Elections*, 50B6.

Goodman, P. S. (2010, August 21). In case of emergency: what not to do. NYTimes.com.

Graham, J. (2007, March 9). Apple buffs marketing savvy to a high shine. *USA Today*, 1B.

Kaufman, J. (2008, June 30). Need press? Repeat: "green," "sex," "cancer," "secret," "fat." NYTimes.com.

Krauss, C. (2010, April 30). Oil spill's blow to BP's image may eclipse out-of-pocket costs. *The New York Times*, B1.

Krauss, C. (2010, May 7). For BP, a technological battle to contain leak and an image fight, too. *The New York Times*, A16.

Lee, C. (2005, March 15). Administration rejects ruling on PR videos. WashingtonPost.com.

Marken, A. (1998, Spring). The Internet and the web: The two-way public relations highway. *Public Relations Quarterly*, 31–34.

McDonough, S. (2005, May 26). Paid promotions sneaking into broadcasts. *San Francisco Chronicle*, C6.

Miller, C. (2009, July 5). Spinning the web: PR in Silicon Valley. NYTimes.com.

Morse, S. (1906, September). An awakening on Wall Street. *American Magazine*, 460.

Newsom, D., & Scott, A. (1986). *This is PR: The realities of public relations*, 3rd ed. Belmont, Calif.: Wadsworth.

O'Brien, T. (2005, February 13). Spinning frenzy: PR's bad press. *The New York Times*, 3-1.

Parekh, R., & Lee, E. (2010, May 10). How to succeed when it's time to make your social-media mea culpa. *Advertising Age*, 1.

Pear, R. (2005, October 1). Buying of news by Bush's aides is ruled illegal. *The New York Times*, A1.

Peters, J. W. (2010, June 9). Efforts to limit the flow of spill news. NYTimes.com.

Pizzi, P. (2001, July 23). Grappling with "cybersmear." *New Jersey Law Journal*, S12.

Randall, C. (1985, November). The father of public relations: Edward Bernays, 93, is still saucy. *United*, 50.

Rutten, T. (2010, February 20). Tiger and Toyota: Rebuilding the brands. LATimes.com.

Seitel, F. P. (1984). *The practice of public relations*, 2nd ed. Columbus, Ohio: Merrill.

Tracy, T. (2010, September 1). BP tripled its ad budget after oil spill. WSJ.com.

Vittachi, I. (2011, June 13). Horse marches through John Wayne Airport to mark air service to Canada. LATimes .com.

White, R. D. (2010, April 30). For BP, oil spill is a public relations catastrophe. LATimes.com.

Chapter 12 News and Information: Getting Personal

Bennett, S. (2003, July 1). How the Iraq War was seen overseas. *World and I*, 62.

Carvajal, D. (2007, March 7). 1,000 journalists killed in ten years while reporting. *The New York Times*, A3.

Charles, D. (2005, September 7). Federal government seeks to block photos of dead. Reuters on AOL News. AOL.com.

Chmielewski, D. C. (2010, May 4). Murdoch to unveil paywall for news content soon. LATimes.com.

Cohen, N. (2010, May 24). Through soldiers' eyes, "The first YouTube war." *The New York Times*, B3.

Daragahi, B. (2011, March 8). Libya keeps foreign journalists on tight leash. LATimes.com.

Faiez, R. (2009, September 9). NYT reporter freed; Afghan aide killed in rescue. SFGate.com.

Fathi, N., & Landler, M. (2009, May 12). Iran releases journalist convicted of spying for U.S. NYTimes.com.

Gans, H. (1985, December). Are U.S. journalists dangerously liberal? *Columbia Journalism Review*, 32–33.

Gans, H. (1986). *The messages behind the news*. In *Readings in mass communication*, 6th ed., ed. M. Emery & T. Smythe. Dubuque, Iowa: Brown.

Garwood, P. (2005, January 21). Deadline passes with no word on reporter's fate. Associated Press on AOL News. AOL.com.

Gerth, J., & Shane, S. (2005, December 1). U.S. is said to pay to plant articles in Iraq papers. *The New York Times*, A1.

Goodman, T. (2011, March 18). Japan disaster shows U.S. journalists unprepared. SFGate.com.

Gordon, M. (2001, October 31). Military is putting heavier limits on reporters' access. *The New York Times*, B3.

Johnston, D. C. (2005, July 11). Most editors say they'd publish articles based on leaks. NYTimes.com.

Just, M., & Rosenstiel, T. (2005, March 26). All the news that's fed. *The New York Times*, A27.

Keller, B. (2011, May 5). The inner lives of wartime photographers. NYTimes.com.

Kuttab, D. (2003, April 6). The Arab TV wars. *The New York Times Magazine*, 45.

Lewis, N. A., & Shane, S. (2007, January 31). Ex-reporter for *Times* testifies for prosecutor who jailed her. *The New York Times*, A1.

Lippmann, W. (1965). *Public opinion*. New York: Free Press.

Liptak, A. (2005, February 16). Jailing of reporters in CIA leak case is upheld by judges. *The New York Times*, A1.

Liptak, A. (2005, June 30). Judge gives reporters one week to testify or face jail. *The New York Times*, A12.

Liptak, A. (2005, July 1). Time Inc. to yield files on sources, relenting to U.S. *The New York Times*, A1.

Liptak, A. (2005, July 11). For Time Inc. reporter, a frenzied decision to testify. NYTimes.com.

Lipton, E. (2007, March 7). Members of a sympathetic jury describe emotional but inevitable conclusion. *The New York Times*, A17.

McDermott, T. (2007, March 17). Blogs can top the presses. LATimes.com.

McFadden, R. D. (2005, July 9). Newspaper withholding two articles after jailing. NYTimes.com.

O'Connor, J. D. (2005, July). "I'm the guy they called Deep Throat." *Vanity Fair*, 86.

Perez-Peña, R. (2010, February 3). Some news sites to try charging readers. *The New York Times*, B2.

Perlez, J. & Schmitt, E. (2011, July 4). Pakistan's spies tied to slaying of a journalist. NYTimes.com.

Peters, J. W. (2011, August 22). Journalists keep in hotel as battle rages outside. NYTimes.com.

Pew Research Center's Project for Excellence in Journalism. *The state of the news media 2011*. Stateofthemedia.org.

Pincus, W., & VandeHei, J. (2005, July 21). Plame's identity marked as secret. *Washington Post*, A1.

Purdum, T. S. (2005, June 3). Three decades later, "Woodstein" takes a victory lap. *The New York Times*, A14.

Purdum, T. S., & Rutenberg, J. (2005, June 2). In the prelude to publication, intrigue worthy of Deep Throat. *The New York Times*, A1.

Quinn, P. (2006, January 7). American journalist kidnapped in Iraq. Associated Press on AOL News. AOL.com.

Raines, H. (2010, March 14). Why don't honest journalists take on Roger Ailes and Fox News? WashingtonPost .com.

Rich, Frank (2005, July 24). Eight days in July. NYTimes .com.

Rutenberg, J. (2003, April 20). Spectacular success or incomplete picture? Views of TV's war coverage are split. *The New York Times*, B15.

Rutten, T. (2003, April 5). A 24/7 war pulls viewers to cable news. *Los Angeles Times*, C1.

Salamon, J. (2003, April 6). New tools for reporters make war images instant but coverage no simpler. *The New York Times*, B13.

Sang-Hun, C. (2009, June 9). N. Korea sentences 2 U.S. journalists to 12 years of hard labor. NYTimes.com.

Schmitt, E. (2005, December 2). Senate summons Pentagon to explain effort to plant reports in Iraqi news media. *The New York Times*, A10.

Schmitt, E. (2005, December 13). Military admits planting news in Iraq. *The New York Times*, A11.

Seelye, K. Q. (2005, March 14). Fewer sources go nameless in the press, survey shows. *The New York Times*, C6.

Seelye, K. Q. (2005, August 1). Newsrooms seek ways to shield identities. *The New York Times*, C1.

Seelye, K. Q. (2005, August 15). Editors ponder how to present a broad picture of Iraq. *The New York Times*, C2.

Seelye, K. Q. (2005, October 4). Freed reporter says she upheld principles. *The New York Times*, A23.

Seelye, K. Q. (2005, November 10). *Times* reporter agrees to leave the paper. *The New York Times*, A21.

Shane, S. (2007, March 8). Debate over possible pardon erupts after verdict on Libby. *The New York Times*, A1.

Steinberg, J. (2005, June 30). Writer in sources case laments threat to jail 2. *The New York Times*, A12.

Steinberg, J. (2005, July 7). Response from journalists is not unanimous. *The New York Times*, A17.

Steinberg, J. (2008, June 8). For new journalists, all bets, but not mikes, are off. *The New York Times*, WK3.

Stelter, B. (2008, August 12). TV networks rewrite the definition of a news bureau. NYTimes.com.

Stelter, B. (2010, March 1). Network news at a crossroads. *The New York Times*, B1.

Stelter, B. (2010, May 1). Job cuts at ABC leave workers stunned and downcast. *The New York Times*, B2.

Stelter, B. (2011, May 10). For journalists, a call to rethink their online models. NYTimes.com.

Stelter, B. (2011, October 3). ABC News and Yahoo News announce deal to share content. NYTimes.com.

Stelter, B. & Preston, J. (2011, May 2). Turning to social networks for news. NYTimes.com.

Stolberg, S. G. (2007, March 7). Libby, ex-Cheney aide, guilty of lying in CIA leak case. *The New York Times*, A1.

Woodward, B. (2005, June 2). How Mark Felt became "Deep Throat." *Washington Post*, A1.

Worth, R. F. (2005, September 20). Reporter working for *Times* abducted and slain in Iraq. NYTimes.com.

Yost, P. (2005, July 6). Judge orders *New York Times* reporter jailed. Associated Press on AOL News. AOL.com.

Chapter 13 Society, Culture and Politics: Shaping the Issues

Alexander, H. E. (1983). *Financing the 1980 election*. Lexington, Mass.: Heath.

Alexander, H. E., & Haggerty, B. (1987). *Financing the 1984 election*. Lexington, Mass.: Heath.

Angelo, M. (2010, May 30). At TBS, diversity pays its own way. *The New York Times*, AR17.

Barber, J. D. (1986). *The pulse of politics: Electing presidents in the media age*. New York: Norton.

Carey, B. (2011, October 18). Parents urged again to limit TV for youngest. NYTimes.com.

Cieply, M. (2007, April 13). Report says the young readily buy violent games and movies. *The New York Times*, C3.

Fairfield, H., & Palmer, G. (2008, July 6). Cashing in on Obama and McCain. *The New York Times*, BU1.

Fetler, M. (1985). Television viewing and school achievement. *Mass communication review yearbook*, vol. 5. Beverly Hills, Calif.: Sage.

Healy, M. (2010, May 4). Toddler TV time linked to poorer fourth-grade classroom attention, math and exercise. LATimes.com.

Hua, V. (2005, June 6). Audience for ethnic media huge. *San Francisco Chronicle*, A7.

James, M. (2010, October 29). TV still the favored medium for political ad spending. LATimes.com.

Krueger, A. B. (2005, August 18). Fair? Balanced? A study finds it does not matter. *The New York Times*, C2.

Liebert, R. M., & Sprafkin, J. (1988). *The early window*, 3rd ed. New York: Pergamon Press.

Lippmann, W. (1965). *Public opinion*. New York: Free Press.

Martindale, C. (1995, August). *Only in glimpses: Portrayal of America's largest minority groups by The New York Times 1934–1994*. Paper presented at the Association for Education in Journalism and Mass Communication Annual Convention, Washington, D.C.

Meyrowitz, J. (1985). *No sense of place*. New York: Oxford University Press.

Mindlin, A. (2007, January 15). Boys and girls use social sites differently. *The New York Times*, C3.

Modleski, T. (1982). *Loving with a vengeance: Mass-produced fantasies for women*. New York: Methuen.

Nauman, A. (1993, April 11). Comics page gets serious. *The Sacramento Bee*, B1.

Patterson, T., & McClure, R. (1976). *The unseeing eye: The myth of television power in national elections*. New York: Putnam.

Pham, S. (2010, November 8). Political TV ad spending sets record. ABCNews.go.com.

Pickler, N. (2007, July 24). Democrats face off in YouTube debate. Associated Press on AOL. AOL.com.

Postman, N. (1985). *Amusing ourselves to death*. New York: Viking Penguin.

Potter, D. M. (1954). *People of plenty*. Chicago: University of Chicago Press.

Reyes, L. I., & Rampell, E. (2007, February 23). Movies' multicultural milestone year. *San Francisco Chronicle*, B11.

Rivers, W. L., & Schramm, W. (1986). The impact of mass communications. In *American mass media: Industries and issues*, 3rd ed., ed. R. Atwan, B. Orton, & W. Vesterman. New York: Random House.

Scott, A. O. (2010, April 18). Brutal truths about violence. *The New York Times*, AR1.

Sidoti, Liz. (2011, April 4). Obama announces 2012 re-election bid in web video. Aolnews.com.

Simon, S., & Stein, P. (2010, September 4). From grass roots to goofball: Politicians pitch on YouTube. WSJ.com.

Spear, J. (1984). *Presidents and the press*. Cambridge, Mass.: M.I.T. Press.

Stanley, A. (2008, June 8). No debate: It's great TV. *The New York Times*, MT1.

Stein, M. L. (1994, August 6). Racial stereotyping and the media. *Editor & Publisher*, 6.

Stelter, B. (2008, March 27). Finding political news online, young viewers pass it along. *The New York Times*, A1.

Stelter, B. (2010, August 1). CBS adds 3 gay roles. NYTimes .com.

Stone, B. (2009, February 8). Disclosure, magnified on the web. *The New York Times*, BU3.

Vanacore, A. (2010, October 29). Sick of campaign ad avalanche? TV stations aren't. SFGate.com.

Vega, T. (2011, September 19). Newsroom diversity groups in partnership. NYTimes.com.

Wright, J. W. (1979). *The commercial connection*. New York: Dell (Synopsis of FTC staff report on television advertising to children).

Wyatt, E. (2009, March 18). No smooth ride on TV networks' road to diversity. NYTimes.com.

Chapter 14 Law and Regulation: Rewriting the Rules

Abrams, J. (2011, May 30). Obama, in Europe, signs Patriot Act extension. Associated Press, SFGate.com.

American Library Association (2007, September 6). Federal judge declares NSL gag order unconstitutional. ALA.org.

American Library Association (2009, September 21). Attempts to ban books in U.S. continue. ALA.org.

Ardito, S. C. (2001, November). The case of Dmitry Sklyarov: This is the first criminal lawsuit under the Digital Millennium Copyright Act. *Information Today*, 24.

Associated Press (2005, January 28). Bush won't appeal media ownership rules. AOL Business News. AOL.com.

Associated Press (2005, December 30). Justice Department opens inquiry into leak of domestic spying. NYTimes .com.

Associated Press (2006, June 8). Fines to rise for indecency in broadcasts. *The New York Times*, C7.

Associated Press (2007, September 6). Judge strikes down part of Patriot Act. NYTimes.com.

Associated Press (2007, December 18). FCC relaxes media ownership rule. NYTimes.com.

Associated Press (2009, May 4). High court throws out ruling on Janet Jackson. WashingtonPost.com.

Associated Press (2010, April 6). Court rules against FCC in "net neutrality" case. NYTimes.com.

Associated Press (2010, April 26). FCC asks court to revisit a ruling against an indecency policy. NYTimes.com.

Associated Press (2010, October 31). Supreme Court to hear violent video game case. NYTimes.com.

Associated Press (2011, October 24). Financial woes may sink WikiLeaks, Assange says. NYTimes.com.

Baker, P. (2007, March 7). For an opaque White House, a reflection of new scrutiny. WashingtonPost.com.

Barnes, R. (2011, October 4). Supreme Court copyright case will decide fate of millions of once-public works. Washingtonpost.com.

Benton Foundation (1996). *The Telecommunications Act of 1996 and the changing communications landscape*. Washington, D.C.: Author.

Birnbaum, M. (2010, March 17). Historians blast proposed Texas social studies curriculum. WashingtonPost.com.

Bode, C. (1969). *Mencken*. Carbondale: Southern Illinois University Press.

Braestrup, P. (1985). *Battle lines: Report of the Twentieth Century Fund Task Force on the Military and the Media*. New York: Priority Press.

Brick, M. (2010, May 21). Texas School Board set to vote textbook revisions. *The New York Times*, A17.

Burns, J. F., & Somaiya, R. (2010, December 7). British court denies bail to Assange. NYTimes.com.

Chu, H. (2011, November 2). Julian Assange ordered extradited in sex case. LATimes.com.

Climan, L. (2001, September). Writers battle media companies. *Dollars & Sense*, 6.

Cloud, D. S. (2011, March 2). Soldier in WikiLeaks case charged with aiding the enemy. LATimes.com.

Coile, Z. (2007, February 17). House Dems back federal shield law. *San Francisco Chronicle*, A5.

Congressional Research Service (2005, March 8). Journalists' privilege to withhold information in judicial and other proceedings: State shield statutes. Library of Congress.

Cowan, A. L. (2005, September 1). At stake in the court, the use of the Patriot Act to get library records. *The New York Times*, A18.

Cowan, A. L. (2005, September 2). Libraries wary as U.S. demands records. *The New York Times*, A21.

Cowan, A. L. (2005, September 10). Plaintiffs win round in Patriot Act lawsuit. NYTimes.com.

Crawford, K. (2005, June 27). Hollywood wins Internet piracy battle. Money.CNN.com.

Davis, J. (2001, April 9). Decision: A defining moment in libel law. *Editor & Publisher*, 9.

Deutsch, L. (2004, January 26). Judge rules part of Patriot Act unconstitutional. Associated Press.

Dombey, D. (2010, December 3). U.S. counts cost in week of leaks. FT.com.

Dunbar, J. (2007, September 11). FCC chair promotes post-digital TV rule. AOL.com.

Dunn, N. (2010, September 23). Banned books week 2010: Which books drew the most fire last year? CSMonitor.com.

Evangelista, B. (2005, April 20). House passes piracy measure. *San Francisco Chronicle*, C1.

Fitzgerald, M. (2001, July 2). "Tasini" reality test. *Editor & Publisher*, 11.

Gerhardt-Powals, J. (2000, November 27). The Digital Millennium Copyright Act: A compromise in progress. *New Jersey Law Journal*, 28.

Greenhouse, L. (2004, December 11). Justices agree to hear case on sharing of music files. *The New York Times*, B1.

Greenhouse, L. (2007, March 18). Free-speech case divides Bush and religious right. *The New York Times*, YT18.

Hakim, D. (2008, June 10). Web providers to block sites with child sex. *The New York Times*, A1.

Hellwege, J. (2001, June). Civil liberties, library groups challenge the latest law restricting web access. *Trial*, 93.

Holsinger, R. (1991). *Media law*, 2nd ed. New York: McGraw-Hill.

Hulse, C. (2005, June 16). House blocks provision for Patriot Act inquiries. *The New York Times*, A17.

Keller, B. (2011, January 26). Dealing with Assange and the WikiLeaks secrets. NYTimes.com.

Khatchadourian, R. (2010, June 7). No secrets: Julian Assange's mission for total transparency. *The New Yorker*.

Kitigaki, P. (2003, September 22). Librarians step up. *The Sacramento Bee*, A1.

Labaton, S. (2003, July 23). Republicans are adding weight to reversal of FCC media rule. *The New York Times*, A1.

Labaton, S. (2007, June 5). Decency ruling thwarts FCC on vulgarities. *The New York Times*, A1.

Lessig, L. (2007, March 18). Make way for copyright chaos. *The New York Times*, WK12.

Levin, M. (2005, January 27). Lawsuits take aim at ads for alcohol. LATimes.com.

Levine, R. (2007, March 12). Old concerts on new media lead to lawsuits. Iht.com.

Levy, L. (1985). *Emergence of a free press.* New York: Oxford University Press.

Lewis, P. (1996, June 13). Judges turn back law intended to regulate Internet decency. *The New York Times*, A1.

Lichtblau, E. (2005, August 26). FBI demands library records. *San Francisco Chronicle*, A5.

Lichtblau, E. (2005, November 19). Extension of Patriot Act faces threat of filibuster. *The New York Times*, A23.

Lichtblau, E. (2006, January 17). Groups file lawsuits over eavesdropping. NYTimes.com.

Lichtblau, E. (2007, September 9). FBI data mining reached beyond initial targets. *The New York Times*, A1.

Lichtblau, E., & Shenon, P. (2008, May 10). From places unexpected, support for the press. *The New York Times*, A11.

Liptak, A. (2007, December 31). In the fight over piracy, a rare stand for privacy. NYTimes.com.

Liptak, A. (2011, October 5). In Supreme Court argument, a rock legend plays a role. NYTimes.com.

McGrath, P., & Stadtman, N. (1985, February 4). What the jury—and *Time* magazine—said. *Newsweek*, 58.

McKinley, J. C. (2010, March 13). Conservatives on Texas panel carry the day on curriculum changes. *The New York Times*, A9.

McMasters, P. K. (2006, January 1). Prying by the press exposes spying on Americans. *First Amendment Center.*

Milliot, J. (2000, November 6). Decision supports web copyrights. *Publishers Weekly*, 56.

National Coalition Against Censorship (1985). *Books on trial: A survey of recent cases.* New York: National Coalition Against Censorship.

New York Times, The (2010, November 28). A note to readers: the decision to publish diplomatic documents. NYTimes.com.

Nohlgren, S. (2010, September 2). Jeff Greene files suit against *St. Petersburg Times*, *Miami Herald*. TampaBay.com.

Peek, T. (1999, January). Taming the Internet in three acts. *Information Today*, 28.

Penenberg, A. L. (2011, January 28). Wikileaks' Julian Assange: "Anarchist," "agitator," "arrogant," and a journalist. WashingtonPost.com.

Pike, G. H. (2001, October). Understanding and surviving *Tasini*. *Information Today*, 18.

Puzzanghera, J., & James, M. (2010, July 14). FCC indecency rule struck down by appeals court. LATimes.com.

Reid, C. (2001, October 15). Writers 2, publishers 0. *Publishers Weekly*, 12.

Reuters (2007, September 11). "Wardrobe malfunction" goes to court. NYTimes.com.

Richtel, M. (2008, February 14). H.P. agrees to settle journalist spy case. *The New York Times*, C5.

Risen, J., & Lichtblau, E. (2005, December 16). Bush lets U.S. spy on callers without courts. NYTimes.com.

Risen, J., & Lichtblau, E. (2009, June 17). Extent of e-mail surveillance renews concerns in Congress. *The New York Times*, A1.

Rousseau, C. (2003, April 23). *Harry Potter* back in schools. *San Francisco Chronicle*, A2.

Salant, J. (2004, January 27). FCC proposes fining Clear Channel $755,000. *Associated Press.*

Shane, S. (2007, July 3). Bush commutes Libby sentence, saying 30 months "is excessive." *The New York Times*, A1.

Shane, S. (2011, January 13). Accused soldier in brig as WikiLeaks link is sought. NYTimes.com.

Shane, S. (2011, December 16). Private in WikiLeaks spying case goes to court. NYTimes.com.

Shields, T. (2000, December 11). Supreme consideration: Free speech vs. privacy. *Editor & Publisher*, 7.

Sisario, B. (2010, December 4). LimeWire to shut subscription music service at year-end. *The New York Times*, B2.

Smith, R. J. (2007, March 7). Cheney's suspected role in security breach drove Fitzgerald. WashingtonPost.com.

Smolla, R. (1986). *Suing the press.* New York: Oxford University Press.

Sniffen, M. J. (2005, December 16). Patriot Act's sunset provisions are limited. Associated Press on AOL News. AOL.com.

Steinberg, J. (2003, May 26). Easier rules may not mean more newspaper-TV deals. *The New York Times*, C1.

Stern, C. (1996, February 12). The V-chip First Amendment infringement vs. empowerment tool. *Broadcasting & Cable*, 8.

Stone, B., & Helft, M. (2007, February 19). New weapon in Web war over piracy. *The New York Times*, C1.

Stout, D. (2009, April 29). Supreme Court backs FCC on indecency rule. NYTimes.com.

Stutz, T. (2010, September 24). Texas Board of Education OKs resolution against pro-Islamic references in textbooks. DallasNews.com.

Swett, C. (2008, January 2). F.C.C. auction may reshape telecom field. SacBee.com.

Ungar, S. (1975). *The papers and the papers: An account of the legal and political battle over the Pentagon papers.* New York: Dutton.

Van Natta, D., Liptak, A., & Levy, C. J. (2005, October 16). The Miller case: A notebook, a cause, a jail cell and a deal. *The New York Times*, A1.

Varian, H. R. (2007, May 31). Copyrights that no one knows about don't help anyone. *The New York Times*, C3.

Woodward, C. & Lardner, R. (2011, June 13). 40 years after leak, the Pentagon Papers are out. Associated Press, SFGate.com.

Wyatt, E. (2010, August 5). FCC Chief opposes fees for Internet priority. NYTimes.com.

Wyatt, E. (2010, December 1). FCC Chairman sets a framework for regulating broadband providers. NYTimes.com.

Wyatt, E. (2011, June 27). Justices agree to consider F.C.C. rules on indecency. NYTimes.com.

Chapter 15 Ethics: Placing Responsibility

Alter, J., & McKillop, P. (1986, August). AIDS and the right to know. *Newsweek*, 46.

Associated Press (2007, March 12). *New York Times* says former reporter's link to source included a $2,000 payment. IHT.com.

Associated Press (2010, November 19). MSNBC suspends host Scarborough for GOP donations. SFGate.com.

Atta, D. (1986, November). Faint light, dark print. *Harper's*, 57.

Barry, D. (2003, May 1). *Times* reporter who resigned leaves long trail of deception. *The New York Times*, A1.

Barstow, D., & Stein, R. (2005, March 13). Government video reports blur media ethics. *The New York Times*, A5.

Brandt, A. (1984, October). Truth and consequences. *Esquire*, 27.

Buettner, R. (2011, February 24). Affidavits say Fox News chief told employee to lie. NYTimes.com.

Calame, B. (2007, March 25). Money, a source and new questions about a story. *The New York Times*, WK12.

Carr, D. (2010, November 8). Olbermann, impartiality and MSNBC. *The New York Times*, B1.

Carter, B. (2010, November 9). Olbermann, on air again, criticizes NBC for its policy. *The New York Times*, B2.

Christians, C., Rotzoll, K., & Fackler, M. (1987). *Media ethics*, 2nd ed. New York: Longman.

Chu. H. (2011, September 6). James Murdoch knew of wider phone hacking, ex-colleagues say. LATimes.com.

Freeman, S. (2005, April 9). Newspaper panel to investigate Mitch Albom. Associated Press on AOL Sports News. AOL.com.

Friedman, J. (2007, March 10). Blogging for bucks stirs uproar over ethics. Reprinted from the *Los Angeles Times* in *The Sacramento Bee*.

Garside, J. (2011, October 10). Campaign grows to oust Murdoch. Guardian.co.uk.

Goldstein, P. (2009, November 13). An embarrassment for Universal: Fabricated news stories. LATimes.com.

Goodman, T. (2007, April 19). Has NBC ushered in a new era for multimedia? *San Francisco Chronicle*, A14.

Halbfinger, D. M., & Weiner, A. H. (2005, June 9). As paparazzi push ever harder, stars seek a way to push back. *The New York Times*, A1.

Hulteng, J. (1985). *The messenger's motives: Ethical problems of the news media*. Englewood Cliffs, N.J.: Prentice Hall.

Ives, N. (2005, April 11). Meeting a deadline, repenting at leisure. NYTimes.com.

Kelly, K. J. (2006, January 13). *People*'s baby scoop: Mag wrote sizeable check for Angelina's pet charity. NYPost.com.

Kirkpatrick, D. D. (2007, January 29). Feeding frenzy for a big story, even if it's false. *The New York Times*, A1.

Kornblut, A. E., & Barstow, D. (2005, April 15). Debate rekindles over government-produced "news." NYTimes.com.

Kurtz, H. (2009, October 18). *Post*'s canceled series of "salon" dinners again called into question. WashingtonPost.com.

Lunzer, B. (2010, October 5). New Hampshire newspaper publishes Afghanistan series with corporate backers. NewsGuild.org.

Lyall, S. (2011, November 14). Pattern of illegality is cited at *News of the World*. NYTimes.com.

Macropoulos, A. (2007, April 2). A misfired memo shows close tabs on reporter. *The New York Times*, C4.

Maerz, M. (2011, January 24). Keith Olbermann's departure and the unanswered questions. LATimes.com.

New York Times, The (2010, February 17). *Times* business reporter accused of plagiarism is said to resign. NYTimes.com.

O'Carroll, L. (2011, December 10). Phone-hacking victims to number 800. Guardian.co.uk.

Prendergast, A. (1987, January/February). Mickey Mouse journalism. *Washington Journalism Review*, *9*, 32.

Preston, J. (2011, March 27). Ethical quandry for social sites. NYTimes.com.

Public Relations Society of America Member Code of Ethics (2000).

Radio-Television Digital News Association Code of Ethics and Professional Conduct (September 14, 2000).

Reuters (2011, November 23). James Murdoch resigns from U.K. newspaper boards. NYTimes.com.

Rich, F. (2005, February 20). The White House stages its "Daily Show." NYTimes.com.

Rubenstein, S., Lee, H. K., & King, J. (2007, April 19). The video: Should it have been shown? *San Francisco Chronicle*, A14.

Sabbagh, D. (2011, October 27). James Murdoch a 'dead man walking' following shareholder vote. Guardian.co.uk.

Society of Professional Journalists Code of Ethics (September 1996).

Sonne, P., Whalen, J. & Orwall, B. (2011, August 17). New issues emerge for News Corp. in Britain. WSJ.com.

Steinberg, J. (2003, June 6). *Times*' top editors resign after furor on writer's fraud. *The New York Times*, A1.

Stelter, B. (2010, November 10). 2nd MSNBC host suspended over campaign donations. *The New York Times*, B1.

Stone, A. (2010, November 5). Keith Olbermann suspended for giving political donations. AOLNews.com.

Chapter 16 Global Media: Discovering New Markets

Abdulrahim, R., & Gorman, A. (2009, August 6). Journalists freed by North Korea back in U.S. SFGate.com.

Andrews, E. L. (2007, April 7). Piracy move on China seen as near. *The New York Times*, B1.

Arango, T. (2008, December 1). Friend, foe or just a fan: World falls for American media, even as it sours on America. *The New York Times*, B1.

Associated Press (2010, January 25). Cable TV station critical of Chavez is shut down. *The New York Times*, A5.

Associated Press (2010, November 10). Rights groups blast Egypt detention of blogger. WashingtonPost.com.

Associated Press (2011, January 30). Egypt bans Arabic broadcaster Al Jazeera. AOLNews.com.

Austen, I. (2007, March 16). Canada: Blackout on early vote results upheld. *The New York Times*, A6.

BBCNews (2010, May 6). "Historic" day as first non-Latin Web addresses go live. News.BBC.co.uk.

Chen, A. C., & Chaudhary, A. G. (1991). Asia and the Pacific. In *Global journalism: Survey of international communication*, 2nd ed. New York: Longman.

Chivers, C. J. (2007, August 29). Russia arrests ten in killing of Putin critic. NYTimes.com.

Committee to Protect Journalists (2011, December 8). Imprisonments jump worldwide, and Iran is worst. Cpj .org/reports/2011/12.

Cowell, A. (2003, July 31). Independent for 81 years, the BBC is facing a challenge. *The New York Times*, A3.

DeGiorgio, E. (2000, April). The African Internet revolution. *African Business*, 30.

Dennis, E., & Vanden Heuvel, J. (1990, October). Emerging voices: East European media in transition. *Gannett Center for Media Studies*, 2.

Fathi, N. (2005, June 29). Women writing novels emerge as stars in Iran. *The New York Times*, B1.

Foster, P. (2010, February 26). BBC signals an end to era of expansion. Business.TimesOnline.co.uk.

French, H. W. (2007, December 7). As Chinese media grow, foreign news is left out. *The New York Times*, A4.

Fuller, T. (2007, April 5). Thailand blocks users' access to YouTube. *The New York Times*, C12.

Garside, J. (2011, July 27). Vodafone under fire for bowing to Egyptian pressure. *The Guardian*, 27.

Gerth, J. (2005, December 11). Military's information war is vast and often secretive. *The New York Times*, A1.

Glanz, J. & Markoff, J. (2011, June 12). U.S. underwrites Internet detour around censors. *The New York Times*, A1.

Hamilton, R. (2010, November 10). In Radio Dabanga raid, Sudan targets last uncensored media outlet on the ground. WashingtonPost.com.

Hassan, A. (2010, June 1). Arabic Web addresses expected to draw millions of new users to Internet. LATimes.com.

Hauser, C. (2011, February 1). New service allows Egyptian voices to be heard. NYTimes.com.

Hays, L., & Rutherford, A. (1991, January 1). Gorbachev bids to crack down on Soviet press. *The Wall Street Journal*, A8.

Head, S. W. (1985). *World broadcasting systems*. Belmont, Calif.: Wadsworth.

Heingartner, D. (2003, June 5). Roaming the globe, laptops alight on wireless hot spots. *The New York Times*, E4.

Hindley, A. (1999, April 23). Breaking the taboos. *Middle East Economic Digest*, 6.

Hindley, A. (2000, February 11). Internet usage, the boom in access. *Middle East Economic Digest*, 27.

Hoo, S. (2004, December 9). Going global: Major foreign expansion is part of China's strategy. *The Sacramento Bee*, D1.

Ivry, S. (2007, April 16). Now on YouTube: The latest news from Al Jazeera, in English. *The New York Times*, C5.

Kim, R. (2007, March 29). Foreign nations take tech title. SFGate.com.

Kirkpatrick, D. D. (2011, May 31). Egypt's military censors critics as it faces more scrutiny. NYTimes.com.

Kirkpatrick, D. D., & Goodman, J. D. (2011, February 3). Reporters in Egypt under broad assault. NYTimes.com.

Kramer, A. E. (2007, March 22). Editor of Russian edition of Forbes guilty of defamation. *The New York Times*, C4.

Kramer, A. E. (2010, November 9). On video, Russian journalist is seen being brutally beaten. *The New York Times*, A8.

Khalil, M., Dongier, P., & Zhen-Wei Qiang, C. (2009). *Information and communications for development 2009: Extending reach and increasing impact*. World Bank Publications.

LaFraniere, S. (2010, January 20). China to scan text messages to spot "unhealthy content." *The New York Times*, A5.

Landler, M. (2010, January 22). Clinton urges global response to Internet attacks. NYTimes.com.

Levy, C. J. (2010, May 18). In culture of graft and impunity, Russian journalists pay in blood. *The New York Times*, A1.

Lowndes, F. S. (1991). The world's media systems: An overview. In *Global journalism: Survey of international communication*, 2nd ed. New York: Longman.

Lyall, S. & Pfanner, E. (2011, April 23). BBC, under criticism, struggles to tighten its belt. NYTimes.com.

MacFarquhar, N. (2006, January 15). In tiny Arab state, web takes on ruling elite. NYTimes.com.

Malkin, E. (2009, September 29). Honduras shuts down 2 news outlets. NYTimes.com.

Markoff, J. (2007, January 29). At Davos, the squabble resumes on how to wire the Third World. *The New York Times*, C1.

Martin, L. J. (1991). Africa. In *Global journalism: Survey of international communication*, 2nd ed. New York: Longman.

McDowall, A. (2001, April 20). Uncorking the bottlenecks. *Middle East Economic Digest*, 45.

Mista, N. (2003, September 15). India's film city is gobbling tribal land. *San Francisco Chronicle*, D1.

Ogan, C. (1991). Middle East and North Africa. In *Global journalism: Survey of international communication*, 2nd ed. New York: Longman.

Paraschos, M. (1991). Europe. In *Global journalism: Survey of international communication*, 2nd ed. New York: Longman.

Pfanner, E. (2011, December 13). O.E.C.D. calls on members to defend Internet freedoms. NYTimes.com.

Picard, R. G. (1991). Global communications controversies. In *Global journalism: Survey of international communication*, 2nd ed. New York: Longman.

Pierson, D. (2010, January 16). Despite censorship, cracks in China's great firewall. LATimes.com.

Pintak, L. (2007, April 27). Reporting a revolution: The changing Arab media landscape. ArabMediaSociety.com.

Richburg, K. B. (2011, April 12). Chinese editors detail censors' hidden hand. Washingtonpost.com.

Richtel, M. (2011, January 28). Egypt cuts off most Internet and cell service. NYTimes.com.

Romero, S. (2007, May 27). Chavez's move against critic highlights shift in media. NYTimes.com.

Sabbagh, D. (2009, March 11). Advertising slump leaves Britain's local newspapers in crisis. TimesOnline.co.uk.

Sabbagh, D. (2009, March 20). BBC must cut spending by £400 million, says Mark Thompson. TimesOnline.co.uk.

Sabbagh, D. (2009, April 16). Digital economy bill to pave way for shake-up of rules governing media mergers. TimesOnline.co.uk.

Saltz, R. (2007, April 21). Using Bollywood ideas to portray today's India. *The New York Times*, A19.

Salwen, M. B., Garrison, B., & Buckman, R. (1991). Latin America and the Caribbean. In *Global journalism: Survey of international communication*, 2nd ed. New York: Longman.

Shadid, A., Addario, L., Farrell, S. & Hicks, T. (2011, March 22). 4 Times journalists held captive in Libya faced days of brutality. NYTimes.com.

Shane, S. (2011, January 29). Spotlight again falls on Web tools and change. NYTimes.com.

Shadid, A., Addario, L., Farrell, S. & Hicks, T. (2011, March 22). 4 *Times* journalists held captive in Libya faced days of brutality. NYTimes.com.

Siebert, F., Peterson, T., & Schramm, W. (1963). *Four theories of the press*. Urbana: University of Illinois Press.

Stelter, B. (2011, February 1). Channels join fight to broadcast Al Jazeera in Egypt. NYTimes.com.

Strobel, W. P. (2005, April 18). Arab satellite channel Al Jazeera goes global. MercuryNews.com.

Stross, R. (2010, April 19). Two billion laptops? It may not be enough. *The New York Times*, BU5.

Tavernise, S. (2010, May 21). Pakistan, citing "sacrilegious content," widens online ban to include YouTube. *The New York Times*, A12.

Timmons, H. (2008, May 20). Newspapers on upswing in developing markets. *The New York Times*, C6.

Tunstall, J. (2008). *The media were American*. New York: Oxford University Press.

Wallace, C. (1988, January 7). Radio: Town crier of the Arab world. *Los Angeles Times*, 1.

Wan, W. (2011, March 4). Egypt's Facebook revolution faces identity crisis. Washingtonpost.com.

Warren, M. (2010, August 28). Argentine president moves to control newsprint. SFGate.com.

Werdigier, J. (2010, November 5). BBC staff strikes over changes to pension plan. NYTimes.com.

Index

NOTE: Page numbers in *italics* refer to photos or illustrations.

C

D

G

N

T

U

X

Y

Z